STUDENTS!
ESSENTIAL ACCESS INFORMATION
FOR HOUGHTON MIFFLIN VIDEO CASES

EXPLORE TEACHING IN ACTION

Are you interested in what happens in actual classrooms? Do you want to know how in-service teachers handle a variety of situations in the classroom? Watch the Houghton Mifflin Video Cases and explore how new and experienced teachers apply concepts and strategies in real K–12 classrooms. Integrated into your text, these 4- to 6-minute video clips cover a variety different topics faced by today's teachers and allow you to experience and reflect on real teaching in action.

TO ACCESS THE HOUGHTON MIFFLIN VIDEO CASES:

1. Using your browser go to **college.hmco.com/PIC/grabe5e**.
2. Select the student website.
3. Click on **HM Video Cases**.
4. You will be prompted to enter the passkey below and to choose a username and password.
5. Select a video case from the list of options.

Passkey: EUSOZAWC0TJP1

Access is provided free with the purchase of a new Grabe/Grabe, *Integrating Technology for Meaningful Learning*, Fifth Edition, textbook, and will expire six months after first use. If you have a problem accessing the website with this passkey, please contact Houghton Mifflin Technical Support at:

http://college.hmco.com/how/how_techsupp.html.

ENHANCE YOUR LEARNING EXPERIENCE

Houghton Mifflin Video Cases are incorporated into your new copy of Grabe/Grabe, *Integrating Technology for Meaningful Learning*, Fifth Edition, through boxed features in the margins of the text. The cases include video clips and a host of related materials to provide a comprehensive learning experience.

Watch textbook concepts come to life through video clips and bonus videos of real teachers applying teaching models and addressing key topics in their own classrooms.

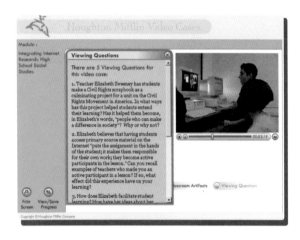

Reflect on the teacher's approach, and assess how you might handle the situation by considering the **Viewing Questions.**

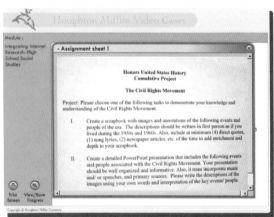

View **handouts and materials** used in the class, and gain ideas for your own portfolio.

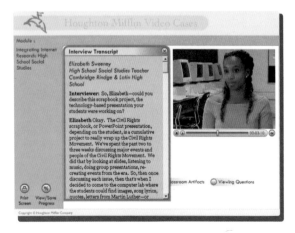

Read **detailed interviews with the teachers** as they explain their approach, how they engage students, and how they resolve issues.

Integrating Technology for Meaningful Learning

Integrating Technology for Meaningful Learning

• • •

FIFTH EDITION

MARK GRABE
University of North Dakota

CINDY GRABE
Technology Facilitator, Grand Forks Schools

HOUGHTON MIFFLIN COMPANY
New York   Boston

Publisher: Patricia A. Coryell
Executive Editor: Mary Finch
Senior Development Editor: Lisa Mafrici
Editorial Assistant: Dayna Pell
Senior Project Editor: Margaret Park Bridges
Associate Manufacturing Buyer: Brian Pieragostini
Senior Marketing Manager: Elinor Gregory
Marketing Associate: Evelyn Yang

Cover image: Matthew Johnson, Mysteries II, 2001

Acknowledgment is made to the following sources for permission to reprint selections from copyrighted material: Preface figure, p. xxxi: Copyright ©1993 and published by Weekly Reader Corporation. All rights reserved. Used by permission. E-portfolios box, pp. 9–11: Reprinted with permission. Figure 1.3 and Focus box, pp. 10, 26–27: Reprinted with permission from www.iste.org, copyright © 2000, ISTE (International Society for Technology in Education), 800–336–5191 (U.S. and Canada) or 541–302–3777 (international), iste@iste.org, www.iste.org. All rights reserved. Permission does not constitute an endorsement by ISTE. Figure 4.1, p. 119: From *Sniffy, the Virtual Rat* software. Reproduced with permission of Brooks/Cole, a division of Thomson Learning: www.thomsonrights.com. Fax 800–730–2215. Figures 4.2 and 4.3, pp. 127, 128: Reprinted by permission of Scholastic, Inc. Figure 4.4, p. 131: Copyright © 2003 Roger Wagner Publishing Inc., a Sunburst Technology Company. All rights reserved. Figure 4.5, p. 133: From *MicroType: The Wonderful World of Paws*, published by South-Western Educational Publishing, a division of International Thomson Publishing Inc. Copyright © 1992 by South-Western Educational Publishing. All rights reserved. Figure 4.6, p. 136: *SimCity 3000* © 1998 Electronic Arts Inc. *SimCity 3000* is a trademark or registered trademark of Electronic Arts Inc. in the U.S. and/or other countries. All rights reserved. Figures 4.7, 4.8, and 4.9, pp. 140, 141, 143: From *Exploring the Nardoo*. Used by permission of The Learning Team. Figure 4.10, p. 149: From *WiggleWorks! Fresh Fall Leaves* by Betsy Franco. Copyright © by Scholastic Inc. Reprinted by permission.
(Acknowledgments continued on page 431.)

Library of Congress Control Number: 2005930266

Instructor's exam copy:
ISBN 13: 978-0-618-73157-2
ISBN 10: 0-618-73157-1

For orders, use students text ISBNs:
ISBN 13: 978-0-618-63701-0
ISBN 10: 0-618-63701-X

123456789-DOW-10 09 08 07 06

Dedication

• • •

Allow me to tell a brief story. I remember a trip my wife and I took to my parents' home during the later stages of Cindy's and my education as graduate students. I happened to awake about six in the morning and went down to the kitchen of our old farmhouse because I was thirsty and needed a drink of water. When I walked into the kitchen, I was surprised to see that the lights were already on and my mother was busy working at the kitchen table preparing her lessons for the day. For some reason, the image has always stayed with me. My mother had taught Home Economics since I was in junior high school, and although I was also preparing for a career in education, I had never really thought much about her dedication to what she did.

My mother used hardware and software too. She had a shallow tray containing a substance that looked like Jell-O, and with this equipment and typed or hand-drawn spirit masters she would turn out dittoed pages about nutrition, sewing, childcare, or whatever she was intending to discuss. It was a slow process. First, the master had to be pressed against the "Jell-O" for a few minutes. It was important to align the master carefully or the final product would be crooked. Then, blank sheets of paper were individually pressed against the Jell-O-like material and carefully peeled away to create the handouts. Try to keep my mom's use of technology in mind as you read about the techniques we describe in this book. The contrast is amazing and provides just one indication of the tremendous change that has occurred in a relatively brief period of time.

This story is intended to get you to think about more than the pace of change in our world. While Cindy and I believe strongly that technology can have a profound impact on our schools, our confidence in technology is justified only in classrooms led by dedicated and skillful teachers. We should be amazed and excited by the power of modern technology, but we should remain impressed by the teachers who begin work at six because last year's lesson may not be good enough. This book is dedicated to Frances Grabe and to all teachers like her.

Brief Contents

• • •

Preface xxi

PART ONE A Teaching and Learning Framework for Integrating Technology in Classrooms 1

Chapter 1 Key Themes and Issues for Using Technology in Your Classroom 3

Chapter 2 Meaningful Learning in an Information Age 38

PART TWO Learning How to Integrate Technology with Your Teaching 77

Chapter 3 Using Tools: Word Processors, Databases, Spreadsheets, and Data Probes 79

Chapter 4 Using Instructional Software and Multimedia for Content-Area Learning 118

Chapter 5 The Internet as a Tool for Communication 170

Chapter 6 The Internet as a Tool for Inquiry 201

Chapter 7 Using Multimedia Tools 242

Chapter 8 Learning to Work with Images, Sound, and Video 271

Chapter 9 Learning from Student Projects: Knowledge as Design and the Design of Hypermedia 314

PART THREE Looking at Issues for the Present and Future 363

Chapter 10 Responsible Use of Technology 365

Glossary 403
References 410
Index 421

Contents

• • •

Preface xxi

PART ONE A Teaching and Learning Framework for Integrating Technology in
Classrooms 1

Chapter 1 **Key Themes and Issues for Using Technology in Your Classroom 3**

Orientation 3
Uses of Technology: An Introduction to Key Themes 4
Physics: Probes and Projects 4
Knowing Nature: Technology as a Tool for the Personal Journey of
 Learning 7
E-portfolios: Reflection and Evaluation in the Middle-School Methods
 Class 9
Themes of Technology Use in the Classroom 11
 Technology Integrated into Content-Area Instruction 11

 Focus: Creative Tension: What Multiple Parties Want from Digital
 Portfolios 12

 A Tools Approach 13
 An Active Role for Students 13
 A Facilitative Role for the Teacher 14
 An Integrated or Multidisciplinary Approach 14
 Standards and Performance-Based Assessment 14
 Cooperative Learning 14

 Spotlight on Assessment: Relating Learning and Assessment 15

Technology in Today's Classroom 16
 Students' Access to Technology 16
 What Students Do with Computers 17
 Resources and Equity 18
Technology and School Reform 19
 Key Elements for Twenty-first-Century Learning 19
 Restructuring Schools 21
National Standards: Goals for Learning and Expectations
 for Technology 22
 What Are Standards? 22

Standards and Reform   24
Standards for Learning with Technology   24
Standards and Educational Equity   25
Changing the Way Technology Is Used in Schools   25

● **Focus: ISTE Technology Standards   26**

● **Focus: How Standards May Be Shaping What You Learn about the Application of Technology   27**

Three Perspectives on Technology and School Reform   29
"Influence of Computer and Internet Use on Teachers' Pedagogical Practices"   29
"High Access and Low Use . . . : Explaining an Apparent Paradox"   30   "The Interplay of Teacher Beliefs, Social Dynamics, and Institutional Culture"   30
Teacher Preparation   31
Teacher Training   31   Teacher Attitudes   32
The Activity-Based Model of Technology Use   32

● **Focus: The National Educational Technology Plan   33**

Early Use of Activity-Based Approaches   34
Today's Use of Activity-Based Approaches and Technology   35
Summary   35
Reflecting on Chapter 1   36
Activities   36
Key Terms   36
Resources to Expand Your Knowledge Base   36

Chapter 2   Meaningful Learning in an Information Age   38

Orientation   38
Cognitive Models of School Learning   39
Fundamental Properties of Mental Activity   39
Memory Stores   40
Short-Term Memory   40   Long-Term Memory   42
Processes: Mental Tools for Doing the Work of Thinking and Learning   46
Metacognition   47
Metacognitive Knowledge   47   Metacognitive Control Functions   48   Using Technology to Improve Metacognitive Skills   49   Mental Activity: A Recap   50
Conceptual Models of School Learning   51
Meaningful Learning   51
Reception versus Discovery   52   Characterizing Typical Learning Activities   52   When to Use Discovery Techniques   54
Constructivism   54

● **Spotlight on Assessment: Performance Assessment   55**

Reviewing the Common Themes   56

● **Focus: Are We Abandoning Truth?   57**

From Theory to Practice: Teaching, Learning, and the Role of
 Technology   57
  Authentic Activities   58
  Inert Knowledge 58   Authentic Activities and Technology 59
  Higher-Order Thinking and Transfer   60
  Ways to Teach Higher-Order Thinking 62   Transfer: The Low Road and the
  High Road 63
  The Social Context of Learning   64

● **Focus:** Using the Internet for Authentic Activities   65

  Cognitive Apprenticeship 65   Cooperative Learning 66   Learning
  Communities 68
  Project-Based Learning   68

● **Focus:** Lev Vygotsky   69

  Previewing Technology Options That May Expand How You Think about
   Student Learning   70
  Computer Tools and Thinking Behavior   70

● **Activities and Projects for Your Classroom:** Ideas for Content-Area
 Projects   71

  Hypermedia Projects   71
Research about Learning with Technology   72
Summary   73
Reflecting on Chapter 2   74
  Activities   74
  Key Terms   74
  Resources to Expand Your Knowledge Base   75

PART TWO   **Learning How to Integrate Technology with Your Teaching   77**

Chapter 3   **Using Tools: Word Processors, Databases, Spreadsheets, and Data
 Probes   79**

Orientation   79
Productivity Tools in the Work of Teachers and Students   79
The Tools Approach   80
Word Processing   81
  Characteristics of Word Processing Programs   82
  Text Input 82   Storage and Retrieval 82   Formatting 82

● **Activities and Projects for Your Classroom:** Word Processing Activities
 for All Grade Levels   83

  Editing 84   Special Tools 84   Document Design Capabilities 85
  The Value of Word Processing Features 85
  Writers, Writing, and Word Processing   86

◉ **Focus: Learning Word Processing Features** 87

  The Writing Process Approach 88
  Keyboarding 89

◉ **Spotlight on Assessment: Electronic Portfolios** 90

◉ **Focus: Using Inspiration to Brainstorm** 92

Spreadsheets 94

◉ **Focus: Publication on the Internet** 95

◉ **Emerging Technology: Inexpensive "Keyboard" Computers** 95

  Comparing Winter Temperatures: A Spreadsheet Project 97

◉ **Activities and Projects for Your Classroom: Spreadsheet Activities** 98

◉ **Focus: Using a Spreadsheet to Help Understand the Solution to an Algebraic Equation** 100

Databases 101
  Developing a Database 102
Investigating Wildflowers: A Database Project 103
  Reflections on Spreadsheet and Database Programs 105
Data Collection Devices 106
  Examples of Data Collection 107
  Using Data Collection to Encourage Higher-Order Thinking 108

◉ **Focus: Using a Data Logger to Measure Stress** 110

◉ **Emerging Technology: GPS and GIS: Interpreting Data in Relationship to Place** 112

  Geocaching: Encouraging Local Explorations Using GPS 113
Summary 114
Reflecting on Chapter 3 115
  Activities 115
  Key Terms 115
  Resources to Expand Your Knowledge Base 116

Chapter 4   **Using Instructional Software and Multimedia for Content-Area Learning** 118

Orientation 118
"Sniffy, the Virtual Rat": An Example of Learning from the Computer 119
Computer-Based Instruction 121
The Process of Instruction 122
Categories of Instructional Software 123
  Tutorials 123
    How Tutorials Function 123 *Evaluating Tutorials 125*

Simulations   125
*Operation: Frog—An Example of a Simulation 127   Attributes of Simulations,
Learning, and Transfer 128   Advantages of Simulations 129*
Drill and Practice   130
Applications of Drill-and-Practice Software 132   Focus of Drill and Practice 133
Educational Games   133
Examples of Educational Games 134   Classroom Uses of Games 137
Exploratory Environments   137
*Characteristics of Exploratory Environments 138   Hypermedia Environments 138
Effectiveness of Exploratory Environments 142*
**Multimedia and Hypermedia in the Delivery of Computer-Assisted
Instruction   144**
What Are Multimedia, Hypermedia, and Hypertext?   144
What Are CD-ROM and DVD?   145
CD-ROM Technology 145   DVD Technology 146
Other Forms of Multimedia Found in Classrooms   147
Talking Books 147   Multimedia References 149
Learning from Multimedia Instructional Resources   150

● **Emerging Technology: The Evolution of Multimedia
Encyclopedias   151**

Strengths and Weaknesses of Multimedia and Hypermedia   152
*Advantages of Multiple Formats and Alternative Perspectives 152   Concerns about
Multimedia in Classrooms 154*
The Evaluation of Computer-Assisted Instruction   157
*Summary of Research on CAI 157   Interpreting Contradictory Research Findings:
The Arguments about CAI Effectiveness 158   Evaluating Software 160
Evaluation Forms 160*
Constructivism and Cooperative Learning with
Instructional Software   163

● **Keeping Current: Locating Appropriate Software   164**

Summary   166
Reflecting on Chapter 4   167
Activities   167
Key Terms   167
Resources to Expand Your Knowledge Base   168

Chapter 5   The Internet as a Tool for Communication   170

Orientation   170
What Is the Internet?   170
What Roles Can the Internet Play in Education?   173
Internet Tools for Communication   174
Internet Tools for Inquiry   174
Internet Tools for Construction   174

Learning by Communicating   174
   E-mail   174

● **Focus:** Making the Connection   175

   Mailing Lists   179
   Conferences   179

● **Focus:** Joining a List Maintained by a Server   180

● **Keeping Current:** Finding Useful Mailing Lists   181

   Chat and Instant Messaging   181
   Videoconferencing   182
   Telecomputing Activity Structures   184
   Advantages and Disadvantages of Computer-Mediated
      Communication   185

● **Focus:** Capitalizing on Volunteerism through Telementoring   186

   CMC's Impact on Discussion 187   Potential Problems with CMC 188

● **Focus:** Netiquette Guidelines   189

Facilitating Online Discussion   191
   Your Technical Role   191
   Your Social Role   192
   Your Managerial Role   192
   Your Pedagogical Role   195

● **Focus:** Key Issues for Online Discussions   197

   Gaining Experience   197
Summary   198
Reflecting on Chapter 5   199
   Activities   199
   Key Terms   199
   Resources to Expand Your Knowledge Base   200

Chapter 6   **The Internet as a Tool for Inquiry**   201

Orientation   201
A Classroom Example of an Authentic Inquiry Task   202
The World Wide Web and Web Exploration Tools   204

● **Focus:** Internet Addresses   205

   Web Browsers   205
   Keeping Track of Online Resources   207
   Making Bookmarks More Informative 207   Exporting Bookmarks 208
Locating Information on the Web: Browsing versus Searching   209
   An Example of Browsing   210
   Types of Search Services   210
   Search Engine and Directory Combinations 211   Index Search Engines 211

Meta-Index Searches 212   Which Type of Search Engine Should I Use? 212
Conducting a Search   212
Using the Web in Your Classroom   213
Categories of Web Resources   216
Online Tutorials   217
Instructional Resources   217
Primary Sources   217

● **Focus:** Doing History: Supporting History Teachers in Promoting
Historical Inquiry   218

● **Keeping Current:** Subscription Information Services   222

Strategies for Using Primary Sources on the Web   222
The Big Six   222

● **Focus:** Issues in Classroom Use of Web Resources   223

● **Focus:** Information Literacy Standards   225

The Big Six and the Internet   225
Information Seeking on the Internet 225   Locating and Accessing Internet Resources 226   Using Internet Information 227

● **Focus:** Citing Internet Sources   228

Evaluating Web Information   228
Editorial Review and Screening of Internet Resources   229
Searching a Database of Reviewed Sites 229   Using Resources Identified by an Educational Portal 229   Digitized Primary Sources from Reputable Institutions 229
Making Your Own Decisions   230
Who Is the Author? 230   Is There an Organizational Sponsor? 231   Additional Evaluation Criteria 231
Using the Web for Active Learning   232
Obtaining Current Weather Data: An Internet Project   232
Scaffolding Web Exploration   233
The Snow Goose Crisis: A WebQuest Example   235
Background 235   Instructional Tasks 236   WebQuest Presentation 236
Conclusion: New Challenges for Teachers   237
Summary   238
Reflecting on Chapter 6   239
Activities   239
Key Terms   240
Resources to Expand Your Knowledge Base   240

Chapter 7   **Using Multimedia Tools**   **242**

Orientation   242
Who Wants to Be a Millionaire?   242
A System for Classifying Student Multimedia Projects   244
  Embellished Documents   244
  Linear Multimedia Presentations or Slide Shows   245
  Hypermedia   246
  Thinking Beyond What Your Projects Will Look Like   246

  ● **Activities and Projects for Your Classroom:** Slide
  Show Activities   247

Software Tools for Creating Multimedia Projects   248
  Creating Embellished Documents with Word Processing Programs   248
  Creating Multimedia Slide Shows   250
  *KidPix Slideshow 250   Presentation Software 252   Example of a Classroom
  Presentation 257*
Multimedia Authoring Environments for Hypermedia   258
  eZediaMX   260
  Elements of the eZediaMX System 260
  Is PowerPoint a Multimedia Authoring Environment?   264

  ● **Emerging Technology: eZediaQTI**   265

  Other Multimedia Authoring Environments   267
Summary   268
Reflecting on Chapter 7   269
  Activities   269
  Key Terms   269
  Resources to Expand Your Knowledge Base   270

Chapter 8   **Learning to Work with Images, Sound, and Video**   **271**

Orientation   271
The Case of the Missing Gerbil   271
Tools for Creating and Manipulating Images   273
  Paint and Draw Programs   274
  *Creating Original Images 274   Modifying Existing Images 274   Saving Images
  That Can Be Used by Application Programs 275   Organizing and Saving Large
  Image Collections 275   Comparing Paint and Draw Programs 275*
  Using Graphics Tools in a Writing Assignment   279

  ● **Focus: Screen Capture**   280

  Understanding Graphics File Formats   282
Tools for Capturing Still Images   284

  ● **Focus: Graphics for the Web**   285

  Flatbed Scanners   286

Digital Cameras   287
Still Images from Video   288

⊛ **Activities and Projects for Your Classroom: Video Images
    to Capture**   289

Locating Image Sources   289
Coloring Books   290
World Wide Web   290
Student Art   291
Clip Art Collections   291
Organizing Your Image Collection   291
iPhoto 292
Working with Video   295
Digital Camcorders   295
Video Production   296
*Planning Phase 296   Collecting Primary Sources and Generating
Interpretive Products 296   Editing 297*

⊛ **Focus: Camcorder Tips**   300

⊛ **Activities and Projects for Your Classroom: Video
    Productions**   301

**Clay Animation: Creating Video by Sequencing Images
    of Clay Characters**   302
Capturing and Storing Sounds for Multimedia Projects   305

⊛ **Emerging Technology: Background Music**   307

⊛ **Emerging Technology: Digital Audio Recording and Podcasts**   308

Learning with Sound and Graphics Tools   309
Summary   310
Reflecting on Chapter 8   311
Activities   311
Key Terms   311
Resources to Expand Your Knowledge Base   312

**Chapter 9   Learning from Student Projects: Knowledge as Design and the Design
            of Hypermedia**   314

Orientation   314
"Is This the Way It Is?": Creating a Geography Project for an Authentic
    Audience   314
Knowledge as Design   316
Looking at Student-Authored Hypermedia   317
Principles of Hypermedia Design: The Process of Developing
    Software   317

Content Organization   318
Experiencing Content in a Variety of Ways 318   Organizational Structure 319
Graphic Design   321
Screen Layout 321
Text Presentation and Writing Style   323
User Interface and Navigation   324
Menus and Maps 324   Buttons 325
Student Cooperation: Fundamentals for Design Teams   326
Going Beyond Factual Information   327
Group Investigation   327
Hypercomposition Design Model   328

● **Activities and Projects for Your Classroom:** Planets   329

Planning   330
Transforming and Translating   330
Collecting Information 330

● **Spotlight on Assessment** Evaluating Projects   331

Generating Knowledge 335
Evaluating and Revising   335

● **Focus:** Experimenting with Different Structures and Linking Systems   336

● **Focus:** Alternative: A Filmmaking Model   337

The Teacher's Role in the Design Process   338
Works of Mind   338
Apprenticeship Method   339
Project Quality   340
Student Projects, Standards, and Restructuring   340
Student Projects on the Web   342
Basic Features and Skills   343
Alternative Ways to Construct Web Pages   345
Word Processing Programs 346   Web Authoring Software for Students 346

● **Emerging Technology:** Blogs and Blogging   347

General-Purpose Web Authoring Software 349
Design Tips for Web Pages   349
Navigation System 350   Page Layout 350   Use of Graphics and Video 351
Text Presentation 352
Learning through Design: The Canada Project   353
Overview and Project Goals 353   Project Specifics 354   Evaluation and Outcomes 357
Summary   358
Reflecting on Chapter 9   359
Activities   359
Key Terms   360
Resources to Expand Your Knowledge Base   360

PART THREE   LOOKING AT ISSUES FOR THE PRESENT AND FUTURE   363

Chapter 10   Responsible Use of Technology   365

Orientation   365
Equity of Educational Opportunity   365
  Equity and SES   366
  Educational Testing Service (ETS) Mathematics Study 369   Role of Educators'
  Perceptions 370   Equity and the Classroom Teacher 371
  Equity and Gender   371

  ● **Focus:** The E-rate as a Solution for Disadvantaged Schools   373

  Equity and Student Ability   375
  Adapting Technology for Equal Access   375
  Adaptations for Mobility Impairments 376   Adaptations for Visual
  Impairments 376   Adaptive Web Page Design 376

  ● **Emerging Technology:** Adaptations for Visually Impaired
  Web Users   378

Copyright Law and Respect for Intellectual Property   378
  Education and Copyright: Issues and Problems   378
  Copyright Law 380   Establishing a Copyright 380   Rights, Licenses, and
  Permissions 381   Copying Computer Software 382   Fair Use 382

  ● **Focus:** Obtaining Permission to Copy   388

  Using Student Work on Web Sites   389
  Rules of Thumb: Suggested Answers for the Copyright Questions   389
Protecting Students from Inappropriate Material and Experiences   390
  Potential Dangers and Reasonable Protection   390

  ● **Focus:** Digital Cheating   391

  Balancing Freedom and Protection 392
  Safe Areas of the Internet   393
  Filtering   394
  Firewall 394   Stand-Alone Filtering Software 394
  Safety Guidelines, Acceptable-Use Policies, and Supervision   396
  Safety Guidelines 396   Acceptable-Use Policies 396   Supervision 397

  ● **Focus:** Rules for the Safe and Appropriate Use of the Internet   398

Summary   399
Reflecting on Chapter 10   399
  Activities   399
  Key Terms   400
  Resources to Expand Your Knowledge Base   400

Glossary   403
References   410
Index   421

Preface

· · ·

Sophisticated technology has become so pervasive and intertwined with many aspects of our private and professional lives that we seldom notice it. We download our music from the Internet into pocket-size devices with enough capacity to let us listen to our music collection all week without having to hear any song twice. We chat online with friends in distant locations at no cost and read blogs. ATM machines, fax machines, cellular phones, caller ID, voice mail, personal satellite dishes, video games, DVD movies, digital cameras, and camcorders—the list of technology innovations we have accepted as commonplace goes on and on.

Technology in Classrooms

We wrote this book because technology seldom plays the same natural role in classrooms that it does in other areas of our daily lives. Prominent commentators on education and technology (for instance, Cuban, 2001; Oppenheimer, 2003) continue to demonstrate that the resources already available in many K–12 classrooms are often severely underutilized. Many new and experienced teachers simply are not ready to take advantage of the resources already available in most K–12 classrooms. We realize that some teachers are uncertain and anxious about computer hardware, software selection, and which technology-supported learning activities are likely to be useful and productive for their students. If you feel that way, we hope the information and suggestions we provide in this book will move you from apprehension to excitement.

This Text's Priorities and Goals

The title of this book is intended to clearly state our commitment to some specific priorities. First, our emphasis is on *integrating technology*. We want to prepare you to use technology as a powerful tool in helping your students acquire the knowledge and skills of the content area or areas you will teach. If you end up feeling more focused on how to use computers, video cameras, and the Internet rather than how to use technology resources to teach reading, mathematics, history, biology, or your specific content area, we have somehow failed to get our most basic message across. Second, our emphasis is on *meaningful (student) learning.* We focus primarily on what students can accomplish with technology and argue that some experiences are probably more valuable than others. We do not ignore your own technology skills, but we emphasize preparing you to provide effective learning experiences to students.

This book is both about technology and about teaching and learning. We feel it is important to consider and discuss both areas together. Our primary goals are to:

· Present the different roles technology might play in your classroom
· Provide specific examples of each type of role
· Inform you of the necessary technical ins and outs of some applications you might use in implementing each role
· Describe typical student experiences and information sources that may change expectations of educational institutions and of the skills students need
· Link proposed classroom uses of technology with content area and technology standards
· Suggest how teachers might initiate and guide particular technology-supported learning activities in classrooms
· Promote critical thinking and reflection about the best uses of technology

As you think about this information, we hope that you also will consider why you and your future students should spend time using technology in the ways we propose. As a teacher, you function in the important role of decision maker. The discussion of classroom learning and how learning is influenced by classroom tasks and activities should help you make decisions about whether you want to devote precious school time to a specific use of technology.

We also hope that as you read this book, you will not assume that school experiences as you know them must remain fixed, with technology somehow finding a way to fit within the existing framework. Some educational leaders are urging both a restructuring of schools and a serious consideration of what schools do. *Technology is functioning as a catalyst* in some of these considerations, and it may serve the same role for you. As you think about how to use technology in your classroom, you will likely find yourself examining broad educational issues. We do not attempt to avoid criticisms of technology. Just remember: In most cases, effective teaching with technology is effective teaching by any means. Criticisms of the way technology has been used also may alert you to more traditional practices that should also be examined. For example, if many experts put down an overemphasis on drill-and-practice computer software, what do you think these same experts would say if asked to address the heavy use of traditional worksheets? We want you to think carefully about teaching and learning with and without technology.

The Cognitive Perspective on Learning

Our intent is to emphasize technology-facilitated classroom activities in an active learning environment—one that strongly engages the thinking, decision-making, problem-solving, and reasoning behaviors of students. We use the term *cognitive* to refer to these behaviors. To implement effective classroom activities, it is critical that teachers understand the connection between learning tasks and the mental activities of students.

Chapter 2, "Meaningful Learning in an Information Age," establishes the foundation for this connection. Chapter 2 focuses on developing your understanding of cognitive behaviors and explains how cognitive behaviors are influenced by learning tasks. Chapter 2 also includes a special emphasis on what are often called higher-level thinking skills—decision making, problem solving, and reasoning. Because we feel that effective education requires learners to go beyond reception of information to cognitive skills involving judgment, interpretation, and application, we offer some general suggestions regarding the types of experiences that promote the development of such skills. We continue to emphasize this connection between learning and meaningful learning activities in nearly every chapter.

Several of the later chapters focus on computer tools that allow students to create multimedia projects. These chapters culminate in Chapter 9, "Learning from Student Projects: Knowledge as Design and the Design of Hypermedia." Chapter 9 integrates several important topics—technology tools, cooperative learning, and learning from the construction of authentic content-area projects. The projects discussed in Chapter 9 and throughout the book represent practical examples of classroom tasks that encourage meaningful learning.

An Approach Anchored in Everyday Classroom Life

We want to assure you that what we propose is practical for you to implement. Our strategy for doing this is to rely primarily on our own experiences within our local school district. We decided that it would be unfair for us to piece together a picture of computer and Internet use originating in grant-subsidized schools, high-tech demonstration sites, or what we have gleaned about the latest and greatest applications from the conferences we attend and the journals we read. Yes, the theory, research, and general instructional strategies we describe in this book draw on contributions from a wide range of educational researchers, policy advocates, and demonstration sites. In contrast, however, most of the classroom examples we include come from teachers we know personally.

A few comments about our own backgrounds may provide a context for what we emphasize. The topics and theoretical perspective of this book result from a blend of the orientations, experiences, and individual interests of the two authors.

Mark Grabe's background is in educational psychology—he is a professor in the Psychology Department and the Instructional Design and Technology program at the University of North Dakota. He brings to this collaboration the theoretical perspectives and research experiences more typical of a university faculty member. Mark has been developing instructional software for approximately twenty years in support of his own research activities. Originally trained to teach high-school biology, he continues to pursue his interest in science education. Some of his first Internet activities involved designing instructional websites to promote the outdoor educational programs of the North Dakota Department of Game and Fish. This work, which you will catch glimpses of throughout this book, has encouraged an interest in hands-on science and the role technology might play in it.

Cindy Grabe's original certification was as an elementary-school teacher; she later earned a master's degree as a learning disability specialist. After she had worked for many years as a reading specialist, her interest and experience in the use of technology in instruction led her to a full-time technology position with the Grand Forks school district. She has been a technology facilitator, a position that in some districts may be described as a computer coordinator, for twelve years. Her position requires that she provide training to district teachers, administrators, and staff members; collaborate on curriculum projects; and conduct demonstration activities with students. She is involved in providing continuing educational experiences for teachers in area schools, and she teaches courses for undergraduate preservice teachers at the University of North Dakota. Recently half of her K–12 contract has been acquired by the university so that she can assist teacher educators with incorporating technology into their classes. Cindy deals directly and continuously with the very practical issues of integrating technology in classrooms. Her own work with students and her associations with many gifted classroom teachers are responsible for most of the classroom examples we provide in this book. Cindy has been recognized as an Apple Distinguished Educator by the Apple Computer Corporation.

Features of the Revision

The first edition of *Integrating Technology for Meaningful Learning* appeared in 1996—and here we are, a little over ten years later, introducing the fifth edition. The rapid transitions between editions have been a necessary consequence of the rapid pace of development and change in technology and some new possibilities for how technology can be applied in classrooms. What has pleased us as we have worked on the various editions has been just how well our original priorities have held up. If anything, themes such as (1) the integration of technology in content-area instruction, (2) authentic technology-supported student projects, and (3) the use of technology to support a more cognitively active approach to learning have become more widely accepted and promoted.

Key Themes

Internet Applications

As we moved from one edition to the next, the growing prominence of the Internet in modern life and the potential of the Internet for education have simply required that we increase our emphasis on Internet tools and classroom applications and pay attention to what students do, and unfortunately what some students are unable to do, using the Internet outside of school. As school and home access have become more ubiquitous and faster connection speeds allow greater amounts of digital material to be transferred, new topics such as the rise of virtual high schools and videoconferencing require attention. Beginning with the fourth edition, two chapters were specifically devoted to learning from the Internet (Chapter 5, "The Internet as a Tool for Communication," and Chapter 6, "The Internet as a Tool for Inquiry"). The Internet is discussed in several other chapters as well. Web page authoring is considered as an outlet for student projects in Chapter 9, and Chapter 10 ("Responsible Use of Technology") contains an extended description of methods for providing safe access to Internet resources, a discussion of copyright issues relevant to using and creating web resources as learning activities, and an analysis of equity issues associated with Internet use both in and outside of schools. This edition adds a discussion of the TEACH Act—new legislation allowing "fair use" activities in distance education.

Reform, Standards, and Legislated Expectations

We continue to explore the connection between technology and educational reform, within the context of increasing emphasis on standards and what might best be described as legislated expectations (such as No Child Left Behind). Although the basic goals of educational reform (Chapter 1) do not require computers or other forms of technology, many connections have emerged. Teachers who make greater use of constructivist teaching methods also make greater use of technology (Chapter 2). Technology tools provide many opportunities for engaging students in learning tasks that allow for collaborative work, authentic student-centered exploration, and performance-based assessment.

We emphasize current national standards for both content learning and technology as these standards have been developed for K–12 students and for those who teach these students. Included in this edition are the new guidelines outlined in the National Technology Plan (Chapters 1 and 2).

As we have written about various expectations that might guide educational practice, we have become interested in the concept of *alignment*. At the most general level, alignment refers to the degree of consistency that exists among components of a model. For example, a simple model might assume that standards guide both the instructional activities selected for the classroom and the topics and skills to be evaluated as indicators of learning. One might also assume that the theoretical positions developed by researchers to explain learning and applied performance would be logically connected to standards, instructional activities, and the emphases present in evaluations. Our nation seems to be engaged in a politically charged debate concerning the effectiveness of education, and in order to distance ourselves a bit from the emotion of this debate, we have found it useful to describe certain points of controversy as the consequence of less than complete alignment.

For example, many complaints about standardized testing might be described as a consequence of the focus of such tests on a subset of the knowledge and skills advocated in standards or in theoretical models of meaningful learning. Because of the pressure exerted by the consequences of performance on such tests, some are concerned that teachers will more closely align classroom experiences with the areas emphasized in such tests than with standards or models of meaningful learning. These are not simple issues, and we try to encourage a more detailed analysis based on the extent or degree of alignment. Coverage relating to standards throughout the text is called out with an icon like the one in the margin at the beginning of this section.

Efficient Use of Technology

The importance of efficiency is another of those ideas that has emerged as we have written over the years about the classroom use of technology. Teachers work under time pressure in complex environments. Given such constraints, the efficiency of an activity seems to influence whether it will be attempted and retained. Improvements in efficiency can be created in a wide variety of ways. The movement from labs of computers to Internet-capable computers in classrooms is one improvement in efficiency. Convenient and spontaneous classroom access seems to be associated with more frequent use of technology. However, in certain situations, involving an entire class in a lab setting may be more efficient than rotating an entire class of students through a small number of workstations in a classroom. In many schools, the combination of wireless Internet access and a portable cabinet containing several laptop computers has become the practical compromise. Assignments that expect students to use technology outside of class save class time but are problematic if a substantial number of students do not have the skills necessary to function independently or do not have access to technology at home or at other times during the school day. We provide statistics describing access issues throughout the book and also address the variability in general technology skills that may result from the resources available to students in the home (Chapter 10).

Our emphasis on the use of technology tools (Chapters 5–9) in content-area projects must constantly involve a consideration of efficiency. Is it worth the time required to learn to use a technology tool (such as digital probes or a multimedia authoring tool) in order to explore a specific topic (such as water quality) or improve a competency (such as literacy)? The time to learn how to use the tool may reduce efficiency, but tools that motivate students may increase their investment and improve efficiency. Technology tools that are easy to learn may be preferred to tools that involve a steeper learning curve. Tools that can be used for many projects may be preferred to tools that have few applications. Tools that engage students in the application of many skills may be preferred to tools that exercise a single skill. We encourage you to consider some of these issues as you read about and hopefully have the opportunity to work with the software we describe in the following chapters.

New Information

Statistics and Research

All chapters include more current descriptive statistics to provide a realistic picture of what resources are available in schools and how teachers are using these resources with students. In addition, all chapters include more recent references to the professional literature and new examples of hardware, software, and instructional activities. We include new classroom examples to illustrate what these resources and activities look like in practice.

Coverage of National Standards and Guidelines

In conjunction with our discussions of educational reform, we emphasize current national standards for both content learning and technology. The National Technology Plan, released since the last edition of this book, outlines action steps intended to position technology to more effectively impact student achievement.

Equity Issues

What has become known as the *digital divide* has emerged as a prominent political issue since the publication of early editions of this book. Our discussion of equity reflects new data and new concerns. Chapter 10 considers how and why gender, socioeconomic status, aptitude, and physical or learning disabilities may influence opportunities to learn with technology.

Coverage of Widely Used Applications

To make this book as useful as possible for classroom teachers, we concentrate on software and applications that are commonly available and, in most cases, relatively inexpensive. As time passes, it is necessary to adjust the specific examples we use. Sometimes superior products emerge. In other cases, a company may go out of business or discontinue a product we had once recommended. (Developing and continually upgrading software designed specifically for the education market is a tough business.) For instance, we now feature the multimedia authoring products eZediaMX and eZediaQTI in the chapters emphasizing student multimedia authoring (Chapters 7, 8, and 9). Coincidentally, during the time this book was being written, the small Canadian company that had developed these products was sold and became a division of SAFARI Video Networks. We hope this change will increase the probability that these products will be widely utilized during the run of this edition.

Learning Features of the Text

Throughout the book you will find special features designed to help you better understand important concepts and use them in your own classroom.

Scenes from Real Classrooms

Descriptions of actual classroom events can provide a powerful way to "see" in action many of the ideas we present. Stories of classroom events and descriptions of actual student projects are embedded in many chapters as demonstrations of teacher or student behavior.

Screen Images and Program Examples

The graphics in this book are mostly images captured as they appear on the computer screen. You may not always have immediate access to the computer tools or the Internet resources we describe, so these images are a convenient way to help you understand what the text explains. Visual examples are one of the best ways to explain topics such as web page design and to present samples from student projects.

Special Features: "Focus," "Spotlight on Assessment," "Keeping Current," and "Emerging Technology"

These highlight boxes allow us the freedom to break away from the main thrust of a presentation and consider a topic in more detail. The topic might involve an extended discussion of an important issue or theory, a suggestion for how a teacher might evaluate a student project, or the description of a new type of application that has promise for classroom use. Setting these discussions apart allows you to consider the topics independently from the main discussion.

Activities and Projects for Your Classroom

We include a large number of application ideas in this book, but we also recognize that teachers work in many disciplines with students of different ages. The features called "Activities and Projects for Your Classroom" allow us to list variations of applications that might be more discipline- or age-specific. The combination of the extended examples and the variations provided within the activity features is a reasonable way to acquaint you with classroom applications.

New Houghton Mifflin Video Case Marginal Features

As we describe later in the preface, this edition includes the integration of Houghton Mifflin Video Cases to illustrate key topics in the text. More than fifteen Video Cases appear on the textbook website that accompanies the text, and they are correlated to the text by a marginal boxed feature and questions for reflection.

End-of-Chapter Activities

Following the text of each chapter, we include several activities we suggest you try. These activities are our attempt to get you to think more actively about important issues presented in the chapters or to try out an application we have described. We have attempted to generate activities that can be accomplished with and without direct access to computer resources, so you should be able to complete at least some of the brief tasks no matter what your circumstances. It would clearly be inconsistent for us to suggest that you can learn meaningfully using only a textbook. We trust that this book will not be the only resource at your disposal and that you will also learn a great deal from teachers and colleagues.

Accompanying Teaching and Learning Resources

As we mentioned earlier, we are making a serious attempt to offer you more than a book. We hope to continue writing textbooks into the future because we feel that traditional books are the most effective way to accomplish certain goals. However, we believe that authors and publishing companies can now use electronic resources, including the Internet, to offer additional experiences that go far beyond ordinary textbook supplements.

Web Resources

Your purchase of this book entitles you to access two websites. The first site, the official online resource for this book, is maintained by Houghton Mifflin Company. You can access it by directing your web browser to **http://education.college.hmco.com/students** and then selecting the specific site for this text. The resources available at this site include:

- Chapter summaries updated to ensure accuracy.
- Direct links to external online resources mentioned in the book, plus a searchable database of web links, which are updated much more frequently than the printed book can be revised.
- ACE self-testing quizzes for each chapter.
- Additional examples of student projects, extending those provided in the book. Some of these include short video segments.
- Numerous essays on special topics, offering self-contained discussions of issues not included in the book.
- New to this edition: Houghton Mifflin Video Cases, which are accessible on the textbook website and correlated to the text by marginal boxed features. Each video case is a four- to six-minute video module that presents actual classroom scenarios depicting the complex problems and opportunities teachers face in the classroom every day. HM Video Cases are accompanied by teacher interviews, classroom artifacts, and reflective viewing questions. Instructors have their own section of the textbook site, where they can access all of the student resources as well as PowerPoint slides and other instructional aids.

 Throughout the book, you will see a marginal icon indicating that material relevant to the topic under discussion can be found on the Houghton Mifflin website. These icons only hint at the resources available, however; there are many features of the website that you will learn about only by exploring the site itself.

You are also welcome to access a second website maintained by the authors (**http://ndwild.psych.und.nodak.edu/book/**). We use our own site to:

- Develop resources that will eventually appear on the Houghton Mifflin site
- Experiment with new ideas, formats, and tools
- Provide examples of products and services characteristic of the Internet technology available in a typical K–12 school

We encourage you to explore the resources provided at both sites and use whatever is best suited to your needs.

WebCT® and Blackboard® Cartridges

Support for online courses is available via platform-ready WebCT and Blackboard cartridges.

Acknowledgments

We owe many individuals our gratitude for helping us bring this book to you. Some years ago, Loretta Wolozin, senior sponsoring editor at Houghton Mifflin, saw in our original proposal the germ of a unique idea and made the trip to North Dakota to talk with us and examine student projects. Putting students in control of powerful tools was not typical, and yet Loretta supported our belief that this theme should be at the core of what teachers learn about the classroom applications of technology. When Loretta retired from Houghton Mifflin, she was replaced by Sue Pulvermacher-Alt, who has continued to encourage and support our approach.

We were assisted in preparing this edition by the guidance of developmental editor Janet Young. We acknowledge that we can be opinionated and stubborn. We respect Janet's gentleness in coping with these personality characteristics and also her guidance in improving the clarity of the information we present. We hope you will find our arguments and explanations clear and our style friendly. Margaret Bridges, the project editor, was responsible for the tedious tasks associated with page and chapter layout, matching hundreds of citations and references, and polishing our prose. Lisa Mafrici, senior development editor, has worked with us now for several years. She helped organize our efforts and kept us focused on deadlines and our revision goals. We would also like to thank the reviewers whose insightful reviews and feedback informed the development of this edition: Marlene A. Bumgarner, Gavilan College; Michael Corry, George Washington University; Harvey C. Foyle, Emporia State University; Frederick B. King, University of Hartford; Sharon Tettegah, University of Illinois, Urbana-Champaign. No book really results from the work of the authors alone, and this book is no exception.

Finally, we owe a giant debt to the many teachers and students who provided the authentic examples we have included. The quality and creativity of the products and the enthusiasm of the individuals who created them impressed us. We hope these examples will inspire your own work, too.

A Final Word

It is not always possible to determine where ideas originate, but we know exactly how we began working with student-authored multimedia. Nearly twelve years ago we were preparing for a workshop in which Cindy planned to introduce KidPix to a group of teachers. The teachers were involved in the decision-making process to select what equipment and software the district would purchase, and we were attempting to develop a convincing argument for the value of tool applications and student-authored multimedia. We were just learning KidPix ourselves and were searching for something that would get the teachers excited. Our youngest daughter, Kim (then in first grade, now in college), had been studying dinosaurs, so we scanned a picture of a dinosaur. We asked Kim to use KidPix to color the picture and then record a song she had learned about dinosaurs. We were pleased with the result and decided to use the product as part of our presentation.

As we continued to work on other parts of the workshop, Kim remained at the computer, singing the dinosaur song over and over. It turned out she was singing as she typed in the lyrics. At the time, it was her persistence and innovation in going beyond our initial request that impressed us. We have since had similar experiences with many learners. We saved Kim's picture and still listen to her song from time to time. Because we have thanked many people in this preface, we should also thank Kim, who is owed some recognition simply for being so tolerant of the work habits of her parents. Her own creative talents and her enthusiasm for learning have served to inspire us for quite a few years. We know students enjoy working in the ways we describe partly because we have had the opportunity to watch and work with them.

my name is stagasurus i'm a funny looking disasaur
for on my back are meny boney platse and
on my tail there,s more

Kim's original multimedia project (converted to grayscale)

A Teaching and Learning Framework for Integrating Technology in Classrooms

• • •

PART ONE introduces you to the roles that technology now plays in education and the roles it is likely to play in the future. The opening chapters present this text's major themes: the "tools approach," activity-based approaches to learning and related performance-based assessment techniques, active roles for students, integrated or multi-disciplinary approaches to learning, cooperative learning, and the role of teachers as facilitators. These chapters also explore some major ideas about meaningful learning and show how technology fits among these ideas.

I Key Themes and Issues for Using Technology in Your Classroom

• • •

In new fields of study, there should always be opportunities to demonstrate vision and encourage optimism and to dream about, imagine, and even predict the future. Thinking about the future is important for educators. And preparing students for that future requires some consideration of the skills that students will need and the rapidly evolving role of technology in educational practice.

In this chapter we introduce you to the key themes that are emphasized throughout this book. We discuss how technology is currently used in classrooms and how it might be used more effectively in the future. We explore the kinds of changes that will need to take place for teachers to make the best use of technology, and we tie this discussion to the much-debated topics of school reform and national standards.

As an educator, you participate daily in shaping the current era of dramatic change. We hope to convey some of the excitement we ourselves feel about the changes in teaching and learning and the role that technology can play. We begin with three examples of classroom projects that highlight some of the themes and applications that figure prominently in this book. As you read, look for answers to the following questions:

Focus Questions

- How is technology use related to school reform?
- How do national educational standards apply to technology, and how do they get translated into classroom practice?
- What are the characteristics of activity-based approaches to learning, and how does technology support these approaches?
- What experiences are influential in preparing future teachers to make use of technology in their classrooms?

Uses of Technology: An Introduction to Key Themes

Throughout this book you will encounter extended descriptions of classroom activities intended to get you thinking about how technology-supported activities can engage students in meaningful learning. In this initial chapter, rather than provide a K–12 scenario, we offer several examples from college courses that relate more immediately to your own experiences as a learner. Perhaps by thinking about how you might learn with technology, you can begin to see how similar activities using technology could benefit the students you will eventually teach.

Over the past several years we have had the opportunity through our university to participate in several projects intended to prepare future teachers to eventually use technology with their own students. We draw on these experiences to provide you with three examples of the uses of technology. We purposely selected these examples because the content of the courses described is not about technology in education. Still, we believe the experiences provided in these courses will influence how these teacher candidates will eventually teach. It seems reasonable that teachers will be more likely to help their students learn with technology if the teachers can draw on their own experiences in learning with technology.

Although higher education faculty members and college students are becoming more and more invested in using technology for "productivity purposes," technology has not been heavily "infused" in the activities of teaching and learning. The examples we provide describe efforts to involve college students in learning with technology. As you read the descriptions, we encourage you to both reflect on your own personal learning experiences and attempt to make connections to content-area courses in K–12 settings.

Physics: Probes and Projects

● ● ●

Larry Watson begins the syllabus for Physics 130 with this statement:

> This course is designed to give you the opportunity to develop for yourself the ideas that model the world. You need not trust what people tell you about science—in fact, it is dangerous to do so. Here you will develop skills that allow you to decide whether or not a model is acceptable. . . . I can only give you the chance to do this—you must participate fully in the "tutorials" and class activities to be successful. Participation means listening to your group members, comparing your ideas to observations, being willing to abandon your ideas if they come into conflict with observation, and writing it all down. I cannot stress this last item too strongly since I will always ask you to "explain your reasoning."

Larry describes the content of his introductory physics course as the study of Newton's laws of motions and of current and potential in circuits using batteries and bulbs. As the brief segment from the course syllabus suggests, the approach is heavily experiential. There is no textbook. Tutorials play an essential role. In a tutorial, students explore the concepts of force and motion or current and potential with basic equipment. Simple tasks are used to produce observable results that confront common student misconceptions. If what students observe seems counterintuitive, the students are challenged to reconcile their personal beliefs about the physical world with their actual observations in the lab. Lab experiences are considered essential.

Several laptop computers and data acquisition probes are available in the lab. The probes, in combination with the data acquisition, storage, and visualization software operating on the computers, offer students several advantages. Students can observe the relationships between key variables (such as acceleration and force) in real time. Large amounts of data can be stored and represented graphically for immediate consideration. Precise measurements are recorded so that students can check the values using formulas describing physical concepts. In general, the equipment allows the students greater flexibility in asking questions they want to ask because there is often a practical, efficient, and accurate way to gather data that might provide answers.

Access to the computers and probes encouraged Larry to add a new experience to his course. Students were organized into teams and challenged to design an experiment that qualitatively and quantitatively demonstrates how physics concepts work in the real world. The project was presented to students as a curriculum development assignment: Students were asked to imagine they were creating a lab task for a high school physics class. The students had to propose a task, identify the theoretical principles that might be involved, define key variables, identify possible misconceptions, describe the equipment setup in detail, and provide sample data. Generating a novel experiment complete with rationale is challenging, and students worked over several lab sessions to create a task that was both unique and informative.

One team of students proposed a task involving an analysis of the changes in energy when a pendulum bounces against a fixed object (see Figure 1.1). The pendulum consists of a length of string attached to a small ball. Potential energy and kinetic energy are interrelated during the cycle of a pendulum. In this case, energy is first added to the system by raising the ball (potential energy = mass of ball x gravity strength x height of ball). When the ball is released, potential energy begins to be converted to kinetic energy (kinetic energy = 1/2 mass of the object x velocity squared). Some of the values for variables in these equations can be obtained by measurement (mass and height of ball). The strength of gravity is a known value. Velocity would be difficult for students to measure without the computer and an appropriate probe.

As the pendulum swings, the ball strikes a force probe (fixed object) positioned at the bottom of the arc of the pendulum. Some energy is lost in deforming the ball and in vibration, but most is returned as the ball rebounds and the pendulum swings upward again. The force probe measures the force with which it has been struck by the ball and sends this information to the computer. Simultaneously, a motion detector gathers data about

FIGURE 1.1

Students' Pendulum
Project: Real-Time Graphs
of Velocity, Acceleration,
and Force, along with
Diagram of Equipment
Setup

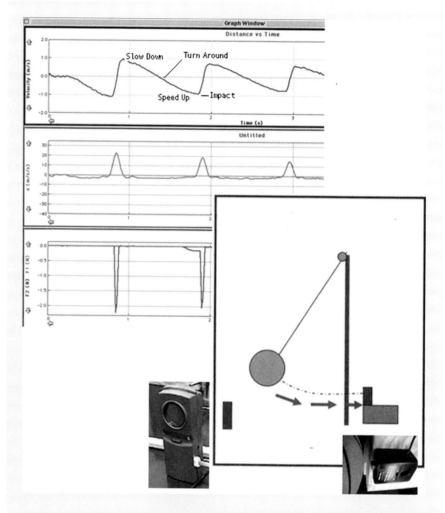

the speed and direction of the ball. The computer software allows data on velocity, acceleration, and force to be linked and studied over time. Specific values can be obtained and used in calculations. Data can be graphed in real time and studied to assist conceptual understanding.

In Figure 1.1, the top panel presents velocity, the middle panel acceleration, and the bottom panel force. If you examine the figure, you can follow the first two passes of the pendulum and see the corresponding decline in the velocity of the pendulum (top panel) and the force with which the ball strikes the force probe (negative spikes shown in bottom panel) as energy is lost from the system. The velocity panel has been labeled to indicate the point at which the ball strikes the force probe and the point at which the pendulum reaches maximum height and begins to fall again. In the graph, velocity is differentiated as positive or negative depending on whether the ball is moving toward or away from the motion probe. When the value for acceleration equals 0, the pendulum has just reversed direction and is closest to the motion probe.

Figure 1.1 also includes the diagram developed by the student team to explain how the apparatus for the experiment is to be arranged. The intended positions of the motion and force probes relative to the pendulum are marked by small rectangles. Adjacent in this diagram are small images of the actual motion and force probes.

Larry bases the grade for each team's project on the creativity of the task and the quality of the description of the procedure and underlying principles of physics. Students must submit and analyze one sample data set and also explain the task in conceptual terms. Although there is a group grade for each project, individual contributions and understanding are assessed along the way to determine if all team members will receive the same grade. Consistent with the philosophy presented in the course syllabus, students must be able to explain the physical phenomenon they now have a new method for describing.

Knowing Nature: Technology as a Tool for the Personal Journey of Learning

• • •

Dr. Glinda Crawford teaches a sociology course entitled "Knowing Nature." She describes the course as involving students in eco-psychology, eco-spirituality, native studies, and bioregionalism. Learners delve into a rich blend of field biology and explore the human experience as part of nature. It is a course for discovering personal connections with the prairie of the upper Midwest and, to some extent, for encouraging activism.

As you might anticipate, Glinda does not feel her goals for "Knowing Nature" can be met by focusing the learner on a single textbook or on lectures. The course has always had a prominent experiential component that involves students in both shared and personal field experiences. For example, students attend a Native American powwow, and they observe the return or temporary visit of birds during the spring migration. Students also explore a place they have personally selected. It might be the family farm, the area around a summer cabin, or a local ecosystem.

Some of the instructional techniques in "Knowing Nature" are unique. After being exposed to the writing of a variety of authors and scientists, students discuss their reading and their personal reactions using an ancient technique that Glinda calls the "council process" or "talking circle." Students sit in a circle that may have an object as a center focal point. Someone offers an initial statement or comment, and the discussion then moves around the circle. Glinda intervenes at intervals to identify the themes that seem to be emerging.

Glinda uses the metaphor of a "personal journey" in describing her teaching methods and her beliefs about how learning occurs. Life is a personal journey. Each individual follows a path that provides different experiences. Meaning making occurs within the context of this personal journey and is

FIGURE 1.2

Webpage Describing the
Prairie Onion by
Stephanie Nelson

shaped by the unique path each individual follows. Consequently what is valued as a learning experience may vary with the individual. Yet, by sharing stories, we can provide insight into our personal meaning making and offer experiences others can integrate into their own journeys.

What does technology have to offer learners in such a course? Glinda admits that at first she could not see a connection with technology, and she certainly did not want students to use technology as a replacement for field experiences. The technological connection came as an opportunity for students to play a role in the development of a small prairie habitat area on the University of North Dakota central campus. The habitat is named the Soaring Eagle Prairie for the large metal sculpture serving as the site's focal point.

Students in Glinda's class develop a website that focuses on the campus project and also explores the prairie habitat and the topic of prairie preservation and restoration more generally. As a contribution to the website, each student selects a particular prairie grass or flower and uses web authoring software to prepare several webpages presenting images and information about the plant. Students explore their plants from a variety of perspectives. They become familiar with scientific information about the plants and procedures for introducing the plants to a new location. They explore what is called ethnobotany—how people of a particular culture use a plant for food, clothing, shelter, medicine, or in religious ceremonies. In all of this research, the students use both printed and online sources. Students also explain their reasons for selecting their plants. Figure 1.2 provides an example from the project.

Images are an important part of webpages. Unfortunately, because the spring in North Dakota arrives late, students have no opportunity to take their own photographs. To supplement their webpages, students have to collect existing images from the Internet. In doing so, students are required to obtain permission from the photographer responsible for each image. The request for permission sometimes sets off an extended series of e-mail messages between the student and photographer.

What is the educational value of such website development? One of Glinda's students observed that when you write a paper as a class project, it is unlikely that anyone but the teacher will ever read it. The website, in contrast, is an opportunity to be part of something larger and long-term. The student felt as though she was making a real contribution to something.

E-portfolios: Reflection and Evaluation in the Middle-School Methods Class

• • •

Gail Ingwalson is responsible for the "Middle-School Curriculum and Methods" course. This time-intensive course (five semester credits) provides future teachers with both university-based and field-based experiences and focuses on strategies for teaching in the middle-school environment. Students in the course are organized into multidisciplinary teams, and each team of future teachers is linked with a team of teachers in an area middle school. The course takes a hands-on approach, with a good deal of individual and group time devoted to the development, implementation, and evaluation of instructional resources (for example, lesson plans, instructional materials). Students, within their multidisciplinary group, also have an opportunity to implement an instructional unit in a middle-school classroom.

The progress that these students are making toward becoming teachers is evaluated through a series of portfolio reviews and based on the INTASC (Interstate New Teacher Assessment and Support Consortium, 1992) standards. Students complete the first review after their introductory course, the second review after completing the remaining coursework required before student teaching, and the final review after student teaching. The portfolio presented at each review consists of items intended to demonstrate progress toward mastery of the ten standards. In addition to the items selected, students must provide a rationale for picking the item, a personal reflection associated with the development or use of the item, and a self-assessment

FIGURE 1.3
LiveText Screen Images:
Student-Created Lesson
with Associated ISTE
Standards (as displayed
when working within the
College LiveText edu
solutions™ online
environment)

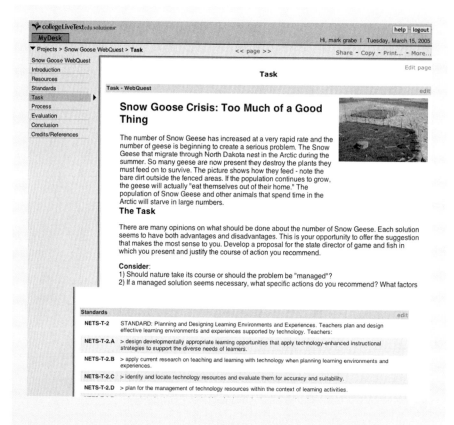

associated with the item. During each review, the student "defends" this portfolio to a panel that asks "portfolio" questions and evaluates the student's responses and work using a rubric. The portfolio review process is independent of any evaluations conducted as a component of individual courses but typically is based on artifacts taken from courses.

At the second portfolio review, students are required to provide two artifacts that demonstrate progress toward each of the ten INTASC standards. The middle-school methods course typically requires the generation of activities and materials that students often use as artifacts in making their case.

As part of a new college technology plan, the college has made a commitment to move toward **electronic portfolios.** This commitment has been implemented gradually in order to ease the burden on the faculty and to allow unanticipated issues to be evaluated as they arise. The middle-school methods course was identified as a "test case" because Gail was willing to confront the unknown technical challenges associated with implementing electronic portfolios and because her course generated many artifacts that students submitted for portfolio review.

Electronic portfolios can be implemented in many ways. Portfolios can be developed using commonly available technology tools (for example, a student can use PowerPoint to organize a collection of word processing documents and short videos). Portfolios can also be developed using online services provided by commercial vendors. The college has committed to using

LiveText, an online service for which students pay a one-time fee for five-year access. Gail claims this approach was selected because (1) students can store a large collection of personal artifacts and know that this collection has been backed up, (2) the service provides powerful online resources (such as a rubric builder and standards used in evaluating content-area preparation and pedagogical preparation) that can be linked to individual artifacts and used by both instructor and student, and (3) the system encourages a longitudinal approach to documenting the development of "emergent teachers." Gail can use the system to encourage students to reflect on course projects, to evaluate student performance on these projects, and to help students think about links among the various standards they must address. Students can select some of their artifacts and related documentation to be part of the portfolio review that precedes student teaching. The online system also has the capacity to make selected materials available to potential employers, although the process has not been in place long enough to be used in this way.

Figure 1.3 demonstrates how a future teacher might use the capabilities of the online portfolio system. In this case, a WebQuest (a technique for engaging students in a structured Internet search, which we discuss in the chapter entitled "The Internet as a Tool for Inquiry") is being proposed as the core task for a classroom project. The project is proposed to demonstrate the teacher's competence in meeting specific International Society for Technology in Education (ISTE) standards for teachers (the bottom of Figure 1.3 shows selected standards). The WebQuest was first created as a webpage and then uploaded into the online portfolio. The standards were selected from a list available on the online site. The template within which this information is organized includes placeholders for other categories of content, such as a project introduction and a proposed method for evaluating the project. Once the proposed project is completed, the student can share it with specifically designated individuals, such as a course instructor or a potential employer.

Themes of Technology Use in the Classroom

These examples illustrate many of the themes we emphasize in this book. Here are some of those themes. As you read these brief descriptions, focus on understanding how the descriptions relate to the examples you have just read.

Technology Integrated into Content-Area Instruction

What it means to integrate technology

In our first two examples, technology was used to explore course content. Whatever the students learned about how to operate the hardware and software systems was secondary to this focus. That is a major part of what we mean by *integrating* technology. Moreover, although the students certainly learned a great deal about technology during their projects, many of their skills associated with hardware and software manipulation could be applied to new content very efficiently.

Focus

Creative Tension: What Multiple Parties Want from Digital Portfolios

When our university was attempting to select a commercial vendor for the move to a digital portfolio system, we contacted Dr. Helen Barrett, an authority on digital portfolios, to determine if she was willing to offer comments on the strengths and weaknesses of the various commercial products being considered. Her reaction was not exactly what we had anticipated. She had some concerns regarding the entire category of applications, not so much for their specific capabilities but because of some of the applications that certain capabilities seem to encourage.

Barrett (2004) differentiates between assessment management systems and electronic portfolios. An electronic portfolio is a collection of artifacts, reflections, and artifact-related assessments assembled by an individual student. The assessment management system extends the more basic electronic portfolio by making use of database technology that allows student artifacts to be linked to other documents (standards, evaluation rubrics, learner reflections). For example, a student might add an artifact, such as a student-authored lesson plan, to the system. The student could then search standards (content area, technology, teacher skill) stored within the system and create links between the artifact and the specific standards the student feels the artifact satisfies. The student might create a document reflecting on her experience in presenting this lesson plan to classmates and link this document to the lesson plan. Finally, the instructor might call up a rubric, use this rubric to evaluate the student's work, and then link this evaluation to the lesson plan. The database-driven assessment management system can provide the capabilities described here to collections of students (for example, all students attending a university or all students taking a specific course) while also allowing the instructor or a program administrator to conveniently access information associated with several students.

An important capability of the database approach is the potential aggregation of various types of data across learners. For example, assume that an education college expects that in the process of acquiring a degree all teacher candidates acquire and be able to demonstrate certain skills in the use of presentation software, such as PowerPoint. The search and organization capabilities of a database system would allow an administrator to query the database to determine which students had or had not met this expectation and to review the evidence (for instance, a project evaluation stored in the system by an instructor) for any student who had attempted to satisfy the requirement.

What could possibly be wrong with a system that provides such convenience? Barrett's concern focuses on the potential consequences of mixing systems involving the personal reflection of future teachers on topics of personal challenge and the institutional need to document competence in specified areas. Shulman (1998) makes a related point in asking whether a portfolio should be about "self-promotion" or "growth" and suggests that self-promotion can become associated with evaluation problems such as the selection of atypical samples of behavior in a way that may misrepresent actual capabilities. Can a system used to argue your qualifications as a teacher also allow you to struggle to overcome self-identified weaknesses?

Concerns such as these are likely typical of many examples of change in long-standing ways of doing things. The issues raised can encourage practitioners to think carefully about goals and practices and seek solutions—a form of creative tension. For example, in defending "management systems," one might note that such systems include opportunities to "set permissions" controlling who can look at what. A teacher candidate might upload and store a document or artifact that can be viewed only by the student and the course instructor. After receiving feedback on a document and making revisions, the student might then set permissions making the revised document visible as evidence that the student has satisfied a specific standard.

As long as potential conflicts associated with the different purposes for creating a portfolio are recognized, it seems reasonable that safeguards can be implemented to isolate the multiple functions a portfolio might serve.

Notice, too, that the technology fits comfortably with the teachers' instructional plans and philosophies. Technology provided a natural extension of each teacher's approach, rather than an alternative or addition.

A Tools Approach

Applying technology to a learning task

Technology can play various instructional roles. A *tools approach* assumes that learners can flexibly apply general-purpose hardware or software—such as the data collection probes and web authoring software—to various topics and tasks. This approach can be contrasted with the use of software developed specifically to teach a particular topic. In a tools approach, students learn by applying the technology to a task rather than by being directly "instructed" by the technology.

An Active Role for Students

Students' constructive mental behavior

The word *active* as used here does not refer directly to the physical activity of the learner, as might be involved in manipulating laboratory equipment. Rather, *active* describes the mental behavior of the students. In the first two examples, the information to be learned was not presented to students in some kind of final, distilled form. Students had to dig for what they learned. They had to pull together bits and pieces of information from several sources, gather data, generate personal interpretations and summaries, and make decisions. Later in this chapter, we say more about the concept of active learning.

A Facilitative Role for the Teacher

Teachers assist students with challenging projects.

When students play a more active role in their own learning, the teacher's role shifts from "dispenser of knowledge" to "facilitator of learning." One assumption behind such a shift is that students accomplish learning, and the teacher's role is to consider how to assist the students. A second assumption is that academic work extends beyond the mere storage of information. In the first two examples described earlier, the instructors did not ladle out information for students to absorb; rather, Larry Watson and Glinda Crawford helped their students undertake challenging projects in which the students themselves gathered information and developed the concepts needed to complete the task.

An Integrated or Multidisciplinary Approach

Using a wide range of skills

It would be difficult to say that our first two sample projects fell within one content area and inappropriate to claim that they had a single objective. Certainly students acquired scientific knowledge; more important, they were involved as practitioners using the methods of science. They used technology tools to acquire information from the physical environment and the Internet, analyzed the data they gathered, and presented their conclusions. As they worked with technology tools, they developed their technology literacy. In working with the data they collected, Larry Watson's students had to use their mathematical skills. In developing multimedia webpages, Glinda Crawford's class made use of reading, writing, speaking, artistic expression, and library research skills.

Standards and Performance-Based Assessment

You are probably aware of the significance of educational standards. Content standards define what every student should know and be able to do. There are standards that define what college students interested in becoming teachers must learn to do (as in the example of Gail Ingwalson's class) and what literacy skills should be present in fourth-grade students. Evaluating mastery of some standards is challenging, especially when a standard focuses on applying a skill. This is when the use of performance-based assessment becomes critical. The digital portfolio system, classroom artifacts, and evaluation rubrics have made it possible to focus on evaluating a learner's ability to put knowledge into action.

Cooperative Learning

One charge that is consistently leveled against using technology in academia is that it isolates students from one another and from the teacher. Nothing could be further from the truth. Technology is a tool and has no inherent or required mode of application. The role of technology in education is always under the control of the teacher and is isolating only if teachers require that

Spotlight on Assessment

Relating Learning and Assessment

In practice, learning and assessment are being interrelated in complex ways. Assessment methods do more than provide information on the quantity and quality of learning. Student experiences with assessment methods carry over into new learning situations, and the types of assessment anticipated appear to influence how and what they learn.

You probably know this from your own experiences. Do you study differently when you are anticipating a multiple-choice examination than, say, an essay examination? Do you review information differently when intending to demonstrate your understanding through a paper in contrast to an examination? If you are a typical student, the way you think about course content is likely to be heavily influenced by how you think your learning will be assessed (Crooks, 1988). Some researchers have claimed that the quickest way to change how students learn is to change the way learning is assessed (Elton & Laurillard, 1979). Others believe that students are more influenced by the method of assessment than by classroom experiences and stated instructional goals (Snyder, 1971).

So what does the research on assessment and learning suggest that teachers should do? The answer, but not necessarily its implementation, is fairly simple: Teachers should think carefully about the knowledge and skills they would like students to develop and make certain that those are emphasized in the assessment process. The research suggests that although some learning outcomes may seem difficult to assess, it is very important that we strive nevertheless to find ways to assess them (Crooks, 1988).

As for the topics addressed in this book, one important implication is that, for optimal impact, some of the more unique learning activities we propose should be accompanied by assessment techniques sensitive to the assumed benefits of those activities. The potential benefits of project-based learning may be undermined if students are then asked to take a traditional test on the content covered by the project or, perhaps even worse, if teachers do not complete an assessment of student project performance because the teachers are unaware of how projects might be assessed.

We will return to the topic of assessment as we consider different types of learning goals and learning activities.

students work on projects or assignments alone. In some cases, independent work is appropriate, and in other cases, cooperative work is desirable.

Technology can enhance interaction among students.

As the first two of our sample projects illustrate, technology can enhance interaction. Students were collaborating *because* of the technology. Students in the physics course developed their lab tasks together and shared responsibility for planning, data collection, and communicating. Students in the sociology course contacted people who would not normally be part of the university community and had extended conversations that contributed to the learning experience. Blaming technology for isolating students or engaging them in passive activity is like blaming the No. 2 pencil for heavy reliance on worksheets.

Technology in Today's Classroom

What uses of technology are typical today?

What we have said so far about the possible uses of technology in education may intrigue you. But whether you are already a teacher or plan to become one, you are probably also interested in what typical schools and classrooms are like. What technological resources—hardware and software—are available to teachers? How does the typical student use technology at the grade level or within the subject area you plan to teach, and how frequently does the student spend time learning this way? If you already teach, you are probably interested in how common your own experiences are. The media sometimes focus on glamorous but atypical examples, and it is easy to assume that things are different from your experiences in other schools or other states.

In addition to examining the current state of affairs, it is intriguing to speculate about the future. Will classrooms change drastically during the next ten years because of technology, or will interest in technology wane? In this section we explore these and related questions.

Students' Access to Technology

The number of computers in schools is increasing rapidly, and these computers are being interconnected so that students can communicate with one another and access information sources available through the Internet. The six-year span ending in 2003 saw the ratio of students to computers change from 7:1 to less than 4:1. The ratio of students to computers connected to the Internet improved from 14:1 to 4.3:1 (Meyer, 2001; Park & Staresina, 2004).

These data may create false assumptions about what any given school may look like. At the level of individual states, the student-to-computer ratio varies from 1.4:1 up to 5.5:1. The student-to-computer ratio for computers connected to the Internet varies from 4.6:1 to 12.4:1. Individual school districts are even more variable (Park & Staresina, 2004). Teachers working in schools at the extremes of this range likely view the potential of technology for their classrooms very differently.

Trend toward wireless and laptops

There have been some other changes in access. Several factors have combined to provide more immediate access. First, there has been a move toward heavier use of laptop computers with wireless access to the Internet. Approximately 12 percent of instructional computers are now laptops. Second, there is an obvious trend to move computers out of specialized labs and libraries and into classrooms. In 2003, the classroom student-to-computer ratio was 7.9:1, down from 9.2:1 in 2002 (Park & Staresina, 2004).

Student computer use not frequent

As we attempt to address the different circumstances that exist in different classrooms, it is important to recognize that the availability of equipment does not determine whether students actually work with the equipment. It is possible that equipment could sit unused in the back of the classroom or computer laboratory.

Let's approach this matter in the following way. Do students make frequent use of school computers? The simple answer for the "average student" would have to be a disappointing "No!" This conclusion is reached by those who question the financial commitment of educational institutions to technology (for instance, Oppenheimer, 2003) and those who believe technology has great, but unrealized potential (for instance, Norris, Sullivan, Poirot, & Soloway, 2003). For example, when a diverse sample of K–12 educators were asked to estimate the amount of time per week their students spent working with technology, they estimated that 59 percent of students spent less than 15 minutes per week in curricular use of non-Internet computer technology and that 90 percent spent less than 15 minutes in curricular use of the Internet (Norris et al., 2003). So, while 81 percent of students report using computers at school (National Center for Education Statistics, 2003), classroom use of technology is often not a frequent experience for many students.

The lack of student use of technology represents a significant challenge, and a variety of explanations have surfaced attempting to explain "the problem." One innovative study asked teachers to report on various factors that some experts have identified as potential causes of differences in technology use (such as years of experience, hours of professional development, gender, access) and then related these potential predictors to reported levels of student use. The study concluded that differences in access accounted for most of the variability in the amount of student use. Teachers with multiple computers in their classrooms or who had frequent access to a computer lab were simply more likely to involve their students with technology (Norris et al., 2003). Perhaps the trends we reported earlier—placing more computers in the classroom and purchasing more laptop computers—will result in more teachers having the immediate access associated with frequent use.

What Students Do with Computers

Computers can play a variety of roles in school. They can be used to teach, facilitate the study of traditional content-area topics, provide opportunities for students to learn how to use technology, or give students general-purpose tools for performing academic tasks more efficiently.

The tutor, tool, tutee model

These distinctions are similar to what was originally called the tutor, tool, tutee model (Taylor, 1980). In the role of *tutor*, a computer application could be designed to teach students (for example, a tutorial program explains how to use a photospectrometer, and a drill-and-practice program helps an elementary-school student become more proficient with number facts). Computer *tools* are more general-purpose applications designed to help users function more productively—for example, word processing programs used to write reports and database programs used to organize and search for information. Applications that allow students to search for information on the Internet are also considered tools. When functioning in the *tutee* role, the student programs (or teaches) the computer.

Recent teacher surveys indicate a shift in how students are using technology. In earlier editions of this book, we reported that the most common experiences involved content-area drill activity and learning about the computer and common computer applications—that is, computer literacy. Now it appears that students are most likely to be applying technology as a tool in their own learning. When researchers asked teachers to identify the categories of computer use that applied to their students, the most frequently mentioned categories of use were word processing, Internet research, and CD-ROM research (National Center for Education Statistics, 2001).

Resources and Equity

New technologies have the potential to both ease and aggravate existing inequalities. If distributed equally and used well, technology provides opportunities to overcome some disadvantages. For example, access to the Internet provides some relief from an inadequate library. Unequal access and differences in patterns of use can also magnify existing inequities. For example, expecting students to search for Internet resources outside of class and after school places those students without home computers at a significant disadvantage.

We tend to be most concerned with inequities when differences in school opportunities compound existing disadvantages, such as low socioeconomic status (SES), and when differences in student experiences within the same school are associated with a student characteristic (gender, for example) that we feel should not influence educational opportunities. In several ways, the SES equity situation has improved a great deal in recent years. For example, programs such as Title I have helped schools with higher proportions of students from low-income families achieve a similar student-to-computer ratio as wealthier schools, and the e-rate, a subsidy helping schools connect to the Internet, has narrowed the gap in Internet access. Differences nevertheless remain. Educators in schools with higher proportions of low-income students tend to have less preparation to integrate technology, work with students with less technology experience, and feel a greater need to focus class time on standard instructional techniques because of pressure to raise test scores. As a consequence, student experiences with technology are more likely to be concentrated on computer basics and support for academic remediation. What students are encouraged to do with technology varies as a function of SES differences in the schools they attend (Warschauer, Knobel & Stone, 2004).

Inequities represent missed opportunities for students needing positive experiences. Our efforts are directed toward acquainting you with the opportunities available in typical schools and some of the inequities, and providing you with strategies for using technology efficiently and solid arguments so that you can become an advocate for technology wherever you work.

Applying technology as a tool

Differences in experiences and opportunities

Technology and School Reform

In addition to being an age of technology, our current era in the United States is certainly an age of school reform. In 1994, Congress passed the Goals 2000: Educate America Act (House of Representatives, 1994). The paragraph introducing this legislation states that its purpose is to improve learning and teaching by providing a national framework for education reform; to promote the research, consensus building, and systemic changes needed to ensure equitable educational opportunities and high levels of educational achievement for all students; to provide a framework for reauthorization of all federal education programs; and to promote the development and adoption of a voluntary national system of skill standards and certifications.

With this legislation, the year 2000 was selected as the target date by which the nation's schools would be systematically reformed to address concerns summarized in the landmark report *A Nation at Risk* (National Commission on Excellence in Education, 1983). This report argued that large numbers of students were passing through the educational system without gaining the knowledge and skills necessary to contribute in a modern technological society. The lost potential of these citizens was seen as a threat to the economic well-being of the nation.

National Educational Technology Plan and twenty-first-century skills

Although the year 2000 has passed without the complete realization of the goals expressed in the 1994 legislation, activities and debates related to the legislation continue to be important. These goals have been declared as a starting point for the effort to fashion a National Educational Technology Plan (Culp, Honey, & Mandinach, 2003) and for recommendations offered by the Partnership for 21st Century Skills (Partnership for 21st Century Skills, 2003). The summary message from these more recent initiatives is simple: Schools must change to prepare students to meet emerging challenges, and technology tools may be of unique value in meeting these challenges. One of these sources claims that "today's education system faces irrelevance unless we bridge the gap between how students live and how they learn" (Partnership for 21st Century Skills, 2003, p. 4).

In this section we look at a number of school reform issues and consider how these issues link to educational applications of technology.

Key Elements for Twenty-first-Century Learning

The Partnership for 21st Century Skills suggests the following priorities:

1. *Emphasize core subjects.* Surprise! The experts suggest that learning in the future will continue to build on the core subjects we teach today (reading, writing, history, math, science). However, what we learn about these subjects, how we learn these subjects, and how we learn to apply basic knowledge will change.

2. *Emphasize learning skills.* The futurist James Naisbett (1984) argued that we must move away from the training of specialists whose skills are soon obsolete to the development of generalists who can adapt. Recently, Gee

(2004) has described the efforts of more insightful and often affluent families to prepare young learners as "shape-shifting portfolio people." Implied in this interesting-sounding phrase is the realization that the jobs of the future may presently be undefined or may quickly change in the skills required. In arguing that they are suited for such positions, successful people will likely be able to draw on a collection (portfolio) of general-purpose academic skills and life experiences demonstrating their ability to adapt.

The Partnership for 21st Century Skills identified some of the general learning skills that should be developed, including information literacy, effective communication, critical thinking and problem solving, interpersonal skills, and self-directed learning.

3. *Use twenty-first-century tools to develop learning skills.* Students need to learn to use the tools that are essential in everyday life and the workplace. The digital tools used to access, organize, integrate, evaluate, and construct new knowledge and to communicate outside school are also appropriate to the work tasks within school.

4. *Teach and learn in a twenty-first-century context.* Learning will be more successful if learning tasks take advantage of real-world examples, applications, and experiences provided both within and outside the school setting. Such experiences will be more relevant and engaging and will increase the likelihood that students will be able to apply what they have learned.

5. *Recognize the need for twenty-first-century content.* While the core curriculum topics have not changed, the world has changed in ways that increase the significance of new skills. Changes in technology are partially responsible. For example, transportation and communication technologies have connected the people of the world as never before. Global awareness must become a greater priority. Internet technology provides access to almost unimaginable amounts of information. For example, on the day these words were written the search engine Google claimed it could provide access to 4,285,119,774 webpages. As access to information becomes easier, skills such as the critical evaluation of information sources and the integration of information in ways that encourage meaningful decisions become more important.

6. *Use assessment methods that measure twenty-first-century skills.* Standardized tests have known limitations and are often not sufficient to evaluate the capacity of students to apply knowledge and skills.

Integrating skills

You might be wondering how students can be expected to acquire more knowledge and develop more skills in the same amount of time—and what classroom teachers should be expected to do in this situation. Part of the response to this challenge might be to recognize that many of the expectations just listed can be integrated. Students can sometimes be expected to apply technology tools to core subject matter topics in ways that rely on the collection of information from the community, involve cooperative learning, require the skills of higher-order thinking, and result in the generation of a product or presentation to be evaluated as an indication of what has been learned. Several of the projects described in this book closely match this set of expectations. It is also important to recognize that not all learning tasks must satisfy all expectations. Perhaps the most fundamental suggestion here is that students should experience a wider range of learning tasks.

Restructuring Schools

Educators are talking more and more about the need to restructure schools. Although restructuring means different things to different people, the basic challenge is to think carefully about what we want schools to do and then to consider how we might most successfully accomplish these goals.

Often you will see a summary table, such as Table 1.1, that contrasts "conventional" or "traditional" education with a reformed or restructured school setting (for instance, Brown, 1992; Knapp & Glenn, 1996; Means et al., 1993). Although such tables oversimplify complex issues, they help us identify critical dimensions. Look at the table carefully. What do you think are the common themes of the restructured school setting as opposed to the conventional setting?

Technology's role in school restructuring

As you read the table, you probably notice an overlap with what you read earlier in this chapter. Key features of the restructured school—active learning, a multidisciplinary approach, student collaboration, and a facilitative or guiding role for the teacher—are the same as our themes of technology use in the classroom. We believe, therefore, that technology can play an important

TABLE 1.1

A Comparison of Traditional and Restructured Schools

	Conventional Setting	Restructured Setting
Student role	Learn facts and skills by absorbing the content presented by teachers and media resources.	Create personal knowledge by acting on content provided by teachers, media resources, and personal experiences.
Curriculum characteristics	Fragmented knowledge and disciplinary separation. Basic literacy established before high-level inquiry is encouraged. Focus on breadth of knowledge.	Multidisciplinary themes and knowledge integration. Emphasis on thinking skills, application of knowledge, and depth of understanding.
Social characteristics	Teacher-controlled setting with students working independently. Some competition.	Teacher functions as facilitator. Students work collaboratively and make some decisions.
Assessment	Measurement of fact knowledge and discrete skills. Traditional tests.	Assessment of knowledge application. Performance of tasks to demonstrate understanding.
Teacher role	Present information and manage the classroom.	Guide student inquiry and model active learning.

part in school restructuring. It can help students learn to think and learn to learn. It can provide ways to cope with today's information explosion. Most of all, it can help encourage meaningful and effective learning.

National Standards: Goals for Learning and Expectations for Technology

Video Case

To listen in on a roundtable discussion about meeting national standards, view the HM Video Case entitled *Teacher Accountability: A Student Teacher's Perspective* on our website. Do you share any of student teacher Caitlin Hollister's concerns?

If educational institutions must move in a different direction, as school reformers insist, one source of guidance may come from national curriculum standards. These goals, which summarize the opinions of content experts, are intended to focus classroom learning and the assessment of student competence on essential knowledge and skills. The attempt to define standards is shaping much of the debate about school reform and hence the role that technology ultimately will play in classrooms.

Here is the approach we hope you will take to learning about standards:

- Become familiar with what standards are and how standards might influence what you do in your classroom.
- Recognize that the emphasis in content-area standards is consistent with the learning theory and the learning activities we emphasize throughout this book.
- Become familiar with the specific standards that apply to what students should know about and be able to do with technology.

What Are Standards?

Standards seek to define what students should learn and thus what teachers should teach. Many practicing teachers are likely to be aware of standards and related concepts such as benchmarks and frameworks. They have probably spent recent summers working on curriculum projects to prepare documents summarizing how state and national standards will be implemented in their schools. You may not have had such experiences, so we begin with a description of what standards are and how they are intended to shape learning activity. We then discuss how standards are related to efforts to reform schools, and we acquaint you with standards that propose what students should learn *about* technology and *with* technology. Finally, we review standards that propose what you as a teacher should know and be able to do to help your students use technology effectively.

Types of standards

The word *standard* is used in several ways. **Content standards** define what every student should know and be able to do. **Performance standards** explain how students will demonstrate their proficiency to establish that a standard has been achieved. Both are important. While performance standards might seem more specific, it is important to understand that the specific demonstrations of proficiency are indicators of more general goals, not goals in themselves.

Benchmarks

Standards are written on many levels of detail. In reading the literature on standards, you will come across the phrase *grain size* used in reference to this

Computer tasks provide meaningful learning activities for all students. Here a diverse group works with a computer and a CD-ROM. (© Michael Zide)

issue. Here is one way to understand how grain size works in practice. On the national level, professional organizations work to establish general educational goals—the general concepts and skills students should acquire. For example, one current mathematics standard requires that students "demonstrate number sense and an understanding of number theory." Immediately you might wonder how this general standard might apply at the grade level you teach or intend to teach. Does this standard define a single expectation, or could it be interpreted as identifying several different levels of accomplishment? **Benchmarks** define a general standard according to a system describing what should be accomplished by the end of several grade-level intervals, say, K–2, 6–8, and 9–12. Benchmarks for our mathematics standard example include "Understand the relationship of fractions to decimals and whole numbers" (grades 6–8) and "Understand characteristics of the real number system and its subsystems" (grades 9–12) (Kendall & Marzano, 1996).

Even when standards are defined in terms of benchmarks, the level of detail—that is, grain size—is not sufficient to specify learning experiences and assessment procedures. In part, this vagueness is purposeful. Telling teachers specifically what and how to teach is a touchy matter that professional organizations formulating standards at the national level have tried to avoid. These organizations have tried instead to establish general goals. Then states and individual school districts are encouraged to interpret these national standards and benchmarks. Here is where curriculum frameworks are developed.

A curriculum **framework** further specifies and organizes the knowledge and skills to be acquired and relates these goals to general instructional processes and assessment techniques (Laboratory Network Program Frameworks Task Force, 1998). Our previous reference to groups of teachers working on standards during the summer encompassed this process of creating frameworks to guide local efforts. Teacher plans, sometimes called lesson plans, could represent a continuation of this planning process. Teachers take frameworks established locally and decide exactly what activities to implement. The classroom teacher takes ideas that began as general standards at the national level and then were expressed as topical units contributing to a suggested sequence of instruction at the local level, and translates them into specific lesson procedures based on specific learning resources. And sample progress indicators at the national level end up moving through a process requiring greater and greater specificity, resulting in the development of learning objectives and related assessment techniques at the classroom level. The teacher usually determines the specific learning activities that students work on and how student understanding will be evaluated (Bartz & Singer, 1996).

Standards and Reform

Most educators, and certainly most preservice teachers, are probably unaware of the role that standards, or at least the discussion of standards, has played in educational reform. We hope that the translation process just described has helped you understand how national standards may end up influencing classroom practice.

Curriculum alignment

You might wonder if standards necessarily lead to a common curriculum in which all students at a given level follow the same course of study. The term **alignment** is sometimes used to promote the benefits of bringing many partners—classroom teachers, those who prepare teachers, companies responsible for the development of instructional materials, and organizations responsible for creating evaluation instruments—together around a common vision. While some would urge an agreement on some very specific content goals (Hirsch, 1988), the standards and the process of implementing standards as we have described them clearly leave room for interpreting goals within a regional and local context. We think alignment and reform are best understood as operating on this more general level, rather than as demanding the same curriculum for all students.

Standards for Learning with Technology

The International Society for Technology in Education (ISTE) has established standards and benchmarks that define general expectations for what students should know about and be able to do with technology. The list of standards is short enough that we can provide it here (see "Focus: ISTE Technology Standards"). We have provided benchmarks for one standard to help you understand how the standards might be interpreted across grade levels (International Society for Technology in Education, 1998).

How should the ISTE standards influence your classroom?

Once you have examined the ISTE standards, ask yourself how such expectations might influence your classroom. There are probably some standards you may not have thought to be your responsibility or perhaps do not see as essential. This book should be helpful in preparing you to address many of these standards, but there are some we ignore. As we have suggested, the translation of standards into classroom practice or, in our case, into what is emphasized in our contribution to the professional development of teachers involves professional judgment, prioritizing, and an understanding of how the learning experiences each of us provides fit within a larger scheme.

If nothing else, standards have prompted discussions among classroom teachers; college of education faculty members; professional bodies advocating for their disciplines, such as the American Association for the Advancement of Science and the National Council of Teachers of English; textbook publishers; local, state, and federal politicians; and many other special interest groups. These discussions concern some fundamental and difficult topics: What are the purposes of education? What should all educated citizens know and be able to do? We encourage you to reflect on these questions and how they apply to your own teaching.

Standards and Educational Equity

The standards that apply to K–12 students emphasize what *all* students should know and be able to do. Hence such standards promote equity. Standards imply that educators are to have similar expectations of students without regard for gender, socioeconomic status, ethnicity, or region of the country.

Equity is also emphasized in the NCATE/ISTE standards that apply to the preparation of teachers. Here are some examples from the NCATE program standards for preservice teachers preparing for student teaching (ISTE, 2000):

Design, manage, and facilitate learning experiences using technology that affirm diversity and provide equitable access to resources.

Create and implement a well-organized plan to manage available technology resources, provide equitable access for all students, and enhance learning outcomes.

Standards emphasize fairness.

Design and facilitate learning experiences that use assistive technologies to meet the special physical needs of students.

Changing the Way Technology Is Used in Schools

If technology, as we have argued so far, can contribute significantly to school reform, and if it is so greatly involved in the development of national standards, why isn't it being adopted more speedily in our schools? Although the 1990s and early 2000s were times of rapid technological growth—when many computers were brought into schools, connected with each other, and connected to the Internet—classroom access to technology is still not universal, and technology is not always used extensively even when it is available. In this section we look at reasons why technology use has lagged in some respects, and then we consider possible remedies for the situation.

Focus

ISTE Technology Standards

Foundation Standards for Students

1. Basic operations and concepts
   - Students demonstrate a sound understanding of the nature and operation of technology systems.
   - Students are proficient in the use of technology.
2. Social, ethical, and human issues
   - Students understand the ethical, cultural, and societal issues related to technology.
   - Students practice responsible use of technology systems, information, and software.
   - Students develop positive attitudes toward technology uses that support lifelong learning, collaboration, personal pursuits, and productivity.
3. Technology productivity tools
   - Students use technology tools to enhance learning, increase productivity, and promote creativity.
   - Students use productivity tools to collaborate in constructing technology-enhanced models, preparing publications, and producing other creative works.
4. Technology communications tools
   - Students use telecommunications to collaborate, publish, and interact with peers, experts, and other audiences.
   - Students use a variety of media and formats to communicate information and ideas effectively to multiple audiences.
5. Technology research tools
   - Students use technology to locate, evaluate, and collect information from a variety of sources.
   - Students use technology tools to process data and report results.
   - Students evaluate and select new information resources and technological innovations based on the appropriateness to specific tasks.
6. Technology problem-solving and decision-making tools
   - Students use technology resources for solving problems and making informed decisions.
   - Students employ technology in the development of strategies for solving problems in the real world.

Communication Tools (Benchmarks)

GRADES 3–5
- Use technology tools (for example, multimedia authoring, presentation, web tools, digital cameras, scanners) for individual and collaborative writing, communication, and publishing activities to create knowledge products for audiences inside and outside the classroom.

Video Case
How can teachers use technology tools to teach problem-solving skills? Watch high-school science teacher Ken Bateman use a multimedia simulation to help students understand a difficult concept in a problem-solving activity in the HM Video Case entitled *Integrating Technology to Improve Student Learning.*

- Use telecommunications efficiently and effectively to access remote information, communicate with others in support of direct and independent learning, and pursue personal interests.

GRADES 6–8
- Design, develop, publish, and present products (for example, webpages, videotapes) using technology resources that demonstrate and communicate curriculum concepts to audiences inside and outside the classroom.
- Collaborate with peers, experts, and others using telecommunications and collaborative tools to investigate curriculum-related problems, issues, and information, and to develop solutions or products for audiences inside and outside the classroom.

GRADES 9–12
- Use technology tools and resources for managing and communicating personal/professional information (for example, finances, schedules, addresses, purchases, correspondence).
- Routinely and efficiently use online information resources to meet needs for collaboration, research, publications, communications, and productivity.
- Select and apply technology tools for research, information analysis, problem solving, and decision making in content learning.

Focus

How Standards May Be Shaping What You Learn about the Application of Technology

You may be using this book in a course that is part of a teacher certification program or an advanced program to prepare technology specialists. If so, there are standards that have been developed to guide the education that you receive. Many institutions preparing K–12 educators in the United States seek accreditation from the National Council for Accreditation of Teacher Education (NCATE). An accrediting agency promotes and monitors quality educational experiences, and standards are an important component of this process. Institutions wanting to list programs as NCATE accredited are required to demonstrate through documentation and periodic discussions with a visiting team of reviewers that established standards have been implemented.

Here are some ways in which NCATE standards shape the preparation of educators to teach with and about technology. As you examine this list, you will note that NCATE sometimes adopts standards prepared by other professional organizations with more focused content-area interests.

- Standards provided by the International Society for Technology in Education (ISTE) or the Association for Educational Communication and Technology (AECT) are used to evaluate advanced programs preparing candidates for computing and technology coordinators, library media specialists, and similar leadership positions. Web addresses for NCATE, ISTE, and AECT are provided at the end of this chapter.
- NCATE standards are also available to describe the skills expected of those serving as technology facilitators (defined as building or campus level facilitators), technology leaders, and those described as computer science educators.
- ISTE standards can also apply to the general preparation of teachers to integrate technology in content-area instruction, and they may define what is necessary to receive **endorsement** in that field.
- Standards that apply to the preparation of candidates to teach specific content areas (for example, math, social studies) are also relevant because these standards establish implications for how technology might best be used in classroom settings.

To give you some idea of how standards are presented, we will use some examples from the NCATE/ISTE standards for Initial Endorsement in Educational Computing and Technology Literacy. NCATE/ISTE expectations are presented as a combination of content standards and performance indicators. The third edition of these standards, developed in 2000, identifies expectations in six categories, provides performance indicators corresponding to each category, and identifies essential conditions that institutions are expected to provide to facilitate development of expected skills. The performance indicators have been developed to correspond to specific landmarks in teacher preparation (such as student teaching, first-year teaching), and you may find it valuable to visit the National Educational Technology Standards (NETS) site to investigate the expectations corresponding to your stage of professional development.

According to the NCATE/ISTE standards, teachers are to develop competency in the following six areas:

I.   Technology Operations and Concepts
II. Planning and Designing Learning Environments and Experiences
III. Teaching, Learning, and the Curriculum
IV. Assessment and Evaluation
V.   Productivity and Professional Practice
VI. Social, Ethical, Legal, and Human Issues

Performance indicators corresponding to these categories cover a wide range of applications, including the use of technology to facilitate personal professional development, to communicate with colleagues and parents, and to improve instruction. A sample of performance indicators associated with the instructional role of first-year teachers follows. The Roman numerals listed after each performance indicator represent the standard category associated with that indicator.

- Arrange equitable access to appropriate technology resources that enable students to engage successfully in learning activities across subject/content areas and grade levels (II, III, VI).
- Engage in ongoing planning of lesson sequences that effectively integrate technology resources and are consistent with current best practices for integrating the learning of subject matter and student technology standards (II, III).
- Teach students methods and strategies to assess the validity and reliability of information gathered through technological means (II, IV).
- Use technology tools to collect, analyze, interpret, represent, and communicate data (student performance and other information) for the purposes of instructional planning and school improvement (IV).
- Demonstrate and advocate for legal and ethical behaviors among students, colleagues, and community members regarding the use of technology and information (V, VI).
- Enforce classroom procedures that guide students' safe and healthy use of technology and that comply with legal and professional responsibilities for students needing assistive technology (VI).

Standards emphasize equity.

Do you find some of these expectations too vague to be very helpful? The NETS website has begun to provide classroom scenarios as a way to exemplify how teachers demonstrate these proficiencies. After you have read most of this book, we encourage you to return to this discussion of standards and see if the expectations now make more sense.

Source: NCATE Program Standards for Educational Computing and Technology Approved in 2000 (International Society for Technology in Education, 2000). See "Resources to Expand Your Knowledge Base" at the end of this chapter for information on how to locate the NCATE/ISTE standards online.

Three Perspectives on Technology and School Reform

Many educators ask whether K–12 learners will soon be using technology more extensively and, if so, how this change may contribute to educational reform. These are questions open to speculation, but this speculation is now based on some data. At an earlier point, we reported that unless educators can provide immediate access to technology only very limited use of technology is likely (Norris et al., 2003). However, what happens when access is less of an issue? We summarize three very different perspectives on the following pages. The headings for our brief descriptions were taken directly from the titles of publications that could serve as examples of each perspective.

"Influence of Computer and Internet Use on Teachers' Pedagogical Practices"

Promoting constructivist practices

An optimistic position holds that as technology becomes more readily available and educators become familiar with the learning experiences that are possible, educational practice will soon change. In particular, this position claims, educators will realize that technology makes some traditional educational goals obsolete, and teachers will move toward more constructivist practices in the classroom, emphasizing active learning and students' construction of personal meaning. (We discuss constructivism in detail in the next chapter.)

This position has some research support. For example, a recent study found a connection between longevity of computer use with students, use of Internet-based teaching activities, and self-reported constructivist change by teachers (Becker & Ravitz, 1999).

"High Access and Low Use . . . : Explaining an Apparent Paradox"

If you had to select a place where you would think technology would be used extensively in classrooms and in ways that changed educational practice, where would that place be? Larry Cuban (2001; Cuban, Kirkpatrick, & Peck, 2001) reasoned that place would be Silicon Valley in California. He undertook a study of several elementary schools, high schools, and colleges from that region to predict what might happen as other schools and colleges matched the conditions already present in the schools he had selected.

Self-perpetuating assumptions hinder technology use.

As you can tell from the title, Cuban failed to find extensive use of technology in what he felt should be fairly supportive institutions. He also found relatively few innovative uses of technology. Cuban speculated that the history and context of educational practice were important factors impeding significant change. Assumptions and practices end up being self-perpetuating. One such cluster of factors evident in high schools includes the isolation of instructors by academic discipline, the fifty-minute class period, and the "transmission" model of instruction. The isolation of disciplines requires that each group be relegated a short period of time so each content area can be covered. Short periods of time with learners encourage a transmission approach. It is difficult to get around to using technology when operating within such constraints. Cuban concludes that the use of technology will gradually increase, but the applications that will become common will be consistent with longstanding methods of teaching and learning.

"The Interplay of Teacher Beliefs, Social Dynamics, and Institutional Culture"

"Laptop" schools—those that provide students with laptop computers—would seem to be a great setting in which to observe how ready access to technology influences classroom practice. The commitment to mobile equipment both offers opportunities and raises expectations. A recent in-depth study of teachers in one laptop school found that some teachers made significant changes in how they approached instruction, but some did not (Windschitl & Sahl, 2002).

Teachers change if they want to change.

Why was there so much difference among these teachers? Interviews conducted by the researchers suggest that teachers have different beliefs and values. Despite this variability, classroom activities have remained fairly similar in most schools because of limited resources and limited awareness of alternative methods. As technology in classrooms offers new opportunities and a growing dialogue among educators creates greater awareness of how technology can be applied, teachers who have been frustrated with traditional approaches have the motivation and now the opportunity to change. In contrast, those who are satisfied with traditional methods see no reason to change. So improving access to technology will be the impetus for *some* teachers to alter their classroom activities, but others will continue doing what they have always done.

Teacher Preparation

One implication of the studies we have just described is that technology use in schools will be slow to improve until teachers are (1) aware of the full range of benefits they can gain from technology and (2) fully prepared to use the technological resources at their disposal. This brings us to the question of how teachers are prepared for the job they are being asked to do.

Teacher Training

Are new teachers prepared to use technology?

The assumption might be that teachers just completing their undergraduate programs would be well prepared to use new tools and model new instructional approaches. In fact, new and practicing teachers say that this is not the case (Moursund & Bielefeldt, 1999).

There are three primary reasons for this lack of preparation. First, colleges of education frequently have no better equipment than K–12 institutions do and only a limited inventory of the types of instructional software used in K–12 classrooms. Second, a large number of college faculty members are unable to make appropriate use of technology in their own classrooms or are unwilling to try because of their own lack of preparation, anxiety, or disinterest. And third, the teacher preparation curriculum typically confines experiences with technology to a single course, one that concentrates on learning to use the technology rather than how to facilitate learning with technology (Panel on Educational Technology, 1997).

Our focus here is on how teachers in elementary and secondary schools can do a better job using technology with their own students, but occasionally we will offer a comment on how future teachers are prepared. It is ironic that the educators of educators persist in employing practices and modeling attitudes that many consider barriers to the effective use of technology in elementary and secondary classrooms. There is probably a positive message for all of us in recognizing this irony: Change at all levels of education, which does not come easily, starts with each of us.

Changing how teachers are trained will not have an immediate impact on school practice. It will take years to place a majority of teachers with extensive college-based technology training into the workforce. Even if teachers have had a college technology course within the past year or so, the field advances very rapidly, and new equipment, programs, and ideas for classroom practice are always emerging. There are many practicing teachers who may have had some exposure to computers but have not worked with authoring software, video production, or digital data probes (we discuss all of these products in later chapters). The World Wide Web has emerged as a powerful and widely used Internet application in an extremely short period of time. While some may find this situation discouraging, we think it is exciting. The tools of many professions are changing at an incredible rate. Why would we as teachers want to be excluded from this progress?

Teacher Attitudes

Teachers are using technology less.

It is easy to be glib about the excitement of new opportunities. It is another matter to deal with the uncertainty teachers face when they suddenly confront sophisticated new equipment in their classrooms. Teachers are used to being in control of their environments and in command of the content they teach. It is not uncommon or even surprising to find them nervous and reluctant to learn how to use technology, particularly when they might be expected to work on it with their students before they feel secure in their own mastery. New teachers face some unique challenges. In a recent study (Bebell, Russell, & O'Dwyer, 2004), researchers used a sample of nearly three thousand Massachusetts teachers to report on multiple categories of technology use. Although the total use of technology did not show differences by years of experience, new teachers reported asking students to use technology *less* during class time. This finding runs contrary to the assumption that younger teachers are more likely to bring change to the classroom. How would you explain this finding? Perhaps less experienced teachers are struggling with many things and do not feel comfortable adding student-centered technology experiences to the mix.

Once teachers work with the equipment and experience different applications, their enthusiasm usually grows, and they begin to develop ideas of their own that they can implement with the new resources. Probably not all teachers would get to this stage if they had to work completely on their own. This is why ongoing training and support of teachers already working in classrooms is so important.

We also try to encourage teachers to recognize that technology can represent a unique situation in which they can learn with their students. When new equipment and software show up in your classroom, you have a tremendous opportunity to model problem solving, persistence when things go wrong, and the joy of developing a new skill!

By this point we have given you much to think about concerning the general role of technology in schools and its connection to school reform efforts. We now leave you to ponder the future for yourself and return to our more immediate priority of orienting you to the perspective taken in this book.

The Activity-Based Model of Technology Use

This book explores the classroom use of technology from a range of perspectives. We do, however, make a special effort to have you consider one particular way of using technology. This approach has been described in a number of ways: activity-based learning (Laboratory of Comparative Human Cognition, 1989), the project approach (Katz & Chard, 1989), using computer

Focus

The National Educational Technology Plan

Among its various provisions, the No Child Left Behind Act of 2001 charged the secretary of the U.S. Department of Education to submit a National Educational Technology Plan. This plan was released in early 2005. Whether in agreement or not, those interested in the application of technology in K–12 settings should be aware of Department of Education priorities. The plan recommends seven action steps:

- Strengthen leadership. Educational leaders at all levels must be more tech-savvy and make more effective use of appropriate expertise in decision making.
- Consider innovative budgeting. Connect the funding of technology to educational objectives and recognize opportunities for innovative restructuring and reallocation of existing budgets.
- Improve teacher training. Improve the preparation of new teachers and ensure online access to development experiences for all teachers.
- Support e-learning and virtual schools.
- Encourage broadband access.
- Move toward digital content.
- Integrate data systems. Use the power of technology to improve efficiency and more carefully track individual student achievement.

An important question is whether the priorities of this plan are consistent with the priorities of this book. While the technology plan emphasizes improving the preparation of teachers and a move toward greater use of digital content, detailed recommendations for exactly how educators should apply technology or what digital resources should be emphasized are not included. The plan is about a wide range of topics that will influence all educators indirectly but may offer little guidance that applies directly.

Material included within the report is more specific and emphasizes (1) the technology skills of "millennials," the interest these students have in "researching and innovating using technology" in their lives, and their high expectations for educational experiences and (2) descriptions of what goes on in exemplary schools, including authentic student projects nearly identical to those we include in this book.

In the cover letter, the secretary of education comments, "Too often, schools have simply applied technology to existing ways of teaching and learning, with marginal results in student achievement." The secretary continues by claiming, "Teachers and students are transforming what can be done in schools by using technology to access primary sources, expose our students to a variety of perspectives, and enhance the overall learning experience through multimedia, simulations and interactive software."

> It is our hope that this book contributes to the national effort to improve the application of technology. As we offer recommendations, we attempt to recognize cultural change in the way technology has been adopted and is used, relevant research on meaningful learning, and the knowledge and skills emphasized in content-area standards. You will have to evaluate the validity of our logic in connecting these foundations to suggestions for practice.

activities as mindtools (Jonassen, 1996; Jonassen & Carr, 2000; Jonassen, Peck, & Wilson, 1999), and design projects (Carver, Lehrer, Connell, & Erickson, 1992; Perkins, 1986). We use all of these terms in this book, but we particularly emphasize the term *activity-based learning* and the discussion of student projects.

Early Use of Activity-Based Approaches

Hands-on, student-centered activities

When activity-based approaches were introduced in the 1960s as a way to reform science and math education (Laboratory of Comparative Human Cognition, 1989), most learning and instruction was based in larger groups and was dominated by teacher presentations. This new approach recommended that at least part of the time available for instruction be shifted to hands-on, student-centered activities and that students collaborate in small groups to work on these projects. The teacher thus became responsible for the following:

- Selecting the activity and providing the materials
- Introducing the activity so that the students' task was set in a meaningful context and had clear goals
- Facilitating the students' work as it proceeded
- Helping the students see the connections between their observations and associated principles or theory

The teacher's role

Without the careful consideration of what the teacher actually must accomplish in this approach, it might appear that the teacher just presents the assignment and then sits at the desk until the students are ready to turn in their work. As you might expect, this is not at all what was intended. Instead, the teacher moves from group to group, participating, probing, and suggesting. A fundamental goal is to help students shift back and forth between theory, principles, and their own observations and experiences. Often the teacher uses questions to guide the students: "Is what you are now observing the same thing you read about?" "What is a good way to explain why this is happening?"

Positive attitudes and better understanding

When evaluations of activity-based learning were made, the results were impressive: Students had more positive attitudes toward science, demonstrated better understanding of the concepts, and were more advanced in using creative and higher-level thinking skills. Yet more than twenty years later, fewer than 10 percent of science classrooms use what was demonstrated to be a motivating and effective curriculum model. As external funds and professional support were withdrawn, teachers were unable to locate the resources necessary for hands-on activities and did not have the time and often the expertise necessary to develop productive learning activities themselves. The explanation for this situation is a good lesson in some of the realities of implementing change in schools.

Today's Use of Activity-Based Approaches and Technology

The role of technology in activity-based learning

Technology may represent the critical element in reintroducing these ideas in a sustainable way and in allowing activity-based learning to play a more prominent role in K–12 education. The hardware and software that many schools already have or that they can acquire at a reasonable cost can be used to involve students in active learning tasks focused on many of the same topics they would otherwise encounter by listening to teacher presentations or reading textbooks.

Tool applications

The activity-based or project-centered approach that this book explores makes heavy use of computer tools: word processing, graphics programs, database programs, spreadsheets, telecommunications software, sound capture and editing software, hardware and software for capturing images and video segments from a variety of sources, and software for authoring hypermedia. Applying these tools to carefully selected tasks encourages the active mental behaviors so necessary for meaningful learning and critical thinking. The same tool can be applied over and over in new ways and in the processing of new information. This flexibility and reusability overcome some of the preparation difficulties inherent in the activity-based approach of the 1960s. Both teachers and students become adept at using the tools, and projects become easier to implement.

Summary

Classroom use of technology is growing and may be changing in its orientation. Many schools are investing in new equipment and purchasing new software. The situation is not without limitations and concerns, however. Growth and enthusiasm are not universal, and equity of resources remains an important issue.

Advocates for education reform provide one perspective on how technology should be used. Among the challenges for educational reform are expectations that students will be required to emphasize new skills needed to function in a world that presents new challenges. National curriculum experts who have established standards for what K–12 students should learn provide a second perspective on how technology should be used and on what technology skills should be developed.

Although individual teachers can have only an indirect impact on the amount of technology available, they can determine how technology is applied. Universities are being challenged to train teachers better in the use of technology, and teachers themselves must adjust their attitudes to take advantage of the new opportunities.

Many of the applications identified in this chapter make efficient use of technology. Technology is proposed as a focal point for activities that engage students actively in collaborative, multidisciplinary learning projects in traditional areas of instruction. We argue that such activities are consistent with the goal of developing learners who have the need to store information, but who must also be more capable of processing information to construct useful, personal knowledge. Teachers will need new skills to help students achieve this goal. There will be due emphasis on presenting information, but also a greater need to model and encourage skills involved in decision making and problem solving.

Reflecting on Chapter 1

ACTIVITIES

- Educators are sometimes asked to reflect on differences in how they and their students might understand the world by identifying objects or events taken for granted by the students but that have changed in a significant way during the lifetime of the teachers (for instance, the removal of the Berlin Wall). Generate your own list of such events and objects, and comment on entries that you feel are most significant in providing you with a different perspective.

- Consider how technology has influenced you as a college student. A recent argument is that future teachers experience few applications of technology as learners and thus lack the experience and insights necessary to make use of technology when they graduate and move into the teaching profession. Have you used technology as a tutor, tool, or tutee? Have you used technology at all? Write a summary of the ways in which you have used technology as a learner during the past year.

- Do you accept the reality of an "information glut"? Generate a list of examples demonstrating changes in the quantity of information available to you. For example, it is possible to watch a television channel solely devoted to providing information about the weather.

- Think of a course you have taken recently that seems especially well suited to preparing you for the Information Age. What specific skills were stressed in this course?

KEY TERMS

alignment (p. 24)
benchmarks (p. 23)
content standards (p. 22)
electronic portfolios (p. 10)

endorsement (p. 28)
framework (p. 23)
performance standards (p. 22)
standards (p. 22)

RESOURCES TO EXPAND YOUR KNOWLEDGE BASE

Many of the topics in this chapter are expanded in later chapters, and additional readings are provided at those points. If you find the idea that technology may change the basic nature of education exciting, you may want to examine the following sources:

Means, B. (Ed.). (1997). *Learner-centered psychological principles: A framework for school redesign and reform.* Washington, DC: American Psychological Association.

Oppenheimer, T. (2003). *The flickering mind: The false promise of technology in the classroom and how learning can be saved.* New York: Random House.

Featured Project Website

URLs listed in this section can be accessed directly from the textbook website. You can visit the Soaring Eagle Prairie website at **http://www.und.nodak.edu/org/soaringeagleprairie/.**

Online Information about Standards

Information about standards can be found at the following websites:

The Association for Educational Communications and Technology (AECT) Standards are available online at **http://www.aect.org/.**

The International Society for Technology in Education (ISTE) Standards, also known as the National Educational Technology Standards (NETS), are available online at **http://cnets.iste.org/.**

The National Council for Accreditation of Teacher Education (NCATE) Standards are available online at **http://www.ncate.org/.**

2

Meaningful Learning in an Information Age

● ● ●

ORIENTATION This chapter considers some key ideas related to the nature of learning. How you use technology in your classroom is determined by your understanding of how students learn and by your expectations regarding the knowledge and thinking skills students should acquire.

It is our intent to help you develop a deeper understanding of how students learn and how technology might contribute to this process. We emphasize a cognitive approach in an effort to help you understand the mental activities of learners and how learning tasks influence student thinking. Theoretical models based on the cognitive tradition suggest that educators can establish learning environments that help students learn more effectively, apply what they have learned, and become more excited about learning. Certain learning experiences also appear important in developing the skills necessary to become autonomous and lifelong learners. Education involves more than the accumulation of knowledge or even the development of understanding. Practical application of knowledge in problem solving and critical thinking—identifiable forms of higher-order thinking—is essential. In all these respects, we believe technology can play a prominent role in providing productive learning experiences.

As you read, look for answers to the following questions:

Focus Questions

- What do assumptions about the structure of long-term memory imply for the successful storage and use of knowledge?
- How do external tasks influence internal mental processes?
- What are authentic tasks, and what is necessary for classroom experiences to be more authentic?
- What are the characteristics of skilled problem solving and critical-thinking behavior, and how does the selection of learning activities influence the development of these characteristics?
- What role can technology play in creating authentic experiences and encouraging higher-order learning?

Cognitive Models of School Learning

As you read about the instructional strategies and learning activities in this book, you will note that we frequently speculate about how an experience influences a learner's mental activities. We believe that understanding how classroom experiences influence mental behaviors can be invaluable to the decisions teachers make about using technology in the classroom. Put another way, we feel teachers' beliefs about what learning is and how it occurs influence decisions they make in their classrooms. What we can do is challenge you to examine your personal beliefs about student learning.

A cognitive perspective   Our approach to examining the mental behaviors involved in thinking and learning is based on a *cognitive perspective.* Cognitive models emphasize how students acquire information and skills, solve problems, and engage in such academic tasks as reading, writing, and mathematical reasoning.

Two approaches to cognition   In this chapter we take two approaches to describing learning and thinking activities:

- The first approach explores some of the fundamental properties of mental activity.
- The second approach explores important issues of school learning at a more conceptual level. By *conceptual,* we are referring to a level of description that classroom teachers may use more commonly to discuss how students learn.

The major distinction between these approaches is in the amount of specificity they use to describe learning and thinking activities.

We present this discussion of school learning because we want you to examine how applications of technology might influence student thinking and learning. You revisit many of these principles in later chapters as we discuss specific applications of technology and describe strategies for using them in your classroom. We encourage you to consider the material in this and the following chapters actively. Discuss the assumptions and proposals with your classmates and instructor.

Fundamental Properties of Mental Activity

Learning and thinking activities can be described in terms of multiple *memory stores,* the *processes* or mental actions that we use as we think and learn, and some *executive mechanisms* that oversee and control the processes and determine whether the processes have accomplished what we as learners have intended. We do not spend a great deal of time exploring classroom learning and thinking at the most fundamental level. However, we do want to familiarize you with some of the most important characteristics of mental behavior and show you some important implications for the classroom use of technology.

Memory Stores

Two memory stores

Memory stores function within the cognitive system to hold information. Once information is taken in through our sensory receptors (for example, our eyes or ears), memory stores come into play. This discussion considers two memory stores: short- and long-term memory.

Short-Term Memory

The most effective way to describe **short-term memory** (STM) is as consciousness: the thoughts, ideas, and images of which a person is aware at any point in time. A moment of reflection will give you some insight into the contents of your STM right now. What ideas are you aware of? These ideas are available in your STM (we hope they include the ideas presented here).

Characteristics of short-term or working memory

STM is also frequently called **working memory.** Learning and thinking activities occur in working memory. Again, a bit of reflection will suggest some important characteristics of working memory. For example, working memory operates within time and capacity limits. That is, there is a limit to how much information we can be aware of and how much mental activity we can engage in at any one time. There is also a limit to how long information will be maintained in working memory without continued attention. How often have you found yourself repeating something or concentrating on it to keep the thought available? Mental *rehearsal* is a way we all attempt to respond to the time limits of working memory.

Many of the characteristics of working memory have implications for explaining learning or thinking difficulties and, as a result, how specific task performance might be improved. Using what you now know about the characteristics of working memory, think about the following classroom scenario:

Jack and his seventh-grade classmates have been receiving keyboarding instruction for several years. Jack can find most of the keys without looking, and he uses the computer to type papers he has already handwritten. However, he is not an accomplished typist. His English teacher has assigned an in-class theme and decides it is important for students to learn to compose at the keyboard. The teacher takes the class to the computer lab and tells the students they must complete their papers by the end of the class period. Jack has great difficulty with this task. Although his typing proficiency clearly limits how quickly he can work, his problems go beyond his ability to get his ideas down on paper. He has an unusual amount of difficulty thinking of what he wants to say and how he wants to organize his paper. The paper he writes is atypically poor.

What does short-term or working memory have to do with Jack's poor English paper? One very likely explanation for Jack's writing problems involves the time and capacity limitations of working memory. If Jack must think to recall the keyboard positions of individual letters, the thinking behavior he must employ in order to type competes for working memory capacity with the various thinking behaviors required to write the paper. The slow speed at which he works only makes matters worse. He is forced to expend his limited cognitive resources to keep thoughts active for a longer period of time.

There are some ways this situation can be improved. An improvement in typing proficiency is a long-term solution, but it has little immediate value. If the teacher insists that the paper be typed in class, Jack might improve his performance by first generating an outline of his ideas and referring to this outline as he works. In this manner, Jack would decrease what he has to accomplish and retain in working memory.

The teacher might also want to think carefully about the goals of the assignment. There may be other ways to accomplish the same ends. If both developing writing skills and composing at the computer are important, imposing a severe time limitation is probably not a good idea for novice typists. Either less demanding assignments should be given or students should have an extended period of time to complete the assignment.

The relationship between word processing and writing is one example of a situation in which the student uses technology as a tool to perform some other academic task. It is helpful for teachers to recognize that in situations like this, an inexperienced student really faces several cognitive tasks. First, the student needs to learn to use a particular computer program. Second, the student needs to perform some academic task using the technology. Under certain circumstances, the combination of these tasks can strain working memory.

The need for well-developed computer skills

The story about Jack provides a worst-case scenario of a student who is still an unskilled typist trying to complete a difficult writing assignment. Both the use of the technology and the academic task are difficult for him and compete for his limited working memory resources. The story also illustrates that challenging classroom assignments become unnecessarily difficult when the computer skills needed to perform them are not well developed. Teachers may also fail to see that the opposite relationship between classroom tasks and technology also holds. Students may have difficulty learning to take full advantage of the power of computer programs when they apply the programs only to challenging classroom problems. We seldom emphasize the development of technology skills without a connection to content-area learning, but we also recognize that the successful application of technology requires some attention to developing technology skills. When the academic task to be accomplished is difficult or must be completed under time pressure, the student is less likely to explore the potential of the technology and, as a consequence, never gets beyond using the technology in the most mundane fashion.

A play phase

To ease the burden of learning to use new programs, students might first be asked to apply programs to very easy or familiar tasks. In other words, it is often useful to allow for a *play phase*. A play phase allows students to explore the capabilities of new software in low-stress settings with low-stress tasks. For example, when students are first learning the features of a word processing program, they should write on a topic such as their families or themselves. This kind of topic allows information to flow freely while the student focuses on features such as fonts, cutting and pasting, and saving the document to disk. Hurrying the process of learning a new program is not always the best long-term solution.

In the chapter entitled "Using Instructional Software and Multimedia for Content-Area Learning" we discuss a type of computer software called *drill and practice*. Drill-and-practice activities are relevant when certain skills (such as typing) need to be learned to the point that executing them takes little working memory capacity so the student's attention can be devoted to other mental tasks (such as writing).

Long-Term Memory

Memory components

Long-term memory (LTM) contains a person's permanent store of knowledge and skills—that is, all the stored products of learning—from both formal education and everyday experiences. Because we all have some sense of what we know, we all have some insight into what LTM contains. How would you describe all the different things you have learned? Different theorists (Anderson, 1983; Gagne & Glaser, 1987) categorize the contents of LTM in different ways. The memory components we discuss here are imagery, episodic memory, and declarative and procedural knowledge. After reviewing them, we describe a model of how LTM works.

Remembering textbooks thirty years later

Imagery Experience tells us that we have the capacity to store imagery of different types (smells, sounds, visual representations). We are capable of recalling very specific smells (Mom's kitchen when she made chicken dinner on Sundays) or visual images (the house we grew up in) from long ago. Researchers, working mostly with visual images, have demonstrated just how remarkable our long-term storage is. In one creative experiment, researchers (Read & Barnsley, 1977) presented pages from elementary-school reading textbooks to adults, who had not seen these books for as long as thirty years. The adults showed a significant level of recognition, especially when a picture was included.

Episodic Memory An **episodic memory** is a stored representation of something you have experienced (Tulving, 1972)—for example, a filmstrip on butterflies viewed in an elementary-school science class, a marketing field trip to a local shopping mall to view store window displays, or a conversation with a friend about today's lunch. Episodic memories are rich in detail, much of which may be of no great significance. They can also be related to a particular time and place. In fact, we often use time and place to help us recall the details of a specific event we have experienced. For example, during a quiz, a student may attempt to recall last Thursday's lecture to locate information relevant to a particular question.

Episodic memories as a mixed blessing

Is such storage of personal experiences an important educational goal? Episodic memories can be a mixed blessing. In certain situations, teachers may not want students to store their academic experiences as episodes. They want students to think about a lecture and store the major ideas rather than the verbatim comments. In other circumstances, however, teachers want students to use experiences from their lives either to discover principles or as a route to a richer understanding of principles. For example, a psychology instructor might ask, "Did your mother ever tell you that you couldn't have dessert until you finished your vegetables? Why do you think she said that?" The instructor hopes that you have had an experience like this and that recalling it might help you understand psychological concepts such as contingency and reinforcement.

Problem solving based on episodic memories

Some instructional strategies ask that educators think about stored experiences in still a different way. For example, advocates of **case-based learning,** pointing to the problem-solving behavior of individuals in professions such as medicine, claim that decisions are often based on the recollection of "episodes" rather than abstract principles. According to this argument, when many physicians encounter a challenging case, their problem-solving behavior first involves the recollection of similar cases they have experienced and then an analysis of common and unique attributes in the cases being considered. The educational implication of such observations has led to a greater emphasis on the accumulation and analysis of "cases" in the preparation of professionals for certain fields.

Personal reflection may demonstrate that life stories play a very important role in your own thinking and problem solving in applied settings. It is not just doctors and lawyers who solve problems in this manner. We all ask ourselves the question, "Has something like this happened to me before?" The recollection of what we or someone else did in a particular situation can be adapted as a solution to a new problem (McLellan, 1996).

An essential point in understanding the significance of educational experiences is that experiences by themselves are not equivalent to knowledge. Much of what we present in this book is focused on this issue: *How do teachers get students to create knowledge and not be satisfied with simply storing information?* Students need to take an active role in working with the information they receive. There are different goals that this active learning might accomplish; for example:

Possible goals of active learning

- One goal might be to acquire principles, rules, concepts, or some other form of abstract knowledge by working with experiences or examples. In this case, learning tasks would be designed to help learners construct personally meaningful abstractions.
- A second learning goal might be to store personal experiences as episodes, but to also associate meaningful labels with these experiences. While experts may recall personal experiences, it is clear that some type of organization is involved. A physician may recall cases based on criteria such as pneumonia in very young children, strange red rashes following a high fever, or an arrhythmic heartbeat in overweight, fifty-year-old males. This labeling system, which some researchers describe as *indexing,* is a very important part of what learners accomplish as they learn from cases (Edelson, 1998; Lesgold, 2001). Learning from cases might be described as processing experiences in such a way that the cases serve as useful personal examples of principles, rules, or concepts.

Technology can play an important role in helping learners achieve both types of learning goals. Many of the tasks we describe throughout this book involve projects requiring learners to process information with the goal of constructing personal knowledge. This processing involves developing and storing personal abstractions and perhaps meaningful systems for indexing personal experiences. Technology may also provide the means to engage learners with experiences (cases) in ways that are more practical and productive (Lesgold, 2001; Schank, 1998).

Declarative and Procedural Knowledge   Many memory theorists have drawn a distinction between verbally based factual knowledge and know-how (Anderson, 1976, 1983; Gagne, 1985). This distinction is often described as the difference between knowing that something is the case and knowing how to perform a certain cognitive process or action. **Declarative knowledge** represents our factual knowledge base, and **procedural knowledge** represents the stored methods we use to do things.

Storing declarative knowledge

Much of school learning has to do with the storage of declarative knowledge. We learn the names of things, significant dates, terms, definitions, number facts, theories of this and that, and many similar categories of facts and concepts. We are also taught to do things: tie our shoes and button our coats, add and subtract, write, solve algebra problems, and argue for a position. In reality, most accomplishments require both declarative and procedural knowledge. It is, for example, difficult to write without having something to say. To engage in an argument, we need the skills of logic and effective communication, as well as factual knowledge.

Procedural knowledge and performance

One final point of clarification: Procedural knowledge is not the same as a verbal account of how to do something. Procedural knowledge is demonstrated by actual performance, not by a description of how something should be done. The stored description of where the letter q appears on a keyboard is declarative knowledge. Pressing the q key when desired is procedural knowledge.

A Network Model of LTM   Most academic and life tasks require the use of several categories of memory contents. Presumably, then, our various elements of memory are organized in a meaningful way, rather than isolated by category of memory unit. Effective educational experiences, therefore, must result in both the accumulation and the organization of memory units. We call this organized structure of memory units a *network*.

Organization of memory elements in a network

The network is a useful way to conceptualize how what we know (our memory) is stored and the ways memory works. **Network models** represent memory in terms of **nodes,** which are cognitive units, and **links,** which establish the relationships among nodes (Anderson, 1983; Collins & Quillian, 1969; Gagne, 1985; Gagne, Yekovich, & Yekovich, 1993).

Figure 2.1 is a graphic representation of what such models attempt to describe. This representation portrays a small part of a high-school biology student's knowledge. Included are examples of the four categories of LTM contents:

1. Imagery: recollections of animals the student has seen
2. Episodic knowledge: the recollection of a hunting trip

FIGURE 2.1

Network of Biological Knowledge Stored in LTM

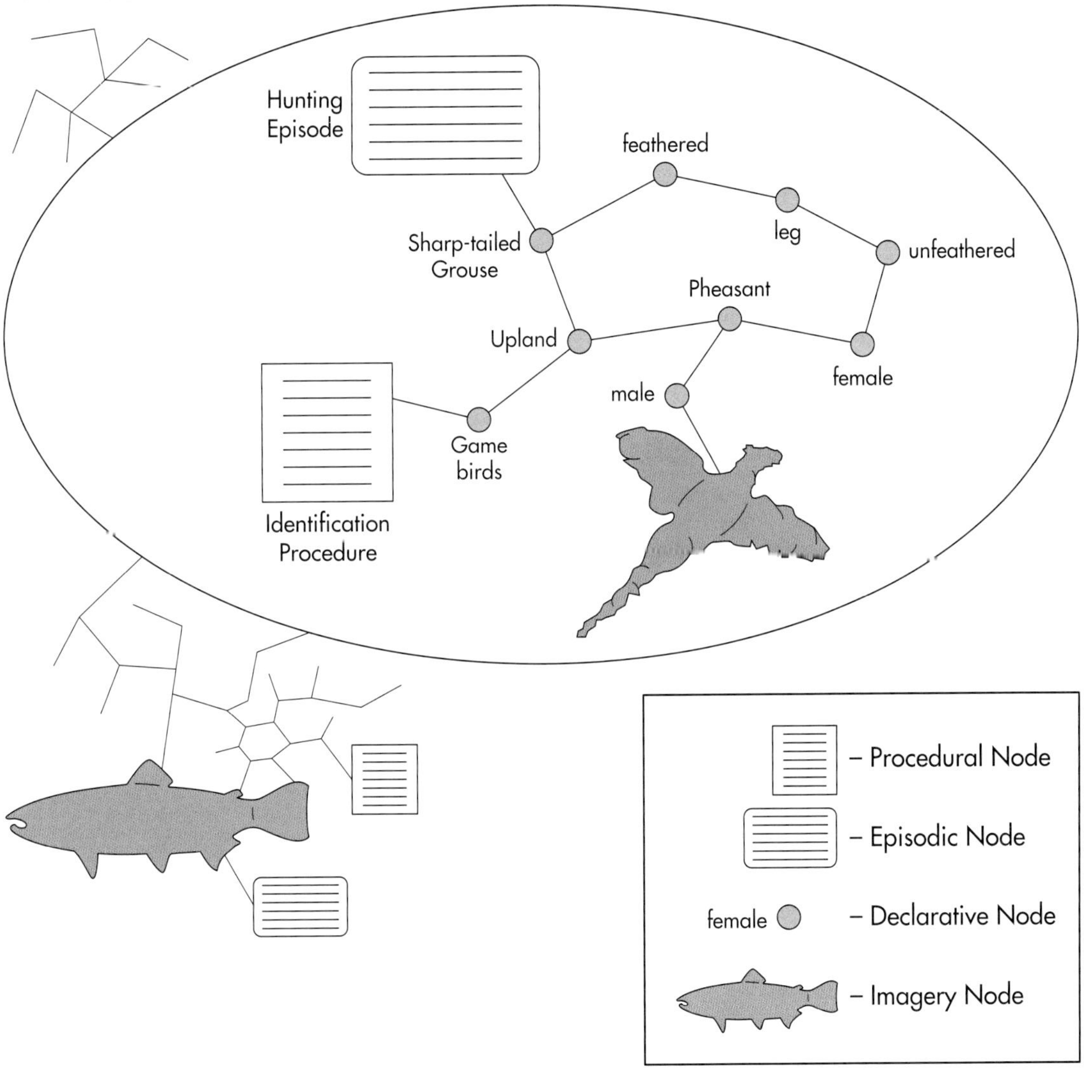

3. Declarative knowledge: conceptual knowledge about pheasants and grouse
4. Procedural knowledge: the stored strategy for identifying particular game birds

Meaningful links among elements

As you can see from the figure, these elements are linked in meaningful ways. For example, the image of a male pheasant is connected with the concepts "male" and "pheasant." (What would you guess is one way to distinguish a female pheasant from a sharp-tailed grouse? One difference is whether the leg is feathered or not.)

The networklike structure of memory explains an important characteristic of human thought. We seldom recall isolated thoughts. One idea seems to make us aware of other ideas, images, or stored experiences. The related nodes that are first activated or brought into our awareness are those that are the most directly linked. Many important kinds of mental performance depend on how individual nodes of memory are linked or organized. Organized elements of memory are more likely to be available to our awareness at any given point than are unorganized elements. Mental tasks will go much more successfully when the memory elements required to accomplish them are well organized.

If LTM consists of a network of nodes, then a major goal of education is to construct and modify this network. One important way to modify the network is to add new nodes (ideas, events, images, or procedures). However, it is also important to organize nodes by adding new links and possibly eliminating other, inappropriate links. The least valuable learning experiences add few nodes or add nodes linked to just a few existing nodes. The most valuable learning experiences encourage students to create rich interconnections among stored elements of knowledge. Creating links is not an automatic process. Students must activate stored experiences and find appropriate connections with new ideas. How all this happens is not fully understood, but we provide further insights as we discuss cognitive processes.

Processes: Mental Tools for Doing the Work of Thinking and Learning

Something very important is still missing in our consideration of what is necessary for learning. Thinking and learning are active. Students acquire information from the world around them and generate personal knowledge; they solve problems; they create new ideas and new things. The cognitive system we have described to this point just sits there. If teachers want to search for more effective learning experiences for their students, they will need to have some general ideas about the mental actions that productive learning experiences should encourage.

The basic actions of the information processing system are often referred to as *processes*. Instead of an extended discussion of the volumes of research on cognitive processes, we use a simpler idea based on this research: the idea of a *mental tool*. Assume that students have at their disposal mental tools they can use to accomplish a variety of cognitive tasks. Here are four hypothetical tool categories:

1. *Attend to:* Maintain certain ideas in consciousness for an extended period of time.
2. *Link/Associate/Organize:* Establish connections between information units stored in LTM or active in working memory.

Categories of mental tools

3. *Elaborate/Extend/Exemplify/Infer:* Create or discover new knowledge from the logical and purposeful combination of active and stored memory components.
4. *Test/Evaluate/Question:* Determine whether a situation is as desired or expected.

We have organized the descriptive verbs in groups to indicate that all verbs in a group describe similar functions. Certainly it would be possible to propose more tools or to explain these phenomena in different terms. The point is, within the cognitive system, there seem to exist mechanisms—mental tools—for operating on the raw information fed into the system from the world and for managing and continually modifying what the system has stored previously. These tools accomplish the work of cognitive activity.

Metacognition

In evaluating the utility of the mental tool metaphor, Paris and Winograd (1990) note that having a collection of tools is not enough. A good craftsperson knows how to use the appropriate tools wisely and independently to complete desired projects. The same is true of effective learners. Effective tool use requires insights into task demands, awareness of personal strengths and weaknesses, and ongoing analysis of whether progress on the task is proceeding well or poorly. The skilled learner can plan to avoid difficulties or compensate for problems. Perhaps a different tool must be used. Perhaps the action of a tool already employed must be repeated until the desired outcome is achieved.

Any model of reading, writing, problem solving, or general study must propose some mechanism to account for the adaptive and strategic nature of actual student thinking and learning behavior. What prominent researchers and theorists have come up with to account for strategic behavior is the admittedly fuzzy and rather poorly operationalized construct of **metacognition** (Brown, 1981, 1987; Flavell, 1987; Garner, 1987; Paris & Winograd, 1990). Metacognition, which is responsible for guiding cognitive behavior, accounts for the strategic use of cognitive tools and for our ability to evaluate the success of our mental behaviors. Metacognition is usually described in terms of a combination of *metacognitive knowledge* and *metacognitive control functions*.

Metacognitive Knowledge

Metacognitive knowledge consists of personal insights into how cognitive tasks such as memory or writing are accomplished, about what makes particular tasks difficult or easy, and about personal cognitive characteristics and capabilities. We all have such knowledge, accurate or not. Students may realize, for instance, that information stored in an organized fashion is easier to retrieve than information stored haphazardly. They may realize that when they can't remember something, they should try to think of related things.

Metacognitive knowledge covers the skills of both academic and professional life. In some cases, this knowledge is the intended result of direct instruction. We are expected to learn strategies for figuring out the meaning of

Side notes

Categories of mental tools

Knowing how to use mental tools

Video Case

View the HM Video Case entitled *Metacognition: Helping Students Become Strategic Learners* to watch middle-school teacher Julie Craven help her students develop metacognitive tools for reading difficult texts. Do you see evidence of planning, regulating, and evaluating in their work?

Metacognition and strategic use of cognitive tools

Ways of developing metacognitive knowledge

an unfamiliar word, to learn how to research and write a position paper, and to learn how to study for an essay examination. Other metacognitive knowledge is picked up less directly. Some students may realize that math is a particularly difficult subject for them, and that is a form of metacognitive knowledge. Students may also figure out that instructors are more likely to ask examination questions on topics covered in class than on textbook topics that were not discussed.

Metacognitive Control Functions

Metacognitive control functions are demonstrated in planning, regulating, and evaluating behaviors (Paris & Lindauer, 1982). Planning concerns decision making before beginning a project; regulating involves adjustments made while working on the task; and evaluating has to do with decisions made once the project has been completed.

Educational significance of metacognitive control functions

Metacognitive control functions have great educational significance. Consider the roles of planning, regulating, and evaluating as they might apply to some of the research and writing tasks involved in a student's preparation of a paper for a history class:

- *Planning:* The student might begin by outlining a rough set of issues to investigate and identifying some sources of information about these issues.
- *Regulating:* As the student examines the sources, she must locate specific information about the issues and determine if enough information is available to attempt writing the paper. If no information turns up related to some key issue, she may decide to find additional sources, modify the initial topic of the paper, or abandon the original idea entirely.
- *Evaluating:* As the student writes the paper, she must determine whether the text meets acceptable standards for spelling and grammar and whether she is presenting the intended ideas in an organized and persuasive manner.

Metacognitive control functions and self-directed learning

Metacognitive control functions also play a major role in self-directed learning. Thomas and Rohwer (1986) describe study behavior as effortful, private, self-managed activities, often operating with little in the way of external guidance regarding what is to be accomplished or what level of mastery is required. If you think carefully about what is (or was) expected of you as a college student, you will note just how much responsibility advanced students must accept. Usually much more material is presented than would be practical to master. Consequently, you must decide what is essential to master and what you can cover more superficially. The nature of future examinations is also vague, and you must make decisions about how your understanding will likely be evaluated. Finally, as you prepare for these examinations, there are few or no concrete ways for you to judge how adequately you have prepared. Do I understand this chapter well enough to go on to the next? Will I be able to solve this type of problem if it appears on the test? All three metacognitive control functions are involved: You must develop study plans, evaluate the adequacy of your understanding, and continually regulate study methods and your allocation of time and attention.

Metacognitive skills related to academic performance often need improvement. Researchers have found that the following problems, among others, are typical:

Metacognitive
functions and study
behavior

- Students' study behavior is often passive (rereading textbook assignments). For organizing and emphasizing important content, students commonly rely on techniques such as note taking and highlighting, which are not the most powerful methods.
- Students frequently use a single study approach, even when course material and evaluation procedures vary considerably.
- Students frequently are unaware that they have failed to comprehend material they have read (Baker, 1985; Markman & Gorin, 1981). They also seem unable to predict accurately how they will do on tests covering the material that they are studying (Pressley, Snyder, Levin, Murray, & Ghatala, 1987). Thus their regulatory functions, the mechanisms that would allow them to adjust their cognitive behavior "on-the-fly," are suspect.
- When students are unable to detect comprehension failures or test preparation difficulties, they are unlikely to use remediation strategies—even simple activities such as rereading or asking the teacher or a classmate for assistance.

Using Technology to Improve Metacognitive Skills

Technology offers several ways to address metacognitive weakness, and there is some debate about which of them is preferable. Much of the controversy concerns issues of learner control versus computer control (Milheim & Martin, 1991).

The tutorial, a form of traditional computer-based instruction (see the chapter entitled "Using Instructional Software and Multimedia for Content-Area Learning"), makes heavy use of questions. Students are presented with several screens of information and then are asked questions about the information just covered. If the student does poorly on the questions, a program using *computer control* might automatically move the student into some material attempting to explain the same information in a different way. A program allowing *learner control* would likely give the learner the option of selecting the review material or continuing to the next section.

Empirical studies of computer-based instruction frequently demonstrate an advantage for computer control over learner control (Milheim & Martin, 1991; Steinberg, 1989). Such findings are frustrating to those who advocate what they believe are motivational and learning advantages of allowing the learner to fine-tune instruction to personal needs. However, allowing the learner a great deal of control does not seem to work in practice.

Balancing computer
control and learner
control

There may be a productive compromise. *Learner control with advisement* is a technique that allows the student to make decisions after considering information or suggestions provided by the computer. In a study evaluating the effectiveness of computer advisement (Tennyson, 1980), students were learning the physics concepts of force, power, velocity, and speed. They first learned formal definitions for each concept. They were then provided with examples and asked to determine which of the four concepts would explain each example. In the learner control condition, students worked with the examples until they felt prepared for the posttest. In the computer control condition, the computer made decisions about how many examples were required, using a mathematical model based on pretest performance and performance on the examples. In the third condition, the learner made the decision to take the posttest but was provided with the same information used in the computer control condition. This study and others have demonstrated that learner control with advisement is superior to unaided learner control (Tennyson, 1980; Tennyson & Buttrey, 1980). Without advisement, students tended to terminate study of the lessons more quickly, possibly indicating that they had overestimated their level of mastery.

A possible advantage of learner control with advisement is that this combination of computer monitoring and learner decision making potentially allows for the development of metacognitive and "learning-to-learn" skills. Students are put in the situation of thinking about the decisions they make as they attempt to master the assigned material. Heightened sensitivity to the processes and the successes and failures of learning may allow the student to develop new planning, regulating, and evaluating skills.

Mental Activity: A Recap

Summarizing information processing and cognition

Before we move on to a more global analysis, let's summarize some of the central ideas covered in the first part of this chapter. We saw that thinking and learning can be described as the movement and generation of information within STM and LTM. The actions learners apply in the effort to move and generate information can be called cognitive tools, and individual students use these tools in a variety of ways and with different degrees of success.

While a good teacher and effective learning environment increase the probability that desirable outcomes will occur, the teacher and environment can only provide information to the learner. Once the student takes in that information, what actually happens to it is the student's own responsibility. This is where issues of skill, motivation, and existing knowledge come into play. Metacognition, the capacity of a student to evaluate and adjust personal behaviors, also plays an important role in adapting thinking and learning behaviors for success.

How technology plays a role

How is technology involved in this perspective? There are at least two ways:

- Technology can present information to students. Mostly this information will be ideas or concepts the student is to master or experiences the student is to think about or index.
- Students may use computers and other forms of technology to complete learning tasks. In this case, technology is not a direct source of information. Instead, the student manipulates information using technology as a tool, and the experiences resulting from this manipulation are what the student thinks about and learns from.

An ongoing interaction

It may seem that what has been described here is a simple serial process: The teacher presents information or provides resources, and the student must take it from there. This is not necessarily the case. In effective teaching and learning, the teacher and student can pass information back and forth. For instance, as feedback to the teacher, the student can produce a product—something as simple as the answer to a question or as complex as a multimedia project—for the teacher to evaluate. The teacher's response then becomes new information for the student to process. The student also acts on the learning environment. In a simple form of action, the student might select an option within a computer-learning activity, and the computer might then inform the student whether the response was correct. In a more complex action, the results of student thinking behavior may take form in the paper being created on a classroom computer. This half-written composition then becomes another information resource for the student to think about. Does this paper make sense? Will I convince a future reader of my point of view? One of the more unique themes in our presentation of the integration of technology is the focus on student use of technology tools to create products. The generation of such products requires the application of the cognitive and metacognitive tools in ways that are likely to result in understanding, and the resulting product provides a powerful way for others to gain insight into the student's understanding and provide feedback.

Although the fundamental concepts we have been discussing are important for understanding the way students learn, both students and teachers tend to think about these matters at a more global level. We will adopt a global level of analysis as we consider the general topic of active learning. Our discussion of conceptual models focuses much more heavily on how effective teachers tend to interact with students and involve students in valuable learning activities. These models reinforce the point that active learning concerns what students do with information, not how much information the teacher and learning environment can provide.

Conceptual Models of School Learning

Several useful models of school learning outline instructional goals, preferred instructional practices, and ideal student behaviors. Here we look at the models of meaningful learning and constructivism.

Meaningful Learning

Meaningful learning versus rote learning

According to Ausubel (1963), **meaningful learning** occurs when new experiences are related to what a learner already knows. It can be contrasted with **rote learning,** which Ausubel describes as the learning of a sequence of words with little attention to meaning, as in simple memorization. In both cases learners are processing information, but their mental activities are quite different. Meaningful learning assumes that:

- Students already have some knowledge that is relevant to their new learning.
- Students are willing to do the mental work required to find connections with what they already know.

Meaningful learning requires motivation.

Learning tasks can contribute to the establishment of these connections by encouraging the student to recognize personal experiences that are relevant or even by providing new life experiences as part of the learning activity.

Because meaningful learning takes work, student motivation is important. Student motivation can be subverted not only by a lack of interest but also by a lack of confidence in the ability to learn meaningfully and by a reward structure that provides too many incentives for rote learning. The teacher's role is to provide an optimal environment that makes the learner feel capable and presents the learner with tasks he or she regards as personally relevant. The student should feel there is some payoff for learning rather than merely memorizing. At a practical level, this might mean that the assessment of learning should require the learner to demonstrate understanding and the ability to apply knowledge as well as recall facts.

Reception versus Discovery

Receiving versus discovering ideas

In addition to meaningful and rote learning, Ausubel differentiated between reception and discovery learning. In **reception learning,** the ideas to be learned are presented directly to students, ideally in a well-organized fashion. In **discovery learning,** in contrast, the student must work to uncover, or discover, what is to be learned. Typically, a large proportion of what is learned in school is acquired through reception learning, and much of what is learned through everyday living is acquired through discovery learning.

Ausubel warned educators not to equate reception with rote learning or meaningful learning with discovery learning. We agree with this warning. The activities connected with discovery are more concerned with generating the ideas to be learned than with relating these ideas to existing knowledge. Rote discovery learning is quite possible, and you can find it in the "cookbook" activities used in some science laboratories. In such activities, a student follows a detailed set of instructions to complete an experiment or task. Technically, the student is using a discovery framework, but because the student makes few decisions and does not have to understand the processes to move from one part of the activity to the next, meaningful learning may not occur. To raise this issue, we sometimes ask the question, "How much chemistry do you learn from baking bread?" The point is that physically manipulating objects and completing activities does not necessarily mean a student is mentally manipulating ideas. "Hands-on" activities must result in active cognitive behavior for meaningful learning to occur. This is one of the dangers when teachers think only in terms of classroom activities and not in terms of how effectively and efficiently the assignments engage the learner. While Ausubel's work is dated, the issue he raised remains relevant. In a recent effort to counter what was described as a misguided return to unguided discovery tasks, Mayer (2004) summarized research on learning experiences and concluded that it is cognitive and not behavioral activity that is essential to effective learning.

Characterizing Typical Learning Activities

Various instructional applications of technology (for examples, see the chapter entitled "Using Instructional Software and Multimedia for Content-Area Learning") fit nicely within Ausubel's framework for categorizing learning ex-

Video Case
See discovery learning in action by watching the HM Video Case entitled *Using Technology to Promote Discovery Learning.* After observing how teacher Gary Simon uses technology in his geometry classroom, why do you think discovery learning is an important component of both learning and instruction?

FIGURE 2.2

Learning Activities Categorized by Two Dimensions: Rote Learning versus Meaningful Learning and Reception Learning versus Discovery Learning. Technology activities appear in parentheses. Descriptions of the technology activities listed are provided in later chapters.

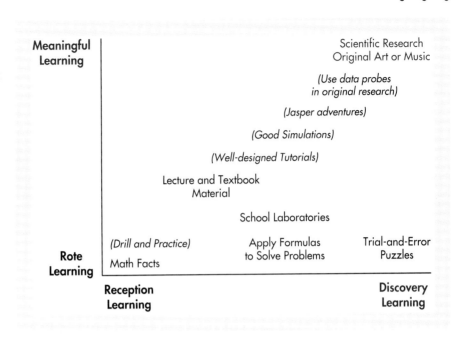

perience. In a computer tutorial, technology presents the critical concepts and rules to be learned in a direct manner, and students working with it are engaging in reception learning. In a computer simulation, the student attempts to identify key concepts or rules by interacting with a simulated responsive environment presented by the computer. The student has to discover the concepts or rules from the experiences that the environment provides.

A graphic representation of Ausubel's framework

The dual dimensions of rote-meaningful learning and reception-discovery learning provide an informative framework for categorizing school learning experiences of all types, as shown in Figure 2.2. The school tasks not involving technology are positioned as proposed by Ausubel (1963). We have added technology-related activities, in parentheses, based on our own perceptions of how these activities engage learners. Of course, the classification of learning activities in this figure requires assumptions about how the typical student will respond to the activities. If you want to draw your own conclusions, you might look up the activities in the index and spend a brief amount of time learning what students do as they engage in these activities. You may also want to test your understanding of this figure by considering where other learning activities would be located.

Different learning activities valuable in different situations

Looking at the figure, you may wonder whether there are some learning activities that should be avoided. A simple answer would be that all types of learning may be appropriate under some circumstances. For example, rote learning may be a reasonable way to approach the learning of basic number facts, but not the historical antecedents of World War II. Concern would probably be appropriate if rote learning were overemphasized or if an instructional activity resulted in a different type of learning experience than was intended. It is unlikely, for instance, that school science laboratories are intended as rote-discovery experiences, and if students are in fact responding to laboratory experiences in a mindless fashion, then this is cause for concern. So part of the task in decision making is to determine what types of mental activities are desired in specific learning situations. Another part is to determine if the learning activities do indeed result in the intended behaviors.

When to Use Discovery Techniques

Discovery techniques are most appropriate when reception methods are unlikely to bring about a high degree of cognitive involvement (Howe, 1972). Such situations include work with younger children and with concepts that are abstract because of unfamiliarity.

Motivation and the choice of instructional methods

Motivation can be highly individualistic. An experienced computer programmer might prefer to consult a reference book about a new technique or command rather than work through a tutorial. On the other hand, students less interested in programming would likely find a book that lists command after command very boring. Instead, they might become quite wrapped up in a book that involved them in using the commands to create an interesting product. The difference here is motivation to perform the necessary mental work. The programmer is already motivated to learn and will process the new information meaningfully as soon as the ideas have been received. The student may need to be motivated by some exciting task before processing the information. When students are motivated and have adequate background knowledge, reception learning can be quite adequate for meaningful learning.

Constructivism

Learning as the building of personal understanding

Like Ausubel's meaningful learning, **constructivism** generally argues that learners build personal understanding and that this constructive process can be facilitated by appropriate learning activities and a good learning environment (see, for instance, APA/BEA, 1995; Brooks & Brooks, 1999; Knapp & Glenn, 1996). There is, however, no single, official explanation for what constructivism represents. The term has been used to address a wide range of issues, from the psychology of individual learning to philosophical reflections on science as a mechanism for pursuing knowledge (Loving, 1997). Some extreme constructivist positions may be disruptive to those of us attempting to bring practical suggestions to classroom teachers, and we are in agreement with those, such as Loving, who advocate a balanced approach.

Probably the two most generally accepted principles of constructivism are these:

■ What a person knows is not passively received, but *actively assembled* by the learner (Jonassen, 1991; Wheatley, 1991).
■ In most circumstances, learning serves an adaptive function. That is, the role of learning is to help the individual operate within his or her personal world.

Video Case

How do teachers implement constructivist principles in the real world? Watch teacher Sarabinh Levy-Brightman as she helps two teams of students prepare to debate Jeffersonian democracy in the HM Video Case entitled *Constructivist Teaching in Action: Classroom Debate.*

Spotlight on Assessment

Performance Assessment

Many educators agree that, to promote meaningful learning, assessment should go beyond a mere testing of factual knowledge. It should focus on a deeper level of understanding and on students' ability to apply what they have learned to new situations. *Performance assessment* is one such approach that has gained ground in recent years.

Performance assessment relies on a variety of methods, all of which require students to demonstrate what they know or can do by creating an answer or a product (Office of Technology Assessment, 1992). One situation in which educators have traditionally relied on performance assessment is the culminating task in graduate education: a thesis or dissertation, which is a formal written presentation of the graduate student's original research. Students must use what they have learned throughout their graduate education to plan and implement a research project, interpret and communicate the results of their research as a written product, and defend their written interpretation in a public forum. Graduate education is intended to prepare advanced students to function as independent scholars, and the process of producing and defending a scholarly product assesses their ability to perform in this capacity.

Other types of performance assessment cover a wide continuum of tasks, ranging from essay examinations to collections of work accumulated over time. You are probably already familiar with essay examinations, in which you have written descriptions, analyses, or summaries to demonstrate your understanding. Research and writing tasks conducted outside class represent a further step along the continuum. Original research and a related exhibition closely resemble the thesis model used with advanced students. A science fair project is a good example. Exhibitions are culminating experiences in which the knowledge or skill gained over many hours of work is displayed. The public nature of the exhibition requires careful consideration of how best to communicate what has been learned, and this additional processing has further cognitive benefits.

At the far end of the continuum, portfolios offer an inclusive summary of student performance. You are probably familiar with the term *portfolio* as the collection an artist or architect puts together to demonstrate his or her skills. Student portfolios are similar, containing samples of the student's best work collected over time. Unlike the items in the portfolio of an artist, those in a student portfolio, such as writing samples, are intended to document improvement. An example of an electronic portfolio was described in the chapter entitled "Key Themes and Issues for Using Technology in Your Classroom."

Technology-supported activities can provide many opportunities for performance assessment. Throughout this book we offer examples and ideas demonstrating how students can use technology as a tool both to learn and to demonstrate what they have learned. The final products that students create are ideal for performance assessment. Thinking of technology in this way is not the most common perspective, but it is clearly one that is gaining attention and credibility.

These two principles of constructive learning lead to at least three significant practical implications:

Students responsible for their own learning

1. *Responsibility for learning.* The student accomplishes learning, and learning is the result of mental work. Learners must mentally act on the information they receive to create personal understanding and transform information into knowledge. Teachers must recognize that the presentation of information by itself may not result in the generation of knowledge. Teachers cannot directly control the mental behaviors that result in learning, but they may be able to model effective learning behaviors for students, and they may assist students by engaging them in activities that facilitate or encourage productive mental activity. Teachers play an important but indirect role.

Learning influenced by context

2. *The context of learning.* Context has a lot to do with what the learner perceives as useful knowledge and how he or she integrates new experiences with existing knowledge. In the most critical sense, does the student see connections between the part of his or her world identified as "school" and the part sometimes referred to as "real life"? A student who perceives little or no connection, constructivists argue, will not build much personal knowledge. (Later in this chapter, we discuss authentic tasks as one way to establish a meaningful context for learning.)

Learning personal knowledge, not abstract truths

3. *The purpose of education.* Constructivists contend that the primary purpose of education is not the acquisition of universal truths. Because each person has different experiences and is assumed to construct an individual interpretation of these experiences, each person's reality is slightly different. Learning means acquiring not abstract general truths but useful personal knowledge.

Reviewing the Common Themes

Rather than get caught up in one particular theory or another, we prefer to focus on the common themes of these various educational theories—themes that have been frequently emphasized by educational reformers (see the chapter entitled "Key Themes and Issues for Using Technology in Your Classroom"). Let's reiterate these key ideas.

First, the theories that we have discussed describe the fundamental nature of the learner as *active.* Active learners seek to build an understanding of their personal worlds that will allow them to function productively. This process requires that learners make the effort to build on what they know in order to interpret and respond to new experiences.

True active learners function in a purposeful manner. They are capable of establishing personal goals, developing strategies for addressing these goals, and monitoring whether the strategies have been successful. By taking such a purposeful, active approach, students make their learning experiences *meaningful.* That is, their new learning relates to their previous knowledge and is relevant to their personal lives. It is deeper than mere rote learning or memorization, and it can be applied not just in school but also in "real life."

Now let's turn to the question of what these theories mean for your classroom practice and how technology can help you apply them.

Focus

Are We Abandoning Truth?

You may be concerned by the constructivist suggestion that universal truths are not the goal of student learning. But before making up your mind, consider a couple of additional points.

First, most of us have held beliefs that we eventually learned were not truths. Some of these beliefs resulted from faulty information, but some were the official truths taught as part of a particular discipline, such as chemistry, physics, or history. Our ideas that passed for knowledge had to be modified later to handle new findings. Can you think of any such examples from your own education? Science "facts" or theories? Historical interpretations?

Second, we obviously do not end up with widely different views of our world. Education is pretty much a social process, and one adaptive purpose of the social context is to confront and negotiate differences in personal perspectives. When others explain their beliefs, we have new information to test against our personal views. Throughout this book, you'll see that we emphasize both learning tasks involving collaboration and tasks that require learners to represent their understanding in ways that allow others to react. Both types of activity are important.

From Theory to Practice: Teaching, Learning, and the Role of Technology

Although educators approach the issue of improving student learning in many different ways, their ideas tend to converge in recommendations for classroom practice. Consider the following general suggestions (Duffy & Bednar, 1991; Means et al., 1993; Partnership for 21st Century Skills, 2003):

1. The catalyst for changing the learning experience at a fundamental level will be centering more of the learner's time on *authentic, challenging tasks.* Students need rich contexts for learning that reduce the emphasis on fact mastery and isolated, discrete component skills and increase the emphasis on *multidisciplinary* tasks that require students to apply and create personal understanding.

2. The social environment should support learning in different ways:
   - Students should have *access to domain experts* who model the skills appropriate to the domain and provide insights into the culture of the domain within what has been described as an *apprenticeship* relationship.
   - Teachers should view their roles differently. The facilitation of thinking and problem solving must accompany the transfer of

information. Teachers may guide student work related to unfamiliar content and acquire new knowledge along with their students.

■ Students should spend a greater amount of time working in *cooperative relationships* with other students to explore alternative perspectives and evaluate ideas. These relationships help provide learning experiences that encourage communication and access to real-world examples.

The collective application of these changes in the social context of learning might be said to establish *learning communities.*

3. A greater emphasis should be placed on *reflective thinking* and *productivity.* The fundamental goal should be the ability to perform relevant tasks with the understanding that not every student will perform the tasks in the same way or acquire the same task-relevant skills.

We see technology as providing an extremely useful set of tools for addressing these goals. Later chapters explore particular uses of technology in greater depth. Here, we isolate a few of the important ideas for more detailed consideration.

Authentic Activities

Authentic activities as everyday acts

Research shows that when learning is accomplished as part of an authentic activity, it is more relevant and more likely to be used in future situations (Brown, Collins, & Duguid, 1989). But what, then, are **authentic activities**? According to one interesting perspective, they are the ordinary practices of a culture (Brown et al., 1989). The term *culture* here refers to what might best be understood as ordinary people doing the ordinary things that readers or writers, biologists, historians, or speakers of Spanish do. Language makes a good example that we can understand from personal experience. Users of a language apply their knowledge as a tool to complete tasks within their everyday environment. By this definition, our use of language is authentic because it has great utility in our daily lives.

Searching for authentic activities in classrooms reveals an interesting insight. In each room there is a recognizable classroom culture, and there are identifiable authentic activities at work within this culture. The problem is that the authentic classroom tasks may not be the ones that teachers really intend. The goals, values, and activities of the school culture and the subject matter culture can be very different (Brown et al., 1989). The student functioning in the culture of a fairly typical classroom uses knowledge to solve problems relevant to the school domain, such as getting the most points possible on the next quiz or pleasing the teacher. But knowledge the student acquires for the school domain may not transfer to any domain beyond the school walls. To state the problem another way, the knowledge students acquire in school is too often inert.

Inert Knowledge

Inert knowledge is knowledge that students have learned but fail to use (Whitehead, 1929). More exactly, it is knowledge that is available in a re-

Naive theories: an example of inert knowledge

stricted set of contexts rather than in all of the contexts in which it might apply. Often the restricted context is extremely narrow. Students may activate knowledge for classroom examinations and then fail to recognize the valuable role the same knowledge could play in other situations. For instance, a student who does well on an arithmetic test may have little practical understanding of prices in a supermarket.

An interesting example of inert knowledge can be found in naive science conceptions. We all function somewhat like scientists in our everyday lives as we develop a wealth of knowledge from our unsystematic and uncontrolled daily observations of the world around us (Bruning, Schraw, Norby, & Ronning, 2004). We form opinions, or *naive theories,* about all kinds of things based on our observations of daily phenomena. Sometimes these naive theories are simply incorrect and contradict more appropriate theories we have learned through formal education. Yet we can maintain incompatible academic and naive theories at the same time (Champagne, Gunstone, & Klopfer, 1985; Linn, Eylon, & Davis, 2004; Clement, 1983; McCloskey, 1983). For example, education students learn about the value of distributed practice, but many still cram for their examinations. The academic theories seem to be applied in the classroom, and the naive theories in the real world. The presence of incompatible knowledge requires that, at any given time, one knowledge source or the other must be inert. To put these ideas into perspective, recognize that the conditions for naive theory and inert knowledge would seem well suited to apply to a profession like teaching. As educators, we have been both formally prepared to apply principles of effective instruction and informally prepared by what we have observed during years of being in classrooms.

How can naive theories be changed? For change to occur, students need to confront the discrepancies between their naive theories and school models of the world. They must be made aware of both ideas at the same time. Hands-on projects conducted in the school environment seem to be a powerful way to activate both naive theories and school models (Shipstone, 1988). Hands-on projects can provide an element of realism that prevents the student from escaping to a purely hypothetical way of thinking. The student sees not just the academic relevance of certain ideas but also their relevance to other aspects of life. When they serve this function, these projects meet our definition of authentic activities, and these are the types of projects this book emphasizes.

Authentic Activities and Technology

We believe that the fundamental requirements for authentic activities are (1) the culture of practice and (2) primary information sources. In both categories, technology can provide many of the resources necessary for authentic activities.

The Culture of Practice The *culture of practice* provides the social contact and the purpose for authentic tasks. We have already described authentic tasks as the ordinary practices of a culture and asked you to consider the activities of the culture of biologists, historians, and Spanish speakers. When used as a model for a productive learning environment, a culture of practice would urge the application of content-area knowledge to the practice of tasks appropriate to the content domain. Students would benefit from occasional opportunities to take on some of the tasks of biologists, historians, and Spanish speakers. See the examples in "Focus: Using the Internet for Authentic Activities" on page 65.

The Internet and the culture of practice

The Internet is a prime example of a technology that can help establish or provide access to a culture of practice. E-mail and web-based projects can connect interested teachers, students, parents, and practitioners who might rally around a particular project. These individuals might be active partners in implementing projects; sources of information, guidance, and feedback; or the audience for whom projects are developed.

Technology and access to primary sources

Primary Sources *Primary sources* represent information or data that learners act on to produce personal knowledge. The Internet offers a vast amount of such information. The sources may exist in digital form (documents, images, sounds), in the form of people willing to provide their opinions or knowledge, or in some cases in the form of equipment that provides a stream of data (such as weather data or images from remote cameras). With its connections to a wealth and variety of sources, the Internet can provide an excellent resource for constructing challenging projects that lead students to confront their own preconceptions and modify their thinking.

Higher-Order Thinking and Transfer

Most educators, we believe, would say they support the development of higher-order thinking skills, but if they were pressed, many would find that their understanding of what they were advocating was vague. This lack of clarity is understandable. Higher-order thinking is not a single process (such as word identification) or even a complex skill that has been designated as a focus of the curriculum at a particular grade level (such as learning to read). It involves many cognitive skills and is potentially involved in every content area. Nevertheless, to be successful, teachers must accept responsibility for assisting students in the acquisition of higher-order thinking skills, understand the nature of the skills they are helping students to develop, and recognize productive options for helping students learn these skills.

It is not easy to provide a simple definition of higher-order thinking, but it is possible to list some of its attributes. **Higher-order thinking** meets the following criteria (Resnick, 1987):

Attributes of higher-order thinking

- It is *complex.* The tasks involved can often be accomplished in several ways, and the entire process often unfolds in stages without a complete course of action being evident from the beginning.
- It is *effortful.* The tasks require conscious effort.
- It is *self-regulated.* Metacognitive planning and monitoring are necessary.
- It frequently involves *judgment*—the evaluation of conflicting information.

Problem solving and critical thinking

These attributes are characteristic of problem solving and critical thinking, two categories of thinking skill that educators frequently emphasize with

TABLE 2.1

Problem Solving, Critical Thinking, and Related Subskills

Higher-Order Skills	Purpose	Subskills
Problem solving	Process involved in overcoming an obstacle to reach a goal	• Recognize problem exists • Represent situation • Select strategy • Implement strategy • Evaluate and repeat if necessary
Critical thinking	Process involving evaluation—in some applications to make a reasoned choice	• Locate information appropriate to a purpose • Analyze arguments • Differentiate verifiable facts from personal beliefs • Evaluate information source credibility • Identify unstated assumptions • Evaluate the logic used in reaching a conclusion • Weigh evidence or options

their students. **Problem solving** and **critical thinking** are thinking processes with identifiable subskills, some of which are outlined in Table 2.1. For the problem-solving process, many theorists have summarized the necessary subskills and the sequence in which they are executed. Critical thinking can also be described as a series of stages encompassing information gathering, evaluation, and usually decision making. The evaluative component of critical thinking varies with the task to be accomplished.

In many situations, problem solving and critical thinking operate in an interdependent fashion. For example, information problem-solving tasks require students to gather and interpret information to solve a problem and thus draw on both problem-solving and critical-thinking skills. As a student, you face an information problem-solving task when your instructor assigns a research paper. You have to locate credible information sources relevant to the assignment, interpret this information, and then integrate the information in a way that satisfies the goals of the assignment. We face many information problem-solving tasks in daily life. For example, we frequently gather and interpret information to achieve a goal when we make major purchases (such as buying a car) or navigate about our world (for instance, determining how to use the bus or subway system to get to an unfamiliar destination). The chapter entitled "The Internet as a Tool for Inquiry" offers an extended discussion of information problem solving.

We have a particular interest in the information problem-solving activities of biologists, historians, writers, and anyone else who might be commonly labeled as active practitioners of content-area skills (biology, history, English). These activities provide one way of defining the authentic tasks that educators might attempt to adapt as learning activities.

Ways to Teach Higher-Order Thinking

There are three distinct approaches to the instruction of higher-order thinking skills within a classroom setting, defined by the manner in which this instruction relates to the instruction of other areas of the curriculum (Wakefield, 1996):

Approaches to teaching higher-order skills

1. *Stand-alone approach.* Class activities are focused on the development of higher-order thinking skills. Instruction in thinking skills is independent of instruction in content-area skills and knowledge.
2. *Dual-agenda approach.* Instruction in higher-order thinking is combined with instruction in another area of the curriculum. Instruction in both areas may be provided independently within the course, but the content-area learning tasks provide an opportunity for practicing thinking skills.
3. *Authentic task approach.* This approach requires the application of higher-order thinking in performing activities that lead to the development of both thinking and content-area skills and knowledge. Rather than being developed independently, thinking skills are learned through the application within domain-appropriate activities.

Table 2.2 summarizes some key points about these three approaches to developing higher-order thinking skills. The following examples, mentioned in the last row of the table, show how technology has been used in implementing each instructional approach:

Using technology to develop higher-order thinking

- The HOTS Project (Higher Order Thinking Skills; Pogrow, 1996) was created as a way to develop higher-order thinking skills in struggling upper-elementary students. It is a pullout program in which a teacher assists a small number of students who need extra attention with instructional software applications that require critical thinking and problem solving. Because the computer experiences and the interactions with the teacher focus directly on the development of thinking skills, HOTS is a good example of the stand-alone approach.
- Teaching computer programming to young students is an example of the dual-agenda approach. The teaching focuses both on learning to use a programming language—a content area—and on the skills of problem solving. (We say more about computer programming in the next section.)
- Data loggers (discussed in the chapter entitled "Using Tools") allow students to collect raw information—for instance, on temperature variations. When these tools are used in authentic student research, the students must not only gather the data but also organize and analyze it to complete the project. Higher-order thinking becomes an essential part of the task they are performing.

The debate over which approach is best is unresolved at this point. By now, though, our own interest in the authentic task approach should be obvious. If it can be assumed that all three approaches have the potential to develop higher-order thinking skills, efficiency may be an issue to consider. How

TABLE 2.2
Summary of Ways to Teach Higher-Order Thinking

	Instructional Strategy		
	Stand Alone	**Dual Agenda**	**Authentic Task**
Focus	Higher-order thinking	Targeted higher-order thinking skills and content-area knowledge	Higher-order skills appropriate to content-area knowledge
Instructional method	Independent course	Process skill instruction added to course	Content course activity selected to require content and thinking skills
Thinking skills	Potential to apply thinking skills in other courses	Thinking skills relevant to content tasks	Thinking skills essential to content tasks
Technology example	HOTS (Pogrow, 1996)	Programming and problem solving (e.g., Salomon & Perkins, 1987)	Use of data loggers in authentic student research (e.g., Albrecht & Firedrake, 1998)

many schools are willing or able to offer a course dedicated only to thinking skills? And is it reasonable to involve students in computer programming, a course that probably is not central to the standard curriculum, because it provides a good opportunity to practice higher-level thinking? For many schools, we believe, the authentic task approach offers the best alternative.

Transfer: The Low Road and the High Road

The process by which specific skills and knowledge learned in one situation prove generally useful in a variety of new situations is referred to as **transfer.** When you think about it, transfer is what formal education is all about. Unless what we teach and learn in our classrooms has some general value in other classrooms and outside the school setting, why bother acquiring the knowledge in the first place?

Low-road transfer

Transfer can occur in two ways, sometimes referred to as low- and high-road transfer (Salomon & Perkins, 1987). In *low-road transfer,* behavior is practiced extensively and in a variety of situations and learned to the point of automatization—that is, to the point at which the person can complete a task without thinking about it. For example, if you drive or are a competent typist, you have practiced the skills involved so much that many of your behaviors have likely become automatized. When you move from your car to someone else's car, your automatized behaviors carry over to the new situation.

High-road transfer

In *high-road transfer,* skills must be *deliberately* transferred from one context to another. For this kind of transfer to occur, two requirements must be met:

1. The individual must be capable of re-representing the original skill at a level that includes a greater range of cases than was covered by the context in which the skill was first acquired.

2. The student must be willing to make a conscious effort to use past experiences to attack current problems. Such an approach requires both motivation and metacognitive skill.

Computer programming and the issue of transfer

Some of the most extensive research on the transfer of higher-order thinking skills has focused on the teaching of computer programming. Programming is nearly a classic problem-solving activity. In fact, descriptions of what experienced programmers do (Pea & Kurland, 1987b) are almost identical to more general descriptions of the problem-solving process (Bransford & Stein, 1984; Hayes & Simon, 1974). Over the years, therefore, various studies have attempted to determine whether students who learn computer programming can transfer their skills to other problem-solving situations. Salomon and Perkins (1987) reviewed a number of such studies to see whether they met the requirements for either high- or low-road transfer. According to this analysis, when students did not (1) spend enough time programming to develop a reasonable level of skill or accumulate enough diverse experiences, (2) consider and discuss how they solve problems when they program, and (3) consider how the problem-solving skills involved in programming might apply to other domains, the research studies were unlikely to demonstrate that students could transfer programming skills to other areas. For more information about the value of teaching computer programming to students, see the textbook website.

Implications for teachers

What are the implications of these findings for classroom teachers? For higher-order skills, we cannot think of many classroom experiences that meet both conditions necessary for low-road transfer (extensive practice, a variety of situations). High-road transfer seems the more practical of the two alternatives. However, high-road transfer establishes clear expectations for educators. Teachers must help students identify and understand the skills being developed and see how these skills might be used in other settings and for other tasks. For example, when students learn to approach a complex computer-programming problem by breaking it down into individual tasks, teachers need to help them recognize what they are doing and understand that the same process can be useful in other situations. In that way, the students will re-represent programming knowledge in an abstract and verbal fashion that can apply to many tasks.

Our general point here is a straightforward one: Technology can make a significant contribution to instruction aimed at higher-order thinking skills, but only if teachers structure the experiences in a way that maximizes the transfer value.

The Social Context of Learning

Learning, particularly learning within educational institutions, is a social phenomenon. Although the learning theories we have emphasized assume individual responsibility for learning, the social environment in which learners function can be essential in modeling, encouraging, and providing opportunities for essential learning and problem-solving behaviors.

Focus

Using the Internet for Authentic Activities

We provide examples of authentic activities throughout this book. Here are a few examples to get you thinking about classroom applications:

- *Winter bird feeder study.* Students in a sophomore biology class position a bird feeder outside their classroom window and make periodic observations of the birds that visit the feeder each Friday. These data are entered into a web form and submitted to the Cornell Laboratory of Ornithology. The students have joined Project FeederWatch, a group of thirteen thousand amateur scientists who are gathering and sharing data in an effort to understand changes in bird populations (**http://birds.cornell.edu/PFW/**).
- *Life of a one-room school teacher.* Eighth-grade students are asked to develop a description of what it was like to teach in a northern prairie one-room school in the late nineteenth century. This description should provide some insights into who these teachers were and what their working conditions were like. For primary source materials, students are asked to use the searchable document and image collection provided by the Library of Congress American Memory website (**http://memory.loc.gov/ammem/**).
- *Spanish-speaking key pal.* Students in a freshman Spanish class are exchanging e-mail with students from Spain to develop their written language skills. The teacher spent a semester in Madrid during college and was particularly interested in locating a companion class from that city. She has a lot of pictures and stories to help her class learn a little more about where their key pals live. The teacher is able to locate a companion classroom using Keypals Club International (**http://www.worldkids.net/clubs/kci/keypals2.html**).

Notice how these activities meet the two requirements of bringing students into a culture of practice and allowing them to use primary sources.

Cognitive Apprenticeship

Reciprocal teaching: an example of cognitive apprenticeship

Educational reformers who want to increase the emphasis on thinking or inquiry skills have tried to develop strategies for teaching such complex mental behaviors. The notion of **cognitive apprenticeship** is one such strategy. Probably the most frequently cited example of cognitive apprenticeship is *reciprocal teaching*, which was designed to teach students how to comprehend written material (Palincsar & Brown, 1984). In this approach, the teacher works with a small number of students. Initially the teacher takes the most active role and models important cognitive behaviors. Because cognitive behaviors (mental processes) cannot be observed directly, important behaviors are defined in terms of behaviors that can be demonstrated: asking questions, summarizing content, identifying and clarifying difficulties, and making predictions.

In reciprocal teaching, the group reads a paragraph together. The teacher then models the target behaviors: asks the students a question, comments about something that seemed difficult to understand, or makes a prediction. Individual students then attempt these activities under the teacher's supervision. Eventually the individual is expected to get to the point of performing all external behaviors and then only the internal equivalents.

Helping learners acquire thinking skills

The goal of cognitive apprenticeship is to help inexperienced practitioners acquire essential thinking skills. The social environment provides the opportunity to learn from more skilled colleagues and to share responsibility so that a demanding task does not overwhelm the learner. Critical to the approach are opportunities to externalize mental behaviors. Teachers and students describe what they are trying to do as they work on tasks that involve the essential thinking behaviors. The descriptions provide less experienced learners something to consider and model. At the same time, they allow the more skilled practitioners to evaluate and offer advice.

The group projects described in the chapter entitled "Learning from Student Projects" provide great opportunities for this kind of interaction. Such authentic technology projects allow teachers frequent occasions to model learning and problem-solving behaviors. By their very nature, authentic technology projects are less predictable and more exploratory than typical classroom experiences. Of course, to engage students in such exploration, teachers themselves need to be flexible and open to new experiences.

Cooperative Learning

Video Case
Watch the HM Video Cases entitled *Cooperative Learning in the Elementary Grades: Jigsaw Model* and *Cooperative Learning: High School* to see how this approach can be used with students of different ages. To what extent do you see Johnson & Johnson's three tasks at work in the videos?

In **cooperative learning,** students work together to accomplish a learning task. They may accomplish this goal by motivating, teaching, evaluating, or engaging one another in discussions that encourage reflection. When all students contribute, cooperative approaches encourage active learning. Cooperative learning also typically encourages inclusion and promotes heterogeneity of participation with respect to ability, gender, ethnic group, and various disabilities. The nature of the task can vary from working together to prepare for an examination, to serving as a tutor to younger or less experienced peers, to completing a classroom project.

Here we are using the phrase *cooperative learning* in a formal way. It refers to methods of student collaboration that have been purposefully structured according to specific and clearly identified principles and have been thoroughly evaluated (for example, Johnson & Johnson, 1999; Slavin, 1991, 1996). Because not every situation in which small groups of students work together will be productive, we believe the details of how cooperation is structured and proceeds are important.

Experts in classroom cooperation (Johnson & Johnson, 1989; Johnson, Johnson, & Holubec, 1991) suggest that three tasks must be accomplished to ensure productive groups:

Three essentials for productive groups

1. Teachers need to help students understand what the desired skill would look or sound like. For example, the teacher may need to explain that a

Cooperative multimedia projects require students to work together to explain content-area topics.
(© Michael Zide)

basic principle of working together is learning to criticize ideas and not people.

2. Students need the opportunity to practice the skill. Role-playing is an effective way to learn social skills.

3. Finally, students new to cooperative projects need to reflect on their use of cooperative skills. Students can benefit from the opportunity to discuss process skills. Did the group encounter conflicts as they worked on the project? Were anyone's feelings hurt because someone misinterpreted the intent of an e-mail message?

Methods of cooperative learning

There is no single cooperative learning method. Some methods are designed to help students master a body of factual material. There are certainly classroom situations in which this is an important goal, and cooperative methods that use group competition to push all group members to achieve have demonstrated value (Slavin, 1991). However, the cooperative methods of greatest relevance for this book are those that involve students in group tasks requiring both the acquisition and the application of knowledge and skill. *Group investigation*, a task specialization method that results in the production of group projects, is discussed in the chapter entitled "Learning from Student Projects." As students work together on a project, they must discuss course content related to the project. As they interact, they acquire knowledge from one another, and they learn from the process of trying to put their ideas into words to allow someone else to understand them. Others in the group may see a problem differently or have a different explanation in mind for some phenomenon. The group process naturally produces a level of cognitive conflict that challenges the personal understanding of group members and encourages more active, self-regulated learning.

Learning Communities

We might define *community* as a social organization created by people who share common goals, values, and practices. If you try to apply this description to the city or town in which you live, you might find it excessively idealistic. We likely would agree that most cities and towns fail miserably in meeting this standard. But a functional community can be any collection of people who have identified themselves with a set of goals, values, and practices. Our interests are in understanding how such communities are formed and in using these mechanisms to build learning communities.

Long-term, authentic, challenging tasks

Communities come together when some form of search process acquaints people who share goals, values, and practices and this group begins to act on its members' common interests. School-based **learning communities** are formed when teachers and students join together to work on long-term projects. The idea is to select authentic and challenging tasks that can be productively approached in a collaborative fashion. The social environment surrounding the project encourages learners of all ages to learn from and teach one another. The task goals of the project shape what knowledge and skills must be acquired, and the nature of authentic tasks usually requires that the learning experiences cross disciplinary boundaries (Gordin, Gomez, Pea, & Fishman, 1997).

Educators do not have to limit themselves to learning communities formed within school walls. Some have argued, in fact, that schools have become distanced physically, emotionally, and intellectually from the core of our traditional communities (Riel, 1997). Students have few experiences directly connecting what they learn with the world outside the school. Moreover, by focusing on the learning needs of citizens of a narrow age range, schools fail to support lifelong learning. For these reasons, many educators are beginning to create work-based learning communities, which allow students to participate in the practices of a discipline or profession.

This brings us back to what we described earlier as the culture of practice surrounding authentic activities. For a student, it is the essential difference between learning about what biologists or historians have produced as information and having the opportunity at some meaningful level to function as a biologist or historian to construct personal knowledge (Gordin et al., 1997).

Project-Based Learning

Student projects provide a practical method for combining many of the elements of authentic activities and cooperative learning. Technology provides many opportunities for classroom projects. Examples of projects and descriptions of how they were developed appear throughout this book. The examples in "Activities and Projects for Your Classroom: Ideas for Content-Area Projects" give you the idea. In all cases, small groups of students use some combination of the computer, printer, various programs, and computer peripherals, such as a scanner or digital camera, to complete the project. In most cases, field or library research is also required.

What good projects do

Project-based learning is based on tasks, groups, and sharing (Wheatley, 1991). The ideal task should confront each student with a problem for which

Focus

Lev Vygotsky

Lev Vygotsky, a Russian developmental psychologist working in the early 1900s, is a classic example of a scholar whose ideas were much more influential after his death than during his lifetime. Here is a brief summary of some of Vygotsky's central ideas (Harley, 1996; Vygotsky, 1978):

Private speech. We have all seen children and even adults talk to themselves as they perform a difficult task. Vygotsky believed this externalized speech was quite functional as an "external" guidance mechanism. Vygotsky also proposed that learners use the speech of others as they solve problems. Gradually these forms of guidance become internalized as silent "inner speech."

Zone of proximal development. Think of a set of related educational tasks positioned along a continuum. At one end of the continuum are tasks the learner can perform with ease. At the other end are tasks that are far beyond the capability of the learner. Between these areas are tasks that the learner can perform with the proper support. This area, called the **zone of proximal development,** defines the tasks where instruction is likely to be most productive. Support usually implies adult guidance or perhaps the cooperation of a more experienced peer. There may be other forms of support that also allow learners to achieve success. With experience, learners become capable of independent functioning.

Scaffolding. **Scaffolding** is doing some of the work for students until they develop the capability to do it for themselves. Such mechanisms might include reminders, pronouncing or explaining words students do not understand, clear step-by-step instructions, and demonstrations of tasks to be performed. Unlike behavioral approaches, which help less skilled learners by creating a simplified version of the task, scaffolding proposes simplifying the learner's role in accomplishing the actual task.

Reciprocal teaching is regarded as a good example of the application of Vygotsky's ideas. Although we did not use private speech, the zone of proximal development, or scaffolding in our discussion of reciprocal teaching, see if you can pick out aspects of reciprocal teaching that illustrate each of these terms. Vygotsky's theoretical ideas are illustrated in several other ideas emphasized in this book—for example, emphasizing the teacher's role as supporting learning rather than dispensing knowledge, the value of learning in cooperative groups, and the importance of engaging students with authentic tasks.

that student has no immediate solution. The task should also be chosen to focus on key concepts from the desired domain of study. The idea is to engage students in an activity requiring them to work with course content that might otherwise be treated more passively. In addition, good projects should (1) encourage students to make decisions, (2) encourage "what-if" questions, (3) require discussion and communication, (4) allow a final product or solution, and (5) be extendible to allow students to move beyond the specific charge they have been given.

Projects seem to be an ideal setting for cooperative approaches. Working with others requires greater attention to understanding. When students work together, they confront the ideas of others and are forced to voice and defend their own beliefs. Trying to explain what you know to someone else, perhaps in several different ways, is a very active way to think through important ideas.

Finally, Wheatley (1991) believes that teachers must allocate time for students to present their ideas, methods, and products. This is important not only at the conclusion of a project but also as the project evolves. Presenting work is an authentic activity that provides an important source of motivation. Presentation also allows groups to gather ideas from other groups and have their own work critiqued. Initial presentations are likely to be made before the teacher and classmates. Later presentations might be made to students from other classes, parents, and even the general public.

Previewing Technology Options That May Expand How You Think about Student Learning

This book explores a full range of ways in which students might use technology in the classroom. We see technology as both supporting traditional methods of instruction and also encouraging experiences consistent with the constructivist perspective. Among the topics we feel are most likely to expand traditional views of productive learning experiences are the role of computer tools and hypermedia projects in encouraging more productive student learning.

Computer Tools and Thinking Behavior

Using computer tools to promote active learning

Computer tools such as word processors, spreadsheets, databases, and multimedia authoring programs may help students learn actively. Computer tools were designed to facilitate certain activities or to create certain products, and engaging in these activities or constructing these products has great potential for generating meaningful learning. Daiute (1983; Daiute & Taylor, 1981) makes such a proposal in discussing the impact of a computer-based word processing environment on the process of learning to write.

Certain word processor features and the way a word processor stores and manipulates text (easy insertion or deletion, moving blocks of text with cut-and-paste functions, alternative edits without time-consuming rewrites) encourage students to revise their work and thus lead to the development of writing skills. It appears that technology encourages students to write more and to revise more frequently (Pea & Kurland, 1987a). If you have used word processing software, this claim may ring true to you. Did you rewrite more

ACTIVITIES AND PROJECTS FOR YOUR CLASSROOM

Ideas for Content-Area Projects

We want to make sure you understand that using technology in content-area instruction can mean something other than learning from the computer in the same way that a student might learn from a book. The student can use the computer to learn by doing. Here are just a few examples to get you thinking about using the computer in this role:

- Second-grade students create alphabet books based on a space theme.
- Middle-school students use clay animation to develop public service announcements focused on healthy choices for adolescents.
- High-school students develop a multimedia presentation to display wild-flowers they observed and videotaped during a nature walk. Special attention is given to a discussion of the habitat within which each species was observed.

---

frequently and try out several approaches rather than attempt to get by with a single, painfully constructed final draft? If the revision power of the computer encouraged you to write differently, perhaps to experiment with different ways of saying something, then it might be said that the external tool (the computer and word processing software) influenced the thinking processes you employed while you wrote. Perkins (1985) describes this potential value of many computer tools in terms of the "opportunities get taken" hypothesis. His argument is that powerful tools encourage thinking and exploration because learners are presented with realistic opportunities that involve minimal risks. (See the chapter entitled "Using Tools" for a more complete discussion of word processing and learning to write.)

Hypermedia Projects

We devote a substantial portion of this book to the proposal that students can benefit from projects incorporating the production of hypermedia. Later chapters discuss hypermedia in detail. For now, we can describe a hypermedia product as a computer-based presentation using some interactive combination of text with pictures, sound, and video. Developing this kind of presentation involves generating the elements of information (text segments, pictures) and creating meaningful links among the elements. We believe that this process and its associated activities (research, collaborative interaction with others working on the same product) encourage many of the desirable learning processes presented in this chapter.

How hypermedia products encourage meaningful learning

To create a hypermedia product, students must represent what they have learned in multiple formats (images, text) and organize information and establish links to demonstrate relationships of various types. Students must understand what they are presenting and think about how they can best represent these ideas to others. Creating the hypermedia product therefore involves several external behaviors that require internal behaviors conducive to meaningful learning. Hypermedia authoring offers many of the same benefits as writing to learn. In fact, it has been argued that writing has a privileged status in education that is not entirely deserved and that other means of representation or combinations of representational systems might be better suited to the content of some disciplines (Smagorinsky, 1995). This would certainly seem possible when the content emphasizes visual elements (as in biology and art), quantitative forms of representation (mathematics), or sounds (music). It has even been claimed (Jonassen, 1986) that hypermedia may represent a superior learning environment because it is similar in structure to human memory (nonlinear presentation of ideas, multiple linkages among ideas, potential to represent ideas using several different formats). Arguably, having students create hypermedia materials requires them to relate images, ideas, and units of meaning in a fashion similar to the actual organization of LTM. In other words, the creation of hypermedia is a useful way to encourage students to search out appropriate relationships among the units of information they are studying. In later chapters of this book you encounter a number of strategies for involving students in the creation of content-area hypermedia projects.

Potential superiority of hypermedia

Research about Learning with Technology

In this chapter, we have developed the theoretical framework for the ideas we address in the rest of the book. Before concluding, however, we want to address the basic question of research support for the value of technology in learning. You may be thinking that our theories about technology sound interesting, but how much direct evidence indicates that they work?

Meta-analyses show benefits

There are literally hundreds of K–12 studies, dating back to the late 1970s, involving computer-based instruction. When a large number of research studies have addressed a topic, a special statistical procedure called *meta-analysis* is frequently used to combine the data from many studies to achieve a general conclusion. These meta-analyses have consistently found benefits for computer-based instruction (Bayraktar, 2001–2002; Christmann, Badgett, & Lucking, 1997; Fletcher-Flinn & Gravatt, 1995; Waxman, Lin, & Michko, 2003). Nevertheless, critics continue to argue that the value of instructional applications of technology has yet to be demonstrated (Clark, 1985; Oppenheimer, 2003). They cite various reasons for their pessimistic position: Research showing either no advantage or a negative effect is less likely to be published; studies have tended to involve only a few classes and supportive teachers; and studies are most frequently short in duration and rely on narrow outcome measures prepared by the researchers rather than long-term studies using a general standardized achievement test.

We explore the research in more detail in the chapter entitled "Using Instructional Software and Multimedia for Content-Area Learning." Here we should point out that, while the general educational use of technology has some relevance, this book really has a narrower focus. Most of the classroom activities we describe fall within a constructivist tradition rather than the direct instruction tradition of computer-based drill and practice or tutorials. While the basic ideas for constructivist activities have been studied for some time in such fields as cognitive and developmental psychology, few actual classroom applications have been thoroughly evaluated using sound research techniques (Panel on Educational Technology, 1997). There are some promising exceptions (Cognition and Technology Group, 1992; Wenglinsky, 1998), but no body of research that would allow a valid general conclusion.

Where does this leave you? At least for the time being, it probably leaves you with access to a moderate collection of technology resources, local expectations that you use these resources productively, and personal responsibility and considerable flexibility for what will happen in your classroom. Specific recommendations for what you should do may be lacking.

The purpose of this chapter has been to provide you with a theoretical foundation for technology-based activities in your classroom. As we discuss each example in later chapters, we will continue to present a combination of theory, research, and suggestions for classroom activities. Our intent is to help you explore options for the use of technology so that you can make your own decisions and feel comfortable implementing them.

Summary

Decisions about classroom use of technology—like all other instructional decisions—should be based on insight into how thinking and learning behaviors function and how external activities and experiences influence these behaviors. This book takes a cognitive perspective in discussing learning, thinking, and problem solving.

At the fundamental level, learning depends on both short- and long-term memory and the way information is organized in memory. It also relies on cognitive processes—basic mental tools for performing cognitive tasks—and on the guidance provided by metacognitive knowledge and metacognitive control functions. Technology can serve as a means of presenting information to students and also as a tool that students themselves use in manipulating information. In either case, the crucial factor in learning is not the amount of information the teacher and learning environment provide, but rather what students do with the information.

At a more global level, several models of learning provide useful insights. Meaningful learning stresses the active role of the learner in creating personal knowledge by establishing links between new ideas and what is already known. Constructivist models also place the learner in the role of creating personal understanding of experience. These theoretical perspectives can help guide the use of technology in ways that engage learners in active mental work.

Authentic activities are important because they provide students the opportunity to apply knowledge as practitioners of the content area they are studying. This kind of task is particularly relevant in efforts to teach higher-order thinking. Because learning in schools is a social phenomenon, concepts such as cognitive apprenticeship, cooperative learning, and the learning community also offer insights into a productive environment for learning. Project-based learning is an ideal way to combine many of the elements of authentic activities and collaborative learning.

All of these concepts, we believe, are important guides for the use of technology in your classroom. Conversely, technology can help you create a learning environment that puts these concepts into practice and encourages the deepest level of cognitive development in your students.

Reflecting on Chapter 2

ACTIVITIES

- Provide an example of inert knowledge. What knowledge or skill was involved? Under what circumstances was this knowledge or skill available, and when was it not available?

- Generate an example of an activity for your content area of interest that satisfies the definition of an authentic activity. Explain what makes this activity authentic.

- Students are sometimes surprised by the scores they earn on course examinations. Propose a practical method that students might use to evaluate their strengths and weaknesses before taking a test.

- Consider the distinction between (1) solving a novel problem by relying on the application of abstract rules or principles and (2) recalling a similar situation you have experienced and then adapting that experience to the new problem. Can you think of personal situations in which you have used each approach successfully? What does this reflection suggest about effective ways to use case-based learning in your classroom?

KEY TERMS

authentic activity (p. 58)
case-based learning (p. 43)
cognitive apprenticeship (p. 65)
constructivism (p. 54)
cooperative learning (p. 66)
critical thinking (p. 61)
declarative knowledge (p. 44)
discovery learning (p. 52)
episodic memory (p. 42)
higher-order thinking (p. 60)
inert knowledge (p. 58)
learning community (p. 68)
link (p. 44)
long-term memory (LTM) (p. 42)
meaningful learning (p. 51)

metacognition (p. 47)
metacognitive control functions (p. 48)
metacognitive knowledge (p. 47)
network model (p. 44)
node (p. 44)
problem solving (p. 61)
procedural knowledge (p. 44)
reception learning (p. 52)
rote learning (p. 51)
scaffolding (p. 69)
short-term memory (STM) (p. 40)
transfer (p. 63)
working memory (p. 40)
zone of proximal development (p. 69)

RESOURCES TO EXPAND YOUR KNOWLEDGE BASE

 An expanded and frequently updated list of online resources is available on the website that accompanies this textbook.

Books on Key Chapter Topics

Hogan, K., & Pressley, M. (1997). *Scaffolding student learning.* Cambridge, MA: Brookline Books.

Johnson, D., & Johnson, R. (1999). *Learning together and alone* (5th ed.). Boston: Allyn & Bacon.

McCaleb, S. (1997). *Building communities of learners.* Mahwah, NJ: Erlbaum.

Tishman, S., Perkins, D., & Jay, E. (1995). *The thinking classroom: Learning and teaching in a culture of thinking.* Boston: Allyn & Bacon.

Wilson, B. (Ed.). (1996). *Constructivist learning environments.* Englewood Cliffs, NJ: Educational Technology Publications.

Learning How to Integrate Technology with Your Teaching

• • •

PART TWO introduces you to categories of software, the most frequently applied computer tool applications (word processors, databases, spreadsheets, e-mail, and World Wide Web browsers), multimedia tools, and the ways these applications support students in meaningful learning and the development of higher-order thinking skills. You look at the advantages of hypermedia and multimedia and how they support students in meaningful learning. We discuss types of multimedia projects you can have your students create and some of the tools and techniques used to produce the sounds and images described in multimedia applications throughout the book. Finally, you explore the concept of design and the learning opportunities that students have when they design and present projects.

3

Using Tools: Word Processors, Databases, Spreadsheets, and Data Probes

• • •

ORIENTATION   In this chapter you read about word processing, spreadsheet, and database applications. These applications are among the most common computer tools in educational use. This chapter also includes a discussion of data probes—specialized hardware devices for measuring characteristics of the physical world. Students are most likely to encounter this type of tool in a math or science class. We discuss these resources together because, as tools, all fill similar basic roles in influencing student behavior. Tools can increase students' productivity or allow them to perform tasks that normally would be beyond their capabilities. They can also help students become more active learners and allow them to acquire knowledge and develop skills in unique ways. You read about ways you can introduce these tools to your students and apply them in your classroom.

As you read, look for answers to the following questions:

Focus Questions
- What are three different levels on which students benefit from applying tool applications in content-area tasks?
- Why are the capabilities of word processing applications especially well suited to teaching writing using the writing process approach?
- What are some classroom word processing, spreadsheet, and database activities that lead to more active processing of course content?
- How might the use of data loggers contribute to authentic research projects?
- What are the general characteristics of tool activities that increase the probability of meaningful learning?

Productivity Tools in the Work of Teachers and Students

In past editions of this book, we have begun this chapter by identifying the many ways in which educators might benefit from opportunities to use productivity tools in their own work. Our assumption was that educators would recognize the general benefits of such tools and then consider how productivity tools might provide similar benefits to students. We have reconsidered the logic of this approach. Several authors (Cuban, 2001; Russell, Bebell, O'Dwyer, & O'Conner, 2003) have noted that teachers are often quite proficient in the use of technology and may frequently use technology to support their own work as teachers, but they make few assignments that would require their students to use technology. In fact, newer teachers, who in general are more confident and capable as technology users, involve their students with technology less than teachers who have been teaching between six and ten years. We and others have begun to consider the failure of the assumption that educators who recognize the personal benefits of technology will push to have these same opportunities extended to students.

What might explain this reluctance to make assignments using technology? Access probably is an important issue (see the conclusions of Norris, Sullivan, Poirot, & Soloway, 2003, described in the chapter entitled "Key Themes and Issues for Using Technology in Your Classroom"). The teacher needs only one computer and probably has some flexibility as to when work can be completed, while in the average school, four students have to share one computer. Still, access alone cannot explain all the findings just described, because first-year teachers and more experienced teachers would have similar access. First-year teachers do face unique challenges in preparing lessons and learning how they will most effectively work with students. This factor would explain lower student use of technology if technology integration was perceived as an instructional goal that was optional rather than a core approach to teaching and learning. Russell and colleagues (2003) also speculate that understanding how to use technology is not the same as understanding how to teach with technology. Perhaps many future teachers now emerge from college with the skills necessary to get their own work done, but without the experiences necessary to prepare them to help much younger students learn to do the same.

This chapter discusses some applications of technology that are probably quite familiar to you and some that you may not have encountered before. No matter what your level of experience may be, it is our intent both to familiarize you with the application itself and also to discuss strategies for classroom integration. We hope to convince you that at least some of the strategies deserve immediate consideration for implementation.

The Tools Approach

The computer can function as many different tools.

A *tool,* by definition, is an object that allows the user to perform tasks with greater efficiency or quality. For example, a calculator allows a student to add a series of numbers more quickly and accurately than the student could add them with pencil and paper. The computer, in combination with different kinds of application software, can function as many different tools. The tool functions performed by the computer can improve the efficiency and quality with which the user manipulates information—much as the calculator does.

Nearly everyone has some occasion to manipulate information every day. Certainly teachers and students are heavily involved with information and could benefit from tools that improve the efficiency or quality of their work. This chapter familiarizes you with some of the basic computer tools that teachers and students might find useful. Other computer applications, such as graphics programs and computer tools used to explore and communicate using the Internet, also meet the general definition of a computer tool, but you will encounter these applications in later chapters. We want you to understand the type of tasks that computer tools allow the user to perform and to gain some insights into what the user does as he or she works with each type of tool.

As you learn about computer tools, consider that working with them may benefit students on several levels (Perkins, 1985). It appears that educational experiences with computer tools result in students:

Ways computer tools may benefit students

1. Learning to use the computer tools
2. Performing certain academic tasks more effectively and efficiently because of the tools
3. Learning domain skills such as writing and problem solving or acquiring content-area knowledge through the application of computer tools to content-appropriate tasks

The concept of mindtool

Sometimes new descriptive terms can help bring new insights. For example, the functions we have just listed have also been described as *technology as tool* and *technology as intellectual partner* or **mindtool** (Jonassen, 1995). The notion that ordinary computer tools can be more than a means to boost efficiency is an intriguing possibility.

In the material that follows, we consider all of the levels on which tool use might be beneficial. However, we continually emphasize that student mastery of how the computer can be used to perform basic tasks is not enough. We need to find ways to allow students to apply the skills they acquire in a variety of meaningful circumstances. As you encounter each computer tool in the presentations that follow, think carefully about its potential applications in your area of interest and about the several levels on which students might benefit from experience with that tool.

Word Processing

Word processing, an application allowing the entry, manipulation, and storage of text, is one of the most popular uses of computer technology in schools, for several reasons (Ravitz, Wong, & Becker, 1999):

■ Word processing is the most widely used computer application in the work and home environments, and educators are sensitive to the development of skills valued in these settings.

Word processing programs may help students write more effectively.

■ Writing is one of the fundamental skills taught in schools. Features of word processing programs may help students write more effectively and develop writing skills more quickly.

■ Writing is a skill that may contribute to the generation and integration of personal knowledge in nearly all content areas. Writing forces students to externalize what they know as they attempt to put ideas on paper (or on the computer screen) and requires an active use of knowledge. Remember that the active processing of information increases the likelihood of meaningful learning.

Characteristics of Word Processing Programs

Most word processing programs allow users to accomplish nearly the same set of basic functions: text input, storage and retrieval, formatting, editing, and printing. Many word processing programs also allow the integration of graphics, audio, and video.

Text Input

Features that optimize text input

Word processing programs have some special features that optimize the writer's ability to input text from the keyboard. One feature that most computer users take for granted is **word wrap.** When working on a typewriter, writers have to pay attention to how close they are coming to the end of a line and decide when to press the return key to move to the beginning of the next line. With word wrap, the computer automatically moves to the beginning of the next line when the word being entered would extend beyond the right margin. Similarly, the computer program also breaks to the next page when the specified number of lines has been entered. Word processing programs also allow writers to insert a forced page break at any time.

Storage and Retrieval

Educational value of saving a document to disk

Storage and retrieval involve the processes of saving a copy of the document to disk and loading a saved document from the disk back into the computer memory. These processes allow work done with a word processor to be extended over time. They have special significance for students who are learning to write with a word processor, because students can submit documents for evaluation and then rework them in response to the comments of peers or their teacher. Storage and retrieval of the original document allow the student to spend time addressing the specific areas of difficulty noted in the comments rather than wasting time regenerating parts of the document that didn't require additional attention.

Formatting

Formatting refers to the physical appearance of the document created with a word processor. Writers may apply formatting features at the level of the character, the paragraph, or the entire document.

Formatting at the character level

At the character level, word processing programs usually allow the user to control font, style, and size. The **font** refers to the design of the character. All characters from the same font share certain design features. For example, this is Univers, this is Palatino, this is New York, and this is Times. Font **style** alters a particular font in terms of slant or thickness. This is **bold,** and

ACTIVITIES AND PROJECTS FOR YOUR CLASSROOM

Word Processing Activities for All Grade Levels

Word processing software can be used even with students in the primary grades. Young children can write stories with software that defaults to a large-size font and prints out on primary-style paper. This software still allows for the complete editing features of deleting, cutting, copying, and pasting. Young children can:

- Write stories using predictable patterns ("The House That Jack Built").
- Create alphabet books (the ABCs of space, winter ABCs).
- Keep a daily journal.
- Create lists of factual information from reference books and write reports with this information.
- Create a class book, with one page of personal information for each child.
- Create content-area class books, such as "Animals Where I Live" or "People in My Community."

In the intermediate grades, students can extend the word processing activities they started in the primary grades. They can:

- Write and revise factual reports using cut and paste and spell-checking.
- Create journal entries using the insert date feature.
- Use the thesaurus to expand vocabulary and eliminate redundancies.
- Write collaborative stories.
- Create cooperative reports, with each member of the group responsible for a different topic.
- Cut and paste to organize the report.
- Write poetry and publish it using center alignment or acrostic poems using a larger-size font for the first letter of each line.
- Write creative stories using different font styles to express emotions such as fear or shyness.
- Publish newspapers.

Middle-school and high-school students can:

- Write scientific reports that include tables and graphs.
- Use outlining features to organize reports.
- Create questionnaires using tab set fills to draw the lines for answers (tab fills draw a solid or dotted line to the next tab that has been set).
- Create lists of information using the column feature to align the list entries.
- Publish newsletters with columns and clip art.

---

this is *italic*. <u>Underlining</u> is also a style. Characters can be displayed in a variety of sizes.

A writer might want to control character formatting for several reasons. Think about the material you read and how character style is used. Newspapers use large, bold type for headlines and article titles. Textbooks use bold print, italicized type, and underlining to bring readers' attention to particular words or phrases. Text written with some variability in character appearance is more interesting and thus allows the author additional mechanisms for communication.

At the paragraph level, formatting typically allows setting **tabs** and **margins,** text **justification,** and line spacing. Tabs, margins, and text justification control the alignment of text on the screen and the printed page. A few formatting features apply to the entire document. For example, some word processors allow the user to designate how many columns of text will appear on a page. Teachers or students who create newsletters may find this feature useful.

Editing

Editing involves modifying text at any time after it has been generated. Most writers composing at the computer notice and correct typing errors as they appear on the computer screen or immediately attempt to improve a sentence that does not sound quite right. Other changes occur much later in the writing process. Some methods of writing instruction require students to have their papers critiqued by the teacher or other students before they write a final draft. In this case, the original material is likely loaded from disk and reworked in response to the comments generated by the original draft.

There are some standard editing features in all word processing programs, including the character-level functions of **insert** and delete and the block operations of delete, cut, copy, and paste. A change in the existing format of a block of text (for example, making plain text bold) might also be considered editing.

Block editing involves making a change to a designated segment of text. The first step in block editing is to **select,** or mark, the segment of text to which the change will apply by dragging the **cursor** over the text with the mouse. Once a block of text has been selected, the writer can execute such commands as delete, cut, paste, or copy. The **delete** function erases the selected text. The **cut** function removes the selected text and stores it temporarily in the computer's memory for insertion at a different location. The process of moving the text from the computer's memory back to the screen at a point designated by the cursor is called **pasting.** The **copy** function temporarily stores the selected text in the computer's memory but differs from the cut command in not removing the text from its original location. Text copied to memory can also be pasted. Writers can use block editing to make major changes in a document; it is particularly useful to reorganize larger documents or to move segments of text from one document to another.

Special Tools

Word processing programs often come equipped with special tools to improve the writer's effectiveness. The most common tools are an outliner, a spell checker, and a thesaurus.

Most students are familiar with outlining. Incorporating an outlining tool in a word processing program allows the writer to plan the structure of the document. Often the outline entries become headings within the document, and the writer can move back and forth between the outline view and the extended text as an aid to organizing a major project. This capability helps the writer to escape the detail level and regain a sense of the overall purpose and structure of the document.

Spell checkers

Spell checkers search text for spelling errors. Most spell checkers identify each word assumed to be misspelled, offer a list of possible alternative words, and then allow the writer to accept a word as originally spelled or to replace the misspelled word or all words in the document spelled in a similar manner with one of the alternatives by clicking the appropriate button. Spell checkers have shortcomings, however. Unique terminology and proper names are initially reported as spelling errors. Spell-checking a list of references is difficult because the spell checker will find an "error" in nearly every line (for example, authors' names are reported as spelling errors). Words that a writer knows are correct can be added to the dictionary to make the spell checker more efficient over time. But spell checkers also cannot detect typing errors that result in a different valid word (*then* instead of *the*, for example), so writers must always proofread their work. Spell checkers have some instructional value in that they point out words that are consistently misspelled. The awareness that you often misspell a certain word—a form of metacognition—can help you learn to spell the word correctly or prompt you to look it up.

Electronic thesaurus

An electronic thesaurus allows a writer to generate a list of words with roughly equivalent meanings. This list allows the writer to find a word with just the right shade of meaning for a specific situation or to search for a different word when the writer feels he or she has been using a particular word too frequently. For example, we considered the word *nuance* for the previous sentence, but the word seemed a bit too formal. The thesaurus recommended eight other words and phrases as potential equivalents, and *nuance* became *shade of meaning.*

Document Design Capabilities

Adding graphics

Word processors typically allow the integration of text and graphics, such as pictures, diagrams, and charts, in flexible configurations. Positioning graphics within text presents a somewhat different set of issues from those applying specifically to text, and some challenges too. For example, once a graphic is inserted, does it remain at a fixed position on the page as new text is inserted above the graphic, or does the illustration slide down the page with the rest of the text? How does a particular word processing program allow text to flow around all sides of a graphic or position the graphic in the middle of a page, with text to the left and right? Mastering all of the options of word processing programs would take students a considerable amount of time, but most programs offer great power and flexibility.

The Value of Word Processing Features

The role of purpose and motivation

Why the concern over such features as fonts, styles, printing multiple columns on a page, and manipulating the position of graphics within text? One initial reaction might be that such features are frills having little to do with the message of the text or the educational benefits of creating the text. But a very different perspective is possible. Consider the importance of purpose and motivation in effective writing and in learning to write. Writers need to be engaged in tasks in which they have authentic opportunities to communicate what they know, want, or feel. Appearance can influence perceptions of authentic authoring and perceptions of importance. The value to young writers of creating a book that really looks like a book or a newspaper that really looks like a newspaper should not be underestimated.

Writers, Writing, and Word Processing

Many people assume that writing with a word processing program will lead to better products and that making frequent use of word processing while learning to write will produce better writers. Perhaps this powerful machine can somehow magically transform all of us into competent authors.

The "opportunities get taken" hypothesis

In learning, as in other areas of life, you seldom get something for nothing. Still, a logical case has been proposed for how simply working with word processing for an extended period may improve writing skills and performance. Perkins (1985) calls this the "opportunities get taken" hypothesis. The proposal works like this. Writing by hand has a number of built-in limitations. Generating text this way is slow, and modifying what has been written comes at a substantial price. To produce a second or third draft with a pencil or typewriter requires the writer to spend a good deal of time reproducing text that was fine the first time, just to change a few things that might sound better if modified. Word processing, on the other hand, allows writers to revise at minimal cost. They can pursue an idea to see where it takes them and worry about fixing syntax and spelling later. Reworking documents from the level of fixing misspelled words to reordering the arguments in the entire presentation can be accomplished without crumpling up what has just been painstakingly written and starting over.

With word processing, writers can take risks and push their skills without worrying that they are wasting their time. The capacity to save and load text from disk makes it possible to revise earlier drafts with minimal effort. Writers can set aside what they have written to gain new perspectives, show friends a draft and ask for advice, or discuss an idea with the teacher after class, and use these experiences to improve what they wrote yesterday or last week. What we have described here are opportunities—opportunities to produce a better paper for tomorrow's class and, over time, opportunities to learn to communicate more effectively.

Do writers take the opportunities provided by word processing programs and produce better products? The research evaluating the benefits of word processing (Bangert-Drowns, 1993; Cochran-Smith, 1991; Goldberg, Russell & Cook, 2003; Owston, & Wideman, 1997) is not easy to interpret. Much seems to depend on the experience of the writer as a writer and computer user and on what is meant by a "better" product. If the questions refer to younger students, it also seems to depend on the instructional strategies to which the students have been exposed. General summaries of the research literature (Bangert-Drowns, 1993) seem to indicate that students make more

Focus

Learning Word Processing Features

Many word processing features can be introduced as needed. The teacher can demonstrate each new feature within the context of a learning activity that will take advantage of that feature. Teachers can also:

1. Create "how-to" posters that can be posted by the computer or small "how-to" cards that can be kept by the computer in an empty disk box.
2. Create text files purposely written to allow students to:
   - Edit paragraphs with punctuation and capitalization errors.
   - Delete unnecessary information.
   - Sequence the events of a story or a set of directions using cut and paste.
   - Use the thesaurus to find alternatives for underlined words.
   - Add charts and graphs.
   - Move and resize clip art.

revisions, write longer documents, and produce documents containing fewer errors when word processing. However, the spelling, syntactical, and grammatical errors that students tend to address and the revision activities necessary to correct them are considered less important by many interested in effective writing than changes that improve document content or document organization.

Many writers bring their writing goals and old habits to the new medium. They revise in ways they already know to fix errors they are aware of. Beginning writers may thus not have the orientation or capabilities to use the full potential of word processing, and their classroom instruction may also emphasize the correction of more obvious surface errors. Thus there are improvements in the products generated when working with word processing tools, but the areas in which younger writers seem to improve are not necessarily the most important ones.

Many of the potential educational advantages of word processing appear only as students acquire considerable experience writing with the aid of technology. Perkins's (1985) argument that writing with word processing programs will improve writing skills because word processing allows students to experiment with their writing makes sense only in situations in which students have written a great deal and experimented with expressing themselves in different ways. The fact that most research evaluating the benefits of word processing has examined performance over a short period of time, with students having limited word processing experience, thus represents a poor test of the potential of word processing (Owston, Murphy, & Wideman, 1992). More recent research based on a three-year study following elementary students as they learned to write with and without access to word processing opportunities has demonstrated a significant advantage for students with ready access to technology (Owston & Wideman, 1997). This study seems to indicate that the technology itself offers some advantages and is consistent with Perkins's proposal that a powerful tool may encourage learners to write in a different way.

Overall, the role of word processing in developing writing skills depends on the goals of the teacher and individual students, the social context provided for writing, and the amount of writing that students do with the assistance of word processing. In the next section we examine one approach that has proved successful for many teachers.

The importance of how teachers and students apply technology

The Writing Process Approach

Stages of the writing process

Features of word processing are particularly well suited to what is often called the **writing process approach,** which encompasses the stages of planning, drafting, editing/revising, and publishing (Graves, 1983). Process models are constructivist in orientation, and the components in the composing process emphasize that the writer's tasks are to create and communicate meaning. The development of composition skills within this orientation often involves collaboration, and writers frequently receive help and feedback from classmates and their teacher during all of the stages. Students are expected to revise, and they learn to critique their own work and the work of others. The publication step implies that student compositions are authentic products prepared to entertain or inform a real audience. The process approach is often described as operating within a writing community in which students write, rewrite, read what others have written, and discuss the activities of writing (Montague, 1990).

Video Case

Step inside a fourth-grade historical fiction workshop with teacher Kristen Nerich and literacy coordinator Patricia Donahue. View the HM Video Case entitled *Elementary Writing Instruction: Process Writing.* What suggestions might you make for enhancing the project with technology tools? For more about process writing, also view the HM Video Case entitled *Developing Student Self-Esteem: Peer Editing Process.*

Word processing fits with the writing process approach in a number of ways. The most obvious application is editing/revising. The recursive nature of process writing—that is, the expectation that ideas will be generated, written, considered, and rewritten several times—is ideally implemented within a system that allows written products to be saved, retrieved, and modified efficiently. Recent research (Goldberg, Bebell, O'Dwyer, Russell, & Seeley, 2003; Russell & Seeley, 2004) has demonstrated a positive relationship between the frequent use of computers in editing written work and the improved development of writing proficiency. Perhaps these findings demonstrate the cumulative impact of revision on the learning of writing skills. Specific strategies for process writing encourage writers to do things such as put what they have written aside for a day and then reread and revise it the next day; exchange papers with a writing partner and request ideas for improvement; or discuss what they have written and what they are trying to say with a teacher, to generate some new ideas for improving their papers. These activities are likely to be perceived more positively if the revisions they lead to can be implemented efficiently.

Word processing and editing/revision

Word processing and planning

Word processing can also contribute to the other writing process stages. For example, a variety of word processing activities can contribute to the planning phase. Students can develop an initial structure using the outlining tool available in many word processing programs or a tool designed specifically to encourage the exploration and organization of ideas (see "Focus: Using *Inspiration* to Brainstorm"). Pon (1988) proposes a variety of brainstorming techniques that take advantage of technology. For instance, the teacher can request story ideas from students and record them in a single file. This list of ideas can be printed and distributed to all students. The teacher can also generate a list of key questions that might help a student come up with ideas for a project. For a paper on friendship, students might be asked to list five qualities of a good friend, briefly describe their good friends (without providing names) and why they like them, and describe how they try to be a friend to others. These tasks could be saved in a file for each student, and each student could be asked to respond individually to the questions. Responses could be discussed in class before students go on to write about friendship.

The publishing stage   The publishing stage is important if classroom tasks are to be perceived as authentic. Younger children need to see their work displayed on the bulletin board or in the halls. They see their stories as even more meaningful when they are compiled into a classroom book that students take home and read to parents. Older students can publish their work in school papers or occasionally send it to local newspapers. Students' informative writing or opinion papers can become required reading in subsequent classes covering similar topics.

Web publishing   The World Wide Web is also becoming a way for students to present their work (see "Focus: Publication on the Internet"). Material written to be communicated to peers through telecommunications has been found to be better organized, mechanically more correct, and more informative than papers on identical topics written to be graded by the teacher (Cohen & Riel, 1989). Having a peer audience seems to be more motivating than the red marks, gold stars, or grade the teacher might attach to the paper.

Keyboarding

One of the long-term controversies over computer use at the elementary-school level concerns whether precious time should be devoted to the development of keyboarding skills (Jennings, 2001). Those who favor making keyboarding part of the curriculum make two points:

- Students must achieve some level of typing proficiency before writing at the computer can be very effective.
- Encouraging students to write at a computer without adequate training allows them to develop bad habits that will be more difficult to overcome when the students do attempt to develop keyboarding skills.

The opposition in this dispute is not really against the development of keyboarding skills, but against holding off access to writing on the computer until students achieve keyboarding proficiency. Also, with the number of computers and the time each student can spend working at the computer each day so limited, some educators question whether allocating time to developing keyboarding proficiency makes sense. There may not be enough time to develop skill, and time might be more productively spent on other activities.

Spotlight on Assessment

Electronic Portfolios

Video Case

To get a better sense of the value of portfolios, view the HM Video Case entitled *Portfolio Assessment: Elementary Classroom* and the bonus video entitled *The Challenges of Portfolio Use.* How can technology assist with the classroom management challenges teacher Fred Park faces?

A portfolio is a systematic and selective collection of student work that has been accumulated to demonstrate the student's motivation, academic growth, and level of achievement. Portfolio assessment is most commonly used in classes in which much of the work takes the form of written or artistic products, but depending on the content area, portfolios can also contain videotapes or audiotapes, computer programs, science laboratory reports, and virtually any other product that can serve to demonstrate learning.

To understand what a portfolio is, imagine a file folder for each student containing carefully selected work samples, the student's comments about these products, and various types of evaluation data contributed by the student, peers, and the teacher. What you have imagined is probably a collection consisting entirely of sheets of paper: written documents and reports, drawings, evaluation forms, and summary evaluation reports. This is a good starting place. Now extend this understanding to include products generated with technology.

Suggestions for Creating and Using Portfolios

Several researchers have suggestions for creating and using portfolios (Paulson, Paulson, & Meyer, 1991; Porter & Cleland, 1995; Tierney, Carter, & Desai, 1991):

- The development of a portfolio should be a joint activity between teacher and student. Teachers might suggest certain categories such as "the piece I am most proud of," "something I had to really struggle to learn," "my attempt to do something very different," and so on. Teachers should also require that certain standard items—for example, the major paper for the course—be included.
- Students should be encouraged to think carefully about the process and purpose of portfolio construction. For each item, students might be asked to write a brief explanation of why the item was selected, what was to be learned from the task, and the student's assessment of his or her success in meeting task objectives.
- Portfolios should allow the teacher and student to evaluate the whole learning process. For example, the portfolio should contain preparatory materials (notes), early drafts or works-in-progress, and the final product. The collection of similar examples over time allows student progress to be assessed.
- With the students' permission, keep sample portfolios that other students can use for ideas for their own collections.
- Attach evaluation instruments, such as checklists and rating scales, to individual items in the portfolio. Periodically enter comments summarizing across portfolio contents to evaluate student progress.

Portfolios and Technology

Certain applications of technology and portfolio assessment are ideally suited to each other. Products generated with technology, ranging from word processing documents to major student-created multimedia projects, can be components of a portfolio. As you think about the writing process, for example, consider how easy it would be to collect and compare multiple drafts a student has generated. Students might be asked to reexamine these drafts and comment on how they worked to create a better final product.

Technology supports the practice of portfolio assessment in another way. Computer products are available to assist teachers and students in creating, organizing, and evaluating portfolios (Barrett, 2000). Some of these products are essentially electronic portfolios (see our example in the chapter entitled "Key Themes and Issues for Using Technology in Your Classroom"). Student work samples (text, scanned images of writing samples and artwork, audio generated from oral reading) are stored electronically and then evaluated using one of several existing modifiable checklists. Students, teachers, and even parents can also attach electronic comments to the work samples.

What level of proficiency is adequate?

How much training a student needs to become an adequate typist depends to some extent on what level of proficiency is considered adequate. Students in the upper-elementary-school grades write with a pencil at a rate of about ten words per minute (Wetzel, 1990). Without keyboard training, upper-elementary-school students will write at the keyboard at about half the rate they can achieve with a pencil. To equal the proficiency elementary students are able to achieve with a pencil requires approximately twenty to thirty hours of keyboard training. After that, students must use their keyboarding skills regularly, or they will regress to an unacceptable level of proficiency. Given what you know about the number of students in a typical classroom, the number of computers available in some schools, and the length of the elementary-school day, you can see what a challenge this requirement represents. Teachers would have to devote a large portion of the time actually spent on computers to keyboarding instruction in order to make students proficient typists. Exposure to keyboarding software without close monitoring by the teacher and without teacher understanding of proper technique also is not likely to produce competent typists (Erthal, 1998).

Cochran-Smith, Paris, and Kahn (1991) give a more optimistic view. They contend that two or three 20- to 30-minute sessions will be sufficient to get elementary-school students familiar with the keyboard and basic computer functions (insertion, deletion, block moves) and into writing. They do recommend a more intensive style of adult–student interaction, called coaching, during writing time. If classroom teachers want to help students develop keyboarding skill, it is also recommended that they seek the advice of business education teachers or others specifically trained to teach keyboarding (Erthal, 1998). Those who focus on the development of keyboarding proficiency identify issues that teachers unfamiliar with the area may ignore.

Focus

Using Inspiration to Brainstorm

Brainstorming, as part of a problem-solving task, might be described as the nonjudgmental process of generating and organizing ideas. A tool suited to this process should make it easy to (1) record ideas as they are generated, (2) organize ideas that have been generated into some type of meaningful structure, (3) record additional comments related to individual ideas without creating a confusing display, and (4) allow easy modification of both content and structure.

Inspiration is a software program designed to encourage the production and organization of ideas. Ideas can be entered in outline or graphical mode (see Figure 3.1). Ideas and the structure of ideas can be treated independently. That is, the ideas can first be generated and then linked in a hierarchical fashion. Once generated, both the idea elements and the structure of the elements can be altered. Text notations can be attached to individual ideas and can be hidden or displayed. Once completed, an Inspiration file can be used to generate a text file, a graphic file, or a webpage.

Inspiration and other outlining tools can prove helpful to individual writers as they think through their goals and generate the structure of a future document. Inspiration in graphic mode can also be a very useful tool for group planning. In this case, members of a group might sit around a large screen or projected display and work to plan a project.

Haynes and McMurdo (2001) propose a different way to apply Inspiration to the writing process. Their instructional approach is based on Inspiration tem-

FIGURE 3.1
Inspiration Screen Image
in Graphic Mode

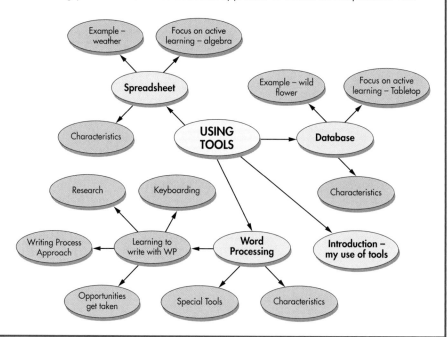

FIGURE 3.2

Inspiration Template with Short Phrases

Source: Based on Haynes & McMurdo (2001).

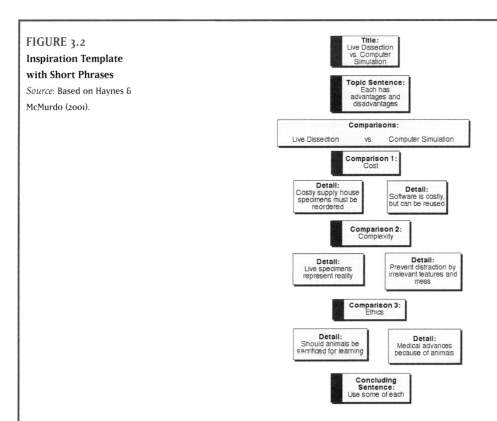

plates that help learners build five different types of paragraphs (such as compare and contrast, classification, reason). Students are provided a specific template as the basis for a writing assignment. The templates for the different types of paragraph originate from a common structure:

Title
Topic Sentence
Supporting Sentence 1
Supporting Sentence 2
Supporting Sentence 3
Concluding Sentence

Variations on this structure address the specific requirements of different paragraph types. For example, the supporting sentences in a compare-and-contrast paragraph identify points of comparison (a similarity or difference).

Figure 3.2 shows one such template. A paragraph based on this template might end up looking like this:

Live Dissection versus Computer Simulations in Biology Labs

Biology teachers can base lab experiences on live dissection or computer simulations, and each approach has both advantages and disadvantages. Lab costs are one factor teachers must consider. Dissection specimens ordered from a scientific supply house are costly and are typically discarded after each student group has completed the dissection assignment. Purchasing several copies of a software program may cost several hundred dollars, but the simulated dissections can be completed many times by many students. A second issue involves the complexity of working on live specimens. Some feel that learners are best served by exposure to the reality of living organisms. In contrast, others feel learners are just distracted by the blood and mess. Finally, there is what some would call the issue of ethics. One position is that animals should not be sacrificed for educational purposes. The opposing position is that many medical advantages have come from work with animals. Perhaps biology teachers should engage students with a few live dissections and with simulations in order to profit from the advantages of each approach.

Templates may help young writers in a couple of ways. The structure of the template eases the process of generating ideas. The required elements give writers a place to start. The structure also helps the writer organize ideas free from the simultaneous demands of crafting prose. Writers get their ideas down first and then focus on writing a paragraph. These advantages are consistent with the concept of scaffolding described in the chapter entitled "Meaningful Learning in an Information Age."

In schools with limited access to computers, it may not be possible to resolve the dispute about keyboarding training. The development of keyboarding proficiency and the application of computers in content-area instruction represent different values, and student use of technology will require value-based decisions about how computers should be used. Access to computers is improving, and inexpensive alternatives to multimedia computers are available (see "Emerging Technology: Inexpensive 'Keyboard' Computers"), but the question of how to spend valuable classroom time remains.

Spreadsheets

Functions of a spreadsheet

Spreadsheets, a common computer application and an important reason for the microcomputer's rapid growth in popularity, are convenient for storing and manipulating numerical data and have long been useful to businesspeople. A **spreadsheet** allows an accountant or a small business owner to organize numerical information; perform calculations on these data; display the results of these calculations in informative ways (charts or graphs); and even ask hypothetical questions about the data, such as what would happen to total profits if three more cents were charged per unit.

Teachers and students recognize that manipulating numbers is part of mathematics. However, storing and interpreting numerical data and asking questions related to those data are also essential to political science, sociology, economics, geology, chemistry, physics, and biology. Consider the following diverse set of questions: What total electoral vote would have resulted if a particular presidential candidate had received 5 percent more votes in a specific bloc of southern states? How much would a 200-pound man weigh if he were

Focus

Publication on the Internet

The World Wide Web (see later chapters for an extended discussion) provides a number of opportunities for student publication. The more formal outlets operate much like print publications. Potential authors submit manuscripts for consideration; an editorial board reviews these submissions. For example, *MidLink* publishes the work of eight- to eighteen-year-old students four times a year. Each edition has an announced theme, and published material is kept online for one year. The decision to include a particular manuscript is made by a student review board with teacher supervision.

The addresses for several student publication sites are provided at the end of this chapter. Contacting one of these sites is also a good way to learn about other opportunities for student publication. Be forewarned: Sites of this type seem to change host machines frequently and may cease to exist if the individuals responsible no longer have the time to maintain them. Sites that change locations can usually be found by searching the World Wide Web for the site name.

There are other opportunities for publication on the Web that are much more immediate and less formal. Many schools sponsor their own websites and provide individuals, classes, and student organizations with opportunities for publication on these sites. An even easier way to get into web publishing is with a **blog.** A blog, a contraction of web log (weB LOG), is a self-expanding webpage that allows individuals with very minimal technology skills to maintain an online multimedia journal. Blogs are typically organized in chronological order, with more recent entries appearing at the top of the page. The entries combine text and an occasional image. Blogs are discussed in greater detail in the chapter entitled "Learning from Student Projects."

EMERGING TECHNOLOGY

Inexpensive "Keyboard" Computers

Immediate and unlimited access to computers is still a distant goal for most schools. There simply is not enough equipment to allow every student to use a computer anytime a computer might be useful. Several companies have recognized this reality and have developed simple computers that can take over some of the demand for computer time. The products look very much like the keyboard of a traditional computer and are designed to perform limited word processing applications. Positioned above the keys is a simple liquid crystal display (LCD) panel capable of presenting eight lines of eighty characters of text each (some models present four lines of forty characters). Again, depending on the model, these machines can store up to eight text documents, for a total of sixty-four pages. Simple editing is possible with all machines, and some are capable of underlining and bolding. Some also include a built-in dictionary and thesaurus. All connect to a computer—either using a cable or, less frequently, by wireless—so stored text can be uploaded for storage, editing, and printing. The machines are much lighter than notebook computers, have a much longer battery life (up to one hundred hours), and are quieter. And the most important feature is that the least expensive of these machines costs approximately $200.

Naturally, the companies producing the machines recommend that schools purchase them in quantity. One company offers a package deal that includes a special security cabinet for storing and recharging forty machines. This storage area is positioned beneath the work space for a full-function computer and printer. This one piece of furniture can be rolled from classroom to classroom as needed and provides an instantaneous word processing lab.

The advantage of such equipment is that activities such as keyboarding or the early phases of writing can become much more familiar without monopolizing the computer lab or classroom computers. In addition, the size and cost of these machines make them transportable.

Students can carry them to the library or to the laboratory to take notes, or even take them home because the risk of damage or loss doesn't carry the same financial burden as with a regular computer. The companies claim these products are extremely easy to use and thus less threatening to technophobes.

Information on two of these products, AlphaSmart and DreamWriter, is included at the end of this chapter.

transported to each of the other known planets? Is it colder in November in Fargo, North Dakota, or in Juneau, Alaska?

How a spreadsheet works

A spreadsheet (see Figure 3.3) is a grid of columns (designated by letters) and rows (designated by numbers). The intersection of a column and a row is a **cell** (designated by a letter and number, such as A2). The spreadsheet user can do two very different things with any cell:

1. *Place a data item in the cell.* Although text elements such as the names of individuals or cities are frequently included to label rows of data, numbers are the most frequently entered data in cells. Each cell typically contains one data element (text or numerical value).
2. *Attach a formula to the cell.* The formula defines what will be entered in a cell and how the data to be entered will be generated. The cell entry is then the product of the formula. Here is an example. The simple formula =C2+C3 defines the cell to which the formula is attached as containing the sum of the values from two other cells (C2 and C3).

FIGURE 3.3
Screen Showing Blank
Spreadsheet

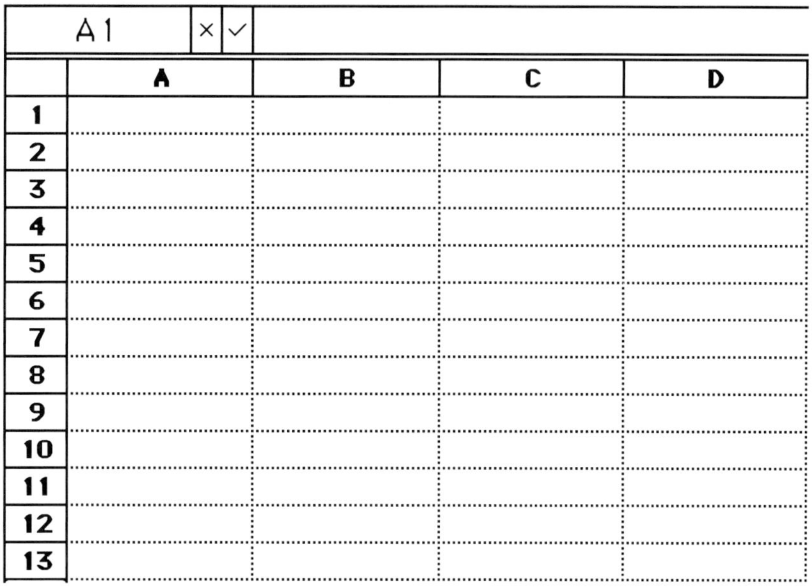

Conventions built into spreadsheets and stored functions allow some very complex operations to be expressed simply. For instance, the expression =average(C2 . . . C200) will generate the average of all the numbers contained in cells C2 through C200 (C2, C3, C4, . . . ,C200) and place the result in the cell to which the expression has been attached. This simple expression combines the convention for identifying all of the values within a range of consecutive values and the stored function for calculating an average.

Functions of a spreadsheet

The functions that can be pasted into a cell allow students to perform a wide variety of calculations or manipulations. Some functions perform statistical calculations, such as the average or standard deviation. Other functions provide mathematical information familiar to secondary-school math students, such as the logarithm of a number to base 10 or the tangent of an angle.

Comparing Winter Temperatures: A Spreadsheet Project

Let's work through a quick classroom example to see how a spreadsheet works. Assume that a seventh-grade class has decided to compare the winter temperatures in various cities. The data here happen to be from cities in North Dakota and Alaska. For a class project, it is easy to examine data from many more cities—perhaps a city selected by each student in the class or a city from each state. (One method for obtaining these data is described in the chapter entitled "The Internet as a Tool for Inquiry.")

Students enter data and attach formulas.

Each day at approximately the same time, students record the temperatures from the cities of interest. Entering these values in a spreadsheet is simple. A student selects the desired cell of the spreadsheet by clicking with the mouse or designating it with the arrow keys and enters the value. The same

ACTIVITIES AND PROJECTS FOR YOUR CLASSROOM

Spreadsheet Activities

Here are some ideas for spreadsheet projects:

- Take surveys on topics such as favorite foods, hobbies, sports, or pets. Graph the frequency with which the more popular alternatives are mentioned.
- Keep track of money earned from classroom projects or schoolwide fundraisers.
- Keep personal grade records.
- Keep records of calorie intake.
- Plan a budget.
- Calculate actual expenditures for different rate mortgages.
- Make conversion tables for weights and measures.
- Calculate age and weight on different planets.
- Plan a trip, and calculate distances for different routes.
- Collect litter for a week. Sort, weigh, and measure the litter. Use charts and graphs to motivate a campaign for recycling.
- Grow bean plants under different conditions (temperature, light), using a spreadsheet to keep track of data and to represent the data with charts and graphs.

process is used to assign labels to the rows (the dates) and columns (city names). Students can attach a formula to a cell in a similar manner. In this example, the intent is to calculate the average temperature for each city. In the software program used for this example (the AppleWorks spreadsheet), the = sign designates a formula. A cell entry beginning with the = sign is automatically understood by the spreadsheet program to be a formula and not data. The easiest way to calculate the average temperature for Juneau is to attach the formula =average(C3 . . . C11) to cell C12 (see Figure 3.4). As soon as the return or tab key is pressed to indicate that the formula has been entered, the result of the calculations appears in the designated cell.

One powerful feature of spreadsheets is that formulas are automatically adjusted when applied to different cells. For example, assume that the students decide to add the temperature for November 29 to this spreadsheet. The Insert command allows a new row of data after row 11, and the average is now automatically calculated for rows 3 through 12 instead of rows 3 through 11. The formula developed to determine the average temperature for Juneau can also be copied and pasted to cell D12, and it now generates the average temperature for Anchorage. When copied to cell D12, the variables C3 . . . C11 in the formula are automatically changed to the variables D3 . . . . D11, to produce the correct result. The capacity of a spreadsheet to make this kind of adjustment may not seem significant in this example, but consider the benefits if the example contained fifty cities and students wanted to compare average temperatures as new data were added each day for a month. Instead of entering

FIGURE 3.4
Spreadsheet Example:
Average Temperatures

	E15	×	✓				
	A	**B**	**C**	**D**	**E**	**F**	
1							
2			Juneau	Anchorage	Bismarck	Fargo	
3		11/20	15	2	37	41	
4		11/21	15	12	18	20	
5		11/22	18	35	9	16	
6		11/23	30	33	3	21	
7		11/24	30	29	9	17	
8		11/25	30	22	10	27	
9		11/26	31	14	19	28	
10		11/27	30	21	20	11	
11		11/28	33	13	33	33	
12			25.77777777	20.11111111	17.55555555	23.77777777	
13							
14							

fifty formulas each day, one formula could be entered one time and quickly copied to the columns for the other forty-nine cities; the formulas would adjust as the rows of data for each new day were added.

Displaying data as charts or graphs

Most spreadsheet programs also allow numerical data to be represented in a variety of chart and graph formats (line graphs, pie charts, bar graphs), as in Figure 3.5. The opportunity to visualize numerical data may provide a useful perspective when students try to interpret the data. Students may also use the charts and graphs generated with a spreadsheet program in reports summarizing their research and analyses. Because newspapers, magazines, and all types of educational materials communicate important data using charts and graphs, learning to interpret and critique them is an important educational objective.

FIGURE 3.5
Bar Graph Summarizing
Average November
Temperatures

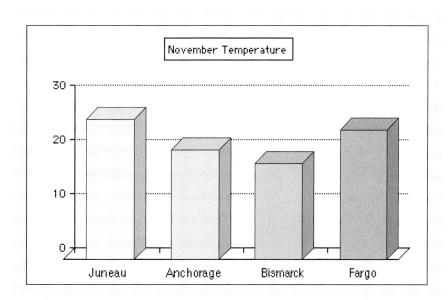

Focus

Using a Spreadsheet to Help Understand the Solution to an Algebraic Equation

Solve the equation $4x - 14 = 4 - 2x$. We expect that you still remember how to do this and that you end up with $x = 3$. How did you find the solution? You probably moved $-2x$ to the left side of the equation (reversing the sign) and -14 to the right side. Then you added and subtracted where possible to generate $6x = 18$. From there you divided each side by 6 and arrived at the answer: $x = 3$.

Now here is a different question: What does $x = 3$ symbolize? What have you found when you solve the equation $4x - 14 = 4 - 2x$? We suspect that many people who can solve the problem we have provided have no idea what the solution represents.

You may not understand what you have found because you were able to arrive at an answer by relying on some well-learned rules. Collectively these rules represent an algorithm: a procedure that generates a correct solution if followed correctly. But rote algorithmic procedures do not ensure understanding, and for that reason national math standards specify that students should learn to solve equations in different ways (National Council of Teachers of Mathematics, 2000). A spreadsheet provides one alternative to the algorithmic approach you have learned to rely on.

FIGURE 3.6

Spreadsheet Used to Solve Algebra Equation

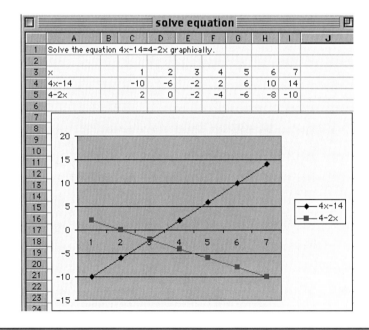

Look carefully at Figure 3.6. In row 3, you see a sequence of numerical values: 1, 2, 3, and so on. These numbers will be used as values for the variable x. The cell entries in row 4 are calculated by substituting the value for x from row 3 in the expression $4x - 14$. Using the spreadsheet, cell C4 would be assigned to the value =4*c3 – 14. Once entered, this formula could be copied to the other cells of row 4 to generate the remaining values quickly. Cell C5 would be calculated as =4 – 2*c3. Again, the formula would be copied to the other cells of row 5.

A spreadsheet (this happens to be Microsoft Excel) usually allows the generation of graphs as an alternative way to represent data. If rows 4 and 5 are transformed into a line graph, the display contained in Figure 3.6 is generated. If you look carefully, you should have a better understanding of what the solution to $4x - 14 = 4 - 2x$ represents. It is the x value at the intersection of the lines defined by $4x - 14$ and $4 - 2x$.

Source: Based on Niess, 1998.

Databases

Database programs are used to organize, store, and search for information. Although different software companies may describe their products using their own terminology, all databases are organized into three hierarchical levels: *fields, records,* and *files.*

Fields

Individual elements of information are stored in fields. Each **field** holds a user-designated category of information: flower pictures, last names, phone numbers, dates of birth, favorite baseball players, bird songs, or virtually any other category of information the user can imagine. Fields themselves are containers. In creating a field, the user establishes a field name, such as zip code, last name, or flower picture, and indicates the type of information that will appear in the field (a zip code would contain a number, a last name would contain text, and a flower picture would contain a graphic).

Records

A **record** is a meaningful collection of fields and is really the defining feature of a database. To understand what a record is, consider some further examples. Commercial databases might be used to describe the attributes of the parts sold by an automotive supply store or the characteristics of potential customers a business might try to interest in its products. For the automotive parts database, fields might include part name, part number, a picture of the part, cost per item, number of items in a minimum order, and the name of the company manufacturing each part. A clerk might consult this database when proposing options to a customer. Schools frequently organize student information using a database. The fields in a school's database might include student name, grade level, teacher, birthday, parents' or guardians' names, home phone number, parents' or guardians' work phone number, and emergency phone number. Students might use a database to investigate the characteristics of different countries (country name, population, size, form of government, primary language, capital city, gross national product, government leaders), or they might create a database for information they have gathered about the nutritional characteristics of different foods that adolescents consume. The total stored information about one automotive part, one customer, one student, one country, or one food represents a *record* within the appropriate database.

The total collection of records making up one of these databases is called a **file**. The file contains the entire collection of information about automotive parts, customers, students, countries, or foods.

Developing a Database

The first and perhaps most important step in developing a database has nothing to do with the computer. The database developer needs to think carefully about the purpose of the database: who will use it, what kinds of backgrounds end users will have, and what questions they will want to ask of the database. People who work with large commercial databases take the planning stage very seriously. Major projects, often involving connections among several databases, require considerable effort to reconfigure, so it is best to think issues through carefully before construction begins. In classroom settings, planning serves more of an educational role.

Consider the relatively popular suggestion of having elementary students develop a database of library books they have read. What would be the purpose of this database? The primary purpose might be either to provide information the teacher can use to evaluate student understanding or to provide a resource that other students can use to find an interesting book to read. This distinction would influence the categories of information included and what specific information students would provide in the database. If the purpose of the database is to interest other students in reading new books, it probably should not provide a complete summary of the books, because this would diminish the excitement of reading mysteries and many other types of fiction. What other categories or fields of information would be important to include? There are many possibilities, including author, illustrator, publication date, topic, genre, storage location of the book, other books by the author, perceived difficulty, and perceived interest value.

Once the database developer has established its purpose and scope, the second step is to use the database software to create a **template** (sometimes called a layout). In this process, the developer specifies the fields and, in some applications, positions them as they should appear on the computer screen. Many database applications also allow the developer to establish attributes of fields. Depending on the program, it may be necessary to specify how much space (that is, how many characters) to set aside for each field and what type of information (text, number, date, picture) to include in each.

Specifying the type of information has a purpose you might not expect. In some programs, a field holding the information 06-09-04 could be identified to the program as containing text or a date. Imagine that this represents the date of a sale by an automobile dealership and that it becomes necessary to locate the owners of all cars sold between January and December 2004. If the field is identified as containing a date, then a search for all sales dates in 2004 will locate every record in that range, including the entry for 06-09-04. But if the information is stored as text, the only way to locate that record would be to search specifically for 06-09-04.

Setting conventions

One final issue is important to consider. The usefulness of a database may depend on how closely the individuals entering and retrieving information follow conventions. In the example in the next section, you will see a database used to organize information about wildflowers encountered on a biology field trip. One characteristic of the flowers noted in this database was color. Different students using this database might have entered information in different ways: "white," "it was white," or "off-white," for example. It is helpful to know that the entry in this field should be a single word and perhaps that it should be one of a predetermined number of alternatives.

Investigating Wildflowers: A Database Project

The wildflower database was the result of a summer biology field trip. The purpose of the database project was to give some structure to the field trip itself and to generate continuing activities that students could pursue once they had returned to the classroom. Before the trip, students decided on the layout, or template, for the database. The purpose of the information collected in the database would be to help the students investigate the relationship among location (open meadow, heavy woods, woods clearing), species of wildflowers identified, and physical characteristics (particularly height and color) of the flowers. The students also decided to record any other characteristics that seemed interesting. With these general goals in mind, the layout was to include fields allowing entry of common name, scientific name, location, habitat, observation date, flower color, and flower size. A general field was also included for extended comments, and a graphics field was included to hold an image of the flower. The layout for the wildflower project appears in Figure 3.7. The database application for this project was FileMaker Pro.

Students went into the field with a wildflower field guide, video camera, notebooks, and insect repellent. They worked in pairs to locate and identify as many wildflowers as possible and used the video camera to record an image of each flower that could later be digitized and inserted in the database. Figure 3.8 shows a sample record from the completed database. You might wonder why we would use a video camera instead of simply collecting specimens. In part, this decision was made because of interest in using the technology and because digitizing images from video allows schools to avoid the cost of developing film. The unnecessary collection of living materials is also an issue that students need to consider; in fact, some species of wildflowers, such as the lady's slipper, are protected by state laws.

FIGURE 3.7
Wildflower Database
Template

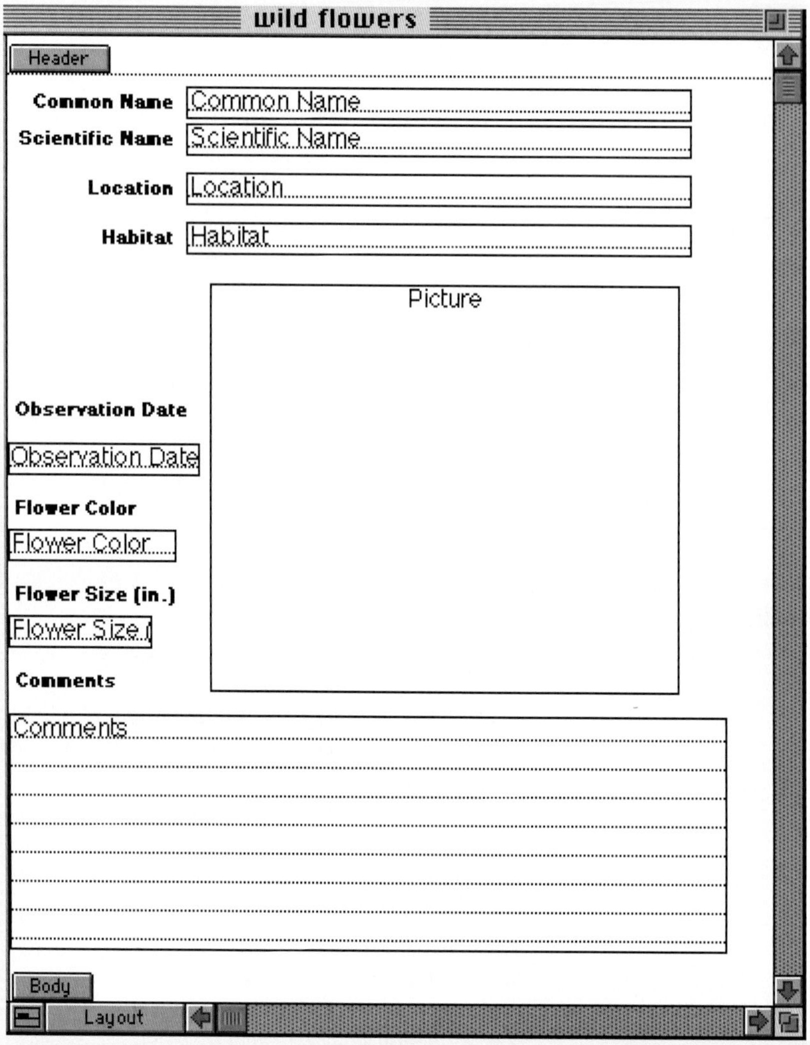

Students use database
functions to analyze
data.

Once the records were complete, students applied sort and find functions to ask different questions of the database. Most database programs allow the output from a sort or find operation to be described in a new version of the original layout. Often it is useful to create a layout containing a subset of the fields in the database and perhaps to organize this layout differently. For example, it is possible to create a two-column display sorted by habitat in which the first column contains the habitat (forest or meadow) and the second column displays the common plant name. In this display format, data from several records are displayed on the screen or printed page at the same time. If the records were sorted alphabetically on the habitat field, the initial rows of this report would list the plants found in the forest and the later rows would list plants found in meadows. This would allow students to discover which plants were unique to the forest and which plants were found in both habitats.

FIGURE 3.8
Record from Wildflower Database

Common Name Dwarf Cornel Bunchberry

Scientific Name Cornus canadensis

Location Webb Lake, Wisconsin

Habitat Forest - Cross Country Ski Trail

Observation Date

06-09-99

Flower Color

White

Flower Size (in.)

6

Comments

This plant was found on a slope along the ski trail. The plant seems to grow in bunches. The white flower is not really a flower - the flower identification book says the white structures are bracts - the flowers are small green structures in the very middle. The book also says the flower grows in cold northern woods and has scarlet berries later in the season. Leaves occur in whorls of 6. The flower blooms May-June. The flower belongs to the dogwood family.

Reflections on Spreadsheet and Database Programs

Spreadsheets and databases underused by teachers

Both spreadsheet and database applications could certainly be used more frequently in classrooms. In a survey (Ravitz et al., 1999), teachers were asked if their students had made use of a database or a spreadsheet in at least three lessons during the past year. Only 8 percent of teachers working in elementary classrooms said their students met this criterion. Middle-school and secondary students made only slightly more use of these types of software. The study indicated that 17 percent of students in science classes, 13 percent in math classes, and 11 percent in social studies classes used a spreadsheet or database a total of three times.

Although it has been argued that creating databases and working with spreadsheets can develop higher-level thinking skills and provide insights in course content (Hartson, 1993; Jonassen, Peck, & Wilson, 1999), researchers have paid little attention to evaluating the impact of experiences with these types of programs. But the findings associated with word processing would likely generalize to the application of the other tools. If this is true, we can say that the mere exposure of younger students to tool applications does not necessarily result in more meaningful learning. At least with modest levels of experience, students will likely apply their traditional approaches to learning when using the tools. To realize the potential of projects based on tool applications, teachers need to provide careful structuring, guidance, and modeling.

Data Collection Devices

Practitioners in many fields are very data oriented. They seek answers to questions through the process of research, which requires the careful measurement of critical variables. Students can engage in a similar process, learning through authentic tasks that model the activities of scientific practitioners.

Educators can now purchase devices that allow students to measure characteristics of the physical environment and store these data for analysis and graphical representation by calculators and computers. The use of a spreadsheet, described in a previous section of this chapter, is one obvious way to work with such data. The cognitive processes involved in deciding how to collect data to provide answers to significant questions, interpreting the data once collected, and communicating conclusions based on this interpretation are the same processes required of scientists and sometimes mathematicians. The processes involve higher-order thinking and allow students to take an authentic approach to the exploration of many content areas.

All data collection devices consist of at least two components:

Components of a data collection device

- A **sensor** that is sensitive to some aspect of the physical environment
- An interface that allows the user to tell the sensor what to do, stores data the sensor generates, and transfers data to a computer, **personal data assistant (PDA),** or calculator for analysis

When the sensor can be connected to and disconnected from the interface, it is often called a **probe.** These two components are present in at least three identifiable types of devices:

- A **microcomputer-based laboratory (MBL)** provides a link between a computer and the sensor. Different sensors can be connected to the same interface device.
- A **calculator-based laboratory (CBL)** provides a link between a calculator and the sensor. Again, different sensors can be connected to the same interface device. Data stored by the calculator can usually also be uploaded to a computer.
- A **data logger** is a freestanding device that contains a sensor, an interface, and a battery. Because data loggers are designed as an integrated unit, they cannot be adapted by attaching different types of sensors. The data logger is connected to a computer for programming and to upload data.

This categorization system actually simplifies some of the options that are available. Some MBLs and CBLs can be detached from the computer or cal-

Force and motion sensors used in a physics experiment.
(© Michael Zide)

culator and taken into the field to gather data. Some portable devices that are neither a calculator nor a full-featured computer (such as the Palm Handheld and DreamWriter) also allow the use of data collection devices.

Types of probes available

To develop an appreciation for the variety of areas that student researchers might investigate, consider a partial list of the probes that schools might purchase. Probes are available for measuring pH, temperature, light intensity, humidity, heart rate, voltage, acceleration, dissolved oxygen, carbon dioxide, and a variety of other variables. Each probe provides a unique type of data and is suited to a certain range of tasks.

Examples of Data Collection

Because temperature is perhaps the most frequently measured characteristic of our physical environment and a familiar concept to nearly everyone, research involving temperature is a great way to begin exploring how educators might make use of data grabbers (Albrecht & Firedrake, 1999). For example, students can:

Projects involving temperature measurement

- Fill different-colored containers with water, place the containers in the sun, and measure how quickly the temperature changes in each container.
- Compare the speed with which a container of cold water placed in different types of insulated picnic coolers warms; compare the speed with which a container of warm sand placed inside different brands of sleeping bags changes on a cold day.

- Compare temperature variability in natural bodies of water (river, shallow pond, deep lake).
- Boil water and record temperature changes relative to time as the water cools; attempt to fit linear, quadratic, and exponential functions to these data.

Temperature is a key variable in many biological and physical reactions. Changes in temperature may increase or decrease enzyme activity (biology), influence the rate of diffusion in a solution (biology, chemistry), and influence the state of matter through freezing, melting, and evaporation (chemistry). Chemical reactions produce or require heat (endothermic or exothermic reactions). The chemical reactions in the breakdown of organic materials produce heat, and proper regulation of this heat is a key factor in successful composting (ecology). Representing the trends in data (exponential functions, asymptote), modeling the influence of several variables, and accounting for some inconsistency in measurements are involved in many types of research (mathematics, statistics).

Startup costs are low.

One of the easiest ways for teachers to gain classroom experience with data collection projects is to purchase a data logger and interface software. The cost for a temperature logger and software should be less than $100. The type that we feel will be of interest to teachers is about the size of a book of matches (see Figure 3.9). The data logger contains a small battery that powers the device for a year. Data loggers need to be connected to a computer only for setup and then later to retrieve the data. The setup might tell the logger how frequently a measurement is to be taken.

A faculty member at the university where we work is interested in the factors that influence the nesting success of grebes, a bird found in wetland habitats. He studies one type of grebe that appears to leave the nest unattended under some circumstances, behavior that is detrimental to the hatch rate of the eggs. He needed a way to measure the frequency and duration the eggs were unattended, and a temperature data logger was the answer. The scientist painted a plastic colored egg to resemble a grebe egg, put a temperature logger inside the egg, and left the egg in an actual nest. Changes in temperature indicated how frequently and how long the eggs were left unattended. By gathering data from many different sites and carefully collecting other data about the sites (for instance, the population of predators), he could test hypotheses about nesting behavior.

Using Data Collection to Encourage Higher-Order Thinking

Components of an authentic project

Data logging is only one component of an authentic project, of course. The other activities that provide the context for this component are just as important in encouraging meaningful learning and the development of higher-order thinking skills. Research activities do not originate in a vacuum; scientists engage in research as a way to extend what they already know about a particular topic. Establishing or activating background knowledge and connecting the research task with this knowledge are important for creating productive content-area learning experiences.

FIGURE 3.9
HOBO Light Intensity Data Grabber

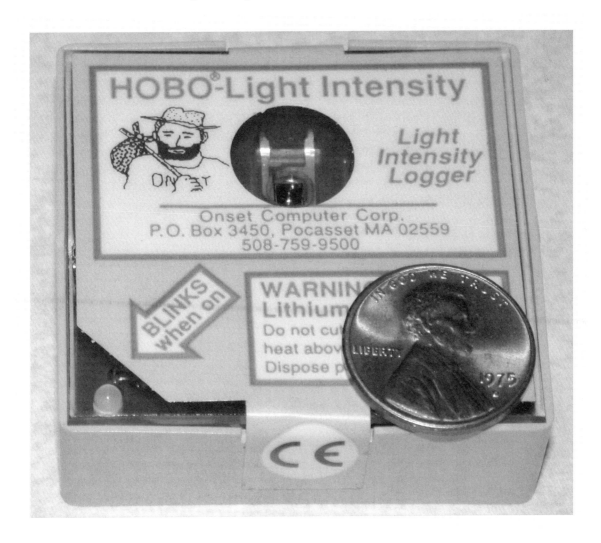

Thinking through the research methodology is an important opportunity for students to develop higher-order thinking skills. You have probably read articles in research journals as part of your own college experience, and you should recognize that each article carefully explains the method used to conduct the research. Most methods have weaknesses, and the goal in designing a research study is to develop a method that allows the strongest test of a particular hypothesis.

Once the data are collected, the scientist must find a way to create meaning from the numbers. Transforming numerical data into a graphic representation, a common method, allows the scientist to contemplate the data in a visual form. Statistical procedures may also be necessary to derive a "typical"

Focus

Using a Data Logger to Measure Stress

Laurie Tweeton, a health and physical education teacher, engages her students in projects that require the collection and analysis of data. Some of her projects use a device that records heart rate data. The device, which consists of a strap worn around the chest and a data recorder worn like a wristwatch, allows complete freedom of activity. The data recorder holds more than eight hours of information and is easily connected to a computer for data transfer.

One of Laurie's favorite projects involves the parents of her middle-school students. She asks for three parent volunteers with three different occupations who are willing to wear the heart monitor during their workday. When they can remember, the volunteers are asked to push a button on the recorder when they change activities and to keep notes identifying the different activities. The data logger marks the time when these transitions occur. Students bring the heart monitor back to school, offload the data onto a computer, create a chart from the data, and enter labels on the chart corresponding to the activities that the parents report. Students then compare the heart rate patterns of each subject and discuss which activities seemed to create the greatest stress.

Having actual data to consider may help you understand the types of investigations that are possible. Laurie allowed us to use the heart rate monitor, and we tried to generate our own authentic investigation. Here is what we came up with. We recently purchased a hot tub (called a spa in some locations) and, in reading the operating instructions, noted some health warnings. Individuals with certain medical conditions are cautioned against using the hot tub. The heart rate monitor seemed a possible way to measure the stress generated by sitting in 104°F water. The design of our experiment was simple: Establish a 20-minute baseline, sit in the hot tub for 20 minutes, and conclude with a 20-minute cooling-off period.

The data generated clearly demonstrate the stress heat imposes on the body (see Figure 3.10). Note the two marks on the x-axis. These marks indicate the transitions between stages of our experiment. The middle segment of the graph, the time during which Mark was in the hot water, demonstrates an elevated and accelerating heart rate. Note irregularities in the data appearing near the transitions between stages of the experiment. During these transitions, Mark was in his swimming suit working to remove and then reattach the hot tub cover with an air temperature of 20°F.

The computer can also store the raw heart rate data as a text file consisting of the numerical values recorded by the data logger. Once this has been done, the text file can be opened with a spreadsheet, and the data can be manipulated and analyzed in various ways. For example, we selected data values for the first and second segments that did not include the irregularities associated with removing the hot tub cover. The spreadsheet average function was then applied to these two sets of numbers. The average heart rate before entering the hot water was 74 beats per minute, and the average heart rate after enter-

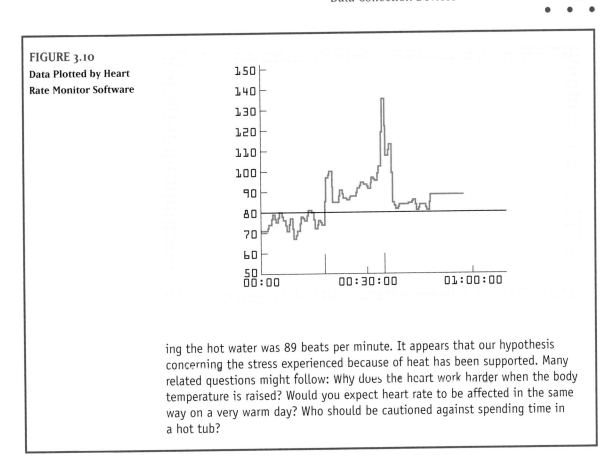

FIGURE 3.10

Data Plotted by Heart Rate Monitor Software

ing the hot water was 89 beats per minute. It appears that our hypothesis concerning the stress experienced because of heat has been supported. Many related questions might follow: Why does the heart work harder when the body temperature is raised? Would you expect heart rate to be affected in the same way on a very warm day? Who should be cautioned against spending time in a hot tub?

outcome from multiple samples. For example, the biologist we mentioned studies several nests from several locations. Calculating a variable such as the average hatch rate from each location would likely be part of the process of attempting to understand differences across the locations. Students might use a spreadsheet to create graphs or calculate statistics based on the data they have gathered.

Finally, the research process is not complete until scientists and student scientists communicate what they have discovered. For students, communication requires interpretation and the use of existing knowledge. Communication can take many forms, and several forms involving technology are considered in this book. A word processing document incorporating tables of numerical information or graphs would be a common communication product. Later in this book we discuss multimedia and online presentations, which represent an exciting way for students to communicate the results of their research. Whatever form the communication takes, learners must attempt to explain the concepts or phenomena they have studied. Students must think through what they have done, what they have observed, and what the data they have collected mean.

 You can find more information about data logging devices, sensors, and related curriculum materials in "Resources to Expand Your Knowledge Base" at the end of this chapter, and on the website that accompanies this textbook.

GPS and GIS: Interpreting Data in Relationship to Place

There is a general model of learning from authentic experiences that might be described as follows:

- Ask meaningful questions.
- Collect relevant data.
- Interpret what the data imply.
- Communicate what has been learned.

The tools we discuss in this and other chapters make contributions to all stages of this model. Inspiration, the organizing tool we discussed earlier, might be used in structuring meaningful questions. Data loggers and probes would be involved in collecting data. Spreadsheets could be used to interpret numerical data. Word processing could be involved in communicating what has been learned.

Here we want to mention two additional tools we see as expanding and interacting with the collection of learning tools we describe in this chapter. **Global Positioning System (GPS)** and **Geographic Information System (GIS)** allow the investigator to search for interpretations of data related to place. GPS uses the signals from multiple satellites to allow an individual with a GPS device (hardware) to determine place in terms of precise latitude, longitude, and altitude. Put another way, a GPS device allows you to determine exactly where you are standing on the earth. Typically, position can be determined with approximately 10-foot accuracy. GIS is a software tool that allows the user to see the relationship between "layers" of information. In most cases, one layer is a map. Other layers could be the presence or quantity of an amazingly diverse set of things—Democratic or Republican voters, cases of a specific disease, fast-food stores, a growth of leafy spurge, nitrate concentration in water. GIS software allows data summarizing the position of objects or "events" to be plotted relative to map coordinates. The general idea is to expose patterns in the data that allow the researcher to then speculate about possible explanations.

A great example of student use of GPS, GIS, probes, and the Internet is the GLOBE program **(http://www.globe.gov/)**. GLOBE is an international program led by a collaborative group of U.S. federal agencies (NOAA, NSF, NASA, EPA). More than 140 colleges and 10,000 schools from more than 90 countries are also involved. GLOBE involves students in authentic projects led by scientists in the areas of air quality, land cover, water quality, soil characteristics, and atmospheric sciences.

In the GLOBE program, students in classes taught by specially trained teachers work with scientists to collect data according to precisely defined protocols. The advantage to the scientists is the massive and distributed data collection system made available by the Internet. Data gathered from precise locations (identified with GPS) can be integrated (with GIS) on an international scale. Students have access to educational materials and learn by contributing to authentic projects.

The projects are presented in ways that have local relevance and have been matched to K–12 standards. While the topics of study most closely address standards in the areas of math and science, the international scope of the project also involves students with world geography, diverse cultures, and several languages (the project homepage is available in seven languages). The data are also available online, and groups of educators are encouraged to propose and pursue related projects.

Geocaching: Encouraging Local Explorations Using GPS

One interesting project that can be implemented using GPS technology is **geocaching.** Geocaching is an activity in which enthusiasts hide or locate small "treasures" using the capabilities of global positioning technology. The cache, typically a small plastic pail or container, holds a log book and sometimes small trinkets. The term *cache* has a historical meaning—it refers to a hiding place for provisions. The location of the cache is shared by the hider, or cache host, as precise longitude and latitude coordinates, and visitors are encouraged to locate the site, observe the surroundings, read and sign the log book, leave and take a trinket, and often claim the success of the discovery on a website.

Consider how a class might take responsibility for establishing and maintaining a cache. The class might create a cache on school grounds or perhaps,

Part of the fun in geocaching is examining the contents of the cache. Often, visitors are encouraged to take and leave a trinket.

Photo courtesy Thales Navigation, Inc. Magellan® eXplorist™ GPS handheld receivers depicted.

with permission, in a nearby park. The coordinates of this cache might be shared with other classes who would be invited to use a GPS device to search for the hidden treasure.

If you are interested in geocaching on a larger scale, you should visit the main geocaching website (**http://www.geocaching.com/**). Geocaches are established to encourage tourism, promote sites of some historical or environmental significance, and just because some people find the adventure associated with this hobby to be intriguing. You might first enter your zip code at this website to discover geocaches that are nearby. You can learn when local caches were last located and sometimes read the comments of visitors. This site also provides advice on creating a geocache and offers the opportunity to advertise your site. As you might expect, it is important to respect the rights of property owners and the environment when establishing a geocache and to understand the long-term commitment that goes along with advertising a site for others to discover. You can find more about geocaching on the website that accompanies this textbook.

Summary

The most common computer tool applications include word processing, spreadsheets, and databases. We have added data collection devices to this tool list because we believe they offer great potential for classroom activities. In general, computer tools allow users to perform tasks with increased efficiency or quality. In addition, the most common computer tools can be applied in content areas in ways that give students a more active role in learning.

You might think of the difference in the purpose of word processing–based writing activities as the distinction between learning to write and writing to learn. Teachers are urged to consider word processing as one component of a writing environment. An effective environment for developing communication skills seems to emphasize coaching, authentic tasks, the writing community, and the writing process approach.

Spreadsheet and database applications are also powerful tools with great potential benefits for exploring content-area topics. Database programs are suited to the organization of factual information and the exploration of potential relationships within this information. Working with a completed database allows students to propose and test hypotheses about different relationships among the stored data. Spreadsheet programs allow many of the same opportunities in exploring quantitative data. Students can manipulate the data, evaluate hypotheses, and visually represent conclusions in the form of graphs and charts.

Data collection devices allow students to measure various characteristics of their physical world in the same manner used by professional scientists. The design, implementation, analysis, and presentation of research based on these data provide the basis for authentic projects.

Reflecting on Chapter 3

ACTIVITIES

■ Create a paper layout for a database on an area of interest. What fields would be included? How would the fields be arranged? What questions should potential users be able to ask of the database?

■ Evaluate the suitability of a particular word processing program for the type of general across-the-curriculum use described in this chapter. Consider such issues as ease of use, cost, formatting capabilities, and the ability to incorporate graphics. Describe to or demonstrate for your classmates what you have learned.

■ Create a simple paper spreadsheet gradebook capable of determining the final percentage for two tests and two quizzes, each worth a different number of points. In your sketch of a spreadsheet, indicate the cells in which student name, test and quiz scores, and final percentage should appear. Write the formula for calculating the final percentage for two students, and indicate the cells to which each version of this formula should be attached. You should be able to complete this task using the sum function =sum(b2,c2,d2) and division =b4/a4. *Hint:* Use one row of your spreadsheet to keep track of the points possible on each test or quiz.

■ Search the Internet for learning activities that make use of CBL, MBL, or data logger technology. Search for CBL, MBL, data logger, or GPS and a term such as *education* or *experiment*. Share interesting classroom activities you locate with your classmates.

■ Connect to **http://www.geocache.com/** and identify the cache closest to your institution. If possible, borrow a GPS device and locate this cache.

KEY TERMS

blog (p. 95)
calculator-based laboratory (CBL) (p. 106)
cell (p. 96)
copy (p. 84)
cursor (p. 84)
cut (p. 84)
database (p. 101)
data logger (p. 106)
delete (p. 84)
field (p. 101)
file (p. 102)
font (p. 82)
formatting (p. 82)
geocaching (p. 113)
Geographic Information System (GIS) (p. 112)
Global Positioning System (GPS) (p. 112)
insert (p. 84)

justification (p. 84)
margin (p. 84)
microcomputer-based laboratory (MBL) (p. 106)
mindtool (p. 81)
pasting (p. 84)
personal data assistant (PDA) (p. 106)
probe (p. 106)
record (p. 101)
select (p. 84)
sensor (p. 106)
spell checker (p. 85)
spreadsheet (p. 94)
style (p. 82)
tab (p. 84)
template (p. 102)
word processing (p. 81)
word wrap (p. 82)
writing process approach (p. 88)

RESOURCES TO EXPAND YOUR KNOWLEDGE BASE

 An expanded and frequently updated list of online resources is available on the website that accompanies this textbook.

Software

AppleWorks is available for the Macintosh operating system from Apple Computer. (**http://www.apple.com/education/k12/products/appleworks/**)

Excel is available for the Macintosh and Windows operating systems from the Microsoft Corporation. (**http://www.microsoft.com/office/excel/**)

Inspiration is available for the Windows and Macintosh operating systems from Inspiration Software. (**http://www.inspiration.com/**) This same company produces a similar product, Kidspiration, for K–5 students. (**http://www.kidspiration.com/**).

Information on Word Processing, Database, and Spreadsheet Applications

The companies selling tool software may also have websites focused on educational applications:

AppleWorks (**http://www.apple.com/education/k12/products/appleworks/**)

Microsoft Corporation (**http://www.microsoft.com/education/**)

Student Publication Sites on the World Wide Web

Global Show-n-Tell exhibits works in a variety of formats created by children up to age seventeen. When we visited the site, a drawing from a two-year-old was included. (**http://www.telenaut.com/gst/**)

KidPub provides opportunities for both classes and individual students to present their work. (**http://www.kidpub.org/kidpub/**)

MidLink is an electronic magazine for students eight to eighteen years old. Theme issues are announced, and student submissions are evaluated for possible publication. (**http://www.cs.ucf.edu/~MidLink/**)

Keyboard Computers

The AlphaSmart is available from AlphaSmart, Inc. Stored files can be transferred to either a Macintosh or a PC with Windows. The company maintains a website at **http://www.alphasmart.com/.**

The DreamWriter is available from Branium Technologies. Several models are available, some capable of connecting to the World Wide Web. Stored files can be transferred to either a Macintosh or a PC with Windows. The company maintains a website at **http://www.dreamwriter.com/.**

Data Logging Resources

Information about data loggers, calculator-based laboratories (CBLs), microcomputer-based laboratories (MBLs), and probes that attach to CBLs and MBLs can be located on the Internet. Some of these sites also sell curriculum materials related to these products. Some sources follow.

HOBO data loggers are available from Onset Computer Corporation. (**http://www.onsetcomp.com/**)

The Polar Heart Rate Monitor is available from HeartMind Heart Rate Monitors. Software associated with this product is available for both the Macintosh and Windows operating systems. (**http://www.heartmind.net/**)

Vernier sells sensors, kits of sensors suited to particular math and science courses, and lab manuals describing a variety of experiments that can be performed with the sensors. The Vernier site also identifies more companies that can use these probes, information that may be useful in extending the small list we provide here. (**http://www.vernier.com/**)

ImagiWorks sells ImagiLab, a product that is designed to work with the Palm Handheld (**http://www.palm.com/**) and various probes. The Palm Handheld (previously known as the Palm Pilot) is a simple, palm-sized computer of the type often called a personal data assistant (PDA). The data from the Palm can be sent to either a Windows or a Macintosh platform computer for further analysis. ImagiProbe for the Macintosh enables students to share data in real time over the Internet. Software that comes with the Palm interface allows annotations and sketches to be stored. ImagiWorks makes available suggested activities to get teachers started. (**http://www. imagiworks.com/**)

Texas Instruments sells a CBL for use with its popular calculators. This is a good site for learning about CBLs as well as probes and activities that can be completed with CBLs. Data from a CBL can also be uploaded to a computer. (**http://education.ti.com/**)

The DreamWriter I.T. is a specialized computer developed for use in schools running the Windows CE operating system. A special data logger and probeware can be purchased to work with the computer. The DreamWriter is a product of Branium Incorporated. (**http://www.dreamwriter.com/**)

GPS/GIS Resources

The following are useful sites for GPS and GIS resources:

GIS in K–12 Education: **http://www.gis.com/specialty/educators/k12.html**
GPS and GIS in Geography: **http://geography.about.com/cs/gisgpstech/**
GLOBE Program: **http://www.globe.gov/**
Purchasing a GPS receiver: **http://gpsnow.com/**

Computers and Writing Instruction

The role that computers play in teaching writing has generated so much interest that it now represents an area of research and practice complete with its own academic journals, professional organizations, annual conventions, college courses on how it should be done, websites, and listservs. There are some very practical issues to address, such as the level of keyboard competence necessary for effective writing, and some areas in which the field is pushing the boundaries of traditional writing, such as the rhetorical elements of web authoring and idea processing software for authors.

The Alliance for Computers and Writing (ACW) is an organization offering support to K–12 and college faculty. The organization has affiliated regional and some state chapters. Its website is a great way to become familiar with the issues in the field, locate a variety of resources, and learn about other groups interested in related topics. The ACW website is located at **http://english.ttu.edu/acw/**.

Computers and Composition is a journal from Elsevier Science (655 Avenue of the Americas, New York, NY 10010) developed for those with special interests in this area. The journal hosts a related website at **http://www.nau.edu/acw/**.

4

Using Instructional Software and Multimedia for Content-Area Learning

• • •

ORIENTATION This chapter acquaints you with computer applications designed for an instructional role. First, we consider what instruction is and look at how traditional instructional activities are being challenged. Then we present a system for categorizing instructional software. Once you understand this system, you should be able to classify new programs that you encounter and understand how each category of software engages learners. For example, you will learn how to determine whether software presents new ideas and develops new skills, helps students become more proficient with skills learned elsewhere, or both presents new skills and provides opportunities for practice.

Our analysis of instructional applications places special emphasis on the attributes and potential benefits of multimedia and hypermedia, which play a large role in commercial instructional and reference resources. We explain how these formats work and describe various ways in which they can be applied. We also offer advice about evaluating educational software for your own teaching purposes.

As you read, look for answers to the following questions:

Focus Questions

- What are the four stages of a complete instructional experience? Which of the stages of instruction do computer-based tutorials, simulations, drill-and-practice software, educational games, and exploratory environments address?
- Why would teachers want students to experience a computer-based simulation rather than the "real thing"?
- When are drill-and-practice activities used inappropriately?
- What are the characteristics of an exploratory learning environment, and what role should teachers play to help students learn from exploratory environments?
- In what ways can multimedia and hypermedia extend traditional instruction and traditional instructional resources?

- What are the unique advantages and challenges in multimedia-supported learning environments?
- Is it possible to apply constructivist principles with instructional software?
- What factors might teachers consider in evaluating software for potential adoption?

"Sniffy, the Virtual Rat": An Example of Learning from the Computer

Allow me to introduce you to Sniffy, the Virtual Rat (see Figure 4.1). Sniffy lives in the virtual version of a Skinner box. The *Skinner box* is named for the famous psychologist B. F. Skinner, who discovered basic principles of operant conditioning by placing animals in carefully controlled environments in order to evaluate the influence of reward and punishment. If you are already familiar with the Skinner box, it is probably because of experiences in a high school or college introductory psychology class.

FIGURE 4.1

Sniffy in Skinner Box with Displays from Cumulative Recorder

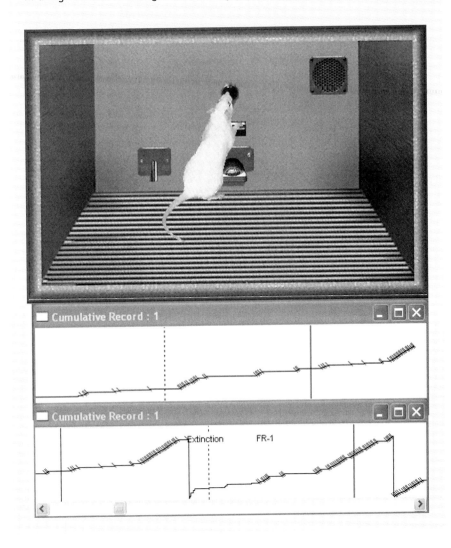

Sniffy has been programmed to exhibit the behaviors of a typical rat. He moves around the cage, sniffs at objects, consumes available food and water, reacts to sounds and light, rears on his hind legs, scratches, and exhibits about thirty typical rat behaviors. Watching Sniffy, you might easily assume that this organism is somehow in control of its own behavior.

The programmers have accomplished much more than creating a convincing visual representation of an actual rat. Sniffy has been programmed to act on the basis of fundamental rules of operant and classical conditioning. In other words, Sniffy can simulate some basic forms of learning and a human "researcher" can test his or her understanding of fundamental learning principles by attempting to train Sniffy.

It is easy to memorize the definitions of terms such as *reinforcement, punishment,* and *shaping,* but it is a different matter to test your understanding of these concepts through application. With Sniffy or a live rat, the first task is typically to teach the animal to press the bar to get food. It is a very simple action, but the rat is unlikely to acquire this response without assistance. Books and lectures typically suggest that new behaviors are most quickly acquired through shaping (the reinforcement of successive approximations to the desired behavior) and through continuous reinforcement (in which a reinforcer is delivered every time a particular action takes place). So, in the situation of your rat wandering about the Skinner box, what do shaping and continuous reinforcement mean? Shaping might require that the rat first be reinforced when it happens to move near the bar and food dispenser. Continuous reinforcement might require that in the early stages of learning his food-getting behavior, the reinforcer be delivered every time the rat wanders near the bar. Once the rat learns to associate the area near the bar and feeding station with food, you must identify another approximation to the final desired behavior. Watching the rat, you notice that from time to time the animal rears up on its hind legs. It does not appear to do this in order to touch objects, because it produces this behavior even in the middle of the cage, but the odds of striking the bar would be greatly improved if the animal could be encouraged to rear up near the bar. So, the next stage of your training program might be to deliver reinforcement if the rat is near the bar and rears up. Increasing the frequency with which the animal rears up near the bar will result in some contacts with the bar and the rat generating reinforcement for itself. As self-generated reinforcement increases in frequency, there is no longer a need to provide reinforcement for anything but the desired behavior: pressing the bar.

Figure 4.1 also shows what are called *cumulative recordings*. This is a format in which those studying operant conditioning often display their data. The recording moves along at a constant rate, and each response by the rat results in a vertical increment in the line. In the top recording, you can view what might be described as the end of the training phase. The animal has begun to respond at an accelerating rate. Once Sniffy has learned to press the bar to obtain food, this response should be maintained by its own consequence. At this point, other operant conditioning concepts can be tested. The reduction in the frequency of a learned behavior that no longer generates consequences is called *extinction*. The software controlling the Skinner box allows the delivery of food to be turned off, at which point a bar press no longer results in access to food. The bottom cumulative recording demonstrates what happens when Sniffy no longer receives food for bar pressing (see the point labeled "Extinction"). The recording shows that several bar presses occur in quick succession and then the rate of responding quickly diminishes. When food is again made available, the occasional bar-pressing behavior is again rewarded, and responding quickly picks up. This quick return of an established behavior after a delay is called *spontaneous recovery*.

You can see that Sniffy can teach a number of useful principles. Still, educators considering the use of Sniffy, the Virtual Rat software might ask several important questions. Why bother to take the time to provide a hands-on experience of any kind instead of presenting the material yourself or having students read about key concepts? If manipulative experiences are important, will working with a computer program serve as an adequate or superior substitute for interaction with the real thing? How do cost, efficiency, and learning outcomes compare? This chapter is intended to help you consider such questions as they apply to the general use of instructional software and multimedia for content-area learning.

Computer-Based Instruction

CBI and CAI

Applications of technology to instruction are often called **computer-based instruction (CBI)** or **computer-assisted instruction (CAI).** If we were to categorize these applications using the traditional tutor, tool, tutee model (Taylor, 1980) introduced in the chapter entitled "Key Themes and Issues for Using Technology in Your Classroom," the applications we discuss here would best fit within the category of computer as tutor. You might remember that the terms *tutor, tool,* and *tutee* refer to the role played by the computer. As a tutor, the computer is directly responsible for instruction. As a tool, the computer makes academic tasks such as writing and calculating easier. When the computer plays the role of tutee, the student instructs the computer by writing programs.

Technology in the role of tutor

In the role of tutor, technology exerts a high degree of control over the information to which students are exposed and over how students interact with this material. It is expected that students will acquire knowledge or skill directly from interacting with the activities provided by the computer. As a teacher or a student, you are no doubt familiar with such instructional activities. You have been exposed to them all of your academic life. The general characteristics of control we just described for technology-based activities could just as easily apply to textbooks, workbooks, and teachers' presentations. Each type of instruction presents information and engages students in specific activities to promote understanding, retention, or skill mastery.

This chapter presents the most traditional view of the purposes of education and the roles of educators and students. This traditional view argues that technology simply provides the means for educators and students to play their roles more effectively. Other advocates of instructional technology argue for drastic reform in both the purposes of education and how these purposes are accomplished; we discuss some of these views in greater detail in other chapters. From this latter perspective, the increasing availability of new and powerful technologies provides both the opportunity and the means to accomplish rather drastic changes in schools.

Instructionism versus constructionism

Some of these changes have been captured in Papert's (1993) distinction between *instructionism* and *constructionism*. Instructionist approaches seek to convey knowledge and skill as effectively as possible and argue that the route to better learning is through the improvement of instruction. The constructionist position holds that students benefit most by finding and generating their own knowledge. The teacher's primary responsibility is to support students in these tasks. Whereas some (Papert, 1993) have urged educators to take a bold step and move strongly toward a more constructionist model of education, we think that a more productive approach, and the model more likely to be implemented in current school settings, will involve students in a combination of teacher-centered (here also used to mean instruction-oriented) and student-centered learning experiences. We believe that the distinction between learning activities seeking to instruct students and learning activities requiring students to take more responsibility for what and how they learn is not necessarily the same as the distinction between passive and active learning. High-quality technology-based learning experiences of any type should engage learners in the active cognitive behaviors we identified earlier in this book.

The Process of Instruction

Four stages of instruction

The complete instructional process takes students through four stages (Alessi & Trollip, 2001):

1. Exposure to information or learning experiences
2. Initial guidance as the student struggles to understand the information or execute the skill to be learned
3. Extended practice to provide fluency or to ensure retention
4. Assessment of student learning

This model is intended as a general description of the components of instruction and not a model specific to instruction delivered with technology. If it can be accepted that all four stages must be present for instruction to be successful, awareness of the stages of instruction can serve several useful purposes. In this chapter, we make use of this model in two ways. First, we use the four stages to identify and differentiate the purposes of different categories of instructional software. We intend that you will develop the capability to assess how many of the stages of the instructional process a given example of instructional software actually provides. Second, we use the stages of instruction to help educators evaluate their expectations for the roles to be played by different types of multimedia.

Analyses of this type can help you recognize some of the misuses of software that often occur in classrooms. For example, teachers sometimes use software designed for the third, or practice, stage as an initial instructional activity. Practice activities provide feedback on the quality of student performance, but this feedback is often not adequate to teach new skills to students who have little understanding of the task. Simple feedback when basic principles are poorly understood is not very helpful.

Another common mistake is the failure to appreciate the distinction between an information resource and an instructional resource or experience. Many multimedia and Internet-based resources provide information that is not specifically designed for instructional purposes. When students are working with such sources, teachers need to help the students locate quality information and process it for meaningful learning. In other words, mere exposure to reference material does not fulfill many of the expectations of the instructional process. In such situations it is unfair to blame the material; the problem is that parts of the instructional process are missing.

In summary, educators must integrate technology-supported experiences within a complete approach to instruction. You will find we rarely describe a technology-supported learning situation that does not include an active role for the teacher.

Categories of Instructional Software

In this section, you will learn the characteristics of five categories of instructional software: tutorials, simulations, drill-and-practice applications, educational games, and exploratory environments. You will become familiar with the stages of instruction that each type of software most frequently covers and see that some categories of learning activities offer students more control and flexibility than others. Once you have completed this section, you should be able to identify some of the strengths and weaknesses of each software category, in theory and in practice. When you reach the final section of this chapter, you can apply your understanding to selecting software to use in your classrooms.

Tutorials

Tutorials adapt instruction to individual students.

High-quality **tutorials** should present information and guide learning—the first two stages of the instructional model (Alessi & Trollip, 2001). We usually think of tutoring as a form of instruction involving a teacher and one or two students. The individual nature of the interaction between tutor and student is assumed to offer certain advantages. In comparison to group-based instruction, tutorials can more precisely tailor the rate of progress and the content of presentations to the needs of the individual student, immediate adaptations in instruction can be made, and students can interact with the tutor. The individual nature of the tutorial approach is frequently proposed as an advantage of computer-based tutorials.

How Tutorials Function
The human tutor usually begins by presenting a small segment of information or demonstrating a specific skill. Then the tutor requires some type of activity

Computer-based projects provide many different opportunities for cross-age interaction.
(© Michael Zide)

on the student's part. Depending on the content being taught, the tutor might ask the student to respond to a question or to demonstrate the skill just presented. The student's performance allows the tutor to judge how well the student has mastered the newly acquired content or skill. This appraisal allows the tutor to do two things: (1) provide motivational feedback ("You're doing very well" or "I think we need to work on this a little more") and (2) use the quality of the student's performance to determine what to do next. Perhaps the student is having no difficulty, in which case it makes sense to move on. Perhaps the student has misunderstood something, in which case the tutor needs to explain a specific concept again.

Students can take an active role in tutorials.

In a tutorial relationship, the student can take an active role by asking for clarification or requesting that the tutor repeat an explanation. Of course, the student can also just ask questions that come to mind. If the questions are relevant to the topic, the tutor can interact with the student to explore the topic, using the student's own curiosity and background knowledge.

High-quality computer tutorials are capable of imitating some of these elements of instruction. Even relatively inexpensive computers can present information using text, sound, animation, illustrations, and video. The powerful multimedia capabilities of the computer provide a fairly satisfactory solution to the requirements of the first stage of instruction. A CD or a DVD offers tremendous storage capacity and can make a great deal of information available to the student. The more subtle and dynamic instructional elements present in guiding student learning are more difficult to mimic, however. Computers can certainly gather information about student understanding or skill mastery by frequently asking questions or requiring that students perform assigned tasks, but computers' information-gathering and interpretation skills are crude in comparison to those of human tutors.

Linear versus branching tutorials

Simply communicating to a student that he or she has missed key ideas in the lesson or has not developed important skills does not satisfy the expectations of guidance. Tutorials attempt to provide additional guidance through hints and remedial explanations. In **linear tutorials,** all students work their way through the same body of information. Students performing poorly may be cycled through a particular segment of instruction a second time. In **branching tutorials,** students having difficulty receive a different instructional approach rather than returning to material that has already proved difficult for them to understand. Branching decisions can also be made based on pretest information. Questions may reveal that some students already know some of the material a particular tutorial was designed to teach. Rather than sending these students through an unnecessary sequence of instruction, they can be routed to the material they need to learn. Branching programs are more complex than linear programs but allow for greater individualization of instruction.

Evaluating Tutorials

A fair question for you to ask when evaluating the instructional potential of computer-based tutorials is: What type of instruction represents a fair comparison? Although computer-based tutorials attempt to model some key behaviors of human tutors, they cannot duplicate all of these behaviors. The human tutor can evaluate student behavior in more sophisticated ways and can respond to student needs more flexibly. Classroom teachers, however, may often be unable to function as tutors because there are too many students and too many different responsibilities in classrooms.

In this context, two points suggest themselves:

Two considerations in evaluating tutorials

1. It is possible that there are some situations in which a less-than-perfect computer-based tutor can productively augment or provide an alternative to what the classroom teacher and traditional instructional materials are able to accomplish.
2. It is neither necessary nor desirable to eliminate the teacher's involvement totally when some instructional functions are provided by technology. It may be possible for teachers to monitor student work as the student interacts with tutorials and to respond to student questions after the learning session.

For these reasons, it is probably irrelevant to ask exactly how the computer compares to a human tutor in most K–12 situations. Instead, the most fundamental questions in evaluating computer-based tutorials concern the clarity, efficiency, and appeal with which important information is presented.

Simulations

A simplified version of the real world

Simulations provide controlled learning environments that replicate key elements of real-world environments. A simulation's focus on a limited number of key elements provides a simplified version of the real world that allows the student to learn a topic or skill very efficiently. A simulation is designed so that the actions a student takes within the simulated environment produce results similar to those that would occur in the actual environment. The student acts, and the simulated environment reacts. Our description of Sniffy, the Virtual Rat provides a good description of this type of interactivity. In order to "train" Sniffy, the student using the simulation has to pay close attention to Sniffy's behavior. In addition, Sniffy is responsive to the actions taken by the student.

Role-playing as simulation

Simulations can be used to learn about properties of physical or biological objects or the principles by which a variety of physical, social, and biological phenomena function. You may already have some experiences with simulations. Role-playing experiences, for example, are a type of simulation. Before student teachers go into elementary or secondary schools to work with students, they commonly role-play such skills as leading a discussion, giving a short lecture, asking questions and providing feedback, and working with a misbehaving student. Instead of dealing with the complexities in an actual classroom, role-playing experiences tend to focus on a particular skill, such as leading a discussion. Computer-based simulations attempt to meet similar instructional objectives.

Simulations can be used before the formal presentation of new material to pique students' interest, activate what students already know about the topic, and provide a concrete example to relate to the more general discussion that follows. Simulations can also be used after students have been exposed to a new topic. In the example, what the student already knew about shaping and continuous reinforcement suggested how to begin the process of training Sniffy. In this approach, the simulation allows students to attempt to transfer what they have learned to an actual application and perhaps to reveal any misconceptions they may have.

Some research (Brant, Hooper, & Sugrue, 1991) suggests that using a simulation prior to formal instruction is particularly effective. In this case, the simulation provides experiences that anchor later concepts and explanations. The simulation serves a similar purpose to a teacher asking students to consider a common real-world experience before beginning instruction. Other research, however, suggests that the best time for a simulation may depend on student background knowledge and the nature of what is simulated (de Jong & van Joolingen, 1998). If learners have little experience with the topic of the simulation, they will be unable to interpret what the simulation demonstrates. For example, a chemistry titration simulation would make little sense to many learners because they lack appropriate background knowledge. Even if the learner were capable of manipulating the software, familiarity with concepts such as pH, acid, and base would be fundamental to what students took away from experience with the simulation.

Varied uses of simulations

Simulations can be used for all four stages of instruction: presentation, guidance, practice, and assessment (Alessi & Trollip, 2001). Although this does not mean that every simulation is intended to provide a stand-alone educational experience, it does imply that simulations are the most versatile of the different categories of CAI.

FIGURE 4.2

Screen Display for
Operation: Frog—
Dissection Pan and
Examination Tray

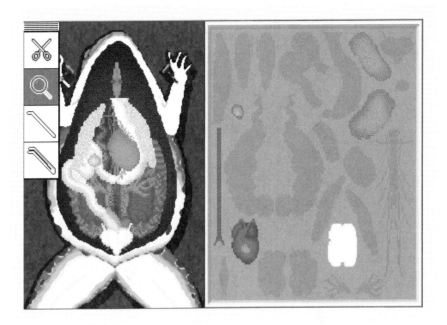

Operation: Frog—An Example of a Simulation

Focusing learners on
key ideas

Do you remember dissecting a frog in high-school biology? Do you remember your reaction and the reaction of some of your classmates when your teacher explained that before you could begin the dissection, you would have to "pith" your frog? (To pith a frog, you use a dissection needle to destroy the connection between the brain and body so that body organs such as the heart will still be functioning and can be observed during the dissection.) Operation: Frog is a computer program designed to allow students to simulate the dissection of a frog. And, no, you don't have to pith the frog before you begin! The program presents students with a set of dissection tools, a dissection tray complete with specimen, and an examination tray for organizing and examining organs removed from the frog (see Figure 4.2).

Informative text, labeled graphics (see Figure 4.3), and digitized photographs from an actual dissection are available for each organ. Occasional animations (for instance, of blood flow) or QuickTime movies are also provided. (QuickTime is a common format for presenting digital video on a variety of computers.)

Operation: Frog exemplifies some of the features of simulations. Simulations tend to present a simplified version of the real thing and attempt to focus learners on key ideas, skills, or components. In contrast to the clumsiness and messiness that comes with dissecting a frog, work with the simulated frog uses simpler procedures and reveals simplified information. When simulated incisions are made at the proper locations, the skin magically disappears. Attempted incisions at other points are ignored. In fact, it is impossible to cut at an inappropriate point or to move a body part that the simulation does not intend the student to move. Developing the physical

FIGURE 4.3
Exported Graphic from
Operation: Frog

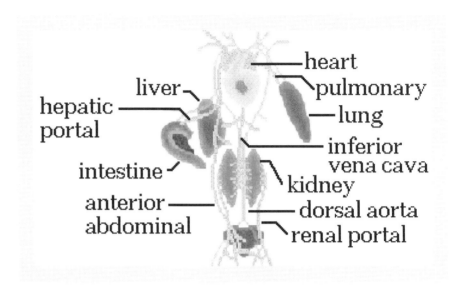

dexterity necessary to use dissection instruments is not a target behavior, so there is no attempt to teach these skills. The organs to be removed at a particular stage of the simulation are designated by color to make them easier to find. There is no need to separate the skin from other tissues or to remove abdominal muscles. Learning about the frog's musculature is not an objective of the simulation, so the abdominal muscles are not present in the simulation. Based on the original description of Operation: Frog, you may be able to list several other ways in which the simulation has been simplified. The simulated dissection clearly focuses the student on the location of specific organs within the body of the frog.

Attributes of Simulations, Learning, and Transfer
The extent to which a simulation mimics reality is called **fidelity** (Alessi, 1988). When you make decisions about instruction or selecting instructional materials, an important issue to consider is how fidelity relates to learning and application.

How does fidelity affect learning?

When looked at beside an actual dissected frog, the various forms of simplification identified in Operation: Frog do result in lower fidelity. Your initial reaction might be that if it is practical, experience with the real thing is always best. But consider, for example, learning to fly an airplane. Would it be ideal to expose a novice to experiences in an actual plane? Even if the issues of cost and safety were ignored or somehow taken care of, the situation of highest fidelity is still not necessarily the best learning situation. The student would be too anxious and the situation too confusing to allow much learning (Alessi & Trollip, 2001). Similar situations may happen in classroom settings more familiar to you. In presenting new concepts or principles, most experienced instructors initially ignore the exceptions and complications that might confuse and increase the anxiety of students. The initial presentation describes concepts and principles with less than perfect fidelity. It appears that a moderate degree of fidelity is best for initial learning.

Now consider the student's ability to apply or transfer what he or she has learned. High fidelity obviously increases transfer of learning to the real situations in which the learning must be applied. We have a dilemma, then: High fidelity appears to reduce learning but increase transfer. At the extreme of very high fidelity, the student—like the novice pilot in an actual airplane—learns very little. At the other extreme, with very low fidelity, we face the problem of *inert knowledge,* which was described in an earlier chapter: Learning has occurred, but the experiences surrounding the learning make it unlikely that it will ever be used.

The best approach, then, seems to involve a moderate degree of fidelity. In such moderate circumstances, learning and transfer both occur, although both are somewhat inefficient. In the initial learning, the student is challenged, perhaps confused at first, but not totally baffled. After the student overcomes this confusion, the relative realism of the learning environment makes it likely that the student will be able to apply what has been learned.

Advantages of Simulations

Simulations have several potential advantages over allowing students to experience the real world. We have already considered how the simplification allowed by simulations can help learners focus on critical information or skills and make learning easier. Simulations can also allow students to observe phenomena that are not normally visible, control processes that are not normally controllable, or participate in activities that would normally be too expensive or too dangerous. Simulations make certain experiences practical and other experiences possible. There are other advantages too.

Concreteness Consider first that many things that students study cannot really be observed. You probably learned about the relative positions of the planets revolving around the sun, how electrons flow in electrical circuits, the movement of glaciers, continental drift, economic principles of supply and demand, how a signal is passed along and between neurons, and the interrelatedness of populations in a food chain. Clearly certain phenomena are difficult or impossible to observe.

Sometimes the object of study has to be made larger (the neuron) and sometimes smaller (the solar system or continents). Sometimes the phenomena have to be speeded up (movement of glaciers and continents; the passage of generations of plants and animals) and sometimes slowed down (movement of electrons within electrical circuits). Sometimes what you view in the real world has to be put in a different form for you to observe it at all. Simulations of different economic principles often represent the relationships among several factors graphically, as with the economic principles of supply and demand or the biological interdependence of predator and prey. Whether the technique involves making the object of study smaller or larger, the phenomena faster or slower, or certain complex relationships more visible, simulations give students concrete representations to ponder.

Opportunity for students to exercise control

Control   A second valuable characteristic of simulations is the opportunity they provide for students to make decisions with logical consequences. Simulations put students in control of situations with which they would seldom be allowed to experiment under any other circumstance.

For example, a simple business simulation might be based on mathematical expressions that define the relationship among such variables as money spent on advertising, the price the customer has to pay for the product, the number of items sold, and profit. As they work with this simulation, students might try to maximize profit and control both the price and the cost of advertising. The computer would inform the student of the number of items sold and the profit earned. As advertising increases and price decreases, customers will buy more of the product. However, total profit will not necessarily increase because of increased expenses (advertising) and a lower profit on each item sold. The ideal solution to the simulation will depend on how the simulation's designers have weighted the value of spending a certain amount of money on advertising and how they have decided changes in price will influence the number of items sold.

Cost-Effectiveness   Sadly, educators have to be constantly aware of how much money educational experiences cost. This reality applies to decisions regarding the purchase of hardware and software, but it also applies to the experiences or materials that simulations might replace.

The components that physics students need to assemble electrical circuits are costly. Certain components, such as transistors, can easily be ruined if students make mistakes in the way they assemble circuits. A computer program allowing students to simulate the assembly of circuits does not require that additional components be purchased when students make errors. In certain situations, simulations provide quality experiences at a reasonable cost.

Safety   There are some things that students should learn that would be dangerous for them to experience directly. Some experiments in chemistry or projects exploring how electrical devices work may be too dangerous for elementary- or secondary-school students. The use of simulators in pilot training is an example of the value of simulation in increasing the safety of training experiences.

Drill and Practice

You probably take your ability to recognize and spell common words for granted. Of course, this was not always the case. Back in early elementary school, you spent a good deal of time becoming familiar with words. Do you remember what you did to learn basic word recognition skills? Obviously you spent time reading. You probably also spent time completing worksheets or some other type of activity that emphasized specific reading skills. The activities focused on specific skills could probably be classified as drills.

An example of computer-based drill

If you have not experienced computer-based drill, you may want to consider the following example. Word Scramble is one of several activities contained on the *Letter Sounds* CD from the Tenth Planet Explores Literacy Series.

FIGURE 4.4
Screen Display from Word Scramble

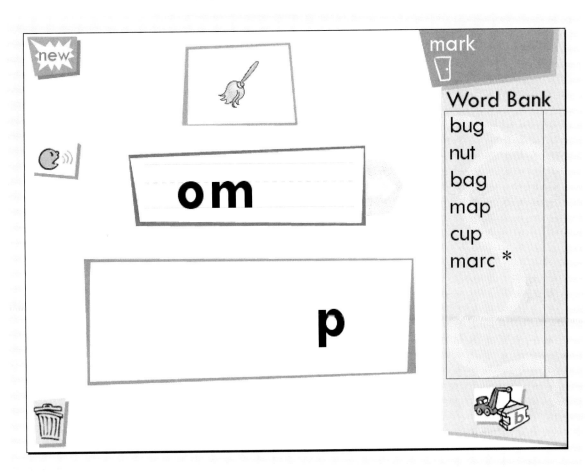

Word Scramble would qualify as a drill activity specifically designed to familiarize the learner with the consonant-vowel-consonant word pattern. Skills in letter-sound correspondence and letter patterns are important components contributing to word identification and spelling.

The Word Scramble program follows a simple repetitive pattern. It presents a picture and pronounces the word the picture represents. The program also presents the letters spelling the word in a scrambled order. The learner's task is to drag the individual letters from the box in which they appear to the word construction box (the box that resembles lined writing paper in Figure 4.4) and arrange them to spell the target word. Clicking the arrow adds the correctly spelled word to the learner's Word Bank. The Word Bank continues to grow as the learner works with the program. The Word Bank also serves as a mechanism connecting several of the learning activities found on the CD.

The designers of the Tenth Planet Explores Literacy Series recommend that fundamental skills be developed through a diversity of learning activities and suggest hands-on activities that can be coordinated with the computer experiences. The designers have given thought to other important issues as well. Evaluating student progress is an important part of any learning activity. The *Letter Sounds* CD comes with a management system that stores data generated by student activity. One particular activity, the Word Building Tool (see the construction equipment image in the lower right corner of the Word Scramble screen in Figure 4.4), encourages students to try to spell words they know. The idea is that students will use the Word Building Tool to try out skills they have developed with the drill activities. Words generated with the Word Building Tool appear in the Word Bank marked with an asterisk to indicate they have been added by the learner and are stored along with entries generated by drill activities for the teacher to examine. As you might expect, words created with the Word Building Tool may not be spelled correctly. However, the teacher can glean a great deal of useful information from the student's efforts. What words did the student try to spell? Do the attempts at phonetic spelling indicate an understanding of letter-sound correspondence? Archiving some of these efforts over time provides portfolio entries documenting changes in student understanding.

Applications of Drill-and-Practice Software

Providing extended practice

Drill-and-practice software is developed to meet the needs of the third stage of instruction: extended practice. Students' initial exposure to academic facts or skills is seldom sufficient for an adequate level of mastery. Extended study is required before the facts or skills can be considered learned. The exact proficiency that students should develop varies with the type of content. For factual information (for example, the product of 2 x 2, the capital of West Virginia), the expectation is that students will be able to retrieve the information from memory quickly, smoothly, and with few errors. Students are also expected to perform many tasks that require mastery of a routine (for example, complete long division problems with accuracy, type 40 words per minute).

Technically, drill and practice are not identical. **Drill** activities concern factual memorization, and **practice** concerns the development of skill fluency (Price, 1991). But we are not considering instructional software in great detail, so we follow the tradition of treating drill-and-practice software as a single category.

Developing skill fluency

Consider an activity designed to develop skill fluency. MicroType (see Figure 4.5) is a popular practice activity for developing touch-typing skills. Students progress through a series of lessons. Each lesson begins with a review of skills from previous lessons and a brief tutorial introducing the skills or letters for the current lesson (such as *f* and *b*). The lesson begins with practice on the individual letters and simple letter combinations (*f b bf fb fib*), advances to simple phrases (to *fib* or *rob*), and then moves to timed lines (see Figure 4.5) and timed paragraphs. Each lesson concludes with a simple game in which the student types lines of text to reveal parts of a picture.

Typing is a skill we want students to be able to perform accurately, swiftly, and automatically. **Automaticity** frees some of the limited capacity of short-term memory for other uses. Usually it is desirable that students not think about their finger placement or the location of the letters as they type. Extended practice is about the only way to accomplish automaticity.

FIGURE 4.5
Screen Display from
MicroType Practice
Activity

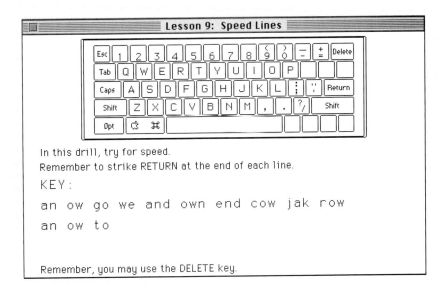

Focus of Drill and Practice

<aside>The timing of drill-and-practice activities</aside>

Whereas other types of instructional software may be used for several of the phases of instruction, drill-and-practice software has a more limited focus. It should not be used to introduce new areas because it has a narrow approach and is not suited to helping students understand new material. Drill-and-practice activities are appropriate after students have advanced past the guidance phase of instruction. Teachers need to be aware of this issue and emphasize drill and practice when fact availability and skill fluency are appropriate goals.

Educational Games

<aside>Edutainment: mixing learning and entertainment</aside>

Instructional activities are categorized as **games** when the activities emphasize competition and entertainment. If the activity has a winner or a loser or focuses the student on competing against established records or standards, the activity has gamelike qualities. Games also employ fantasy, action, uncertainty, and similar features to make the activity interesting for the players. You will probably recognize that many of these same features were present in the activities already described as examples of other CAI categories. Commercial instructional software often combines elements of several different categories of software. If software is to be labeled, it is often necessary to determine subjectively the degree to which certain characteristics are present. Is some entertainment used to motivate learning, or does some learning result as a byproduct of play? Many people describe some types of game activities as **edutainment.**

<aside>Why are games so effective?</aside>

Researchers, educators, and software developers have grown increasingly interested in digital games and how games might be used in education. This interest arises from a variety of perspectives. Some researchers recognize that video games have achieved a high level of commercial success and represent a preferred method of recreation for many young people. Understanding why games are so voluntarily engaging for extended periods of time, how they motivate participants to create online communities of practice, and how they appear able to scaffold the development of complex motor skills, rules, and factual knowledge may suggest insights for those interested in improving classroom learning (Gee, 2003). Other researchers suggest that the extended focus on interactive digital entertainment, in combination with a preference for fast-paced television (for instance, MTV, *Blues Clues*), has created a strong preference for these styles of interaction and presentation that may have resulted from brain restructuring. As a consequence, researchers are concerned that students may regard conventional methods of "noninteractive, show-tell" instruction as extremely boring and possibly even incompatible with the needs of a brain prepared to respond to stimuli presented in a different way (Prensky, 2001). Developers and researchers are using these perspectives to explore ways to use fantasy, interactivity, challenge, competition, and fun to improve instructional software.

Examples of Educational Games

Certain educational games have been popular for a long time and seem to embody characteristics teachers find of value. The Oregon Trail and Where in the World Is Carmen Sandiego? fall into this category. The Oregon Trail was first released in 1978 in a text-only format.

Educational use of The Oregon Trail

The Oregon Trail   The Oregon Trail, now a CD-based multimedia product, takes the student on a covered wagon journey from Independence, Missouri, to Oregon in 1865. The game puts the student in the role of expedition leader, and the outcome of the journey depends to some degree on the decisions he or she makes along the way. What items should be purchased to outfit the wagon as the trip begins? How far should the wagon attempt to travel in a day? Should the wagon stop at a fort for supplies? Stops at landmarks, forts, and towns engage the leader in "conversations" that can be useful in revealing obstacles that are likely to be encountered and in suggesting ways to survive these difficulties. The leader may learn how to cross the river or when to hunt for food.

We categorize The Oregon Trail as a game rather than as an authentic simulation because of its emphasis on entertainment and the general nature of its historical experiences. The game does provide a sense of the experiences of the early pioneers and may be a useful way to generate interest in a unit about this time period. Educators have taken to supplementing the game activity in a number of ways. One approach is to have students keep notes as they play the game and then write diary entries compatible with their notes. The Oregon Trail is so popular that Internet sites have been developed or located to accompany the game. Such sites may provide current scenes along the route of the trail, related historical information, or the perspective of Native Americans from the region.

Complex activities in the Carmen Sandiego series

The Carmen Sandiego Series   The Carmen Sandiego series (Where in the World Is Carmen Sandiego?, Where in the USA Is Carmen Sandiego?, Where in Time Is Carmen Sandiego?, and others) puts the student in the role of detective. A crime has been committed, and the thief is dashing from city to city or country to country (this aspect varies with the version of the game). As the detective, the student must attempt to trail Carmen or her partners, using the clues that are revealed (for example, the kind of currency the villain is using, some characteristic of the city). Reference materials (*World Almanac Book of Facts* reference guide) supplied with the software help students interpret the clues. The newest CD-ROM version includes colorful graphics and allows the detective to question a witness, search the crime scene, compare notes with other detectives, log evidence in a database, and issue warrants. Students can play the game over and over again without encountering the same case. The game acquaints students with several aspects of geography (location of cities and countries, factual information about specific places), requires the use of reference materials, and encourages note taking.

SimCity Now consider something a bit more exotic. SimCity, a popular game that has been evolving since the late 1980s, assigns a player the role of mayor. In this capacity, the player must develop and oversee the operation of a city. The cities can be created from scratch, or the player can accept the challenge of operating one of the major cities of the world. The goals of the game are basically to maintain or grow the population of Sims, the fictional citizens of the city, and to do so while responding to a wide assortment of issues and problems that emerge dynamically as the many facets of the simulated environment interact. If you build an inexpensive coal power plant, the Sims complain about pollution. But if you build solar power generators in an effort to be environmentally conscious, the Sims complain about the cost.

A player can set as a goal the development of any type of community that can be imagined—industrial center, metropolis, or rural town. As developer and mayor, the player controls many factors, including:

- The position of the city within the available terrain
- The development of transportation, utility, and public services infrastructure
- The zoning of land for residential, commercial, and industrial use
- The lending of money for special projects
- The levying of taxes
- Enactment of ordinances to allow or disallow certain behaviors

In SimCity 4, a recent edition in the SimCity series, you can even explore the role education plays in a community. You learn by structuring the educational environment and then considering the consequences. For example, there is an opportunity to explore the different issues associated with private and public institutions by controlling the options available to citizens. What role is played by informal educational facilities such as public libraries and museums? What are the advantages and disadvantages of a community college in contrast to a university?

The SimCity games provide the player with many types of data. The sophisticated physical appearance of the city provides one type of feedback (see Figure 4.6). The Sims come out of their homes and places of work and move about the city. Cars, buses, and trucks move over the streets and roads. Buildings are developed and fall into disrepair. This activity is not random, but

FIGURE 4.6

Screen Image of SimCity, Showing City and User Controls SimCity 3000 © 1998 Electronic Arts Inc.
SimCity 3000 is a trademark or registered trademark of Electronic Arts Inc. in the U.S. and/or other countries.

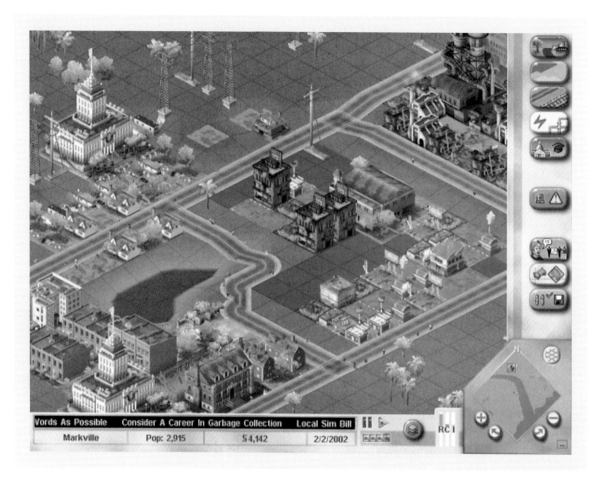

based on the characteristics of the city. The player can zoom in or out depending on the level of visual detail that is desired. Other forms of information are always accessible. A News Ticker constantly streams information across the bottom of the screen. Any item that seems interesting can be clicked on to obtain greater detail. The mayor can consult a variety of ledger sheets, charts, and graphs to obtain data on many variables and to see how variables interact. The mayor can also call on a panel of advisers to obtain specialized input. All of these sources of information are dynamically adapting to the changing characteristics of the city.

Critical thinking and problem solving in SimCity

How SimCity can be entertaining may be obvious, but it may not be apparent why the experiences provided by the game have educational value. At the level of general skill development, accepting the challenge of being mayor involves the player in both critical thinking and problem solving. The game provides a complex environment in which there are embedded data and problems and no perfect solutions. The way to survive is to establish priorities and then manipulate what can be manipulated in response to these priorities. If environmental sensitivity is a priority, one will find that it may not be feasible to expand the population beyond a certain point. At the level of specific skills and knowledge, the game provides insight into how cities and city government function.

SimCity has generated an online community of devotees. It is possible to exchange cities with other players and to download suggestions and utilities related to the game. For example, there is a utility that converts contour maps published by the U.S. Geological Survey into terrain maps for SimCity. You can locate an area familiar to you and attempt to populate it with Sims. Resources of this type allow for some interesting classroom adventures.

Classroom Uses of Games

Making the best use of educational games

Teachers use educational games in several ways. Some, such as The Oregon Trail and SimCity, provide interesting ways to initiate related areas of study. Like simulations, carefully selected games may activate existing knowledge and pique student interest in the more traditional academic work that follows. The challenge in working with games is not in the potential for meaningful learning, but in the approach students bring. The fundamental question is whether students will be producing knowledge by analyzing data and testing ideas or whether they are manipulating the game at a superficial level, just clicking buttons or selecting options to see what will happen (Henderson, Klemes, & Eshet, 2000). In our opinion, the perspective students take is greatly influenced by how teachers interact with them in response to student experiences with the game.

Although games are often equated with competition, they can also be used to enhance cooperation. SimCity, for example, encourages extensive record keeping and planning. Students can share these tasks and benefit from opportunities to discuss strategy or evaluate game consequences. The Carmen Sandiego games make heavy use of travel guides and almanacs, and several students can work together to look up information.

Finally, teachers may also use educational games to reward hard work or achievement. There is nothing wrong with using technology in this way, but you should be aware of potential problems. Sometimes students who always get their work done first are the only students who get to spend time with the computer games. Teachers need to take care that computer games do not become an exclusive opportunity for certain categories of students. Teachers must also be aware of the proportion of precious computer and classroom time devoted to games. Game use must be kept in check, and care must be taken that time on the computer does not become play time.

Exploratory Environments

Computer-based worlds to explore and manipulate

Exploratory environments provide manageable and responsive computer-based worlds for students to explore and manipulate (Hsu, Chapelle, & Thompson, 1993; Joyce, 1988). These computer-based activities have also been described as intentional learning environments (Scardamalia, Bereiter,

McLean, Swallow, & Woodruff, 1989) and interactive environments (Kozma, 1991). In a way, exploratory environments attempt to place the learner in a "real world" situation and require the learner to engage in tasks authentic to that situation.

An exploratory environment offers elements for students to work with and a setting in which the manipulation of these elements allows students to explore a cohesive body of information or a rule system (Hsu et al., 1993). The specific nature of the elements, information base, or rule system depends on the content area the environment was developed to represent. Exploratory environments present information, but they are not directive in the manner of tutorials. The material that students spend time examining or manipulating is largely self-selected. Some, but not all, exploratory environments contain a task, goal, or problem to be solved.

One difficulty with these nondirective environments is that a rich database of information is not always enough to engage many students in active learning. So whether an assignment is embedded in the exploratory environment or suggested by a teacher, guided interaction with the environment appears to be most productive. This issue is raised again after you have had an opportunity to become more familiar with exploratory environments.

Characteristics of Exploratory Environments

Common features of exploratory environments

It is difficult to list an exact set of requirements for an exploratory environment, but the following features are common:

- *Learner control.* Clearly, exploratory environments encourage and may actually require that students exercise control over their experiences.
- *Flexibility.* Students can typically do many different things. They can even do the same thing in several different ways, revisiting the same concepts from different perspectives or using different approaches.
- *Active learning in a realistic situation.* Exploratory environments are designed to provide opportunities for active learning that are anchored in realistic situations, experiences, and goals.

Hypermedia Environments

Exploring settings that are rich in information

Environments developed using hypermedia technology resemble simulations in many ways and allow the student to explore settings rich in information. Some environments of this type allow the student to exercise control only through movement. The student moves from setting to setting, and each setting reveals certain information or makes certain experiences available. Settings may reflect different physical locations (different regions of a state) or points in time (important dates in history).

Other environments allow the student to select an action from among a specific set of actions. The student selects this action in a particular setting and then experiences the consequences of that action. Programs of this type are useful in representing social situations. For example, a brief scenario might describe a social dilemma such as a classroom disciplinary situation. The software might then present alternative courses of action the teacher could take. When the student using the software selects one of these alternatives, the social interaction moves to some kind of conclusion based on the alternative selected.

The Adventures of Jasper Woodbury The Adventures of Jasper Woodbury is a series of learning activities based on a combination of video, text, and computer software. Originally developed by the Learning Technology Center of Vanderbilt University as a research program focused on contextualized learning, the adventures are now available commercially to schools.

Students solve a complex problem.

The Jasper adventures present students with believable stories, each ending with a challenge. The challenge is a complex problem that includes several subproblems. The typical classroom approach is to have the entire class view one of the adventures and then have small groups of students work to propose solutions to the challenge at the end of the adventure. To solve the challenges, which require a problem-solving approach and focus on mathematical concepts, students have to examine the content of the video carefully for data relevant to the problems. The developers of the series argue that this "embedded data design" improves the transfer value of skills that students develop.

In The Big Splash, one of the Jasper adventures, a high-school student decides to help the school fund the purchase of a video camera by setting up a "Dunk a Teacher" booth at the school carnival. Because the dunking booth will cost some money, the student approaches the principal for a loan. The principal agrees to provide the loan if the student can produce a business plan demonstrating the likelihood that the project will make a profit. To produce the business plan, the student must estimate the potential revenue and probable expenses. Surveying students to determine whether they would spend money to dunk a teacher and how much they would be willing to pay for the chance determines the potential revenue. Consideration of how to conduct a survey provides an opportunity for the exploration of research methodology and statistics.

The student eventually locates a dunking machine and a pool. Because the pool must be rented by the day, the time the pool is in the possession of the school is an issue. The dimensions of the pool, but not the capacity, are known. The amount of time required to fill and drain the pool poses another problem to take into account. Several methods for filling the pool are available and vary in cost and risk. The school hose is available but slow. A water truck is available, but it charges by the mile and has an added fee each time it is filled. The water truck also cannot carry enough water in one trip to fill the pool. The fire chief volunteers the local fire truck but warns that the truck will not be available if a fire should occur. This list should give you some idea of what would have to be considered in producing the business plan.

Extending the Jasper adventures

The Jasper adventures have also been developed to be extended to analogous problems and other content areas. The analogous problems modify the original story to create opportunities for students to transfer what they have learned. For example, students can consider whether a Jell-O slide would generate more income than the dunking pool. To extend the Jasper adventures into other content areas, teachers are given suggestions for further study following up on some issue raised in the adventure. For example, The Big Splash

FIGURE 4.7
The Water Research Centre in Exploring the Nardoo

raises the issue of taking out a loan. Students might explore how to apply for a loan at a bank, how the bank makes money on the loan, what collateral is, and other concepts related to the lending of money.

Authentic learning activities in a realistic setting

Hypermedia Exploratory Environments: Exploring the Nardoo Exploring the Nardoo is an exploratory environment that allows students to conduct biological, geological, and chemical investigations of an imaginary Australian river. Problems and the information to suggest solutions to these problems are embedded within a complex hypermedia environment. This learning environment attempts to create authentic learning activities that are situated in a realistic setting (Brown, Collins, & Duguid, 1989; Harper et al., 2000). The software was developed by a team of instructional designers at Australia's University of Wollongong in collaboration with the New South Wales Department of Land and Water Conservation.

The logical place to begin our description is at the Water Research Centre (see Figure 4.7). Here the student meets three scientists who describe their own investigations and provide assistance. Most of the items visible in the Research Centre serve as links to information sources. For example, the River Investigations board at the rear of the room explains the details of thirteen investigations that are in progress. The filing cabinet (not visible in Figure 4.7) contains files of documents related to many of the issues raised by the embedded investigations. The clipboards (above the computer) provide access to

FIGURE 4.8

Personal Digital Assistant Used to Measure River Flow and Turbidity in Exploring the Nardoo

Students explore the environment and collect and analyze data.

radio and television programs, and the office computer provides a way to search all of the embedded resources.

Explorations are not confined to the information sources located within the Water Research Centre office. Learners explore the river itself. They can visit four regions of the river as it flows from mountains to plains and can explore each region during four time periods covering sixty years. Learners are provided with a multipurpose tool, the personal digital assistant (PDA), which allows them to move about the hypermedia environment (for instance, between the river and Research Centre, or among regions of the river), collect and organize data, and generate reports. In Figure 4.8, you can observe one use of the PDA. In this case, the PDA's data-gathering tool (the eyedropper) is being used to gather two types of data (river flow rate and turbidity) from the middle of the river channel. These are two of the many measurements of stream quality that can be taken.

We have become interested in factors that influence flooding because of personal experiences in our own community. The river simulation allowed a test of a hypothesis that we have heard debated: that farming practices that reduce natural vegetation and encourage rapid drainage of water from the land increase the likelihood of flooding. One way to test this hypothesis within the Nardoo environment was to attempt to gather data on river rate and turbidity at approximately the same river location before and after the land was heavily farmed. In Figure 4.8, you will note that much of the vegetation has been cleared on the right-hand side of the river, and the data indicate greater turbidity and a more rapid flow of water than when these same measurements were taken at an earlier time period. The PDA shows these data recorded after visiting two eras in the history of the river. As expected, both the rate at which the river flows and the turbidity are greater after land along the river has been developed for farming. In reality, you cannot travel back in time, but time travel might be possible in an exploratory environment.

Tasks that promote meaningful learning

It is important to consider how students might use this rich, interactive information environment so that meaningful learning occurs. Without a task or problem to solve, students might simply move within the hypermedia environment, seeing what they can find and what the various tools do. The richness and interactivity of the software are entertaining to explore, but do not guarantee meaningful learning. Fortunately, the investigations embedded within the hypermedia environment do provide tasks for individual students or groups of students to accomplish. For example, in one task students are told, "A conference is being held dealing with the sustainability of current farming practices and the effect they have on the environment. Students from your school have been invited to make a multimedia presentation at the convention dealing with the impact of farming practices on the river environment. In your presentation you should provide a summary that shows the variety of farming types present in the Walloway region."

The investigations that students are asked to complete are challenging in several ways. Students may lack the background to anticipate the types of data that may be relevant to the tasks they have been asked to accomplish. They also may be inexperienced in crafting the required product to summarize what they have learned. The hypermedia environment provides several mechanisms for supporting students in accomplishing these tasks (see the discussion of scaffolding in the chapter entitled "Meaningful Learning in an Information Age"). For example, the scientists from the Water Resource Centre assigned to the investigations are available to offer advice. The software even provides scaffolding for the authoring tasks that students are to accomplish based on their explorations. Students can load genre templates that provide advice on how to structure presentations of various types (see Figure 4.9). Exploring the Nardoo was designed not only to engage students in demanding investigations, reflections, and communication tasks but also to support student work in ways that allow them to take on these authentic challenges (Gordon, 1996).

Effectiveness of Exploratory Environments

With the exception of evaluations conducted with the Jasper Woodbury interactive video materials (Cognition and Technology Group, 1990, 1996; Goldman et al., 1996), exploratory environments and the learning tasks they enable have not been thoroughly evaluated. The focus on embedded authentic learning emphasizes skills not easily evaluated using traditional research methods (Greeno, 1998). Nevertheless, the exploratory work conducted with

FIGURE 4.9

Scaffolding to Support Student Authoring Tasks in Exploring the Nardoo

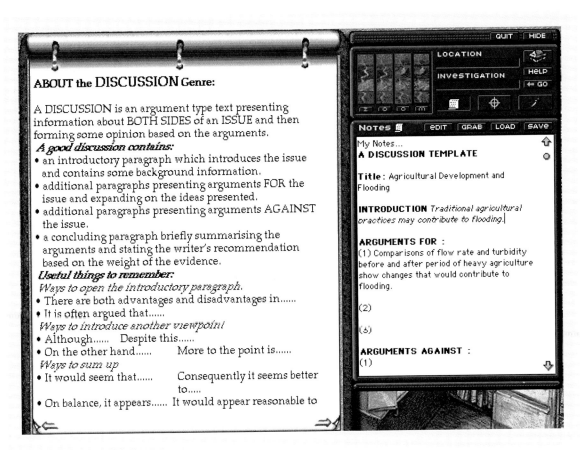

the Jasper Woodbury adventures is encouraging. Learning in the Jasper Woodbury environment is described as being anchored in realistic problems and experiences provided through interactive video, and it does appear that the video experiences encourage students to develop mental models to account for the phenomena they have observed.

The importance of structuring tasks or problems

Work with the Jasper Woodbury adventures and with the hypermedia environment of Exploring the Nardoo suggests that the presence of structuring tasks or problems is important. It should not be assumed that students will engage in the most desirable types of active exploration or generative thinking when exposed to exploratory environments (Gordon, 1996; Hsu et al., 1993). One proven method for increasing the involvement of learners in active exploration and generative thinking is to have them work within the exploratory environment in small groups. Research comparisons of individual and small-group use of the Jasper Woodbury tasks have demonstrated the advantage of cooperative grouping for knowledge acquisition and the transfer of problem-solving skills (Barron, 2000).

Multimedia and Hypermedia in the Delivery of Computer-Assisted Instruction

We have already used the terms *multimedia* and *hypermedia* several times in this chapter. These terms appear many more times in later chapters where we explore how students learn from Internet resources and by authoring projects that summarize their learning activities. It is time to describe multimedia and hypermedia in greater depth and to consider the benefits and limitations of these information formats as instructional resources.

What Are Multimedia, Hypermedia, and Hypertext?

While the term *multimedia* and, to a lesser degree, *hypermedia* are encountered frequently, those with a need for official definitions will be disappointed. There are no industry standards, and different people use the terms differently. Educators sometimes use the terms interchangeably, even though the terms are intended to describe different combinations of media and communication methods. For our present purposes, we offer definitions based on a logical identification of product characteristics.

Multimedia and hypermedia defined

If a product uses more than one modality (say, visual and auditory), at least two symbol systems within a modality (words and pictures), or at least two genres within a symbol system (prose and poetry, a still image and video), the product includes multiple media—that is, multimedia. **Multimedia** thus translates as "many formats." By this definition, a series of slides with musical accompaniment is multimedia. To maintain our intended focus, this book concentrates on forms of multimedia in which a computer is involved.

Hypermedia allows multimedia to be experienced in a nonlinear fashion. In this format, units of information—such as individual words, segments of text, or segments of audio, pictures, animations, and video clips—are connected to each other in multiple ways. Hypermedia environments are often described as *interactive* because the hypermedia user must direct the software and hardware environment to present the next unit of information to be experienced. Because control is vested in the user, different individuals potentially have very different experiences as they work in hypermedia environments. When the information in hypermedia consists entirely of text, the term **hypertext** is used. Hypertext was actually the first form of hypermedia but now is seldom seen in educational settings.

Linear versus nonlinear organization

The idea of an organized yet nonlinear system might be a bit confusing. Here's a comparison that might help explain how hypermedia works. Traditional books are organized in a linear fashion. As you read, you encounter a series of ideas. An author orders the ideas in this series based on his or her opinion of the structure that will make the information most interesting, most persuasive, or easiest to understand. If you were to read a section of a chapter a second time, you would obviously encounter the same series of ideas in the same order.

Now consider how a book, perhaps a science textbook, might be presented in a hypermedia format. From a particular segment of text describing scientific discoveries, the reader might be able to access the definition of any term appearing in boldface print, view a picture of the famous scientist responsible for each discovery, read a short biographical sketch of the scientist, and review the scientific principles on which scientific breakthroughs were based. Some scientists and some scientific principles might be associated with several different discoveries. Different students might explore this environment in different ways. Some might just review the scientific discoveries. Some might read all of the biographies of the scientists. Some might take each discovery in turn and learn about the discovery, the scientist, and the principles associated with the discovery. Some might review everything available about a famous scientist's work. In contrast to the predictable pattern of readers' working with a textbook, the exploration of a hypermedia environment offers much more variety.

Although multimedia and hypermedia are distinct, a separate discussion of each would be unnecessarily complicated. In this book, we use the term *multimedia* to discuss issues that apply to both multimedia and hypermedia. We use the term *hypermedia* only when an issue relates exclusively to hypermedia. The information that follows will acquaint you with the characteristics and potential benefits of multimedia as applied in educational settings.

What Are CD-ROM and DVD?

Discussions of multimedia and hypermedia always seem to include some reference to CD-ROMs and DVDs. There is a practical reason for this association: These storage systems offer the capacity necessary to hold a lot of information and, in particular, information that takes up a great deal of disk space (such as video). Multimedia and hypermedia require tremendous amounts of information, and the connection between the applications and storage media is thus a very logical and necessary one. Some basic information about CD-ROMs and DVDs should help you understand how these storage methods work and when they can be of particular value in classrooms.

Advances in CDs and DVDs

Because this chapter emphasizes commercial instructional applications, our descriptions in this chapter typically assume that CD-ROMs and DVDs will be purchased already loaded with data. **CD-ROM** stands for *c*ompact *d*isc–*r*ead *o*nly *m*emory. In other words, information stored on a CD-ROM can be read from the disc into the memory of the computer but cannot be erased or modified. (Notice that optical discs are spelled with a *c* and magnetic disks are spelled with a *k*.)

CD-ROM Technology
A CD-ROM holds about 600 **megabytes** (1 megabyte equals 1 million bytes) of information on a disc that costs less than 25 cents. New computers usually come with a CD-ROM player/burner already installed, and on some computers, the CD-ROM is the only storage device other than the computer's hard drive.

Difference between digital and analog format

CD-ROMs store information in digital form. It has become challenging to contrast the digital format with earlier storage formats because the digital format is now so common. Ten years ago video and audio were often stored on tape in an **analog format**. To be used by a computer, such material would have to be converted or "digitized" before the video and audio could be combined with other media types (see the techniques described in the chapters entitled "Using Multimedia Tools" and "Learning to Work with Images, Sound, and Video"). Now that camcorders store video on tape in a **digital format** and most people purchase music CDs rather than tapes or records, you may have little experience with the difference between digital and analog formats. The digital format, which essentially represents all forms of information as strings of 1's and 0's, can be used to store audio, video, and images as well as computer programs. The advantage of the digital format is that the computer user can bring data of this type into the memory of the computer and work directly with the information. There is no need for conversion. For example, a picture from a CD-ROM can be modified using a graphics program or can be inserted into a word processing document.

The CD technology you use to store information on your own computer is a little different from that used on a commercial CD. The commercial process generates a master expensively and then stamps many individual CDs cheaply. With a personal computer, a laser is used to "burn" digital information onto a special CD blank. The blank is called a CD-R if it can be written once or a CD-RW if it can be rewritten multiple times. This process is much less expensive for producing individual CDs, but very expensive and slow if you want to create thousands.

Surprisingly, CD-ROMs do not offer enough capacity for some applications. Collections of high-quality images exceed the capacity of a single CD. Digital video applications also frequently exceed the capacity of a CD. For such purposes, users must move to DVDs.

DVD Technology

Characteristics of a DVD

A **digital video disc (DVD)** looks very much like a standard CD, but the DVD player uses a more sophisticated laser system that allows the disc to contain more tracks and more densely packed pits, and to spin faster. In addition, a DVD potentially allows two layers of information to be stored on both sides of the disc (a CD has one layer of information on one side). These differences allow a great deal more information to be stored. The lowest-capacity DVD holds several gigabytes, and the high-end DVD holds 17 gigabytes. The most obvious benefit of this amount of storage is in the delivery of high-quality video for entertainment or educational purposes. A standard movie of the type you are used to renting on videotape fits comfortably on the lowest-capacity DVD, and you probably own a DVD player to play rented DVDs.

Educational applications of DVD technology probably have not emerged as quickly as some had hoped. The version of DVD (DVD-ROM) that holds computer data has received less attention than the version used to distribute commercial video, even though combination CD/DVD drives are available for most new computers. One exception might be in the area of reference materials such as products offering a combination of an encyclopedia, atlas, fact book, and so on.

A **DVD-RAM** (or DVD-RW) gives users storage with a capacity of at least 4.7 gigabytes at a cost of less than $2 for each disc. This low-cost storage or

Uses of DVDs

backup capacity is very useful in an educational setting and encourages the increased use of the DVD format.

Those who have stored projects on 2-megabyte disks may not be able to imagine how they would ever make use of several 4.7-gigabyte DVDs; each DVD would offer as much capacity as 2,400 disks. First, consider that computer hard drives are fallible, and backing up the contents of a personal computer is a wise practice. Copying valuable contents from a hard drive to a DVD-RAM is convenient, quick, and inexpensive. Second, certain types of projects require large amounts of storage. For example, we work with students who do video editing on a computer. They edit together segments of video to create a documentary about their field trip, a memento of season highlights for members of the basketball team, or perhaps a tour of the school building for new students. The amount of disk space required for such projects can strain the capacity of a hard drive, and for a while the stored material had to be erased once the videotape had been created and the project was over. The large capacity of DVD-RAMs allows the digital information to be stored in case there is some reason to work with certain elements of the project again. Finally, consider a possibility now available to preservice teachers. A preservice teacher involved in student teaching might videotape classroom presentations and place examples of his or her best work on a DVD for distribution to potential employers. There are possibilities here that are just starting to emerge as educators begin to imagine applications that require large amounts of storage.

Other Forms of Multimedia Found in Classrooms

The multimedia storage systems we have just described can be used as delivery systems for the various types of CAI activities discussed earlier in the chapter. There are also some unique types of multimedia software that are not necessarily CAI materials in themselves but may be adapted for CAI use. This section presents two such applications—talking books and reference materials—and the classroom situations in which you might choose to use them.

Talking Books

The storage capacity of CD-ROMs has made possible the creation of talking books. These products are most commonly based on popular and award-winning children's literature and are characterized by colorful artwork, optional access to narrators who read the story "in character," access to pronunciation and definitions by clicking on words, and objects within the artwork that perform simple actions when clicked. The CD-ROM is important because it provides the capacity necessary for the high-quality sound, graphics, and simple animations hidden in the artwork.

Helping children develop a relationship with books

Teachers can often appreciate how this use of technology, the high-quality narration, and the fun of looking for the hidden treasures in the artwork might intrigue young students. The questions teachers often ask are, "Is it worth spending this much money when you could buy the actual book for much less?" and "Will students be less interested in reading if the computer

Video resources can play a valuable role in many classroom activities.
(© Michael Zide)

will read books to them?" The value in talking books is in helping children develop a relationship with books and in building excitement about reading (Chomsky, 1990).

Content-area reading materials for young readers have also been developed using the talking book approach. For example, the *National Geographic Wonders of Learning CD-ROM Library* explores topics such as "The World of Plants" from science, nature, and geography. Like the previous example of children's literature, the content-area reading materials appear as a colorful book on the computer screen. Such resources allow the user to select from a number of features in addition to basic narration. Individual words can be pronounced and explained in context, in either English or Spanish. The Spanish-language option is intended to assist students learning English as a second language.

Language arts instruction with talking books

The talking book concept has also been developed into a system for language arts instruction. WiggleWorks is based on a series of lavishly illustrated stories and nonfiction works for young children published by Scholastic. The students have the option of reading the "books" to themselves or having the computer read the books to them. Each student's oral reading can be recorded,

FIGURE 4.10

Sample Screen from the WiggleWorks "Coloring Book" Activity

Fresh fall leaves . . .

played back, and contrasted with the narrated version. The materials take an approach that emphasizes the connections between reading and writing. In one option available for each selection, students are presented a "coloring book" version of the original book. This coloring book version can be modified in a variety of ways with several different types of tools. The text from a particular page can be retained, and paint tools and image stamps appropriate to the theme of the story can be used to create a new illustration. Or the image can be retained and "colored," and the student can add new text suited to the image (see Figure 4.10).

The WiggleWorks materials contain sophisticated management and assessment tools. The computer keeps track of what students do with each text selection (listen, read, write) and saves any products that the student creates (written samples, recordings of oral readings). The teacher can review this information, add notes for archival purposes, and export any of this information for inclusion in a student portfolio.

Multimedia References

School libraries, and to a lesser extent individual classrooms, make certain reference sources available to students. Reference materials such as encyclopedias, almanacs, globes, and atlases have general value in many content areas. Some books and magazines are also purchased because of their value as reference material. Most schools have a subscription to the *National Geographic Magazine* and possibly to the more youth-oriented *National Geographic World*. School libraries also may have books that might be described as multimedia collections—for example, *Birds of North America, Wildflowers of the Northern*

Plains, or images from World War II. Alternatives to all of these examples are available on CD-ROM. Similar products are emerging on DVD.

Advantages of technology-based reference sources

Technology-based multimedia reference material offers several advantages. In some cases, the CD-ROM version is less expensive. All volumes of *National Geographic* (more than 110 years' worth) are available on CD for approximately $160. CD-ROM versions of popular encyclopedias cost approximately $50 (see "Emerging Technology: The Evolution of Multimedia Encyclopedias"). Multimedia resources offer a second advantage in making information available in multiple formats. Some information sources cannot be presented in text format, and some information sources that could be presented as text are more motivating when presented in other ways. For example, reading about the cry of a loon is not the same as hearing it. Reading the words of President John F. Kennedy's inaugural address is less moving than hearing the speech in his own voice.

Multimedia encyclopedias allow powerful search features. CD-based encyclopedias have hypertext links among articles that allow powerful searches using individual terms or various combinations of terms. Searches using multiple terms are often called Boolean searches. Boolean searches refer to the logic involved in defining when certain conditions have been met. (See the discussion in the chapter entitled "The Internet as a Tool for Inquiry.")

Finally, CD-based references often allow a copy-and-paste capability. These two procedures allow material to be copied from the reference and then pasted into another application. (This is sometimes described as cut and paste in manuals accompanying reference software, but this description is inaccurate because nothing is actually removed, or "cut," from the original source.) The availability of copy and paste allows students to use pictures, maps, and tables from other sources in their own documents. You may be concerned that this option encourages students to copy when they are usually asked to summarize and organize the material they take from references. However, because copying is so obvious in this case, it actually gives teachers a convenient opportunity to explain students' responsibilities in using information from other sources.

Learning from Multimedia Instructional Resources

This chapter has outlined the categories of instructional software and described the use of multimedia in such learning experiences. What you have read to this point has been more descriptive than evaluative. Now that you understand the basics of multimedia, hypermedia, and computer-based instructional experiences, it is important to consider what is known about their effectiveness. Our analysis begins with an evaluation of the strengths and weaknesses of multimedia and hypermedia. We then turn to what is known about the effectiveness of the different categories of instructional software. As is so often the case, there seem to be no simple conclusions. However, we do feel we can identify issues that educators must consider and situational variables associated with more and less productive learning experiences.

EMERGING TECHNOLOGY

The Evolution of Multimedia Encyclopedias

CD and DVD technology has changed the way we think about encyclopedias. Multimedia encyclopedias, which cost less than $40, are more than the contents of an encyclopedia stored on a disc. For example, the two-CD *Microsoft Encarta Encyclopedia 2005* includes 63,000 articles, 20,000 photos and illustrations, 200 video segments, 2,000 sound or music clips, and nearly 36,000 web links. The companies creating computer-based reference tools have always had vast stores of information to draw on, but competition and consumer interest have led to products that are both more powerful and augmented by activities and tools intended to involve students with information in a more active manner. The "old-style" encyclopedia on a disc made limited use of powerful search features or true hypermedia. Now encyclopedias offer more sophisticated searches (that is, Boolean searches) and embed links to related articles, images, interactive activities, and even games both within the CD or DVD and on the Internet. Companies may also develop thematic approaches that present a topic at a more general level or a historical approach based on a time line and then provide links to a number of individual encyclopedia articles.

No matter how sophisticated disc-based reference materials become, they have one inherent weakness true of all reference material: Once published, they are immediately at least partially out of date. New discoveries that may negate long-held beliefs and important events occur daily. Companies developing multimedia encyclopedias are making use of the Internet to keep the content they offer as current as possible. One approach uses the Internet to provide online access to a continually updated version of the encyclopedia (for example, *Grolier Online, Encarta Online Deluxe*). Other approaches rely on what have been described as hybrid strategies: various combinations of the CD and the Internet. For example, Microsoft provides a feature called "Update Encarta" that allows owners of the CD to access and download new articles and article updates written for the encyclopedia. Owning the CD provides access to these services for a specified amount of time, and continued access can be purchased as a subscription service.

Finally, companies use the Internet to offer educators opportunities to build learning activities around the CD or Internet-based reference materials. For example, the web-based Encarta Schoolhouse provides Internet links based on a series of themes. Each theme, covering a topic such as the Civil War, life in the ocean, or earthquakes, is supported by suggested activities and links. Current events are also explored in ways that involve the existing reference materials.

The resources described here should provide teachers with some powerful opportunities to engage students in meaningful learning. The theme-based activities would provide great opportunities to develop WebQuests, as described in the chapter entitled "The Internet as a Tool for Inquiry." Teachers would need only to review some of the Internet resources and establish scaffolding activities. The links established between current events and more standard encyclopedia content offer a different kind of opportunity. In that case, students could use experiences that are more immediate and specific to understand issues and content that are likely to be more remote and abstract.

You can find more information about these products in "Resources to Expand Your Knowledge Base" at the end of this chapter, and on the website that accompanies this textbook.

Strengths and Weaknesses of Multimedia and Hypermedia

Multimedia instructional resources present information in more formats than is typical, and hypermedia allows such resources to be explored with greater flexibility. Experts have identified both strengths and weaknesses in such resources. Here is our summary of these issues.

Advantages of Multiple Formats and Alternative Perspectives

Multimedia and hypermedia provide an efficient and cost-effective way to deliver effective learning experiences to which students otherwise would not have access. These experiences range from direct support for verbal instruction to students' active exploration of new information.

Multimedia as an effective supplement to verbal instruction

Support for Verbal Instruction   The availability of text, sound, animation, video, and still images for presenting information and the easy transitions among these formats can increase the clarity of explanations. Different methods of representation are potentially suited to explaining or demonstrating different concepts or skills, and multimedia and hypermedia make it easy to give students these different experiences. For example, it is more effective to give a basic explanation of mitosis and then step through a time-lapse video of cell division than to struggle through a verbal analysis of how the chromosomes align themselves along the equatorial plate or how the spindle fibers pull the chromatids toward the centrioles. A teacher can easily point out these phenomena in the images displayed on a screen. The teacher might first talk the students through the stages of mitosis by advancing the video a few frames at a time, describing changes and pointing to interesting developments as they appear. Then the teacher might run the entire sequence so students will have an opportunity to appreciate how the process unfolds.

Multimedia can support verbal instruction in other ways. Consider the challenge of helping students understand the form of musical composition called a fugue. It is easy to give a verbal definition, but will terms like *theme, imitation,* and *counterpoint* mean much to students? Of even greater importance, would students be able to identify a fugue if they heard one? Again, the teacher's definition or the definition in a tutorial could be supported by listening to a musical selection, such as an appropriate passage from Beethoven's Ninth Symphony. The teacher might play a few seconds of music, pause to ask if the students are able to hear different voices imitating each other at different pitches, perhaps hum a few bars to identify the imitation, and then play the brief selection again. The appropriate CD and related software (such as *Analysis of Beethoven Symphony #9*) make this type of demonstration easy to implement.

Encouraging students to think about complex issues

Authentic Learning and Depth of Learning Experience There are other kinds of content that multimedia can present in particularly powerful ways. Kozma (1991) argues that multimedia, particularly combinations involving video, are very useful when the content has to do with social situations, interpersonal problem solving, foreign language training, or moral decision making. Multimedia can encourage students to think about complex issues. Kozma uses the example of *A Right to Die? The Case of Dax Cowart* (Covey, 1990). This social documentary examines the actual experience of a young person who had been burned over 60 percent of his body and lost his sight. He would always be disabled but could survive if willing to submit to a long and painful treatment. The patient found the treatments unbearable and wanted to have them stopped. The video provides actual comments from the patient, mother, doctor, nurse, and lawyer. As the student works with this material, he or she is asked to make decisions. The student's decision making and the presentation of opposing perspectives, in the words and images of real people, provide a depth of experience that would be impossible without interactive multimedia.

Realistic experiences

A similar argument has been made in support of providing authentic learning tasks anchored in realistic settings (Bransford et al., 1990). The video format provides experiences that are both more complex and more like situations outside the classroom, exposing students to realistic experiences they may not have encountered directly. Video provides more information to sort through and think about, and video material can often be examined from multiple points of view. Working to process such a rich information source is one way to engage students in more active learning. Learning experiences that combine extended video segments and other resources and activities allow students to anchor what they learn in realistic goals, activities, and situations.

Activating two types of memory

Dual-Coding Theory The capability of efficiently offering related experiences in different forms may have other advantages. Paivio's (1986) **dual-coding theory** is often cited as support for exposing students to both pictures and verbal information. Dual-coding theory argues that imagery and verbal information are stored in different ways. Experiencing something verbally and through imagery offers advantages because the experiences may result in two memory codes instead of one. Students exposed to pictures or video and verbal input may store and retrieve information more effectively than students who do not have these multiple inputs.

It is possible to be even more explicit about the conditions under which multiple formats are advantageous (Mayer, 2001). When you are explaining relatively complex phenomena, dual codes are most beneficial when students are able to interrelate the codes. For example, a computer animation with narration was found to lead to better understanding of how a bicycle pump works than allowing students first to hear the narration and then to watch the animation. Access to both sources of information also resulted in an advantage over access to only one source of information.

Meeting Individual Needs Both interactive multimedia and hypermedia offer students some degree of control over the information they experience. Students can get help when they need it. When they have difficulties, they can get supplementary information or experience information in a different format.

Other needs are also important. Sometimes a student understands the information but wants to know more. Imagine a learning environment in which a student can quickly ask for more depth, greater detail, or additional examples when encountering something of great personal interest. The control allows students working in responsive environments to meet their own needs.

You may recall from the previous discussion of talking books that these CD-based products allow readers to click on unfamiliar words to have words pronounced and defined. Students struggling with English can even listen in Spanish. The frequency with which these options are used and the individual words with which students need assistance vary greatly. Multimedia and certainly hypermedia programs often leave the decision to display a video segment, diagram, or supplemental text to the student. In theory, students who need access to a different type of explanation or are likely to find a visual representation helpful have opportunities to customize their learning environment. As multimedia and hypermedia environments become more sophisticated, options for students will become even more varied.

Motivational Benefits Finally, the variety of formats that multimedia and hypermedia offer is motivating. For many students, seeing a human take the first steps on the moon or hearing Dr. Martin Luther King Jr.'s "I Have a Dream" speech results in very different affective reactions than simply reading about the lunar landing or reading Dr. King's speech. Emotion is part of school learning and part of what makes learning exciting.

Concerns about Multimedia in Classrooms

Experts have raised a number of concerns related to the multimedia and hypermedia programs that are currently available and to some of the assumed benefits of multimedia and hypermedia. We want you to have a realistic sense of how multimedia applications are used in classrooms and to understand that there are potential problems. Such awareness will help you recognize classroom situations in which problems might develop and help you make more informed decisions about how to use multimedia with your students.

Duplication of Existing Instructional Materials Talking children's books and CD-based atlases, encyclopedias, and almanacs are clearly similar to the books already common in classrooms. Images of artwork, plants, whales, and other collections of photographs on a CD or a DVD are similar to slide collections. Is this redundancy necessary? Or is there nothing wrong with duplication?

Certainly there is nothing wrong with taking a good idea and making it available in a different form. Computer-based resources are sometimes less

---

Student control helps learners meet their own needs.

Appeals to senses and emotions

Cost-effectiveness as an issue

expensive than printed ones, have greater durability, and may be perceived as more interesting by students. Counterarguments can be offered, however. Computer-based resources are not always less expensive. And a CD may be a cost-effective replacement for an encyclopedia, but is it a cost-effective replacement for a children's book?

Another issue concerns how educators should use a valuable limited resource. If a limited number of computers or DVD and CD players are available, why not make certain that these resources are used for unique purposes? Perhaps the emphasis should be on using technology in ways that offer students experiences they do not have now.

Need for new learning skills

Inadequate Student Skills Learning from any information source requires that students have skills suitable to both the format and the particular method in which information is made available. Multimedia and hypermedia are new learning environments. It makes sense that if they offer an alternative to learning from traditional sources, these new formats will also require the development of new learning skills.

For example, it has been demonstrated that approaches combining text with extensive video can sometimes result in poorer learning. In one informative study, junior-high earth science students worked with multimedia containing interesting video from the Great Quake of 1989 (Levin, 1991). When presented with text only, students seemed to be in a familiar element. When presented with text and the opportunity to watch interesting video, the students appeared to become distracted by the video and retained less essential information. This problem, which is appropriately described as being distracted by *seductive details,* has been demonstrated in multimedia containing unnecessarily redundant or superfluous text, video, or animations (Mayer, Heiser, & Steve, 2001). It appears that more is not always better.

By the way, this is not really a new phenomenon. It has been known for some time that pictures in books can interfere with the performance of young readers (Schallert, 1980). This early work with traditional reading material offers some additional insights. Pictures in any medium must serve a purpose. Pictures interfere when they do not convey useful information. As readers gain experience, they seem to learn to ignore pointless graphics. As students become experienced users of multimedia, they may adopt similar strategies. We can only hope that multimedia designers will use graphics and video effectively, and that students will have a reason for giving these sources of information careful consideration.

The choices available in hypermedia offer another challenge to learning skills. Hypermedia allows students to move freely among ideas and information sources. There may be some ways in which the richness of resources and the freedom of exploration allowed by hypermedia are problematic. For example, it is not well established that students can make effective decisions regarding their own learning. Given what is known about general metacognitive competence and students' control of their learning with technology (see the discussion of metacognition in the chapter entitled "Meaningful Learning in an Information Age"), inconsistency in taking advantage of potentially helpful learning experiences is not surprising.

Categories of learners

Research that has studied the approach learners take as they explore hypermedia has identified several categories of learners (Lawless & Brown, 1997; Locatis, Letourneau, & Banvard, 1990):

- *Knowledge seekers:* Learners who use a strategic approach concentrating on the examination of material consistent with an assigned goal
- *Feature explorers:* Learners who seem captivated by special effects and gravitate toward options such as movies and sound files
- *Apathetic users:* Learners who spend very limited time interacting with instructional material, moving through what is available in a rapid and linear fashion

These categories suggest that when learners use hypermedia ineffectively, it may be for a variety of reasons. They may wander off, get lost, or simply lose interest.

The value of experience

It appears that experience plays an important role in determining how effectively learners use a hypermedia environment. With poor background knowledge, learners have little insight into what might be important to examine carefully. They may be unaware of holes in the understanding they are creating. Learner control is ineffective if learners are unable to make wise decisions. Learners with poor background seem to be more easily distracted by attractive but nonessential features and to face greater danger of becoming lost and frustrated (Dillon & Gabbard, 1998; Gay, 1986; Lawless & Brown, 1997).

When learners do have unproductive experiences with hypermedia, is the problem in the learning environment or in the learner? Both learners and software design may be at fault.

Cognitive load makes demands on short-term memory.

The concept of **cognitive load** provides a way to think about several issues associated with learning from hypermedia. Remember from earlier in this book that comprehension and learning activities occur within the time and capacity limitations of short-term memory. Cognitive load can be thought of as the various stresses imposed on short-term memory. When the combination of stresses imposed by individual capabilities, media resources, and learning tasks exceeds the capacity of short-term memory, performance will deteriorate. It may be useful to recognize that although the navigational potential of hypermedia provides some opportunities, it also imposes certain demands not present in linear materials such as books. Keeping track of where you are within a hypermedia learning environment requires some cognitive resources not required when following the linear format that an author builds into a book or a videographer builds into a video. These unique demands may be tolerated by experienced hypermedia users and good readers, but perhaps not by learners who are inexperienced in navigating hypermedia or who are already struggling with comprehending the text components of the learning materials (Lee & Tedder, 2004).

Developers of multimedia continue to become more sophisticated in recognizing the unique demands and advantages of hypermedia (Mayer, 2001). There are clearly better and poorer ways to design learning environments so that learners appreciate the structure of information and examine it systematically (Jonassen & Grabinger, 1990). Effective hypermedia provides an easy-to-use navigation system and convenient ways for learners to return to key landmarks in the instructional content. Effective hypermedia also combines media types in ways that recognize the limits of cognitive resources (Mayer, 2001).

The Evaluation of Computer-Assisted Instruction

A great deal of research has been conducted to evaluate the effectiveness of computer tutorials and other forms of CAI. In this section we briefly survey the research, suggest a perspective that may help you decide how to interpret the research findings, and then discuss how you can evaluate software for yourself.

Summary of Research on CAI

Studies suggesting a moderate advantage for CAI

Because of this huge volume of information, it is common to rely on reviews in evaluating the effectiveness of CAI (Bayraktar, 2001–2002; Christmann, Badgett, & Lucking, 1997; Fletcher-Flinn & Gravatt, 1995; Liao, 1992; Waxman, Lin, & Michko, 2003). Tutorials and drill activities have been studied most extensively. These studies have found that technology seems to offer a moderate advantage over traditional instruction, with tutorials somewhat more effective than drill activities, particularly for younger and less able students (Lepper & Gurtner, 1989). The effect is labeled "moderate" because 66 percent of students taught using CAI performed better than the average for a group taught more traditionally.

One of the more recent reviews compared more current CAI research with older studies and suggests that the advantage of CAI may be increasing. However, the general benefits are still described as moderate (Fletcher-Flinn & Gravatt, 1995). A review of the research evaluating simulations reached a similar conclusion (Thomas & Hooper, 1991). With the exception of the work done with the Jasper Woodbury interactive video materials, research evaluating exploratory learning environments is much less extensive.

Critics of CAI

Even the moderate advantage for CAI instruction has been questioned, however. Critics point out that studies producing no advantage for CAI are less likely to be published, that many studies involving CAI do not control study time to make certain that students receiving CAI do not work longer, and that computers in many situations are so novel that students may respond to them more positively because of the uniqueness of learning with technology. A recent meta-analysis determined that short-term CAI experiences produce a larger advantage over traditional instruction than comparisons involving instructional programs of longer duration, and the author interpreted this trend as supporting the novelty or motivational explanation (Bayraktar, 2001–2002). Others accept the findings that CAI may offer an advantage but argue that CAI materials are often just more carefully developed and that there is no intrinsic advantage in the actual method of instruction (Clark, 1985; Fletcher-Flinn & Gravatt, 1995).

The U.S. Department of Education, acting under the authority of the No Child Left Behind Act of 2001 and the Education Sciences Reform Act of 2002, has funded its own rigorous evaluation studies, conducted according to exacting standards. Core factors in defining "rigorous" research were the randomized assignment of students, classes, or schools to treatment or control conditions and the use of standardized achievement test scores as the main dependent variable. A large-scale research study implemented in the 2004–2005 academic year focused on the evaluation of sixteen commercial products targeting grade 1 reading, grade 4 reading comprehension, grade 6 pre-algebra, and grade 9 algebra, with special emphasis on schools having a high proportion of students from low-income families. The commercial products were selected through a competitive process allowing vendors to propose their products for consideration (U.S. Department of Education, 2004). Like the existing research, the results of this study, when available, will also likely generate controversy. The large scale of the research, the focus on a small number of commercial products, and the use of standardized achievement tests will provide results that are regarded as more rigorous but will also likely be criticized as narrow in terms of the instructional methods explored and the manner in which effective math and reading skills were evaluated. It will be interesting to follow how this government-sponsored approach plays out, how the results determine government funding priorities, and the reaction that both the results and the policy decisions generate.

Interpreting Contradictory Research Findings: The Arguments about CAI Effectiveness

Most teachers do not follow the research reports that appear in research journals; nevertheless, they should pay some attention to the general conclusions of educational researchers because these findings should eventually be translated into changes in classroom practice. Authors less directly focused on determining the effectiveness of CBI (for instance, Cuban, 2001; Healy, 1998) have also raised questions that educators need to consider. For example, educators advocating large investments to increase student access to technology are asked to defend these requests, given the lack of research demonstrating consistent benefits to students. The issue in this case is the limited resources of schools and the cost-effectiveness of technology resources (Healy, 1998).

Those advocating computer-supported instruction must also recognize that even in those schools with abundant technology resources and technologically savvy educators and parents, students still have very few experiences with CBI in core content areas (Norris, Sullivan, Poirot, & Soloway, 2003). Despite all of the research, the general encouragement of government and commercial interests, and increasing awareness on the part of educators, the culture and methods of the classroom have proven very resistant to change (Cuban, 2001).

Making sense of conflicting views

So what should you make of these confusing and conflicting views of CAI effectiveness? At present, teachers should not expect miracles from technology (or from any other approach to instruction, for that matter). However, when used thoughtfully and with common sense, many commercial products make learning opportunities available to students. The "big question"—Is it better?—is probably naive and very difficult to answer, given the complexities of classroom learning. Researchers and educators might most productively focus instead on how best to use computers to support learning by asking general questions about what factors improve learning (Hannafin et al., 1996):

TABLE 4.1
Potential Software Effectiveness, by Stage of Instruction Note: We have ranked effectiveness on a scale of 0–3.

Applications	Components of Instruction			
	Presentation	Guidance	Practice	Assessment
Tutorial	* * *	*		
Simulation	* *	*	* *	* *
Drill and Practice			* * *	
Educational game	*	*	* *	*
Exploratory environments	* *	*	*	*

General questions to ask

- How can learners be most effectively oriented to important lesson content?
- What are the most effective ways to use multimedia sources to encourage learning and understanding?
- How can learners be assisted in detecting and responding to errors in their understanding?
- How can the sequencing of content be best adapted to individual learner needs?
- How can learners develop the ability to apply what they know?
- What factors motivate learners?

Clearly, instructional and multimedia software do not eliminate the need for teaching, nor do they eliminate the need for teacher supervision. Students will have questions in response to a learning activity presented by the computer just as they may have questions during a science laboratory or about a social studies reading assignment. Teachers need to take an active role in structuring the learning environment, and this includes the use of instructional applications.

Relating software to the four stages of instruction

We suggest that teachers keep the four phases of instruction in mind as they consider instructional software. Table 4.1 summarizes our comments regarding how different types of software benefit students. In general, the ratings indicate that instructional software provides positive but incomplete experiences. The summary also suggests that guiding students, especially in ways necessary to develop complex mental skills, is frequently beyond the current capabilities of technology. Teachers must continue to provide some of the guidance necessary for effective learning, which will often mean that teachers and students may want to interact together with the technology.

Situations in which technology has unique value

There may be some situations that lend themselves especially well to CAI (Alessi & Trollip, 2001). Many of the following suggestions appear throughout this chapter but are summarized here for emphasis. Technology is often of unique value when:

- Prolonged individual practice is necessary (math facts, typing).
- Traditional approaches fail to make the content exciting (history).
- Learning the skill presents a significant danger to the learner (flying an airplane).
- Concepts to be learned are difficult to visualize or conceptualize (calculus, physics).

■ Students progress at significantly different rates and need to proceed at their own pace (any content area that builds heavily on prerequisite knowledge).

■ Practical limits of time, space, or money make certain experiences impractical (genetics experiments).

You might use this list as you think about the experiences you want to provide your students.

Evaluating Software

Variations in teachers' reactions

The process of selecting software is subjective. If you have the opportunity to serve on a curriculum committee charged with selecting software, you will soon discover that committee members often have very different opinions. Nevertheless, a subjective decision should not be confused with an arbitrary one. The curriculum committee participants are likely to have plenty to say in support of their recommendations. Teachers have different styles, philosophies, and insights into how students learn, and they may value certain learning outcomes over others. These differences account for some of the variability in the classroom behaviors of teachers; they also explain why reactions to a particular piece of software can be so different. One teacher might value the methodical and organized way in which a particular tutorial presents information, and another teacher might feel that the same tutorial leaves too little room for student independence. Teachers will use techniques and materials that are consistent with their values and beliefs (Hannafin & Freeman, 1995).

Teachers consider many factors when selecting software. However, the discussion of things to think about and the lists of things "experts" suggest ought to be valued should not obscure one essential question that all teachers examining software must ask: Would I be able and willing to integrate this activity into my existing curriculum? To help yourself answer that question, you may want to use a software evaluation form or checklist.

Evaluation Forms

Using an evaluation form

Evaluation forms can be found in many sources (Alessi & Trollip, 2001; Ring, 1993). The form shown in Figure 4.11 begins with open-ended questions requesting the reviewer's descriptive and subjective comments and follows with a checklist of important program characteristics. This is fairly typical. The program title, publishing company, cost, and other general information are included for archival purposes. The curriculum standards and benchmarks that instructional materials address are likely to be significant. Certain items are included to remind the reviewer to check system and hardware requirements. Some packages require additional memory or add-on hardware items such as a speech synthesizer, or function only with the most recent operating system. It is all too easy to purchase software that will not run on existing equipment.

The remainder of the form asks the reviewer to consider how students might use the software and to comment on certain characteristics of the software that could influence how productive and valued student experiences might be. One item now included on many such forms for teachers is a listing

FIGURE 4.11

Software Evaluation Form with Open-Ended Questions and Weighted Checklist of Program Characteristics

Review Summary Sheet

General Information

Reviewer _____

Title _____

Publishing company _____

Publication date _____

List price _____

Availability of site license _____

Site license agreement _____

　　　Price _____

Hardware and Operating System Requirements

Host microcomputer _____

Operating system compatibility _____

Requires _____ MB of memory

Is product network aware? _____

Storage _____ Hard drive _____ MB approximate capacity required _____

CD-ROM player _____ DVD player _____

Other hardware requirements _____

Curriculum Integration _____

Standards and Benchmarks Addressed _____

Program Format

_____ Drill Practice _____ Tutorial _____ Simulation _____

_____ Other (Describe:) _____

_____ Combination (Describe:) _____

Brief Description _____
_____
_____

Curriculum Compatibility

Subject area _____

Grade level _____

Specific topics _____

Reviewer Recommendation and Comments _____
_____
_____

Checklist

Rating: Extent to which the software successfully meets objective

Weight: Extent to which the objective is important to the rater

Total: Product of rating and weight

(Higher values are intended to indicate greater quality and importance.)

EVALUATION CATEGORY	RATING (0–5)	WEIGHT (0–5)	TOTAL (0–25)
CONTENT			
Easily integrated with existing content	_____	_____	_____
Software satisfies district standards	_____	_____	_____
Content presented accurately	_____	_____	_____
Content presented efficiently	_____	_____	_____
Content presented effectively	_____	_____	_____
Presentation approach is motivating	_____	_____	_____
Program encourages active thought	_____	_____	_____
Content avoids offensive representations	_____	_____	_____
Quality of content justifies cost	_____	_____	_____

Comments: _____

PROGRAM FUNCTIONS	RATING (0–5)	WEIGHT (0–5)	TOTAL (0–25)
Program is easy to operate	_____	_____	_____
Pace is appropriate	_____	_____	_____
Student can save work in progress	_____	_____	_____
Student can control rate of progress	_____	_____	_____
Student can change shift among activities	_____	_____	_____
Feedback is appropriate	_____	_____	_____
Saves data on student performance	_____	_____	_____

Comments: _____

SUPPLEMENTS	RATING (0–5)	WEIGHT (0–5)	TOTAL (0–25)
Quality of student supplemental materials	_____	_____	_____
Quality of instruction manual	_____	_____	_____
Useful suggestions for program use	_____	_____	_____
Useful follow-up ideas	_____	_____	_____

Comments: _____

Total score			_____

of the standards the software could be used to address. The assurance that commercial software would be useful in addressing required standards is helpful to teachers concerned with this issue.

On the checklist, the weight for the perceived importance of each characteristic and the rating of the extent to which the program satisfies the characteristic fall on a six-point scale (0 to 5). The product of the weight and the rating results in a score for each characteristic. You will notice that the weight of each item is blank; that is, the form itself does not identify how important any given characteristic or issue should be in the final decision. The reviewer needs to make such value judgments.

We hope you will have an opportunity to apply this evaluation procedure to a number of software products and to discuss your conclusions with your classmates and instructor. This process should help you clarify what you will eventually look for when you find yourself in the position of purchasing software for your students' use.

A number of websites offer reviews of educational software that often prove helpful. You will find several in "Resources to Expand Your Knowledge Base" at the end of this chapter, and on the website that accompanies this textbook.

Constructivism and Cooperative Learning with Instructional Software

We have one final, and very important, question to ask in this chapter: Do the types of software we describe here allow a constructivist approach? This is a tricky question, and we think that the answer depends on how you define *constructivism* and which category of instructional software is being considered. It also depends on how software is used.

Broadening the way software is used

In an interesting way of making this point, Squires (1999) proposes the phrase *subversive use,* which refers to situations in which the teacher may imagine a creative use for a learning activity not considered or promoted by the original developers. A related point is that a student's experience with instructional software does not define the total learning experience, and the teacher can incorporate the computer task into a broader activity. When we suggest that a student might be asked to create a diary based on his or her experience with The Oregon Trail, we are suggesting a subversive use of The Oregon Trail—that is, one not required by the software designers.

Working on an instructional program with a partner represents one way to broaden the experience. In many situations, assigning two students to a computer is a matter of practicality, but it also represents a way to change the nature of the learning experience in a constructivist direction. Research suggests that cooperative learning seems to benefit students working with tutorials (but not drills) and that students should receive some training in how to learn cooperatively to benefit from cooperative experiences (Susman, 1998).

Cooperative problem-solving activities

Exploratory environments offer excellent potential for cooperative learning. As we mention earlier, teachers who use the Jasper Woodbury adventures typically ask small groups of students to propose solutions to the challenge.

Keeping Current

Locating Appropriate Software

A tremendous amount of commercial instructional software is available today. In purchasing software for your own classroom or for your school, you should develop an awareness of a reasonable sample of the products that are available and then proceed to gather more detailed information about the quality and curriculum appropriateness of specific products that seem most interesting. This process is probably more difficult than inexperienced individuals might anticipate. Unlike the tool applications discussed in other chapters, individual instructional software products target niche markets. Consequently, compared to a major word processing program, an instructional software product will likely have a smaller marketing budget, will be harder to find on shelves, and will be reviewed in fewer publications.

So how do you become acquainted with the software you might purchase? Here are several suggestions:

- *Attend conferences and conventions.* State teachers' conventions frequently have sessions on instructional technology, and many vendors' booths are devoted to product demonstrations. It is also possible there will be a conference in your region devoted specifically to educational computing. Such conferences provide an excellent opportunity to meet other teachers interested in technology and to see what vendors have to offer.
- *Take a class or workshop.* If you are using this book as part of a college course, you are already in a setting in which you are likely to work with a variety of software products. This experience will be valuable in developing your awareness of useful software. If you are an undergraduate student, many new products will be available by the time you are working in a school and in a position to recommend software for purchase. Many colleges and universities sponsor brief workshops for practicing teachers. Sometimes teachers gather for a special session at a local college, and sometimes people from the college go out to the schools. School districts able to fund a position for a computer coordinator may provide their own staff development activities. In most locations, workshops must cater to a cross-section of teachers to be cost-effective and will be unlikely to discuss a large number of individual instructional software products. Still, workshops are an effective way to develop a background about effective instructional software and refine your ideas.
- *Browse through magazines for educators.* A number of magazines are written specifically for computer-using educators (see a list in "Resources to Expand Your Knowledge Base" at the end of the chapter). Teachers may subscribe to these publications themselves, schools may purchase the magazines and make them available through school libraries, or teachers may find them in a local college library. It is often informative to read reviews by many different authors, keeping in mind

that they have biases just like anyone else. Reading several reviews will provide some balance in the information you gather.

- *Interact with other teachers using telecommunications.* The Internet and commercial network services allow teachers to interact with other teachers. The teachers participating have already selected themselves as computer users. It is common to see messages such as, "We have $4,000 to spend on software for the science department. Do you have any recommendations?"
- *Communicate directly with software companies.* Software companies have a vested interest in making sure that educators are aware of their products. Contacting a company can be especially useful if it is willing to provide a review copy. Usually the best way to obtain an examination copy is through an administrator or computer coordinator who approaches the company. Some companies provide free sample programs with certain functions disabled. Finally, companies are beginning to offer previews of their products—program descriptions and samples of what the student would see on the screen—on websites.

Other multimedia applications have been developed specifically for cooperative problem-solving activities. In tasks developed by Tom Snyder Productions (Great Ocean Rescue, Great Solar System Rescue, the Decisions, Decisions series), several subproblems are set within a single scenario, and students work through these subproblems to resolve the central problem. The activities follow a carefully structured approach to ensure efficiency, make managing the classroom easier, and scaffold the students' approach to solving the complex problems that are presented.

In the Decisions, Decisions series, groups of students take on a hypothetical role and make a series of decisions. Each decision has consequences that create the situation for a new decision. For example, in Decisions, Decisions: The Environment, students put themselves in the role of a mayor who must deal with a pollution problem during a reelection campaign. The mayor must confront the complex public policy issues that can occur as a consequence of the conflicting agendas of low taxes, cost-effective manufacturing, and the desire for clean air and water. Students are given individual responsibilities for developing knowledge relevant to decisions, and this collective knowledge is then called on in the problem-solving process. As the group integrates the information, they are often required to reach consensus on the next step. The need to come to an agreement generates a great deal of class discussion.

Clearly, software of this complex type fits more easily into a constructivist approach than an approach focused on the presentation of information. Whatever the type of software, however, it is important to remember that software does not totally control the learning environment. The teacher remains in control. The teacher can and should take responsibility for deciding how the software is used.

Summary

A complete instructional experience takes the student through four stages: (1) the presentation of information or learning experiences, (2) guidance as the student struggles to develop knowledge and master skills, (3) extended practice, and (4) assessment. Not all activities, computer or otherwise, should be expected to provide all four stages of instruction. Often lower-quality instruction occurs because it is assumed that an experience satisfies the expectations of all four stages or because a task suited to one stage of instruction is used inappropriately to provide the experiences of a different stage.

Tutorials, simulations, drill and practice, games, and exploratory environments are categories of CAI. Commercial products seldom represent a pure example of any single category.

Tutorials are designed to present information and guide learning. Teachers must participate actively when students are working with tutorials.

Simulations attempt to replicate the key elements of an actual experience. Although it is unlikely that any one product will provide for all four stages of instruction, simulations can provide for all of them. Fidelity, the exactness of the match between a simulation and reality, influences both learning and transfer. The relationships between fidelity, learning, and transfer are complex, and the best situation for rapid learning is not always the best situation for effective transfer. Simulations offer potential solutions to a number of instructional problems and can make learning experiences more concrete, more controllable, less expensive, and safer.

Drill-and-practice activities have a bad reputation. Nevertheless, they are appropriate when information and skills need to be learned to the point of fluency and automaticity. Care must be taken not to emphasize memorization unless it is actually the intended objective of instruction.

Games put a premium on motivation, entertainment, and competition and can engage students with appropriate academic content. Educators might consider games as a way to introduce students to new topics or as ways to motivate. When a game is used to motivate work independent of the game itself, care must be taken for all students to have a realistic chance of receiving this reinforcement so that students do not view technology as only for play.

Exploratory environments allow a student-centered approach to learning in a specified domain. For best productivity, teachers need to remain involved as students work with this software.

Multimedia and hypermedia often play an important role in CBI. Definitions of *multimedia* and *hypermedia* can be confusing because the terms are used inconsistently. In this book, *multimedia* describes a communication format implemented with a computer and integrating several media, such as text, audio, video, still images, and animation. *Hypermedia* is an interactive, nonlinear form of multimedia in which the units of information are connected to one another in multiple ways. The hypermedia user has considerable freedom to choose which links to pursue and in what order.

Because information in the form of sound, high-quality pictures, or video requires large amounts of space, multimedia and hypermedia often make use of the large storage capacity of CD-ROMs or DVDs.

Multimedia and hypermedia offer both advantages and disadvantages. Multimedia presentations allow students more diverse experiences that may be more motivating or present information in ways that are more informative. Dual-coding theory holds that the redundancy present in multiple formats can allow more effective storage in and retrieval from memory. Critics lament the cost of multimedia and recognize that some students may not have the academic skills to handle the decisions allowed by hypermedia. Some students may be distracted by superfluous sounds or graphics and learn less efficiently.

Research evaluating the effectiveness of CAI in general has been extensive. Overall, comparisons seem to demonstrate a moderate level of success. Teachers should not, however, expect miracles from technology. In evaluating specific software, subjectivity is unavoidable, but a careful appraisal is still important. In making purchasing decisions, teachers are encouraged to consider carefully their own instructional priorities and to determine how they would integrate the software into their curricula.

Finally, teachers should remember that they themselves determine how students will use instructional software and multimedia resources. Even traditional presentation software can be incorporated into a broader learning task that encourages students to construct personal understanding.

Reflecting on Chapter 4

ACTIVITIES

■ List simulations, computer or otherwise, that you have experienced. What principles or causal relationships was each simulation constructed to represent?

■ Identify how principles of concreteness, control, cost-effectiveness, and safety might apply to the example of Sniffy, the Virtual Rat.

■ Analyze several games, and list the specific characteristics you feel make each game enjoyable.

■ Compare a paper and CD-based encyclopedia (preferably from the same publisher, such as Grolier). Look up the same topics in each source, and write a summary of what you observe.

■ Review the description of WiggleWorks presented earlier in the chapter. What examples of scaffolding (structured support for learning) do you detect?

■ Use Figure 4.11 to evaluate a commercial software product. Discuss your evaluation comments with your classmates.

■ Locate one of the journals mentioned in "Resources to Expand Your Knowledge Base" as providing useful information for teachers. List the types of information you discovered in reviewing one issue. Share this information with your classmates.

KEY TERMS

analog format (p. 145)
automaticity (p. 132)
branching tutorial (p. 125)

DVD-RAM (p. 146)
edutainment (p. 133)
exploratory environment (p. 137)

CD-ROM (p. 145)
cognitive load (p. 156)
computer-assisted instruction (CAI)
   (p. 121)
computer-based instruction (CBI)
   (p. 121)
digital format (p. 146)
digital video disc (DVD) (p. 146)
drill (p. 132)
dual-coding theory (p. 153)

fidelity (p. 128)
game (p. 133)
hypermedia (p. 144)
hypertext (p. 144)
linear tutorial (p. 125)
megabyte (p. 145)
multimedia (p. 144)
practice (p. 132)
simulation (p. 125)
tutorial (p. 123)

RESOURCES TO EXPAND YOUR KNOWLEDGE BASE

An expanded and frequently updated list of online resources is available on the website that accompanies this textbook.

Technology Journals

A number of journals are written to inform K–12 teachers about issues related to classroom applications of technology. These journals can be helpful in several ways. Teachers can learn about new developments in hardware and software and can also learn how other teachers are applying technology. These periodicals frequently carry critical reviews and side-by-side comparisons of hardware and software products. Information about the strengths and weaknesses of products can be very helpful when planning purchases.

Children's Software and New Media Review (**http://www.childrenssoftware.com/**)
Journal of Computers in Mathematics and Science Teaching (**http://www.aace.org/
   pubs/jcmst/index.html**)
Learning and Leading with Technology (**http://www.iste.org/L&L/**)
MultiMedia and Internet@Schools (**http://www.infotoday.com/MMSchools/
   default.shtml**)
Technology and Learning (**http://www.techlearning.com/**)

Software

The Adventures of Jasper Woodbury. Jasper Woodbury was developed by the
   Learning Technology Center, Vanderbilt University. Six adventures were
   copyrighted in 1992 and are available through Lawrence Erlbaum.
   (**http://www.erlbaum.com/jasper.htm**)

Exploring the Nardoo. This CD-based program, distributed in North America by
   Learning Team, is accompanied by an instructor's manual prepared by a
   team of teachers. The manual explains how tasks encouraged by Exploring
   the Nardoo meet specific science standards and provide activities that teachers
   can use to provide related learning experiences within the classroom and community. (**http://www.immll.uow.edu.au/immll/Nardoo/nardoo.htm**)
Operation: Frog. Operation: Frog Deluxe is available from Tom Snyder Productions.
   (**http://www.tomsnyder.com/**)
The Oregon Trail. The Oregon Trail, from the Learning Company, exists in several
   formats for several different computers. The latest version is available on CD-
   ROM. (**http://www.learningcompanyschool.com/**)

SimCity. SimCity 3000 is a product of Electronic Arts. (**http://simcity.ea.com/**)

Sniffy, the Virtual Rat. Sniffy, the Virtual Rat, from Wadsworth Publishing, is available for both Macintosh and Windows platforms. (**http://www.wadsworth.com/ psychology_d/special_features/ext/sniffy/**)

Where in the World Is Carmen Sandiego? Where in the World Is Carmen Sandiego? (1992) and other games in the Carmen Sandiego series are products of Broderbund. Software is available for Macintosh and Windows machines. The latest versions of these products come in deluxe CD-ROM versions. (**http://www.broderbund.com/**)

Word Scramble. Word Scramble is one activity from the Tenth Planet Explores Literacy Letter Sounds CD. This product is available for both Macintosh and Windows platforms from Sunburst Communications, Inc. (**http://www.sunburst.com/**)

Talking Books

WiggleWorks. The Scholastic Beginning Literacy System is a K–2 language arts system available on CD-ROM for Windows and Macintosh from Scholastic New Media. (**http://teacher.scholastic.com/readingprograms/wiggleworks/ index.htm**)

Multimedia References

The Complete National Geographic. 112 Years of National Geographic Magazine on DVD-ROM or CD-ROM is available from the National Geographic Society. (**http://www.nationalgeographic.com/**)

Encarta Encyclopedia for Windows is available from Microsoft Corporation. (**http://encarta.msn.com/**)

Grolier Multimedia Encyclopedia (CD-ROM and DVD) for Macintosh and Windows computers is available from Scholastic, Inc. (**http://www.scholastic.com/**)

Cooperative Problem Solving

The Great Solar System Rescue, The Great Ocean Rescue, and Decisions, Decisions are group problem-solving activities available on CD-ROM from Tom Snyder Productions. The online version of Decisions, Decisions, which is focused on current events, is free to the public and available from this same address. (**http://www.tomsnyder.com/**)

5

The Internet as a Tool for Communication

• • •

ORIENTATION   The Internet is arguably the most important technological innovation of our generation, and it offers what some feel is the potential to reshape many facets of society. Within the educational domain, how, where, and possibly what we learn and teach may change. In this chapter, you first encounter an overview of the multiple educational roles the Internet can play; we prefer to describe such roles as different *tools* for learning. In the later sections of the chapter, we concentrate on the Internet as a tool for communication.

From the outset, it is important to recognize that the Internet is a shared resource that provides opportunities for commerce, entertainment, and education. No single entity is developing it, and certainly no single entity is paying for it. Educators must understand that they are tapping into a resource not designed specifically for their benefit. But it is a resource of unparalleled potential nonetheless.

As you read, look for answers to the following questions:

Focus Questions

- What are the different types of Internet tools available to teachers and students?
- How might educators make use of e-mail, mailing lists, chat, and video-conferencing as tools for learning?
- What are some e-mail activities that can be adapted for the content area you plan to teach?
- How is online communication different from face-to-face communication? What characteristics of online communication represent an educational opportunity and what characteristics are likely to cause problems?
- What can educators do to increase the effectiveness of online discussions?

What Is the Internet?

The **Internet** is an international collection of computer networks with more than 800 million users worldwide—a number that continues to grow daily

(Global Reach, 2004). To put the Internet's rapid growth in perspective, look at these statistics:

Growth of the Internet

- In 2002, when we were preparing the fourth edition of this book, the estimated number of Internet users was only 500 million.
- It took 38 years for 30 percent of the U.S. population to acquire personal access to the telephone and 17 years for 30 percent of the population to acquire access to television. For the Internet, the same level of commitment was achieved in 7 years (UCLA Center for Communication Policy, 2000).

Think of the Internet as a meta-network—that is, a network of networks. There are huge networks providing a high-speed regional backbone, and there are small networks within individual office buildings. One of these networks might be located at your university or local school district. By running the right software on one of the computers on any one of the networks, you become an active part of the entire system.

TCP/IP

Members of the Internet community have made a commitment to share resources and to transfer information over the network in an agreed-on manner. This method of transferring information from computer to computer is called **transmission control protocol/Internet protocol (TCP/IP).** Rules associated with TCP establish how small amounts of digital information called packets are sent from place to place and how the system should respond when an expected packet does not arrive. The system works the same if the information is part of an e-mail message, a webpage, or streaming video. The IP rules establish a system for addressing and forwarding the packets. Each computer on the Internet has a unique identity or address called an **IP number.** Typically the same computer also has a **domain name.** The difference between the two is that the IP number is expressed as a series of numbers and the domain name as an easier-to-remember series of abbreviated words. For example, the IP number for one of our desktop computers, 134.129.172.88, gets translated as grabe.psych.und.nodak.edu.

A special computer, a *domain name server (DNS),* keeps track of the domain names corresponding to the various IP numbers. The unique designation for each computer is important, ensuring that data sent over the Internet get to the right place. You don't have to understand how TCP/IP functions to appreciate what it allows users of the network to accomplish. Files can be quickly sent and received by different kinds of computers over great distances with great accuracy. Messages and files end up where they are supposed to, at a specific computer with a specific IP number.

Classrooms with Internet access

Investment in Internet connectivity has been increasing so quickly that it is impossible to report accurate statistics. Even the common indicators used to demonstrate trends in school access to the Internet have changed. For example, when we wrote the second edition of this book, the common indicator was the proportion of schools with Internet access. In 1996, about 50 percent of schools had Internet access. Now, with school access over 98 percent, the individual school is no longer a useful unit of measurement for understanding the rate of change. Changes in access are now quantified in terms of the proportion of classrooms with Internet access or even the proportion of classrooms with a certain number of computers connected to the Internet (four seems to be the current standard). Nationwide, by 2004, the ratio of students to computers with Internet access was 4.3:1, and the ratio of students to classroom computers with Internet access was 8.4:1 (Park & Staresina, 2004). Laptop and wireless access may be partly responsible for improved classroom access to the Internet. Twenty-seven percent of schools have invested in wireless networks. If these statistics are surprising, either elementary and secondary schools may have changed more than you realize, or your recent personal experience has been in schools that depart from what is now typical. We anticipate that this process of change will continue and suggest that you connect to the National Center for Education Statistics (**http://nces.ed.gov/**) for more current data.

Focusing exclusively on school access provides an incomplete picture of the educational significance of the Internet. Both parents and students also connect from home, libraries, and other public locations. Insight into this broader perspective on Internet use is important for several reasons. First, the Internet offers a way to communicate with parents, to provide information about academic assignments, and to keep parents informed of important school events and issues (Huseth, 2001). Second, students use the Internet from home or community sites to complete school assignments. An awareness of how frequently students do work from home and which students may not have this opportunity is crucial for teachers. Finally, it is important for educators to appreciate how extensively the Internet is used by average citizens. Educators can help students develop skills that are needed for functioning in the larger society.

Home access to the Internet

Sixty-five percent of U.S. citizens can access the Internet from home, and the average user spends 12.5 hours online per week. If access from work and other community locations is also included, 75 percent claim to be Internet users. Twenty-four percent of home users have high-speed access (see "Focus: Making the Connection"), and it appears that high-speed access makes a qualitative difference in how the Internet is used. Even though those with high-speed connections can get the information they need more quickly, they spend 4 hours more per week online than those with dial-up connections. It appears that the speed and convenience of access encourages an even greater reliance on the Internet as a source of information and services. Home users use the Internet most frequently for e-mail, but also commonly search for information and visit sites providing news (Center for the Digital Future, 2004).

Unfortunately, family income is an important determinant of whether students and parents have Internet access at home. Teachers in high-poverty schools have to take home access into account when considering Internet use. When teachers from high- and low-poverty schools (more than 75 percent versus less than 35 percent of students eligible for free or reduced price school lunch) were asked to report whether specific issues were barriers to the use of technology, 77 percent of teachers from high-poverty schools, compared to 37 percent of teachers from low-poverty schools, listed access to technology outside school as a significant barrier. Teachers from high-poverty schools also more frequently listed student skill in using technology as a barrier. So it

Whether or not students have home access to the Internet has important implications for what teachers can assume in making classroom assignments.

is important to recognize that students from low-income families have less access to technology outside the school and that one consequence of this lack of opportunity may be a difference in the skills these students bring to the classroom. When teachers were questioned whether they asked their students to use technology to complete assignments outside the classroom, 34 percent from high-poverty schools and 54 percent from low-poverty schools said they gave such assignments. We discuss equity issues in greater detail in the chapter entitled "Responsible Use of Technology."

What Roles Can the Internet Play in Education?

Three types of tools

There are many ways of organizing information about the educational uses of the Internet. Various writers have created schemes based on content areas (such as language arts or science), grade levels (elementary, secondary), or categories of software (web browsers, e-mail, and so on). We take a different approach. Throughout this text, we frequently refer to technology as a *tool*. This metaphor provides a very important perspective for educators. Proficiency with a tool is valuable only when the tool is used to accomplish a meaningful task. Similarly, we want to emphasize that Internet applications— and all other varieties of technology—become valuable when your students use them to learn the skills and knowledge appropriate to the content area you teach. The system we use recognizes that the Internet can provide (1) tools for communication, (2) tools for inquiry, and (3) tools for construction (Bruce & Levin, 1997).

Internet Tools for Communication

By *tools for communication,* we mean efficient methods for exchanging information and communicating with others. This chapter provides detailed descriptions of e-mail, mailing lists, chat, and videoconferencing, along with examples of the types of Internet projects that can be accomplished using these types of software. We pay special attention to the positive and negative characteristics of online communication and to what instructors might do to facilitate productive communication among learners.

Internet Tools for Inquiry

The term *tools for inquiry* refers to methods for solving information problems. The chapter entitled "The Internet as a Tool for Inquiry" shows how learners can make efficient use of the major Internet tools that promote student inquiry, such as the web browser and searchable information embedded in the World Wide Web. In addition to acquainting learners with these technology tools, educators must accept the challenge of providing learning tasks that encourage content-area learning and the development of inquiry skills. We provide the structure for one type of problem-solving task that is practical for educators to develop and that scaffolds student inquiry learning. We also acquaint you with online sources for other meaningful learning tasks.

Internet Tools for Construction

The phrase *tools for construction* refers to the Internet as a vehicle for presenting products that students create to summarize a learning activity. This theme is emphasized in the chapter entitled "Learning from Student Projects," as well as in the chapters on multimedia tools and working with images, sound, and video.

Learning by Communicating

One of the most powerful uses of technology is putting people in touch with other people. Students and teachers can convey ideas and information nearly instantaneously or in ways that allow those at the other end of the conversation the freedom to respond at a convenient time, when they feel prepared. Technology allows individuals with common interests to interact over great distances, but it also allows learners who may see each other every day to interact in ways that increase the commitment to careful reflection and thus to learning.

E-mail

Electronic mail, commonly known as **e-mail,** is an Internet access system for sending, receiving, and storing messages. It was one of the first Internet applications, and it remains the most frequently used. It is estimated that 90 percent of U.S. Internet users take advantage of e-mail and 62 percent check their e-mail at least once a day. This means that 76 percent of U.S. citizens have an

Focus

Making the Connection

To understand how a computer on your desk connects with the Internet and with resources on thousands of other computers throughout the world, it helps to think of the system as involving several components: the Internet service provider, the transfer line, the hardware device connecting your computer to the transfer line, and your computer and its software.

Internet Service Provider

An **Internet service provider (ISP)** is a company or organization that connects multiple users to the Internet backbone. Some of the largest ISPs are companies whose names you probably recognize (MCI and AT&T) and others whose names are less familiar (UUNET). A local ISP may be operated by your university or a small private company in your community (check the phone book under "Internet"). The connection to the Internet may also be provided through an online service provider such as America Online (AOL) or Microsoft Network (MSN). These companies offer proprietary information resources, available only to members of the service, but they also connect members to the Internet at large.

Transfer Line

To get from your school or home to the ISP, digital information must travel over some kind of transfer line. This link may be a regular copper phone line—a setup often referred to as a *dial-up connection* or *dial-on-demand connection*. An **integrated services digital network (ISDN)**, **digital subscriber line (DSL),** or cable connection provides a faster connection. Special requirements for these access methods tend to limit the use of such systems to higher-population areas.

Leased fiber optic lines, sometimes called dedicated connections, come in different bandwidths. The *bandwidth* indicates the amount of information that can be moved in a fixed amount of time. Some common fiber optic lines transmit information at 56/64 Kbps (kilobits per second). T1 lines at 1.5 Mbps (megabits per second) are also common. Schools sometimes lease part of a T1 line, known as a *fractional T1*. Many school districts using a leased line also use a service called frame relay, which allows multiple buildings to connect to a single leased line. Leased fiber optic lines are currently the most practical way to provide the bandwidth necessary to serve a large number of students.

Other options are available and may be used more heavily in the future. For example, commercial community-wide wireless access allows connection over a distance of several miles.

Connecting to the Transfer Line

To send data through the transfer line, your computer needs a device to connect to that line. The type of device varies depending on the nature of your connection.

A **modem** is a hardware device connecting the computer to a copper phone line or other type of transfer line (such as digital cable). A modem is necessary because the signal understood by the computer may have to be converted to a form acceptable to the transfer system. When phone lines are used to transfer the signal, the computer and telephone communicate using different types of signals. A computer uses a digital signal, and a telephone an analog signal. An **analog signal** is continuous, and the digital signal is discrete (either 1 or 0). An **analog modem,** the more popular type currently, functions by converting the computer's digital signal into an analog signal that can be sent over a standard phone line. The term *modem* stands for "modulate/demodulate," which represents the processes of changing a signal back and forth between the digital and analog forms. Most modems today offer transfer rates of at least 28.8 Kbps. ISDN lines, which use an all-digital technology, are capable of transfer rates up to 128 Kbps, but they require a different type of modem and supporting hardware when the distance to the ISP is several miles. DSLs provide transfer rates between 384 Kbps and 1.5 Mbps, and cable connections, which use a special cable modem, are typically in the range of 500 Kbps to 1.5 Mbps for downloads (although upload speeds are slower).

For a still faster connection using fiber optic cable instead of standard phone lines, your computer must have a special hardware device called an *Ethernet card,* which is installed in the computer itself. But it would be highly unusual for a single computer to be connected to one of these more expensive fiber optic lines. Usually several computers are first joined together in a **local area network (LAN),** and then the LAN is connected to the dedicated transfer line through a device called a *router.* The computers in a school lab or in different classrooms would likely be connected in this fashion.

Wireless Connections

One recent development replaces part of the LAN with a wireless access point and wireless interface cards added to individual computers. With this system, it is no longer necessary to link individual computers into the LAN with Ethernet cable. The access point, a radio frequency (RF) hardware device operating on what is referred to as the 802.11 standard, is connected to the LAN, and multiple computers (usually ten to fifteen computers in a school setting) can then wirelessly connect to the Internet through the access point. Computers can move around within a range of approximately 150 to 250 feet and still maintain an Internet connection.

Twenty-seven percent of schools now have some form of wireless access. There are several advantages in wireless access for schools. Wireless systems allow schools to reduce some of the construction costs associated with pulling cable through walls. This is particularly true in older buildings in which asbestos abatement procedures must be part of any construction project. Also, when wireless is combined with the use of laptop computers, schools have much greater flexibility in how they use technology. Schools are purchasing more laptops; these computers now account for 12 percent of the machines available to students (Park & Staresina, 2004). Students can take computers with them when they move about. For example, students can carry their computers from a desk to a lab station in chemistry or biology or from the class-room to the school library.

One popular mobility option makes use of what might be described as a mobile lab. A mobile cart equipped with an access point, printer, and a dozen or so computers is wheeled into classrooms as needed. The access point is connected to the LAN, and a large number of students can then work online simultaneously. Even a lunchroom or commons area can be transformed into a computer lab when not needed for other purposes. If the equipment is stored near the multipurpose room, it can be brought out whenever the space is available for student work. Using technology in this way offers schools greater flexibility in how they use existing space, and the immediacy of access raises the likelihood that teachers will make extensive use of technology.

The User's Computer and Its Software

Several different types of software must be installed on the computer you use to access the Internet. First, your computer must have TCP/IP software. As mentioned earlier, this software, which typically comes as part of the operating system (Windows XP, for instance), allows each computer to conform to the common protocol that makes it possible for all computers to share resources over the Internet. Second, your computer must have application software appropriate to the type of work users want to do on the Internet. That is, if you want to send and receive e-mail, you need e-mail software. If you want to browse the World Wide Web, you need a web browser.

If you are connecting through an analog modem, the modem requires its own software. Most Internet applications operating over a modem require **point-to-point protocol (PPP)** software. A computer running PPP effectively becomes part of the Internet. (Another protocol, serial line Internet protocol, or SLIP, is now fairly rare.)

e-mail account and most use the account on a regular basis (Center for the Digital Future, 2004).

A teacher or student using e-mail composes a message and then sends it to the address of another individual. When this individual logs on to his or her account and searches for mail, the message is detected and brought to the computer screen to be read. Exchanging e-mail messages sounds simple, and it is. And many creative projects based on the simple process of exchanging messages have demonstrated the educational potential of correspondence with other teachers, students, parents, scientists, politicians, and potentially anyone else in the world with access to a computer, a modem, and the Internet.

Applications of e-mail

Among the more common e-mail projects are exchanges of correspondence with other students to learn about a different culture or to practice foreign-language skills, projects that allow the collection and integration of data (for instance, on water quality) from many different locations, and projects that involve sharing student-generated literature or newsletters. Many students also seem to enjoy more informal opportunities to strike up friendships and correspond with a key pal. E-mail systems also allow a file to be attached to a message. Users with compatible systems can thus exchange whatever computer files they can create. We say more about projects later in this chapter. The intent of this section is mainly to acquaint you with some of the technical issues associated with the use of e-mail.

The client-server model

E-mail functions on what is called a **client-server model.** Individuals have e-mail accounts on a computer known as a *server*. The server may be maintained by a school, a local ISP, or a large commercial entity such as AOL or Yahoo!. Your e-mail address includes a personal identifier and the domain name of the server. The two components are separated by the @ symbol. For example, Mark Grabe's e-mail address is mark_grabe@und.nodak.edu. He uses mark_grabe as his personal identifier (the underscore is required because addresses cannot include spaces), and und.nodak.edu is the name for the mail server responsible for the account.

An e-mail *client* is software on your computer that interacts with the mail server to send and receive e-mail. This interaction can take either of two forms:

1. In one approach, the client software does most of the work. The server accumulates mail until the mail can be downloaded to the client, and the server also sends a message on to the intended recipient. But downloaded messages are stored on the computer running the client software and can be read even when the computer is not connected to the Internet.
2. In the second approach, the client software functions only to upload and download e-mail messages to and from the server. A common approach of this type uses a web browser as the client; messages are displayed and entered within the fields of a webpage. In this approach, much of the work is actually done by the mail server, which is generating the necessary webpages and interpreting data entered by the user. Accumulated messages remain on the server until each is purposely deleted.

Free or inexpensive e-mail clients

The first method allows for more powerful software and more sophisticated e-mail capabilities because the work is accomplished by a dedicated personal computer rather than a shared remote server. Powerful e-mail clients can automatically sort incoming mail into different folders, identify probable spam (unwanted junk mail), search for individual stored messages by keywords, and create an address book that stores a variety of descriptive information. There are several free or inexpensive products offering these capabilities, such as Eudora, Microsoft Outlook, and Netscape. In addition, because each user stores information on a different machine, the storage capacity for sent and received messages is limited only by the capacity of the hard drive.

The main limitation of this type of e-mail client arises from the same basic fact—that each user has a different machine. The user must be in possession of his or her computer to access the information stored on it. This presents a difficulty for students and teachers, who often use multiple computers. Students may work on a computer at home, and then at school they may use several different computers. In this type of situation, it is best to use the server to store accumulated e-mail rather than download the messages to a personal computer.

Most people who make heavy use of e-mail take advantage of both methods. If you are not familiar with accessing and sending e-mail using a web browser, you might want to establish a free account on a system that relies on this approach, such as Hotmail or Yahoo!.

Mailing Lists

Sending a message to a group of readers

Because there are many situations in which a group rather than an individual is the target of communication, some online applications have been designed for this purpose. In one such application, users may send an open message to a defined group of readers. The user sends an e-mail message to a designated address, where it is relayed to the entire list of readers. Applications of this type are often called **mailing lists** or **listservs**, and the site from which the list originates is called the **list server**.

Members of active lists may receive several dozen messages a day. If you join such a list, a lot of information will come your way, and relevant messages may provide some useful piece of information or identify an individual you can contact for further discussion. Of course, some of the questions and messages sent through a list will be of little interest to you. These you can quickly scan and delete.

Mailing lists relevant to teachers

Many mailing lists address both general and specific topics relevant to teachers. For example, a school Internet administrator might send a message asking for information about what other schools have done to keep students from accessing inappropriate material. Each person or institution on the list would receive the message, and many might reply. Each reader would also see the responses of other members of the list.

Threads: sequences of messages on one topic

Often discussions focus on a specific topic until the topic is exhausted and then move on to something new. The sequence of messages on one topic is called a **thread.** A thread is created when a user replies to a previous message. Most e-mail systems have a reply option that preserves the **header** (a descriptive phrase) from the previous message, and this allows all the messages on one topic to be stored together. Archived files of list discussions allow you to a follow a thread and ignore unrelated messages.

Conferences

A different approach to the exchange of messages within a group does not result in a large number of messages being sent directly to you. Instead, the messages are "posted" to a network location, where users go to review the material electronically. To understand how this works, think of departmental bulletin boards in high schools that inform students of activities and news. Information on the upcoming orchestra concert, notice of band instruments for sale, and a notice of jazz band auditions would be found on the bulletin board near the music department. Other bulletin boards serving similar functions would be located throughout the school.

Electronic equivalent of a bulletin board

The electronic equivalent of the bulletin board, called a **conference** or **forum,** can hold hundreds of messages and can be read by people from all over the world. Often many conferences are available through the same electronic source. People who participate in conferences are encouraged to start relevant

Focus

Joining a List Maintained by a Server

It is not difficult to join a mailing list. Some lists are associated with a website and allow users to subscribe by filling out a form appearing on a webpage. Other lists rely entirely on e-mail. When this is the case, the list usually has both a submission address and an administrative address. The submission address is the one to use to send messages you want included on the list. To subscribe to the list, however, you typically need to send a message to the administrative address. Your subscription request should have a blank subject line (that is, nothing in the e-mail field that asks for the subject) and should include the simple statement SUBSCRIBE LISTNAME FIRSTNAME LASTNAME as the main body of the message—that is, the word *subscribe* followed by the name of the list, your first name, and your last name.

When you first subscribe to a list, you may be sent a summary of the procedures that apply to that list. Often the procedures explain what to do if you are going to be away from your computer for a while and don't want your e-mail inbox to be filled with mail from the list. You also may be told how to receive the individual messages as a digest (a single file instead of many individual messages) and how to remove yourself from the list.

One of the major problems is that users frequently forget the administrative e-mail address or the address for the website associated with the list. Although they constantly receive e-mail messages, the messages come from the submission address, and the administrative address is not mentioned. Since you will need to have the administrative e-mail address or be able to return to the administrative webpage to implement any of the procedures, be sure to save the instructions you receive when you first subscribe.

One more hint about using mailing lists: Often telecommunications services have an automatic reply feature, which allows you to send a message in response to one you have just received. When reading a message on a mailing list, remember that the immediate source of the message is the list server, not the person who actually wrote the message. Using the reply feature will send what you may intend to be a private message to all members on the list. More than one person has been embarrassed by such an error. The message author's address will appear somewhere in the message; this is the address to use when private correspondence is desired.

new discussions with a question or comment, respond to a posted comment, or just read the existing comments to glean whatever useful information might be available. Obviously the more participants there are, the more material will be available.

Conferences are potentially of greater value than mailing lists for some educational goals because the structure of the discussion topics, responses, and responses to responses is very evident and easy to explore. Conferencing

Keeping Current

Finding Useful Mailing Lists

Most days we all have discussions that draw on the knowledge of our colleagues. Such casual conversations allow us to request help from experienced associates and to check out what others might think of our new ideas. Imagine having similar access to hundreds of experienced colleagues, and you can begin to appreciate the potential of mailing lists.

 There are many mailing lists you may find helpful. You can find some listings in "Resources to Expand Your Knowledge Base" at the end of this chapter, and on the website that accompanies this textbook. On this frequently updated website we offer both resources for locating lists on a wide range of educational topics and a few specific recommendations of our own.

As we mentioned previously, it has become common to develop a webpage associated with major listservs. Using a search engine to search for the list name (see the chapter entitled "The Internet as a Tool for Inquiry"), we were able to locate most of the lists we included in our online resources. The website often provides a convenient way to subscribe and to access list archives.

applications are built into popular web-based course management systems such as Blackboard and WebCT. You may have already used a conferencing application in a university course. School districts that want to make conferencing available to teachers and students do not need to purchase such a comprehensive system; instead, they can purchase simpler software that will provide basic conferencing functions.

Chat and Instant Messaging

Synchronous versus asynchronous communication

E-mail, mailing lists, and conferences involve forms of communication in which messages are composed and made available to the reader at one point in time with the assumption that the message will be reviewed by the reader at a later point in time. Because of the time gap between sending and receiving messages, this form of communication is described as **asynchronous.** Real-time or **synchronous** exchanges are also possible. Sometimes this form of interaction is referred to as **chat** (although "keyboard conversations" might be a better description because the interaction takes the form of typed text).

There are now many opportunities for students, educators, and others to engage in chats. The necessary software might include a standard web browser running a Java applet (a small piece of software your browser automatically downloads to allow interactivity within the browser window) or a stand-alone chat client (such as AOL Instant Messenger, known as AIM, or iChat, the chat system for the Macintosh operating system).

If you intend to make use of chat as a learning activity, you should make certain the method you use allows for private discussion. A system for limiting access is important both as a way to bring together learners with similar goals and for security reasons (see the discussion of potential online dangers in the chapter on responsible use of technology). Access can be controlled in different ways; for example:

Ways to ensure the privacy of chat

- Web-based course management systems such as Blackboard or WebCT offer chat as a tool available only to those students enrolled in an individual course. The instructor or system manager has to intervene to include others. You may have personal experience with such systems in your college or university. These systems are also being used in K–12 settings.
- Many chat systems offer the ability to define a private chat room and to limit access to those individuals who appear on a preapproved buddy list. The terminology (such as *room* and *buddy list*) may vary. When using this type of chat system, the instructor identifies the participants and informs them of the time the chat is to occur and the name of the chat room they should enter. The instructor also prepares a buddy list corresponding to those who have been contacted to participate. Shortly before the chat is to begin, the instructor launches a chat client and sets up a private chat room with the designated name. Only those students whose names appear on the buddy list can gain access.

Instant messaging

Instant messaging has become very popular among young Internet users. Instant messaging provides for synchronous communication between just two individuals. The typical instant messaging system, such as AIM, is automatically enabled when a computer running the appropriate software is turned on and connected to the Internet. Instant messaging software makes use of a self-determined list of buddies (friends) and keeps the user informed of which individuals from the list are also online. When an instant message is sent to a buddy, an alert sound indicating that a message has arrived is generated by the remote machine. The buddy can then read the message and perhaps begin an exchange of messages. Often chat and instant messaging are used together. During a group chat, participants sometimes engage in side conversations with one individual using instant messaging.

Videoconferencing

Videoconferencing: synchronous video and audio

Videoconferencing is synchronous video and audio communication; that is, participants send and receive video and audio simultaneously. Videoconferencing can be accomplished in a number of ways, and, as is often the case, the amount of money you have to invest will influence the quality of the experience. With high-end videoconferencing equipment and a high-bandwidth Internet connection, an instructor can teach a course to a remote site or to individuals scattered about a state or country. At the low end of the scale, two individuals might communicate through two fairly typical classroom computers augmented with inexpensive video and audio input devices. While there are useful applications at all points along this continuum, we focus on low-end applications that are more likely to be available in your classroom.

Inexpensive videoconferencing options

Inexpensive, cross-platform audio- and videoconferencing is now possible. Using America Online Instant Messenger (5.5 or later) with the Windows XP operating system or iChat AV with the Macintosh operating system (10.3.5

FIGURE 5.1

Mark Grabe and Student Using iChat. In this configuration, the image being sent appears as a small inset.

or later), educators who have an Internet connection, a video input device, and a microphone can participate in videoconferencing (see Figure 5.1). Special video cameras, often called web cams, are available for the single purpose of feeding a video signal into computers and can be obtained for less than $100. A high-speed connection to the Internet is likely to be the most common barrier. Faster connections increase the number of video frames sent and received per second and make it less likely that the audio will break up.

The videoconferencing tool described here is designed for **point-to-point** communication. A point-to-point application connects one computer with one other computer, in contrast to an application such as chat, in which many computers are able to send messages to many computers. Even so, it is possible to use point-to-point videoconferencing for conferences in which all members of a class participate. As one example, the teacher might want to engage the class in a conversation with a subject expert. The video and audio from the expert would be sent to just one computer, but the sound could be turned up high or amplified through external speakers, and the video could be displayed on a large screen with a video projection system. Students who wanted to ask the expert a question would have to move to the connected computer so the microphone on that computer could pick up the question.

Sense of adventure needed

Finding ways to use inexpensive videoconferencing tools requires teachers and students with a sense of adventure. Classroom videoconferencing is unlike tuning into either a television news program or the interactive television you may have experienced in a college class. Sometimes the sound is garbled beyond recognition. The visual image can also be lost or change so slowly that parts of two images appear jumbled together. Still, videoconferencing is functional, and it allows some very interesting opportunities. Videoconferencing can be used effectively in any situation in which a visual or auditory signal would add to the authenticity of a project.

Telecomputing Activity Structures

Internet communication provides the opportunity for many kinds of activities and projects. Frequently magazines written for computer-using educators provide descriptions of classroom projects. Harris (1995) suggests that instead of looking for projects they can duplicate in their own classrooms, teachers should understand the properties of different kinds of projects—Harris calls them "activity structures"—and then apply these structures to the content being studied. Harris contends that this approach makes it more likely that classroom content is emphasized. Similarly, we suggest that understanding these instructional strategies allows teachers to adapt the strategies to meet specific educational standards. Here is a brief review of the activity structures Harris identifies:

- **Interpersonal Exchanges.** "Talk" among individuals, between an individual and a group, and among groups.
  - *Key pals.* Unstructured exchange among individuals or groups (for example, exchanges to develop cultural awareness or language skills)
  - *Global classrooms.* Study a common topic and exchange accounts of what has been learned (for example, themes in fairy tales)
  - *Electronic appearances.* E-mail or chat interaction with a guest, perhaps after some preparation (for example, a local engineer responds to questions from students in a physics class)
  - *Electronic mentoring.* Ongoing interaction between an expert and a student on a specific topic (for example, college education majors offer middle-school students advice on class projects)

Basic structures for projects

  - *Impersonations.* Participants interact "in character" (for example, correspondence with a graduate student impersonating Benjamin Franklin)
- **Information Collections.** Working together to collect and compile information provided by participants.
  - *Information exchanges.* Accumulation of information on some theme (for example, favorite playground games, recycling practices)
  - *Electronic publishing.* Publication of documents based on submission by group members (for example, publication of a district literary magazine of short stories submitted by elementary students)
  - *Tele-field trips.* Share observations made during local field trips (for example, visits to local parks; a special case could be expeditions undertaken by experts, such as a bicycle trip through Central America)
  - *Pooled data analysis.* Data collected from multiple sites are combined for analysis (for example, cost comparison of gasoline prices)

■ **Problem-Solving Projects.** Focus of interaction involves solving problems.
- *Information searches.* Solve a problem based on clues and reference sources (for example, identify state landmarks or cities in response to a progression of clues)
- *Electronic process writing.* Post written work for critiques before revision (for example, composition students comment on classmates' papers)
- *Parallel problem solving.* Groups at different sites solve the same problem and then exchange and discuss methods and conclusions (for example, compare ideas to improve school spirit)
- *Sequential creations.* Work on sequential components of an expressive piece (for example, add a stanza to a poem about friendship)
- *Social action projects.* Groups take responsibility for solving an authentic problem and share reports of activities and consequences (for example, cleaning up the environment, helping the homeless)

Advantages and Disadvantages of Computer-Mediated Communication

Online communication is sometimes referred to as **computer-mediated communication (CMC).** As the opportunity to communicate by way of the Internet has become more practical, it has become important to understand the educational advantages and disadvantages of CMC in contrast to face-to-face communication.

Advantages of CMC

At first, you may not be able to imagine any possible educational advantage of interacting by way of the Internet when compared to meeting in the same classroom. However, if you take a broad view of education, some advantages of CMC are obvious. CMC is place independent—that is, individuals do not have to be in the same location to communicate. Some forms of CMC, such as e-mail and conferencing, are also time independent and do not require the participants to interact at the same point in time. For these reasons, CMC offers practical solutions to some very real educational problems relating to time and location. For example, some teachers in our state who want to take a graduate course live more than one hundred miles from the nearest university. Some are in the situation of having to take additional courses to achieve the "highly qualified" status required by the No Child Left Behind Act of 2001. They cannot drive to a class after they finish teaching for the day. An Internet-based course offers a practical option for students faced with such circumstances.

Students in K–12 classrooms may also face challenges of time and place that CMC can address. Consider some of the activity structures described in the preceding section. While we would encourage students to take advantage of the opportunity to spend time in other countries to learn a second language or experience another culture, the reality is that such experiences are rare. Key pal and global classroom activities take advantage of the place independence of CMC. A teacher we know is very interested in the Iditarod (the Alaskan dogsled race). She has brought mushers to her class, and her class has also communicated with mushers online. We would guess that fourth-grade students in

Focus

Capitalizing on Volunteerism through Telementoring

Volunteers play important roles within K–12 institutions. They may serve as crossing guards, sell popcorn at athletic events, or help students deal with academic or personal challenges. **Telementoring** offers a new way for volunteers to offer their services. The idea of telementoring is simple: E-mail, chat, or videoconferencing systems are used to link adult volunteers with students when face-to-face interaction is not practical. Telementoring does not offer solutions for traffic control or staffing the concession stand, but it may provide access to personnel willing to apply their expertise and experience to assist young learners.

Using estimates of the number of U.S. citizens volunteering an average of at least three hours per week in educational institutions and the percentage with Internet access, proponents claim that more than 2 million individuals have the commitment and access necessary to serve as telementors. The size of this pool could be increased substantially by adding the number of college students seeking volunteer experiences or credit for experiential learning courses. Telementoring may be especially appealing to organizations such as corporations, colleges, museums, professional groups, and healthcare providers that want their employees or members to provide service in the community in ways that are cost- and time-effective. For these reasons, telementoring would seem to offer great potential (O'Neill & Harris, 2004).

One of the most significant challenges in realizing the potential of telementoring is coordination, in terms of the various components that must come together for a successful learning experience. The two most obvious components of a telementoring experience include (1) students and (2) at least one mentor with task- and situation-appropriate knowledge and skills. Other possible components include a well-developed curriculum project, specialized online tools to support project activities or mentoring, technical support, and training and support for mentors. How many of these components would be involved and who would take responsibility for organizing each component will vary from situation to situation. Sometimes the classroom teacher will be able to take total responsibility for the project. The teacher may have a specific project in mind, know an individual or individuals willing to correspond with students, and have access to and be comfortable with the technology to be used (for instance, the school e-mail system). But it is unlikely that telementoring will become very common if individual teachers must take sole responsibility for the success of such ventures. There are simply too many issues to be addressed and tasks to be accomplished. Luckily, several organizations that have taken on the cause of telementoring have developed "telementoring portals." Through a website, these organizations offer descriptions of successful telementoring activities, propose large collaborative projects involving telementors, attempt to identify and describe the qualifications of individuals willing to serve as telementors, offer suggestions and training resources to those willing to serve as telementors, and develop special tools to facilitate the online mentoring process. Brief descriptions of several of these portals are included in the website that accompanies this textbook. Take the time to explore these sites. You will learn much more about the potential of tele-mentoring and perhaps become interested in either implementing a project as a teacher or volunteering as a mentor.

You can learn more about telementoring by connecting to the International Telementor Program (**http://www.telementor.org/**), Electronic Emissary (**http://www.learningrelationslab.org/**), or the On-Line Learning Relationships Lab (**http://www.learningrelationslab.org/**).

Florida have few visits from mushers, but connecting to Iditarod Internet sites during the annual race and participating in online chats would still be possible.

The issues of time and place come into play in some other important ways. Class time is precious, especially time devoted to class discussion, and it turns out that CMC may have a significant positive impact in that area.

CMC's Impact on Discussion

The nature of classroom discussion has some startling characteristics. When classes are involved in what is defined as discussion, teachers speak between 40 and 80 percent of the time, and most communication is between the teacher and a student rather than among students (Costa, 1990; Dunkin & Biddle, 1974). Such discussions tend to draw in students who are good at developing quick responses and are able to gain the attention of the teacher and group within a time-dependent environment (Althaus, 1997). Quick responses are also rewarded because most teachers pause for less than two seconds after asking a question before speaking again to call on another student, rephrase the question, or provide an answer (Tobin, 1986, 1987).

CMC encourages diverse participation.

Reviews of research with college students indicate that the properties of CMC change some of these patterns of interaction. It appears that online discussions encourage greater and more diverse participation. A higher proportion of students tend to be involved when given the opportunity to contribute comments by e-mail or conferencing. One research group found that student comments in the classroom averaged 12 words, but contributions to an e-mail discussion averaged 106 words. Students obviously have more time to construct an e-mail message, so it is not surprising that the messages are longer. Also, e-mail messages are more complex than classroom comments and range over several topics. As you might expect, message complexity in chat sessions is more similar to that found in face-to-face classroom discussions (Althaus, 1997; Black, Levin, Mehan, & Quinn, 1983; Olaniran, Savage, & Sorenson, 1996; Quinn, Mehan, Levin, & Black, 1983).

Two factors may contribute to these advantages:

1. In chat, conferencing, and e-mail discussions, any number of students can work on the preparation of their comments at the same time, and each can be assured that the comments will eventually be added to the discussion. The first student to click "Send" does not block out other participants.

2. CMC reduces a variety of classroom cues (sounds and visual information) that may inhibit some students. Even the visible presence of the teacher as authority figure may cause some students to take less initiative.

In summary, CMC may encourage more productive discussion by increasing the number of active student participants and extending the time available for discussion. It can help those who cannot think as quickly as others, may not be as proficient in using the language, or may be apprehensive of sharing when in the physical presence of peers (Althaus, 1997). Even for those who have no difficulty expressing themselves in class, the writing activities involved in e-mail allow the time for reflection not available in a fast-paced classroom discussion.

Potential Problems with CMC

Need for keyboarding skills

Despite the advantages of CMC, there are some difficulties that are important to recognize. Although, as we have noted, some forms of CMC make use of interactive audio and video, the most common forms rely on keyboarding skills. Keyboarding speed varies greatly. Participating in a chat can be frustrating even for those used to entering text at a keyboard, and students with poor keyboarding skills may even be challenged by course requirements that demand the construction of e-mail.

Does CMC promote inappropriate comments?

Some difficulties of CMC derive from the same basic attributes that are perceived as advantages. While some researchers find that fewer cues encourage greater student participation, others think that the lack of cues can be associated with immature, insensitive, and unproductive behaviors. Inappropriate comments may become more frequent when a student cannot see classmates frown or turn red when he or she says something that is inappropriate. A classmate may interpret a remark incorrectly when he or she cannot see the speaker smile to indicate that the comment was intended as a joke. There is also some indication that CMC results in more evaluative comments, including comments that are too critical (Smilowitz, Compton, & Flint, 1988). If you participate in mailing lists, you may have experienced this already. When we read the comments that some people post, we wonder if they act this way with the people they see at work.

Importance of netiquette

The exact reason a lack of cues results in inappropriate behavior has been explained in several ways. One theory proposes that a lack of external cues leads to greater focus on the self and a corresponding self-centeredness in behavior. In contrast, a second theory proposes that fewer social cues result in a lessening of the focus on the self, with a corresponding increase in anonymity and reduction in sense of responsibility. Research evaluating competing theoretical models may eventually offer suggestions for reducing inappropriate online behavior (Joinson, 2003). Students involved in CMC can be sensitized to these limitations, learning to become more careful in the construction of the messages they send. Schools frequently provide students with a code of online conduct, often called **netiquette** (see "Focus: Netiquette Guidelines").

In our comments in the next section about the roles of the instructor in online discussion, we recognize the importance of a positive social environment and suggest methods of intervention for students who are being insensitive.

Focus

Netiquette Guidelines

Internet etiquette, commonly referred to as *netiquette,* consists of conventions for proper online behavior. Conventions are important in facilitating group interaction and allowing groups to function efficiently, fairly, and in ways that allow individuals to feel good about their participation. By following these guidelines, both in personal communication and in class work with your students, you minimize problems and show others that you are knowledgeable and caring.

Monitor Your E-mail Account

If you intend to communicate with e-mail, you should monitor your account on a regular basis and respond to messages promptly. Responding promptly is courteous and lets the sender know the message has been received.

Watch Grammar and Spelling

Proper grammar and accurate spelling should be an obvious expectation for educational applications of CMC. Online messages are often informal, but they still offer students the opportunity to practice good habits. For you, too, spelling and grammar are important; your words leave an impression, especially in the absence of other cues. So take the time to reread your messages before you send them, and encourage your students to do the same. Some e-mail software comes equipped with a built-in spell checker, and software can also be purchased that will monitor text as you type.

Create a Context for Your Comments

"Go ahead, George. I think it is a good idea." If you walked up to your friend George on the street and said this, he might be pleased, but he would probably have no idea what you were talking about. The same thing frequently happens online. Someone makes a comment or asks a question. Someone else reads the comment or question and replies. But the passage of time increases the likelihood that the person asking the question will forget what was asked or who was asked to respond.

The easiest way to establish a context for a reply is to connect your reply to the original message. Most e-mail clients allow the original message to be included in a reply. Usually the best approach is to retain only the sections of the original message that are relevant and merge your new comments with the original comments that prompted your reply. You can preface this section of combined material with a short introduction and explanation.

Compose the Subject Line Carefully

The subject line is the first thing the recipient of your message sees. If the subject or your e-mail address does not attract attention, the recipient may delay reading the message or even delete it. The subject line also provides a context for the rest of the message. With people you do not know, the best policy is to write a subject line that accurately describes the content or purpose of the message. "Question about PEP Grants" is better than "Important Question." While you can enter a long phrase for the subject, short phrases are generally preferable because the e-mail client may display only the first few words.

Ask Yourself: Would You Say It Face-to-Face?

One way to evaluate messages for appropriateness is to consider whether you would make the same comments in a face-to-face setting. If you would not, because the comments would be considered unnecessarily harsh, the message should be rewritten in less offensive language.

Be Careful with Sarcasm and Humor

Without the benefit of the cues present in face-to-face communication, sarcasm and poking fun at another person can easily be misinterpreted as criticism.

Remember That CMC Messages Can Be Permanent

Once your message is sent, it continues to exist, no longer under your control. The recipient may save it indefinitely or forward it to others. While forwarding without permission is considered inappropriate, you should recognize that almost anyone might see what you have written. If you would not be willing to make your comments public, carefully consider sending them over the Internet.

Listen Before You Speak

You might think that the Internet would be a great setting in which to ask whether you should purchase computer brand X or computer brand Y. True, but don't assume that this question would be welcomed in all settings. If you ask this kind of question on the wrong mailing list, you will immediately set off howls of protest. Computer users are very loyal to brands, and many lists have tired of the debate over which brand is better.

Another good example involves making recommendations for commercial products. Some lists and chat rooms encourage the exchange of information about books, programs, and services, and some actively oppose it. How do you know what behavior is appropriate? Sometimes the only way is to observe before you participate. This behavior, often called **lurking,** allows you to become familiar with the topics and communication styles that are acceptable.

Reply to the Proper Person

This guideline sounds obvious, but it is commonly abused. Sometimes the problem results from a simple mistake. Often mailing list participants forget that an e-mail message came from the list and not from the person authoring the message. Attempting to reply to the author results in a message sent to all members of the list. A similar problem can be created by accidentally "responding to all" in response to a message that was sent to some people as a cc.

See Virginia Shea's book *Netiquette* (San Francisco: Albion Press, 1994) for additional ideas.

Facilitating Online Discussion

As you gleaned from the preceding section, online discussion is not foolproof. While researchers have demonstrated its benefits (Scardamalia & Bereiter, 1996; Schacter, 2000), secondary and college instructors report that their students sometimes generate few comments and that those few are sometimes neither detailed nor insightful. Use of online discussion requires more than pointing students toward the discussion tool and giving them a general topic to discuss. Successful student discussions are more likely to occur when instructors offer a structure for online interactions and apply some basic skills as moderators.

Teachers who want to engage learners in productive online discussion should recognize that they will play at least four identifiable roles (Berge, 1995):

Four roles for the teacher

1. Technical
2. Social
3. Managerial
4. Pedagogical

The following comments explain these roles and provide strategies that experienced online educators have found to be successful.

Your Technical Role

To participate in online discussions, students must operate a computer and some type of software (browser, chat client), successfully connect to the Internet, and manipulate the specific communication system made available by the educational institution or commercial provider. As a classroom instructor, you are seldom responsible for technical chores; yet when a student cannot get something to work, you are likely to be the first person contacted. Here are some suggestions for dealing with students' online problems:

Tips for handling students' online problems

■ Become personally familiar with all aspects of the communications system and software. Try using the system in different ways—from your computer lab or office and from home over a modem. When sophisticated systems such as Blackboard and WebCT offer you unique privileges as the instructor, you should nevertheless add yourself to the system as a student so you can discover any limits placed on the other participants.

Ideas for creating a social setting online

- Create an FAQ (a list of Frequently Asked Questions with answers) and make it available to students. The initial entries might be based on personal insights—the issues you have encountered as you learned the system. Later additions to the FAQ can arise from difficulties encountered by the students. The FAQ should be available online and as a handout.
- Engage learners with the system immediately and in a way that allows them to focus on becoming familiar with the system rather than on content. If the discussion experience is an extension of a face-to-face class, take the entire group through a quick overview.

Your Social Role

Online discussions involve some unique social challenges. In distance education courses or some of the projects we described previously, students may even be interacting with others they have never met. Even when online discussion is used to extend traditional classroom discussions, the absence of face-to-face cues reduces feedback, as we have already mentioned. One of the instructor's roles, therefore, is to help the participants create a social presence (Kemery, 2000).

When students are unable to meet in person, you might do the following:

- As an icebreaker, pair students up and have them interview each other online. Summaries of the interviews can be presented to the group.
- Collect photos of all the students and brief self-descriptions and present these as simple webpages. The pages can be password protected if security is a concern.
- Begin the discussion by posting a greeting to students and perhaps by sending a private message to each student with an invitation to respond.

When the discussion is an extension of a face-to-face class, you still need to create an awareness of social presence to inhibit insensitive comments. One suggestion is to use student names and quotes from their previous contributions in related replies.

Your Managerial Role

The instructor as manager assumes responsibility for assuring that learners understand the goals and procedures of the discussion, that all learners have the opportunity to participate, and that the goals of the discussion are accomplished efficiently (Kimball, 1995). Because the managerial and pedagogical roles are important even when working with students in your own classroom, we explore these roles in some detail.

As a discussion manager, you should accomplish the following five tasks:

1. *Identify the purpose for the discussion.* Making the purpose of a discussion clear helps participants shape their comments and decreases the likelihood that inexperienced participants will misunderstand what is expected of them. The purposes of a discussion may include:

- Offering help to those experiencing difficulty
- Exchanging information on a specific topic
- Persuading others of the value of a personal opinion
- Carefully and logically exploring important ideas to achieve understanding
- Evaluating knowledge or understanding to award a grade or alter the course of instruction
- Exploring options and reaching consensus on the course of action the group would like to take to address a problem

How to explain a discussion's purposes

Though not exhaustive, this list illustrates the activities you may eventually have to explain to your students. Consider how you would explain the purposes listed here to learners of different ages. As an example, imagine you are teaching seventh graders. How would you explain the expectations of an information exchange focused on experiences in one-room schools? Here is one possibility:

> We want to gather together what all of us have learned about what it was like to attend a one-room school. If we think about several different stories, we should be able to create a list of the ways in which being a student has changed over the years. Were you able to find a relative who attended a one-room school? Do you remember anything interesting from the material I asked you to read? Who has a story to tell?

As another instance, how would you explain the purpose of a discussion intended to generate personal understanding? Our example involves a controversy over grazing rights on public land:

> Let's see if we can put together an explanation of the disagreement between the ranchers and the environmentalists over whether the ranchers should be able to graze cattle on land owned by the government. Why does each group feel it is right? What one disagreement do you feel will be most difficult to fix? Who wants to explain what the ranchers believe?

Providing a structure for the discussion

Another way to help learners understand the purpose of a discussion is to provide a structure that the discussion will follow. The structure identifies the intended stages in a discussion and gives learners an indication of activities appropriate to each stage. One example of a structured online discussion is called **collaborative argumentation** (Jonassen, 2000). This structure is appropriate to situations in which the group has to reach a decision in spite of differences of opinion. Collaborative argumentation involves three stages in which participants are given time to:

1. Offer proposals with supporting arguments
2. Evaluate and compare the proposals offered
3. Attempt to reach consensus

As a facilitator, you might first familiarize participants with the structure and then refer to the stages in encouraging comments from participants. For example, you might indicate that in the first phase of the discussion the goal is for participants to present proposals without having to defend them against criticism. When the generation of proposals slows, you might make one last call for new proposals, indicating that it is about time to move on to a comparison of the proposals.

2. *Define the instructor's and students' roles.* It is helpful to clarify who plays what role in a discussion. As instructor, you might be an information provider, evaluator, or facilitator. As participants, are students supposed to provide information and personal opinions, evaluate the comments of others, or ask questions? If you want students to discuss issues based on assigned readings or on their understanding of other presentations, this represents a different approach than expecting students to offer personal opinions requiring no preparation.

Discussing roles with the students

A short discussion of roles can be helpful. You might explain that you will be responsible for presenting new information or, alternatively, that you intend to offer a couple of leading questions and then you expect students to carry the conversation. To clarify the students' role, you might say, "Your comments should reflect what you have learned from readings or from class. Try to explain where your ideas are coming from."

3. *Keep the discussion fresh by altering the techniques you use.* From time to time, you can modify the format of a discussion to provide some variety. Here are some options:

Using a variety of techniques

- If it appears that students are taking sides on an issue, conduct a simple poll to determine how mixed the opinions are.
- If the discussion seems to be proceeding at an abstract level, present an example from personal experience and ask the group to determine whether the principles advanced during the discussion apply to that example.
- Assign students to specific pro and con positions and have an online debate.
- Assign students to small groups and ask that they consider a specific issue and then offer a summary to the group.

Clarifying what students are expected to do

4. *Establish basic expectations for student participation.* There are many simple expectations that can be clarified for students and that limit later disagreements. For example:

- What are the expectations regarding spelling and grammar? Are students expected to proofread before submitting their comments?
- If the discussion takes the form of a conference, how often are students expected to check for new messages?
- If discussion performance will be graded, what variables will be considered: frequency of contributions, thoughtfulness of contributions, attempts to respond to the comments of others?

Guiding and reinforcing student behavior

5. *Respond to productive, disruptive, or passive behavior.* As a facilitator, you must take responsibility for encouraging and discouraging specific discussion behaviors. If a student is "lurking"—that is, following a discussion but failing to participate—you should encourage him or her to participate. If a student is being overly caustic in responding to the com-

ments of others, it is appropriate to ask the student to try to offer a different perspective without being so critical of other people. If, on the other hand, a student has made some especially useful comments, you should encourage him or her with direct praise.

For these types of issues, it is often helpful to address participants individually via private e-mail or a face-to-face meeting. If you send a private e-mail, your message might take one of the following forms:

- "Thanks for providing such a thoughtful comment on underage drinking. Your contribution was very useful in getting the group to consider why some of their peers drink."
- "Your enthusiasm for this discussion topic is great, but you are beginning to dominate the conversation. Other students seem to quit responding when you offer so many comments. Perhaps you could cut back the number of comments a little and see if others will become more active. Thanks."
- "We have not heard from you in some time. Try to offer at least one new comment each week."

Your Pedagogical Role

As the teacher, you expect discussions to deepen learners' understanding of course content and to help them develop higher-order thinking skills appropriate to the course. To achieve these goals, you must make decisions and take action to shape the discussion. The following list offers some suggestions:

1. *Evaluating discussion performance.* One of the most fundamental and well-founded principles of the behavioral model of learning is that our behaviors are altered by consequences. Behaviors that generate what a learner regards as reinforcements are continued, and those that generate either punishment or a lack of any consequence decrease in frequency. Even though we perhaps are focused on the internal cognitive behaviors of learners, we should recognize that certain external behaviors encourage thinking and learning and that we as teachers can establish consequences that influence these behaviors. For instance, we control many of the consequences that learners experience for participating in classroom discussions, completing homework assignments, and engaging in other external tasks that influence their learning.

   Consider the consequences you might use to encourage participation in online discussions. Would you grade student participation? To instructors who daily engage their classes in face-to-face discussion, awarding points for discussion may seem unnecessary. Online instructors, however, often establish evaluation procedures for their class discussions. They might announce that students should post at least one message each week, and this level of activity might guarantee a certain number of points toward the final grade. Some online instructors also evaluate the quality of student comments, though this requires a more sophisticated and more labor-intensive evaluation system. For such purposes, online instructors have an option not available in face-to-face situations: They

Using consequences to encourage participation

have a permanent record of the discussion that they can use as part of their evaluation process.

Evaluation practices do appear to influence students' online performance. MacKinnon (2000) created a categorization system for student comments. Irrelevant comments were awarded no points. Simple statements of information taken from course material received 1 point. Comments involving application, linking examples with principles, linking principles with examples, and cause and effect were awarded 2 points. Students could accumulate up to 10 points toward their course grade during each discussion session. MacKinnon followed the pattern of comments through multiple discussion sessions. Information statements dominated the first session. Following this session, the researcher coded the comments of each participant and returned this summary to the students. Two-point statements became significantly more common in the later discussion sessions.

Think about this issue. Whether or not you feel discussion performance should determine part of a student's grade, you should recognize that your pedagogical role includes some responsibility for consequences.

Asking timely questions

2. *Using key questions to encourage and direct student thinking.* Timely probing questions are an effective technique for increasing the productivity of discussions. Questions are one way to scaffold thinking behavior, and you can use them online just as you would in a face-to-face setting:

What reasons do you have for saying that?
Do you think you and Sue agree on this point?
How would you explain what by you mean by unethical?

3. *Modeling and developing skills for meaningful learning.* The pedagogical goals of discussion often include having the learner build a personal understanding of the topic by actively integrating the ideas raised in the discussion with existing knowledge. The moderator can engage the discussion participants as cognitive apprentices (see the chapter entitled "Meaningful Learning in an Information Age") by externalizing important cognitive behaviors so that students can observe the skills and then practice them. Two behaviors that help in this process are weaving and summarizing (Kimball, 1995).

Modeling the skills of weaving and summarizing

Weaving is the activity of bringing together ideas raised during a discussion. It demonstrates connections that the commenter has observed. *Summarizing* is a broader integration of ideas that might occur at the end of a discussion or at transition points. It provides a structure for the key ideas that have been identified. Here are two examples:

Sam, your comments seem similar to Sally's. You have both provided instances of teachers who used images taken from the Internet without permission from the copyright holder, setting poor examples of ethical behavior for their students. [*weaving*]

Let's see: Our examples of abuses of copyright now include the use of videotaped television programs, distributing copies of sheet music, and using images taken from the Internet. [*summarizing*]

Focus

Key Issues for Online Discussions

Our brief summary of online discussion techniques necessarily simplifies or passes over some important matters. When you have a chance to use online discussion with your own classes, you will probably confront issues like these:

- *Asynchronous versus synchronous discussion.* Most of our comments do not differentiate between asynchronous discussion lists and real-time chats. Some instructional techniques will vary from one setting to the other.
- *Age of learners.* Because the use of online discussion in K–12 settings is very new, most of the actual data come from studies of college students. Matters such as the extent to which the instructor should control the course of a discussion probably need to be approached differently if the students are sixth graders rather than college students.
- *Type of class.* If a class meets only online, never face-to-face, the roles outlined here probably must be approached even more conscientiously than we recommend.
- *Differences of opinion among experts.* There are differences of opinion on many issues. For instance, should proper grammar and spelling be required? Should lurkers be prompted to participate? Should participation be graded? Should the instructor structure the discussion?
- *Ongoing research.* Most of our recommended practices are based on suggestions of experienced online educators rather than on specific research. Researchers have only begun to investigate these questions in depth.

The idea in cognitive apprenticeship is to first demonstrate key skills in the context of an authentic task and then allow learners to attempt the same behaviors. For instance, after demonstrating the skills of weaving and summarizing, you might ask one student to comment on connections he or she has observed and ask another student to summarize key ideas.

Gaining Experience

Taking an online course to learn how it works

The suggestions we offer should help you reflect on some of the issues educators must address when involving students in online discussions. We hope you have some experience with online discussion as a learner before you attempt to moderate discussions as a teacher. This perhaps is our most important recommendation: Experiment with online discussion before you offer it to your students. If you have not participated in online discussion during your regular classes, think about signing up for a short online course on a subject you would like to explore. The experience you gain as a student can be invaluable when you are guiding your own students online.

Summary

The Internet, the vast web of interconnected computers that spans the globe, has been growing at a phenomenal rate. Educational interest in the resources of the Internet has heightened, too. Most schools have some form of access to the Internet, and the way schools are compared now tends to focus on the level of access from the classroom. As schools have begun to take greater advantage of the Internet, home access has become a more important issue. Students with home access gain more experience in using technology and also have an easier time completing assignments that rely on the Internet. Family income is an important variable in determining home access.

The Internet can provide students with three basic types of tools for learning: (1) tools for communication, (2) tools for inquiry, and (3) tools for construction. Internet communication is the main focus of this chapter; the other tool applications are considered in later chapters.

Of all the tools available for computer-mediated communication (CMC), e-mail is the most popular because it is so versatile and easy. E-mail also has the advantage of being a tool widely accepted by the general population. Mailing lists, also known as listservs, are an adaptation of e-mail that allow an individual to communicate with a group. If you become a member by adding your e-mail address to a mailing list, all messages sent to the list's submission address will be forwarded to your e-mail account. Conferences offer another method for group interaction; they differ from listservs in that participants connect to the server and determine which comments to examine instead of receiving all comments automatically as e-mail.

Chat sessions offer a synchronous text-based communication format. Chat sessions have become a common feature of online courses because they provide an opportunity for class discussion. For synchronous communication between only two individuals, instant messaging has become popular.

Videoconferencing offers synchronous video and audio communication. More expensive versions of videoconferencing allow participants to join the conference from several different sites, but inexpensive alternatives are available for connections between two standard computers. The imperfect reliability of low-end videoconferencing means it is most suitable to those willing to engage in more adventurous teaching methods.

Online communication provides the opportunity to engage learners in a wide variety of projects. Teachers new to technology may want to begin with well-tested class projects, but as you gain experience we urge that you adapt the common project types to your own curriculum priorities and student interests.

The advantages and disadvantages of computer-mediated communication in educational settings are still being investigated. Two important factors are (1) the greater time CMC allows students to think and compose messages and still be certain that the messages are presented to the group and (2) the limited number of cues available from communication partners. Depending on your perspective, these factors may have positive or negative consequences. The more leisurely pace and the limited number of cues available in CMC allow more students to participate, provide more time for reflection, and shift the balance from a teacher-dominated discussion toward more equal participation. However, discussion may be less organized, without clear lines of authority, and perhaps less sensitive in addressing the comments offered by other participants.

Instructors who want to make use of online discussion should recognize the need to play technical, social, managerial, and pedagogical roles. The technical role involves assisting participants with technical problems that may arise. The social role requires the ability to develop and maintain an environment that encourages positive interactions. The managerial role involves helping learners understand the goals and procedures of the discussion and providing an opportunity for all to participate. The pedagogical role involves motivating student effort, engaging students in activities that promote learning, and modeling productive discussion behaviors.

Reflecting on Chapter 5

ACTIVITIES
- Subscribe to one of the listservs described in this chapter or in another resource for educators (make sure you take note of the procedure for unsubscribing). After one week, summarize the topics discussed on the list, and evaluate how helpful you feel the list would be to educators.

- Locate an existing communication project that might be relevant for your area of interest (see the project resources in "Resources to Expand Your Knowledge Base"). Classify this project according to the scheme provided by Harris (1995). Summarize the project for your classmates.

- Using a free chat client (such as AOL Instant Messenger or MSN Messenger) or the chat tool from a web-based course management system (such as Blackboard or WebCT), participate in a chat on a topic designated by your instructor. Were you able to follow the flow of the discussion? Did your typing skills affect your ability to communicate your ideas? Did certain individuals dominate the discussion? (*Note:* Your institution may block the use of chat clients.)

KEY TERMS

analog modem (p. 176)
analog signal (p. 176)
asynchronous (p. 181)
chat (p. 181)
client-server model (p. 178)
collaborative argumentation (p. 193)
computer-mediated communication (CMC) (p. 185)
conference (p. 179)
digital subscriber line (DSL) (p. 175)
domain name (p. 171)
electronic mail (e-mail) (p. 174)

Internet (p. 170)
Internet service provider (ISP) (p. 175)
IP number (p. 171)
listserv (p. 179)
list server (p. 179)
local area network (LAN) (p. 176)
lurking (p. 190)
mailing lists (p. 179)
modem (p. 176)
netiquette (p. 188)
point-to-point (p. 183)
point-to-point protocol (PPP) (p. 177)

forum (p. 179)
header (p. 179)
instant messaging (p. 182)
integrated services digital network
   (ISDN) (p. 175)

synchronous (p. 181)
telementoring (p. 186)
thread (p. 179)
transmission control protocol/
   Internet protocol (TCP/IP) (p. 171)

RESOURCES TO EXPAND YOUR KNOWLEDGE BASE

An expanded and frequently updated list of online resources is available on the website that accompanies this textbook. It includes websites for all software described in this chapter, as well as a collection of online projects related to this chapter.

Software for Online Communication
E-mail through the Web. *Some companies provide a free e-mail account that can be accessed using a web browser:*

Gmail (**http://gmail.google.com**)
Hotmail (**http://www.hotmail.com/**)
Juno (**http://www.juno.com/**)
Yahoo! Mail (**http://mail.yahoo.com/**)

Internet Chat Opportunities
There are many ways to chat online. This brief section includes only a few of the available methods, sites, and software.

Web-based course management systems with chat tool. These multicomponent environments provide both chat and conference tools. Your educational institution will have to be using one of these systems for you to have access to the communication tools.

Blackboard (**http://www.blackboard.com/**)
WebCT (**http://www.webct.com/**)

Instant messenger/chat clients. Instant messenger systems allow person-to-person real-time private communication (instant messaging) and chat. Access is typically controlled by identifying a list of buddies (friends).

AOL Instant Messenger (AIM) (**http://www.aim.com/**)
iChat AV (**http://www.apple.com/macosx/features/ichat/**)
Microsoft Network (MSN) Messenger (**http://messenger.msn.com/**)
Yahoo! Messenger (**http://messenger.yahoo.com/**)

Videoconferencing Software
NetMeeting, a videoconferencing tool developed by Microsoft, is available free of charge for the Windows operating system. Information and the opportunity to download the software are available online. (**http://www.microsoft.com/ windows/netmeeting/**)

IChat AV, available as part of the Apple Macintosh operating system, offers videoconferencing opportunities for up to four participants. (**http://www .apple.com/macosx/features/ichat/**)

6

The Internet as a Tool for Inquiry

● ● ●

In this chapter you learn what you and your students need to know to make efficient use of the Internet as a tool for inquiry. The web browser and the World Wide Web are responsible for the tremendous surge of interest in the Internet. We explain the techniques involved in operating the browser and in searching for useful resources.

One of the concerns associated with student use of the Internet is that some resources are misleading or inappropriate. We describe how to involve students with quality resources and help students learn to evaluate resources for themselves. You also learn how the Big Six, a model of information problem solving, can be used as a model for inquiry tasks. Finally, the chapter examines how you as a teacher can develop and structure learning activities, such as WebQuests, that efficiently involve students with Internet resources.

As you read, look for answers to the following questions:

Focus Questions

- How can learners take advantage of online services to locate needed information through the processes of browsing and searching? What can learners do to improve the efficiency of their searches?
- How can teachers and students keep track of the valuable web resources they have located?
- What are the differences between instructional resources and primary sources, and what roles do these resources play in a learning environment?
- What guidelines might be applied to evaluate the information found on webpages?
- What information problem-solving skills are emphasized in the Big Six model, and how do these skills apply to an Internet inquiry task?
- What are the components of a WebQuest? How can you use a WebQuest with your students?

A Classroom Example of an Authentic Inquiry Task

Imagine you are a second-grade student, and your teacher decides that she will allow you and your classmates to purchase a class pet. She will contribute $30, and you will be allowed to make the selection. But there are some issues beyond cost that you have to consider. Some pets are dangerous, and some students are allergic to certain animals. (You understand this because you have a cat at home, and your aunt says it makes her sneeze.) The pet will have to stay in a container of some sort and remain at school over weekends. There is one more thing: Your teacher says the entire class will make the decision. You have to gather information and then explain to other students what kind of pet you would like the class to buy and why.

Does this sound like a good project? Ellen Knudson, a second-grade teacher at Solheim Elementary in Bismarck, North Dakota, thought so. Mrs. Knudson has a history of keeping pets in her classroom. She also likes to involve her students with technology projects—particularly projects in which the students are in control and make their own decisions. It seemed natural, then, to let her students research possible classroom pets on the Internet. Even younger students could be challenged to use the Internet to solve an authentic information problem.

Preparing for the Project

To prepare for this project, Mrs. Knudson had a lot of work to do. To keep the students' research focused and efficient, she decided to ask them to consider just three potential classroom pets: a budgie (a type of bird, more formally known as a budgerigar or parakeet), a sugar glider (a marsupial), and a leopard gecko (a reptile). Even for just these three animals, finding Internet resources appropriate to second graders was a challenge.

Certain factors, such as the use of scientific nomenclature (*Melopsittacus undulatus* for budgie), did not bother her because she felt her students should learn to cope with real-world information. But she was concerned about whether the web resources would be concise, contain the specific details students would be asked to locate, and be presented at a level that the young readers could understand.

Sometimes, she discovered, a single Internet page provided all of the information needed for an animal, and sometimes a page provided a great opportunity to investigate a particular issue. She made a careful selection of both types of sites. The varied experiences would be good for her students.

Introducing the Project

Mrs. Knudson used class discussion to introduce her students to the project. Then she directed them to a series of webpages she had created. The following information appeared on the introductory page:

Class Pet

Mrs. Knudson wants to buy a new pet for the classroom. She needs help in selecting the right one. Click on the pet names below to find out more about each animal. As you are reading, keep these guidelines in mind:

- It must not be a mammal because of allergies to animal hair and fur.
- It must be $30 or less in price.
- It must be able to live in the 10-gallon aquarium or birdcage in our room.
- It must be easy to feed. Food must be easy to get and fairly inexpensive.

After you have read through the information, write out your choice, listing the price, the cage or equipment the animal needs, the group the animal belongs to, and the animal's diet. Also explain why you think this pet would be interesting to study and care for.

The Project Develops

The classroom had just one computer connected to the Internet, but Mrs. Knudson could take her class to the school's computer lab when group work was necessary. During this project, students worked on the lab computers in pairs and took notes they would use in their discussions.

After the initial information-gathering phase, students continued the discussion back in the classroom. Because the students sat at tables rather than individual desks, each table of three to four students formed a convenient discussion group. The course of discussions was unpredictable.

Mrs. Knudson listened to each group, asked questions, and answered some of the students' questions. When the students puzzled over scientific names, she reviewed several general strategies for dealing with unfamiliar words. One group attempting to estimate food costs wanted to know how large a teaspoon was. Students at each table were asked to write out their group's recommendation before the entire class discussed the issue. Figure 6.1 illustrates the recommendation of one table of students.

FIGURE 6.1

The Classroom Pet Project. The recommendations of one group of students after their Internet research and discussion.

> BEST PET by Table 3
> We recomend the Budgie because it costs 10 dollar to 20 dollars.
> They eat green vegtables. And they eat 2–3 teespons of seeds a day.
> They need a cage.
> The budgie is in the bird family.

An Authentic Activity

You can see from Mrs. Knudson's example that carefully prepared Internet projects can serve as excellent, authentic learning activities even for very young students. We make frequent references to authentic tasks throughout this book and provide an extended discussion in the chapter entitled "Meaningful Learning in an Information Age."

In the case of Mrs. Knudson's class, the students learned about various animals, not just to store the information, but also to use the information to solve a meaningful problem. Each group needed to make a strong case for a certain class pet in the hope of persuading classmates to agree.

This introductory example was intended to get you thinking about the use of the Web in authentic inquiry tasks. We find it helpful to describe the experience of completing such tasks as information problem solving, a concept we develop later in the chapter. To solve problems with online information, it is necessary to understand the basics of operating a web browser, to use online directories and search tools to locate useful online resources, and to evaluate, interpret, and apply online information. In the example from Mrs. Knudson's classroom, very young students completed a sophisticated task because Mrs. Knudson performed some specific subtasks for them. This type of support and structure—*scaffolding,* to use the term introduced earlier in this book—allows students to efficiently complete appropriately challenging authentic tasks while concentrating on the development of core knowledge and skills. You will find that some of the most important decisions the teacher makes in engaging students in authentic inquiry tasks concern which tasks will be completed by the teacher and which by the students.

The World Wide Web and Web Exploration Tools

The resources available on the Internet are disorganized because they have resulted from the efforts of many institutions and individuals operating independently and contributing whatever they think might be useful. Because the Internet lacks a central directory, it can be challenging for inexperienced users and time-consuming for anyone to pull together resources related to a specific topic.

The Web: a vast variety of interconnected resources

The **World Wide Web** (**WWW,** or simply **the Web**) represents a significant improvement on the original Internet because it allows a variety of information sources to be interconnected through a special type of hypertext or hypermedia link. These information sources might be text documents, graphics, sounds, or even other websites. To find information on a particular topic, you can use online directories or search engines, or you can begin at a website on which someone else has provided a list of helpful links for that topic.

Focus

Internet Addresses

You may have noticed that throughout this book, we include Internet addresses for your use. Most look something like this: **http://ndwild.psych.und.nodak.edu/book/default.html.** This address, called a **universal resource locator (URL)**, provides a program that is running on your computer the ability to request a specific file from a specific remote computer located on the Internet. This remote computer you have asked to send you a file or files is called a *server.*

The URL consists of three components:

- The protocol, which defines how the file will be sent
- The name of the server making the file available
- The location of the file on the server

For our example, the protocol is **hypertext transfer protocol (HTTP),** which identifies the information requested as a webpage. You may encounter other protocols, such as file transfer protocol (FTP), when using the Internet for other tasks. The server name in our example is ndwild.psych.und.nodak.edu; the file on the server is located in the directory named *book* and has the name *default.html.*

To visit the websites we mention throughout this book, you will have to enter the URLs in the field located near the top of the web browser. (Depending on the type and version of your browser, the area in which you enter this information may be labeled "Address," "Location," or some similar name.) You will not have to enter long URLs repeatedly. Luckily, browsers have the capacity to store a list of URLs—known as bookmarks or favorites—that users may want to visit again. We discuss bookmarks later in this chapter.

Web Browsers

Special client software, called a **browser,** is required to connect to and interpret the protocol used by web servers. A browser provides a graphic interface and allows interactive involvement with the full range of hypermedia—text, pictures, sounds, and movies. You can follow links from resource to resource in a variety of ways, including using the mouse to click on specially marked pictures or words that serve as links to other resources.

HTML tags

The exciting multimedia displays you encounter when exploring the Web are sent to you in pieces and then assembled by your web browser. The one essential piece among the assortment of file types is a simple file containing plain text. This file has no large headline-sized fonts, no centered headings, and not even mandatory paragraph breaks. This simple text document has one unique characteristic. Embedded within the text are the special tags making up the

hypertext markup language (HTML). The tag
tells the browser to break and start a new line of text. The tag set <I></I>surrounding text would cause that text to appear italicized. The IMG tag causes an image to be transferred and displayed (for example, <IMG SRC="mark.gif">). SRC provides the location of the image. You can view samples of HTML by asking your browser to show the source code for a webpage. Look for the source option under one of the browser menus. (You learn more about HTML and how to construct webpages in the chapter entitled "Learning from Student Projects.")

A web browser interprets—or, more accurately, tries to interpret—the HTML tags and builds the webpage before your eyes. Because different browsers may do this work in different ways, the appearance of a webpage may vary a little depending on the browser you use. HTML is also constantly evolving, and there are differences of opinion over which functions should be included. If your browser is out of date or is not designed to implement one of the newer functions, some features that the webpage author included will not be displayed.

Formats available on the Web

The variety of formats available over the Web is constantly expanding. We have already mentioned text, pictures, sounds, and movies. Some other options include:

- Three-dimensional virtual experiences based on **virtual reality modeling language—VRML—**or on a format called **QuickTime VR**
- Streaming video and audio, interactive animations (for example, Macromedia Flash)
- **Portable document format (PDF),** for preserving the format of complex documents
- Small programs, called **applets,** that are transferred to your computer and run within your browser (for instance, Java applets)

Streaming technologies

With so many formats constantly emerging, it is difficult to predict which will take hold and become standards. We think that online video and audio offer some exciting educational possibilities, and **streaming** technologies may make these formats practical. In the past, the great volume of data required to present digital video made transferring, storing, and then displaying lengthy video segments impractical. Instead of saving a large data file, the streaming approach continuously caches (temporarily stores) part of an audio or video segment for presentation on your computer. The computer needs to store only enough data to keep ahead of what is being presented at the moment. The quality of this format is improving rapidly, and extended "video on demand" seems to have many educational applications. We discuss new video formats in greater detail in the chapter entitled "Learning to Work with Images, Sound, and Video."

Plug-ins

The great variety of web formats is available because of special software applications called plug-ins. A **plug-in** is a special type of software developed to function within another software application. Within a web browser, plug-ins can perform various roles—for example, by presenting a movie within the browser window rather than in a separate window. The browser downloads a file (such as a QuickTime movie), and the plug-in presents it (in this case, plays the movie).

Plug-ins must be obtained independent of the browser. This usually means they must be downloaded from a different Internet source, which can often be accomplished using the browser. You connect to the website sponsored by the company responsible for the additional software and select an option that will send the software to your computer over the Internet. Plug-ins are almost always free and are made available to increase sales of the software used to create and serve new formats of Internet content. Sometimes when a web author uses an uncommon multimedia element (such as a VRML scene), the author will also point you to a website from which the player for that element can be obtained.

 Browsers themselves are typically free. You simply connect to the host site of the company that developed the browser and download it. You can find more information about locating and using browsers on the website that accompanies this textbook.

Keeping Track of Online Resources

Bookmarks and favorites

All browsers have the capability to store the location and perhaps even a brief description of webpages you have visited and may want to find again. Depending on the browser, this list of important URLs may be referred to as *bookmarks* (the term we use) or *favorites*. Adding a bookmark to the stored list is as simple as selecting the Add Bookmark option from one of the browser menus.

Browsers all have some system for categorizing the list of stored URLs. A common system is to allow the user to create and name file folders and then to move individual URLs into the appropriate folders. An organized system becomes helpful when you have located hundreds of sites you want to remember. Knowing how to keep track of useful sites is an essential skill in conducting Internet research.

Making Bookmarks More Informative

Changing a bookmark title

One of the long-term problems in working with bookmarks is interpreting the bookmark titles. The original bookmark takes on the title that the author has attached to the website. Authors may use uninformative titles such as "Home Page" or even forget to attach a title. Luckily, browsers allow you to replace the title provided by the author with a phrase you find more personally meaningful. For instance, when using the Firefox browser, you would select the menu item Manage Bookmarks and then choose the option Bookmark Properties. Figure 6.2 illustrates how useful it can be to rename a bookmark.

Adding descriptive information

The figure also shows how an extended description—a brief paragraph of information—can be added to the bookmark. This descriptive information provides one seldom-used advantage. When the bookmarks page is open, the information associated with each bookmark can be searched. This can be a valuable tool to any teacher who has stored hundreds or thousands of bookmarks and now wants to locate the sites related to a particular topic. With some experience, you learn to add descriptors based on personal needs. For example, if you like to keep track of interesting lesson plans you find on the Web, you might label bookmarks with descriptors such as "Ecology Lesson

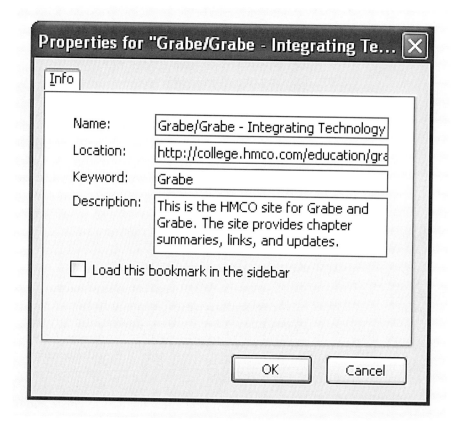

Plan," "Cell Lesson Plan," and "Mitosis Lesson Plan." Searching for "ecology" or "mitosis" would then lead you to specific bookmarks.

Exporting Bookmarks

It is possible to "export" or save a list of bookmarks as an HTML document. There are several reasons you may want to learn to do so. Once you have created an organized system of bookmarks, you should make a backup just to protect your investment of time. Another reason—a very important one for teachers and students—is to transfer your bookmark collection (or at least the part of it that relates to a particular topic) to another person.

When you consider the environment in which students use the Web, you can see the importance of this function. Students work on different machines—multiple machines in the school, or sometimes one machine at school and a family computer at home. Teachers also may do computer work both at home and at school, and they may want to prepare resources for students to use on different computers. When you save bookmarks as an HTML document, any annotations associated with the bookmarks will appear on this page.

Options for exporting bookmarks

Browsers that allow bookmarks to be exported require that the bookmark collection be open before the export and import options are available. Selecting the export option generates an HTML file that you can move about. To add such a file of bookmarks to an existing set, you would select the option with a name such as Import or Import Bookmarks. This command allows two bookmark lists to be merged.

A simple alternative to exporting the entire bookmark list is to drag individual web addresses to the desktop. This is accomplished by dragging the small icon located adjacent to the address; look for the @ sign or a small icon representing the site to be visited. The result is a very small file with a label corresponding to the webpage name. Students can collect these files in a folder and store them on a personal disk for use on another computer. You can change the file label if you feel another short phrase might be more meaningful, and you can even annotate the file if storing additional information about the web address would be helpful. When you click on this file, the web browser is launched and you are returned to the site.

Locating Information on the Web: Browsing versus Searching

The sheer magnitude of the part of the Internet known as the Web is difficult to comprehend. In fact, it may be impossible to calculate the total holdings of the Web because a significant amount of content, sometimes called the *deep Web*, is stored in large databases or is not available for unpaid public access. The automatic search techniques used to gather data on various characteristics of the Web cannot access these sites. The public Web, estimated to comprise approximately 35 percent of websites, consists of nearly 3.1 million websites, each providing access to an average of 441 webpages. The number of websites actually appears to be shrinking, but the number of pages per site is expanding (O'Neill, Lavoie, & Bennett, 2003).

Browsing a hierarchical directory

Browsing is based on a web index or directory consisting of a hierarchical system of subject headings and subheadings. As you move down through this hierarchical system, you reach a level at which links to specific sites are provided. The links have terse but descriptive titles and are sometimes accompanied by a sentence of additional information. This system is useful when you are exploring a topic and trying to gain an understanding of its ramifications.

Searching a database

Searching, the second approach, is based on the use of a **search engine,** an online database that contains information about a large number of websites. A search engine accepts a user's request or **query** and searches through its body of stored information to identify potentially useful websites. Then a list of these addresses—known as *hits*—and brief content descriptions are returned to the user. Searching is most useful when you begin with a specific goal in mind and generate a query targeted fairly precisely to this goal.

Online services cannot be neatly divided into those offering browsing and those offering search engines. Because the online services are competing to attract as many users as possible, many commercial sites now offer a combination of methods. Let's look at some examples both for browsing and for searching.

An Example of Browsing

For a demonstration of how you might browse a directory to solve an information problem, we can use Yahoo!, one of the most popular web directories. Assume you want to research the topic you are now reading about: locating information on the Web.

The Yahoo! directory

The Yahoo! homepage offers fourteen basic subject categories that are very broad: "Health," "Science," "Society and Culture," and so on. For our topic, the category "Computers and Internet" is obviously the most relevant. This link leads to a new page containing approximately forty-five new subject headings, several of them potentially useful: "Information Technology," "Internet," and "World Wide Web." As this example shows, it is sometimes difficult to know which subject to select. You will sometimes have to try several different options. Let's assume we choose the category "World Wide Web."

Selecting this link brings us to more than three dozen new subject headings. Among them is the promising topic "Searching the Web." Selecting this subject reveals a number of subheadings, including "How to Search the Web," "Indices to Web Documents," and "Search Engines and Directories." Each of these options finally produces a long list of links to individual webpages. The links are the titles from the webpages. Sometimes an additional sentence provides a better hint about the site's contents. Sometimes, though, the title is not very helpful, and you have to visit the site to see if it will be useful.

Our browsing has taken us through four levels of subject headings, and we have ended up with three groups of links to webpages. To put what we have accomplished into perspective, Yahoo! is subdivided into at least 25,000 categories that link to more than 3 million websites. The procedure we described did not require a great deal of time, and it located a large number of informative websites appropriate to our initial question.

As you can see, browsing in a well-organized system can be quite productive, and we encourage you to try the process on your own.

Types of Search Services

There are many search engines bidding for your attention. Universities maintain a few experimental ones as part of research projects, but most are commercial. This does not mean that you have to pay to use them. As soon as you connect to a commercial search engine, you will realize that it is supported by advertising dollars. You have to maneuver around the colorful product displays to get your work done.

Differences among search services

The major services all offer some form of a searchable database, but they differ in how sites are added to the database and what information about each site is stored in the database. New servers and new webpages may become known to the online service through nominations received from the public (mostly from people who are themselves page authors). Alternatively, the service can identify new sites by using a software *robot* (also called a *bot, spider,* or *crawler*) that continually roams the Internet looking for new servers and new pages.

Web librarians—people who examine web documents and classify material they think might be useful—can generate the information stored in the database. Or, as an alternative, the service can use indexing software that automatically examines designated parts of webpages and identifies keywords. Some indexing software generates keywords by examining a limited amount of information, such as the page title and the first hundred words of text. Other indexing software reads and processes *all* of the text found on each webpage.

The indexing process is especially important, and it accounts for some noticeable differences among the search services. For example, computerized indexing methods are less expensive than web librarians and generate larger databases. Also, indexing methods that use the entire webpage link more descriptive terms with each page. Therefore, searching with a service that has built its database from computerized searches of entire webpages tends to generate a longer list of sites to examine. In some cases, this may be an advantage. In other cases, however, you may find it much more useful to examine a list of ten quality sites rather than a list of one hundred sites that vary greatly in quality.

Because of the differences among search services, you will want to become familiar with several of them. The following sections offer some guidance.

Search Engine and Directory Combinations

Several search services are based on a cataloging system very much like that maintained by conventional libraries. Human editors examine web material and organize content within what they consider to be a useful classification system. You can browse the classification system or search the cataloged material using key terms.

Browsing and searching combined

You can also use a combination of browsing and searching to improve the quality of your search, a unique advantage of this type of service. Let's say you want to learn more about the type of spider that wanders about the Web searching for new webpages. If you were to connect to Yahoo! and search for "spider" from the homepage, you would find several hundred sites, including pages that address a cartoon character, a type of car, eight-legged arthropods, as well as the Internet search robot. However, if you first select the Yahoo! subject heading "Computers and Internet" and then perform the same search in this category alone, the return would be approximately fifty links, nearly all of them appropriate to the topic of interest.

This type of search system provides access to less of the Web than do search services that rely on a computer-generated database, but it might be argued that the overall quality of material is a little higher. Examples of this type of search service are Yahoo! and the Open Directory Project.

Index Search Engines

Index search engines rely on a computer-generated index of the contents of websites. Thankfully, the techniques used are more sophisticated than a simple list of all the webpages containing a specific word. Some form of proprietary artificial intelligence system is used to determine which webpages are most relevant to your query. For example, search engines that index entire webpages use variables such as how many times keywords are mentioned in an article and how close to the top of a document a keyword appears. When the search engine responds to your query with a list of sites, the ones deemed most relevant appear at the top of the list.

Google: an index
search engine

Google, a search engine claiming to offer a database of more than 8 billion webpages, has a unique method for ranking the sites located during a web search. Google's data-gathering process takes into account not only the information appearing on webpages but also the links among webpages. A simple way of explaining the approach is that links to a webpage are counted as votes for the value of that webpage. The assumption is that those who create webpages will link their pages to other content the authors feel is useful. Google uses this "collective intelligence" as a way to order the listing of sites found during a web search. The sites at the top of the list generated by a query are the most frequently referenced and are assumed to be of more general value.

Index search engines tend to provide access to huge numbers of webpages. Google found more than 21 million sites for the search term "spider." Other examples of this type of search service are Yahoo! and MSN Search.

Meta-Index Searches

Combining results
from several search
engines

Some search tools activate and cross-reference the results from several search engines. These meta-index searches take a little longer because various individual searches must be initiated, the results integrated, and duplicates eliminated. However, a meta-index search does not accumulate all the sites generated by all of the search engines. To keep things more manageable, the search tool takes only the top ten to fifty sites generated by each search engine.

You might suppose that a meta-index search would always be the most productive. However, as you'll see later in this chapter, search engines offer certain advanced search methods that can help you in many situations, and these methods differ from one engine to another. For this reason, meta-index search tools can use only basic search procedures, consisting of combinations of keywords. Examples of this type of search service are MetaCrawler and Search.com.

Which Type of Search Engine Should I Use?

Every experienced user of the Web seems to have an opinion about which search engine is most useful. From time to time, articles in computer magazines compare the different search engines on a standard set of search tasks. Despite authors' recommendations based on these analyses, the actual search data show that search engines differ in effectiveness from one assignment to another. If anything, reading such articles has caused us to try different search engines than we might normally employ.

The value of trying
multiple search
engines

We suggest that you too take the time to explore several search engines to gain some familiarity to make your own decisions. At the end of the chapter, we explain how you can locate the search services we have mentioned and several more. Whenever the results from your favorite search engine are disappointing, it is worth trying both a different engine and a different combination of search terms.

Conducting a Search

Web search engines usually present users with a very simple and easy-to-use interface. An unfortunate consequence is that many users never really learn to take advantage of the powerful search features that are available. It is so easy just to type something into the little text field, click Submit, and see what you get. While this often works just fine, some types of searches require a more sophisticated approach, and it is useful to know how to employ more advanced search techniques.

Why advanced searches are useful

Here is an example. Educators in our state paid special attention to the bicentennial of Lewis and Clark's journey of discovery because the explorers spent so much time in North Dakota. Educators and students in the state created webpages (containing lesson plans, student projects) related to this celebration. Consider how we might search for these webpages. A search using a phrase such as "Lewis and Clark in North Dakota" generates more than 800,000 pages. Because the type of material we are searching for was created by teachers and students and is seldom used as a resource by other widely viewed sites, the links to these pages are not likely to appear near the top of the list returned by a general search. This is the type of situation in which advanced search techniques become useful.

Many of the search services we describe offer easy ways to conduct advanced searches. To get to these advanced search options, look for a link on the search site homepage with a label such as "Advanced Search."

How to perform an advanced search

The advanced search options available through HotBot will serve as our example. The top portion of the HotBot advanced search page is shown in Figure 6.3. An advanced search allows you to specify the desired target in a more precise way, by adding multiple filters to a basic search. As you can see in Figure 6.3, we modified our general search "Lewis and Clark" by adding a "date" filter to limit the results to pages created within the last two years and a "domain" filter to limit the results to pages with a server address ending in k12.nd.us (designating a North Dakota K–12 site). This search generates just 210 hits—a list that is much more manageable and appropriate to our specialized goal.

HotBot offers several other types of filters. The "word" filters allow searches to be limited by the presence or absence of words. For example, by adding the words "lesson plan" as a word filter, the "Lewis and Clark" search was narrowed to five hits containing lesson plans. A word filter can be applied as any of the words, all of the words, none of the words, or an exact phrase. Searches can be filtered to generate pages in a specified language and containing designated content types (for instance, video, images). For example, a "Lewis and Clark" search might be modified to locate images of the Shoshone guide Sacajawea by adding a contents filter for image and a word filter for "Sacajawea."

Using the Web in Your Classroom

The skills associated with the use of a web browser and search engine are necessary to access information on the Web. Now what? What should students be doing now that they have access to the vast and varied resources of the Web?

Answering this question is not easy. Rather than starting from a purely idealistic position, we begin with an analysis of the challenges teachers face in integrating Internet tasks in the classroom. The rest of the chapter covers a

FIGURE 6.3

Some Search Options Available from the HotBot Advanced Search Form

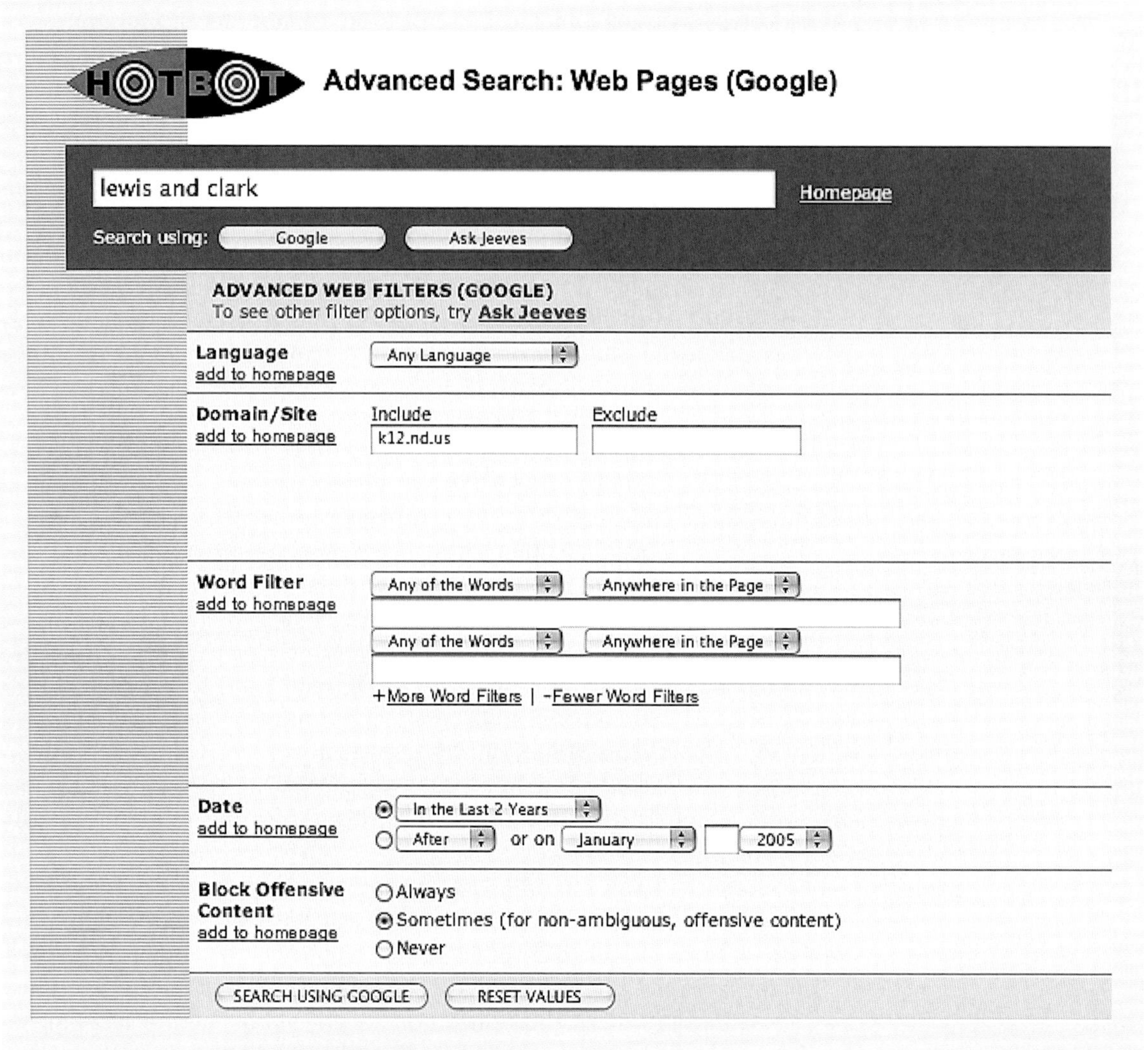

range of learning tasks that take advantage of Internet resources with suggestions for how the tasks can be implemented in ways that acknowledge the instructional challenges that are raised here.

How the Internet may challenge teachers' comfort zone

Deviating from tradition incurs a certain amount of stress. Attempting to incorporate use of the Internet into instruction can make additional demands on pedagogical content knowledge in ways that push some educators beyond their comfort zones (Wallace, 2004). **Pedagogical content knowledge** refers to those instructional skills that can be unique to the teaching of - discipline-specific knowledge and skills. Educators face four continuing challenges to their pedagogical content knowledge: (1) knowing the subject matter, (2) knowing what students know and can do that is relevant to the knowledge to be taught, (3) keeping track of the progress students are making, and (4) presenting learning experiences in ways that coherently link ideas and skills.

With traditional instruction, commercial curriculum materials and textbooks can be used to reduce the demands on a teacher's personal knowledge. Teachers tend to assume they can master the content and skills emphasized by the books they use. They also assume that the material presented in these books is written at a level appropriate to their students, is based on the standards and benchmarks that students are expected to address (assuming the curriculum materials are recent), and introduces ideas and skills in an order supported by expert opinion. By requiring students to complete readings and activities from these textbooks and using recommended questions or techniques for assessing understanding, teachers can track how well students can do what experts expect students to be able to do.

Reliability and other challenges

In contrast to commercial instructional materials, some Internet resources—namely, primary sources—are more up-to-date and wide-ranging, but also sometimes unreliable and unstable. Many of them were not prepared as instructional resources or developed for younger learners. Resources may not consider all sides of important issues or be linked to other resources in ways that provide context or present implications. Sometimes sites are not maintained, and links embedded within the sites no longer function. Wallace (2004) suggests that such realities may present teachers with challenges they do not encounter with traditional instructional materials. For example, what happens when students locate online information sources that are outside the teacher's existing knowledge base? Is this information merely something the instructor is not aware of, or is it faulty information? How does the teacher integrate online resources with more traditional instructional materials? How does the teacher orchestrate instruction when different students have located different online information sources and studied different content that may come from different perspectives? How should student learning be evaluated when students have learned different things?

Perhaps a productive way to frame the issue we are raising is to ask the question, To what extent do you want to function in the role of an instructional designer? One answer to this question may lie in the data we presented earlier (see the chapter entitled "Key Themes for Using Technology in Your Classroom") indicating that new teachers are less likely than more experienced teachers to involve their students in learning with technology. These data may indicate that the collective challenges facing many beginning teachers encourage reliance on prepackaged materials that are both efficient and "safe."

Teachers need not rely totally on traditional commercial resources. The remaining material in this chapter outlines a range of Internet approaches that are useful in the classroom. Some applications clearly require more of the teacher than others, but some of the more adventuresome applications also involve students in unique learning tasks.

The rest of this chapter addresses three topics we feel can help you make decisions about using web resources in your classroom:

1. How can web information be categorized for use as instructional resources? We present a category system that differentiates types of web

Helping students locate and evaluate information on the World Wide Web can sometimes challenge a teacher's content knowledge. "Information problem solving" can help.

content and identifies corresponding roles to be played by teacher and student.

2. Most content on the Web is not designed to serve an instructional purpose and might best be described as information, primary source material, or data. We discuss what is involved in the process of working with and learning from such raw resources, using the general approach of information problem solving.

3. Finally, we provide some suggestions for classroom projects involving web resources. We present a basic approach that can be applied across many grade levels and content areas.

Categories of Web Resources

Categorizing Internet resources

The Internet—particularly the large body of information available through the Web—is a tremendous educational resource. The quantity and breadth of what can be explored is impressive, and educators should be excited by the potential. To help you think through some of the different approaches to instruction that might be taken, we propose a simple category system, shown in Table 6.1, that identifies types of educational resources that can be found on the Internet. Think of the categories as points along a continuum differentiated in terms of the amount and type of involvement expected of the classroom teacher. Our purpose is to create a point of departure for discussing how teacher and student activities might vary when learning from different types of resources.

TABLE 6.1

Categories of Instructional Resources Found on the Internet and Related Teacher Responsibilities

	Online Tutorial	Instructional Resource	Primary Source
Description	Resource takes responsibility for instruction.	Resource outlines activity but does not provide instruction.	Resource provides raw materials on which learning activity might be based.
Teacher role	Teacher troubleshoots when student encounters problem.	Teacher is responsible for facilitating and evaluating learning.	Teacher locates source, creates related activity, facilitates and evaluates learning.
Examples	Online tutorial; online class.	Online curriculum activities.	Teacher-created WebQuest based on general-purpose webpages.

Online Tutorials

The online equivalent of a computer-based tutorial, an **online tutorial,** is located at one extreme end of the continuum. The Internet now makes complete courses—even complete degrees—available. Here we focus, however, on learning activities rather than courses.

Characteristics of online tutorials

Online tutorials are designed for independent learning with well-integrated learning sources, explanatory segments, and evaluation activities. Most activities of this type are likely to be available through subscription services—companies that provide educational resources as a business. Of course, any educational use of technology may shortchange learners on at least one of the components of instruction (presentation, guidance, extended practice, and evaluation). This is why we suggest that the classroom teacher should be involved as a troubleshooter when students are using online tutorials.

Instructional Resources

Lesson resources for a teacher to implement

Instructional resources are at the midpoint of our continuum. Internet resources of this type provide the components of a learning activity but leave the teacher responsible for implementation and evaluation. Someone else has identified the lesson goals, located and developed the information resources, proposed learning tasks related to lesson goals, and, in some cases, arranged online experiences to support the classroom learning activities. Often, the site provides possible evaluation rubrics (guidelines) as well. The teacher clearly is not starting from scratch; nor is the teacher turning control of the learning experience over to the organization responsible for the resources.

Primary Sources

Our emphasis in this chapter is really on the end of our continuum—primary sources—because this final resource category provides the opportunity to take advantage of a tremendous amount of Internet content and because

Focus

Doing History: Supporting History Teachers in Promoting Historical Inquiry

It is probably fair to claim that not all content areas receive the same priority in schools. For example, contrast the study of history with that of language arts and mathematics in elementary school and with mathematics and science in middle and high school. The time dedicated to the content area in a typical school day, the amount of targeted federal funding available, and whether the content area is evaluated on "high stakes" tests would be indicators of the priority schools place on each subject area.

There may be a number of reasons for the fact that not all content areas receive the same attention. Some (reading, writing, mathematics) may be regarded as more central because they provide the basis for developing a wide range of other academic knowledge and skills. It would be difficult to study history without a solid foundation in reading and writing. Other content areas have been linked systematically with the goal of maintaining a competitive national advantage in the international economy. To decision makers, an emphasis on science and mathematics appears to be essential for achieving this goal.

Those interested in the teaching of history face some other challenges. Historians have long grappled with the issue of what the most fundamental goals of teaching history in K–12 classrooms should be. Some see history in schools as the vehicle for preserving traditional versions of the past and developing patriotism. Others see the teaching of history more in terms of developing the skills necessary to perform historical inquiry: namely, analyzing and interpreting the past by rigorously weighing and judging evidence from a variety of original sources. Not only do these conflicting agendas emphasize different knowledge and skills, but the second viewpoint argues that the first tends to favor an official history that ignores both multiple perspectives and the reinterpretations brought on by the application of new and more sophisticated methods of inquiry. This controversy is not new; in the history of teaching history, it goes back more than one hundred years (Nash, Crabtree, & Dunn, 1997).

Without getting into the controversial issue of whether the teaching of history perpetuates falsehoods and stereotypes, it may be enough to claim that what most students learn about history is highly factual in nature, and that the facts tend to be learned in a manner that gives students little insight into the causal links among the facts they happen to remember. Students fail to grasp what historians focus on the most: explanations for why and how historical events unfolded (McKeown & Beck, 1990).

A case can be made that the study of history offers unique opportunities to develop higher-order critical thinking skills (see the chapter entitled "Meaningful Learning in an Information Age"). Historical inquiry involves reasoning that is less dependent on the kinds of quantitative data that typify math and science. It also recognizes that different individuals and groups experience history differently and thus have different perspectives. Many important issues that face all of us require skill in conceptualizing ill-defined problems, carefully analyzing nonquantitative information, recognizing bias in the perspectives of oneself and others, and generating logical arguments for positions when certainty is impossible (Voss, Carretero, Kennet, & Silfies, 1994). However, in the typical approach to teaching history, there is a limited emphasis on historical inquiry.

History teachers who want to involve students in historical inquiry face the kinds of challenges we discussed earlier. Although structuring the history course around a textbook would be less demanding, the Internet does offer opportunities for involving students with historical documents and artifacts and for supporting teachers who want to involve students in inquiry activities. Online tutorials, instructional resources, and primary sources are available. The *WebQuest,* a strategy for structuring student inquiry projects that we discuss later in this chapter, offers a great approach for managing student inquiry. If you are interested in teaching history or see similar opportunities for developing higher-order thinking skills in your particular content area, we hope the classroom examples presented in this chapter are helpful.

Website: Engaging Students in American History

With funding from a Department of Education "Teaching American History" grant, the school district in our community has developed a website that provides instructional resources for history teachers. The resources created through this project have been added to the vast collection of material made available by other commercial and private organizations; examples are included on the website that accompanies this textbook. Teachers seeking ways to supplement their existing collection of resources will find many great opportunities on the Internet.

The collection of lesson plans provided through the Engaging Students in American History website can be searched by topic, grade level, time period, or standard. The identification of learning activities appropriate for an age group or to suit required standards addresses the challenges we discuss in the section "Using the Web in Your Classroom." The learning activities are presented as lesson plans supported with links to several categories of additional resources (teacher resources, student resources, general bibliography, suggestions for modifications, and so on). Most of the resources are primary and secondary sources (text documents, images, audio segments) that can be accessed online. Selecting the "printer-friendly versions" results in the generation of a webpage integrating various resources into a single document that can be printed from the browser or saved to a computer. The resources are available to anyone connecting to the site. Participants in the grant-funded project are provided access to some additional tools that allow them to customize and store lessons for delivery to students.

The site offers instructors several kinds of support. Some information is provided to help instructors develop knowledge appropriate to the topic of

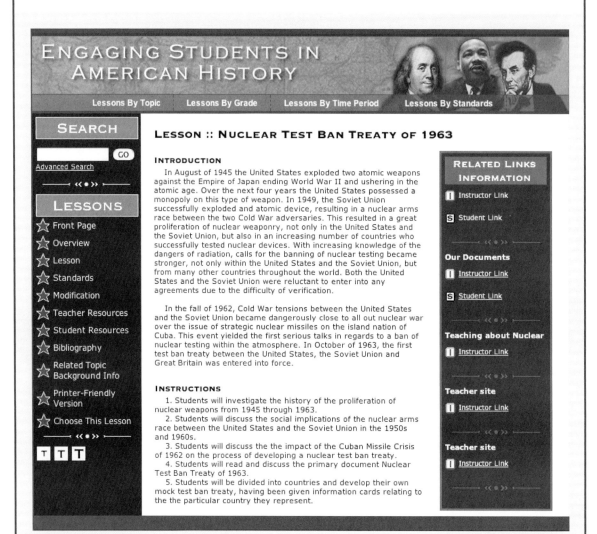

FIGURE 6.4

Instructional Resources from Engaging Students in American History Web Site

the lesson and to connect the main topic addressed by the lesson with a larger context. For example, the lesson shown in Figure 6.4 places the nuclear test ban treaty of 1963 within the framework of the Cold War. The site also suggests resources that students might use to complete the lesson assignment (such as a link to an image of the original treaty from the Library of Congress).

working with this content engages learners in unique and authentic information processing activities.

Primary sources are raw information sources, not necessarily developed to meet educational needs or even to provide a fair or unbiased treatment of a particular issue. Many sources of information we encounter daily fall into this category. Newsmagazine articles (*Newsweek, Time*), newspaper articles (*New York Times*), and encyclopedia entries qualify, and so do interviews that students might conduct with members of their community. Most library books—even some of the ones in school libraries—are not specifically packaged to meet educational goals. The online equivalents of commercial news sources are becoming more and more common in school libraries (see "Keeping Current" to learn more).

Raw information sources

Practitioners of many disciplines work with primary sources. Historians work with information in the form of photographs, documents, maps, diaries, and similar artifacts. Biologists have access to preserved specimens and genetic maps. Meteorologists can tap databases of weather data from around the world. Social scientists have access to census information and the archived data from various surveys. More and more of these data sources are being digitized, and many are available for public access through the Web (see "Keeping Current" to learn more). Then, of course, there are the millions of free World Wide Web pages and downloadable files that the first part of this chapter was intended to help you learn to search and access. Such raw information sources are typically developed independent of any curriculum standards and often not with the K–12 age group in mind.

Teachers must orchestrate how students in their classes will use these web resources. They might require that students "study" specific web resources (for example, visit specific URLs). Working with the Web in this way might provide an **incremental advantage** over existing practices in that students have access to many more resources and can access these resources more efficiently than is now the case, but this method does not offer a **transformational advantage**—an alternative approach to student learning. Student experiences would still emphasize similar classroom activities and the same cognitive skills, even without the Internet. The transformational advantage of Internet activities would be realized if students were engaged in *different* learning activities emphasizing cognitive skills that have some *unique* value. These skills might be unique in emphasizing new areas, such as information literacy, or in finding ways to target skills that have always been valued but are difficult to develop in some content areas, such as critical thinking and problem solving.

A transformational advantage in learning

In our view, to develop the search, inquiry, and critical thinking skills necessary to solve the problems they encounter in both school and daily life, students need more opportunities to work with information in challenging ways. To this end, we think students would benefit from more tasks requiring (1) that they use primary sources rather than prepackaged instructional resources and (2) that they apply information from these primary sources in solving authentic information problems.

The next section explores strategies that will help you guide your students in using the Web for this purpose.

Video Case

For more about using online primary sources to teach history, watch the HM Video Case entitled *Integrating Internet Research. High School Social Studies*. You've already learned that educators differ in their stated goals for teaching history. What goals does high school teacher Elizabeth Sweeney bring to her class?

Keeping Current

Subscription Information Services

Online commercial information services are becoming more and more common. These services range from providers offering the online equivalent of a library (full-text versions of many books, magazines, and newspapers) to the online version of a single source, such as a major newspaper.

Schools purchase access to such services because of the quantity and selection of materials, the search tools, and the reasonable cost. The quantity of information available is impressive. The resources available from each of the general services vary, but it is common to have access to the full-text version of hundreds of magazines and newspapers, maps, and photo collections. Some sites provide access to news wire services. The resources are selected to meet the information needs of educational institutions, and the search features give students important aids in finding the information they need. Although schools must pay for access, the cost is typically less than that of subscribing to several newspapers and magazines.

You can find additional information about subscription services in "Resources to Expand Your Knowledge Base" at the end of this chapter, and on the website that accompanies this textbook.

Strategies for Using Primary Sources on the Web

Information problem solving

Many terms are used to describe the skills needed to function in an information-rich society. We are accustomed to the term *literacy* being used in reference to skills associated with print materials. Some have used the phrase *media literacy* to indicate that learners need to be able to understand and evaluate the message from several types of media (print, TV, radio) (Johnson, 2001), and *digital literacy* has been used to target the special demands of gleaning information from the Internet (Gilster, 1997). *Information literacy* (Doyle, 1999) would seem the most general of this family of similar concepts.

Our own preference is to take a slightly different perspective. The applied skills students will need to locate, interpret, and apply information to authentic inquiry tasks can be defined as *information problem solving*. To help you better understand information problem solving and the skills students must develop to become effective information problem solvers, we turn to a model known as the Big Six.

The Big Six

Many life tasks require information problem solving.

The **Big Six** is a clearly articulated and interrelated set of skills. Because of their concreteness, these skills provide an especially useful way of conceptualizing—and teaching—the skills necessary to use the Web as a tool for inquiry.

Focus

Issues in Classroom Use of Web Resources

A recent National School Board Association publication addressed the importance of locating "quality" websites and recommended that educators and students develop search and evaluation skills to avoid becoming "overwhelmed by the pointless, the prurient, and the perilous" (Abdal-Haqq, 2001). We could point to many articles, chapters, and books that combine comments on the tremendous educational potential of the Internet with similar cautions regarding the variable quality and appropriateness of some online information. It is a confusing combination of messages that may leave educators wondering whether web resources have a place in the classroom.

The real world of information has never been a perfect place. There have always been hucksters selling copper bracelets to cure arthritis and scholars who have somehow parlayed their admitted scientific expertise in one area into an opportunity to publish pseudoscientific or outrageous positions on completely unrelated topics. Misleading and inaccurate information sources did not originate with the Internet. Extreme examples, such as websites denying the reality of the Holocaust or explaining the virtues of the Aryan Brotherhood, generate concern among parents and educators, but the problem of slanted, deceptive, or self-serving communication is much more general. For young people, the pervasive influence of television and magazine advertising in shaping inappropriate values and encouraging pointless consumerism represents a more serious "information" problem. Many of the information sources we encounter outside the school environment are intended to persuade us to make certain consumer, political, or personal decisions, and the individuals or organizations offering this information have no obligation to be objective or fair.

To convince you to allow students to venture into the world of online information as part of learning tasks and to use such experiences to help them learn to think critically about information sources, we offer two further observations:

1. Students already consistently use the Internet as a source for information. A recent survey of twelve- to seventeen-year-olds with Internet access indicated that 71 percent claimed to have used the Internet as the major source for their most recent school project (Levin & Arafeh, 2002).
2. Students are already deluged with information from many unofficial sources and should learn to think critically about what they see and hear. Students in grades 7–12 with Internet access at home report spending seven hours a week online (Doherty & Orlofsky, 2001). The time they spend exploring the Web is distributed across a broad range of topics. Some of the most frequently accessed content involves topics such as popular culture (music, entertainment) and personal issues (relationships, fashion). Students are heavily involved with content that was not developed with educational goals in mind (Center for Media Education, 2001).

> In sum, students live in a world filled with information they encounter in many forms and from many sources. To interpret this welter of information, they need to develop good critical thinking skills. Activities and projects that involve primary web sources can be an excellent way to guide them in their development.

The individual skills comprising this approach enable a learner to identify the nature of an information problem; locate, process, organize, and apply information resources to generate a solution; and finally, evaluate the success of this solution (Eisenberg & Berkowitz, 1990).

The originators of the Big Six have always argued that many life tasks require these skills. Problems such as figuring out how to get from one location to another using the subway system in a strange city or even determining which movie you might find most enjoyable on a Saturday evening are commonly solved through the acquisition and processing of information. Critical thinking and decision-making skills that might apply in making an informed decision to purchase one product instead of another or to vote for one candidate rather than another also involve the gathering and evaluation of information. Information problem solving is a great way to understand the research activities of scientists, historians, and economists. All of these examples involve gathering, interpreting, and acting on information. Let's look in more detail at the skills involved in this useful model.

The Big Six skills

The six interrelated information processing skills include:

1. *Task definition.* Define the problem, and identify information resources needed to solve it.
2. *Information-seeking strategies.* Identify the range of possible information resources, and prioritize those resources for investigation.
3. *Location and access.* Find the information sources and the relevant information within them.
4. *Use of information.* Process (read, view) the information, and extract relevant ideas.
5. *Synthesis.* Organize and create a product (a decision, a paper) from the core ideas.
6. *Evaluation.* Consider the product and the effectiveness of the problem-solving process.

The Big Six skills can also be expressed as a series of questions (Jansen & Culpepper, 1996):

1. What needs to be done?
2. What can I use to find what I need?
3. Where can I find what I need?
4. What information can I use?
5. How can I put my information together?
6. How will I know if I did my job well?

Focus

Information Literacy Standards

Information Literacy Standards have been proposed to identify crucial skills needed by independent learners (American Library Association & Association for Educational Communications and Technology, 1998). The following standards deal specifically with information literacy goals:

Standard 1: The student who is information literate accesses information efficiently and effectively.

Standard 2: The student who is information literate evaluates information critically and competently.

Standard 3: The student who is information literate uses information accurately and creatively.

Source: From *Information Power: Building Partnerships for Learning* by American Association of School Librarians and Association for Educational Communications and Technology. Copyright © 1998 American Library Association and Association for Educational Communication and Technology. Reprinted by permission of the American Library Association. Available: **http://www.infolit.org/definitions/9standards.htm.**

You may already have some experience in applying these skills at your college library and in many of your college classes. How would you find a book containing information about the possible relationship between the destruction of the rain forest and global warming? How would you use this information as part of a paper advocating international subsidies for alternative economic ventures in countries likely to resort to massive deforestation?

Although developing information problem-solving skills has always been part of a solid education, technology provides new opportunities for access, manipulation, and expression that should increase the attention paid to these skills and broaden how educators think about them.

The Big Six and the Internet

Let's examine three critical stages of the Big Six to determine how they apply to web-based inquiry.

Information Seeking on the Internet

We want students to consider Internet sources among the various information sources that might be used to address a problem. Before they do so, students have to know that the teachers who will evaluate their work will respect their use of such resources. You might contemplate your own experiences in this respect. When you receive a class assignment, do you include the Web among other possibilities, such as visiting the library to search for relevant books or journal articles? Has your approach changed in the past few years? How do your instructors react?

Students also need to achieve a certain familiarity with the various information resources available on the Internet. One obvious instructional approach is to *require* that some problems be handled using Internet resources. However, after familiarity has been achieved, students should also be able to evaluate the strengths and weaknesses of online resources and use them when appropriate to the task.

Guiding students in online information seeking

In guiding students at this stage, you will have to consider whether to point students toward resources you select or that others have screened, to allow them to find their own resources, or perhaps to require some combination of prescribed and self-selected resources. In the long run, we feel students need to be prepared to use both types of resources, and at some point your role as teacher will include helping your students become capable of locating and evaluating resources. In a structured approach proposed by McKenzie (1997), students first use carefully selected commercial resources (material provided through subscription services), then explore and synthesize web resources selected by the classroom instructor. In this way, students gain a more formal and traditional background in a subject before considering resources that have not been vetted with the same editorial scrutiny.

Locating and Accessing Internet Resources

We would equate *locating and accessing* with some of the processes we outline earlier in this chapter—using a directory or search engine, conducting efficient searches, quickly examining sites, and bookmarking potentially useful sites for later use. The development of these skills takes some time. Later in this chapter, we describe a scaffolded curriculum project called a WebQuest that can be used to involve students in content-appropriate web projects and to support the development of search and evaluation skills.

The intention in any scaffolded task, as we mention in the chapter entitled "Meaningful Learning in an Information Age," is to assist students so that they can work on meaningful tasks and then to turn more and more of the responsibility over to the learners as they grow more proficient. You can recognize this process in grade-to-grade changes in traditional information-intensive projects. A third-grade teacher who wanted students to complete a project on butterflies would likely bring in appropriate resources from the school library. A high-school biology teacher, on the other hand, would likely send students to the library to locate their own resources. In the transition years, classroom teachers and librarians work with students to develop the skills necessary to identify and access appropriate resources.

Helping students develop Internet search skills

The same kind of transition and continual instruction should be applied to the development of Internet search skills. Students need to be introduced gradually to various search tools and procedures. Although activities of this type can be taught in an isolated fashion (as in Internet treasure hunts, in which search skills are taught by requiring students to answer unrelated trivia questions), we prefer integrating instruction and learning within a more authentic task. As part of an inquiry project, students might be directed to explore the use of several search engines and different search strategies. Students would document their results and discuss with other class members the tools and strategies they found to be most productive. Resources that seem particularly useful can then be added to the list of required resources the teacher has already identified. With experience, students should be able to take total responsibility for some projects.

Using Internet Information

At the stage of *using information,* students carefully process the web resources they have located and then extract the information that is important to the problem-solving task. This part of the process is roughly equivalent to traditional reading and taking notes. Because the resources exist in a digital format and are Internet-based, the skills involved may be slightly different, however. For example, web resources typically exist as hypermedia rather than in the linear format found in books. Working through material in which you can make decisions about the order in which you explore the content requires some experience. It can be helpful to have different students compare what they have learned from the same website to assist them in summarizing what the document had to say.

Collecting information from the Internet

Students can take notes from online resources using traditional paper-and-pencil methods. However, relevant information (text and images) can also be collected and stored using technology. Students can learn to copy critical text segments and images from the online document and paste this information into a word processing document to be saved or printed. Students do need to appreciate the copyright issues that govern this behavior, and they must provide proper credit to the original source when they use the information in a school product.

Educators are legitimately concerned that the ease with which computers allow information to be copied will contribute to plagiarism. Some fear that they may be unable to detect when students use copied material in their projects. Probably the best defense against such abuse is to take a proactive approach—clearly explain how students are to make use of intellectual property they locate online and perhaps require that students demonstrate how they have used their notes and the material they have extracted to create their own projects.

Judging the quality of information obtained online is a special concern. If you have chosen the sites for your students, you likely have ignored sites you feel would be unreliable. But as students do more of their own exploring, they must be prepared to carefully evaluate what they encounter. Part of using information should include rejecting what is unreliable or at least differentiating opinions that appear to be contrary to the most commonly held positions. The freedom the Internet offers to express personal opinion and the lack of editorial oversight for many sites make critical thinking skills essential.

Critical thinking, as we indicate earlier in this book, requires a combination of intentions, dispositions, and skills. Learners must be willing to reflect

Focus

Citing Internet Sources

Research is one of the most common reasons that secondary and elementary students use the Internet. Students need to learn to provide citations for Internet resources just as they cite the sources of other information. Some believe that citing Internet sources is especially important because the nature of the Internet makes it so easy to copy and paste material. Providing accurate citations makes students aware of their responsibilities and provides teachers a way to follow up on the resources students have used (American Psychological Association, 2001).

Here is a basic citation format that is widely considered acceptable:

Author/editor. (Year). *Title* (edition). Producer (optional). Retrieved [access date] from Protocol (for example, FTP, HTTP)://Site/Path/File.

The following is a sample citation in this format:

American Psychological Association (2001). *Publication manual* (5th ed.). Retrieved November 27, 2004, from http:www.apastyle.org/elecgeneral.html.

on information they encounter, have a desire to understand, and consider options and opinions with an open mind. Some of the skills that apply include the following (Beyer, 1988; Ennis, 1987):

Types of critical thinking skills needed

- Analyzing arguments
- Differentiating verifiable facts from personal beliefs
- Identifying the perspective or bias of a source
- Identifying unstated assumptions
- Detecting critical ambiguities
- Evaluating the inductive or deductive logic used in reaching a conclusion

The question of evaluating Internet information is important enough that we explore it further in the next section.

Evaluating Web Information

Assuming you have accepted our claims that the quality of Internet information is both a concern and an opportunity, how can you maximize your students' opportunities for authentic inquiry while minimizing the risk that they will be seriously misled? Let's consider the tools and criteria for screening web sources.

Editorial Review and Screening of Internet Resources

Filtering software

While there are few barriers to making information available on the Web, there are ways to screen or filter information that students access. Many schools have invested in filtering software. This software, which works primarily by refusing to allow browsers to access material from certain targeted sites, is useful as a way to block access to objectionable material. The companies selling this software continually update their list of potentially offensive sites and make these revised lists available to schools that have purchased the software.

Online dangers and coping mechanisms are considered in greater detail in the chapter entitled "Responsible Use of Technology." Our focus here is on the more general issues of information quality and educational suitability. For these purposes, blocking objectionable sites is not sufficient. If you want your students to access only educationally appropriate material, you can use the resources described in the following sections.

Searching a Database of Reviewed Sites

Databases screened for K–12 users

In our description of Internet directories, we explain that directories are compiled and organized by human editors and that the online database developed from this review process is often searchable. In some cases, the selection process includes the criterion that the resource must be appropriate for K–12 students. Searchable databases of web resources are provided as a service by commercial search sites (such as Ask Jeeves for Kids and Yahooligans!) and sometimes as the product of a funded program to identify web resources for K–12 students (for instance, KidsClick!).

Using Resources Identified by an Educational Portal

The basic idea of a *portal* is to consolidate access to important information resources and services within a single online location. The intent is to encourage users to connect to a single site that provides them with what they need to do their work and meet their personal needs. Commercial sites such as Yahoo! and America Online would like you to use them as a portal because their business model depends on a high volume of users. An educational portal attempts to achieve somewhat the same objectives for educational resources and tasks.

Educational portals

Some educational portals try to offer such valuable resources that school districts will pay a subscription fee for students and teachers to have access. Others are subsidized by advertising, federal grants, or organizations willing to support educational services. Educational portals may either generate educational materials or develop lists of existing online resources appropriate for educational purposes. Either way, it is in the best interest of educational portals to be associated with quality web content. A list of educational portals is provided at the end of this chapter. Examples include ProQuest K–12 and Blue Web'n.

Digitized Primary Sources from Reputable Institutions

If the Internet were not available, what might classroom teachers use as primary sources? Obviously, it would depend on the subject area, but teachers would likely use traditional library resources such as books, newspapers, and magazines. History teachers might take their students to a local museum to examine artifacts, and biology teachers might take their students to a zoo. Teachers probably trust the credibility of these resources because of the sponsorship of a reputable institution (publisher, museum, zoo).

Resources from major institutions

Many such reputable institutions are working to make their resources available through the Internet. Most major newspapers and many magazines offer their content directly or through subscription services. For example, OnlineNewspapers.com offers links to thousands of newspapers throughout the world, providing many sources that are probably not available in your school library. If your class is studying the weather, you can access weather maps, satellite images, data such as pressure, wind direction, temperature, and much more directly from the National Weather Service (**http://weather.gov/**). Major museums are also offering digitized versions of resources for public inspection. The Smithsonian's American Memories Collection is a great example. Ironically, you can view many resources online that you would not have access to if you were to visit the museums.

The commitment to expanding access to digital data and artifacts is going to increase. The National Science Foundation is putting millions of dollars into the Digital Libraries Initiative to make a wide range of resources freely available. Everyone from university scholars to fourth-grade students will have access.

So, one effective strategy for locating quality information resources is to connect through websites maintained by institutions or organizations you already trust. You can find information on these sites in "Resources to Expand Your Knowledge Base" at the end of this chapter, and on the website that accompanies this textbook.

Making Your Own Decisions

How do you decide?

For a typical project you will find many useful resources available through the options just described. However, reviews exist for only a small proportion of Internet content, and in many cases you may want to go beyond the pre-screened sources. In such cases, how can you decide which websites to trust?

Although evaluating information is a subjective process, the following criteria can be helpful. Besides using these criteria yourself, you can teach them to your students as part of the critical thinking that ought to be applied to any information resource.

Who Is the Author?

The primary question in evaluating a resource is: Who is responsible for this information? A variant of this question, which all too often applies to web resources, is: Does *anyone* claim authorship of this information? The identity of the author is useful in establishing the credibility of the information.

Looking for information about the author

Often, the author's name on a webpage also functions as a link to the author's homepage. Information on the homepage or perhaps on the original document may indicate the author's affiliation with an institution or organization. This affiliation may reveal something about the author's qualification or bias. Additional links or references may point to other work by the author. Authors with a body of work in a variety of sources, particularly sources requiring editorial approval, are traditionally regarded as greater authorities than those who have published less or more narrowly.

Is There an Organizational Sponsor?

Reliability of the organization

If the information appears under the sponsorship of an organization, you may be able to draw some additional inferences. Is the organization an official academic or scholarly one? Is there a logical connection between the organization and the type of information offered at the website? Would such a connection indicate a possible bias or just a commitment to support work in a particular area? Does the organization advertise products or services related to the information provided? Does the site supply a connection to a webmaster who may be able to provide additional information?

Remember that sites ending in .edu and .gov are sponsored by educational institutions and government agencies. Sites ending in .org are sponsored by organizations of various sizes and purposes. The suffixes .com and .biz denote commercial entities.

Additional Evaluation Criteria

Some further criteria may be helpful in evaluating the verifiability, accuracy, and objectivity of the information provided on a website (Alexander & Tate, 1999; Descy, 1996):

Other useful evaluation questions

- If the document is an attempt to summarize the findings from other sources, are the conclusions adequately referenced or linked to other work?
- If the document presents data, is there a clear description of how the data were gathered?
- If the document addresses issues or provides data that are time sensitive, does it include a publication date?
- If the document argues for a particular position, does it acknowledge other positions in an evenhanded manner?
- If the document is essentially an editorial, does the author acknowledge that it expresses a personal opinion?

Some search engines allow you to search for sites that link to a designated web address (for instance, HotBot has a search option called "Links to This URL"). Information about the number and characteristics of other sites with links to the site you are reviewing can be informative.

Relying on multiple sources

Finally, perhaps the best advice is to rely on multiple sources in developing an understanding of any issue. Gilster (1997) suggests that users think in terms of accumulating and integrating information rather than in terms of learning from a specific website. This idea is based on the observation that web authors make individual contributions of information *and* link to the contributions of others. You can best use the power of the Web by gathering ideas and perspectives from multiple sources and integrating them into your personal way of understanding.

Using the Web for Active Learning

From retrieving information to solving authentic problems

The intuitive nature of browsers and the power of search engines allow students to find information easily on almost any topic imaginable. The quantity and breadth of what can be explored are impressive, and educators should be excited by the potential. Yet, as we emphasize repeatedly, exposure to information is not the same as meaningful learning. We want students to go beyond retrieving information—we want them to use the Web to solve authentic information processing problems. This is a good way to integrate the use of technology into nearly any content area and a way for students to take on challenges that they can attack collaboratively.

In this section we explore strategies you can use to stimulate active, meaningful learning with web resources. We begin with an example of a project that uses the Web as a source of authentic scientific data.

Obtaining Current Weather Data: An Internet Project

Working with data allows students the opportunity to use knowledge and skills in ways that are appropriate to a particular subject matter domain. Consider a project based on the question, "Are winter temperatures in Alaska colder than winter temperatures in North Dakota?" This question might seem relatively simple, but determining a valid way to find the answer requires some careful thought. Are there places in Alaska that are colder than places in North Dakota? Are there places in North Dakota that are colder than places in Alaska? Is Alaska the coldest state? What would be a reasonable way to summarize winter temperature as a single variable? Why might people hold stereotypes about what places they have not actually experienced are like?

Finding weather data online

One way to begin is to explore what information is available. The Weather Underground website has provided current weather data on the Internet for years. After examining the city list for each state, students would know that they could obtain weather information for a number of cities in both Alaska and North Dakota. (See Figure 6.5.) It might occur to them that to provide a complete answer to the question, they would need to gather information related to more than one location in each state. How many cities and which ones to include are important questions. Perhaps it would be enough simply to select every other one on each list. Perhaps it might be useful to examine a map and select cities from different parts of each state or cities reflecting different geographic characteristics.

To continue this example, assume that students have selected Fargo and Bismarck in North Dakota and Anchorage and Juneau in Alaska. The data gathered from a single day in mid-December indicate that the current temperatures were Bismarck, 21; Fargo, 17; Anchorage, 26; and Juneau, 30. At this point, students might want to determine whether they can now answer the original question. There are always abnormally warm and cold days during the winter. Perhaps the data are not representative of typical winter temperatures. Perhaps Juneau is having an unusually warm spell. A more scientific approach might be to gather data over several weeks and then calculate an average.

FIGURE 6.5
Weather Underground
Information for Alaska

City	Temp. (F)	Humidity	Pressure (in)	Conditions
Anchorage	26°	44%	30.36	blowing snow
Barrow	-15°	77%	30.64	Clear
Fairbanks	-9°	77%	N/A	light snow
Juneau	30°	100%	N/A	Clear
Ketchikan	35°	89%	29.66	Clear
Kodiak	32°	45%	N/A	Clear
McGrath	-22°	74%	30.85	Mostly Cloudy
Nome	19°	87%	30.54	light snow
Valdez	38°	28%	30.16	Mostly Cloudy
Yakutat	26°	100%	29.91	Mostly Cloudy

Using a spreadsheet to record and average data

At this point, students could use a spreadsheet to record the data from several cities over several days and calculate an average temperature for each city (see the illustrations of spreadsheet use in the chapter entitled "Using Tools"). In this way, they might discover that some parts of Alaska are warmer and others are colder than the typical winter temperatures in North Dakota. The teacher and students might then want to know why this is the case. Finding out why would require that students go to the library or the Internet and do more research.

Scaffolding Web Exploration

In a project like the one just described, the teacher's role is critical. To begin, he or she must help students propose questions that are interesting and appropriate to their backgrounds and abilities. As the project unfolds, the teacher should challenge students to think deeply about what they are doing and guide them to learn the skills of thoughtful inquiry.

Supporting students in challenging tasks

One approach to such teaching is based on cognitive apprenticeship and scaffolding, concepts you encounter in the chapter entitled "Meaningful Learning in an Information Age." The basic idea is to ease students gradually into what are likely to be challenging tasks by creating a supportive structure to guide their work. In other words, as the teacher, you would initially do some of the work for students.

To see how the scaffolding process might work, let's consider another sample project. Assume that you would like your students to write a position paper on a controversial topic, using web resources. If they were working independently, each student would have to find resources related to the topic, examine a number of these resources to determine both the opposing positions and the basic arguments for and against each position, select a position to defend, find particularly good sources related to that position, carefully review the sources to obtain key data and develop sound arguments, and then write the paper. Consider just a couple of areas that might cause difficulty. Students might lack the experience to use a web browser in a sophisticated way, such as to conduct an advanced search or bookmark potentially relevant resources. Students might be unable or unmotivated to find truly good sources among the many that are available, or they might lack the reading or inquiry skills necessary to identify different positions or the arguments for and against these positions.

Ways to guide students   How would you assist the students? You might conduct an initial web search, generate a list of potential sites, and then designate three helpful sites for students to review. For each of these sites, you might offer guiding comments, such as, "This resource presents a good description of the general problem and outlines positions A and B," or "This site provides some very persuasive arguments for position B." You could also deal with some computer skill issues by authoring a simple webpage that presents this background material to the students and links them to the more productive sites (see the chapter entitled "Learning from Student Projects" for a discussion of web authoring). If the students have even the most basic competence in using a browser, this webpage would allow them to connect directly to the suggested resources. The cognitive apprenticeship model assumes that students will gradually take on more and more of these skills. To encourage this development, you might have students search for their own resources to augment those that you have provided, or you might ask students to review key resources without suggesting specific things they should try to learn from each resource.

The WebQuest model   Bernie Dodge (1995) has proposed that educators provide scaffolding through what he describes as WebQuests. A **WebQuest** is a document (usually prepared as a webpage) consisting of:

1. A brief introduction to a topic
2. The description of an inquiry task related to that topic
3. A set of primary web resources students can use in performing the task
4. Suggestions for how students might use the web resources in performing the task

Many teachers who develop WebQuests simultaneously prepare a rubric to guide evaluation of the students' responses to the inquiry task.

Because the structure of a WebQuest is simple and relatively easy to describe, it helps teachers understand how they might create learning tasks based on Internet content. However, the WebQuest is probably also an example of an instructional strategy that requires experience and careful preparation to achieve optimal results. The purpose of a WebQuest is not just to use web resources to locate specific factual information to answer specific factual questions. Rather, the goal is a learning activity that promotes genuine information problem solving. To create such an activity, you need to identify an interesting and appropriate topic, define a task that requires problem solving and reflection, and locate web resources that provide information for processing rather than preprocessed conclusions. The next section offers an example of a WebQuest intended to promote this kind of meaningful learning.

The Snow Goose Crisis: A WebQuest Example

The Snow Goose WebQuest originated in a magazine article that described how a rapid increase in the population of snow geese was threatening the fragile ecology of the Arctic tundra. The article went on to consider whether this was a situation that biologists should attempt to address and, if intervention was appropriate, what possible actions might be taken. This seemed an interesting problem for a middle-school or high-school WebQuest, and because we live in the middle of a goose migration route, it was also an authentic issue for students in our schools to address. Students could be asked to examine information related to the snow goose crisis and to propose what, if anything, should be done. The problem seemed complex enough that students might realistically argue for several different courses of action.

Background

To understand the situation, students would need background information. To help you see why we think this WebQuest involves inquiry and information problem solving, we will explain some of that background here.

Because of the extreme climate, tundra vegetation grows very slowly. Geese use the tundra as a breeding ground, and the parents and young rip plants out by the roots as they feed around the nesting areas. Once an area has been destroyed in this manner, geese, other wildlife that feed on the vegetation, and animals that feed on the plant eaters will not be able to inhabit the area for many years. There is a very real threat of a population crash in which many birds and animals will die from malnutrition and related diseases.

Issues for the Snow Goose WebQuest

One of the most basic issues in such a situation is whether humans should intervene to alter a process of nature. Noninterventionists argue that nature will find a solution even though the process may be harsh. In contrast, biologists favoring active management of natural resources assume that intervention can avoid extreme swings in populations. Those favoring intervention also argue that some of the causes for the existing situation are the result of human actions. For the snow geese, these human causes include changes in farming practices that leave a great deal of waste grain on the ground following harvest, making it easy for birds to feed during the fall and winter, and the development of a system of protected areas that allow geese to avoid hunters and predators during the fall and spring migrations.

If biologists choose to intervene, there are many possible, but untested, approaches. One interesting question is whether economic benefits should be considered. For example, a solution that extends the hunting season and increases the bag limit (the number of birds that can be shot each day) may attract more hunters and money to certain areas of the United States and Canada. Reducing food and habitat in areas in which geese overwinter would also reduce the population, but with no economic benefits. There is also the matter of expense and who pays for the intervention (taxpayers, nature lovers, hunters). Finally, there is a question of personal values regarding such issues as intervention and killing wildlife for sport.

Instructional Tasks

A major part of creating a structured inquiry task of this type is locating task-appropriate Internet resources. When we initially conducted a web search with the phrase "snow goose," we received more than 4,200 hits. Listed among the first four sites were the titles "Snow Goose with White Wine," "Snow Goose Hunting in Nebraska," and "Snow Goose Inn." Even using the phrase "snow goose crisis" resulted in seventy hits.

Put yourself in our place and assume that you are developing this activity for middle-school students. Even if your students are experienced enough to generate targeted searches, the amount of material to examine will be formidable and will require a great amount of their time. Thus, although students do need to learn to conduct their own web searches, you may decide in this case to locate useful sites in advance. You may also want to find particular web resources that lend themselves to thinking through different positions on the issue.

Scaffolding the WebQuest

In general, WebQuests are described as scaffolded because the teacher assists the student in ways that allow the student to address challenging problems with an acceptable level of effort and a reasonable opportunity for success. This is particularly important for younger students. As a teacher, you set the stage for your students, allowing them to focus on key issues and encouraging them in their critical thinking and problem solving.

WebQuest Presentation

Preparing a multimedia presentation

Figure 6.6 shows most of our finished WebQuest prepared as a webpage. The introduction, intended to establish a background for the activity and generate student interest, contains a photograph showing the devastation caused by the feeding habits of snow geese (note the difference between the fenced and unfenced areas) and explains that snow geese and other Arctic species are in serious jeopardy. The task, which is to generate a multimedia presentation, requires the student to propose and defend a course of action that federal and state biologists might take in responding to overpopulation of snow geese. In preparation for this task, students are directed to some specific websites (only three are visible) that offer information relevant to the assigned task. You will note from Figure 6.6 that these links are annotated so that students know what they might attend to most closely when studying a particular site. What does not appear in the figure is the list of secondary resources. In addition to the webpages we wanted every student to visit, we provided a list of supplemental sites that contained additional information some students might find helpful.

The WebQuest does not have to take this exact format. Some WebQuests offer students a choice among multiple tasks. We believe that once teachers understand some of the basic principles exemplified by the WebQuest model, they will be able to extend the model in a variety of ways.

In some of our own work, we have tried to foster information problem solving by including primary sources of three separate types: Internet-based,

FIGURE 6.6

Snow Goose WebQuest Presented as a Webpage

Snow Goose Crisis: Too Much of a Good Thing

The number of Snow Geese has increased at a very rapid rate and the number of geese is beginning to create a serious problem. The Snow Geese that migrate through North Dakota nest in the Arctic during the summer. So many geese are now present they destroy the plants they must feed on to survive. The picture shows how they feed - note the bare dirt outside the fenced areas. If the population continues to grow, the geese will actually "eat themselves out of their home." The population of Snow Geese and other animals that spend time in the Arctic will starve in large numbers.

The Task

There are many opinions on what should be done about the number of Snow Geese. Each solution seems to have both advantages and disadvantages. This is your opportunity to offer the suggestion that makes the most sense to you. Develop a proposal for the state director of game and fish in which you present and justify the course of action you recommend.

Consider:
1) Should nature take its course or should the problem be "managed"?
2) If a managed solution seems necessary, what specific actions do you recommend? What factors were involved in your solution and which of these factors were most important? The factors you consider might include ethical considerations, scientific findings, economic benefits, and others. Just make sure your plan identifies the factors you feel are important.

The Resources

General introduction; Description of the problem; Possible explanation of the problem

Suggestions for repelling geese on private land

Fish and Wildlife Service priority recommendations

---

school-based, and community-based. For example, a history activity, which focused on the different experiences of male and female teachers in one-room schools, included online primary sources from the Library of Congress American Memory Collection, an article from an edited collection published by the State Humanities Council and found in the school library, and interviews with older citizens from the community who had taught in or attended one-room schools.

Conclusion: New Challenges for Teachers

Meeting instructional challenges

This chapter offers what might at first appear to be contradictory messages. On the one hand, we recognize that teachers may feel overwhelmed when the challenges of teaching with the Internet are added to the many existing challenges educators face. In response to this reality, we propose that teachers (1) become familiar with online instructional resources and (2) locate or create curriculum-appropriate WebQuests. The first suggestion recognizes that quality and grade-appropriate resources already exist. The second suggestion provides an approach that gives teachers a reasonable level of control over the materials students will encounter and an efficient way to structure a learning task for a group of students. There are very practical ways that teachers can use Internet-based activities to augment traditional learning experiences.

On the other hand, having made recommendations that reduce the demands of integrating Internet experiences, we do propose that teachers take responsibility for helping students develop new technology skills and increase the emphasis on higher-order thinking skills. We propose that it is important for students to acquire the skills necessary to search for online information, to evaluate the quality of this information, and to take on projects requiring them to solve authentic information problems with information they locate online. We add such expectations to what has traditionally been expected of teachers because it appears that online resources will play an increasingly important role in daily information problem-solving tasks and because struggling with authentic information problems can contribute to all academic areas.

We urge you to carefully consider the range of options we have described and make an effort to understand the strengths and weaknesses of each. With this awareness, you will be prepared to make decisions concerning which activities are best suited to your instructional goals and circumstances.

Summary

The World Wide Web is largely responsible for the great interest in the Internet. The quantity of information resources and the ready access from classroom computers offer a great potential for using the Web as a tool for inquiry.

The browser is the software application that provides access to web information as well as tools for navigating within this content and keeping track of important sites. The bookmark feature is one browser tool that teachers should master. While creating bookmarks is very easy, bookmarks are most useful when they are organized and annotated. Learning to create and export topic-specific bookmarks is a useful technique for guiding students' web explorations and a useful skill for anyone who must work on several different computers.

Learning to locate useful web resources is another essential skill for web-based inquiry. Search services provide opportunities for both browsing and searching. Often it can be useful to try several services. Teachers and students should also try to master a few of the more advanced search techniques that allow targets to be pinpointed more accurately.

We suggest that educators think of web information as forming a continuum from online tutorials to instructional resources to primary sources. Online tutorials attempt to offer a complete activity for independent learning, incorporating learning sources, explanatory segments, and evaluation activities. Instructional resources provide components specifically prepared to meet educational goals but leave the teacher responsible for implementation and evaluation. Primary sources offer "raw" information not specifically intended for educational use and thus, when used in the classroom, require more preparation and experience on the part of the teacher. Even though primary sources can be biased and insensitive to the background of the learner, working with them prepares students to solve authentic problems outside of a protective classroom environment. Evidence on the increase in Internet use outside of school settings argues for the importance of developing such skills.

The Big Six provides a model of the skills required to solve problems that rely on the gathering and processing of information. The six general skill areas involve (1) task definition; (2) information-seeking strategies, or identifying possible resources; (3) locating and accessing these resources; (4) using the information (that is, processing it and extracting relevant ideas); (5) synthesizing and organizing the information and executing the problem's solution; and (6) evaluating the solution and the experience of solving the problem. Applied to the Internet, the Big Six can help you identify particular skills your students need to acquire.

The quality of web material is an important issue. Educational portals and databases of reviewed websites can help you identify resources useful for your students. Many reputable institutions, such as major newspapers, magazines, and museums, offer online access to their content. Frequently, however, you will have to make your own decision about the quality of an Internet resource. Useful criteria for evaluating web documents include the author's qualifications, the reliability of the organizational sponsor, and the adequacy of the document's references. You can help your students learn critical thinking by teaching them to apply such criteria on their own behalf.

Using web resources for active, meaningful learning typically involves some degree of scaffolding by the teacher—that is, taking responsibility for organizing the process for your students and completing some of the more difficult or time-consuming tasks. The WebQuest is one type of scaffolded, web-based inquiry task. A WebQuest proposes a decision-making, problem-solving, or information-integration task and then directs students to specific webpages that provide the necessary resources. WebQuests offer an excellent format for curriculum projects that teachers can accomplish within a reasonable amount of time.

Reflecting on Chapter 6

ACTIVITIES

■ Generate an annotated bookmark (favorites) list on a topic of your choice using the technique described in this chapter. Export this list to simulate the process of creating a resource list for students.

■ Compare the productivity of several web search methods. Submit the same request to a browsing service such as Yahoo!, a service for younger users such as Yahooligans!, and a search service such as Google. How many "hits" did you generate with each service? Did the same pages appear at the top of the list? Could you detect any difference in the educational quality of the resources you generated?

■ Explore one of the subscription project sites listed in "Resources to Expand Your Knowledge Base" (under the heading "Sources for Structured Internet Activities"). Create a summary of the project, its intended grade level, the content area it emphasizes, and its cost, and share this information with other students in your class.

■ Design a WebQuest (or a "paper equivalent"). That is, describe a problem, propose an inquiry task and a related product, identify key web resources, and develop a rubric for evaluating the inquiry product.

KEY TERMS

applet (p. 206)
Big Six (p. 222)
browser (p. 205)
hypertext markup language
  (HTML) (p. 206)
hypertext transfer protocol
  (HTTP) (p. 205)
incremental advantage (p. 221)
instructional resource (p. 217)
online tutorial (p. 217)
pedagogical content knowledge
  (p. 214)
plug-in (p. 206)

portable document format (PDF)
  (p. 206)
primary source (p. 221)
query (p. 209)
QuickTime VR (p. 206)
search engine (p. 209)
streaming (p. 206)
transformational advantage (p. 221)
universal resource locator (URL) (p. 205)
virtual reality modeling language
  (VRML) (p. 206)
WebQuest (p. 234)
World Wide Web (WWW) (p. 204)

RESOURCES TO EXPAND YOUR KNOWLEDGE BASE

Here are addresses for the search services mentioned in this chapter. The number of search engines is continually expanding as both commercial and experimental services are added. An expanded and frequently updated list of online resources is available on the website that accompanies this textbook.

Google (**http://www.google.com/**)
HotBot (**http://www.hotbot.com/**)
MetaCrawler (**http://www.metacrawler.com/**)
MSN Search (**http://search.msn.com/**)
Open Directory Project (**http://dmoz.org/**)
Search.Com (**http://www.search.com/**)
Yahoo! (**http://www.yahoo.com/**)

Web Resources
Reviewed Sites
Ask Jeeves for Kids (**http://www.ajkids.com/**)
Yahooligans! (**http://yahooligans.yahoo.com/**)
Educational Portals
ProQuest (**http://www.proquestk12.com/**)
Blue Web'n (**http://www.kn.pacbell.com/wired/bluewebn/**)
MarcoPolo (**http://www.marcopolo-education.org/**)
Subscription Information Services
EBSCO Information Services (**http://www.ebsco.com/**)
HighBeam (**http://www.highbeam.com/**)
ProQuest (**http://www.proquestk12.com/**)

Sources for Structured Internet Activities

Global Grocery List, an ongoing e-mail project, especially good for Internet beginners, asks students to visit their local grocery stores and record the prices of items on the grocery list. Through sharing this information, data are collected from students all over the world. No fee for participation. (**http://landmark-project. com/ggl/**)

JASON Project sponsors an annual scientific expedition to engage students in science and technology and to provide professional development for teachers in grades 4 through 8. Classes can participate individually or receive further services through statewide-sponsored networks. Fee for participation. (**http://www. jasonproject.org/**)

The Journey North is a yearly adventure that engages students in a global study of wildlife migration and seasonal change. No fee for participation; a charge for associated curriculum materials. (**http://www.learner.org/jnorth/**)

NASA Quest, sponsored by NASA, allows students to share in some of the excitement of authentic scientific explorations, such as high-altitude astronomy, Antarctic biology, and robotics. Resources include television broadcasts and videotapes, printed workbooks, and online interaction. No fee for participation. (**http://quest. nasa.gov/**)

Newsday encourages students to produce their own newspapers based on the news articles submitted to *Newsday* by student reporters all over the world. No fee; two projects a year. (**http://www.gsn.org/GSH/project/newsday/**)

North American Quilt is an interactive online project designed to bring an interdisciplinary approach to the study of geography. Students study their local geography and share their research on the World Wide Web. Sponsored by Online Class; fee for participation. (**http://www.onlineclass.com/NAQ/**)

One Sky, Many Voices provides the opportunity for K–12 students to use technology tools to investigate environmental themes related to weather. Projects run from four to eight weeks. Nominal fee for participation. (**http://onesky .engin.umich.edu/**)

ThinkQuest is an annual contest that challenges students and teachers to create web projects that harness the power of the Internet. The archives create a library of Internet educational materials for use in the classroom or at home. Project competitions include an international division for students ages twelve through nineteen, a junior division for U.S. students in grades 4–6, and a teacher division for U.S. teachers. No fee to participate; contestants compete for cash prizes. (**http://www.thinkquest.org/**)

7

Using Multimedia Tools

● ● ●

ORIENTATION This chapter has two broad goals: (1) to develop a simple system for classifying student multimedia projects and (2) to describe some of the software authoring tools students can use to produce multimedia projects. You have read about multimedia tools in other chapters, but here we present these tools more systematically and describe their capabilities more completely. After reading this chapter, you will know about and be able to recommend several specific software tools that students can use to generate each category of multimedia project. In addition to reviewing multimedia tools, this chapter introduces the concept of multimedia authoring environments.

As you read, look for answers to the following questions:

Focus Questions

- What is an embellished document, and what are some examples that students could create for a content-area course?
- What is a linear presentation or slide show? What are some examples of assignments that could result in a student-created slide show?
- What is interactive hypermedia?
- What options and issues do you need to consider when you choose authoring software?
- How do students' multimedia projects encourage meaningful learning?

As you know, we believe that student projects often encourage meaningful learning. Students engage in active learning and thinking as they work to complete projects appropriate to the content they are studying. Let's start this chapter by looking at an actual multimedia project.

Who Wants to Be a Millionaire?

● ● ●

Whatever you may think of the current emphasis on major standardized examinations that evaluate elementary student understanding using multiple-choice questions, such tests are a fact of life. Students must become familiar with this method of assessment and review large amounts of material to prepare for important examinations. Here is an activity that Cindy

FIGURE 7.1

Million Dollar Question

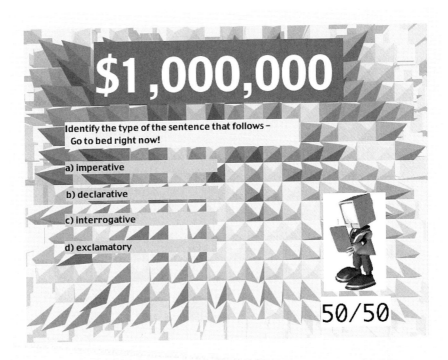

Lovas of Kelly Elementary used to help her fourth-grade students become more sophisticated test takers and also review the major content areas covered in fourth grade.

The basic idea was to create a review activity roughly based on the popular television program *Who Wants to Be a Millionaire?* The class was divided into groups, and each group was given the responsibility of developing a series of questions for one area of study: science, math, social studies, language arts, and word of the day. Using the material they were reviewing as a source, each group of students generated multiple-choice questions appropriate to their area of responsibility. Students knew that part of the task involved creating questions with a great range of difficulty, and this challenge led to some interesting discussions of what makes a question easy or difficult.

Once all of the questions were written, each group used a multimedia authoring program to prepare their version of the game. The game worked like this. Each question is presented as a separate screen (see Figure 7.1). The player selects an answer by clicking on it. Incorrect responses are greeted with a buzzer or some other noxious sound. Correct responses generate applause, a congratulatory message appearing on a transition screen, and a button to take the player to the next question. Students playing the game did not have to quit if they answered a question incorrectly, and the challenge became to determine how many questions in the series could be answered correctly.

Of course, the television version of *Who Wants to Be a Millionaire?* has some features that are not practical in the classroom. Because the classroom game was designed to be played by individual students, "ask the audience" or "lifeline" did not seem practical. Students did create a version of "50/50."

Each question display contained a 50/50 button, and selecting this button took the player to another screen with two of the answers removed.

When all of the groups had completed their work, the sets of questions were integrated through a start page that contained an image and music associated with the television program. All students then had the opportunity to play the game. The game was also shared with another fourth-grade class. In case you are curious, here is one example of a "million dollar" question:

Science: What is a filament?

(a) wire in a light bulb

(b) metal side

(c) stator

(d) rotor

A System for Classifying Student Multimedia Projects

We emphasize and differentiate three types of multimedia projects in this chapter: (1) embellished documents, (2) linear multimedia presentations (often called slide shows), and (3) hypermedia. (Video, because it integrates visual and auditory information, might also be considered multimedia. We delay a discussion of video projects until a later chapter so we can focus on the techniques in greater detail.) Knowing about the different categories of multimedia projects should help you think about which multimedia projects to use in your teaching. Figure 7.2 contains visual representations of these different project types.

Embellished Documents

An **embellished document** is a text document that has been enhanced with other multimedia elements. Student authors might add pictures, sounds, or video segments to text because information in these alternative formats seems more informative or more interesting than text alone. Students can prepare some form of embellished document with nearly every word processing program and with other tools such as paint programs and web authoring programs.

Ease of sharing embellished documents

If an embellished document is to include sound or video, the audience will have to view the document using a computer. The author does not have to be present or use his or her own computer to show this kind of document to a reader. It is as easy to send someone a word processing file on disk as it is to send a letter, and embellished documents can usually be sent as an attachment to an e-mail message. Students in other classrooms or schools can easily view the document containing sound and video that you or your students have created. If the document contains text and still graphics, students can print and distribute it. Common examples of embellished documents are student-authored newsletters, reports, and instructional manuals. A single

FIGURE 7.2

Categories of Student-Authored Multimedia

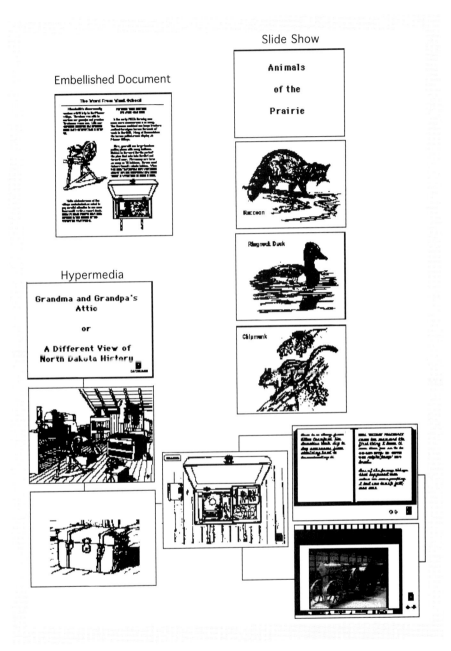

webpage might also be considered an embellished document. Most authoring programs also have a "web" or HTML format. We comment on using common authoring tools to produce web content in the chapter entitled "Learning from Student Projects."

Linear Multimedia Presentations or Slide Shows

Using presentation software

A **slide show** is a **linear multimedia presentation** that might be used as a self-contained presentation or may accompany a speech or lecture. The defining attribute of this format is the linear nature of the presentation. Slide shows can be viewed on the computer screen or by using a projection system, recorded on videotape for presentation, printed to produce a series of overhead transparencies, or made available on the Web. Like all the other projects discussed in this chapter, a slide show can incorporate text, several types of graphics, and sound. You may have seen presentations of this type as a college student. It is fairly common for college instructors to use what is frequently referred to as *presentation software* to prepare and present multimedia material as support for their lectures. Students can also use the same software to prepare their own presentations. See "Activities and Projects for Your Classroom: Slide Show Activities" for more suggestions for student-authored slide shows.

Hypermedia

User-controlled pathways

A **hypermedia** project differs from embellished documents and linear multimedia in the complexity of the pathways that are available through the information and the degree of control that users can exercise in navigating those pathways. As you discovered in earlier chapters, hypermedia authors segment information into meaningful units and create pathways among the units. In creating the units of information and establishing the links, authors attempt to anticipate the types of information different users might find helpful and provide convenient ways for these users to explore. Users decide which of the options provided by the author they want or need to experience.

Thinking Beyond What Your Projects Will Look Like

How might we sum up all of this information? Clearly, the three formats we have described differ in complexity. Embellished documents or slide shows can be used in any situation in which reports are used to develop communication skills and encourage students to think about course content. Nearly all classes require students to write reports or research papers or to give oral presentations of some type. Incorporating a few graphics or a short video segment takes a little additional time and new skills but does not require a serious deviation from existing activities. On the other hand, creating an interactive hypermedia project does involve committing a significant amount of time to developing some new skills in using technology and developing the project itself. In deciding to embark on involving students in developing hypermedia, you need to be committed to something that is currently quite out of the ordinary.

Questions to ask about a multimedia project

One of the greatest challenges in introducing student-authored multimedia projects is to get teachers to think beyond what finished projects will look like. We want teachers to think about the skills that students will develop and draw on in completing the projects. Think about the following questions too:

- Why would you have students spend their time developing these projects?
- How will students gather and transform information as they prepare to create their multimedia project?

ACTIVITIES AND PROJECTS FOR YOUR CLASSROOM

Slide Show Activities

Many classroom activities traditionally done with paper, pencils, and crayons can easily be converted to slide shows incorporating text, color graphics, and sound. Slide shows can be either a whole class activity, in which each student is responsible for one or two slides, or an individual or small group activity, in which the individual or group is responsible for the entire presentation. The following examples should get you thinking about the many opportunities for using slide shows in your classroom.

Here are some examples of whole class slide shows:

Getting to Know You

- A parents' night introduction of class members

Theme-Based Alphabet Books

- *The ABC Book of Space,* for example, or *The ABC Book of Birds*

Recycling Posters

- Student-created slides to encourage recycling

Parade of States

- Student-created slides depicting important facts about states

Seasonal Poetry

- Scary poems for Halloween

Our Favorite Books

- Student-created slides depicting favorite books could be kept in the library and viewed by other students

Memories of Junior High

- Slides created by current students as an orientation for future students

Here are examples of individual or small group slide shows:

- Book reports
- Creative stories
- Modern fairy tales
- Autobiographies
- Historical portraits
- Geographic travelogues
- Cartoons
- Animal reports
- Stages of meiosis or mitosis
- Stages in the development of a thunderstorm
- Chronology of world events, such as the breakup of the Soviet Union
- Differing viewpoints on controversial issues such as welfare

- ■ How will you encourage active student involvement with the central course ideas that you want to emphasize in a particular project?
- ■ How will you assess student projects?

We hope that we can help you interconnect all these issues. Unfortunately, the linear format of a textbook does not allow us to interweave these ideas very effectively. It would be nice if we could insert buttons that would let you instantly return to our chapter on meaningful learning to review how external activities, such as projects, can stimulate valued mental behaviors or just as instantly glance ahead to later chapters, where we make the point that many important behaviors in project development have nothing to do with the computer. But because a textbook is not hypermedia, the best alternative seems to be to remind you constantly of the value of projects and the ways to integrate them into the social setting and curriculum of your classroom.

Software Tools for Creating Multimedia Projects

A basic set of software tools can be used to construct the entire range of project types, and the project types can be applied to a variety of content areas, at many levels of sophistication, by students at all grade levels. The time that students spend learning how to use the software tools and to design each category of multimedia will be spent efficiently if they continue to use similar software tools to design similar projects. Whether students will eventually communicate with multimedia the way many adults now communicate with text remains to be seen, but it is reasonable to predict that multimedia—very possibly student-authored multimedia—will play an increasingly important role in academic settings.

General-purpose tools with multimedia capabilities

For many multimedia projects, no specialized software is required because many of the most widely used software tools have built-in multimedia capabilities. For instance, general-purpose tools such as word processing and paint programs targeting the K–12 market also emphasize integrating graphics, sound, and video segments. In the following pages we show you what you can do with some of these general-purpose tools. We also consider a few more specialized tools that offer more powerful options. As an educator, you will need to balance this additional power against the added cost and training time required by the more specialized tools.

It is important for you to feel confident that you would know where to begin in helping students develop their own projects. After you complete this section, you should be able to suggest several specific programs that could be used to author each category of multimedia projects. You should also be able to describe in general terms what the author does in working with each type of software.

Creating Embellished Documents with Word Processing Programs

Most word processing programs are capable of producing multimedia. Some allow users not only to combine text and graphics but also to integrate video

FIGURE 7.3

**Simple Embellished
Document Created with a
Word Processing Program**

Rabbit
in the
Rock

*You never know what you will find when you spend time
walking outdoors. When we were on our field trip, I noticed
a strange looking rock beside the trail. The rock was
different because it was hollow. When I looked inside, this
is what I saw. Have you ever seen a rabbit in a rock?*

segments and digitized sound. These more flexible programs are used mainly
to produce printed documents, but they have the potential of creating a file
containing information stored in the other formats. This file can be shared
with others who own the same program.

A small embellished document appears in Figure 7.3. This simple document consists of three elements: a title, an explanatory text segment, and an
image. The image was taken from a videotape (we describe the specific technique in the chapter entitled "Learning to Work with Images, Sound, and
Video"). The document shown in Figure 7.3 was prepared using the type of
word processing program likely to be available in most schools (in this case
AppleWorks). Short QuickTime segments (audio or video) can also be incorporated into embellished documents prepared with standard word processing programs.

**Desktop publishing
features**

Computer applications capable of integrating text and graphics, using
different text styles, and arranging text in columns are often described as
desktop publishing programs. Historically, word processing programs and
desktop publishing programs were distinct, but now they are much less
clearly differentiated, and standard word processing programs can be used to
generate all but the most complex documents. The expanded capabilities can
add value. Sometimes, adding extra features can do a great deal to increase
student pride in authorship and encourage more student reflection.

A text object

A core concept in the design of embellished documents is to treat segments of text and graphics as objects that can be individually edited and positioned. Think of a **text object** as a rectangular frame containing text. The

sides of the frame are usually not visible. Any time you work with a word processing program, you are actually entering text into a frame of a sort. The frame is established by the left and right margins, and the text frame changes if you decide to change the margins. In desktop publishing, one text object does not cover the entire page, and there are likely to be several text objects on each page. The author can position text and graphic objects on the page and move these objects around to determine which arrangement is most effective.

If a teacher wants to emphasize multimedia applications, it may not be enough for him or her simply to know that a particular program is capable of desktop publishing applications. Often a decision will have to be made about trade-offs among ease of use, the desktop publishing functions available, and price. There are a number of very useful products available, but teachers should have their own objectives and budgets in mind when making a decision.

Creating Multimedia Slide Shows

Multimedia slide shows can be created using either general multimedia authoring tools or tools designed specifically for linear multimedia presentations. We will present good examples of tools that teachers and students have used to do some interesting things, but we are not claiming that they are the best. Your instructor and your own investigations may lead you to other applications that you prefer. Nevertheless, these examples should start you thinking about this category of multimedia tools and give you a better understanding of how students use a slide show tool to create a project based on a class topic. As you read, try to develop your own examples of slide show projects for your content areas.

KidPix Slideshow

Capabilities of KidPix Deluxe 3

KidPix Slideshow was designed specifically to generate slide shows. As its name implies, it is a feature of KidPix (in this case KidPix Deluxe 3), a popular and inexpensive paint program designed for younger children. KidPix Deluxe 3 consists of two components: Paint Zone and Slideshow. KidPix Paint Zone allows a multimedia author to create images, include text with the image, and attach sound. The images can be created within the Paint Zone or loaded from another source. The sounds attached to the images can be recorded using a microphone or imported from another source. Each screen image is saved as a separate file. Additional information about the KidPix Paint Zone is provided in the chapter entitled "Learning to Work with Images, Sound, and Video."

Students collaborate to create a series of slides.

KidPix Slideshow allows several individual image files to be organized into a slide show (see Figure 7.4). This system of creating and then integrating separate files works well for school projects. In a fairly common application, individual students or student teams are assigned to create one slide in a series. Each student or student group might provide information about one butterfly, one fish, one classmate, or one low-fat food to become part of an integrated series dealing with biological organisms, the class, or nutrition.

FIGURE 7.4
KidPix Slideshow
Assembly Area

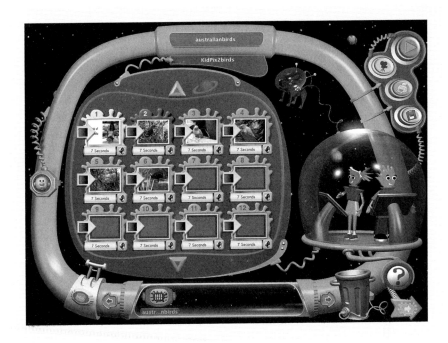

As the project proceeds, students may work simultaneously on several different computers to develop their contributions to the final product. When the individual files have been completed, KidPix Slideshow allows the teacher or the students to integrate and organize the individual files.

KidPix Slideshow is an easy product for students to work with. If you look carefully at Figure 7.4, you will notice miniatures of several "slides" and three icons associated with each slide. The icons are used to set properties of the slide show.

■ The transition icon (arrow) separates the images. Selecting this icon allows the author to select the visual and auditory transition that will accompany changes from one image to the next when the slide show plays. Transitions show how one image appears to replace another on the computer screen. One image may appear to slide over the image on the screen, emerge and expand out of the middle of the existing image, or replace it in a number of other possible ways. Authors may use transitions to convey the relationship between the two images, such as whether the information on the new slide continues the presentation on the same level or provides greater depth about what was presented on the previous slide. Transitions also help to keep the presentation a little more interesting. Inexperienced authors, however, often use such a great quantity and variety of transitions that the effect becomes distracting; in this case, teachers have to decide whether to encourage a more systematic approach.

■ The page advance icon (the box below each slide) allows the author to establish how quickly the slide show will advance from one slide to the next. The default is a seven-second interval, but one of the options allows the user to select a different interval. The advance can also be based on a mouse click or the time necessary for the computer to play the sound associated with the slide.

■ The sound icon (to the right of the page advance icon) controls whether the sound associated with each slide will consist of the sound stored as part of the slide and/or the computer "reading" the text appearing on the slide.

The miniature pictures in Figure 7.4 show birds of Australia. This slide show was prepared to chronicle observations made during a visit to a zoo. Narration accompanying the images describes the surroundings and identifies the birds. KidPix Slideshow is perfectly suited to this kind of project. Once the images have been isolated and stored as individual files (techniques are described later in the book), it takes just a few minutes to bring the individual images into KidPix Slideshow. Students can quickly learn all they need to know to work with the program and can spend their class or homework time developing the comments to accompany the images.

Presentation Software

The multimedia slide show has become an extremely common format because speakers frequently use it to support their presentations. The category of software that has been developed to support this type of application is described as **presentation software.**

Software that helps speakers communicate information

Presentation software provides a set of tools specialized for the purpose of helping communicate information to others in a way that is structured, forceful, and transitory. The word *helping* is critical to this definition. Presentation software is seldom totally responsible for delivering information by itself; rather, it is intended to support the efforts of a speaker. Presentation tools produce and present the computer-based equivalent of overhead transparencies. Although presentation tools can be used to create transparencies, the more popular method of delivery is probably with a large-screen monitor or a **video projector** (a piece of equipment that projects a screen image onto a larger screen).

Presentation tools are designed to help users perform three tasks: (1) organize the ideas for a presentation, (2) generate the visual materials, and (3) deliver the presentation.

An outlining tool

1. *Organizing ideas.* Often presentations are initially created with an outlining tool. An outliner allows the user to get ideas down quickly and to cluster and reorganize ideas efficiently. Projected presentations place a premium on the expression of ideas in a succinct fashion. An outliner provides a good way to prepare and organize precise statements.

Common features for generating slides

2. *Generating the visual materials.* The visual components of presentation images—think of them as projected slides—consist of text, multimedia elements (images, video, and sound segments), and a background. A presentation tool allows these components to be combined into the

Students making a PowerPoint presentation to the class (© Michael Zide)

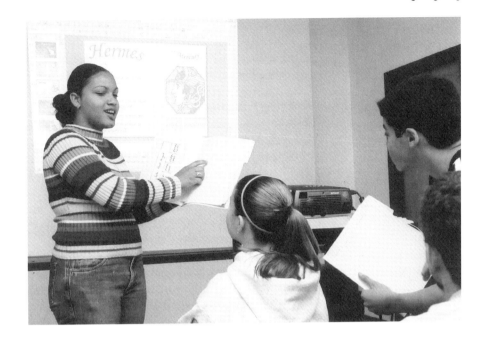

Video Case

Watch seventh-grade teacher Gretchen Brion-Meisels instruct students in making PowerPoint presentations as part of their unit on Costa Rica in the HM Video Case entitled *Multimedia Literacy: Integrating Technology into the Middle-School Curriculum.* How does she integrate technology instruction with the cooperative learning strategies you learned about earlier?

composite images the audience will eventually view. Common features include the following:

- For easy reading, text statements are often presented as **bulleted charts,** using a large, legible font.
- Often the presenter uses a technique called a **build,** which reveals bulleted items one at a time against a fixed background so the significance of each idea can be stressed as it is revealed. A similar approach is sometimes used with graphics. This procedure is useful when an author wants to demonstrate stages, such as those in the metamorphosis of a butterfly, or to call attention to individual parts of a whole, such as the parts of a frontier fort.
- So that the presentation is easy to view, the text and graphics are typically placed on some type of colored background. It is easier to read white lettering against a colored background than vice versa. A single background color and perhaps simple graphic elements (for example, a project title) may remain across the entire presentation.
- Most presentation programs allow the preparation of a **master slide** that contains all elements common to all slides, a technique that greatly increases preparation efficiency. Only the text and some graphics change from slide to slide. Many presentation tools provide templates to make the creation of the master slide even easier.

Projecting or printing slides

3. *Delivering the presentation.* Finally, presentation tools are used for the actual delivery of the presentation. While this primarily means controlling the projection of each slide, it is usually also possible to print out miniature images of the slides. Copies can be distributed to the audience so that they can follow along, read the slides if they don't happen to

have a good view of the screen, and take notes. Most presentation tools allow the presenter a method for coordinating a set of more detailed notes to use while presenting, and these notes, too, can be made available to the audience.

Widespread use of PowerPoint

Preparing Presentations with PowerPoint Microsoft PowerPoint is the most commonly used presentation software, and it has also become a popular choice for a variety of multimedia tasks in K–12 schools. This software is likely to be available in schools as part of the Microsoft Office Suite, which also includes Word, Excel, and other productivity tools. In addition to the prototypical functions of presentation software we have just described, PowerPoint has capabilities that expand its utility to include hypermedia authoring (discussed later in this chapter) and creating content for the Web (see the chapter entitled "Learning from Student Projects").

Templates available in PowerPoint

PowerPoint allows the user great versatility in putting together a presentation. When establishing the look and feel of the presentation, the user can rely on templates available within PowerPoint or create everything from scratch. The templates exist on two levels:

1. Design templates allow the selection of a visual theme and color scheme. If you have watched PowerPoint presentations, you may have noticed the way in which color patterns and the placement of small elements of clip art carried through the many slides you viewed. This consistency probably existed because the person who developed the presentation made use of a design template.

2. Page templates offer suggestions for the appearance of different types of pages—a title page, a page presenting a list of bulleted points, a page presenting an image or video segment with title, and so on. The idea is that the user will select a page template and then "fill in the blanks" with the text, image, or other multimedia elements appropriate to the presentation under development (see Figure 7.5). Once inserted, the elements making up a given slide can be adjusted as needed.

Figure 7.6 presents an example of what PowerPoint looks like while users are in the process of preparing a presentation (the appearance varies somewhat with the version of PowerPoint used). There are three panes within which the user works:

1. *Outline pane.* On the left is the outline pane, which shows the order of slides and major text elements from each slide. If you prefer, you can begin the process of generating a presentation by working entirely in the outline pane (the size of the pane can be expanded by selecting outline view from the View menu). The idea is to concentrate on the structure of your presentation and worry about the details later.

Working in the outline pane

When text is entered in this mode, each time you press the return key PowerPoint assumes you intend to enter another major heading of the outline. If you want the new text to be nested under a heading, you press the return key and then the tab key. Once you embed text, the outline tool assumes new entries are to be made at the same level of the

FIGURE 7.5
Some PowerPoint Page Templates

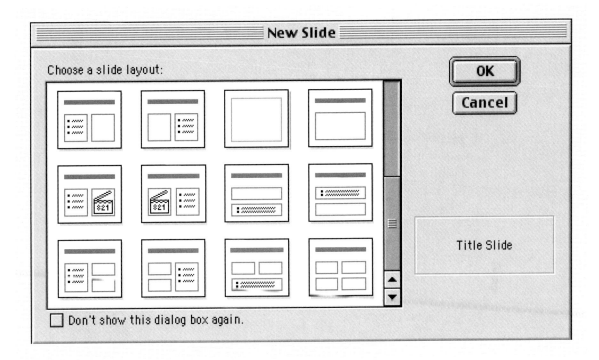

outline. To enter text so that it appears at a higher level of the outline, the user must use the shift and tab keys. An entry of text at the highest level of the outline also signals the creation of a new slide. Outline mode can be used extensively or it can be ignored. If you like, you can identify only slide titles in outline mode and then work out the details in the slide pane.

2. *Slide pane.* The slide pane is the area of the display that shows the appearance of the actual slide. The example in Figure 7.6 includes a title, an image of a human brain, and a label associated with the image. This pane allows the developer the greatest control over the layout of an individual slide. The developer adds objects (text box, image, video segment) within this pane, aligns the objects, and alters object characteristics (such as text size, font, and color; image size and location; and whether a video segment will have a controller or play automatically). Many characteristics of the presentation can be controlled.

Preparing builds in the slide pane

Builds are prepared by positioning all elements on the slide and then using the animation feature to control the order in which elements will appear and the effect that will announce the appearance. Text can simply appear in place, it can swoop in from any direction the producer chooses, it can "dissolve in," and so on. Another menu option allows the selection of visual transitions that will mark the change from one slide to the next.

FIGURE 7.6
Screen Image Showing the Three PowerPoint Panes and the Tool Bars

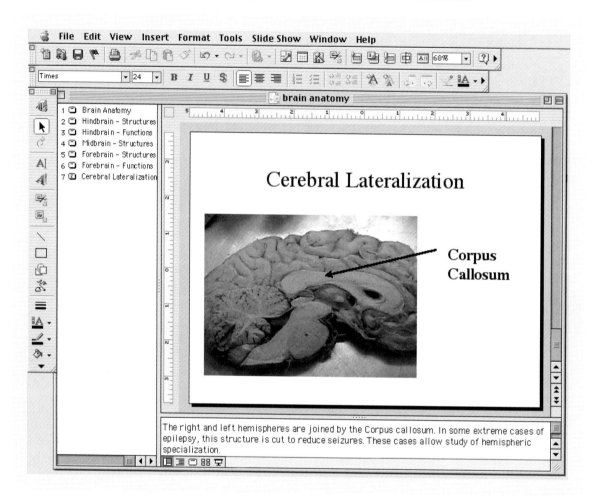

One feature that increases the versatility of PowerPoint for student projects is Hyperlink. The feature can be applied from the Insert menu. Hyperlinks allow PowerPoint to deviate from a strict slide show format. Any object (image, text phrase) can serve as the origin of a hyperlink, and the destination of the link can be another slide in the PowerPoint presentation, a website (a browser is launched to present the site), or other documents (the appropriate software application is launched to present the document). We say more about this feature in the later discussion of using PowerPoint for hypermedia projects.

Using the notes pane

3. *Notes pane.* The third pane, located below the slide pane in Figure 7.6, is used for entering notes to be associated with the slide. These notes may be used by the presenter or distributed as part of a handout to those

who will eventually watch the presentation. PowerPoint offers options for printing materials associated with a presentation.

Presenting with PowerPoint The most basic method for presenting with PowerPoint uses the same software used to prepare the presentation and requires only that the software be switched to Slide Show mode (Slide Show menu). In this mode, the slide is the only thing visible on the screen. Slides are advanced by using the space bar or forward arrow or by clicking the left button on the mouse. If necessary, using the right mouse button or keyboard arrows allows the presenter to move back to an earlier slide.

Other presentation options include the addition of narration so that a presentation can be experienced without the physical presence of a presenter and the translation of the slide show into format appropriate for web delivery.

Example of a Classroom Presentation

To give you a better idea of how slide show presentations can be used by teachers or students, we next describe one example in detail. In this case, the presentation tool is Keynote.

A recent controversy in our community focused on the decision of whether to construct a large events center. This building, named the Aurora, has since been constructed and is used for college football games, concerts, and other events that draw large crowds. When constructed by a small city, a building of this size is very expensive, and the decision to fund such a project with local money was not an easy one. The issue of whether to build the Aurora was put to a vote several times before the necessary citizen consensus was achieved.

The Aurora controversy created an opportunity to follow local politics and consider the various issues presented for and against an issue of local importance. A classroom teacher might take advantage of this situation by dividing the class into small groups, asking individual groups to adopt a pro-Aurora or anti-Aurora position, and then assigning each group the task of preparing a presentation in support of its position for a public forum. While public meetings would probably be much too heated for student presentations, presenting to classmates would be realistic enough to generate enthusiastic discussions. Arguments would have to be well thought out because claims for or against the project would be vigorously challenged.

Figure 7.7 is an example of a typical presentation slide that students might create. The slide presents a set of reasons that a new events center would be valuable to the community. This slide was the result of time spent gathering and interpreting information to identify persuasive arguments favoring the construction of the Aurora.

Themes and templates establish recommended color schemes, font and text styles, and object arrangements. The sample slide in Figure 7.7 was created by using the "title and right bullet" template that goes with the "crayon" theme. All master slides created with the crayon theme have a textured tan-colored background and a horizontal crayon slash. The template used to create this slide has a title text box at the top and a bullet text box on the right-hand side. The left-hand side of the slide is blank. Creating the slide

FIGURE 7.7
**Page Created with
Keynote Page Template**

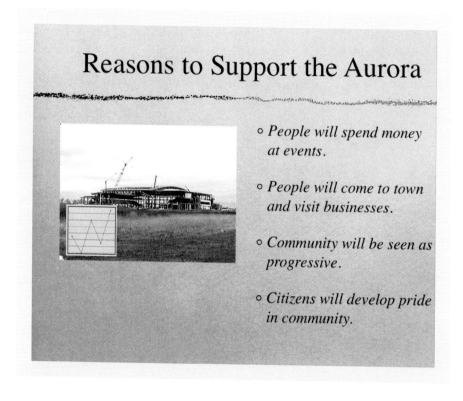

shown in Figure 7.7 was a matter of filling in the blanks. The image was inserted and resized to fit the blank space. Text size and style was determined automatically as text was entered into the title and bullet text boxes. After the bulleted entries were added, a "dissolve" build style was assigned to the entire set. When initially presented, only the title and image appear. Each additional click results in one of the bulleted points gradually becoming visible.

**Benefits of using
presentation software**

You can see how presentation software is valuable for this type of classroom activity. The use of a presentation tool can focus students on the creation of an organized product and encourage a careful consideration of the arguments to be made and the structure that would make these arguments most persuasive. During the presentation itself, the slides help the listeners follow the speaker more effectively. The slides can also provide multimedia elements that allow the speaker to present information that would be difficult to describe or less interesting if presented orally.

Multimedia Authoring Environments for Hypermedia

**Characteristics of a
multimedia authoring
environment**

A multimedia authoring environment often achieves the following results:

- Integrates a variety of tools frequently used to produce multimedia products
- Allows basic multimedia functions to be included in products without requiring the author to engage in detailed programming

- Allows one or more authors to store and organize multimedia components for use in preparing multimedia products over an extended period of time

The combination of these characteristics gives teacher or student multimedia authors a great deal of support and power.

Let's look at what each of the characteristics of a multimedia authoring environment contributes:

- Remember that at a basic level, multimedia is a combination of text, graphics, and sound. A multimedia authoring environment provides tools for manipulating and perhaps creating all of these types of information. It should be possible to enter and edit text, import or create graphics and video segments, and import or record sound.

- Once the basic resources are available, the authoring environment should allow you to integrate and rearrange the different types of information easily. For example, the multimedia authoring environment should allow you to combine text and graphics and position these elements of information exactly as you would like to have them appear on the computer screen.

- Finally, the component that most clearly distinguishes multimedia authoring environments from the other applications we have discussed is the ability to create the means by which users will interact with the multimedia content. The author may create presentation methods that range from giving the users no control over what or when anything is experienced to allowing the users always to select what is to be experienced next.

Multimedia authoring environments can generate embellished documents, linear presentations, and interactive multimedia, but it is the production of interactive hypermedia projects that most clearly demonstrates the full capabilities of authoring environments.

Creative application of basic computer skills

A number of multimedia authoring environments are appropriate for teachers and students, and even more products of this type are likely to appear in the near future. Here, we will review several products so that you will have some idea of what authoring environments are like and what can be done with them. Do not worry at this point if you think that you are not learning enough to develop multimedia materials on your own. You learn more in the chapters that follow. There are also many how-to manuals and websites available to help teachers learn both the basics and advanced techniques. However, you will also see that you do not need a lot of know-how to start experimenting with simple projects. Keep in mind from the beginning that if your intent is to use a multimedia project to involve students in meaningful content-area learning, they should not have to spend a long time developing computer skills. The creative application of a reasonable number of simple skills should give them powerful experiences. Such experiences are available through eZediaMX, one of the most popular multimedia environments in school settings.

eZediaMX

Like other multimedia authoring environments, eZediaMX might be described as a multimedia construction set. It contains elements that can be seen as multimedia building blocks and others that provide the tools to work with these building blocks. EZediaMX documents are created within the eZediaMX workspace. A separate program (eZediaPlayer) is used to view the document. The completed document and document resources can be duplicated and distributed with a copy of the player as part of the purchase agreement.

Elements of the eZediaMX System

Multimedia products are assembled from individual objects. The word *object* implies certain things in reference to computer software. Think of an **object** as a building block with a defined purpose or function. Creating products from objects has many advantages. Objects are reusable, and the opportunity to make copies of objects or to copy an object and make small modifications to the copy greatly increases efficiency. Objects are also independent. This property allows the developer to isolate and finish specific tasks. The objects used to assemble eZedia products include, among others:

- Document
- Frame
- Background
- Media objects (text, graphics, video)
- Interactive objects (button, video controller)
- Logic objects (branch)
- Special objects (path, speakme)

This list is hierarchical: Documents are made up of frames, and frames hold backgrounds, buttons, text objects, graphics, and other objects. Some objects add a capability to another object; for example, "linkto" allows one object, such as a button, to activate another object, such as to display a graphic.

Frame The **frame** is the fundamental unit of the eZediaMX system. You can usually think of a frame as equivalent to the object holding what you see on the computer screen at any one time. What users see are sources of information, such as text, graphics, video, and some of the other elements of the multimedia system. Figure 7.8 shows the eZediaMX "workspace" with a frame containing a graphic, two text objects, and buttons providing access to other frames.

If you look carefully at Figure 7.8, you will note that the surface of the frame has been covered with a background object (see the label "parchment brown" in the upper-left corner of this object). A collection of objects of all types comes with this authoring program. Users can either use these objects or make their own. Note that all of the objects in Figure 7.8 have a label or tab attached to the upper-left corner. Clicking on the tab provides the opportunity to set a number of properties associated with that category of object. (We describe these properties later.) The label and tab are visible only while the project is being constructed.

FIGURE 7.8
eZediaMX Workspace with Frame

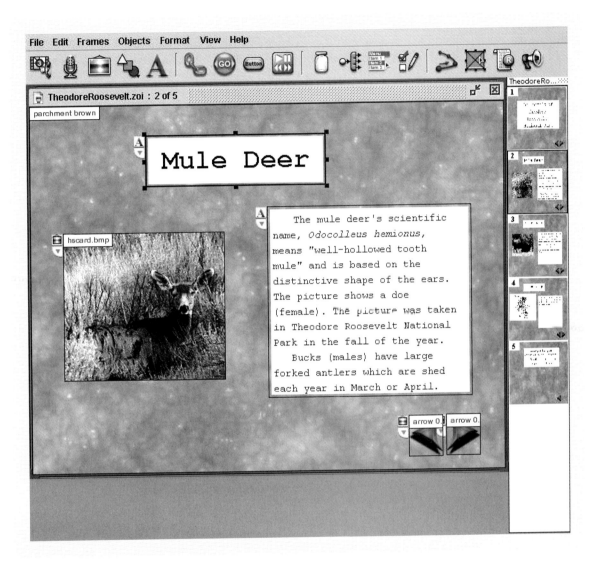

The document: a "pile" of frames

Document An eZediaMX file is called a **document** and consists of a series of frames. You might find it helpful to imagine a document as a pile of note cards, just like those you would use to prepare a speech or study for a test. You would likely organize your note cards so that you could move through them in a sequential order. Because eZediaMX is a hypermedia environment, frames can be linked together in complex patterns. A sequential arrangement is easy to implement, but the real power in hypermedia is to create multiple links among frames and then allow the user to choose how the material will be explored.

Frames in a document do not necessarily contain the same categories of information or look the same. The appearance of each frame and the objects each frame contains can be uniquely crafted, or some elements can be held constant to decrease construction time. Projects can take on whatever form the author desires.

Text Objects   When you enter text in a text object, most of the editing features of a typical word processor are available. You can easily make font changes; delete and insert text; cut, copy, and paste between text objects or between applications; and check for spelling errors.

Adding a text object is easy. Icons representing most objects appear in the icon menu bar. The "A" icon is used to add a text object (see Figure 7.8). When you select this command, an object appears in the middle of the frame. You may drag this object to the position you want it to occupy within the frame and then drag it by the edges to make it the size you want.

Working with text objects

Many attributes of the text box and of the text in the box can be modified. The various attributes and associated options are displayed when you click the tab attached to the upper-left-hand corner of the text box. For instance, it is possible to set the font and the size of the text and to establish the color of both the text and the background. It is also possible for the text to appear with a transparent background, or for the text box to be totally invisible until the user clicks on a button.

Buttons

Buttons   **Buttons** allow the author to prepare optional actions for the eventual user of the document—for example, moving to other frames, revealing and hiding pictures and QuickTime movies, playing sounds, launching a browser to view a specified website, triggering an animation, or revealing a hidden text message. Buttons, in other words, can give users the opportunity to choose the information they will encounter next. Learning to use buttons greatly expands the diversity of projects student authors can develop.

Assigning attributes to buttons

Adding a button is similar to adding a text object. Selecting the button icon positions a generic button in the middle of the frame. The author can then move the button to the intended position, assign desired attributes, and attach other functions (such as links). There are several options students should understand. First, you can attach a name to each button. It is particularly useful for the button's name to describe its purpose. A button labeled "Song" near a bird picture, for example, suggests to most users that the button will provide that bird's song. The button name may be visible or invisible.

A very important button attribute is its visibility. The capability of creating a button that the user cannot see may at first seem confusing. The advantage in using invisible buttons—usually several different buttons—is to cover different objects or parts of an object. By clicking on the area the button covers, the user initiates any action attached to the button. Often the object to be covered is a graphic or part of a graphic. By carefully positioning invisible buttons over critical features of the graphic, a software author might allow users to reveal text describing each selected feature or to move to another frame with a larger, more detailed image of the selected part of the original image. Or, instead of using buttons to present information, invisible buttons can be used as part of a method for evaluating understanding. Buttons can be used to program testlike events ("Click on the carburetor," for example, or "Click on the part of the weather map showing the cold front") and to provide feedback.

FIGURE 7.9

**Menu and Example of
Dialog Box (Get Object
Info . . .) Used to Assign
Button Attributes**

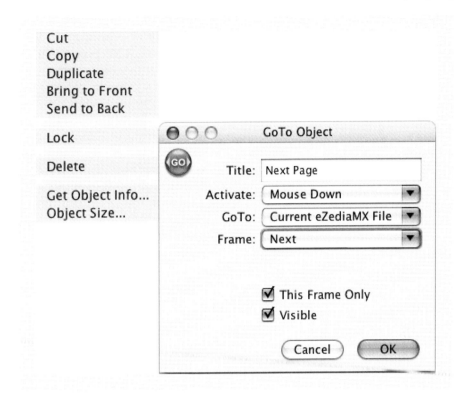

User-controlled actions to be triggered by a button can be set in several ways. First, there are several button types. The GoTo button is intended to link the user to another frame within an eZediaMX document, to a designated website, or to a different type of document, such as a word processing document. When a link leads to a resource outside the eZediaMX environment, the link causes the application (web browser, word processing program) associated with the resource to launch and present the resource. The most common use of this button is to link to a possible destination within the document. Multiple buttons are used to offer multiple destinations (next frame, previous frame, final frame). The Control button allows the author to designate the controls the user will have available while viewing a video (play/pause, stop, rewind). The generic "Button" in combination with the "linkto" object is used to control the activation of another object. Depending on the object that is the target of this link, activating it may cause a graphic or text object to appear, a video to begin, or an object to move along a designated path. You can easily identify the icons associated with these button types in Figure 7.8. You can assign attributes to a button by clicking the button tab, selecting an option from the menu, and then, if necessary, entering information in the dialog box that appears. Figure 7.9 displays the button menu list and the dialog box that appears when the "Get Object Info . . ." menu item is selected. The entries in the dialog box determine that clicking on the button named "Next Page" will take the user to the next frame in the document.

Adding audio or video

Multiple Media A multimedia authoring environment should offer powerful ways to create with many forms of media. In addition to text objects, video, audio, and still images are other object types that can also be added to frames (note the first three icons in the icon menu at the top of Figure 7.8). The sound icon opens a special window allowing sounds to be recorded using the computer's built-in microphone. Sounds from other sources can also be added. (Sources for royalty-free sound clips are included in the chapter entitled "Learning to Work with Images, Sounds, and Video.")

Adding attributes to media objects

Media objects are treated in much the same way as text or button objects. The author adds a media object by clicking on the corresponding icon or dragging the media file into the frame, positions it, and then sets the attributes of the object. There are multiple ways to display images and start video or audio segments. The presentation of the objects can be triggered by opening the frame on which they appear or by clicking on a button. The end of a video or audio segment can also be used to trigger the display of another object.

Other Features EZediaMX offers other features that some young authors will find useful:

- A **path-based animation** is a method for moving an object around the screen following a path established by the author. The author draws a path, links an object to the path, and links an object (such as a button) to start the animation. Attributes of the animation include whether it will be repeated and how fast it will move.
- The **speakme** object will read text from a linked text object.
- EZediaMX offers methods for generating simple surveys or quizzes. The combination of a **multichoice** object and a **logic** object can be used to send the user to different frames, depending on the response to a question. A correct response might move the user forward to new material; an incorrect response might return the user to previous material for additional review.

Is PowerPoint a Multimedia Authoring Environment?

Specially designed software, or PowerPoint?

We have concentrated on eZediaMX because it is available for both Windows and Macintosh platforms and because it is a multimedia authoring environment developed for educational applications. EZediaMX is a good example of a category of authoring software designed for the K–12 environment (see the website that accompanies this textbook for more examples). Our experience observing K–12 multimedia authoring suggests that educators who want to involve their students in multimedia authoring fall into two camps: One camp makes use of software designed for the K–12 environment, and the other uses PowerPoint. Those who use PowerPoint tend to explain their approach in two ways. The argument is either "This is the type of software students will encounter outside school" or "This software was already available so I used it." There is merit both in developing powerful tools geared to the needs of learners and in advocating the use of general-purpose tools for a variety of applications. We do not feel it is our place to contend that one of these approaches

EMERGING TECHNOLOGY

eZediaQTI

EZedia has a second product for K–12 multimedia authors. This product, eZediaQTI, is unique, and we feel it has great potential. QTI stands for Quick-Time Interactive. QuickTime, a cross-platform format developed by Apple Computer, is probably most typically used as a web video delivery format (see the chapter entitled "Learning to Work with Images, Sound, and Video"). What makes the QuickTime format interesting is that it can store more than just audio and video information. Here is one way to understand what the format offers: You may already realize that your experience when watching video results from the rapid display of many individual images. Video is often displayed at 30 frames per second, but slower presentation rates are typically used with video sent over the Internet. Instead of thinking of frames as the source for the series of still images that simulate continuous motion when viewing a video, think of frames in the way we have used the term in understanding the functioning of eZediaMX. At a simple level, this is how eZediaQTI works. Each frame contains objects (text, images, buttons, video), and instead of being displayed at a fast and constant rate, a frame is displayed and then the application running QuickTime waits for an action from the user. The action of the user not only can display the next frame but also can trigger an action within the frame or send the viewer to a designated frame. QuickTime can even use a frame to contain a video, effectively embedding a video within a single frame of another video.

The QuickTime format is efficient in terms of size, can easily be sent over the Internet, and can be displayed within standard web browsers. In other words, once a document has been authored in eZediaQTI, any computer user with access to a web browser would already own the software necessary to explore the document. This product could be embedded in a webpage and experienced over the Internet, or it could be burned onto a CD.

The eZediaQTI workspace is displayed in Figure 7.10. We have attempted to duplicate the project used in explaining the capabilities of eZediaMX. If you compare the icon tool bar for eZediaMX (Figure 7.8) with the one in Figure 7.10, you will notice that fewer icons are available in eZediaQTI. At this time, eZediaQTI does not allow some of the advanced capabilities of eZediaMX. You will also notice that eZediaQTI has a different and easier way of assigning attributes to an object. When an object is selected, a dialog box opens (see the right side of Figure 7.10) and allows the attributes of this object to be manipulated. In this case, the button has been named "Forward," the color of the button has been selected, and the action of the button has been defined as taking the user to the third frame in the document when the button is clicked.

FIGURE 7.10

eZediaQTI Workspace

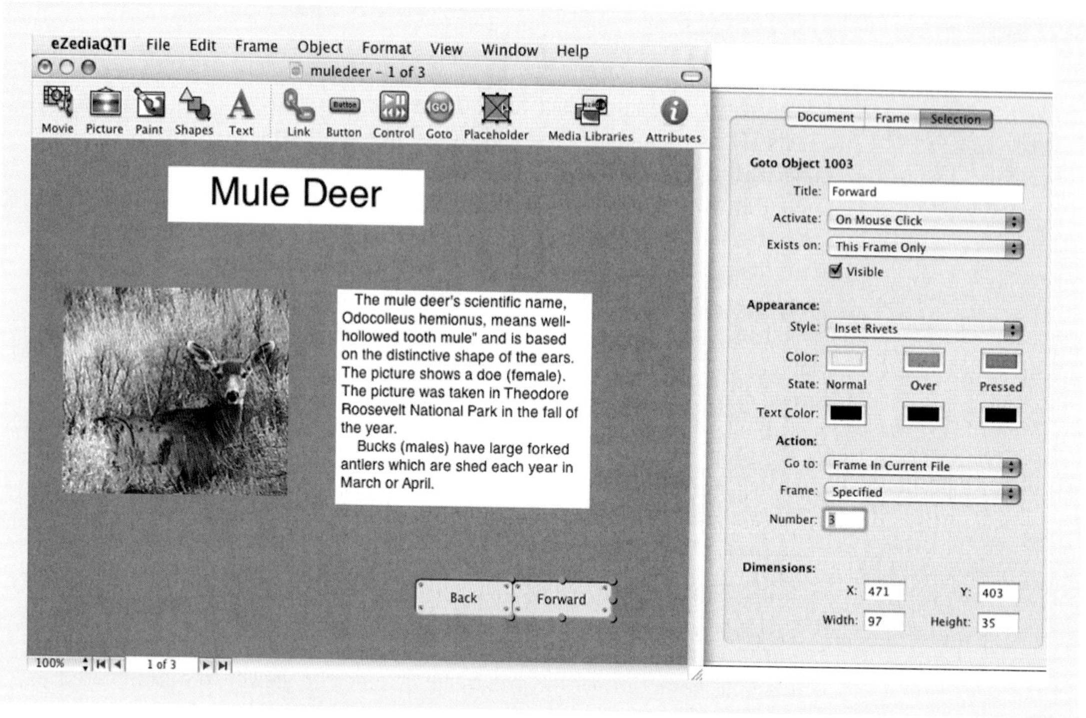

This product is exciting because it is easy to use, powerful, and designed for easy display over the Internet—qualities that make it ideal for a wide range of classroom multimedia authoring projects. Additional information about eZediaQTI and demonstrations can be found on the website that accompanies this textbook.

is superior. Instead, we hope to give future and practicing teachers the basic information they need to make personal decisions.

Because Microsoft Office products are so widely available and you probably have access to PowerPoint on a laboratory computer or possibly your own personal computer, we suggest you explore the question "Is PowerPoint a multimedia authoring environment?" as we describe some of the capabilities of this program. Let us begin by establishing some of the capabilities we would expect in an educational multimedia authoring environment: It should be capable of incorporating multiple media (text, images, video), and it should be able to generate a product that the user can explore as hypermedia. If you carefully read our earlier description of PowerPoint as a presentation tool, you already realize that PowerPoint presentations can incorporate a range of media types. So, it is the hypermedia capability—the creation of a product that the user can explore in multiple ways—that is still in question. Again, we cannot possibly provide a complete description of the capabilities of the many software programs we use as examples; instead, we will demonstrate several ways in which interactivity can be added to a PowerPoint document.

Open PowerPoint and select the option "blank slide." Duplicate this slide several times using the "duplicate" option appearing in the Insert menu. What you have created is very similar to the multiple-frame document we described earlier when discussing eZediaMX. In PowerPoint, you can move to each of these slides (similar to frames) and add text boxes, images, or other multimedia elements. What is missing are ways to turn what would normally be a slide show into a hypermedia document.

Solutions to the interactivity challenge can be found in the Slide Show menu. The "Action buttons" option allows you to insert buttons to which various actions can be assigned. These actions allow you to control movement to a specific slide, to play a video or audio segment, or to open a document or Internet site in another application, such as a web browser. Also in the Slide Show menu is the option Action Settings, which allows the same actions to be assigned to other objects (see Figure 7.11). For example, an action setting could be attached to an image. Clicking on that image might result in the user being taken to another slide that provides additional information or plays an audio segment associated with the image.

The "custom" action button warrants additional comment. In our discussion of eZediaMX we discussed the value of invisible buttons. For example, sometimes it is desirable to have an action occur when the user clicks on a specific part of a large image. The custom action button can play this role because the transparency of the button can be set to 100 percent; then the button can be sized and positioned on top of other objects.

By positioning several action buttons or attaching actions to other objects on individual slides, the author provides the viewer with multiple options to pursue. While PowerPoint does not duplicate all of the capabilities found in more dedicated multimedia authoring environments, it does offer capabilities that meet the basic expectations for presenting multiple media in a way that users can actively explore.

Other Multimedia Authoring Environments

Several other high-quality authoring environments appropriate for student projects have been developed, and more appear to be on the way. You can find more information in "Resources to Expand Your Knowledge Base" at the end of this chapter, and on the website that accompanies this textbook.

FIGURE 7.11
PowerPoint Action Settings

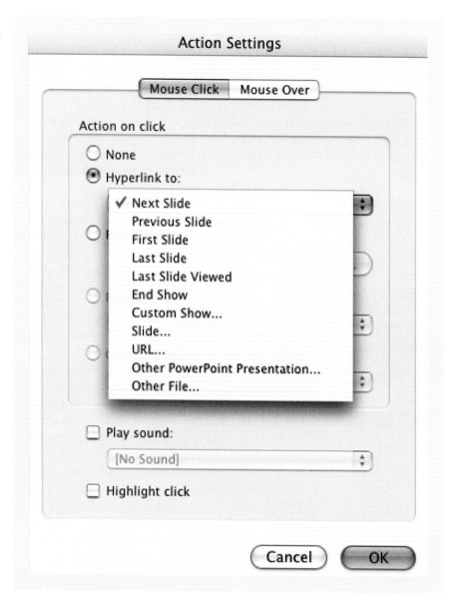

Summary

Student multimedia projects can be classified as embellished documents, linear multimedia presentations or slide shows, or interactive hypermedia. An embellished document is a text document that has been enhanced with images, video, or sound. A classroom newsletter printed and sent home to parents or shared with other students is a common example of an embellished document.

A slide show is a linear multimedia presentation. Using elements of text, sound, still images, and video, the author prepares a series of multimedia slides to inform and entertain an audience.

Interactive hypermedia, the most complex of the multimedia formats, offers users choices instead of binding them to a single type of experience. The user has greater control over which sources of information to consider and perhaps the formats in which information will be encountered. Developing hypermedia is complex because the author has to prepare a much more extensive body of information to explore.

Teachers have many options available when selecting software tools that students might use to create multimedia projects: both general and common software tools such as word processing programs, more specialized multimedia tools designed to create slide shows, and powerful hypermedia authoring environments, or a combination of all of these.

The authoring environments offer project developers a variety of tools for creating and linking information resources. When teachers consider the various ways in which multimedia projects can be created, they might think about a number of issues. How is the project intended to encourage thorough consideration of information? Does the project include additional objectives, such as the development of interpersonal skills, problem-solving skills, or communication skills? Finally, teachers might want to consider whether students are likely to use the same software to create other projects in the future.

Reflecting on Chapter 7

ACTIVITIES

■ Consider the unique advantages and disadvantages of slide show and hypermedia applications. Describe a classroom project most appropriately presented as a slide show and one most appropriately presented as interactive hypermedia.

■ Familiarize yourself with a word processing program capable of integrating text and graphics. Demonstrate the capabilities of this program to your classmates.

■ Familiarize yourself with a slide show application. Demonstrate the capabilities of this program to your classmates.

KEY TERMS

build (p. 253)
bulleted charts (p. 253)
button (p. 262)
desktop publishing (p. 249)
document (p. 261)
embellished document (p. 244)
frame (p. 260)
hypermedia (p. 246)
linear multimedia presentation
  (p. 245)

logic (p. 264)
master slide (p. 253)
multichoice (p. 264)
object (p. 260)
path-based animation (p. 264)
presentation software (p. 252)
slide show (p. 245)
speakme (p. 264)
text object (p. 249)
video projector (p. 252)

RESOURCES TO EXPAND YOUR KNOWLEDGE BASE

 An expanded and frequently updated list of online resources is available on the website that accompanies this textbook.

Software Resources

AppleWorks: Available for the Macintosh and Windows platforms. Apple Computer Corporation. (**http://www.apple.com/appleworks/**)

KidPix products (KidPix Deluxe 3): Available for the Macintosh and Windows platforms. Broderbund Software. (**http://www.broderbund.com/**). There is also an official KidPix website. (**http://www.kidpix.com/**)

Hypermedia Authoring Environments

eZediaMX and eZediaQTI: Available for the Macintosh and Windows platforms. Safari Video Networks. (**http://www.ezedia.com/**)

MediaBlender: Available for the Macintosh and Windows platforms. Tech4Learning. (**http://www.tech4learning.com/mediablender/**)

mPOWER: Available for the Macintosh and Windows platforms. Multimedia Design Corporation. (**http://www.mPower.net/**)

Presentation Tools

Keynote: Available for Macintosh. Apple Computer. (**http://www.apple.com/keynote/**)

PowerPoint: Available for the Macintosh and Windows platforms. Microsoft Corporation. (**http://www.microsoft.com/powerpoint/**)

Presentations: Available for Macintosh and Windows as part of AppleWorks 6. Apple Computer Corporation. (**http://www.apple.com/appleworks/**)

8

Learning to Work with Images, Sound, and Video

● ● ●

ORIENTATION   This chapter explores some of the tools and basic techniques that allow students and teachers to produce the kinds of images, sounds, and video segments described in multimedia applications throughout this book. After reading this chapter, you should understand how these information resources are represented digitally and how some examples of software and hardware can be used to create these representations. As always, actually working with the applications is likely to provide a much fuller understanding. We encourage you to supplement your reading with hands-on experiences.

As you read, look for answers to the following questions:

Focus Questions

- What distinguishes paint programs from draw programs, and what are some educational applications of each?
- Why must teachers pay attention to the file format used to store graphic images and sounds?
- How can teachers and students capture images for use in their own projects?
- How can teachers and students combine video segments and other multimedia formats into an integrated video production?
- Where might teachers find prepared images to use with computers?
- How do students benefit from the collection and manipulation of sounds and graphics?

The Case of the Missing Gerbil

● ● ●

Cully Gause, a science teacher at South Middle School in Grand Forks, North Dakota, wanted to provide his students a laboratory experience involving electrophoresis, a procedure in which a weak electrical current is used to carry molecules through a special gel. The size of the molecule determines how quickly the molecule moves. Over time, differences in the speed with which molecules travel separate the different molecules from an unknown

271

FIGURE 8.1

Images from the Missing Gerbil Movie

substance into distinctive bands. Comparing the pattern of bands produced by a known and an unknown substance (for example, a blood sample) is the basis for DNA fingerprinting and other techniques in which it is necessary to separate protein or other molecular fragments.

Cully realized that his students had some awareness of this procedure through television shows and would be interested in the procedure if he could present it in the right way. Lecturing about electrophoresis was probably not going to be an effective approach. But he was not able to purchase enough materials to allow many small groups of students the opportunity to perform a hands-on experiment.

Faced with this dilemma, Cully decided to create a movie based on a crime investigation. The movie chronicles the adventures of Cully and his assistant (the student teacher) as they investigate the disappearance of a classroom gerbil. As the movie begins, the investigative team is exploring the crime scene. Soon Cully is off to interrogate various school personnel, who give both logical and illogical reasons that they could not possibly be the gerbil snatcher. During a more thorough investigation of the crime scene, Cully's assistant locates some drops of what appears to be blood. Perhaps the culprit was cut dragging the gerbil from its cage or perhaps the gerbil bit the abductor before being subdued! Cully is soon off to collect samples from his prime suspects. Were teachers really willing to donate blood for "the cause"? No; that would have been asking a bit much of even the most dedicated teacher. The samples were actually the demonstration solutions that came with the electrophoresis kit.

This complex scenario was established purely to create a background for the demonstration of the electrophoresis technique. With the exception of labeling the comparison samples with the names of the suspects, the demonstration proceeds pretty much as described in the laboratory manual. At the conclusion of the demonstration, the students are shown the gel slab (see Figure 8.1) and asked to identify the culprit.

Students knew the video was a spoof, but it still engaged them in a way that a scientific documentary would not. The use of their own school as the setting allowed students to recognize and hypothesize about the crime scene. The suspects in the video were familiar school personnel, and watching their teachers and others they knew behave in rather uncharacteristic ways seemed to maintain the attention of these middle-school students. Cully was also able to mix in a lot of humor. For instance, after asking the head cook if she could account for her whereabouts during the hours before school began, he asked her if there were any unusual meat entrees on the day's lunch menu.

We normally emphasize student use of technology in this book. We made an exception in this chapter because we felt this was a highly creative application that took advantage of available technology resources to engage students. Cully Gause's video production put what might have been a standard teacher demonstration into a much more interesting and thought-provoking context. Creating your own video is quite feasible, and you may be surprised at what can now be accomplished with a camcorder, a computer, and some ingenuity. Video production is one of the topics we discuss in this chapter, and we encourage you to consider this activity as the basis for student projects.

Tools for Creating and Manipulating Images

Created versus captured images

Images can be brought into the computer environment in a variety of ways. To differentiate those applications in which images are created using technology from those in which images are captured using technology, think of the more familiar examples of an artist using paints and canvas to create a painting and a photographer using a camera to capture a photograph. Both processes require creativity and technique. The same is true in the application of technology. In the discussion that follows, we describe paint and draw programs as tools for creating and manipulating images. In later sections we describe scanners, digital camcorders, and digital cameras as tools to capture images.

Paint and Draw Programs

Student access to a graphics program is essential to the multimedia project approach frequently mentioned in this book. Graphics programs are traditionally differentiated as paint or draw programs. **Paint programs** store images as records of the individual dots of color, and **draw programs** represent what appears in an image mathematically. We consider this distinction in greater detail at a later point. Paint programs are generally more useful for multimedia projects. No matter what type of graphics program or programs students are using, they will benefit from tools that allow them to do the following:

- Create graphics from scratch
- Modify graphics from other sources
- Save images in the format required for other application programs
- Annotate, organize, and search large image collections

Creating Original Images

Most students can create informative displays.

All graphics programs allow users to produce original artwork. The quality of what they create depends on their talent and experience and the tools the program makes available. People who are accustomed to creating art with a pencil or paintbrush may find their initial attempts to draw or paint using a computer program and a peripheral device such as a mouse frustrating and unsatisfactory. Yet, with experience, artists do learn to work with the tools of technology to produce some remarkable products. Even students with limited artistic skill and experience can generate informative displays.

Modifying Existing Images

Often, as you will see in later sections of this chapter, students can find or capture images of a higher quality than they could create themselves. To use these images in multimedia projects, students need graphics tools that can manipulate and modify the images.

The most frequently used tool capabilities are:

Loading graphics files

- *Loading, or opening, existing graphics files.* Although this may seem an obvious function, not all graphics programs were developed for the purpose of modifying graphics files created by other programs or methods. Files can be stored in many formats, and programs differ in how many different file types they can access.

Copying and pasting

- *Copying and pasting parts of images.* Frequently students want to use part of an existing picture to create a new display. Students may want to take parts of several individual images and combine them into a new composite image to demonstrate stages in some process or to make various comparisons. Perhaps they want to show the stages in a butterfly's development: egg, caterpillar, chrysalis, butterfly. Or they may want to contrast the painted lady butterfly with the monarch.

Enhancing images

- *Enhancing an existing image using a variety of tools.* Students may want to use the text tool to label parts of an image or create a composite image of several small color pictures and a line drawing they have created themselves.

Saving Images That Can Be Used by Application Programs

Saving in a suitable format

Students generally use a paint or draw program at an intermediate stage of a project. For the final stage, the images that have been created or modified are integrated into a larger product—a multimedia presentation, webpage, word processing document, or the like. Thus the paint or draw program should be able to save images in a format suitable for the final authoring or presentation program.

You may want to consider the issue of file compatibility before your students begin to work on projects. Most graphics programs allow images to be saved in at least a couple of file formats, typically a format specific to the program plus one or more other formats. High-end graphics programs allow files to be saved in a large number of formats, but less expensive programs designed specifically for classroom use may offer a minimum of options. This can be an issue when students create an image in one application (such as a graphics program) and on a computer with one type of operating system (such as Macintosh) and then need to use the image in another program (such as a web authoring program) on a computer with a different operating system (such as Windows). If you are aware that file compatibility is an issue, you would want to have students save their work using a format that will work across applications and operating systems (for example, JPEG). We provide more information on file formats later in this chapter.

Organizing and Saving Large Image Collections

How to save and organize?

It has become so easy to collect large quantities of digital images that it can be a challenge to locate an image you need. If you have your own digital camera, you have probably encountered this problem already. If not, imagine a classroom project in which four or five teams of students spend a day taking digital pictures on a field trip. More difficult still, imagine keeping track of the images accumulated from field trips taken over several years. Collections can easily grow to include hundreds or thousands of images. Specialized tools help users annotate, organize, and search through large image collections. Subsets of images can be identified and separated for use in specific projects. While organization may be the main function of programs of this type, such software may also contain simplified paint tools that meet all requirements for some classroom projects. We review an example of this type of software application later in this chapter.

Comparing Paint and Draw Programs

Now that you understand the basic functions of graphics software, we can consider the differences between paint and draw programs. Each of these two categories has advantages and disadvantages.

Pixels

Paint programs are used to create and manipulate **bitmapped** images. With such programs, an image is created on a "page" that contains a set number of visual elements. You might think of visual elements as the individual points or dots that make up the image and background. A bitmapped image is "painted" on the background by changing the color of these individual dots, or **pixels.** Working at the level of individual pixels offers the greatest flexibility in creating an image, but paint programs also have some disadvantages when modifying, storing, and printing images. There are problems in effectively adjusting the size of images, and the images tend to take up more disk space than images created by draw programs.

Draw programs, in contrast, are used to create and manipulate **object-oriented images.** Object-oriented programs define the elements (points, lines, circles) making up these images in terms of mathematical equations. When an object-oriented image is saved to disk, it is this mathematical information, not a record of the color of individual pixels, that is saved. This does not mean that a young student working with a draw program needs to know the equation for defining a circle and locating the circle at a particular spot on the computer screen. The program takes care of the mathematics. Because object-oriented programs are composed of individual objects and these objects can be isolated and modified, certain editing functions are much easier with draw programs.

Draw programs also tend to store images much more efficiently and display images with higher quality than do paint programs. The display quality of an image in a draw program is limited only by the quality of the computer screen or printer used to produce the display. At issue is how much information—that is, **dots per inch (dpi)**—the screen or printer is capable of presenting. The mathematical formula defining draw objects can be used to produce basically the amount of information that the display device is capable of representing. The quality of bitmapped images is defined when the images are created and thus may be lower than the quality of image that the display device can present.

In this chapter we give more attention to bitmapped images than to object-oriented images because the devices that students use to capture images from other sources, such as camcorders and digital cameras, produce files in the bitmapped format. Moreover, the simple type of editing students are likely to do—for example, cutting a picture from one source to display it in another application—is easier in the bitmapped paint format than in the object-oriented draw format.

AppleWorks One effective way to demonstrate some of the differences between draw and paint programs is to consider an application such as Apple-Works that makes both types of tools available. You will notice in Figure 8.2 that the paintbrush, pencil, paint can, airbrush, and eraser are available as paint tools but not as draw tools. Paint tools allow the manipulation of individual pixels with great flexibility. The pencil tool provides a good example of this flexibility. A pencil can be used to sketch or to scribble. The complexity of either of these images would be difficult to represent efficiently in a mathematical equation. All of the other tools that are unique to the paint format can be applied with the same flexibility.

You will also note from Figure 8.2 that both paint and draw palettes offer tools for creating basic shapes, such as rectangles, lines, and polygons. Even when draw and paint tools are used to create identical images, the properties of the images are still very different. Compare the two rectangles on the right side of Figure 8.2. The rectangle created with the draw tool is a single unit. If the user decides to remove it from the computer screen, it will be deleted as a

FIGURE 8.2

Paint and Draw Palettes from AppleWorks

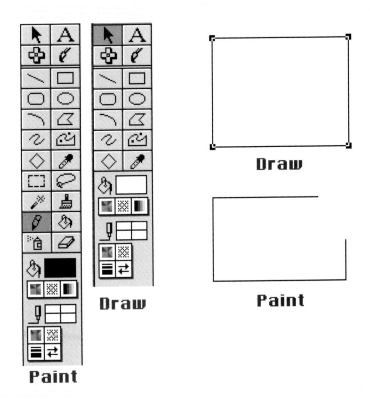

unit. The small, dark squares appearing at the corners of the rectangle are handles the user can drag (click with the mouse and move with the mouse button held down) to change the shape of the rectangle—for instance, to make it long and thin, short and fat, or a perfect square. The handles disappear as soon as the user selects another tool or begins work on another part of the computer screen. In contrast, the rectangle created with the paint tool is not a single unit; it is actually made up of pixels that can be manipulated independently. To demonstrate the difference between rectangles created with draw and paint tools, the eraser tool has been used to eliminate a corner of the painted rectangle in Figure 8.2. A set of pixels has been removed, and the rest of the rectangle remains. The eraser is not available when working on draw objects because they must be treated as whole units. Similarly, because the painted rectangle is not one unit, it cannot easily be reshaped into a square.

Distortion of enlarged paint images

One other unique problem that users of paint programs encounter is the distortion that occurs when the size of an image is changed. The individual pixels that make up an image are like tiny blocks. When an image is enlarged, these blocks are simply magnified. In some cases, particularly with diagonal lines, this magnification results in a distortion that is often called **jaggies** (see Figure 8.3).

Do schools need both draw and paint applications? There are some very useful applications for object-oriented images in the fields of design and

FIGURE 8.3
**Bitmapped Line Magnified
Four Times**

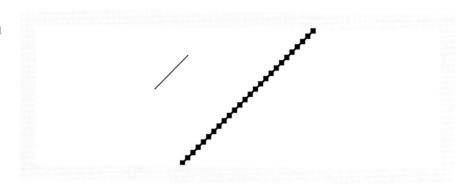

engineering, and educational experiences related to these areas offer opportunities for draw applications. However, these applications are relatively infrequent in comparison to the opportunities to use paint programs. The flexibility of bitmapped graphics is extremely important for the general computer tool approach we advocate here.

KidPix Deluxe—A Paint Program KidPix is one of the best examples of a paint program developed specifically for younger users. This inexpensive program combines a set of functional graphics tools, an interface intended for young users, and some quirky tools and features just for fun.

A graphic user interface for young users

The KidPix interface was designed to make the program's options apparent even to inexperienced users. The idea is to use icons that visibly suggest what can be done with each tool so that the user does not have to learn or remember complicated procedures. Although most users have to experiment a bit to become familiar with what some of the options actually do, this **graphic user interface (GUI)** makes it easy to learn and remember how to use the program.

Tool icons and related options

If you have had little previous experience with computer paint programs, the structure of the KidPix interface might serve as a convenient model for understanding more complicated programs. As you examine a monitor displaying KidPix (see Figure 8.4), you will see a column of icons down the left side of the screen and a row of options associated with the selected tool icon across the bottom of the screen. The user can easily choose among paint tools, color options, and tool options. Although not all paint programs make these choices visible simultaneously to the user, other paint programs work in approximately the same way. The user selects a paint tool to work with; when applicable, the color the paint tool is to apply; and an option for the specific effect the tool will have. In KidPix, when a tool is selected, the tool options available for that tool appear automatically; the young user does not have to remember the options that are available or how to implement them. In some cases, all of the available options cannot fit in a single row. When this is the case, a numbered arrow at the end of the row informs the user that more options are available. The user can view the additional options by clicking on the up or down arrow.

FIGURE 8.4
KidPix Deluxe 3 Monitor Display

Using Graphics Tools in a Writing Assignment

How are the various graphics tools used to construct a picture? The following description takes you step by step through the process of creating a simple image, which was the cover for a writing assignment, "My Pet," by Kim. (The finished image is provided later in Figure 8.6.) This image combines the picture of a dog, captured using a video digitizing technique, with simple line art and text created in KidPix.

The process begins with the original picture of a dog sitting under a kitchen table. To get just the part of the image that is needed, the area around the dog is carefully erased. One useful approach when doing very detailed work is to magnify an image several times. Working on an enlarged image calls for much less delicate control of a tool such as the eraser. It would be very easy to slip and erase a paw if it were necessary to work on a same-size image.

For detailed work, magnify images

Focus

Screen Capture

Screen capture is the process of saving the screen image or part of the screen image (even if the screen contains text) as a graphics file. The process is very much like taking a picture of the screen. Screen capture capabilities are built into the Macintosh and Windows operating systems. In Windows, the keyboard command is Alt-Print Screen. A copy of the screen is saved to the **clipboard,** a computer memory buffer from which it can be loaded into a paint program such as Windows' own Paintbrush. The Macintosh equivalent is Command-Shift-3. Executing this command should result in the reassuring sound of a camera shutter click that lets the user know the computer has taken the requested action. Screen capture for the Macintosh saves the screen image as a file on the computer's hard drive. A paint program can then be used to load and work with the captured image. Command-Shift-4 changes the cursor to crosshairs and allows a selected area of the screen to be stored as a PDF (portable document format) file.

It is also possible to purchase small programs (sometimes called *utilities* and often available as shareware) that extend the basic screen capture techniques. For example, such utilities usually allow the user to select and then capture any part of the image that appears on the entire screen and then to print or save the designated segment.

Screen captures can be used for many different purposes. One important use is capturing screens from application programs to use in material that explains to others how to use those programs. Many images in this textbook were captured from the screen for this purpose. Teachers may have opportunities to use this technique to prepare instructional materials for their students. If you wanted to prepare handouts explaining to students how to use a new program, this would be a useful way to display what the computer screen would look like at certain critical points.

Once the picture of the dog has been isolated from the background, it is moved to the bottom of the screen, out of the way.

The first step in constructing the doghouse is to generate a large rectangle using the rectangle tool. (The shape tool options, such as the rectangle, become available across the bottom of the KidPix display when the user clicks on the pencil icon shown in the middle of the left column in Figure 8.4.) After it is selected, the rectangle tool is positioned in what is intended to be one of the corners of the finished shape. The mouse button is then depressed, and the rectangle tool is moved toward the opposite corner of the intended shape. If the user starts in the upper-left corner, the mouse can be moved on a downward diagonal or over and then down (see Figure 8.5). As long as the mouse button remains depressed, the rectangle tool will draw a rectangle between

FIGURE 8.5
Technique for Using Paint
Rectangle Tool

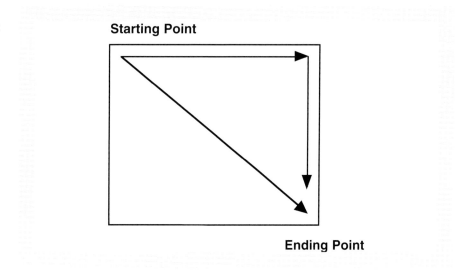

Starting Point

Ending Point

the initial point and the point to which the tool is moved. When the mouse is released, the size of the rectangle is fixed. If the image does not meet the user's expectations, it can be removed with the undo tool and redrawn.

When you examine Figure 8.6, the fact that you no longer see a complete rectangle may at first confuse you. The oval tool was used to generate a large oval on top of the rectangle. Because the opaque tool was selected from the fill options appearing across the bottom of the screen (see Figure 8.4), the oval obscures part of the line making up the original rectangle. The technique for creating an oval is exactly the same as for creating a rectangle. Start at a point on one boundary and move the tool toward the corresponding point on the opposite side of the figure. With a little practice, users learn to create ovals of different shapes. Of course, you also do not see a complete oval in Figure 8.6. The bottom part of the oval was erased using the erase tool, beginning at the points where the oval intersected the rectangle. The result is the entrance to the doghouse.

Using fill and undo features

Kim created the roof by using the line tool to draw three lines and the paint bucket to fill the enclosed area with a pattern selected from the available options. It is important when using a fill procedure to make certain there are no gaps in the boundary of the area to be filled. If an opening is present, the fill color or pattern will leak out across any open area of the picture. If this should happen (and it happens to everyone because breaks in lines are not always easy to see), the key is not to panic. Simply use the undo tool to delete the last action taken. It is also good practice to save your work every few minutes, so that you will never be in the position of losing work that has taken a long time to create.

To finish the picture, text is added using the text tool, and the student's signature is added using the pencil tool. The image of the dog is then moved to its intended position at the side of the doghouse. Because KidPix moves only rectangular areas, some of the lines on the doghouse were covered up

FIGURE 8.6

Sample KidPix Picture

with the "white" space that surrounded the picture of the dog. These lines had to be redrawn. Obviously, some of the mechanical techniques used in computer graphics are a little different from those used with pencil, crayons, and paper. Learning these techniques is just a matter of awareness and practice.

It is difficult to describe the process of creating a picture with a paint program. Some processes are best learned by experience; if you have the opportunity, you should certainly take the time to acquaint yourself with at least one paint program.

Benefits of a higher-end program

Because of its modest cost and intended users, KidPix does not have some of the tools or tool options that are available in full-featured graphics programs and does not meet all the needs of educational settings. For instance, it cannot open all types of image files, shrink or enlarge an image, or change brightness and contrast. For these purposes, students and teachers would need a higher-end program. It is not necessary to invest in many copies of a higher-end program, but at least one workstation with additional tools and features should be available so that students and teachers can perform more sophisticated functions. You can find some suggestions for graphics software in "Resources to Expand Your Knowledge Base" at the end of this chapter, and on the website that accompanies this textbook.

Understanding Graphics File Formats

When a graphics program stores a graphic image, the resulting file has a characteristic format. Users may encounter a bewildering array of graphics file formats. This situation exists for several reasons.

Why so many file formats?

1. Certain file types are associated with different hardware platforms. For example, BMP (we explain this term and others shortly) is a common format on computers running the Microsoft Windows operating system, and PICT is a common Apple Macintosh format.
2. Certain file types were designed to accomplish certain tasks. The TIFF format, for example, was developed for scanned images, and the GIF format was designed for exchanging graphics through the Internet.
3. Many graphics programs have a native format. This means that programs of this type save graphics files in a format that is intended to be loaded only by the same program. In most cases, however, programs offering a native format also allow files to be saved in other formats.
4. Some graphics file formats allow higher-quality **compression.** Conversion to a compressed file format results in a file that takes less disk space and consequently can be transmitted over the Internet more quickly. There are two basic types of compression:

   - **Lossless compression** methods store data with greater efficiency and generate a smaller file without a reduction in image quality.
   - **Lossy compression** creates a smaller file that approximates rather than exactly matches the original. Typically, the small differences are difficult to detect and not essential.

Why should teachers using computers in their classrooms bother to become aware of the characteristics of various graphics file formats? Here are some situations you might encounter:

- An elementary-school teacher wants to scan some line art from a coloring book and then have his students paint the images using KidPix. The school's older scanner saves the scanned images as TIFF files. (Scanners are discussed later.) KidPix cannot load this file format. What should the teacher do?
- A high-school science teacher finds some breathtaking photographs on the Internet from a recent space mission. The photographs are in JPEG format. The school has Macintosh equipment. Should the teacher download the files?
- You have a great collection of free clip art stored on a Macintosh CD. A teacher friend of yours has ideas for using some of the images in a classroom newsletter, but the teacher uses a Windows machine. Is there some way to make the images available to her?

Translators

There are several ways to deal with the various file formats you might encounter. If you are lucky, you will be able to ignore them. Many programs have built-in **translators**—small utilities that allow the program to accept a variety of file formats. Programs of this type can also be used as an intermediary. For example, KidPix accepts PICT, BMP, and JPEG files. Photoshop is a much more powerful and flexible program that allows files to be opened and saved in a variety of formats. If it were necessary to get a TIFF image into KidPix, Photoshop could be used to open the image in TIFF format and save the image in PICT format. KidPix could then work with the image. This is one of the reasons we recommend that schools invest in a more powerful graphics program even if students would only rarely use such a program. There are also utility programs that are designed primarily to convert files from one format to another.

Here is a brief explanatory list of graphics file formats you may encounter; they are usually called by their abbreviations (in parentheses):

Common graphics file formats

bitmap (BMP) Common bitmap format for the Windows platform.

encapsulated PostScript (EPS) A format commonly used for storing object-oriented graphics files.

graphics interchange format (GIF) A format created by CompuServe for efficient transfer of bitmapped images over the Internet. The GIF format continues to be popular for this purpose.

Joint Photographic Experts Group (JPEG) A lossy compression format that produces high-quality images while drastically reducing file size. This is presently the most common Internet format.

PICT A generic file format for the Macintosh that allows a mixture of bitmapped and object-oriented graphics. (*Note*: "PICT" is not a group of initials—it's just short for *picture.*)

portable network graphic (PNG) An efficient format for the Internet, developed as a replacement for GIF. This format is lossless.

RAW Another lossless format, available on some digital cameras. RAW is intended for camera storage only; the images should be converted once they are moved to a computer. (*Note*: Raw is not an acronym).

tagged image file format (TIFF) The most flexible format for bitmapped (not object-oriented) graphics and often the standard output file for scanning. It can be used across Macintosh and Windows platforms.

Tools for Capturing Still Images

Capturing images from paper or surroundings

There are several ways in which students can capture images for use in projects. Here we will describe how students can use scanners to transfer images from paper and use digital cameras and camcorders to capture images from their surroundings.

Scanners working in combination with a computer were developed to convert an external image into a digitized graphics file. This means that existing images, such as a crayon line drawing created by a young student or a secondary-school student's original pencil illustration, can be converted into the kind of digital information that a computer can use. Information in the form of a graphics file can be saved to disk, loaded back into the computer later, displayed on the computer monitor, or printed. Once an image is present in a form the computer can manipulate, tool software can be used to cut sections from a larger image to form smaller images; integrate images from several sources to form a new composite image; add text to label parts of an image; add color to black-and-white drawings; and modify, combine, and manipulate the stored images in many other ways. Once brought into the computer, and perhaps enhanced with graphics software tools, images captured

Focus

Graphics for the Web

Preparing images for presentation on webpages presents two challenges:

1. Images that are part of webpages are viewed with different browser software used on a variety of hardware platforms.
2. Transfer speed across the Internet can be a problem, particularly when users are connecting by modem. It is important to keep the file size of images as small as possible.

The current solution to these challenges is to use file formats that are **cross-platform**—meaning that the format is accepted by different types of computers—and to take advantage of techniques that minimize file size. Nearly all web graphics are sent over the Internet in one of three file formats: GIF, PNG, or JPEG. Anyone wanting to include graphics on their webpages needs to know how to convert existing images to these formats and to understand the strengths and weaknesses of each format type.

Large graphics files can be a problem because users become impatient when files take a long time to transfer over slow Internet connections. As more and more users have access to high-speed connections, our expectations for how quickly webpages should load also have changed. One way to control the size of graphics files is to restrict the number of colors that are used. For example, GIF files rely on 256 or fewer colors rather than the thousands or millions of colors allowed in JPEG or PNG files. Using 256 colors works just fine when you are creating your own images, but it is not an adequate solution when you are using images captured with a scanner or digital camera. In generating a GIF file, the graphics software must convert many of the colors present in the image to one of the 256 colors that are available. This conversion process creates some distortion as shades of color are simplified into fewer colors. As the web has matured, we have come to expect higher-quality images.

PNG and JPEG image files make use of the full color palette available on the computer and save file space in other ways. Because JPEG is presently the most widely used file format on the Web and is the only Internet-ready format available with many authoring and graphics programs designed for the education market, we focus our comments on attributes of the JPEG file format.

There are two attributes of JPEG image files you might want to consider when preparing images for Internet presentation. The first is image **resolution.** Resolution is the number of pixels per unit of measurement. The term might be used to describe the number of pixels captured per inch by a digital camera, the number of pixels per inch displayed on a computer monitor, or the number of pixels per inch put on paper by a printer. One issue that can confuse web authors is the conflict between the resolution capabilities of a computer monitor and the resolution, or *pixel density,* at which a digital image was captured by a camera. Pixel density is typically described as a pair of numbers representing the number of pixels in the width and height of an image. A 3.34-megapixel digital camera is set to capture high-quality images at approximately 2048 x 1536 pixels and 300 pixels per inch. This generates an image of 6.83 x 5.12 inches when printed on a quality printer. Your computer monitor cannot display this resolution. If you have uploaded a digital camera image into your computer and attempted to display it using a web browser, you know what happens—the image is huge. Instead of each pixel taking 1/300 of an inch as was assumed when the image was stored by the camera, it is displayed as 1/90 of an inch. This translation greatly expands the size of the image. You may be fooled if you open the image in some graphics editing programs, such as KidPix, because the programs will compensate for differences in resolution to display images in a standard-size window.

More advanced graphics programs allow the user to adjust the pixel density of an image while holding the dimensions of the image constant. This capability is typically the way digital camera images are prepared for web presentation. Reducing the resolution of an image reduces the size of the image file and increases the speed with which the image file can be sent over the Internet. You can force a browser to display a high-resolution file in a smaller size by adding some commands to the HTML code displaying the image (we comment briefly on HTML code in the chapter entitled "Learning from Student Projects"). However, sending unnecessarily large files as part of a webpage is not recommended.

The second attribute of a JPEG file that is important for web presentation is the level of compression that is applied. JPEG files are saved with lossy compression technique, thereby introducing a small amount of error, or visual noise, into an image to save file space; that is, the stored image is a simplified replica of the original. The noise is more subtle than that associated with GIF images. When the image is complex (with lots of colors and a complex pattern), the noise is difficult to detect. More advanced graphics programs allow the user to control how much compression is applied, and the user can experiment to find the most acceptable trade-off between file size and image quality. This is one more advantage that a more costly and specialized advanced graphics program would have over a less costly graphics program using a single standard compression setting. When experimenting with compression settings, it is always important to save a copy of the original image. Once an image has been compressed and the file saved, it is not possible to recreate the original image from this file.

from an external source can become part of the multimedia products discussed in several other chapters of this book.

Flatbed Scanners

Operating a scanner

If you have ever copied documents with a photocopying machine, you are well on your way to being able to operate a flatbed **scanner.** You begin by lifting the lid of the scanner and placing the sheet of paper with the image you want to scan face down on the glass. When the scanning process begins, you will notice the familiar light source moving along the length of the image beneath the glass plate. In a scanner, a lens or mirror system beneath the glass plate focuses the light reflected from the original image into the charge-coupled device (CCD). The output from this device is translated within the scanner into the digital form acceptable as input to a computer.

Digital Cameras

It may surprise many to learn that digital cameras have been around for some time. These devices may appear similar to traditional cameras, but instead of capturing images on film, digital cameras use a CCD like that used in a camcorder. The older versions kept images on a special video floppy disk, and the method of storage was similar to that of videotape. These images were not digitized. The images stored on this type of disk still have to be converted to a digital format with a video digitizing card before they can be used in multimedia applications. The digital cameras available over the past few years store images in a digital format. Both the quality of the images captured by these cameras and the price have improved dramatically, and many schools are purchasing digital cameras.

Image quality   There are several things to keep in mind when purchasing a digital camera for school use. The quality of the captured images is a big issue. Currently, the more you are willing to pay, the higher-quality images you will be able to store. Probably the most significant factor in image quality is the pixel density the CCD is able to capture; as we indicated earlier, the more tightly packed the dots of color are, the higher quality the image is. Present digital cameras are also described by the number of megapixels the CCD is capable of capturing in the image as a whole. The more pixels used to represent the same area, the higher the quality of the image. The current standard is probably the 3- (actually 3.34-) megapixel camera, but 5- and 7-megapixel cameras can be purchased for well under $500. Cameras are changing rapidly, and it is difficult to predict the cost and capabilities of the cameras that will be available to you as you read this book.

There are some other factors that determine image quality. Such factors include the quality of the lens system and the algorithm used to process the image for storage. Lens systems differ in quality and also in whether the lens allows the photographer to zoom in and out. If a zoom feature is available, it may be either an electronic zoom or a true optical zoom. With the electronic zoom, the digital image is simply magnified, much like the action you might use to increase image size with a paint program. This type of magnification causes some distortion. The true optical zoom produces images of much better quality. Some storage methods use a lossy method to allow more images to be stored, and this results in images of somewhat lower quality. Camera manufacturers are willing to degrade the quality of images because of the practical limits of storage. A camera that can hold only eight images and then needs to transfer the images to a computer does present some practical challenges when working in the field.

Storage and transfer methods   The storage method and the related issue of how you transfer the images to a computer for student use are important issues to consider. Storage mechanisms include RAM (memory chips much like those contained in a computer), **flash memory** (a kind of removable memory cartridge), disks, and even CDs. There are advantages and disadvantages to each. For example, RAM memory is the least expensive but requires that the camera be frequently linked to a computer to offload pictures. This system is typically used in only the most inexpensive cameras.

For those familiar with traditional cameras, working with a digital camera takes a little adjustment. One thing you will probably notice is a delay. The camera does not record the image the instant you attempt to activate the shutter. In most cases it takes a couple of seconds, and this makes photographing moving images or pictures that require a quick reaction difficult. It also takes a little while for the camera to process and store the image. You cannot click away as you can with traditional 35-mm cameras.

Fitting the camera to its intended use

As you can see, purchasing and using a digital camera requires that a number of issues be considered. It is important to determine how the camera will be used and what features are necessary for that type of use. You can purchase a camera capable of taking digital pictures that rival what you could generate by taking photographs with a traditional 35-mm camera. A 7-megapixel camera can presently be purchased for about $750. Would it be better to purchase two 3-megapixel cameras for the same total amount? Which would be the better choice for the situation in which you will use technology? Some suggestions for learning about digital cameras are included on the website that accompanies this textbook.

Still Images from Video

A good option for still images

A camcorder can serve as a convenient source for still images. There are two ways to do this. Some camcorders have the built-in capability to capture images and store them to tape. If you have access to a camcorder, check to see if it offers this capability. Typically, there is a separate button for this specific purpose. You can also use a video recording as a source for still images. In this case, the video needs to be downloaded to a computer and accessed with a video editing program. Editing video on a computer provides the opportunity to step through the video one frame at a time. Video editing programs typically offer an option that allows a frame to be captured as a still image. For example, iMovie, the application we describe later in this chapter, has a menu command Save Frame As. Note that the quality of camcorder images tends to be much lower than all but the most inexpensive digital cameras (about 72 pixels per inch).

It is important to be aware of these options for two reasons. First, there is the simple issue of access to equipment. You may have access to a camcorder but not a digital camera. Or you may have access to both, and bringing along the camcorder simply offers a way for another student to collect visual data. Second, we think there are some situations in which video is an effective way for less skilled individuals to collect material that will be used to generate images. For example, situations that occur quickly and without warning (such as a whale breaching) are difficult to capture with a still camera. While video may be a convenient way to capture an entire experience or to capture a lot of

ACTIVITIES AND PROJECTS FOR YOUR CLASSROOM

Video Images to Capture

Once you understand the basics, it is easy to generate a list of the types of video images students might capture. The opportunities to provide examples, demonstrate something, or just liven up your writing are limitless. Here are a few ideas to get you started. Video-capture techniques can be used to generate images that:

- Contrast proper and improper weightlifting techniques
- Reveal geometric shapes in your environment
- Personalize a language board (a device used to communicate by pointing at pictures) for a seriously language-impaired student
- Recall experiences from field trips to a farm, factory, museum, lakeshore, or local business
- Show the birds that have visited your bird feeder
- Expose instances of local pollution
- Exemplify merchandise displays you consider interesting and effective
- Show the many ways computer technology is used in the workplace
- Illustrate some of the things that make students happy

---

information, the still images within the video may be the most useful and perhaps most efficient way for students to reflect on and communicate what they have learned.

Locating Image Sources

Huge range of multimedia resources

Searching for multimedia resources will take you into new territory. It has led us to carry our camcorder down wooded trails and into county historical museums. We have become acquainted with student artists at all educational levels. We have scoured bargain bookstores and museum and zoo gift shops in search of unusual coloring books, as well as the backs of computer magazines for the ads of small companies offering collections of sounds, video clips, and pictures.

Increasingly, resources are becoming easier to find. The market for multimedia resources has started to expand, and inexpensive collections are now available in every educational supplies catalog. Nevertheless, we urge teachers not to rely completely on such material and to make project-by-project decisions about how best to gather resources. The convenience of providing students access to commercial multimedia collections should be balanced against the fun and educational value of searching for your own resources.

Because scanners are used to capture images that already appear on paper and because teachers tend to be familiar with many sources of this type, it may be most productive to comment on a few resources teachers may overlook.

Coloring Books

Coloring book images ideal for scanning

Coloring books provide images that are nearly ideal for scanning. Because the images are drawn simply, emphasizing only the essential details, the quality of the captured images tends to be very high even when they are scanned with inexpensive equipment. Also, the images are already drawn in line mode, so images captured from coloring books can be saved in files that do not take up very much disk or memory space. Coloring book images also lend themselves to a more active role for students. Students can label, color, and incorporate parts of the images into their own artwork.

Theme coloring books are published for a variety of audiences. College students enrolled in human anatomy or neuroanatomy, for example, frequently use specialized coloring books to study the subject matter of these courses. The students are asked to use colored pencils to indicate certain structures or differentiate organ systems in a complex line drawing. Other coloring books emphasize specific topics, such as butterflies, mammals, plants and animals of Rocky Mountain National Park, or Native Americans of the northern plains. Coloring books are frequently published by organizations such as state historical societies, groups with an interest in wildlife management or preservation, the national park system, and major museums. These coloring books are found most easily by visiting shops run by the organizations. Several publishing companies also offer a variety of publications in coloring book form. These resources are most likely to be found in large bookstores. Often bookstores have only some of the coloring books available and may need to special order the ones you are interested in.

Checking copyright limitations

Those producing or sponsoring coloring books have different motives. In many cases, their intent is to make money, and scanning images from the books would be regarded as copyright infringement. Teachers might be surprised to learn that companies have different policies on this matter. A careful reading of the copyright information, which is usually located on the inside of the front cover, may yield the requisite information. Many companies deny access to the entire contents of the coloring book. Others allow a specific number of images to be used for projects. It is also sometimes worth the time to write to the organizations that sponsor coloring books you are interested in using; some allow images to be used for educational purposes. (We discuss this topic in more depth in the chapter entitled "Responsible Use of Technology.")

World Wide Web

You know the Web provides access to hypermedia and is rich in high-quality images. Although web browsers allow you to save any image that strikes your fancy, actually doing so is a questionable practice. If you see an image you would like to use, you should contact the owner of the webpage before taking it.

Online image collections

The Web offers an alternative you might consider. Several sites specialize in organizing collections of images for public use. Try using a search engine and the words "clip art" to get started.

Student Art

Another scanning resource to consider is student artwork. Students can draw or paint images relevant to a particular topic, and these creations can be scanned for inclusion in projects.

Creating multi-disciplinary links

Two factors particularly recommend this source. First, working with student art provides an opportunity to create a unique multidisciplinary linkage. Art can contribute to other content areas, and the work in content areas can provide opportunities for artistic expression. This relationship may be informal, created simply by extending the typical content of a science or history course, or it may involve a more formal cooperation between two classes and two instructors.

Engaging students with artistic talent

Second, drawing on student artistic talent showcases the unique abilities of some students who may otherwise receive little attention in a science or history classroom. Artistic talent is far from perfectly correlated with the other academic talents teachers encounter. Providing artistic students an opportunity to contribute may also engage them more actively with the course content.

Clip Art Collections

Image collections on CDs

Many collections of images are available to computer users. These collections have generally been targeted at desktop publishers, but the collections about places, cultures, land formations, historical events, or biological organisms also have relevance for classrooms. It is possible to purchase CDs containing 100 butterflies, mammals, scenes from Germany, and many similar collections for about $20. A collection containing more than 100,000 images is available from another vendor. These resources are often advertised as royalty free. Owning a collection of royalty-free clips allows the use of these resources for classroom projects without concern for copyright restrictions. Personal computer catalogs are a good source for these CDs.

These resources are not always marketed in ways that emphasize educational applications. Products of this type will eventually become more prevalent for the education market, however, and will be offered through outlets familiar to teachers. A few specific suggestions for locating these resources are included at the end of this chapter.

Organizing Your Image Collection

Commonsense labeling may not be sufficient.

During a field trip or other occasion for collecting a large number of images, or when combining the images collected by several individuals, you can accumulate hundreds of image files. While stored within the camera, the image files are assigned incremental filenames (for instance, DSCN0715.jpg, DSCN0716.jpg). How do you go about organizing and making sense of a large collection of images? Once they are copied to the computer, your first step is probably to open each file, discard the poor-quality images, and relabel the "keepers" in a more meaningful way. Because the length of filenames is limited, it is difficult to generate descriptive file labels, and pretty soon what seemed like a good label (zootrip01) demonstrates limited value. It might occur to you to create a series of folders, label each folder (zootrip2005), and then label each image file assigned to each folder in a more meaningful way (bears01.jpg). At some level, however, such a system simply becomes overwhelming and inefficient. Specialized software applications are available that provide powerful tools for organizing and making use of large image collections.

iPhoto

IPhoto offers a variety of capabilities for importing, organizing, editing, and publishing digital images and video clips. While the strength of this application is in the powerful ways in which large collections of images can be organized, annotated, and searched, the less sophisticated editing and publishing tools may be useful as convenient substitutes when more expensive dedicated editing and authoring tools are not available. Accordingly, we will concentrate on iPhoto's organizational functions but offer brief comments on its editing and authoring capabilities.

Load, edit, annotate, locate, generate

One way to understand the use of iPhoto in creating projects is to think in terms of a sequence of the following activities: (1) load images, (2) edit images and eliminate rejects, (3) annotate images for future reference, (4) locate images relevant to a specific project, and (5) generate and publish a multimedia project. This sequence of activities may actually unfold over a long period of time, involve different participants in completing different stages, involve iPhoto alone or iPhoto in combination with other applications, and require that participants break from this sequence when difficulty in completing one activity requires that an earlier activity in the sequence receive more attention. We will follow this sequence in briefly describing how iPhoto works.

IPhoto will accept images directly from a digital camera or from any storage device the computer can access (CD, hard drive, flash drive). All images appear in a general "library" that is subdivided into "rolls." A roll represents a collection of images loaded at one time, and each roll is automatically dated when loaded. If you wish, you can assign a more meaningful title to the roll (field trip to Getty Museum). The user interface for iPhoto is shown in Figure 8.7.

Culling images

One of the great things about digital photography as opposed to using film is that you can take a large number of pictures without increasing your expense. Photographers can cull images at two stages. If there is time, the images stored in the camera can be examined using the camera's display, and images that are obviously of poor quality can be deleted. This activity may be necessary to free up space on the limited-capacity storage medium. Once loaded into the computer, images can be examined more carefully and the selection process continued, You will want to eliminate images of no value and see if you can salvage images that are poorly composed or improperly exposed. Eliminating the unsalvageable images is easy: Select the image and hit the delete key. Improving images is easy as well. IPhoto offers editing tools that can be used to crop out an unwanted portion of an image; fix "red eye," which occurs so commonly with digital flash photography; and automatically adjust color balance and brightness. If you wish, you can also manually adjust brightness, contrast, exposure, sharpness, and several other image characteristics. This product is not intended as a substitute for high-end image editing products, but it will meet student needs for most classroom activities.

FIGURE 8.7
iPhoto 5 Album

Using titles and comments

    A program such as iPhoto also offers multiple ways to organize your collection and improve your ability to find images and remember what they show. While image collections and individual images tend to come into iPhoto with meaningless titles, it is easy to attach a label to both rolls and images. In addition, you can attach keywords and annotations to individual images. IPhoto operates under the assumption that there will be a limited number of keywords and that each keyword will be used multiple times. The idea is to create meaningful subsets of images. For example, a high-school teacher involved in teaching chemistry and physics might have a keyword ("chemistry" or "physics") to identify images potentially useful in each class. The user creates a list of keywords and then assigns one or more keywords to individual images. In contrast, comments are intended to be wordy and unique. If you have ever examined a collection of old photos, you may have noticed short descriptions written on the back of some of the photographs or below the photos in an album. Think of comments in the same way. If you examine the information pane of Figure 8.7 (lower left), you will see the location where titles and comments for individual images are added. The other information appearing in this pane is automatically assigned when the images are downloaded from the digital camera.

Annotating for active learning

Image titles and comments are useful in several ways. The iPhoto search feature (note the Search field in the lower-right corner of Figure 8.7) can be used to locate images by keyword or by words appearing in a comment. With large image collections, this feature is critical. Linking text information with images is valuable for another reason. The title and comments can help you or someone else understand what the image displays. Returning to our comparison with old photo albums, you may have occasionally used the comments appearing on the back of some photographs to identify relatives you have never met; the images alone were not particularly meaningful. Adding notes is helpful even when the images you are storing are based on your own experience. It is very easy to forget important details. You may have had the personal experience of visiting a zoo, taking pictures of the animals and birds, and then later not knowing for certain what type of gorilla, chimpanzee, or ape an interesting image represents. Keeping notes as you collect images, and then using these notes to add comments as you store the images, makes the development of an image collection a more active and meaningful learning experience.

Publishing options

To use iPhoto to create a product, you first identify the images to be included in a project. This is done by creating an album, dragging the desired images into the album, and then sequencing the images in a way that tells a meaningful story. The images visible in Figure 8.7 are part of an album. Images appearing in an album are not physically removed from the library, and the same image may be included in several albums. With the help of templates available in iPhoto, albums can be used to generate slide shows, books, and webpages. The images in an album can also be exported as a collection for use in projects created with other multimedia authoring applications.

We would like to encourage educators to explore the features of iPhoto and identify ways in which this application could support classroom projects. For teachers wanting to have students develop a project within a single application, we suggest that teachers consider the book templates available in iPhoto. These templates seem intended for use in creating high-quality picture books that can be uploaded for commercial printing and then displayed on a coffee table. Teachers might use the same templates in a different way. Identify the book templates that allow the inclusion of text boxes and text pages, and then consider printing the books on your classroom computer. Projects that encourage students to reflect on experiences using a combination of writing and student-collected images would seem most likely to encourage meaningful learning.

Working with Video

As you have seen in earlier chapters, many class projects can incorporate video segments. Here is a list of desirable resources for such projects:

- *Camcorder.* The video camera is the most essential feature for video projects. Cameras range in price (from $300 up).
- *Camcorder accessories.* Certain accessories improve the quality of what can be captured with a camcorder. Our suggested accessories are a good tripod, light source, and remote microphone. Quality sound is often one of the most difficult challenges, and a $25 mike and 25-foot cable or a somewhat more expensive wireless mike are wise investments.
- *High-end computer with large storage capacity.* The computer must have a fast processor and large amounts of RAM to work with the real-time processing of video and audio. Video requires large storage capacity, so the larger the hard drive the better. If using a computer with the Windows operating system, make certain the computer has a FireWire adapter (look for the label "IEEE 1394"). Windows XP and ME support FireWire, but the hardware is not present in all computers.
- *External storage.* No matter what the capacity of the computer hard drive, it will be necessary to consider some form of external storage for archiving video products. One of the easiest solutions is to send any finished products back out to videotape. Another solution is to store video products on CD or DVD. Large external hard drives in sizes ranging from 80 to 160 gigabytes can be purchased for between $200 and $300 and are good investments if a school intends to do a lot of video editing. The less expensive models connect using USB or FireWire cable and can be easily moved from location to location and computer to computer.

Resources for video projects

- *Video-editing software.* Video editing software is used to combine the video and audio segments downloaded from a camcorder with other information sources (still images, music). Although video editing software ranges greatly in cost and power, it is possible to create high-quality productions with software costing very little and perhaps already available with recently purchased computers. Several video editing applications are included in "Resources to Expand Your Knowledge Base" at the end of this chapter.

In the sections that follow, we explore some of the techniques, software, and hardware involved in working with video.

Digital Camcorders

We are writing this book at what appears to be a transition point in the camcorder industry. Most of the camcorders purchased by schools now seem to be digital rather than analog. With a digital camcorder, the video stored to the tape is already in digital format. We believe that digital camcorders now represent the standard for school-based video products.

Students explore their community by capturing images. (© Michael Zide)

Advantages of digital video

The transition to the digital format makes the production of classroom video much easier. Digital video does not degrade each time it is copied from one location to another, and this characteristic improves the quality of video productions generated with inexpensive equipment. Also, because the visual and audio inputs are converted to a digital format in the camera, special hardware does not have to be added to the computer.

Video Production

The generation of a polished video product might be described as video production, a process that encompasses far more than taking some footage with a camcorder. When it is done as a learning task, the other steps in the process contribute to making the experience active and authentic.

The process of video production is typically accomplished through a sequence of three steps. We use educational terminology in describing these steps, but the activities are roughly equivalent, whether engaged in for commercial or educational reasons.

Planning Phase
Video projects typically begin with a planning phase. Planning establishes goals for the project and identifies the resources that will be needed.

Collecting Primary Sources and Generating Interpretive Products
Video productions are constructed from both raw materials—primary sources—and interpretive products generated to explain or integrate these

raw materials. What qualifies as raw material and interpretive product varies with the type of video production. If a class decides to create a drama depicting the initial meeting of the explorers Lewis and Clark with Sacajawea and her husband, Toussaint Charbonneau, at the Knife River Village, the students would have to use online and library resources to research the Lewis and Clark expedition. From these primary sources, the students would write a script and then tape a short play. The script and the video production would represent their interpretive products.

If students have decided to create a documentary focused on their community's recycling efforts, primary sources would include the raw audio and video resources collected on location. Additional information might be extracted from books, newspapers, interviews, and other sources. This information may be directly included in the video product or used in making decisions about whether other resources will be included. Other resources may also have to be created or collected. For example, video productions often include still images such as photographs and charts to illustrate specific positions. This type of production would likely require that a narrative script be written to integrate the various information sources. This script would serve to interpret the multiple primary sources.

Editing

Video editing is the process of integrating multimedia elements (text, audio, video, images) into a video production and making changes to these elements or the integrated product to improve quality. Video editing environments should provide the capacity to accept different types of media (video, audio, images), edit existing media (add text, delete unneeded portions of video or audio), create some basic resources (record narration), add video and audio transitions (fades between video segments, fade audio in and out), and create an integrated final product.

FireWire data transfer A basic video editing system appropriate for K–12 classroom projects includes a digital camcorder and a computer that is FireWire enabled and runs a recent version of the platform-appropriate operating system. **FireWire** (sometimes called the IEEE 1394 standard) is a system for high-speed data transfer between a computer and peripheral devices such as a digital camcorder or an external storage device. The FireWire system consists of a specific type of cable and appropriate hardware resident on the computer and peripheral. Newer Macintosh and some Windows systems come FireWire enabled, meaning the necessary hardware is already included. Special cards can be purchased to add FireWire capability to other computers. FireWire is important not only for its speed, but also because it allows the computer and digital camera to interact.

Once connected, the digital camera can be controlled from the computer. The same play, fast forward, and reverse functions you may be used to implementing by pressing buttons on the camera or using a hand-held controller can be controlled through software running on the computer. This capability is particularly useful when editing video because the editor concentrates on manipulating one device (the computer) rather than attempting to manually coordinate the actions of two devices (the computer and the camcorder).

Video editing software Our preferred editing system includes a recent version of the operating system because the software tools necessary to perform the video editing functions we have listed and many more are now included with the operating systems at no additional cost. IMovie comes with recent versions of the Macintosh operating system, and Movie Maker comes with recent versions of the Microsoft Windows operating system. If you are using a fairly recent computer but are not using a version of the operating system recent enough to include iMovie or Movie Maker, the capabilities of these video editing programs in the school environment may be worth the cost of an upgrade. Our brief description of video editing software concentrates on iMovie, because iMovie and Movie Maker are similar enough that a description of both products would be largely redundant.

IMovie functions in three modes. The first is used to move selected video content from the digital camcorder to the computer, the second is used to create a video product from these video clips and other multimedia resources, and the third is used to save the final video product.

Collecting video clips with iMovie

Gathering Video Clips from the Camcorder Collecting video clips from the camcorder and moving them to the computer is a relatively easy process. The camcorder is manipulated through the iMovie software using the simple controls described previously. The camcorder video is played through the computer, and the image appears within the iMovie interface within the area called the monitor. The monitor is the large area in the upper-left-hand corner of Figure 8.8. When the editor locates a segment of video she wants to store, the editor clicks the import button both to begin and to end the capture process. (*Note*: The camcorder control buttons and the import button do not appear in Figure 8.8 because the software is shown in edit mode.) As clips are captured, the image associated with the first frame of the clip appears within the area of the interface called the shelf (see the upper-right-hand portion of Figure 8.8). The shelf stores the items available for use in constructing the new video product. In addition to importing video clips from a camcorder, items such as digital images, audio clips, and video from other sources can also be added.

Assembling Video Clips into a Finished Product Once the editor has collected the raw content to be used in preparing the video, the editing process begins. It is not assumed that the clips that have been collected will be used as is. Individual clips can be divided into smaller segments and useless material discarded.

Organizing clips and adding new items

The new video product is first organized by dragging items from the shelf to the Clip View/Timeline, which appears at the bottom of Figure 8.8. In Timeline mode, the user has access to more features and has more precise control. If you look closely at Figure 8.8, you will note that you have one track containing video clips (and other visual components) and two tracks for audio. Audio that is brought in from the camcorder is not displayed in a separate track. If you want, you can separate the audio from the video, and the audio associated with the video clip will then appear in one of the audio tracks. You might want to do this to exercise greater control over the original audio. For example, you might want to fade the original audio in and out between segments of narration added to the second audio track. Other visual information (still images or video segments) can be added on top of existing clips on the

FIGURE 8.8

iMovie Interface in Edit Mode

Timeline (the command is Paste Over at Playhead). You might do this when it would be useful to continue the audio but to substitute a specific still image for a segment of the original video. When the time allocated to the still image ends, the original video would again be visible. Other iMovie editing features include the ability to insert text headings and to insert a variety of visual transitions between segments so one scene moves more smoothly into the next.

Exporting the video for storage

Saving the Finished Product Once the video product has been assembled, it can be displayed in full-screen mode using iMovie. However, iMovie is not intended to be the software used to repeatedly display the finished product. The usual procedure is to export the movie to another storage device and probably to another file format.

Focus

Camcorder Tips

Students of all ages can use a camcorder effectively, but that does not mean that teachers should take their camcorder skills for granted. Some opportunities, such as a major field trip, might come only once a year, and scant experience can mean that students return from such a trip with little in the way of a permanent record. If we were to offer only one suggestion, it would be to allow the students to practice using the camcorder before they attempt to record an important event. Give students some fun and simple recording assignments, such as a favorite cook in action, the school's messiest locker, plants on the school grounds, or close-ups of the contents of a pocket, and then take the time to critique their work.

There are many books that explain basic camera techniques to hobbyists, and you will find it worthwhile to thumb through one. If you intend to use the video primarily to capture individual images for computer projects, here are some additional suggestions to consider:

- Show students how to identify what is informative or interesting and get a tight shot of it. Students seem to capture video images that are too distant and too general. There is nothing wrong with capturing images from a variety of distances, but generally the close views are most useful.
- Do not pan a scene and assume you will be able to capture later what is useful. Capturing still images from video works best when you have a still image to work with. Pause for ten to fifteen seconds when recording individual scenes you expect to be useful.
- For the best close-up shots, students should set the camera to extreme wide angle and move it toward the object until they get the image they want. Most students intuitively take the wrong approach to capturing close-ups. They tend to stand at a comfortable distance from the object and then zoom in with the telephoto. Getting close to an object with a wide-angle setting will increase the amount of the image that will be in focus. The students may find themselves on their hands and knees in the dirt, with the camera two inches from a wildflower, but the picture will be great.
- Always carry an extra battery.
- Read the instruction manual so you know, among other things, how to stop the camera from stamping the time and date on the recording.

One of the most obvious reasons for exporting and then moving a movie is storage space. Raw digital video requires approximately 1 gigabyte of storage space for five minutes of video. While new computers typically have hard drives with at least 40 gigabytes of storage space, it is not practical to use the computer's hard drive to collect video over an extended period of time. A simple and inexpensive solution is to simply send the finished product back out to the digital camcorder. The video is then stored in digital format on tape.

ACTIVITIES AND PROJECTS FOR YOUR CLASSROOM

Video Productions

Here are some ideas to get you started thinking about classroom video projects:

Training tapes. Create a videotape explaining to the next class how your class did something (for example, using the computer to create T-shirt iron-on transfers).

Video storytelling. Create a video with no words, and then have students make up stories to go with the video.

Regional news broadcasts. Create news segments that summarize school or local events. Language classes might use this activity as a way to make practical use of the language skills they are learning.

Conversational language situations. Have students prepare videos to demonstrate conversational German, Spanish, or another language through meeting the family of a friend, ordering in a restaurant, buying a bus ticket, or asking directions to a local historical site.

Extending classroom resources or opportunities. Bring an experience to students that would not be possible for them to experience directly, as Cully Gause did in the Case of the Missing Gerbil described at the beginning of this chapter.

Interviews with local experts. Arrange to video local people who have specific expertise.

Portfolios. Accumulate segments of oral reading over the course of a year.

Documentaries. Present a local issue, and examine both sides of it.

Video autobiographies. Students present themselves, including comments from significant people in their lives.

Public service announcements. Create appeals for community action or awareness on such issues as alcohol abuse or household recycling.

Time-lapse studies. Record the process of a major local construction project or the development of a butterfly, for example.

Critique performances. Record musical, theater, or athletic events for later analysis and evaluation.

Video yearbook. Publish a video version of the yearbook.

Extracurricular highlights. Provide a summary of the experiences of an athletic team, the group responsible for a play, or a senior trip.

You might also want to save video to a CD or DVD or prepare it for delivery over the Internet. Here the export process must involve some form of compression. You might remember from an earlier chapter that the capacity of a CD is less than 1 gigabyte. Without compression, a CD could hold only a few minutes of digital video. The Internet presents even more severe challenges because present bandwidth constraints prevent data from moving fast enough to generate a high-quality display on a distant computer. Compression techniques and a reduction in the size of the image are necessary to export video for Internet distribution. IMovie exports video in the **QuickTime** format with various compression techniques appropriate for CD or Internet applications.

IMovie is intended to be both easy to use and powerful. While more sophisticated software exists (some examples are listed at the end of the chapter), the low cost of this software, the ease of use, and the fact that it runs on low-end Macintosh computers makes it an ideal candidate for classroom projects.

Multimedia projects that can incorporate video

Incorporating the Movie into Other Products Short video segments can be added to many types of multimedia projects (see the chapter entitled "Using Multimedia Tools"). For example, video segments can be included as part of:

- An embellished document created with a word processor
- A multimedia slide show generated and displayed by a presentation tool, such as Microsoft PowerPoint
- A hypermedia project, such as an eZediaMX document or a webpage

Longer movies are typically created to stand alone. The next section describes some innovative video projects undertaken by a multidisciplinary team of middle-school teachers.

Clay Animation: Creating Video by Sequencing Images of Clay Characters

Laurie Tweton, a middle-school health teacher, has become an advocate for student projects based on a technique called clay animation. If you are unfamiliar with the role clay animation might play in classrooms, you may be surprised to learn that you have experienced clay animation projects in another setting—the movie theater. Clay animation has been used to produce several recent full-length movies. In the hands of students, it is a method for generating short videos that serve as the culminating and focusing activity for various learning experiences.

During a typical clay animation project, small groups of students work to create clay characters and use these characters to tell a story or convey a message. The range of possible topics is unlimited. The characters could be genes and the story could be meiosis, or the characters could be historical figures and the story the portrayal of a historical event. For one such project, the multidisciplinary middle-school team Laurie works with selected the theme of "Respect," and individual student teams worked on projects involving respect for self (for example, smoking), respect for others (for example, racism), and respect for the environment (for example, recycling). The student projects concluded with the planning, production, and sharing of one-to two-minute public service announcements based on clay animation movies. The middle-school team approach allowed the teachers to schedule large blocks of time on specific days for the clay animation project.

The team of teachers Laurie works with is associated with the areas of math, language arts, health, and science. All of these curriculum areas were represented in the work of students. Part of clay animation projects involves the development of the sets within which the clay characters "perform." The sets, characters, and props should be in proper proportion. If the three-inch adult character is assumed to represent a six-foot-tall adult, how tall should the clay character representing an average fourth grader be? What would be proper dimensions for the door? Students were expected to perform such calculations. Students were also expected to develop outlines for their projects and to submit written scripts. Developing and evaluating the written products represented the language arts component. The areas of health and science provided the content background for the student projects.

Once students have completed their research, developed a story line and script, and created their stage, characters, and props, it is time to create the animation. Laurie describes the process as take a picture, move a little, take another picture. Characters and props are positioned on the stage. The digital camera or digital camcorder used to take a picture is positioned on a tripod or in some other secure position. A digital camcorder capable of taking and storing individual pictures was used in the "Respect" project.

Once a picture has been taken, the characters are moved. The animation process requires that only a small change be made between pictures. It takes students a while to understand the subtleties. Laurie tells students to anticipate taking 100 to 200 images to create their short movies, but she also says some experimentation always seems to be necessary.

Once the images have been collected, the images are brought into iMovie. IMovie not only allows the images to be sequenced but also allows the eventual addition of narration or possibly a musical background and titles. To complete the production process, the components are saved as a QuickTime movie.

If you are interested in trying clay animation with your students, here are some of the key areas to consider:

- Classroom clay animation movies are likely to be brief. Instead of an elaborate plot, these movies are likely to have a central message. What will that message be? The creation of a storyboard—a series of simple sketches depicting the major action sequences to be animated—can be a helpful planning activity.

- Characters are created from clay because the material is relatively inexpensive and easy to shape. Some animators use special tools to shape the clay. For more elaborate projects, clay is shaped over a wire skeleton called an armature. The wire (sometimes heavy "pipe cleaners") makes it easier and quicker to pose the characters for the many pictures that must be taken. Sources for clay, armature material, character details (for example, eyes), and other clay animation products can be found on the Web (see the resources listed at the end of the chapter). A small industry has sprung up to meet the needs of teachers and hobbyists interested in this method for creating movies.

- The stage, set, or background for a clay animation project can be created in many ways. Figure 8.9 shows a black background that focuses attention on the characters and props. Backgrounds can be painted or created from photographs. Props can be fashioned from clay or construction paper, or they may consist of small objects such as toys. A lighting source for the set should also be considered.

FIGURE 8.9
Sample Clay Animation Set, Characters, and Props

- The many pictures used to create an animation can be captured in many ways. We have already mentioned the use of a digital camera or a digital camcorder. Another way to capture images is with the type of simple and inexpensive video device used to feed a digital signal directly into the computer. This type of device typically is used in videoconferencing, has no storage mechanism of its own, and can be accessed by software that allows individual pictures to be captured. These devices and software can be purchased for under $100.
- In addition to video, clay animation can also be used to produce animated GIFs and simple animations.

In addition to the "Respect" project, Laurie's students have recently completed projects such as these:

"Dare to Be Different": Three figures jump off a cliff on a dare, while one shakes his or her head and walks away.

"Terrorism": A plea for international unity.

"Say No to Drugs": A young person refuses to respond to the suggestion that drugs are the way to have fun.

"Please Buckle Up": A car accident results in injury because of failure to use seat belts.

"Stamp Out Pollution": A comment on factory waste.

One observation teachers often make in working with such projects is that some students who often go unnoticed have a rare opportunity to play a central role in a classroom activity.

Capturing and Storing Sounds for Multimedia Projects

Using a video editor to capture sound

The process of capturing sound bears many similarities to the process of capturing video. In fact, one convenient way to generate an audio file is to use the video editing software we described at an earlier point to separate the video and audio tracks recorded by a digital camcorder, discard the video track, and save the audio. This ends up being a practical solution for capturing sound from remote locations because educators are likely to have access to a camcorder and because the method is simpler than techniques for bringing audio from a portable device such as a cassette recorder into the computer.

Using an authoring program and a microphone

Another option is to use programs such as PowerPoint and KidPix, which have built-in capabilities for capturing sound. If the computer contains the appropriate hardware capabilities, one need only plug in a simple microphone (many laptop computers have built-in microphones), click the record button within the software program, and then speak, sing, play a musical instrument, or in some other way generate an audio signal for the program to capture. In this case, the actual process is very similar to the process of capturing video from an analog signal. The microphone brings an analog signal into the computer, and specialized hardware then converts the analog signal into digitized sound.

Issues in converting analog sound to digital

Several variables come into play in converting analog sound to digital sound. The first concerns the accuracy with which the analog signal is converted to a digital signal. Analog sound is represented as a continuous sound wave. The conversion to a digital form is accomplished by representing this continuous wave in discrete steps. The more steps there are, the more accurately the original information can be represented. A digital representation allowing 16-bit sound divides the sound wave into 65,536 steps. Hardware allowing 8-bit sound allows only 256 steps in the sound wave to be differentiated and thus produces a lower level of accuracy.

Another variable associated with sound digitizing is the **sampling frequency,** which is the number of times per second that a digital representation of the analog signal is produced. Sampling frequency is usually described in thousands of samples per second, or kilohertz (kHz). Both the bit depth (8-bit versus 16-bit) and the sampling frequency influence quality and storage requirements. The CD-recorded music that you listen to is probably stored at a bit depth of 16 and a sampling frequency of 44.1 kHz. The sound recorded in the applications described in this chapter would more likely be recorded at a bit depth of 8 and a sampling frequency of 11 kHz. The difference in sound quality is noticeable but acceptable for most purposes. One advantage of the lower-quality sound is that it requires less storage space. A ten-second sound recorded at the lower-quality settings would require only about 115 kilobytes of disk space. The connection between sampling frequency and file size is an issue you may also encounter when saving audio tracks in video applications. For example, iMovie allows the user to select sampling frequencies from 8 to 48 kHz and mono or stereo tracks when saving a movie. Saving audio at a lower frequency and in mono would reduce file size and might be important in creating a reasonable product for web presentation.

FIGURE 8.10

KidPix Audio Palette

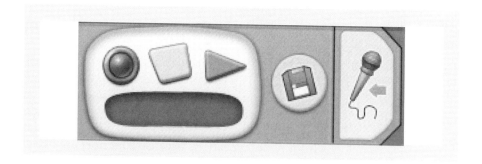

Audio file formats

The method for recording sounds can be fairly simple. For example, Macintosh computers have sound capabilities built in and do not require an extra board. Some other computers require the addition of a sound card. Software applications that support sound usually open an audio palette when the user selects the menu bar option allowing sound to be recorded. Figure 8.10 shows the audio palette from KidPix. The simple interface is appropriate for young users: one button to record, one button to stop recording, one button to play, and one button to save. The audio recording is stored with the image file.

Sounds can be stored as independent files or as resources (a component that is part of a mixed file format). When you create a multimedia program with KidPix, any sounds that are included are usually incorporated as resources within the stack or the multimedia file. Applications also store sounds as independent files; that is, the file contains nothing but the data necessary to reproduce a sound. For example, eZediaMX has a simple sound capture system that generates a Quicktime audio file. Like graphics, sounds can be stored in several different formats. The audio interchange file format (AIFF) is used by many software applications that produce files to be loaded by other programs and other hardware platforms. Windows sound applications frequently use the Waveform Audio (WAV) format. There are even generic formats intended to be shared through the World Wide Web. For example, the (mµ-law) format is commonly used as a component of webpages because it can be interpreted by web software running on several different hardware platforms.

The MP3 format

In addition, teachers should be aware of the MP3 format. MP3 is an audio layer of the more general MPEG-1 standard and is often used to compress the audio tracks from CDs. Originally, MP3 files were played through a computer using free software. Now, specially designed CD players and other hand-held devices are also available to play this format. A CD containing only MP3 files can hold the music from at least half a dozen regular CDs. Because MP3 files are easily created from commercial music CDs and burned to blank CDs or sent over the Internet, there are many copyright concerns associated with this format.

Promoting students' motivation and active involvement

It is easy to become so enamored of sounds that you clutter a presentation with a lot of useless noise. The skillful use of sound is another of those design-related matters for which there are probably no hard-and-fast rules. Our ap-

Background Music

Students often have a strong interest in using music to embellish their multimedia projects. Music can create an emotional background for presentations, and the message in carefully selected popular songs often seems a way to emphasize the intended message. However effective in accomplishing student goals, unrestricted use of music violates copyright restrictions. The restrictions are most extreme when the multimedia project is to be presented on the Internet. Specific copyright issues are addressed in the chapter entitled "Responsible Use of Technology."

It is possible to purchase soundtracks in much the same way as it is possible to purchase clip art. You will not be able to locate tunes from the most recent Top 40, but you will be able to find tracks that will serve as an effective background for presentations. In addition to background music, collections of sound clips often provide specialized sound effects.

SmartSound from Sonic Desktop Software takes a unique approach. The Maestro component of this software allows the user to select from a series of options to locate an appropriate musical selection. The basic CD allows the user to indicate how the music will be used—for example, as an opener, to accompany action, or as a background. The user then indicates how long a segment is desired. After several more choices (including style and instrumentation), the program offers and opens the proposed composition in the editor. If the composition is satisfactory, the editor allows the music to be exported in several different audio formats.

The editor also provides another very interesting opportunity. The musical compositions are made up of many small individual segments—musical phrases. The user can work directly with these segments to modify the existing composition or create an entirely new composition from scratch. It is something like having your own musical construction set. This basic approach can be expanded by purchasing additional CDs that focus on specific themes (for example, holidays, drama and documentary, classical masters).

proach is a little different. Although student projects should be tasteful, our priority is the kinds of experiences that motivate students and help them work with information actively. Putting together a thirty-second speech about a butterfly or a fish can be a useful experience for a second grader. Agreeing to record a short poem that an elementary-school student writes to accompany a drawing can increase her motivation to write the poem. As a teacher, you will need to consider specific situations and determine when working with sound would meet the criteria of increased motivation or more active involvement with information.

Emerging Technology

Digital Audio Recording and Podcasts

People are probably much more aware of the possibility of developing personal collections of digital images and video than of the possibility of collecting digital audio. This might simply reflect a general lack of insight into the value of recording the audio component of our daily experiences. We are aware of digital audio and video because many more people we know have purchased the equipment to develop such personal collections. Inexpensive devices for collecting digital audio and transferring this content to a computer have been available for years, but unless you prowl the aisles of local business supply or electronics stores you may not realize this is the case. The inexpensive devices for recording audio tend to be marketed as a way to keep audio "notes."

However, there may be a number of ways these devices can be used by your students. Having students interview members of their community can offer useful opportunities for gaining insight into educational topics such as history. The information gained from these interviews can be used in many ways. A student might write a paper based on her grandfather's personal recollections of serving in the Vietnam War or create a multimedia project containing descriptions in his voice. The digital audio recorder provides the opportunity to move audio sources to the computer for use in such projects. The generation of simple Internet "radio broadcasts" is also a possibility. You may be familiar with the term **podcast.** It is formed from the words *broadcasting* and

FIGURE 8.11
iPod with iTalk Voice Recorder

iPod (the name of a popular Apple digital music player). People who podcast create audio commentary and make this content available on the Internet. It is kind of an audio version of blogging (see our description of blogs as an example of simple web publishing in the chapter entitled "Learning from Student Projects"), and people who write blogs may also offer podcasts. The idea of podcasting is close to what we are proposing here. Imagine a sixth-grade current events project in which students select what they feel to be the most significant current event of the week, read what they can about this event, and then create a three-minute audio summary and analysis. Imagine that this audio product is available to parents and anyone else who cares to visit the class webpage.

You do not need an iPod to create or listen to podcasts, but if you already happen to own this device, the addition of an inexpensive recorder (see Figure 8.11) allows a very convenient way to collect audio. Most iPod users download music from a computer to the iPod, but you can just as easily upload audio you have recorded to the computer. These audio segments can be integrated into multimedia projects using the applications we describe in the chapters entitled "Using Multimedia Tools" and "Learning from Student Projects."

Additional information about these devices appears in "Resources to Expand Your Knowledge Base" at the end of this chapter. Information about integrating audio collected in this fashion is available on the website that accompanies this textbook.

Learning with Sound and Graphics Tools

Up to this point, the discussion in this chapter has focused mainly on techniques of getting sound and pictures into the computer and manipulating these sources of information once they have been transformed into digital form. These are obviously very practical skills for anyone who wants to work with multimedia. What may not be obvious, though, is what these skills have to do with learning more traditional content knowledge. We hope that the background from other chapters has provided some insights into how these skills may facilitate the active manipulation of information. It may also be useful to take a more direct approach and list some of the ways in which working with sound and graphics can contribute to traditional learning.

In the chapter entitled "Meaningful Learning in an Information Age," two important proposals were that (1) certain external tasks or activities increase the probability that students will engage in desirable cognitive behaviors and (2) those external activities can provide a purpose and meaningful context for important thinking and learning behaviors. To illustrate these possible links, let's identify some of the actions required when students use sound and graphics tools in projects.

Activities conducive to meaningful learning

Projects can require that students search for sounds or graphics that exemplify a particular principle or justify a particular argument. To find appropriate examples, they must thoroughly understand the principle or argument to be demonstrated and evaluate alternative sources of information to find an appropriate illustration. What pictures could be collected at a zoo to provide examples of carnivores, and which would illustrate herbivores? Which poem demonstrates the rhythm of iambic pentameter?

Teachers may also require that students identify the features present in visual or auditory information. Students may be required to find the esophagus in a dissected frog or the point at which the oboe begins to play in a piece of music. When a student is asked to use computer tools to label images or mark the point at which a specific sound is present, identification skills are likely to be engaged.

Images and sounds lend themselves to comparisons and contrasts of many types—for example:

- Illustrate the difference between a moth and a butterfly.
- Illustrate the difference between a cocoon and a chrysalis.
- Compare the sounds of an oboe and a bassoon.
- Discriminate among major thirds, minor thirds, major sevenths, and minor sevenths (musical chords).

Opportunities to manipulate and explore information

As we note at the beginning of this chapter, education presents students with information in the form of sounds and graphic images, but students often do not have opportunities to manipulate information in these formats. Students are inundated with graphics and sounds, but they seldom act on this information directly. Sound and graphics tools provide opportunities for manipulation and exploration.

Summary

Students normally play a receptive role when relating to information represented in the form of images or sounds. Tools for manipulating images and sounds allow students to relate to these forms of information more actively.

Technology allows users to create original images or capture representations of existing images. Software applications that allow images to be created and modified can be categorized as paint and draw programs. These applications differ in their representation of images.

Because a paint program allows the manipulation of images at the individual pixel level, it is probably the most general educational application. Draw programs are used to create and manipulate graphic objects rather than individual pixels. Draw programs may be of special value when precision illustrations are required.

Paint programs differ widely in cost; more expensive programs tend to offer more tools. If a school decides to purchase many copies of a less expensive program, it should also consider making available a small number of copies of a more expensive program. One useful feature of more expensive programs is the ability to open and save files in different file formats. Unfortunately, different kinds of computers and different software programs store graphic images in different ways. It is sometimes necessary to convert an image stored in one format to a different format so that other computers or programs can access the image.

Image capture can be accomplished with a scanner or digital camera. Scanning is used to capture images that already appear on paper. Digital camcorders store audio and video in a digital format, and this information can then be transferred to a computer without the need for conversion. Combining video segments into video productions is now a real possibility using inexpensive video editing software and the computers available in most school settings.

Sound capture is similar to video capture. Software and hardware are used to convert an analog signal to a digital signal. The quality of sound resources and the capacity required to store them are influenced by the bit depth and sampling frequency used in the conversion process.

Reflecting on Chapter 8

ACTIVITIES

■ Locate an example of a commercial image collection you might use. Describe the properties of this collection, the tools you would use to work with the images, and some projects that might incorporate these images.

■ Construct a list of criteria to use in evaluating a graphics tool designed for younger students.

■ If your students had access to video-capture equipment, what types of graphics collections would you have them compile?

■ Propose a three-minute video you would like to make. What primary sources would be involved?

■ Familiarize yourself with a paint program. Demonstrate the program's capabilities to your classmates.

KEY TERMS

bitmapped (p. 275)
clipboard (p. 280)
compression (p. 283)
cross-platform (p. 285)
dots per inch (dpi) (p. 276)
draw programs (p. 274)
FireWire (p. 297)
flash memory (p. 288)
graphic user interface (GUI) (p. 278)
jaggies (p. 277)
lossless compression (p. 283)

lossy compression (p. 283)
object-oriented image (p. 276)
paint programs (p. 274)
pixels (p. 275)
podcast (p. 308)
QuickTime (p. 301)
resolution (p. 285)
sampling frequency (p. 305)
scanner (p. 286)
screen capture (p. 280)
translator (p. 283)

RESOURCES TO EXPAND YOUR KNOWLEDGE BASE

 An expanded and frequently updated list of online resources is available on the website that accompanies this textbook.

Books

Heid, J. (2004). *The Macintosh iLife '04 in the classroom.* Berkeley, CA: Peachpit Press.

Herrell, A., & Fowler, J. (1998). *Camcorder in the classroom: Using the video camera to enliven curriculum.* Upper Saddle River, NJ: Prentice-Hall.

Theodosakis, N. (2001). *The director in the classroom: How filmmaking inspires learning.* Calgary, Canada: University of Calgary Press.

Hardware Resources

IPod is a digital audio device from Apple Computer Inc. that can be used in combination with either the Macintosh or Windows operating system. Additional information can be found at **http://www.apple.com/ipod/**.

ITalk Voice Recorder is available from Griffin Technology. Additional information can be found at **http://www.griffintechnology.com/products/italk/**.

Image Collection Software

IPhoto is available for the Macintosh operating system. (**http://www.apple.com/iphoto/**)

Picasa 2 is available for the Windows operating system from Google, Inc. (**http://www.picasa.com/**)

Image Editing Software

KidPix: Available for Macintosh and DOS computers from Broderbund Software. (**http://www.broderbund.com/**). Information about KidPix products can be found at **http://www.kidpix.com/**.

Photoshop: A high-end graphics editing program available for both the Macintosh and Windows operating systems. From Adobe Systems. (**http://www.adobe.com/**). Adobe also offers PhotoDeluxe and Photoshop Elements, less expensive products that will satisfy most classroom needs.

Audio and Image Collections

Although you can buy CDs of royalty-free photographic-quality images and clip art through most software catalogs, we would encourage you first to explore free online resources to determine whether they meet your needs. A search using the word "clipart" should generate a large number of options. Here are some suggestions to get you started:

DiscoverySchool.com Clip Art Gallery (**http://school.discovery.com/clipart/**)

Pics4Learning, provided by Tech4Learning (**http://www.pics4learning.com/**)

TeacherFiles.com Educational Clip Art (**http://www.teacherfiles.com/clip_art.htm**)

Many programs likely to be used in school settings (word processing programs, web authoring programs, multimedia authoring programs) come with clip art collections.

To provide background audio for classroom movies, we suggest Smart-sound for Multimedia (**http://www.smartsound.com/**) from Sonic Desktop Software. This product allows users to choose selections of royalty-free music or to piece together original compositions by selecting and organizing small chunks of music. This company also offers collections of sound effects.

Video Editing Software
Low-End Products
iMovie: Available for the Macintosh platform. Apple Computer Corporation. (**http://www.apple.com/imovie/**)
Movie Maker: Available for the newer versions of the Windows platform (Windows ME, Windows XP). Microsoft Corporation. (**http://www.microsoft.com/windowsme/using/video/articles/**)
MovieWorks and MovieWorks Deluxe: Available for the Macintosh and Windows platforms. Interactive Solutions. (**http://www.movieworks.com/**)
High-End Products
Adobe Premiere: Available for both the Macintosh and Windows platforms. Adobe Systems. (**http://www.adobe.com/premiere/**)
Final Cut Pro: Available for the Macintosh platform. Apple Computer Corporation. (**http://www.apple.com/finalcutpro/**)

Resources for Clay Animation
Tech4Learning provides clay animation resources for the education market. These resources include books, kits providing clay animation materials, and software (Spin PhotoObject). (**http://www.tech4learning.com/claykit/**)

Learning from Student Projects: Knowledge as Design and the Design of Hypermedia

● ● ●

In this chapter we explore a major concept in both hypermedia and learning: design. It is typical to think of design as the process by which professionals construct useful products. Architects design buildings, for example, engineers design bridges or cars, and educational software developers design software. It also seems that motivated and active students design their own meaningful representations of their experiences. Design is thus a general concept that recognizes the importance of skilled behavior applied to the accomplishment of a meaningful goal.

The product of a design process is also called a design. A bridge is a design resulting from a design process. So are buildings, computer programs, and knowledge. Our focus here is on student-designed hypermedia and the learning opportunities when students participate in such projects.

As you read, look for answers to the following questions:

Focus Questions

- What organizational, graphic, text, and interface design principles should students be aware of as they develop hypermedia projects?
- What student and teacher activities are typical of the various stages in a cooperative group project?
- How can the design of hypermedia facilitate the design of knowledge?
- How does the teacher interact with students to make the creation of projects valuable learning experiences?

"Is This the Way It Is?": Creating a Geography Project for an Authentic Audience

Chris Douthit, a seventh-grade world geography teacher from Schroeder Middle School in Grand Forks, North Dakota, has been looking for ideas related to an important segment of his course in which students learn about

Canada. Although Grand Forks is located approximately ninety miles from the Canadian border and this proximity results in economic, political, and cultural ties that should be important to his students, Chris struggles to find good instructional resources. Evidently, in the generic approach required to develop world geography curriculum materials for U.S. students, Canada does not receive a lot of attention. In addition, Chris feels that the treatment offered by the traditional textbook does not provide the perspective or depth that will generate much student enthusiasm. Doing a better job is important: Because of the way the social studies curriculum is laid out, the month he spends on the study of Canada may be the only opportunity many of his students will have to learn about their northern neighbors until they graduate from high school.

Monte Gaukler, technology facilitator, is aware of Chris's frustration and has been looking around for ideas. She finds an example of a "country report" on the eZedia website (see the description of eZedia products in the chapter entitled "Using Multimedia Tools") and thinks some version of such a project may make a productive addition to Chris's Canada unit. EZedia happens to be a Canadian company, and she decides to contact the company about the sample country report project and to inquire about multimedia components (such as royalty-free images, songs) that might be used in a project about Canada. Somewhere in this conversation, a very creative idea emerges.

Student multimedia projects about places are common. In our experience, such projects take one of two approaches. In the first approach, students learn about another place, create a multimedia product about this place, and then present this product to classmates as a way of sharing what they have learned. For example, groups of students might create travel brochures about other countries and then present their brochures to classmates. A second approach involves an exchange of information between groups of students located in different places. For example, students from "sister" schools in the United States and Japan create webpages about local industries. This might be described as the "I'll tell you about me and you tell me about you" model. Here, however, is the twist that made the Canada project distinctive: What if students from the United States learned about the Canadian provinces, created websites summarizing important information about the provinces, and then sought a reaction from students who live in those places? "Here is what we think it is like to live in Manitoba. Here are lists of the most important economic and cultural influences. Here are some of the most unique or important geographic features. Is this the way it is?" Take a minute to think about this approach and how it might differ from the other approaches we described in influencing how students tackle the study of another place.

We return later to Chris's classroom to follow the development of this project. You will learn how active learning, student collaboration, and technology come together as students prepare for and craft their project. As we describe how students can design projects relevant to many content areas, we try to instill one important perspective: meaningful learning as the result of a student's personal cognitive process of design. Useful knowledge itself can be considered a design (Perkins, 1986). The more traditional concept of design may also be important here, because one way to involve students is by challenging them with a design project. In other words, designing a tangible product appears to facilitate the design of personal knowledge. As we proceed, we explore both the design of products and the design of knowledge, as well as connections between these two types of tasks.

Knowledge as Design

Knowledge as information

How we think about knowledge can strongly influence our behavior as teachers and learners (Perkins, 1986). At least two perspectives are possible. The first views knowledge as information. Information is basically factual knowledge—ideas that are accumulated from various academic and life experiences and are known for the sake of knowing. Information is stored with the assumption that it will eventually prove useful. The perspective of knowledge as information is consistent with the metaphor of learning as transmission. A more knowledgeable person passes knowledge on to a less knowledgeable person.

Knowledge as design, adapted to a purpose

In contrast, **knowledge as design** is knowledge adapted to a purpose. In the context of the model of active learning used throughout this book, knowledge as design is a probable product of meaningful learning. It is information generated by a student as a tool to accomplish some purpose. The perspective of knowledge as design is consistent with the metaphor of learning as construction. The learner with a purpose takes advantage of the information available to build personal understanding. A more knowledgeable person may facilitate the process of knowledge construction in a less knowledgeable person, but the person doing the learning must perform the acts of knowledge construction.

What the learner does with knowledge

It is important to understand that the distinction between knowledge as information and knowledge as design is inherent not in the raw facts and experiences that learners encounter, but *in what the learner does with these raw materials.* You can test this position by considering content that most people would regard as basic factual information. What about those names and dates we all attempted to learn in history classes? What is the purpose of knowing that Columbus reached the New World in 1492? If you asked a middle-school student this question, you would likely hear that the purpose in knowing this date is to answer a question correctly on the next exam. We might smile at the naiveté of this response, but do we have anything better to offer? Perkins (1986) proposes that even historical dates can represent a design. To understand how this works, think about the work of professional historians and how they might use landmark dates. For the historian, dates become tools of organization. A date can be a way to connect several simultaneous events, perhaps as a precursor to exploring possible cause-and-effect relationships. Dates can also serve to sequence events over time. Students can use dates the same way, but they are more likely to think like the middle-school students described here and not like apprentice historians. It is unfair, though, to place the blame totally on the student. The teacher may be as focused on the upcoming test as the student is.

Design as a tool with a purpose

A **design,** in this sense, is a tool developed to accomplish a purpose. Both concrete designs and knowledge as design fit this framework. What is significant here is that a purpose exists and is recognized from the outset. One of Perkins's (1986) favorite examples of a tool is a screwdriver. He suggests the absurdity of someone fashioning an object and then wondering what might be done with it. "Oh, this might be useful for mixing cookie dough. No, I think I'll use it to turn screws." Strange? Yet school learning often proceeds in just this way. A student often learns or memorizes information, thinking that this fact or idea should be useful for something, but at the time the student is often not exactly certain what. Perhaps you can sense where we are going with this logic. In the major example we use in this chapter, middle-school students are learning about Canada with an immediate purpose: The knowledge becomes a tool they apply in designing a multimedia product.

Active, purposeful learning

Emphasizing knowledge as design implies that students should spend a good part of their school time in active, purposeful learning. Some activities work particularly well to provide design experiences. For example, what if students designed useful products instead of studying them? What if they were able to play the roles of engineers, biologists, or historians and had to design a new piece of playground equipment, evaluate the pollution of a local pond, or develop a historical account of a past event? What if students designed software—in particular, instructional software?

Looking at Student-Authored Hypermedia

This chapter emphasizes student-authored hypermedia. Design projects could also be based on the development of databases, projects requiring the analysis of data with a spreadsheet, and various kinds of writing activities. (The idea of learning through design is versatile and does not require technology, but our focus in this book, of course, is on technology projects and on suggesting productive ways that teachers and students can use technology.) Possibilities for hypermedia projects abound.

Many possibilities for projects

We begin with some guidelines for the development of hypermedia projects and then return to the topic of meaningful learning as design, emphasizing the opportunities for meaningful learning inherent in hypermedia projects.

Principles of Hypermedia Design: The Process of Developing Software

What is hypermedia design?

Hypermedia design is the purposeful process of developing a hypermedia product that is informative, interesting, and easy to use and understand. The production of truly professional and high-quality products that meet these standards is both science and art. In this section, we concentrate on some basic guidelines that apply to multimedia design projects: content organization, graphic design, text presentation, and development of the user interface. The intent is to cover some of the basic principles that might be immediately useful in student-generated projects using a product such as eZediaMX (see the chapter entitled "Using Multimedia Tools"). Many of the principles described here are also relevant if students have the opportunity to author hypermedia materials for the World Wide Web.

Content Organization

An author in any medium exercises a fairly substantial degree of control over the sequence in which the reader or user encounters the various elements of information. For example, in a typical textbook, the author creates a structure so that the reader encounters ideas in a certain order and interrelates them in a certain way. From the textbook author's perspective, ideas flow into each other in a logical way, and the author's intention is to communicate this logical sequence to the reader. Illustrations are placed close to text ideas that they explain or exemplify.

Linear organization

In such a linear format, access to ideas or illustrations in other chapters or even earlier in the same chapter can be somewhat cumbersome for the reader. The reader can override the structure imposed by the author, but the reader will then have to search about blindly (thumbing back through a chapter to reread a section) or use a general guide (table of contents) or a specific guide (index) to find related material. The extent to which the author has planned for these alternate ways to interrelate ideas is likely to have been very limited. It is usually not assumed to be the author's responsibility to encourage or expedite nonsequential reading of the book. Books must be organized in a linear style, and the author must commit to a single organizational structure to accommodate this limitation. In hypermedia, by contrast, the structure can be much more variable.

Experiencing Content in a Variety of Ways

One of the advantages (and, some might say, curses) of hypermedia is that it allows the author to present content that users can experience in a variety of ways. The medium does not impose the limits. The user could theoretically move from any unit of information (called a **node**) to any other unit of information. As we mentioned earlier in the book, the connections between nodes are called **links.**

Navigation through nodes and links

Although it is a bit of an exaggeration to claim that all nodes in most hypermedia applications are interconnected, it is fair to claim that multiple linkages among ideas are available. To maximize the effectiveness of the presentation, the hypermedia author designs a structure by allowing some subset of all possible links. **Navigation** is user-controlled movement through hypermedia content. The navigation system defines the way users can move about within the hypermedia content. The structure the author imposes on the information shapes the environment in which the user can explore. The structure of linkages should be based on the author's analysis of the purpose of the software product and the possible logical connections the content expert sees in the material. The extent to which the user is allowed to control access is closely related to the product's intended purpose.

FIGURE 9.1
Common Organizational Structures for Hypermedia Projects

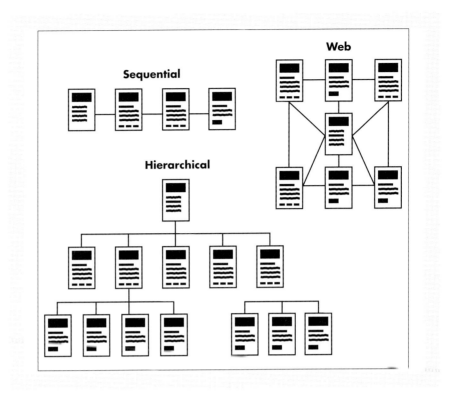

Organizational Structure

Organizational structure concerns the pattern in which nodes are linked (Jonassen & Grabinger, 1990). Here we examine three common structures: sequential design, hierarchical design, and web design. (They are shown in Figure 9.1.) These models describe pure forms. In practice, the structure of hypermedia is often some variation on or integration of these structures.

Sequential Design The most basic way to present information is with a **sequential design,** in which each element leads directly to the next in logical sequence, with no other options for the user. You are already familiar with this structure because it is typically used in print media to present short descriptions or explanations. Television programs and educational videotapes also use this organizational structure.

Organization by simple, logical sequence

The major advantage of a sequential design is simplicity. Users are familiar with this format, and it is also relatively easy for the designers because there is no need to set up a complicated navigation system. The designer can concentrate on communicating a specific message logically, informatively, and interestingly. This may be the best structure for younger or beginning hypermedia designers. The sequential structure is especially useful when the purpose is to train the viewer in a specific skill.

Organization by categories and subcategories

Hierarchical Design A **hierarchical design,** as you can see in Figure 9.1, organizes content as a system of categories and subcategories. A user interacts with information of this type by moving through a series of choice points—that is, **branches.** Each branch narrows the user's immediate focus in some way.

The Yahoo! web directory, described in the chapter on the Internet as a tool for inquiry, is a good example of an extensive web project organized in this manner. One purpose of a hierarchical structure is to organize information so users can find what they need without inspecting all the available information. A hierarchical structure also allows users to reorient themselves if they become lost. When they get disoriented, it is a simple matter to move back up the hierarchy and gain a sense of the structure for the entire site.

Structure is important in a second way. Even if the user is intended to process all of the information provided, the structure of the hypermedia can help the user organize what is learned. For example, certain systems for classifying biological organisms (remember phylum, class, order, family, genus, and species from high-school biology) have a theoretical rationale. The student may develop an appreciation for such a classification system while navigating the structure to explore individual animals. The biologist's design for classification is integrated into the design of the hypermedia.

Organization by a complex set of links

Web Design   A **web design,** as Figure 9.1 illustrates, takes fuller advantage of the potential of hypermedia by creating a complex set of connections among nodes. The intent is to provide users as much freedom as possible to follow links that address their interests and needs.

A web design, also known as a network structure, allows the user the greatest flexibility in examining the content provided, and it allows the hyperauthor the related opportunity to create more open-ended, exploratory information environments. The World Wide Web is a good example of the power and problems of a network structure. Because the Web has been created by thousands of different authors who do not have to commit to a single design model and who can link to other resources as they see fit, the structure of the Web is freeform and complex.

The practical value of this flexibility depends to some extent on the user's ability to navigate the content effectively. It is quite possible for the user to become lost within the network because the richness of the many interconnections and the lack of a simple organizational structure can be confusing. Even when working within a hypermedia application intended for use on a single computer, the user may be able to move among definitions of keywords, alternate documents making a similar point, illustrations, other illustrations providing greater detail of segments of earlier illustrations, selections from speeches or music, and short video pieces. Each of these items might be considered a node, and when it is understood that the user can enter and leave many nodes using different links, the difficulty some users might have in using the network becomes apparent. A user who gets sidetracked can have difficulty picking up the initial theme again. The human factors issue of how to assist the user in navigating complex hypermedia systems has become an interesting area of inquiry. You might recall that we discussed how some learners had difficulty with hypermedia in the chapter entitled "Using Instructional Software and Multimedia for Content-Area Learning."

FIGURE 9.2
Layout Grid

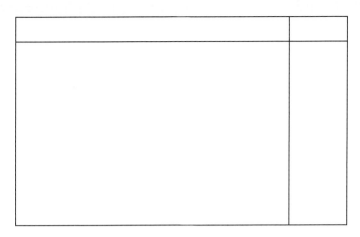

Graphic Design

Graphic design is an area of study that concerns the relationship between the appearance and the content of material, in this case material appearing on the computer screen. The purpose of careful graphic design is to make this displayed information as informative, easy to understand, and interesting as possible. This section provides an overview of selected topics likely to be applicable to student developers. While these are sound principles that can guide the graphic design process, truly outstanding products also arise from experience and creative talent.

Screen Layout

Using a grid

Objects—buttons, pictures, or text fields—should be placed and grouped in a way that facilitates the user's activities. One way to develop a strategy for screens of a certain type is to make use of a **grid:** a pattern of lines that organizes the placement of objects and maintains consistency across similar screens (see Figure 9.2). A grid does not have to be complicated to be effective; it may be merely a line dividing the screen into two main areas. The layout

FIGURE 9.3
Sample Screen Layout

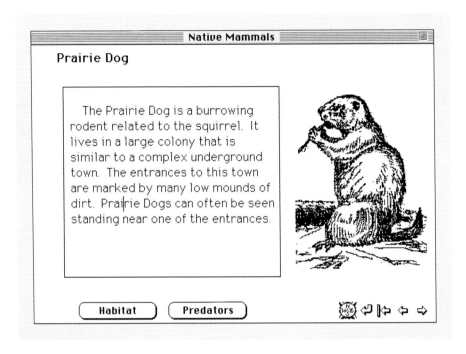

used in Figure 9.2 might be used to present a series of illustrations. As you can see in the figure, the lines designating key areas of the screen do not have to appear on the screen.

Here are some guidelines for screen layout:

Guidelines for screen layout

- Buttons should usually appear along the edges of the screen. Make an exception when a button has an impact on just part of the screen. This might be the case when the button would reveal some hidden information such as labels for a diagram. The button should then appear adjacent to the object or area it influences.
- Group together buttons that serve similar functions. Buttons that appear throughout a hypermedia presentation should also be separated from buttons that only appear in specific situations.
- Use size to control the user's attention. Allocate the most grid space to the most important elements.
- Do not abandon the grid concept just because the screen displays only text. A screen of solid text is dull and hard to read. Organizing text elements on the screen can increase both readability and interest (see the next section on design principles for text; Apple Computer, 1989).

Try evaluating the principles of screen layout as they apply to the example in Figure 9.3:

- Could you sketch the grid that was used to organize this screen?
- Would you organize a set of screens containing a picture, text information, navigation buttons, and buttons establishing topical links in any other way?
- Have the general guidelines for screen layout been followed?

Text Presentation and Writing Style

Small blocks of text

Principles for using text in hypermedia emphasize clear communication, legibility, and motivation. In general, hypermedia will not present the user screen after screen of continuous text, for several reasons. First, screens of solid text are difficult to read, so designers are encouraged to present text in chunks surrounded by space for greater legibility. Second, hypermedia is based on the notion of connecting specific idea units in complex ways. Small blocks of text rather than continuous screens of text are best suited to constructing these connections. Usually the text component of hypermedia prepared for younger readers will read differently from extended text.

Text layout goes beyond writing style and statement length to encompass the placement of text on the screen and the appearance of the text itself. Briefly summarized, the text on the screen should be easy to read, and special embellishments (special fonts, bold type, size) should be limited to situations in which it is important to draw the user's attention to something unique and specific. Teachers introducing any kind of program allowing text display (word processing, a paint program, eZediaMX) are likely to find that students will manipulate text characteristics unnecessarily at first. It is great fun to experiment with the many elements of text appearance, and this process of experimentation is one way for student designers to become familiar with the possibilities. However, at some point, the student as designer needs to consider how these different options might be used most productively to communicate with the user. Following are some general guidelines for designers of text (Apple Computer, 1989):

Guidelines for text design

- Text messages should be concise. When it is important to communicate complex ideas or large amounts of information, consider identifying the important ideas and presenting them as separate but linked nodes. Avoid the use of scrolling fields except for special circumstances. (Scrolling fields allow the user to control the display of a large document using a mouse or the keyboard. The text scrolls, or moves up and down on the screen, as directed by the user. Only part of the total document is visible at any one time.)

- Text should be easy to read. Consider issues such as font size, line spacing, and margins. Lines should be neither too long nor too short. They should not stretch from one edge of the screen to the other, nor should they be so narrow that they consist of only a couple of words.

- Consider presenting text in several different fields within the same screen display. A title or heading can be separated from the main body of text, or distinct ideas can be separated from each other.

- Do not overuse multiple fonts, font sizes, or font styles. Use larger fonts, bolding, or underlining to bring attention to titles, important ideas, or key terms. When techniques for distinguishing text are used too frequently, specially designated text is no longer special.

- Use special fonts sparingly. For example, script is comparatively difficult to read, but it might be used to designate entries from a special source such as a diary.

■ Keep in mind that the user of a hypermedia document may interact with the document on a different machine from that on which the document was created. If a particular font is not available on the user's machine, unexpected results may occur. For example, the default font may be larger than the intended font, and, as a result, part of the intended message may no longer be visible.

All of these design principles emphasize using text in a controlled fashion—for example, keeping text segments short and simple. Teachers may want students to write more extensively. Thus, in some situations, the goals of learning from the project and of meeting ideal design guidelines may be in conflict. One solution to this dilemma is to realize that the hypermedia product does not need to contain all of the writing the student has done related to the project.

User Interface and Navigation

Careful development of the interface

If a user is to exercise a substantial degree of control over interaction with the material in a hypermedia product, he or she must have some idea what the hypermedia product is about and how the material is organized. At any given point, the user must know what actions are possible and what the consequence of each action is likely to be. The user must also have some idea of where he or she is within the total body of information and how to get from one location to another. Finally, the mechanisms by which these goals are accomplished should either be intuitively obvious or require very little learning time. The goal is to allow the user to think about the material, not about what must be done to interact with it. As hypermedia authors, you and your students must give considerable thought to the practical mechanisms by which the potential user will interact with the information provided. Earlier you learned the term *graphic user interface* for a presentation that employs icons to help students select the appropriate tools or content. The general term for all the mechanisms that allow the user to interact with the information is **user interface.** Careful development of the user interface is important any time the structure of the hypermedia is going to allow the user to make choices about what will be experienced.

Menus and Maps

It is often helpful to provide a main screen that identifies the major topics covered by a hypermedia product. With World Wide Web projects, this is a common way to use the homepage. By identifying the topics, the author gives the user a sense of the scope of the material available and a way to identify what has and has not been covered.

Ways to identify major topics

A **menu** provides a list of the topics. This list might be presented using text or perhaps some form of graphical representation (see Figure 9.4). In contrast, a **map** identifies the components of the presentation, as well as the main links among the components. Maps are of particular value when the hypermedia product has a complex structure and allows the user many choices.

FIGURE 9.4
Graphical Menu
Developed by a Middle-
School Student

Buttons

**Buttons controlling
actions**

In most forms of hypermedia, user actions are usually initiated by clicking a button. As we mention in the chapter on multimedia tools, buttons are areas of the screen that respond to commands issued by the user, such as clicking with a mouse, touching the screen, or pressing a designated key. Buttons offer an intuitive method of taking action. This is why buttons and the touch-sensitive screen are used in situations when instruction must be minimal and inexperienced users are many (as at kiosks in a museum or shopping mall). Buttons also provide a useful way for both the hypermedia author and the user to exercise control. By programming the allowable actions as buttons, the author can offer the user a specified set of alternative actions and allow the user to control when an action will be initiated and which action will be taken.

These guidelines should acquaint you with basic principles that can guide the creation of hypermedia. Obviously, our guidelines here are more concerned with the quality of the hypermedia product than with the learning experience students might have in creating such products. Nevertheless, teachers must be sensitive to areas in which product design and learning opportunities may be in conflict and to the amount of time necessary to develop high-quality hypermedia products.

In the next sections, we integrate the theoretical ideas of learning through the process of design and concrete suggestions for how to accomplish one type of design project—hypermedia—in classroom applications. For reasons related to practical matters of teacher time and resources and to the design of learning environments likely to encourage active learning, these classroom applications often require that students work together in cooperative groups.

We like to think of these groups as design teams. We start with a short general discussion of cooperative learning.

Student Cooperation: Fundamentals for Design Teams

You have encountered cooperative learning a number of times in this book. We have presented cooperative learning as (1) an essential component in many plans for restructuring the mission and methods of schools, (2) a way to make learning active and meaningful, (3) a partial solution when technological resources are in short supply, and (4) a productive way to implement multimedia projects. You will also learn that cooperative learning provides a meaningful way to involve students with varying levels of skill and with special needs. Cooperative methods can play a highly important role in learning with technology. We feel it is worthwhile to explore cooperative learning more directly. Here we want you to consider the basic principles of cooperative learning and acquire some concrete ideas for using cooperative approaches to student projects. This material should acquaint you with conditions that are essential to productive cooperative environments and leave you with the sense that you would know where to start should you decide to use cooperative methods.

Cooperative learning techniques are hardly new. In elementary school, you probably took turns quizzing a classmate with flash cards. You may have encountered situations in college in which an education instructor divided your class into groups and asked you to discuss a topic, generate possible solutions to a teaching problem, or practice a specific teaching skill. You probably participated in these experiences with little training and with mixed results.

Some cooperative methods better than others

What has changed is that more formal cooperative learning methods have been proposed and carefully evaluated at different grade levels and in different content areas. Details can be important. Not every situation in which one student interacts with another is effective. What has come from this research are some concrete and practical learning methods and an understanding of key components that influence student learning. We cannot review this entire body of work or present all of the many successful strategies that have been developed, but if the ideas presented here appeal to you, there are some very helpful sources you might consult to learn more (Johnson, Johnson, & Holubec, 1991; Slavin, 1991, 1995). See "Resources to Expand Your Knowledge Base" at the end of the chapter.

Principles of cooperative learning

At the most basic level, **cooperative learning** refers to a classroom situation in which students work together to help one another learn. The idea is to create an environment in which students want each other to succeed and work to motivate and teach each other, to accomplish this goal. Typically, cooperative groups consist of two to five students and are often purposely made heterogeneous, that is, mixed with respect to ability, gender, and ethnic group. Cooperative groups provide a way to include students with special needs.

Team rewards and individual accountability

Research indicates that *team rewards* and *individual accountability* are especially important for success. **Team rewards** are some form of recognition for a group's success. These rewards can take many different forms: certificates, posting pictures of outstanding teams, and special activities, for example. **Individual accountability** means that team success is based on the individual accomplishments of all team members. For example, each team member may be expected to take a test on the content covered, and team performance is based on all of the scores earned. Sometimes scores are compared with past performance so that each team member has an equal opportunity to contribute to team success (Slavin, 1991).

Going Beyond Factual Information

In considering specific cooperative methods, it is important to recognize that different methods are best suited to different learning goals. Some cooperative methods were designed to help students master content typified by single right answers, and other methods focus on more open-ended problems requiring data acquisition, analysis, and synthesis. Some methods retain a fairly typical role for the teacher; that is, the teacher presents the content. Other methods require the teacher to focus on facilitating the learning process and to allow students to take more responsibility for the content.

Task specialization methods

The cooperative methods of greatest relevance here are those that have been developed to involve students in group tasks requiring both the acquisition and the application of knowledge and skill. These approaches, referred to as **task specialization methods** (Slavin, 1995), require that individual students contribute in unique ways to the accomplishment of a group task. Task specialization methods require individual accountability and team rewards. In task specialization methods, the quality with which the task is completed determines the team's reward. Individual accountability is accomplished through task specialization. Each student must accept unique responsibility for some aspect of the assigned task, and the group's performance thus depends to some extent on the contribution of every group member. The Tom Snyder products described in our earlier discussion of cooperative problem solving (see the chapter entitled "Using Instructional Software and Multimedia for Content-Area Learning") use this approach.

Group Investigation

Group investigation is a task specialization method that results in the production of group projects associated with a general theme proposed by the teacher (Sharan & Sharan, 1992). There are three principal reasons to consider this approach:

- Concrete strategies for group investigations have been developed, and some very useful guidelines have been established to help teachers implement group projects in their classrooms. (For an example, see "Activities and Projects for Your Classroom: Planets.")
- The group investigation model can be easily adapted to technology-based projects. Group investigations are intended to result in an informative summary report and presentation, and a multimedia project can serve as the summary report or support the group's presentation to the entire class.

Advantages of the group investigation method

■ The effectiveness of the group investigation method has been carefully studied. Because the research base in support of technology-based group projects is limited, demonstrations that projects of a similar nature result in effective learning experiences are reassuring. Research demonstrates that group investigations result in significantly better performance than traditional learning activities (Slavin, 1995).

The group investigation model has been worked out in detail (Sharan & Shachar, 1988; Slavin, 1995), and you will probably stick close to this model when you implement group projects for the first time. With experience, you will discover what works in your classroom. Substituting a multimedia project for the final report may require some alterations. The system may also require some tweaking to meet the needs of your students, fit your teaching style, and be feasible within the amount of time you can allot.

Mixing different learning experiences

When you decide to approach a topic using group investigation, you do not have to limit student learning opportunities to those provided through cooperative group experiences. You might decide to initiate the unit of study in a traditional way. Perhaps students will work with a textbook and whole group instruction at first. These experiences might be used to establish background and develop some of the issues that might then be pursued through group investigation. Or you might decide to jump right in and initiate the study of a new unit with the group investigation process. Then as you think about the topics students have selected, you may feel the need to provide supplemental experiences. As the class moves through the time period allowed for the unit, it is appropriate to mix in other learning experiences and assignments. The group investigation process does not have to be the sole learning experience you use.

Hypercomposition Design Model

The *hypercomposition* design model (Lehrer, 1993; Lehrer, Erickson, & Connell, 1994) provides a concrete way to integrate many of the themes we have developed throughout this book. **Hypercomposition** deals specifically with hypermedia projects as content-area learning experiences and comfortably incorporates meaningful learning, cooperative learning, knowledge as design, and many other themes we emphasize. The model is intended to guide teachers in the implementation of hypermedia projects. Although we feel it is important to offer concrete ideas that teachers can relate to, we are not suggesting that teachers must implement projects exactly as we have described them. Examples and models should provide you with principles, strategies, and ideas. Your own experiences will determine how you integrate these elements into classroom practice.

General framework based on the writing process

The hypercomposition design model was developed by observing and interviewing students as they completed hypermedia projects. The observations were then incorporated into a general framework to help other teachers facilitate hypermedia projects. The general framework for the model was based on a widely accepted model of the writing process (Flower & Hayes, 1981; Hayes

Planets

Students study the planets at many grade levels. Let's take a look at how group investigation could be applied to this unit using a presentation tool for the final project. We trace the project through the six stages of the group investigation model (Sharan & Sharan, 1992).

Stage 1: Identify the topic and form student groups. After viewing an introductory video on the planets, have students submit the name of the planet they would be interested in studying in greater depth. Divide the class into groups based on their choices.

Stage 2: Team planning. Once the groups have been formed, the members of each one must decide on a plan for how their group will function. Will each member choose a special area to research, such as the planet's geology or its weather? Or will the team members gather information, come back to the group to share what they have learned, and then divide responsibilities?

Stage 3: Team members conduct inquiry. As the group members gather resources, ongoing decisions must be made as to what information should be included in the project. In this phase, it is important that students take detailed notes they will be able to share with group members. They should also keep in mind visual images that might help illustrate the concepts being summarized. For example, students might use the Tom Snyder product *The Great Solar System Rescue* and show clips that give graphical representations of the sizes of the planets.

Stage 4: Prepare the final report. The students in each group must now map out the project. Each group member can take on a specific role, such as being responsible for the graphics, entering the text, connecting the visuals, or developing the navigation system. Or each student can take responsibility for one planet feature, such as the makeup of the atmosphere, and be responsible for organizing all of the information sources related to that feature. When each group has its planet report put together, the class as a whole can decide how to integrate the different team projects. In what order should the planets be presented? What kind and how many introductory screens are needed? How will the project end?

Stage 5: Present the final report. The students in the class can view the finished project and question group members about information that may not be clear or that seems of special interest. The project can then be shared with other classes or with parents. The project could be recorded on videotape and saved in the library for future classes to use as a resource.

Stage 6: Evaluation. Although we call this the last step, it is important to realize that assessment comes into play throughout the project. The teacher should meet periodically with the groups and discuss what is happening. What kinds of resources have been gathered? How was the information organized? How were decisions made as to what information should be included? Who took responsibility for what? What difficulties were encountered, and how did group members attempt to solve problems? What suggestions do the group members have to improve future projects?

& Flower, 1980) and shares many features with the model for group investigations you have just encountered. To create guidelines for hypermedia design, Lehrer (1993) extended the writing process approach (described in the chapter entitled "Using Tools") to include the generation of knowledge (it is not assumed that hypermedia authors have already learned what they will eventually present), attention to the special features of hypermedia, and the requirements of collaborative authorship. Note that hypermedia design is not proposed as a strictly linear process. In general, authors do work from the beginning to the end of a project, but a good deal of looping back occurs as work at later stages reveals the weaknesses of work completed at earlier stages. The model proposes that projects incorporate the major elements of planning, transforming, translating, and evaluating and revising.

Planning

The topics teachers propose to guide their students' hypermedia projects are usually broad. The intent is to allow the members of student groups to explore a bit and then concentrate on what interests them. In the initial planning stage, group members should attempt to define major topics, establish the basic format of the presentation, and work out how the group will function.

Guiding students in the planning stage

It is very possible that students will be so inexperienced with the general topic that the group will be unable to make effective decisions. In this case, the teacher must offer advice. You may tell students to do some initial research and give them some sample sources of information. More specific decisions about topics and responsibilities may result from this initial investigation. This would be a great opportunity to propose a WebQuest (see the chapter entitled "The Internet as a Tool for Inquiry").

Students also might not function effectively in a group setting. Some students may dominate the decision making and leave others out. Others may not know how to listen, criticize, or accept criticism. The teacher might need to establish some guidelines for group functioning and monitor performance in this area.

The general tasks in planning the group project require the group to do the following:

1. Develop major goals.
2. Propose topics and the relationships among topics.
3. Propose a presentation format to fit this organizational scheme.
4. Establish team member responsibilities.

Transforming and Translating

The transformation and translation phase consists of two general processes: collecting information and generating knowledge.

Collecting Information

Search and recording strategies

To collect information relevant to project goals, students must identify potentially relevant sources through the use of effective search strategies, locate the information relevant to project goals, and employ some process to retain

Spotlight on Assessment

Evaluating Projects

If authentic tasks are to achieve their potential benefits, student performance must be evaluated in ways that students both find informative and perceive as fair. Here we look at two assessment devices you might use to communicate expectations to students, guide your evaluation of projects, and communicate feedback to students. The specific components of these assessment devices (some authors have used terms such as *assessment rubrics* and *analysis guides* in a similar way) will vary with the nature of the project and with what you want to emphasize. What you want to emphasize might also be worked out in the project planning stage through negotiation with your students.

To provide a context for this discussion, let's propose a sample project:

> *Task:* Create a multimedia product that presents your team's analysis and recommendation regarding beverage container recycling. This hypermedia product will be viewed by the general public in the city library and will urge the public to support the recycling plan you propose.

We will gloss over all of the activities required of you to facilitate this project and get right to how you might create useful assessment devices.

Continua of Descriptors

Generating continua of descriptors allows you to specify the competence areas to be used in the assessment process and to define specific levels of accomplishment within each competence area (Tierney, Carter, & Desai, 1991). The intent of the continua is to help the evaluator and those being evaluated identify levels of quality in prescribed areas. In implementing this approach, it is useful to create a form to present the assessment guidelines and communicate areas of strength and weakness clearly. The form might take the following general structure.

Project Title

Strong Performance		Needs Improvement
	Competency 1	
Descriptor 1A	Descriptor 1B	Descriptor 1C
	Competency 2	
Descriptor 2A	Descriptor 2B	Descriptor 2C
	Competency 3	
Descriptor 3A	Descriptor 3B	Descriptor 3C

Because one of the goals in creating this type of form is to present information concisely, you might feel it is necessary to add material in which the descriptors are laid out in more detail.

Now let's develop continua of descriptors for our sample project. Again, in practice, we would urge you to develop assessment devices in collaboration with your students.

The project example might require evaluation in several general areas: domain knowledge and procedural skills, design skills, and team skills. Specific competencies could involve content coverage, argument communication, screen layout, graphics, user interface, involvement level of team members, and team support. Each area of competency would then be defined in terms of concrete levels of accomplishment. For example, for content coverage, the following categories might be used:

Exhaustive coverage of multiple issues bearing on local recycling situation
Adequate presentation of main recycling issues
Incomplete coverage of important issues

The form built from these continua might look something like this.

Beverage Container Recycling Project

Strong Performance		**Needs Improvement**
	Content Coverage	
Exhaustive coverage of multiple issues	Adequate coverage of issues	Incomplete coverage of essential issues
	Argument Communication	
Persuasive use of logic and data	Adequate presentation of position	Unpersuasive or unclear argument
	Screen Layout	
Interesting display with proper and predictable placement of buttons and graphics; text attractive and easy to read	Understandable positioning of buttons and graphics; text readable	Confusing or disorganized placement of screen elements; text difficult to read
	Graphics	
Informative and interesting, with proper placement	Adequate information value	Graphics often unrelated to message or improperly placed
	User Interface	
Easy to understand; functions without error	Error free	Confusing or occasionally fails
	Team Involvement Level	
All students contribute in a meaningful way	All students active	Some students involved

Holistic Scoring Guide

The holistic scoring method differs from the continua technique in the assignment of each project to a summary category. In making a holistic judgment, the evaluator could consider the same competency areas used in the continua method, but the descriptive statements associated with the competency areas have been organized to reflect different holistic levels of accomplishment. The evaluator has to determine which cluster of descriptors best describes the project and the process generating the project. The labels assigned to the categories are intended to reflect the nature of the holistic evaluation. Sets of

terms—*beginning, intermediate, advanced; exceptional, adequate, marginal*—
that seem suited to the nature of the project and to the type of feedback
intended are used as category labels (Tierney et al., 1991).

A form is useful in guiding evaluators and providing expectations and feedback to students. A holistic guide for the beverage container recycling project
might look something like this:

Beverage Container Recycling Project

Marginal Project. Projects may be classified as marginal because of the quality
of the project or the process producing it. Marginal projects might be incomplete or inaccurate or might not function as they should. The process associated with a marginal project might not involve all team members, or team
members might treat each other poorly. Specific characteristics might include
the following:

- The project does not establish sufficient background describing general
  problem of waste disposal and specific problems associated with the
  disposal of beverage containers.
- The proposed recycling plan is sketchy and difficult to understand.
- The arguments supporting the recycling plan are not persuasive.
- Placement of buttons is haphazard
- Text segments ramble and make it difficult to identify key points.
- Message of graphics is frequently unclear.
- An unfamiliar user would find it difficult to use this product.
- Buttons strand user without a way to move on or do not work at all.
- The project was completed by only some of the team members.
- Comments of team members were frequently critical or did not provide
  constructive advice.

Adequate Project. Projects are described as adequate when they indicate a
reasonable understanding of the problem and propose a logical solution. The
entire team should make some contribution to the completion of the project.
Specific characteristics might include the following:

- The project presents an overview of the problem of waste disposal
  and provides specific information on difficulties created by beverage
  container disposal.
- A reasonable plan for beverage container recycling is proposed.
- Buttons controlling the presentation appear in a consistent screen
  location.
- Text segments are concise and informative.
- Graphics contribute to the message of the presentation.
- Use of the project requires little instruction.
- Buttons and other control devices function as intended.
- All students make a unique contribution to the completion of the
  project.
- Team members are positive in remarks made to other team members.

Exceptional Project. Projects are described as exceptional when the information provided is extensive, the arguments advanced are particularly

persuasive, and the proposed problem solution is insightful. The project should be interesting for viewers and exhibit exemplary design principles. Team members should work to bring out the best in one another. Specific characteristics might include the following:

- The project provides an extensive overview of the problem of waste disposal and specific information on difficulties created by beverage container disposal. An effort has been made to provide information that defines the problem at the local level. The presentation is well organized and interesting.
- Multiple suggestions are provided for recycling beverage containers. The argument for recycling is persuasive.
- Buttons controlling the presentation appear in a consistent screen location.
- Text segments are concise and informative.
- Graphics are informative and interesting.
- Graphics are used to increase the impact of the basic message.
- Use of the project requires little instruction.
- Buttons and other control devices function as intended.
- All students make a unique contribution to the completion of the project.
- Team members go out of their way to encourage and assist one another.
- Team members teach one another needed skills.

Online resources are available to assist educators in understanding and developing rubrics. Teachers can examine sample rubrics constructed for different categories of student projects and use web-based tools to create rubrics for their own classroom projects. You can find suggestions in "Resources to Expand Your Knowledge Base" at the end of the chapter, and on the website that accompanies this textbook.

the information for later use. Search strategies could encompass methods as diverse as electronic searches of the card catalog in the school or local library, use of the index in books covering the general area of interest, and asking questions of people who might know something about the topic. Once good sources are located, students might use photocopying, note taking, audio recording, or video recording to collect the information. These skills could be novel, and some training might be necessary. Not all students know how to operate a camcorder, for instance. Students might also need to learn effective note-taking skills.

Creating information
    The potential for creating information should not be overlooked. Students can conduct original experiments or replicate established procedures to gather original data, develop questionnaires to give to students from their school or local residents, or conduct structured interviews.

You will probably want to review samples of student work (notes, sources selected) to provide feedback and offer suggestions. One advantage of a project approach is the opportunity to help students learn to learn. Projects put more responsibility in the hands of students and require them to engage in diverse self-guided activities. Projects provide great opportunities, but students need guidance to profit from these opportunities. Students are likely to have the most experience processing information that a textbook author or a teacher has already organized and thought through for them. Be careful that students are not left to drift aimlessly as they encounter new expectations.

Generating Knowledge

Organizing, summarizing, interpreting

Once they have gathered the raw information, students will need to organize, summarize, and interpret it. Some specific academic skills could be introduced at this point. Students might benefit from learning to outline, generate concept maps, or write summaries (Day, 1986). Also, some basic statistical procedures might be applied to quantifiable data. Statistical procedures can be as basic as determining the frequency of an event or finding the average of multiple measurements. Perhaps these data can be graphed in informative ways. This might be an opportunity to introduce students to spreadsheets and related data visualization capabilities. Students need to interpret what they have discovered. What are the major ideas? What are the causal factors that appear to be present? What alternative interpretations might be possible?

Publication

The other major task of knowledge generation is the publication of what has been learned. One decision is determining the format for publication. The formats of desktop publishing, electronic slide shows, and hypermedia have been discussed previously. The decision you and your students make will depend on the type of information to be conveyed, the equipment and time available, and the students' skills.

To summarize, the stage of transforming and translating includes processes involved in the collection of information and the generation of knowledge. Students working on projects would:

- Search for and collect information
- Develop new information
- Select and interpret information
- Segment information
- Link information

Evaluating and Revising

Authoring is not a one-pass process. Sometimes the product does not meet expectations. A variety of difficulties can occur within the product itself or in the way the product conveys information to users. In some cases, a problem is obvious as soon as a button does not take the user to the intended destination. In other cases, problems may be more subtle or even hidden from the author. For example, the author may assume an unrealistic level of background knowledge on the user's part and thus present new information too rapidly or briefly.

Recognizing and fixing problems

Evaluation is the process of searching for all of these difficulties and many more. It is impossible to list all of the things that might go wrong; even experienced developers continually encounter new problems. We are always amazed when we attend technology demonstrations to see just how frequently experts encounter difficulties demonstrating the products they have created

Focus

Experimenting with Different Structures and Linking Systems

Because students will likely have little experience in browsing or authoring hypermedia, teachers might want to consider the following suggestions for introducing the ideas of nodes and links. Professional instructional designers use a process called **storyboarding,** in which they rough out the sequence of displays and activities to be incorporated in the software.

Students can do the same thing. They can represent nodes with sketches or brief statements entered on note cards. Each node might be thought of as the information the eventual user will view or hear at one time. These note cards can be tacked to a bulletin board and linked with lengths of yarn. It shouldn't be too difficult to imagine representing the different organizational structures presented earlier in this chapter in this manner. One interesting variation is to use sticky notes instead of note cards. These notes can be easily positioned on a blackboard and connected with chalk lines.

---

and worked with for hundreds of hours. We have found ourselves in the same situation several times. Because problems seem unavoidable, here are some suggestions for how to make the problems surface so that you or your students can understand and fix them. Note that we use the term *problems* to refer to problems in both the software and the content that the software was developed to present:

Guidelines for identifying problems

- *Software developers can learn to test systematically all planned and unplanned actions within programs that have been created.* It is sometimes users' unintended actions that cause problems. A developer can easily become focused on what he or she thinks should happen and forget that the eventual user does not have this same insight. When confused or without the benefit of knowing exactly what to do, users may do something that was not intended and cause a problem. So test a product for the unanticipated. For example, if the user is asked to type a number into a box, try typing "one" and not just "1." If you developed this product, you probably assumed the user would use a digit and not a word to represent a number.

- *Developers can ask naive users to try out products and carefully observe what happens.* Do naive users try to do things that were not intended? Do they become confused or say that they cannot understand the ideas presented? Listen carefully to what they have to say. You have probably done the same kind of thing with papers you wrote for college classes. You asked a classmate or a friend to read your paper and tell you what he or she thought. Consider a hypermedia product as another way to inform or communicate, and ask others what they think.

Focus

Alternative: A Filmmaking Model

We emphasize the hypercomposition design model because it can be related to process writing and because we assume the connection with writing projects will offer a comfortable connection for educators. Our discussion of this model is intended both to put our recommendations for multimedia authoring into a well-formed theoretical context and to offer a concrete description of the various tasks that must be accomplished as the author creates a multimedia product. The model provides a general framework educators can use to structure and support the "authoring as learning" process for students. There is at least one other media design model that has been adapted as a guide for student multimedia projects. This second model is based on the filmmaking process.

Nikos Theodosakis (2001) approaches learning through design from the perspective of a filmmaker. He advocates the educational value of cooperative video production in much the same way we have promoted multimedia authoring. His model outlines a media production process broken down into stages (development, preproduction, production, postproduction, and distribution) and accomplished by student teams (director, writer, camera operator, editor, producer). Working within the context of a content-appropriate challenge, the basic idea is that a production team must plan and "pitch" a project to the teacher and, upon gaining approval, implement the proposed project. Depending on circumstances, the project might be designed to create a video product that argues for a cause or provides a brief educational experience. Tasks are assigned that are consistent with the role of each team member. For example, the writer might develop a script, create scene breakdowns, record sound, write voice-over narration, and develop press releases as the team moves through the stages of the production process. The camera operator might research possible visual topics, generate a shooting schedule, operate the camera, locate additional needed images and video, and select key still images from the video. The individuals working on a team might stay in the same roles or switch roles as the project progresses.

Some educators may find this approach very helpful because it offers a great structure for those new to media projects. Others may explore the descriptions of stages, roles, and activities as a way to develop new insights that can be woven into the teacher's way of doing things. Theodosakis's website is **http:// www.thedirectorintheclassroom.com/.** You can find more information on the filmmaking approach to hypermedia in "Resources to Expand Your Knowledge Base" at the end of this chapter, and on the website for this textbook.

■ *Test out products on different equipment* (preferably the exact equipment your target audience will use). Different equipment is the cause of most difficulties that experts encounter in novel situations. Programs have a nasty habit of not working exactly the same way on different machines or on machines using different versions of the operating system. Often the equipment used to develop software is more powerful (more memory, larger monitor) than the machines software users work on. A variation of this recommendation for webpage authors is to test the webpages with different browsers.

■ *Ask a content-area expert to review the product.* Commercial developers of educational software do this all the time. For example, if the product is in the area of history, history teachers and historians not associated with the project are asked to review it. As a classroom teacher, you might end up serving as the content-area expert responsible for this type of review. It might be useful to have several teachers participate in the review of hypermedia projects. One teacher might evaluate how effectively the product meets standards of effective communication (organization, clarity, grammar), and another might evaluate the factual accuracy and logic of arguments. Each of these procedures might identify limitations that the design group will want to take into account in upgrading the product's quality.

The Teacher's Role in the Design Process

Now that you are familiar with some basic design principles, some of the fundamental ideas of cooperative learning, and at least one general model for student hypermedia projects, let's look at some of the implications of bringing such projects into your classroom. You may have already generated your own implications after considering some of the sample projects.

Works of Mind

When teachers incorporate projects, many will need to adjust what they do and, in some cases, what they teach. Perkins (1986), who advocates the concept of learning as design, justifies the need to engage students in a different type of learning activity this way. His concern is that schools seldom allow students to do "works of mind" (original projects or investigations that are largely the responsibility of the learner). Schools teach students about mathematics, history, and biology but do not allow students to do mathematics, history, or biology.

Learning by doing
One of the few exceptions Perkins notes to the principle of "learning about rather than doing" is in art. Students at most grade levels do works of art. Why? As educators, we recognize that a design like a picture can exist at a very elementary level. Even kindergarten students draw, paint, and sculpt objects from various materials. But most other content areas seem different. We often cannot think of what an elementary design in biology or history would look like. One reason is the assumption that an accumulation of information is required before a work of some form is possible. In many cases, however, the nature of the problem is scalable, and background knowledge can be ac-

quired. Students can design a history of their own families or study the ecology of their classroom aquarium. Students can acquire project-relevant knowledge and skills as they proceed.

Lehrer and his associates (Carver, Lehrer, Connell, & Erickson, 1992; Erikson & Lehrer, 1998; Lehrer, 1993; Lehrer et al., 1994), as well as others (Brown, 1992; Harel, 1991; Harel & Papert, 1990; Pearlman, 1991; Resnick, Bruckman, & Martin, 1999; Toomey & Ketterer, 1995), have proposed that projects in which groups of students attempt to explain or teach with technology qualify as works of mind. In a typical classroom activity of this type, the teacher coaches small groups of students as they pursue projects that fall within some general domain. The general domain refers to the topic designated for study by the curriculum: the Civil War, the life cycle of the butterfly, and so on. Individual projects prepared by different groups pursue the general topic in different ways or emphasize different aspects of the overall theme, depending on the interests and abilities of group members and the information that students encounter as they research the general topic. To maintain a student focus, teachers should intervene to redirect students only after careful consideration. Instead of direct intervention, teachers would be more likely to influence students by asking leading questions such as, "Why do we have historians? What do they do?" Carver and her associates (1992) use Sheingold's (1991) phrase "adventurous teaching" to describe the tolerance teachers must exhibit to allow students the necessary freedom to construct knowledge. Students cannot truly function as junior biologists, historians, writers, or political advocates if teachers make key decisions for them.

Giving students freedom to construct their own knowledge

Apprenticeship Method

Students as apprentices

If teachers do not transmit information and do not tightly control student activity, what do they do? It is useful to view the teacher's function as initiating students into the community of scholars appropriate to the area or areas being investigated (Lehrer, 1993). To develop domain-appropriate learning and thinking processes, students are engaged in tasks authentic to the domain within an apprenticeship relationship with the teacher and perhaps with other domain experts (people within the community). Students, as a result, experience activities as authentic tasks that might confront domain experts, and they acquire knowledge and problem-solving skills associated with these tasks.

For example, a historian uses primary sources (original maps, diaries, letters, newspaper accounts, legal documents, pictures, personal interviews) to describe past events and explain past behaviors. The historian must locate sources, analyze the material for important information, integrate ideas into a logical account of behavior, and communicate an effective description and explanation of past events to others. Students can take on similar tasks using similar sources and engaging the same cognitive processes. The issues could resemble the topics covered in traditional textbooks (battles of the Civil War) or could be more unusual or local in orientation (for example, early education in your community—the first teacher, building, student characteristics). Often activities are multidisciplinary because scholarship of this type frequently does not confine itself to a single traditional content area, such as reading, mathematics, or science.

We discussed cognitive apprenticeship earlier in this book. To review briefly, it concerns not the transmission of factual information but the development of cognitive skills. In developing cognitive skills, the role of the teacher shifts over time from demonstrating (modeling), to coaching the student through early efforts, to a more passive role in which the teacher may observe and intervene only occasionally. The coaching stage is especially critical. A key component of coaching is the provision of support devices—such as reminders, conventions (common techniques or strategies for performing expected tasks), or constraints—that help the apprentice to approximate the complex behavior of the expert. When the skills to be learned are cognitive, it is also important to find some way to externalize these behaviors so that the internal cognitive behaviors can be observed and discussed. Often the expert must attempt to explain what he or she is thinking to provide the novice some awareness of internal behavior.

Project Quality

The quality that should be expected of student-generated products is the subject of some debate. Some contend that students should develop only prototypes and not strive to produce products of high quality (D'Ignazio, 1990). This position might imply that students should learn only the most basic software design techniques and not spend time on embellishments or refinements. In some respects, it is clear that there is a diminishing return on time spent in polishing a presentation.

Importance of students' pride in their work

However, there is also a somewhat different perspective. Much of our rationale for student projects includes the idea of involving students in authentic activities. A student's sense of scholarship and authorship comes with producing something of which he or she can be proud. Students know what a real newspaper, a real video production, and authentic computer software look like. Student designers want to develop projects others would use and appreciate.

A realistic classroom goal

A realistic classroom goal is probably to familiarize students with some fundamental principles of design that apply to their particular project. These fundamental principles will vary with the nature of the project, the age and experience of the students, whether the project is an individual or a cooperative venture, and the teacher's goals. Even if the principles taught to younger students are fairly simple ones, they can help the students generate projects of very respectable quality.

Research following middle-school students involved in multiple hypermedia design projects over a two-year period has demonstrated that students moved toward higher self-imposed standards both in the questions their projects were developed to address and in the quality they expected of the hypermedia products (Erickson & Lehrer, 1998). Students working on multiple collaborative projects used their experience to raise expectations for knowledge building and for the associated products used to communicate what they learned.

Student Projects, Standards, and Restructuring

Advocates of engaging students in sophisticated design projects often slip into arguments for restructuring schools (Lehrer et al., 1994; Thomas & Knezek,

1991). When educators talk about restructuring, they are in part proposing changes in the curriculum, the roles played by teachers, and the learning activities provided for students (Thomas & Knezek, 1991). Our discussion of reform and educational standards earlier in this book recognizes the growing pressure for valuing a wider range of domain-appropriate performance skills. Certainly design projects engage teachers and students in unique activities, have them play somewhat different roles than they did in the past, and use school time in different ways. Hypermedia design projects change the teacher's role from dispenser to facilitator. In many cases, students are expected to find information themselves and then construct knowledge from it. Students may encounter situations and discover information that teachers have not experienced directly. They may try to do things that their teachers have not done. The information they use will not always be found in traditional textbooks or even in the school library. Often it will be found outside the traditional school setting—in the community, biological habitats, work settings, and other nontraditional but content-appropriate settings. More activities will be group based. Activities will have to be graded in different ways. Spending fifty minutes each day in the classroom may not provide the optimal setting for many activities. Traditional school practices are difficult to change, but some exciting proposals seem to be emerging.

Need for flexibility, spontaneity

Using technology-based projects to explore content you might normally teach in a traditional manner will require flexibility on your part. You cannot expect to approach a project with the same high degree of structure possible with textbook-related instructional materials. Even a project that echoes an activity already implemented by another teacher or replicates a project you did with last year's class is an adventure in learning. You will likely find that some uncertainty is desirable and that a degree of flexibility creates a more active learning environment. Uncertainty provides opportunities for students to make decisions and allows you the opportunity to model problem-solving skills. Some spontaneity is necessary. If students run into an idea that fascinates them, they should be encouraged to pursue this opportunity and find a way to integrate their experiences into the project.

As you have progressed through the various topics in this textbook, new ideas may have caused you to recall and reconsider projects you first encountered some time ago. You may have found yourself recalling projects from earlier chapters when we discussed techniques such as scanning, video digitizing, and sound capture or when hypermedia and paint tools were presented. Now you have a better understanding of how those projects were created. The discussions of cooperative learning or design principles may also have encouraged you to reconsider some of these projects. You may already have judged some of the projects against basic standards of design or thought about more effective ways that groups of students might have studied the same content areas. Examples represent raw information; we hope you have taken the opportunity to work mentally with these examples to create personal knowledge.

We devote the rest of this chapter to some of the practical issues involved in implementing classroom projects. We first discuss the development of World Wide Web pages as an option for student projects. We then look at an extended example of a hypermedia project.

Student Projects on the Web

The Web offers an alternative outlet for multimedia projects. Most of the projects we describe throughout this book could have been implemented in some form as webpages. Web projects also offer some powerful and unique opportunities. The capacity to link your multimedia projects with other Internet resources can be useful. The process of searching the Internet for good resources serves as a way to involve students actively with content. The Web also allows an efficient means for collaboration with students from other locations.

Skills not difficult to learn

As we suggest in our discussion of other forms of multimedia, the skills necessary to produce web-based multimedia can be learned in a reasonable amount of time and can be used repeatedly as an efficient and creative way to explore and process course content. In the pages that follow we describe web materials and the mechanics of web authoring simply but accurately. The capabilities of the Web are expanding daily, and some functions are quite complex. We cannot hope to help you grasp the entire potential of authoring for the Web, but we will give you the background necessary to do useful work. We propose that you adopt a minimalist approach to web multimedia (D'Ignazio, 1996), learning as few new software tools and as few new technology skills as possible. If this experience is productive and exciting, there will be plenty of related techniques and ideas you can explore.

Components of webpages

Think of webpages as consisting of a combination of (1) multimedia elements (text, graphics, sounds, movies, and such), (2) the special command language called hypertext markup language (HTML) that informs the browser how to organize these multimedia elements for display, and (3) links allowing access to other pages. You already have considerable knowledge of multimedia elements from previous chapters. You have also learned that an Internet link can be expressed in the form of a URL. The element of web authoring you have yet to experience in depth is HTML.

You have already used one type of markup language, perhaps without realizing it. If you have word processing experience, you have probably underlined and bolded text, centered and enlarged a segment of text to serve as the title for a paper, and perhaps inserted a picture at a specific location in your document. You did not type any detailed codes to make text bold; rather, you probably selected a segment of text and then used a keyboard command (Command-b or Control-b depending on the operating system) or the equivalent menu option. The specific codes needed to create bold text were then inserted in the word processing file you created. Although the codes were not visible, the results were.

Similarity of web authoring to word processing

You can now create web documents in exactly the same way. As you will see, certain web authoring programs allow you to control the appearance of a webpage by positioning multimedia elements on a blank page and manipulating various aspects of their appearance (such as size, justification, and text appearance). The markup language that creates this appearance is not visible on the screen; it is saved in the file that is eventually sent to the machine that serves your webpages. These commands that are not visible to the user but are interpreted by the browser are called **tags.** You could also create the same file by entering all of the markup tags and the text content of the webpage directly from the computer keyboard. There are some reasons you might want to do this (more options become available or control of screen appearance is more precise), but the time required to learn the unique tags necessary to perform these various functions is not worthwhile for most individuals.

Basic Features and Skills

One way to help you understand the possibilities and demands of authoring for the Web is to outline some of the fundamental skills student authors should have. Think of these as the building blocks of webpages. When students combine these components in different ways, they will be able to create a wide variety of projects. Following is a list of actions and a brief description of how each action is implemented. Several web authoring programs are listed at the end of this chapter. All of the programs we have included (and several more we did not) are capable of doing the following actions without requiring the user to enter HTML tags:

Typical actions in creating a webpage

- *Set background color.* Select the menu option, and then select the color from a palette to control page color.
- *Add text to the page.* Type or open a text-only file created by some other application.
- *Set the size of headings.* Select the text with the mouse, and then select heading size from the menu to create bold page headings of different sizes.
- *Create lists.* Select lines of text, and then select a menu option to create hierarchical lists.
- *Add graphics, sounds, and movies to the page.* Drag the image file, sound file, or QuickTime movie file to the page, and drop or open the file using the menu bar option.
- *Link the text or a graphic to other pages.* Select the text or graphic; then use the menu option, and select the file for a link. For pages at other sites, select the text or graphic, and then use the menu option to type in a URL for the link.
- *Horizontal rule.* Use the menu option to draw a horizontal line to separate areas of the page.
- *Table.* Use the menu option to add a table of cells to the page. The boundaries of the cells can be manually adjusted using the mouse to create cells of different size. Tables provide a convenient way to define a webpage template (see Figure 9.7 later in the chapter).

Many of the techniques described here were used to create the page in Figure 9.5 from two graphics files and a text file. (The logo at the top of the page is a graphic image created in another program.) Some comments have been added to the figure to point out noteworthy features. All underlined text and the smaller graphic serve as links to other webpages. When the web authoring program saves the page, the resulting HTML file consists of the text, the HTML tags, and information that will allow a browser to load and position the graphics and follow a link to another location. To make this information

FIGURE 9.5
Sample Webpage Showing Common Elements

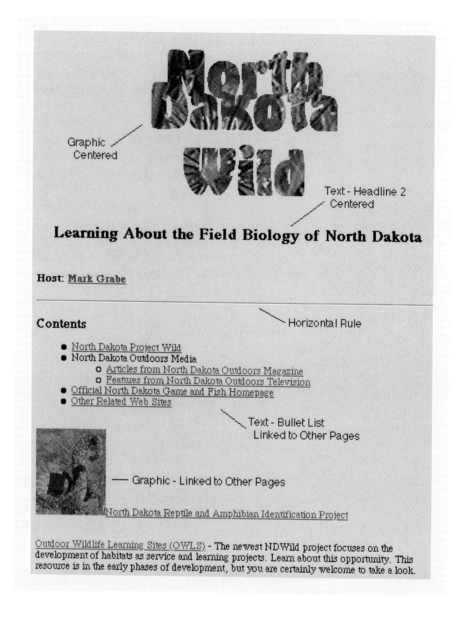

available to users, the HTML file and the two graphics files would have to be loaded to a server. We won't explain what is necessary to operate a server or how to load files to the server; operating the server requires some computer experience and is usually left to someone with special training. Loading files is not difficult, but the technique will vary with the kind of server a school uses.

An example of HTML
The raw HTML document responsible for what you see in Figure 9.5 looks like this:

```
<HTML>
<HEAD>
    <TITLE>North Dakota Wild</TITLE>
```

```
</HEAD>
<BODY>
<CENTER><IMG SRC="pics/ID.GIF"</CENTER>
<BR>
<H1><CENTER>Learning About the Field Biology of North Dakota
</CENTER></H1>
<BR>
Host: <A HREF="/dept/grabe">Mark Grabe</A>
<BR>
<HR>
<H3>Contents</H3>
<UL>
<LI><A HREF="instmat.html">North Dakota Project Wild</A>
<LI>North Dakota Outdoors Media
     <UL>
     <LI><A HREF="media.html#anchor37399">Articles from North
Dakota Outdoors Magazine</A>
     <LI><A HREF="media.html#anchor38708">Features from North
Dakota Outdoors Television</A>
     </UL>
<LI><A HREF="http://www.state.nd.us/gnf/">Official North Dakota
Game and Fish Home Page</A>
<LI><A HREF="others.html">Other Related Web Sites</A>
</UL>
<BR>
<A HREF="keyhead.html"><IMG SRC="pics/rattleS.GIF">North Dakota
Reptile and Amphibian Identification Project</ABR>
<BR>
<BR>
<A HREF="http://ndwild.psych.und.nodak.edu/owlshome.html">Outdoor
Wildlife Learning Sites (OWLS)</A> - The newest NDWild project focuses
on the development of habitats as service and learning projects. Learn about
this opportunity. This resource is in the early phases of development, but
you are certainly welcome to take a look.<BR>
</BODY>
</HTML>
```

Alternative Ways to Construct Webpages

As a webpage author, you can choose to work with HTML or ignore it. It exists in either case. No matter how you choose to develop web content, it is helpful to understand the basics of what HTML does and to recognize that with the exception of text, multimedia elements presented by webpages are not actually part of the HTML file. Just these insights can be helpful. For example, one of the most common problems beginning web authors encounter is having pages they have designed on a classroom machine fail to present graphics when loaded to a server. The problem occurs because the graphics files cannot be located. Perhaps the author has loaded the HTML file but forgotten to load the graphics files to the server. Perhaps the files have been loaded but have been stored in the wrong place. "Disappearing images" are a common problem, but a little understanding of how HTML functions goes a long way toward knowing what to look for in finding a solution.

In most educational settings, web projects are developed using some type of authoring software. As the author, you concentrate on what should appear on the page and where the elements of your page should be placed. The authoring software generates the necessary HTML codes. Here are some authoring software options.

Word Processing Programs

Saving a word processing document as HTML

The same word processing program you use to write term papers probably has the capability to create webpages (a partial list of such programs is included at the end of the chapter). Some functions are performed automatically, and all you have to do is indicate that you want to save the document as HTML. To do this, select Save As instead of Save from the menu bar of the word processing program, and determine if HTML is one of the options you are given. (It is always a good strategy to save the document first as a traditional word processing document. If the webpage does not come out looking like you had hoped, it will be easier to make adjustments to the word processing file than to the HTML file.)

When you save a word processing document as HTML, the program recognizes certain features in your document and attempts to duplicate these features in HTML. For example, images embedded in the document will be converted and saved as JPEG files, and text that appears in bold type will be saved in the HTML document surrounded by the <B> and </B>tags. Some important features of webpages, such as links to other pages, are not created automatically. Instead, the word processing program will offer you a method for creating these features directly. For example, a link is usually created by selecting a phrase of text and then selecting a menu option that allows a web address to be associated with that phrase. When the word processing document is saved as HTML, the selected phrase becomes a link.

Take a careful look at the capabilities of the word processing programs available to you. If you are interested in creating simple webpages, you probably already have the software you need to complete the task.

Web Authoring Software for Students

Software companies, taking note of the potential for student web authoring projects, have created products that attempt to simplify and focus the process of creating webpages. EZediaQTI, the product used in the example project we describe in this chapter and one of the authoring environments we described in the chapter entitled "Using Multimedia Tools," is a good example. EZediaQTI would not be a likely candidate for commercial web developers but does allow students many creative options. You can find more information about this application and other products for student use in "Resources to Expand Your Knowledge Base" at the end of this chapter, and on the website that accompanies this textbook.

EMERGING TECHNOLOGY

Blogs and Blogging

The term *blog,* a simplification of the phrase "web log," typically refers to a webpage consisting of chronologically ordered entries, with the most recent entries appearing at the top of the page. Sometimes, blogs are described as online diaries or journals to help those unfamiliar with this form of web publishing understand the format. Depending on the blog software and the inclination of the blogger, entries may consist of text, text and web links, or almost any combination of the media types we have discussed in this book.

The authoring of a blog can be accomplished with very little technical skill and without having to purchase specialized software. A blog author creates individual entries using a web browser to connect to a specialized, password-protected website. The software that generates and serves blog pages runs on a remote server and can be accessed by many different users.

Figure 9.6 displays what an author might see while generating a blog entry. Information is submitted using a web form. The text information is entered in text fields (Title, Post). Other components (such as a link or an image) are added by clicking on buttons. Each button opens a dialog box for accepting a specific kind of information. This system of buttons and related dialog boxes allows the blog software to write HTML code. For example, you may not know the HTML codes necessary to insert a link in a webpage. Figure 9.6 displays the dialog box that appears when the Links button is selected. The web address you would like associated with the link is entered in this dialog box. When the dialog box is closed, the HTML code for this link appears in the Post text box (see Figure 9.6). A similar process is used to upload an image file and then automatically generate the HTML necessary to display the image. The blogger clicks the Publish button to finish the process and upload the entire entry for general viewing.

Blogs are not intended to be elegant websites. For the author, the advantage is in ease of use. Blogs are for those who want to either offer comments frequently or spend their time crafting what they have to say rather than designing webpages. Those who read blogs are looking for constantly updated content, and it is the information rather than the stylish design that encourages them to return. This ease of use and focus on content are what make blogs so well suited to educational applications. Students can learn to use a blog application very quickly, and once they have mastered the application, time spent on blog entries is mostly spent on writing.

There are all sorts of blogs. Some bloggers seem to find value in creating a running account of the nuances of their own lives. Other blogs are maintained by professional journalists who seem motivated to extend their professional comments to another medium. Some blogs provide a series of entries related to a common topic and offer a good way to keep current if you happen to be interested in that topic. We maintain a blog that comments on issues in the application of technology in education. In part, this gives us a way to write

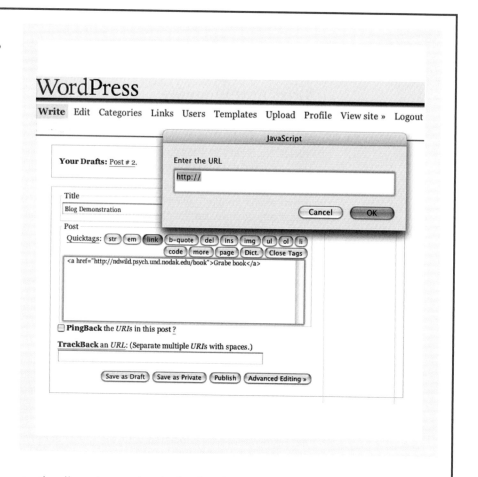

FIGURE 9.6

Web Form Completed to Generate Blog Entries Using WordPress Blog System

continually and generate a body of work we can tap for other projects (such as this book). Our blog is like a notebook we allow others to view.

Some student teachers maintain a blog as a way to reflect on their experiences and to share their experiences and reactions with a supervisor back at the university. Blogs do not have to be the property of a single individual. A group of students can take turns submitting entries to a class blog.

Educators might consider two ways to involve students in blogging. The first is to take advantage of a free service made available for public use. Blogger.com (now owned by Google, Inc.) has been in existence for several years and is very easy to use. However, it is important to understand the limitations of using a site like Blogger. Commercial sites may include ads, may not offer features we have described (such as an easy method for including images), and may not offer a method for limiting the access of viewers. It is the last issue that educators may find most troubling. Because bloggers typically want to attract readers rather than keep them away, sites offering free blogs do not invest effort or resources in eliminating readers of any kind. While blog entries are safe from modification, educators and parents may feel uncomfortable allowing student writing to be viewed by the general public. If educators involve students with a public blog site, they must be vigilant to ensure that personal information does not appear in blog entries. Alternatively, a school can host its own blog site. If a server is available, the school can add a free or low-cost blog system. If a school operates its own server, there are ways to provide security that will reduce concerns about student-generated content—for instance, protecting the site with a password or allowing access within the school intranet only.

This book explores several different approaches to what might be described as multimedia authoring. These approaches share the assumption that students learn from the process of designing multimedia products. One potentially important difference among the examples we explore might be described as *efficiency*. Blogs can be a very efficient way to generate a multimedia product; some of the other approaches to multimedia authoring require the investment of more time in the assembly of the product. Because different approaches may trade efficiency for flexibility, it is not possible to draw a simple conclusion as to which is the most desirable approach. We find some support for the value of efficient approaches in a recent summary of research on "writing to learn" (Bangert-Drowns, Hurley, & Wilkinson, 2004). This review concluded that frequent, short assignments produced the greatest benefit to students. This description would seem to suit the general approach taken by bloggers.

General-Purpose Web Authoring Software

Instead of purchasing web authoring software developed specifically for educational settings and younger learners, most educators rely on general-purpose web authoring software. This software is readily available through retail outlets or catalogs and in some cases can be obtained at no cost. A list of some of the less expensive software is included at the end of this chapter.

Trends in authoring software

The trend in web authoring software is toward more sophisticated products. As each new version of a given product has been released, the software has offered more features and more options. Also, some companies that at one time had both a low-end and a high-end product have abandoned their low-end product. With the exception of classes focused on media production or technology applications, general-purpose software offers far more options than are needed for the projects we describe. You cannot really blame companies for attempting to offer the larger segments of their market more powerful tools in the hope that users will pay a relatively small amount of money for an upgrade, but the move toward products of greater and greater complexity may make the products less well suited for classroom use. We hope you will have the opportunity to work with several methods for creating web content and evaluate this concern for yourself.

Design Tips for Webpages

Student web projects have become so common that we highlight some of the specific design guidelines educators should consider as their students create webpages. Here are general design categories that apply to web projects and some specific issues associated with each category.

FIGURE 9.7

Example of a Webpage Template. This template consists of two tables, each made up of three cells. The areas identified as title, image, and narrative are not actually defined in the HTML but are suggested components to be included for this example.

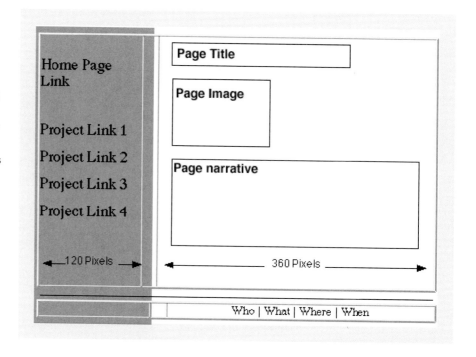

Navigation System

Helping users orient themselves

The basic mechanism allowing navigation is the collection of links the designer embeds within the pages making up the site. Creating a navigation system that allows users to orient themselves easily and return to main choice points can be very helpful. Links to these choice points might consistently appear in a cell along the left margin of pages or at the bottom of pages. At the very least, users should have frequent access to a link allowing them to return to the last major choice point they encountered.

Page Layout

Objects on a webpage should be grouped in a way that facilitates the user's activities. An object could be a segment of text, a picture, links serving a specific purpose, or any multimedia element that can be presented on a webpage. In general, the placement of objects should be predictable, and objects important to the purpose of the page should appear in prominent locations.

Creating a template

One way to develop a strategy for pages of a certain type is to create a template. This is very similar to the idea of a layout grid mentioned earlier. The template shown in Figure 9.7 was developed for a project in which individual teams would develop a single page to be incorporated into a class project. (Figure 9.8 shows a finished webpage based on the template.) Our sample template incorporates a navigation system and identifies the common elements that students are to provide. Its organization is based on two tables, each made up of three cells. We strongly suggest that teachers wanting to help students create webpages learn how to structure the pages using the table tool, which is available in most webpage authoring programs. Tables offer a convenient way to create a page template.

FIGURE 9.8

Example of a Finished
Webpage Based on the
Template in Figure 9.7

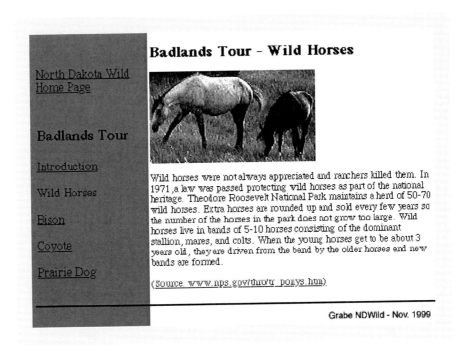

Use of Graphics and Video

A high proportion of webpages include graphics. Some sites now offer video. There are several issues to consider when incorporating such features on your webpage.

Considering file size

The size of web images and movies should be a consideration. The text and individual images that make up a webpage are sent over the Internet as separate files, and the browser integrates the files to form the page you see on the computer screen. Image files tend to be much larger than the HTML (text) file and take longer to transfer. Movie files are far larger yet. With a slow connection, the wait for several images to load can be significant. Web designers wanting to make heavy use of graphics often try to offer alternatives for users without a high-speed connection.

One alternative makes use of thumbnails rather than large images. A **thumbnail** is a small version of a large image. The small image provides an idea of what the larger image looks like and serves as a link to a page containing the full-size image. Following the link to the page containing the full-size image results from a conscious decision and allows users with slow access to spend the additional time only when they think that viewing the full-size image is essential. There is really no equivalent alternative when providing video content. Video that appears in a small window (for example, 240 x 180 pixels) requires that a smaller amount of data be sent over the Internet. However, even at this size, a modem connection will not be practical. A series of still images and text can be offered as an alternative for those with slow connections.

For the best image quality, remember the advantages and disadvantages of GIF and JPEG images. Use JPEG with complex images such as photographs that have many colors in a complex pattern. Use GIF for images containing

Working cooperatively, these two students use a scanner to create a digital image file for their project.
(© Michael Zide)

large areas of solid color, as might be the case in logos, simple illustrations, or large decorative text.

When you are preparing graphics for the Web, always save your original image file when creating new images of a different size or a different file type. If you decide to change your mind, starting over with the original image will result in a better final product than trying to work backward from an altered image.

Text Presentation

Breaking up long text passages

Although long segments of text are difficult to read from a computer screen, there are situations in which the content to be presented consists mainly of text. The solution is not to ask users to move through many webpages containing small segments of text. The usual recommendation is to present webpages containing at least three pages of text. You can break up the extended text in a variety of ways: blocking text messages and surrounding them with space, using headings to organize and separate blocks of text, and reworking text information in the form of numbered or bulleted lists.

Width of tables

Remember that many users will print longer segments of text rather than read the material from the screen. If you use tables to control the appearance of your webpages, the total width of your table should be approximately 500 pixels. Wider tables will not print properly on standard paper. Web authoring programs allow authors to specify the height and width of the cells that make up a table.

Although we suggest that educators make the effort to learn some design fundamentals, it is also important to remember that student web projects may sometimes require different priorities from those emphasized by design experts. For example, educators might encourage students to use extended text or many images when such information sources would be consistent with the goals of the project.

Learning through Design: The Canada Project

To bring together many of the themes we have just considered, let's return to the middle-school geography classroom we described at the beginning of this chapter. Chris Douthit and Monte Gaukler are helping seventh-grade students learn about the Canadian provinces and territories by asking the students to conduct preparatory research and then generate multimedia summaries for web presentation. As we noted earlier, the most unique characteristic of this project is the collaboration of Canadian students as project evaluators.

Consider this example with both an open mind and a critical eye. Perhaps it is very different from anything you have experienced personally or discussed as part of your professional training. As you read, we do not ask you to assume that things always worked smoothly or that all students were optimally involved. What we ask is that you attempt to imagine a variation of these techniques as they might be applied to topics you would teach.

Overview and Project Goals

To counter "thinness" of geography textbook

It is important to understand at the outset that Chris is not a traditionalist. He does not use a textbook. He considers the typical middle-school geography textbook as too "thin"—covering too many topics, with most topics receiving far too little coverage, and some of the topics he prefers to emphasize receiving a couple of columns at best. However, his approach is not idiosyncratic or without a philosophical foundation. He pays attention to standards, benchmarks, and frameworks in developing the experiences he provides. He also claims that students need a variety of learning experiences, an approach that gives students with different needs a greater chance to find something that appeals to them and also encourages all students to take on different challenges. Chris had not used eZedia's multimedia authoring software before, but student projects, presentations, and collaborative experiences were already a part of his approach.

Early decisions needed

Some of the first decisions educators have to make before involving students in a multimedia project are practical ones: What skills or topics will be emphasized? How much time will be allowed? How much structure will be provided? To some extent, these questions are interrelated. If the range of topics is narrow and precisely defined for students, the amount of time needed to complete the project will likely be shorter. However, very tight guidelines may also restrict the amount of exploration and decision making required of students. Remember that Chris allows one month for the study of Canada and considers this an important topic because students do not necessarily return to this subject matter in later courses. Accordingly, he planned to set aside six class periods for this project—two days in the library gathering information and four days in the computer lab becoming familiar with the software and creating the multimedia products.

Project Specifics
Each student was assigned to a two-person team, and each team was assigned a Canadian province or territory to investigate. Chris made the assignments himself so that he could (1) use his knowledge of student characteristics to match team members and (2) be assured that all areas of Canada would be included. The decision to use the smallest possible cooperative group was based on his experience in the computer lab and with cooperative projects. Because each team would be working on a single computer when creating the multimedia product, using the smallest possible team meant that most students would actually have a chance to be involved. With larger groups, it would be too easy for some students to be become disengaged and wander about. Chris also feels that smaller groups encourage a more effective sharing of responsibility and a more intense social experience. Student activity—both research and multimedia authoring—was carefully scaffolded. Students went to the library with an outline of the topics to be addressed in their multimedia presentations. Major headings included history, major cities, economic factors, important physical features, and tourism. Specific questions were included under each heading. Under the topic of history, for example, students were asked to find out when the province was officially recognized, how the province was named, and three historical facts that have shaped the unique identity of the province.

When students were in the lab and ready to begin creating their projects, they were also asked to follow certain guidelines in order to generate a multimedia product that would follow the same general format and contain some common elements. The goal in both research and design was to encourage efficiency.

Students used eZediaQTI to create their projects because of the ease with which multimedia products created with this software can be shared on the Internet. Presenting the project as webpages was critical to being able to receive comments from Canadian students. Since the plan was to keep the structure of the project simple and to minimize what students needed to learn about the authoring software, another reason for choosing eZediaQTI is that it allows the author to create content for web delivery without having to learn HTML or a software application for designing webpages. (Some of the features of this authoring tool are described in the chapter entitled "Using Multimedia Tools.") These middle-school students were familiar with using computers to create multimedia projects, but not all had used eZediaQTI before.

Storyboarding in practice

Teachers are often encouraged to engage students in storyboarding as part of the process of developing a multimedia project. The basic idea in creating a storyboard is to identify key elements in a multimedia project and then determine how these elements will fit together. The storyboard is intended to help developers think through the structure of a project and then guide the creation of the project. It is something like writing an outline before you write a paper. In this project, however, student teams did not create a storyboard for their work, because each group was asked instead to organize the information they had to present using a structure provided for them. This approach increased the efficiency of student work and assured that the components of the final product would follow a consistent pattern. The basic structure is illustrated in Figure 9.9, which shows a storyboard for the entire project.

Planning with buttons and frames

The entire collection of content was accessible through a "homepage" in which the flags of provinces and territories functioned as buttons. Each button was linked to a "province" frame. This frame displayed the license plate of that province or territory as a title and provided buttons linking to the work of the different teams who had researched that province, as well as a button linking back to the homepage. Each team product began with a frame containing the map of the province and buttons linking to categories of information for that province. Each category was presented as one or more frames of information, with buttons linking either back to the start point for the team's project or forward to another frame of information. In Figure 9.10, the image is one of a series providing information on tourism in Ontario. Students were allowed to use their creativity and productivity to determine how many frames they would use and how the individual frames would be designed—the selection of information, the segments of text, and choice of images.

A rubric for evaluation by audience

While this project did not involve a large number of Canadian schools, participation was sufficient to provide Chris's students a sense of writing for an authentic audience. Probably the most innovative response to the request for feedback was provided by Barb Makowsky's sixth-grade class. Barb works in the Lord Selkirk school district in St. Andrews, Manitoba. After a quick examination of the online content, Barb created a simple evaluation rubric by adapting the rubric she uses to evaluate her students' writing assignments. The rubric provided the opportunity to rate specific project qualities (such as interest, reading difficulty, navigation, links) on a numerical scale and to respond to open-ended questions (Any incorrect information? Any incorrect spelling or poor grammar? One thing you enjoyed? One thing that could be improved?). She then paired up the students in her class and had each pair evaluate the work of one team from Chris's class. Although Barb's students were familiar with rubrics, the opportunity to apply a rubric in the role of evaluator was unfamiliar.

Reading the completed rubrics, you get the feeling that students can be quite thorough in evaluating surface-level features. They find spelling errors and buttons that do not work. They report that text is hard to read when it is superimposed on a busy graphics background. Occasionally they challenge a factual statement. For example, one project stated that "The first settlement on P.E.I. was in 9000 BCE" but included no additional information. This statement did not seem accurate to the pair evaluating the project. There was also evidence of a deeper level of thinking. Several review teams commented that the pictures were nice but sometimes did not match the topic. Some teams noted that the frames associated with some topics, such as the history or climate of a province, did not contain much information. It seemed like a polite way of saying, "You should have been able to find out more." It is

FIGURE 9.9

Storyboard Showing Structure of Canada Project

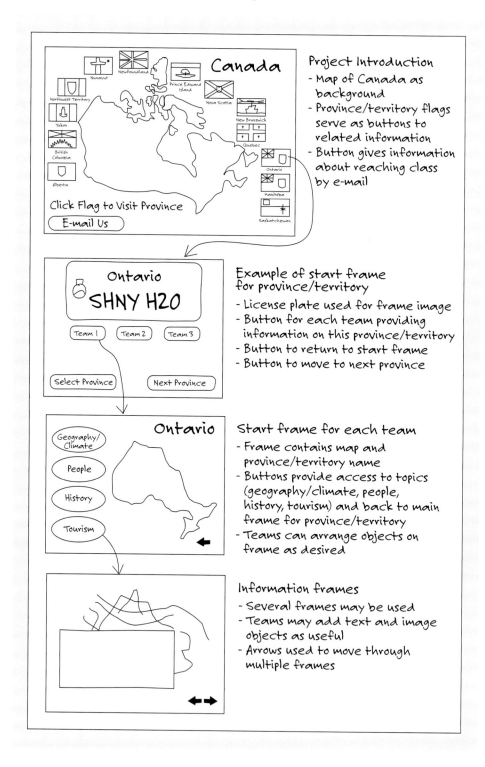

FIGURE 9.10

Sample Information Frame from Student Project Listing Tourism Options in Ontario

interesting to note that some expert adult observers (Cuban, 2001; Oppenheimer, 2003) have also expressed concern that some student multimedia projects do not actually contain much content.

Evaluation and Outcomes

Multiple skill areas assessed

How was student work on this project evaluated? Chris critiqued student performance in several different categories. First, did students locate the information required by the project outline? Second, what was the quality of the product? Was the writing grammatically correct? Did the buttons work? Were the frames neat or sloppy? Finally, what was the teacher able to observe in terms of each student's behavior? Did the student stay on task? Did the student work well with his or her partner? In other words, his evaluation approach did not involve a rubric, but it did recognize multiple skill areas that should be considered and used to provide feedback.

Students excited about research

As you recall, the original plan was to accomplish the project in a total of six class periods—two for library research and four for training and project authoring in the computer lab. However, when the opportunity to interact with Canadian students became available, Chris and his students decided to invest more time to produce a project of higher quality, and the final project ended up taking eleven class periods. Underestimating the time required is common when students take on a project using a specific authoring package with which they have limited experience. (The instructor had to take time to learn the software as well.) In this case, more time was also required because students did additional research, in the library and online, and spent more time working on the appearance of their project than might normally have been the case. Chris noted that as students began to work on the project, they learned that they needed more information, and the Internet provided an important source in this secondary search for more material. For example, the Internet offered the most current population data and provided an opportunity to learn about Nunavut (which became a Canadian territory in 1999).

Time investment a big issue

The time required to complete multimedia projects is an issue that has been raised by some researchers who are critical of the inefficiency of this type of student project (for instance, Cuban, 2001; Oppenheimer, 2003), and it is clearly an issue teachers need to consider. Was Chris concerned about the scheduling change? Yes; because the project took longer than expected, he felt the need to reduce the amount of time he normally devoted to Canadian history. Would he do a similar project in the future? Definitely, but he would have to think carefully about the time involved. This was a unique situation, and a project that had generated so much student enthusiasm was worth the time spent. Next time, he might try to involve students with the software at an earlier point so that all the training time won't need to be concentrated during just one topic in the course.

The value of authenticity

One of the major areas of emphasis in our discussion of the integration of technology has been on multimedia authoring as a way to explore content-area topics. Chris and Monte would be the first to say that they might do some things a little differently next time. However, projects provide authentic experiences. The frustrations some students encountered in using the software to implement their ideas, as well as the visible differences in quality brought about by assembling student work, provide a little taste of the way things tend to work in the "real world." The teachers feel confident that the project generated an enthusiastic response from most students and allowed some students to display skills that had remained hidden under more traditional circumstances.

In considering this project, you get a glimpse of a multimedia authoring tool in student hands, but you can also see the application of concepts such as cooperative learning, learning through design, and performance-based assessment. Our goal was not to show you an optimal demonstration of each of these concepts. Instead, we hope that thinking through an authentic example will allow you to imagine projects you might implement in your own classroom.

Summary

This chapter integrates two views of design: design of products and design of personal knowledge. Design involves constructing or structuring a product for a purpose. For computer software, the purpose might be to help the user accomplish some task more efficiently, learn something, or have an entertaining experience. The design of knowledge also stresses the connection between structure and function. Knowledge as design helps the learner do something. Without purpose, learning becomes focused on the accumulation of information, not its application.

Student-authored hypermedia represents a concrete integration of the design of knowledge and the design of a public product. In this unique situation, students are designing knowledge to generate a product. The hypermedia product provides a purpose for the hypermedia author's construction of personal knowledge.

To create products that are informative, interesting, and easy to use and understand, hypermedia authors should attend to the organization of content, basic principles of graphic design, clear writing, and the development of an effective user interface.

Hypermedia design projects might be considered a special application of a cooperative learning model called group investigation. In a group investigation, students identify aspects of a general theme that interest them and then join teams to study these individual topics. The teams are expected to determine how they will gather, analyze, and summarize information relevant to their topic. Individual students are expected to assume some independence in contributing to this process. Each team identifies the essence of what the members have learned and presents this information to the entire group.

Hypermedia design uses a complex set of processes that can involve young hypermedia authors in the construction of personal knowledge. Learning is situated in a task that provides a purpose for student activities. The design model presented here bears a strong resemblance to a popular model for the writing process. Identifiable components of this model include planning, information collection, knowledge generation, and evaluation and revision.

Within this model, the teacher involves the student as an apprentice and takes responsibility for coaching both the knowledge design and the hypermedia design skills. In the early stages of a project and especially when working with inexperienced designers, the teacher may be required to provide some direct instruction, demonstrate procedural skills, model cognitive processes by externalizing thinking behavior, and stimulate cognitive behavior with leading questions. As students become more experienced and the project takes shape, teachers will play a less direct role. Students will take on a great deal of responsibility for their own learning.

Reflecting on Chapter 9

ACTIVITIES

- Consider the content and skills you intend to teach as they might be used by "practitioners"—that is, actual historians, biologists, and the like. Identify who might be considered practitioners, and propose tasks appropriate to the capabilities of your students that would put the students in the roles of these practitioners.

- Briefly outline a potential hypermedia project. Develop a holistic scoring guide and continua of descriptors appropriate to assessing the project and important project-related skills.

- Develop a storyboard for a simple hypermedia project appropriate to a content area that interests you.

■ Determine if the word processing program you usually use is capable of generating HTML. If so, transform a document you have already created into HTML to see what the product looks like.

KEY TERMS

branch (p. 320)
cooperative learning (p. 326)
design (p. 317)
graphic design (p. 321)
grid (p. 321)
group investigation (p. 327)
hierarchical design (p. 319)
hypercomposition (p. 328)
individual accountability (p. 327)
knowledge as design (p. 316)
link (p. 318)
map (p. 324)

menu (p. 324)
navigation (p. 318)
node (p. 318)
sequential design (p. 319)
storyboarding (p. 327)
tag (p. 343)
task specialization methods (p. 327)
team rewards (p. 326)
thumbnail (p. 351)
user interface (p. 324)
web design (p. 320)

RESOURCES TO EXPAND YOUR KNOWLEDGE BASE

 An expanded and frequently updated list of online resources is available on the website that accompanies this textbook.

Web Design Principles
Lynch, P., & Horton, S. (1999). *Web style guide: Basic design principles for creating webpages.* New Haven: Yale University Press. (**http://www.webstyleguide.com/**)
Tollett, J. (2000). *The non-designers web book* (2nd ed.). Berkeley, CA: Peachpit Press.

Resources for Cooperative Learning
Johnson, D., Johnson, R., & Holubec, E. (1991). *Cooperation in the classroom* (rev. ed.). Edina, MN: Interaction.
McConnell, D. (2000). *Implementing computer supported cooperative learning* (2nd ed.). Sterling, WV: Stylus.
Putnam, J. (Ed.). (1993). *Cooperative learning and strategies for inclusion: Celebrating diversity in the classroom.* Baltimore: Brookes.
Sharan, Y., & Sharan, S. (1992). *Expanding cooperative learning through group investigation* (3rd ed.). New York: Teachers College Press.
Slavin, R. (1991). *Student team learning: A practical guide to cooperative learning* (3rd ed.). Washington, DC: National Education Association.

Thematic Instruction, the Project Approach, and Project Ideas
Counts, E. L. (2004). *Multimedia design and production for students and teachers.* Boston: Pearson.
Fredericks, A., Meinbach, A., & Rothlein, L. (1993). *Thematic units: An integrated approach to teaching science and social studies.* New York: HarperCollins.
Harel, I. (1991). *Children as designers.* Norwood, NJ: Ablex.
Katz, L., & Chard, S. (1989). *Engaging children's minds: The project approach.* Norwood, NJ: Ablex.

The Director in the Classroom

Resources associated with the work of filmmaker Nikos Theodosakis can be found in several ways:

Online—http://www.thedirectorintheclassroom.com/

Theodosakis, N. (2001). *The director in the classroom: How filmmaking inspires learning.* San Diego, CA: Tech4learning Publishing.

Web Authoring Software

Word Processing Software Capable of Generating HTML Documents

AppleWorks: Available for the Macintosh and Windows operating systems. Apple Computer Corporation. (**http://www.apple.com/appleworks/**)

Microsoft Word: Available for the Macintosh and Windows operating systems. Microsoft Corporation. (**http://www.microsoft.com/office/**)

Software Developed Specifically for Educational Settings

MediaBlender: Available for the Macintosh and Windows operating systems. Tech4Learning. (**http://www.tech4learning.com/mediablender/**)

eZediaQTI: Available for Macintosh and Windows operating systems. eZedia (**http://www.ezedia.com**)

General-Purpose Web Authoring Software

Adobe GoLive: Available for the Macintosh and Windows operating systems. Adobe Systems. (**http://www.adobe.com/golive/**)

Macromedia Dreamweaver: Available for the Macintosh and Windows operating systems. Macromedia, Inc. (**http://www.macromedia.com/dreamweaver/**)

Microsoft FrontPage: Available for the Macintosh and Windows operating systems. Microsoft Corporation. (**http://www.microsoft.com/frontpage/**)

Netscape Composer: Available for the Macintosh and Windows operating systems. Netscape. (**http://www.netscape.com/**)

Blogging Systems and the Educational Application of Blogs

Blogger.com (Google, Inc.) is a popular free host for many blogs. (**http://blogger.com**)

WordPress (the example used in this chapter) is a free blog software that runs on any server that supports PHP (a scripting language) and MySQL (a database). (**http://wordpress.org**)

WEBLOGG-ED is a good blog about educational blogs. (**http://www.weblogg-ed.com/**)

Online Resources for Rubric-Based Evaluation

RubiStar is an online rubric construction tool made available by the High Plains Regional Technology in Education Consortium (HPR*TEC). Rubrics for different types of student projects are also available at this site. (**http://rubistar.4teachers.org/**)

Rubric Builder is an online rubric construction tool made available by the Landmark Project. (**http://landmarks4schools.org/**)

Looking at Issues
for the Present and Future

• • •

PART THREE looks at issues and concerns related to using technology responsibly. These issues include equity, fair use of intellectual property, and protecting students from inappropriate content and personal harassment or harm. Classroom applications of technology will not find support among parents and community members unless these important issues are addressed. When problems arise in these areas, you can explore ways to create solutions to them.

10 Responsible Use of Technology

• • •

ORIENTATION   This chapter discusses three topics related to responsible use of technology: equity, copyright law, and the protection of students from inappropriate content and experiences. After you complete your study of this chapter, you should be able to explain important issues associated with each of these areas and list some concrete ways that teachers and schools might use to ensure that students will use technology in a responsible manner. The areas of responsible use that we discuss in this chapter represent challenges that must be met for technology to find broad success in classrooms. We must find ways for all students to take advantage of the learning opportunities technology offers, provide appropriate recognition and copyright protection for those who create these resources, and make certain that students have experiences that are safe and productive.

As you read, look for answers to the following questions:

Focus Questions

- What inequities exist in student access to technology and in the learning activities students experience? What factors appear responsible for these inequities?
- What adaptations can be implemented for students with special needs?
- What is copyright law designed to protect? What resources can be used in student and instructor multimedia projects? What are key guidelines that determine what can be taken from the Internet and what can be placed on the Internet?
- What are some safety guidelines that all Internet users should know?
- What are some options schools might use to protect students from inappropriate Internet content?

Equity of Educational Opportunity

Effects on students' future lives

We believe that technology already plays an important role in K–12 education and that it will play an increasingly important role in the future. Clearly technology has become an indispensable part of the way we live and work, and our educational system must accept some responsibility to prepare students for this reality. Students who move through the educational system without having access to technology not only are limited in the ways they can approach traditional academic subjects, but also are missing out on experiences that would enhance their future ability to work and learn in a world more and more dependent on technology. The phrase **digital divide** is used to refer to the gap between those who are able to benefit from digital technology and those who are not. The term applies to the group differences mentioned in this chapter (such as gender and income) and to even broader distinctions involving international economic and political differences.

To gain some perspective on equity issues, think of the technology trends of the past two decades. During the 1980s, schools became involved for the first time with computers and various computer peripherals. The 1990s served a similar function for the Internet. Early in each decade, funding the newer forms of technology was fairly experimental, and some districts moved ahead more quickly than others. As computer or Internet applications became more commonplace, not having access to these opportunities became regarded as a deficit. Lack of access was viewed with particular alarm when it perpetuated or exacerbated existing inequities.

A number of descriptive studies have attempted to identify inequities in technology access. They examine whether variables such as student-to-computer ratios, classroom Internet access, or what students do with technology can be associated with factors like gender or differences in student ability. Some focus on links with low **socioeconomic status (SES),** a measure based on income, education, and occupation. Although we offer some numbers generated by these studies, we focus more on trends than on the numbers themselves. Variables such as student-to-computer ratios and classroom Internet access change quickly; the overall trends are of much more lasting significance.

Equity and SES

A number of factors must be present before students are likely to experience the benefits of technology we have described in this book. The schools these students attend have to invest in the necessary hardware and software, connect computers to the Internet, and provide teachers with the background and support necessary to provide students meaningful learning experiences. Teachers, administrators, and parents have to place a priority on learning experiences that allow students the time to create multimedia products or engage in community-based explorations. These factors have not always existed, been implemented in a coordinated fashion, or been applied consistently in all settings or with all students. Schools have been spending money on computers for years. More recently, attention has shifted to providing Internet access. Teacher support and training traditionally have lagged behind. While student experiences with technology depend on these resource issues, experiences also vary with instructional priorities.

Inequities in speed of progress

One simple way to describe equity issues is to suggest that schools with a higher proportion of advantaged students seem both to have progressed through this list—from computers to Internet access to teacher training and support—at a more rapid pace than schools with less advantaged students, and to have placed a greater emphasis on using technology to support the development of higher-order thinking skills and technology-based student projects. Here are some findings that support this notion:

■ Access to computers in schools, usually measured as the ratio of students per computer, once showed sizable differences when schools with high proportions of students from low-income families were compared with schools with low proportions of such students. Fortunately, these differences have now narrowed substantially. The ratio of students to Internet-connected computers is 4.1:1 nationwide and 4.3:1 in high-poverty schools (Park & Staresina, 2004).

■ In 2004, it was reported that the percentage of schools with Internet access from one or more classrooms was 92 percent nationwide and 89 percent in high poverty schools. In 1999, the values for the same comparison were 64 percent and 39 percent (Park & Staresina, 2004).

■ SES differences in schools were a predictor of whether teachers reported receiving professional development in the use of computers in the past five years (Wenglinsky, 1998) and whether a school hired a full-time computer coordinator (Jerald & Orlofsky, 1999).

■ Contrary to what many probably expect, teachers in high-poverty schools (defined as schools in which 75 percent of students are eligible for free or reduced price lunches) were more likely than teachers in low-poverty schools (schools with less than 35 percent of students eligible for free or reduced-price lunches) to report frequent instructional use of computers. The major differences were that teachers in high-poverty schools were more likely to report the use of technology for practice drills and as a free-time or reward activity (U.S. Department of Education, 2003).

Inequities in home resources

What students do with technology in school is not the only issue of concern. The resources available outside school influence the skills students bring to school and the academic work they can do on their own. Here the trend is more discouraging, and SES differences seem to be increasing as technology becomes important in a greater number of higher-income occupations. Eighty-five percent of families with incomes in excess of $75,000 have access to the Internet. In contrast, 38 percent of families with an income of less than $25,000 have Internet access. In addition, 42 percent of high-income Internet users have high-bandwidth access, in contrast to 28 percent of low-income Internet users (National Telecommunications and Information Administration, 2004). Broadband access (DSL and cable) provides more than just greater download speed; it appears to significantly alter how the Internet is used. Those with broadband access spend four hours more per week online, often have the opportunity to simultaneously access the Internet from multiple computers, and use the Internet for a greater variety of tasks (Center for the Digital Future, 2004). Online services and the sophistication of technology continue to advance but are not free. Children from families with more income simply have an advantage in accessing and making use of these advances. Figure 10.1 provides a graphical representation of some of these data on income and Internet access.

FIGURE 10.1

The Digital Divide at a Glance: Socioeconomic Status and Internet Access *Sources:* U.S. Department of Education (2003), Park & Staresina (2004), National Telecommunications and Information Administration (2004).

What determines "high-poverty" status for a school?

Low-Poverty School

Less than 35% of students eligible for free or reduced-price lunch

High-Poverty School

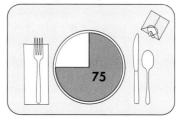

At least 75% of students eligible for free or reduced-price lunch

Narrowing the gap?

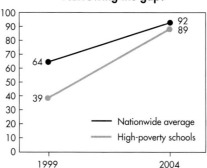

Percentage of schools with Internet access from at least one classroom

Home matters, too

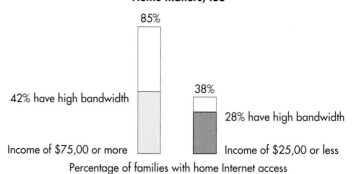

Percentage of families with home Internet access

Community access centers

Recognition of the significant differences that exist in home access has led to an interest in developing **community access centers.** For example, because schools have already made the investment in technology and Internet access, programs are being developed to make these resources available to students and members of the community after traditional school hours. In some cases, students not only learn in these centers but also serve as mentors to community members needing to learn about technology or accomplish such concrete tasks as visiting an Internet site describing employment opportunities (National Telecommunications and Information Administration, 2002).

Are these SES differences important? We think so. Students with fewer technology-related experiences would seem less prepared to use technology in future work and learning settings. Lack of experience may also narrow a student's range of vocational aspirations. Of course, we also assume that lack of access will affect student academic performance. Is there more to offer on this subject than logical arguments? A recent major study provides an interesting perspective on some of the equity issues that we have just outlined.

Educational Testing Service (ETS) Mathematics Study

Relating standardized test scores to technological access

The ETS mathematics study (Wenglinsky, 1998) was based on data gathered from fourth- and eighth-grade students who took the 1996 National Assessment of Educational Progress (NAEP) exams in mathematics. This research is unusual because it relates achievement data gathered using a major standardized test and a national sample of students to variables providing information about the students' schools and the students' uses of technology. The students and their schools provided the following information:

- How frequently technology was used in the study of mathematics
- Student access to technology
- The professional development of teachers
- What students did with technology that was relevant to the study of mathematics
- The social environment of the school

The study's results

Several of these variables (access, student use, professional development, and social environment) are similar to ones we have already emphasized. The ETS study identifies equity differences similar to those mentioned earlier; more important, the study provides some possible connections between these equity issues and student achievement. The fundamental conclusion was that the most significant inequities did not lie in how frequently computers were used but in what students did when they used the computers:

- Mathematics achievement benefited when eighth graders used computers to work on content-area-appropriate simulations and applications. Mathematics achievement was lower when students used computers to work on drill-and-practice activities.
- Students in schools with a higher proportion of less affluent students or more minority students were more likely to use computers to work on drill activities.
- Teachers in schools with a higher proportion of less affluent students had received fewer professional development experiences with technology.

The impact of
professional
development

■ Teachers with fewer professional development experiences were more
likely to emphasize drill and practice.

The fact that several variables are interrelated does not necessarily demonstrate a causal relationship among them. Even when we take this caution into account, however, one way of interpreting the ETS mathematics data is clear: Some students do not do as well in mathematics because teachers engage them in less powerful uses of technology, and one reason that teachers are likely to use less powerful methods is the lack of appropriate professional development experiences. This lack of teacher preparation is a greater problem in schools with higher levels of low-income and minority students. These data also suggest that what students do with the technology available to them is a more serious equity issue than differences in how much time students spend using technology.

Role of Educators' Perceptions

A focus on
remediation

Other studies have also found that what students are asked to do with technology is related to student economic background (George, Malcolm, & Jeffers, 1993; Meyer, 2001; U.S. Department of Education, 2003). However, teacher preparation is not the only explanation provided for why student experiences differ. A second interpretation focuses on educator perceptions of the type of learning experiences that would be most helpful to students. According to this view, educators working with large numbers of students from less affluent backgrounds assume that these students lack basic skills and fundamental knowledge. Therefore, the educators conclude, the most productive use of school time and resources is to focus on the remediation of such fundamentals. The assumption is that the opportunity to apply knowledge and skills, problem solving, and authentic student projects must build on basic skills and will not be productive until students have first developed an adequate background.

A related explanation, but one focused on a different source of teacher motivation, notes that the pressure to raise standardized test scores and cover standard curriculum material has influenced how much time educators in low-SES schools feel students should spend using technology and the types of activities that should be emphasized (Warschauer, Knobel, & Stone, 2004).

It is indeed possible that many educators hold the view that there is a greater need to focus on basic skills in student populations with a high proportion of students from low-SES families. Yet this hierarchical view of classroom tasks is not universally accepted. Many educators believe that even for students lacking certain basic skills, a more productive approach is to embed the practice of these skills within activities that students find to be personally meaningful. As you have seen throughout this book, using technology to facilitate activity-centered projects in content-area instruction is one way to provide such experiences. Students can be inspired by the opportunity to use technology in interesting and challenging ways, and it would be unfair to limit the involvement of any student who would profit from this source of motivation (Laboratory of Comparative Human Cognition, 1989).

Equity and the Classroom Teacher

Not all studies have found the SES differences identified in the ETS study. For example, a survey of schools participating in the National School Network, a group of schools committed to Internet use, indicated that, if anything, schools with a higher proportion of students from low-SES families were more involved in activities such as collaborative online projects and student web authoring (Becker & Ravitz, 1998). How can these studies come to such different conclusions? First, the schools participating in each study were not selected in the same fashion. Moreover, the schools and teachers involved in the National School Network may view the role of technology differently.

Think about the possible connections among such variables as student background, teacher training, teacher beliefs about what is best for students, pressure to raise scores on standardized achievement tests, variations in access to technology, and variations in how students use technology. All of these may affect your students and the way you teach in your classroom.

Teacher training and support

For classroom teachers, two issues particularly concern us. First, learning experiences of the type we describe in this book—inquiry and construction experiences in which students use technology to go beyond the passive reception of information—may be less frequently available to some students because their teachers do not have the training and support necessary to guide them. One solution might be to provide practicing teachers with ongoing opportunities for professional development, perhaps through interaction with a full-time computer coordinator. Unfortunately, without external support, this is just the resource that is least likely to be available in school districts in low-income areas. Perhaps our observation that investments need to move from computers to Internet access and then to professional development will hold true, and eventually the support for staff development will be improved.

What you can do

Our second concern is that teachers will focus disadvantaged students exclusively on the accumulation of information. The solution to this challenge is not a financial one; it is something you can address in your own teaching. Throughout this book we encourage you to consider applications that lead students to evaluate information thoughtfully and to use it to address personally meaningful problems. The matter is in your hands as a teacher. We hope the activities outlined in this book will provide you with some ideas.

Equity and Gender

Gender differences in choices and experiences

There are other inequities that cannot be explained in terms of differences in access or teacher preparation. Despite the fact that males and females have increasingly similar attitudes toward the importance of computers and have similar access at home and in school, the sexes have some different experiences with technology as a result of educational and career choices, and these differences in experience may affect future academic or vocational opportunities (Volman & van Eck, 2001; Weinman & Haag, 1999). Here is a sample of the types of indicators that concern some educators:

■ Differences exist in the technology-related courses that males and females select. Females dominate courses focused on clerical skills, which

• • •

The Telecommunications Act of 1996 called for subsidizing Internet access for poor schools. Rural high-poverty schools were eligible for the highest subsidies.

Bill Ridder / *The Paris News* / AP-Wide World Photos

Video Case

To learn about teaching approaches that can help overcome gender barriers for girls in the sciences, view the HM Video Case entitled *Gender Equity in the Classroom: Girls and Science.* Middle-school teacher Robert Cho reflects on the importance of mentors and role models who can encourage girls to pursue careers in nontraditional fields.

Possible explanations

are regarded as being associated with careers that are less technologically advanced.

- A very small proportion of high-school females take the computer science Advanced Placement examination.
- Only about 25 percent of college undergraduate computer science degrees are awarded to women.
- Females rate themselves as having lower computer abilities than males and are less likely to believe that computer skills help them do better in school. This difference in confidence in personal computer skills appears despite efforts to account for differences in experience, and it appears in teachers as well as students (American Association of University Women Educational Foundation, 2000; Gehring, 2001; Volman & van Eck, 2001).

Why might males and females have different experiences, and why might they feel differently about themselves as potential users of powerful applications of technology? Several factors frequently appear as explanations:

- Stereotypes of computer use and computer users are perpetuated in popular media. Males are commonly represented as "power users," or those who use computers for more sophisticated tasks.
- Recreational software that may create an interest in computers is strongly slanted toward males.
- Educational game software often encourages competition, requires eye-hand coordination, and rewards speeded-up responses as ways to increase motivation. Such features may provoke anxiety in females, possibly decreasing interest in other computer-based activities.

Focus

The E-rate as a Solution for Disadvantaged Schools

The **e-rate**, a subsidy for the costs of providing Internet connection to schools and libraries, was established by the Telecommunications Act of 1996. The more general purpose of this law is to ensure "universal telecommunication and information services" to all citizens of the country regardless of income or location. This legislation specifically targets elementary and secondary schools, healthcare providers, and libraries for access to "advanced telecommunications services" (Federal Communications Commission, 1997).

The e-rate is funded by charges to the telecommunications industry. Some argue that this charge represents a "back-door tax" levied without providing citizens the opportunity to approve the tax or control how the money is spent. Supporters argue that the intent was not to have the telecommunications industry pass on the cost to consumers, but to have the industry absorb these additional costs out of the savings allowed by regulatory changes that reduced access charges previously paid by long-distance companies. Thus the funding mechanism for the e-rate is controversial (Department of Education, 1998). Recently, the program has also been subject to reports of fraud and waste, which resulted in a temporary halt to the distribution of funds (Office of the Inspector General, 2004). Unfortunately, these concerns make the future of the program somewhat uncertain.

The e-rate is intended to provide discounts on hardware and services essential to the transmission of information, such as:

- Telephone connections
- Wiring for Ethernet connections
- Internet access charges through dial-up or leased line connections
- Equipment for wireless access
- Hardware required for Internet connections—routers, hubs, and computers used as servers

Schools are eligible for subsidies ranging from 20 to 90 percent, depending on the proportion of low-income students attending the school. Schools receiving the lowest reduction (20 percent) have less than 1 percent of the student body eligible for reduced-price lunches. Those schools eligible for the 90-percent reduction must have more than 75 percent of the students eligible for reduced-price lunches. Rural schools are eligible for slightly higher discounts because their telecommunication costs tend to be higher.

The e-rate is administered for the Federal Communication Commission by the Universal Service Administration Commission. This organization receives applications and decides how the available money will be awarded. Applying for e-rate money is not a trivial exercise. Schools need to file a technology plan that explains how the e-rate money will be used to improve educational services. This plan must also include an assessment of communications needs, provisions for staff development, and a strategy and budget for maintenance.

A school must also take steps to show that eligible vendors will have an opportunity to compete to provide the services that the school is requesting (Department of Education, 1998).

In 2001, Congress attempted to impose mandatory filtering as a new requirement for e-rate funding. The Children's Internet Protection Act (CIPA) mandated that school and library authorities must certify that they are enforcing a policy of Internet safety that includes measures to block or filter Internet access for both minors and adults to certain visual depictions. These include visual depictions that are (1) obscene, or (2) child pornography, or, with respect to use of computers with Internet access by minors, (3) harmful to minors. An authorized person may disable the blocking or filtering measure during any use by an adult to enable access for bona fide research or other lawful purpose (Children's Internet Protection Act, 2001).

CIPA also required that schools establish an Internet safety policy and hold a public meeting to discuss the proposed safety policy. Among other requirements, the safety policy must explain security measures protecting students during their participation in e-mail and chat as well as actions taken to prevent minors from disclosing personal information.

CIPA guidelines have generated considerable controversy. Many public libraries, which were expected to comply because of e-rate funding, see the measures as overly repressive or demanding of too much attention from librarians who serve mainly adult patrons. Some see the requirements as violating First Amendment rights. Others complain about the imperfections of screening software and the lack of precision in the phrase "harmful to minors" (American Library Association, 2002).

- The computer is viewed as a tool for math, science, and programming—subjects that, sadly, may be of less interest to many females.
- The more aggressive nature of young males may offer an advantage in gaining access to computers or the Internet when there is not enough equipment for everyone.
- Computer activities such as programming and competitive gaming emphasize mastery rather than social motives and may be more likely to appeal to males (Cooper & Weaver, 2003; Sanders & McGinnis, 1991; Weinman & Haag, 1999).

Benefits of the project approach

In contrast to past classroom applications of technology, it seems reasonable that the project approach we recommend offers some advantages in involving students with technology in a more equitable fashion. Female students feel equally competent in the use of computer tools (Gallup Organization, 1997), and focusing on applications rather than technology may encourage gender equity. Tool applications exist for all disciplines, offer the opportunity to engage all students, and can offer opportunities for collaboration and social interaction as well as opportunities for independence and competition. Moreover, the development of skills associated with tool applications can lead students toward vocational opportunities.

The American Association of University Women (American Association of University Women Educational Foundation, 2000) encourages experiences that move students beyond what they describe as simple application experiences (such as PowerPoint presentations). They suggest increasing the opportunities to use technology in "tinkering" activities, arguing that such activities develop higher-level thinking skills as well as a deeper interest in technology. Our interpretation of this position would involve students in technology-based activities that encourage experimentation and flexibility as part of authentic projects. Many of the applications we have described (data probes, GPS, advanced multimedia authoring, and video production, for instance) offer opportunities for moving far beyond basic technology functions as part of student projects. Our approach in this book tends to focus on ease of use and simplicity. However, there is usually much more power and flexibility in the software and tools than we have described. If desired, the opportunity is there for learning a great deal about technology and exploring the use of technology in accomplishing authentic tasks.

Equity and Student Ability

A number of studies have demonstrated that more and less able students have different experiences with technology. Less able students use computers less frequently, have fewer Internet experiences, and tend to spend a greater proportion of their time in drill-and-practice activities (Becker & Ravitz, 1999; Schofield & Davidson, 2004). These differences may exist because more able students are assumed to be more trustworthy and capable of independent activity (Becker & Ravitz, 1999), because the academic needs of less able students are assumed to require remediation focused on the development of basic skills and knowledge (Laboratory of Comparative Human Cognition, 1989), or because teachers assume that lower-achieving students will struggle with the technology skills necessary to engage in technology-supported tasks (Schofield & Davidson, 2004).

Provide meaningful activities for all.

However, a strict bottom-up model of instruction has been challenged because it cannot be assumed that the isolation and practice of lower-level skills is the most productive way to teach (for example, Laboratory of Comparative Human Cognition, 1989). The alternative is to embed the practice of individual skills within more meaningful activities. Activity-centered projects offer this opportunity and also frequently take advantage of cooperative groups that involve students of various levels of ability. Technology skills are less of a barrier when tasks are implemented cooperatively. In addition, students can be inspired by the opportunity to use technology in interesting and challenging ways, and it would seem unnecessary to limit the technology-based experiences of less able students to drill and computer tutorials.

Adapting Technology for Equal Access

This book is based on the premise that technology can provide meaningful learning experiences for the benefit of *all* students. However, more than 50 million Americans have some type of disability that requires that adaptations be made to take advantage of what technology has to offer.

Video Case
In an *inclusion classroom*, children with cognitive, affective, and psychomotor issues can succeed cooperatively with typical students. Watch the HM Video Case entitled *Inclusion: Grouping Strategies for Inclusive Classrooms*. Where do you see technology fitting into the inclusion picture? What kinds of technologies can you imagine that could still be developed to address the needs of inclusion classrooms?

These individuals may have mobility impairments that make it difficult to operate a mouse or use the keyboard. They may have visual impairments that make the computer screen useless as a device for presenting information or serving as the interface for user input. Learners may have auditory impairments or learning disabilities that present challenges. The computer and the Internet can provide great independence and compensate for many traditional obstacles. However, without meaningful access, technology can also impose new barriers.

Adaptations for Mobility Impairments

Mobility impairments make it difficult for learners to interact with technology. The problem may be difficulty in manipulating input devices (keyboard, mouse) or even basic physical tasks associated with operating a computer or peripheral device (turning on the computer, inserting a diskette or CD). Here are some ways to respond to mobility impairments:

- A power strip can be used to turn all equipment on and off with a single switch.
- Alternative keyboards position the keys farther apart and disable repeat keys so that users with slower and less precise movements have less difficulty.
- Special software, which causes the cursor to scan across a screen representation or across program choice buttons, allows individuals capable of controlling a switch (using a knee, the mouth, or the head) to make selections.

Adaptations for Visual Impairments

Visual impairment should not hinder learners from taking advantage of technology. Some of the following adaptations can be made:

- Blind individuals can use a standard keyboard. Braille key labels may be helpful to some of these students.
- Special **screen reader software** can "read" the screen to the learner (earphones can be used to reduce the distraction to others). Basic speech synthesis from text is fairly standard, but screen reader software can also "describe" menus, windows, and screen icons.
- Special software can allow magnification of the screen image for learners with limited vision. Some programs allow screen content to be enlarged sixteenfold.

Adaptive Webpage Design

The adaptations we have described so far address the general use of computers, and they certainly apply to helping students make use of the Internet. In practice, though, challenges and solutions are often unique to a particular combination of learning limitation and computer application. The use of the Web by blind students offers a good example.

For blind students to use the Web, the adaptations we have already discussed, such as screen reader software, are essential. However, there are some other challenges that cannot be met through modifications in software or hardware. The way that webpages themselves are designed is important.

Consider the issue from the perspective of the designer. Most web designers recognize the need to accommodate limitations such as older versions of browsers and relatively slow modems. But designers often forget that some Internet users face very different challenges. Visually impaired students cannot read a webpage or scrutinize images and illustrations. Less obviously, these students cannot use the mouse to point at a text link or click on an image map hot spot. The hot spots of an image represent the areas of the image designated to serve as links. The browser usually takes different actions according to which hot spot is clicked.

Some basic design suggestions can make a big difference, and web designers of any age can implement many of these features (Adaptive Computer Technology Centre, 1998; World Wide Web Consortium, 1999). Often it is helpful to begin with the question: Could the webpage be interpreted totally by listening? This question does not imply that the author must create an audio version of each webpage; rather, the page design should allow the user's special software to "read" the screen to the user. Here are some principles to follow:

Principles for adaptive web design

- If some page information is not presented as text—for example, if important content information is contained in images, illustrations, or video—consider offering alternative sources of information. An image map should be accompanied by text links that can be used as alternatives to the map's hot spots. A link to a separate page containing a text segment can be offered as an alternative to an explanatory illustration. Video can be supplemented with an audio track to provide descriptive information.

- Take advantage of the built-in opportunities to provide redundant information. HTML provides opportunities to include supplemental information, but designers frequently ignore these opportunities. Imagine, for example, that a webpage uses a graphic forward arrow as a link to the next page in a sequence. Many visually impaired students, who have no use for graphics, set their browsers to avoid loading graphic images. The designer can use the ALT attribute to specify text that will appear as a replacement for an image. In this case, specifying ALT="Next Page" would allow the text phrase "Next Page" to appear in place of the arrow. This kind of supplemental information is very easy to add when using a web authoring program.

- Information presented in tables or multiple columns can be confusing when "read" by older screen reader programs, because the reader attempts to follow the text horizontally across the entire page. We do advocate the use of tables as a way to construct webpages, but tables with side-by-side columns of lengthy text are especially problematic for users dependent on a screen reader. The best solution may be to insert a link at the top of the page providing access to a single-column, alternative version of the page.

- Careful punctuation is important. Screen readers identify punctuation marks, and these can be critical for a user's understanding of the content. On many webpages, items in lists do not end with punctuation marks, and this lack of punctuation can make them more difficult to interpret.

EMERGING TECHNOLOGY

Adaptations for Visually Impaired Web Users

To comprehend web content and make effective use of the navigational and interactive elements built into webpages, visually impaired users need more than a spoken version of webpage text. They need to hear a description of other elements appearing on a page, they need to know when text segments serve as links, and they need access to some of the alternative descriptive information that may not be displayed automatically. If the page author has done a conscientious job, all of this information is embedded in one way or another within the raw HTML; what is required is a different way of interpreting the HTML and presenting information to the user. A different type of browser or an enhancement for existing browsers could allow HTML to be interpreted and the embedded information presented in a different way.

Home Page Reader is an example of a program that extracts and presents supplemental information. This product:

- Reads text in a male voice and text links in a female voice
- Reads ALT text and HTML 4.0 (a more advanced version of HTML with an expanded set of capabilities) information provided by webpage authors
- Describes tables, frames, and forms
- Summarizes page links and allows the selection of links using the number keypad
- Allows visually impaired users to create "readable" bookmarks

Advances in HTML, hardware, and software are coming together to allow visually impaired users to benefit from web resources. Although these tools have been available for several years, they are still finding their way into the K–12 classroom.

Copyright Law and Respect for Intellectual Property

All teachers need to be aware of their personal obligations regarding copyrighted materials, and they need to teach their students to respect the intellectual property of others. It may be helpful to think of these responsibilities as interrelated. A powerful way to develop any behavior in your students is to model this behavior yourself.

Education and Copyright: Issues and Problems

Why is copyright important in education?

Copyright is the body of legal rights related to the reproduction, distribution, and performance of original works. Copyright is such an important issue in education because the process of education relies heavily on instructional materials (including textbooks, films, and computer programs) and other resources that can serve an educational purpose (newspapers, television programs, videotapes, music CDs, reference books). We now must add Internet resources as a new option for both instructional material and general information. These essential information resources were purposefully created through the intellectual efforts of others—often as a way for these individuals to make a living. If we want creative individuals to spend their time preparing instructional materials, they must be compensated when their materials are used.

Educators can violate copyright law in various ways, for example:

Examples of copyright violations

- A music teacher copying orchestra sheet music so each child can take a copy home to practice
- A biology teacher developing a personal collection of informative television programs on videotape for use in class
- An English teacher who has purchased a new word processing program copying it to all three computers in his room
- A college professor printing out an article from a subscription Internet information service, making copies, and distributing them to her students

Because teachers are not, as a rule, prone to breaking the law, why do they sometimes violate copyright law? Some may want to help students but lack the resources they think are necessary to do so. A second reason may result from a combination of easy access to the means for making copies and sketchy knowledge of when copying is appropriate. Nearly every teacher has access to a photocopier, tape recorder, video recorder, scanner, and computer with blank disks. These are available in schools and in most public libraries. Most users of the Internet probably realize that if you hold down the mouse button while clicking on a webpage image (or click with the right button when working on a Windows machine), the browser will ask you if you would like to save a copy of the image. If it were illegal to copy documents, television programs, computer programs, web images, and the like, would the methods and equipment for doing so be so readily accessible?

The answer is yes. The methods and materials are available even though some of the copying they are used for is illegal. Of course, schools, libraries, and the companies creating products that enable copying are not advocating theft of intellectual property. These organizations assume that those who use their products and resources understand when copying is appropriate and when it is not. When violations occur, it is sometimes because teachers or students assume that the opportunity to copy something implies more than it does. In this situation, teachers and students need a thorough understanding of what is appropriate.

False assumptions about Internet materials

For the Internet in particular, one final problem may be caused by a different set of false assumptions. Access to a tremendous amount of Internet material is free, and often there are no obvious indicators such as a copyright symbol or a statement that the material is protected. Are you stealing when you use something that has no posted price and that no one has openly spoken for? Yes, for these reasons:

- The assumption that you are not taking revenue away from an author by copying content from a webpage may be wrong. The individual responsible for the web content may be paid by others—advertisers, for example—when the information on the page is accessed. If your behavior prevents others (such as your students) from visiting a webpage, it is possible you are limiting the income of the website author.

■ The intent to make money is not necessary for intellectual property to be protected. The author has the right to control who displays what he or she has created.

■ The absence of a copyright statement is not an indication that the author has given up his or her rights.

Again, teachers and students may simply need a better understanding of what is appropriate. Our goal in the following sections is to make you aware of some of the general issues regarding copyright and then to take a more specific look at issues pertaining to the Internet.

Copyright Law

The government's authority to develop copyright law is established in the U.S. Constitution in Article I, section 8, which grants Congress the authority "to promote the progress of science and useful arts, by securing for limited times to authors and inventors the exclusive right to their respective writings and discoveries." This section of the Constitution is responsible for what we know as copyrights and patents.

Scope of the law

The current copyright law was written in 1976 and has since been amended to make the law more specific. Congress has also formed committees to offer suggestions on such topics as copying from books and periodicals, copying of music, off-air videotaping, and, more recently, multimedia. This collected body of information does not address every possible situation, but the original law was written to be very open-ended and defines as copyrightable "original works of authorship fixed in any tangible medium of expression, now known or later developed" (Copyright Act of 1976, Title 17 of the U.S. Code, Section 102, included in Salpeter, 1992). Nearly any type of instructional material you can think of is probably included: print materials, software, pictures, recorded music, musical scores, television broadcasts, works of art, and Internet webpages.

Copyright encourages progress.

It is easy for educators to see only one side of copyright law: as telling teachers what they cannot do. However, if you read and think carefully about the statement from the Constitution authorizing copyright laws, you may gain a different perspective. Copyright law is intended to encourage "the progress of science and useful arts." In other words, if educators expect others to create and improve instructional materials, educators should also expect that mechanisms must be put in place to allow these individuals to make a fair profit on their work. For example, if subscription-based web services become perceived as a market prone to frequent copyright violations, commercial developers will not put effort into creating high-quality products for that market.

Establishing a Copyright

Automatic nature of copyright

How exactly does a work's creator establish copyright under the current law? In fact, the creator does not need to take any specific steps to claim copyright because any author's work is automatically protected from the time it is created. This principle applies not only to written works but also to music, photographs, artwork, and so on.

An author can provide notice of copyright with a notation in the following form: © year name—for example, © 2006 Cindy Grabe. The word *copyright* can also be used in place of the copyright symbol. You are probably aware that there is a U.S. Copyright Office and that authors can register their works with this office. But the fact that a work has not been registered or even that it does not carry a notice of copyright should not be interpreted as a waiver of copyright.

Rights, Licenses, and Permissions

Copyright law grants authors or owners five basic rights:

Basic rights covered by the law

1. *The right to make copies.* If you are the creator of the work, you can make as many copies as you want.
2. *The right to create derivations.* A derivation is an adaptation of the original. For example, a painter might create prints from an original painting, or an author might create a movie script based on a book.
3. *The right to sell or distribute copies.* The author can make a profit by copying and selling his or her works to others.
4. *The right to perform a work in public.* Generally the author of a work controls the presentation of the work to the public. The performance right covers, for instance, live performances of music and the presentation of a play.
5. *The right to display a work in public.* This right covers situations such as the display of a painting or the presentation of original artwork on the Internet.

Transfer of rights

The author or creator of a work can transfer some or all of these rights to others. If the copyright itself is assigned to someone else, that means that all rights are transferred. For example, a large software company may pay an independent developer a large sum of money to be assigned the copyright for a computer program the developer has written. From that point on, the company can do whatever it wants with the program. In an alternative arrangement, the granting of a **license,** only the rights specified in the agreement are transferred (Fritz, 1992). Although the term *license* may not always be used, this is a common type of agreement, and it may or may not involve money.

License agreements for schools

Examples of license agreements in education are common. You may have heard of a software **site license,** which allows a school or other organization to make copies of software it has purchased. The license may limit the number of copies, or it may allow unlimited copying as long as the software is used on a machine that the school owns. A license of this type does not allow the school to distribute copies outside the site. A site license offers some advantages to both parties. The school is allowed to purchase the software for less than the standard price per copy, and the company selling the software usually saves on packaging and manuals.

When you ask a copyright holder for permission to copy a work in a specific way for a certain context, you are in effect applying for a mini-license. For example, you may ask an artist for permission to scan a painting or drawing that you want to include in a classroom project. In instances of this sort, only very specific and limited rights are granted. For advice on acquiring permission, see "Focus: Obtaining Permission to Copy."

Copying Computer Software

When is it permissible to copy software?

The copyright law was amended in 1980 to address the copying of computer software (section 117). Illegal copying of computer software, often called **software piracy,** is rampant; estimates are that software authors lose $2.6 billion annually in U.S. sales (Business Software Alliance, 2002). Section 117 of the copyright law states that legitimate owners of software can copy the software in two situations. First, they can copy the software when making a copy that is essential in allowing the software to run on their own computers. This usually means that the owner of the software will have a copy of the program on the disks or CD he or she purchased and also on the hard drive of a computer. Section 117 also allows the individual purchasing the software to make a backup or archival copy. The backup is a safeguard against the loss or corruption of the original program. The backup legally should not be used on a second computer while the original is still in use.

The owners of a software copyright can also grant a site license allowing software to be copied. This agreement allows the purchaser to make a specified number of copies or to allow a specified number of copies to be active on a local area network (LAN) of interconnected computers. Copying software to multiple machines (multiple loading) and allowing several users to use a program simultaneously over a network without a site license are violations of copyright law. Sometimes violations of this type are quite purposeful, as when a business purchases one copy of a spreadsheet program and loads it on every employee's computer. In other cases, violations are more innocent. A teacher may purchase a program for her home computer and then decide to take the program to school so that her students can use it. If there is only one original, two individuals should not be using a program at the same time.

Fair Use

Libraries provide easy access to photocopiers, so it is very easy for anyone to copy material from books, journals, and magazines. This does *not* mean that all types of copying are legal; yet because libraries do not want to promote copyright violations, there must be some situations in which material can be copied without seeking permission from the author or creator.

In fact, you are allowed to make photocopies in the library because of a provision called **fair use,** defined in section 107 of the copyright law. The guidelines governing fair use can be confusing, and it is important for you as a teacher to understand what they mean. Essentially, section 107 provides some exceptions to the general principle that the creator of the work holds exclusive rights to copy and distribute it.

For purposes such as teaching, scholarship, and research, section 107 specifies four "factors to be considered" in determining whether a particular act of copying represents fair use:

Factors determining fair use

- *Purpose of the use.* Generally, copying is more acceptable if it is for non-profit purposes than if it is done for profit.
- *Nature of the copyrighted work.* The copying of factual material, such as a summary of historical events, is more likely to be fair use than the copying of original poetry or fiction.
- *Amount and substantiality of the portion used.* Copying a small part of the original is more likely to be tolerated than copying the entire work.
- *Impact on commercial value.* Copying should not harm the commercial value of the original or deprive the creator or publisher of permission fees. For instance, copying of workbooks is not considered fair use because workbooks are intended to be purchased and used only once. A related consideration for many kinds of material is the number of copies made; obviously a large number of copies would have a greater impact on a work's commercial value than a small number.

These four factors were intended to be balanced against one another in particular cases. The overall intent was to create a law that is flexible and applicable to many situations, reflecting the great variety of copyrighted material and the equally great variety of possible uses. For many educators and other professionals, however, the result has been uncertainty about what they can and cannot do.

Meaning of fair use varies with the medium.

To make matters even more complicated, the meaning of *fair* in *fair use* sometimes varies with the medium (Major, 1998; Martin, 1994; Salpeter, 1992). For example, video is a common way of delivering educational content, and video players are common in most schools. Specific guidelines have been developed to guide the taping of television programs for classroom use. Television programs offered free of charge for viewing by the general public can be recorded and used for nonprofit instructional purposes, but a number of conditions must be met:

- Recorded material must be used within the first ten school days of the forty-five calendar days following the actual broadcast. Material recorded in June, for example, could not be used in October because the time period extends beyond forty-five calendar days. A program recorded on December 27 might legally be used with a class on January 12 because consecutive school days do not include weekends or holidays. Recordings are to be erased by the end of the forty-five-day period.
- Schools cannot record a variety of programs and then make them available to teachers. Recordings can be made only by or at the request of an individual teacher, to be used by that teacher. A teacher cannot request that the same program be re-recorded, no matter how many times the program is broadcast.
- Teachers do not have to show entire programs, but the content of the programs as broadcast is not to be altered. For example, combining small segments from several programs is not allowed. Any copy of a broadcast program must contain the broadcast copyright notice.
- Educational institutions are to accept responsibility for implementing adequate control measures to see that recorded material is used within

the established guidelines. Schools allowing teachers to use recorded television programs in their classrooms are expected to take an active role in guaranteeing compliance with copyright law.

The companies responsible for some television programs have adopted a more lenient set of guidelines related to instructional use of the programs. See the description of Cable in the Classroom in "Resources to Expand Your Knowledge Base" at the conclusion of this chapter.

Fair Use as Applied to Multimedia and the Internet There are many areas for which specific fair use guidelines such as those just described for the use of content from television programs do not exist. Multimedia and webpage authoring, two areas emphasized in this book, are examples. We think there are some important areas in which teachers need guidance:

Four questions for teachers

- Can students and teachers take resources from websites for use in learning and instructional activities?
- Can students and teachers use the material developed by others on their own webpages?
- Can teachers post student work on the Web?
- What should teachers do if they want to protect online resources they have developed?

Without specific guidelines in these areas, the reasonable approach is probably a conservative one, drawing on existing policies that apply to other media.

Because of the matters left unresolved by the copyright law, there have been various attempts to bring interested parties together to negotiate more specific guidelines. One of the earliest such negotiations focused on the issue of photocopying of printed works, and a set of guidelines was worked out specifically for that medium. Let's look at what those rules entail. A key point to remember is this: The guidelines that apply to copying material for your own professional use differ from the guidelines for preparing multiple copies for your students.

Liberal allowances for personal photocopying

Copying for Your Own Use In general, as an individual, you are allowed to copy rather extensively in preparing for your classes or conducting scholarly work. For example, your college or university library will likely allow you to copy an entire journal article or book chapter as part of your research for a paper. The same is true when you are doing research to prepare for teaching a class. Fair use guidelines for individual scholarship are fairly liberal.

This does not mean, however, that there are no limits. For example, when Mark Grabe's university library honors his request to copy a chapter from a book, the library records his name and the book title. The library will not allow him to copy a second chapter from the same book. This is the point at which the library feels copying might be perceived as a substitute for purchasing the book.

Making Multiple Copies for Classroom Use Guidelines for making multiple copies for class use are much more conservative than those controlling personal use. For books and periodicals, the multiple-copy fair use guidelines include these points:

Guidelines for
multiple photocopies

- *Brevity.* A teacher is allowed to excerpt and distribute 1,000 words or 10 percent, whichever is less, from a written document. Similar guidelines have been set for other media, as we describe in the next section.
- *Spontaneity.* Copying a particular work must be the "inspiration" of the teacher who wants to use the work. For example, a librarian is not supposed to collect material for a teacher. The decision to use the work must occur so close in time to its actual use that it would not be practical to obtain permission.
- *Cumulative effect.* Material is to be copied for a single course, and the time period during which the material may continue to be used is restricted. To control the cumulative effect of the copying, limits are placed on how many items may be taken from the works of a single author or artist.

These are the guidelines that were developed to contend with the technological innovation called the photocopier. Now let's consider what headway has been made in dealing with more recent advances in multimedia and distance education.

CONFU

Guidelines for Creating Multimedia and for Distance Education In recent years, individuals from various parties with a vested interest in fair use (such as the U.S. government, publishing companies, the Software Publishing Association, and the Association for Educational Communications and Technology) have met to propose guidelines for technological applications in educational contexts. These meetings evolved into the **Conference on Fair Use** (commonly referred to as **CONFU**). After two years of work, CONFU's suggestions for teacher- or student-created multimedia and for distance education were finalized in 1997. The full text of the documents prepared by this committee is available on the Internet (CONFU, 1997a, 1997b), and the preamble to each document includes a good discussion of fair use in general.

Guidelines for distance
learning

The CONFU guidelines still do not provide the focus on Internet resources or issues that we would prefer. When the CONFU meetings occurred, only a few colleges and schools were beginning to explore uses of the World Wide Web for teaching their students. Another attempt to deal with emerging copyright issues, the Technology, Education, and Copyright Harmonization Act of 2002 (Technology, Education, and Copyright Harmonization Act of 2002, 2002), or **TEACH Act,** was implemented to provide guidance for distance education. The CONFU guidelines are probably the most useful for classroom teachers interested in how fair use applies to the type of projects we described in previous chapters. Let's examine these guidelines in some detail. We then briefly outline some of the new opportunities made available by the TEACH Act.

Guidelines for
multimedia

CONFU's multimedia guidelines address student use of copyrighted work as part of course-related multimedia projects and teacher use of copyrighted work in the creation of "noncommercial" multimedia for instructional purposes. CONFU attempts to suggest the applications, time frame, portion, copying, and distribution limits that would comply with established fair use standards.

Application

- *Students.* Students may create and present multimedia projects containing copyrighted material for educational purposes within the course for which they were created, and they may save these projects as examples of their academic work for future job or academic interviews.
- *Teachers.* Teachers may use multimedia that includes copyrighted material conforming to fair use for purposes of (1) face-to-face instruction, (2) student self-study, (3) remote instruction to enrolled students on a network providing controlled access, or (4) evaluations of teaching performance or job interviews.

Time, Copying, and Distribution Limits

- *Time.* Teacher-created multimedia may be used in instruction for up to two years. (If the teacher cannot prevent duplication of copyrighted material, the material can remain available for only fifteen days.)
- *Copying and distribution.* It is suggested that only two copies, the original and a backup, should be created. Only one copy should be available to users, and students should not be allowed to make personal copies. When the product has been the result of a collaborative effort, each participant may keep a copy for archival purposes.

Portion Limits

The portion limitation defines the amount of material that may be taken from a copyrighted work. These limits apply cumulatively to projects created by students or teachers. For example, a teacher who creates multimedia resources to be used in conjunction with daily lectures must consider the total material used in all lectures in determining what resources may be taken from a given source.

- *Video.* Users are allowed to use up to 10 percent or three minutes, whichever is less, of material from a video work.
- *Text material.* Users are allowed to use up to 10 percent or 1,000 words, whichever is less, from a copyrighted work. Poetry represents a special category. A poem of 250 words or less may be used in total, but no more than three poems by one poet or five poems from a published anthology may be used.
- *Music.* Users may use 10 percent or thirty seconds, whichever is less, from an individual musical work.
- *Photographs and other illustrations.* No more than five images by an artist or photographer may be used. For images from a collection (such as a book), the limit is 10 percent or fifteen images, whichever is less.

Additional guidelines   There are some additional expectations. Students and educators are required to cite all sources carefully when using copyrighted material. Providing credit includes listing a full citation for the original work and any copyright notices displayed in the original source. With the exception of copyright information related to images, this information may be consolidated in a single section within the multimedia product (for instance, it may appear as a list at the end). For images, however, information about the source and copyright should accompany each individual image. Finally, students and teachers should include in the introduction to their multimedia product a statement indicating that material is incorporated in this product under the fair use exemption of the U.S. copyright law and is restricted from further use.

TEACH Act removes some limitations.

TEACH Act The TEACH Act was pushed forward because Congress recognized the potential significance of distance education, the role that digital media could play in distance education, and some of the inherent limitations imposed on distance educators compared with educators working in a face-to-face classroom environment. So, one way to understand the purpose of the TEACH Act is to think of its provisions as removing some of the copyright limitations uniquely placed on online educators. For example, your instructors may from time to time include small amounts of copyrighted material in classroom presentations. Perhaps a graph from the textbook is scanned, incorporated into a PowerPoint slide, and projected on the screen during a lecture. Perhaps a verse from a poem is excerpted and presented in the same fashion. These uses of copyrighted material would be allowed as fair use. Until the TEACH Act, making these same resources available over the Internet would not have been allowed without permission.

The TEACH Act proposes that distance educators can make limited amounts of copyrighted material available as part of "mediated instructional activities." Unfortunately, the meaning of the phrase "mediated instructional activities" has been left somewhat vague, never fully creating an equivalence between face-to-face and online teaching. The implication appears to be that instructors will organize content into units much like lectures or classes and make them available to students for a limited amount of time. Although these expectations would be difficult to implement in online courses in which individual students work their way through units of content and activities at drastically different rates, the guidelines will offer new opportunities for online educators working with a group of students who move through the course together.

The TEACH Act identifies strict guidelines for institutions and instructors. The institution bears responsibility for developing appropriate policy and helping educators understand how the policy can be implemented. Instructional resources can be accessible only by students enrolled in the class. The institution might meet these requirements by requiring that distance education instructors use a course management system that identifies enrolled students and protects course resources with a student-specific password system. The instructor then bears responsibility for the appropriate use of copyrighted materials and for using such materials during a period of time that is relevant to a class session (Crews, 2002).

Unresolved questions

The meaning of legal concepts tends to become more concrete as cases related to laws are considered by the legal system. Some of the uncertainty we have described will likely be resolved within the next few years.

Focus

Obtaining Permission to Copy

The first step in obtaining permission is to determine who owns the copyright. With books, journals, and documents, the copyright notice usually appears near the front of the publication. Also check the acknowledgments page. Pay special attention to information about multiple copyrights. With music, the lyrics and musical score may be protected separately. This is also frequently the case with the text and illustrations in documents. Websites may include a "terms and conditions" statement that explains the author's position on the use of site contents.

A list of items to include in your request for permission follows. This list assumes that you want to copy material from a document, and some of these items may need to be modified slightly if another type of material is involved. Circumstances may also require that the form of the letter or e-mail message be modified. Be sure to include the following elements in your request:

- The full name of the author or artist responsible for the work you propose to copy
- The exact reference for the source material
- Page number(s) or the URL (for web content) for the material you want to copy
- The number of copies you propose to make
- A full description of how the copied material will be used, including:
  - The nature of the project
  - Whether the material will be used alone or combined with materials to be obtained from other companies
  - Who will assemble the project
  - Who will view the finished project
  - How long the material will be kept, and what will happen to the project after the intended academic task has been completed
- A description of the course in which the material is to be used
- Your name, position, institutional affiliation, full address, and telephone number

Some companies may expect you to pay a royalty fee for using their material. You may feel it is appropriate to acknowledge that this is a possibility and ask what the fee will be. For example, you might say, "If a royalty fee applies to copying the material that has been described, please notify me so that I can determine if funds are available."

It is important to allow several weeks for your request to be considered. It may take a month to process your request, and you will want to allow time to develop an alternate plan in case your request is denied.

Remember to be courteous. What you are requesting is a privilege.

Source: Based on suggestions provided by Long, Risher, & Shapiro (1997). We have added other suggestions based on our own experiences.

Using Student Work on Websites

Students' possible rights as authors

Before we sum up our outlook on copyright issues, there is one more area we want to address. It is common to view student work on school websites. Do students have rights as authors? Copyright law is clear on the issue of ownership. Unless a student has been hired to create material and is operating under a formalized work-for-hire agreement, a student owns any work he or she has created.

Getting signed permission

Does this mean that the teacher cannot keep or make copies of a student's work? According to one opinion (Burke, 1993), a teacher may have an implicit license to make copies to be used as an example for later classes. For example, teachers sometimes save outstanding research papers so that students in later classes can see what the teachers expect. However, the instructor would not have the right to use student material in a derivative work—something like a book authored by the teacher in which the student work appears as an example. Because placing work on a website can clearly be considered a form of distribution, web publication of a student's work raises similar concerns. Therefore, we make this recommendation: The best policy is to treat student work in the same way you would treat the work of any other artist or author; that is, request signed permission to use the work.

Note that because most K–12 students are minors, certain situations may also require permission from a parent or legal guardian. Often the best option is to work out the publication arrangements at the beginning of a project, obtaining the necessary consent from both students and parents.

Recognizing student work in this manner helps the student understand the concept of authorship. It also develops an appreciation for the rights accorded those who produce intellectual and creative works.

Rules of Thumb: Suggested Answers for the Copyright Questions

The four questions answered

We have told you as much as we can about how copyright and fair use apply to the Internet. Obviously these are complex topics without definitive answers. Still, educators do want guidance, and if definitive answers are not available, they need rules of thumb. Returning to the four fundamental questions that we posed at the beginning of this discussion, here are our suggested answers:

- Can students and teachers take resources from websites for use in learning and instructional activities?

  Check the website itself for terms and conditions governing usage. In the absence of guidelines on the site itself, a convenient way to think about fair use has been provided by Georgia Harper (1997), who recommends that educators follow the suggestion of "small parts, limited time, and limited access." The CONFU guidelines may provide a way to interpret this suggestion.

- Can students and teachers use the material developed by others on their own webpages?

  We believe that the use of copyrighted resources on "unprotected" webpages without permission is questionable and should be avoided. Certainly the activities we emphasize in this book do not require this type of material. The Golden Rule provides a useful way to think about this issue. As a teacher, would you want other teachers to "borrow" some of your best lesson plans or classroom materials without at least asking?

The TEACH Act does allow "fair use" applications on protected websites available to enrolled students in connection with what is defined as "mediated instructional activities." Note that our suggestions for multimedia authoring often assume a potential audience such as parents or students in other classes, and such groups would fall outside the group defined as enrolled students.

■ Can teachers post student work on the Web?

We encourage schools to use the Web to present student work, but to do so in a way that recognizes the creative talents of the student. In any decision to publish student work, the students and parents should be involved.

■ What should teachers do if they want to protect online resources they have developed?

There is no guaranteed way to protect your work once it is online. What you can do is to indicate that you regard your work as copyrighted and that it should not be used without your permission. (Be aware, however, that in some cases, the institution you work for, such as your school or school district, may believe that it owns the rights. You may want to check your district's policies.) If your work is intended for a specific audience such as students involved in a distance education experience, you can limit access through the use of password protection.

Protecting Students from Inappropriate Material and Experiences

The Internet compared with other media

Educators must recognize that the Internet does not exist specifically to support educational goals. In this regard, the Internet is similar to other information systems we encounter in our daily lives. Cable television has the capacity to bring sporting events, congressional testimony, educational programming, and sexually explicit content into our living rooms. The telephone can be used to chat with Grandma about Thanksgiving dinner or with a paid psychic about your future. For adults, all are acceptable forms of "information." If we want to benefit from powerful communication systems, we must both recognize and find ways to adjust to the multiple purposes and audiences the Internet serves.

It is true that there are risks in allowing students to use the Internet. Both educators and students must recognize these risks so that protective measures can be taken. In this section we explore the dangers and outline what we consider reasonable responses to them.

Potential Dangers and Reasonable Protection

Possible risks from Internet access

What are the possible risks of Internet access? Students may encounter the following (Magid, 1998; National Center for Missing and Exploited Children, 2000):

Focus

Digital Cheating

Recent anonymous surveys of students indicate that cheating is rampant in K–12 and college institutions. Even a high proportion of the most academically able students admit to cheating (for instance, Bushweller, 1999b). While academic cheating takes many forms, our primary concern is **plagiarism**— representing someone else's work as your own. Plagiarism is certainly not dependent on technology, but technology makes the mechanical act of copying another's work easier.

Plagiarism takes many forms. Students may cut and paste from websites or CD-based encyclopedias. In some cases, such plagiarism is unintentional and results from the inappropriate assumption that "borrowing" small amounts of material is allowed. Some students, for example, assume that adding a citation allows copying paragraph-length excerpts. Most students know better and "borrow" material, recognizing that it would be extremely unlikely their teachers would ever be able to locate the original source. The vastness and informality of Internet resources probably reinforce this perception.

The most blatant form of digital plagiarism involves the purchase of complete essays or term papers from a commercial online provider (Bushweller, 1999a). While many of these sites include disclaimers encouraging students to use the downloaded material for "research purposes only," the general tone of the sites and even site names (several contain the word *cheat*) suggest a very different purpose.

What can teachers do about this problem? Some urge the use of more effective methods of detecting plagiarism. Plagiarism.org offers a detection service to college instructors. Student papers are submitted online, and each is compared against a database of manuscripts. Segments of text identified as possibly copied are highlighted for the instructor to investigate. Teachers might also try searching for suspicious phrases using a standard search engine.

Part of the solution is to establish clear guidelines and possibly make the generation of scholarly works a more interactive process. Students should learn how to cite their sources accurately and how to personalize and interpret primary sources in creating their own products. Students can begin to learn these skills at an early age. One second-grade teacher we know helps her students learn to take notes in their own words by having the students close the reference book before they write down any information. Writing can be made a more interactive process by asking students to submit intermediate products (for example, notes, printouts of webpages they intend to focus on) or by asking students to discuss their projects before or after the paper has been submitted for grading.

- *Inappropriate content.* Students using the World Wide Web may encounter material displaying sexual acts and violence, promoting the hatred of specific groups, or encouraging dangerous or unlawful activities.
- *Physical molestation.* Students using e-mail or chat areas may encounter individuals who wish to do them harm, such as pedophiles. Some individuals, often representing themselves deceptively, use Internet communication tools to become acquainted with students and eventually attempt to arrange a meeting. In a study of ten- to seventeen-year-old Internet users, 3 percent reported that during the year they had an encounter in which a solicitor had asked to meet them somewhere, called them on the phone, or sent them money or gifts (National Center for Missing and Exploited Children, 2000).
- *Harassment.* Students using e-mail or chat areas may be subjected to harassment, becoming the target of demeaning or threatening messages. Twenty percent of ten- to seventeen-year-old Internet users indicated that they had been sexually solicited online within the year. Most had been approached by another youth (National Center for Missing and Exploited Children, 2000).
- *Legal and financial threats.* Students may knowingly or unknowingly become involved in situations with legal or financial consequences. For example, an attempt may be made to deceive students into providing a credit card number.

Balancing Freedom and Protection

Putting the dangers in context

In light of these potential dangers, the general public and educators are justifiably concerned about abuses of the Internet. However, exercising proper caution must be distinguished from paranoia. There is some level of potential danger involved in openness to any means of communication. Pornography, hate literature, descriptions of how to create explosive devices, and the open discussion of drug use certainly exist, and educators cannot guarantee that students won't find such material on the Internet. But educators also cannot guarantee that such materials are not being stashed in a student's locker and passed around during school. Similarly, a small number of individuals seek to take advantage of young people through Internet conversations, but such individuals may also hang out near play areas after school.

One issue that educators face in trying to regulate students' Internet access is a clash between the democratic ideal of a right to personal expression and the desire of parents and educators to protect young people from harmful experiences. At least at an abstract level, most people would agree that both personal expression and individual safety are fundamental rights. The challenge is to create an Internet environment that does not impose censorship and yet allows adults to control what minors in their care experience.

Conflicts of this type are often resolved without major difficulty in other situations. For example, local grocery stores and gas stations carry magazines containing nudity. Publishers have a right to sell this material, and adults have a right to purchase it. The solution is for the magazines to be enclosed in a plastic envelope that cannot be opened until the magazine has been purchased, and the business establishments will not sell the magazines to minors.

In this situation, reasonable measures have been taken to satisfy the conflicting values.

In the case of Internet use, how can educators provide a similar balance between freedom and protection? What would constitute reasonable measures? To answer this question, consider a parallel situation.

A parallel situation

We have always allowed our children to answer the telephone even when we are not at home. The telephone is a valuable communication tool, and we recognize that our children have friends they want to talk to. We certainly want them to answer when we're calling them. However, we do recognize that there are possible dangers. We cope with these dangers in the following ways:

- *Technology.* One of our responses is technological: We have caller ID and voice mail. Our children can see who is calling or allow the caller to record a message. If we are calling from a phone that is not recognized by caller ID, our daughter may pick up the phone when she hears us talking to the voice mail system.
- *Instruction.* We supplement the technology with instructions we have given our children. For example, if a strange caller asks for one of us, our daughter is not supposed to say that her parents are not home. Instead, she says that they can't come to the phone right now and asks that the caller leave a message or call back in a little while.

A three-pronged response

The Internet presents a different set of challenges, but the goals are basically the same, and a similar combination of measures can be used. Educators can (1) direct students toward safe areas of the Internet, (2) take advantage of filtering systems that screen Internet content, and (3) directly intervene with students through supervision, instruction in safety guidelines, and the administration of an acceptable use policy. We believe that educators need to consider all these methods rather than assuming that a single approach will be sufficient.

Learning life skills

These mechanisms are necessarily self-serving in meeting the legal responsibility of schools to provide a safe learning environment. However, it is also important to recognize that providing this safe environment is not enough. Schools must prepare students for a world in which use of the Internet is increasingly prevalent and in which protective measures often will not be in place. Students will need knowledge, skills, and a sense of personal responsibility in order to function safely and ethically. The discussion of safety guidelines intended to supplement a school's less-than-perfect filtering and supervision strategies provides the opportunity to develop awareness and strategies useful outside the school. Careful consideration of the acceptable-use policy (which we discuss later in this chapter) and the rationale for such a policy prepares students to understand expected behaviors in work settings.

Safe Areas of the Internet

Internet sites that have been screened and operate under supervision may be thought of as "safe areas." We have mentioned several of these areas throughout this book, and we will attempt to organize and summarize them here. Additional information about these resources is provided at the end of the chapter.

Here are some ideas for identifying and using safe areas:

Guidelines for finding
and using safe areas

■ Search for websites using a directory that rates websites and allows searches to be limited to sites approved for students and younger users. A good example of a directory of this type is Yahooligans!, an offshoot of Yahoo!. The searchable Yahooligans! Database provides links only to sites appropriate for student exploration (see Figure 10.2). Ask Jeeves for Kids offers a similar service.

■ Focus most student web experiences on well-tested curriculum projects. For example, Pacific Bell sponsors Blue Web'n, a very large, annotated, online database of educational websites.

■ Use chat and e-mail services that provide supervision. For example, Kidlink, a service that establishes communication opportunities among students, sponsors supervised chat areas. Gaggle, an online e-mail system intended for K–12 users, allows teachers to control who is provided access, domains that are to be blocked, and words that are prohibited.

■ Emphasize e-mail or videoconferencing projects that are organized through other teachers.

Filtering

Two approaches to
filtering

Filtering helps control what Internet users are able to access. Filtering is accomplished in different ways, but the basic idea is to block access to material and activities that have been judged to be inappropriate or dangerous. We describe two approaches schools might consider: a firewall and commercial stand-alone filtering software.

Firewall

Functions of a firewall

A firewall is a computer and sophisticated software that control the flow of data between two networks. A firewall might be used to separate the Internet and the network connecting the computers within a school district. In such a situation, the barrier created by a firewall could serve two functions: (1) protecting the information maintained by the district's computers from being damaged or accessed from any computer external to the district network or (2) determining what someone within the district could request from the Internet.

Data flow across a firewall can be filtered on the basis of either IP address or protocol. This means that students can be prevented from downloading information from certain designated websites (identified by IP address) or from using specific services such as Internet relay chat or e-mail (identified by protocol). A firewall is also capable of gathering information on attempted external breaches of the security system or keeping a record of the webpages requested by each computer in the district. An individual with advanced technical skills would manage a district firewall.

Stand-Alone Filtering Software

How filtering software
works

Commercial stand-alone software has been around for several years and is popular for both schools and homes. This software works primarily by refusing to accept material sent from certain targeted sites. The companies selling

FIGURE 10.2

Yahooligans!: A Safe Online Information Site

these products continually update their lists of sites that provide offensive material and make these lists available to those who own copies of the software.

These systems do not offer perfect protection. Offensive material can be added to an existing site at any time, and new servers are always being connected to the Internet. However, this software does provide a reasonable means of protection from established sites that offer material not appropriate in a school environment.

Filtering programs offer some other interesting strategies for controlling access. Several companies provide those who purchase their filtering software with lists of disapproved and approved sites. Using a list of approved sites would offer protection against inappropriate material contained on new servers. Some filtering programs can also keep track of which sites students have visited.

When a system gathers information about students' or teachers' use of the Internet, it is important that these users be aware that such information is being collected. A clear statement should appear in the acceptable-use policy (which we discuss in the next section) and possibly on any login screen that identifies a user to the system. It is probably best to take the position that the goal of a system for tracking individual use is to prevent inappropriate use of school resources rather than to surprise those who might be "caught" by such a system. Clear warning would establish this priority.

Additional filtering strategies

You can find a list of the more popular commercial filtering programs in "Resources to Expand Your Knowledge Base" at the end of this chapter, and on the website that accompanies this textbook.

Safety Guidelines, Acceptable-Use Policies, and Supervision

Because technological mechanisms are not foolproof, schools cannot rely totally on them to control how students will use the Internet. Preparing students to be responsible users of the Internet also involves helping them learn what is safe and appropriate behavior.

Safety Guidelines

The need for clear rules

Students need to know that inappropriate material exists on the Internet and that someone might attempt to exploit them through Internet conversations. They need to know what content and situations they are to avoid. It is especially important that younger students be informed in concrete terms of behaviors they should avoid.

For a summary of some common rules as they might be presented to younger students, see "Focus: Rules for the Safe and Appropriate Use of the Internet." Classroom teachers should take the time to present and explain guidelines of this sort. In addition, it is helpful to post them in a visible location.

Acceptable-Use Policies

Schools need to establish clear standards that go beyond a simple list of rules. It is useful to formalize such guidelines in a written document, often called an acceptable-use policy (AUP).

Functions of an AUP

An AUP typically establishes expectations for how students and sometimes faculty will use school resources, procedures they are expected to follow, and consequences when expectations and procedures are violated. If you are a student, we suggest you search through your room to find your institution's guidelines for student behavior. This document may be referred to as the "Code of Student Life" or some similar title. Somewhere within this document you will find policies relating to the use of computer and Internet resources and a general explanation of various actions the institution can take against you for violating these and other stated policies.

An AUP for a K–12 institution accomplishes similar goals, but with these differences:

- It is likely to exist as an independent document.
- It will emphasize instructional as well as regulatory goals.
- It will recognize that K–12 students are minors.

Rather than reproducing a complete AUP, we outline some of the issues that typical AUPs address. Finding real examples of AUPs is easy: They are commonly included as webpages within school websites. If you use any search engine and request "acceptable-use policy," you will find many examples.

AUPs usually address the general use of technology in schools. Here we focus just on issues concerning the Internet. Typical AUPs treat the following subjects:

Issues that AUPs address

- *Purpose.* Student learning is the reason the school provides access to technology. Many AUPs begin by explaining that access to the World Wide Web, e-mail, and other Internet tools is provided in order to help students learn. This statement of purpose establishes boundaries that can then be used to set priorities or exclude certain activities. Playing online games, for instance, may be perfectly good fun, but such behavior is outside the established priorities. After connecting Internet resources with valued educational experiences, the statement of purpose often continues by explaining that certain rules and regulations are necessary to ensure that learning occurs in a safe and productive environment.
- *Access to services.* Most AUPs explain the services the district provides and what is necessary for students to use these services. For example, the school may make the Web available to all students, but students in the elementary grades may have access to e-mail only through a common class account. Middle-school and high-school students might be given individual e-mail accounts, provided the student and parents sign a user agreement form.
- *Unacceptable behaviors.* After making the point that many uses of technology are a privilege and not a right, most AUPs list behaviors that are not allowed and indicate sanctions that may be applied if students engage in unacceptable behavior. The common areas of concern include personal safety; violations of system security or purposeful attempts to damage system functions or online content; academic violations such as plagiarism; purposeful efforts to view online materials identified as inappropriate; and harassment of other people. Sanctions typically involve loss of access privileges; in severe cases they may include more severe punishment, such as suspension or even criminal prosecution.
- *Position on privacy.* Will school officials examine student or faculty e-mail, monitor websites that have been visited from a particular computer, or open data files saved in student accounts? If such practices are regarded as necessary, the AUP should state clearly that all accounts are considered school property and may be examined to ensure safe and responsible use.

Supervision

Monitoring students as you participate

The clear statement of rules and careful documentation of policies are not enough. Classroom teachers, librarians, and other school staff members need

Focus

Rules for the Safe and Appropriate Use of the Internet

Following are some sample rules for Internet use, worded as they might be presented to students. The wording could be adjusted depending on the age of the students.

1. I will not reveal personal information in e-mail or chat messages. Personal information includes:
   • My home address
   • My home phone number
   • The names of my parents, my teacher, and other students in my class
   • The name and address of my school
     Note: Schools may also decide that students should not reveal their full names, perhaps using only a first name and last initial, such as "Cindy G."
   If I am asked for any item of personal information, I will ask my teacher what I should do.
2. I will never agree to talk on the telephone or meet in person with anyone I met through chat or e-mail without first talking with my teacher.
3. I will tell my teacher if I find any information that I should not see or that makes me feel uncomfortable.
4. I will not share my e-mail password with anyone, including my best friends.
5. I will not make fun of other students in e-mail messages. If anyone sends me an e-mail message that makes me feel uncomfortable or angry, I will not respond. I will report e-mail messages that make me feel uncomfortable to my teacher.
6. I will not visit websites that are inappropriate for school use. If I accidentally load this kind of site, I will leave it immediately. If I have questions about whether I should be looking at certain websites, I will ask my teacher or librarian. I understand that viewing inappropriate sites may result in the loss of Internet privileges.

Source: Based on Magid (1998).

to be willing to monitor students' use of computers and the Internet. Teachers should participate actively when students work with technology. Supervision is yet another reason to remain involved, not sit at a desk while students under your charge do their work.

This combination of honest concern, clear standards, and appropriate supervision is how schools customarily teach and maintain appropriate behavior. Although absolute protection cannot be guaranteed, these measures do seem a reasonable response to the potential dangers.

Summary

This chapter examines several issues under the general heading of the responsible use of technology. Accepting responsibility is a matter of acknowledging, understanding, and meeting obligations to the laws of our society, to parents and students, and to our colleagues.

Educational equity defines responsibilities educators have in providing fair and equal experiences for all students. Not all students have equal opportunities to use technology. Schools with a large number of less affluent students do not allow equal access to the Internet and engage students in different technology-supported learning experiences. Federal programs are beginning to address the issue of access, but access alone will not provide equal experiences. Varying amounts of teacher preparation and support, along with assumptions regarding what type of experiences students from less affluent homes require, appear to be at the root of differences in what students experience. Researchers also indicate concern regarding differences in how males and females are involved with technology in educational settings. The communication, inquiry, and construction tasks the Internet allows may contribute to an improvement in female interest in technology. Students with physical, sensory, or cognitive limitations also may be at a disadvantage in taking advantage of Internet resources and experiences. In many cases, adaptations in hardware and software can provide improved access and opportunity. A more thoughtful approach to web design can also be helpful.

Responsible Internet users respect copyright law. Both teachers and students need to know what resources they can take from online sources or present online as part of instructional or learning activities. Understanding what are called fair use guidelines is not always easy, and a familiarity with general principles and a willingness to ask permission are what must be expected of a responsible user.

Recognizing the potential dangers of Internet access and experiences and taking steps to protect students against such dangers are other responsibilities that educators must accept. Educators can direct students toward safe areas of the Internet, employ filtering systems that provide some barriers to the display of inappropriate materials, and directly intervene with students through supervision and instruction in safety guidelines.

Reflecting on Chapter 10

ACTIVITIES

■ Investigate some of the equity issues discussed in this chapter. Check out a general-purpose computer magazine from the library and make a tally sheet to evaluate the advertisements. How many white males appear in the ads? How many women? How many members of minority groups? Try to classify the role that each person in the ads plays. Is one group consistently more active or more in control than others? Be prepared to compare your observations with those of your classmates.

■ Write a "Responsible User" contract that students and parents must sign before the student will be allowed an e-mail account.

■ Review the acceptable-use policies for several K–12 schools. You should be able to locate many AUPs through the use of any search engine. What areas are addressed consistently? Were issues raised in this chapter that are not mentioned in some of the AUPs you reviewed?

■ Try the following as a simulation of what visually impaired students experience when they use the Internet. First, modify the browser so that it does not display images. Second, use only the keyboard to explore the Web (use a Windows machine and the tab and return keys to select and follow links). Did you encounter pages that you could not comprehend? Were there situations in which you were unable to navigate?

■ Several software products are sold for the purpose of downloading individual pages or entire websites. On the basis of your interpretation of fair use, argue for or against the legality of using this software to collect resources for (1) personal scholarship, (2) access by your class within your classroom, and (3) worldwide access from a server located in your school.

KEY TERMS

community access center (p. 369)
Conference on Fair Use (CONFU) (p. 385)
copyright (p. 378)
digital divide (p. 366)
e-rate (p. 373)
fair use (p. 382)

license (p. 381)
plagiarism (p. 391)
screen reader software (p. 376)
site license (p. 381)
socioeconomic status (SES) (p. 366)
software piracy (p. 382)
TEACH Act (p. 385)

RESOURCES TO EXPAND YOUR KNOWLEDGE BASE

An expanded and frequently updated list of online resources is available on the website that accompanies this textbook.

Safe Areas of the Internet

Directories and Search Sites

Ask Jeeves for Kids was created as a version of Ask Jeeves for younger users. (**http://www.ajkids.com/**)
Yahooligans! was created by Yahoo! as a specialized and separate directory of sites for younger web users. (**http://yahooligans.yahoo.com/**)

Educational Content Databases and Content Lists

Blue Web'n, a database of "blue-ribbon" educational learning sites sponsored by Pacific Bell, provides access to reviewed, high-quality educational sites. (**http://www.kn.pacbell.com/wired/bluewebn/**)

Supervised Chat Environments

The Kidlink organization matches students from all over the world for e-mail and chat. The chat rooms are supervised. (**http://www.kidlink.org/**)

Teacher-Controlled E-mail

Gaggle provides a web-based e-mail service intended for K–12 users. There is a free version that includes advertising or a subscription service that is ad free. (**http://www.gaggle.net/**)

Filtering Internet Content

Internet Filtering and Control Products

Cyber Patrol: Available for the Windows and Macintosh platforms. SurfControl. (**http://www.cyberpatrol.com/**)
CYBERsitter: Available for the Windows platform. Solid Oak Software. (**http://www.cybersitter.com/**)
Net Nanny: Available for the Windows platform. Net Nanny Software International. (**http://www.netnanny.com/**)

Adaptive Software

Home Page Reader, a screen reader with special capabilities for Internet tasks, is available from IBM for the Windows operating system. (**http://www-3.ibm.com/able/solution_offerings/hpr.html**)
JAWS, a screen reader for the Windows operating system, is one of the most popular products for personal computers. It is available from Freedom Scientific. (**http://www.freedomscientific.com/**)

Guidelines for Accessible Webpages

World Wide Web Consortium. (1999). *Web content accessibility guidelines* [Online]. Available: **http://www.w3.org/TR/WAI-WEBCONTENT/** [May 2002].

Gender Equity

The American Association of University Women promotes education for gender equity. (**http://www.aauw.org/**)

Digital Divide

The Harvard Center for International Development and Massachusetts Institute of Technology cosponsor a website focused on the range of topics concerning the digital divide. (**http://www.digitaldivide.org/**)

Copying Television Programs for Classroom Use

Cable in the Classroom is a massive public service venture supported by a large number of national cable companies. This organization provides information on cable programming with educational relevance, supplemental materials to accompany selected programs, and information on programming made available with liberalized provisions for copying. Cable in the Classroom has an informative website. (**http://www.ciconline.com/**)

Plagiarism

Plagiarism.org offers a web-based service that allows instructors to compare a student paper against a database of papers available through the Internet. (**http://www.plagiarism.org/**)

Glossary

● ● ●

alignment The process of using standards to create consistency in what is emphasized in learning resources, instruction, and evaluation.

analog format Variations in a signal represented as continuous; a sweep secondhand in contrast to a digital clock.

analog modem A device that transforms a digital signal into an analog signal for transmission via telephone wires.

analog signal A signal having the capability of being represented by continuous values. For example, there is no set number of colors in the visible spectrum. One shade blends gradually into the next.

applet A small program that operates within a browser.

asynchronous (communication) Communication in which a message is sent at one time and received or read at a later time (for instance, e-mail).

authentic activity An activity that people perform in their daily lives.

automaticity Process by which well-learned skills are executed with minimal mental effort.

benchmarks Carefully selected examples of student performance that characterize specific levels of achievement. They are often used to exemplify what would be expected of students in meeting a standard at different grade levels (for example, fourth or eighth) but may also be used to establish other points along a scale of accomplishment.

Big Six A series of six activities involved in solving an information problem: (1) task definition, (2) information seeking, (3) location and access, (4) use of information, (5) synthesis, and (6) evaluation.

bitmapped (image) Represented as rows and columns of pixels in which each pixel is represented by a number to indicate color or shade.

blog A web publishing method in which participants use a standard browser to add comments to a self-expanding webpage (shortened from "web log").

branch A choice point that narrows and focuses the information available to the user.

branching tutorial Tutorial in which the sequence of content a learner encounters is determined by the quality of performance on the previous step.

browser Software used to connect to web servers and to display information on the local (client) computer.

build A presentation technique in which related items are revealed in succession to emphasize the significance of each idea.

bulleted chart A series of text statements arranged in a list format, often preceded by a bullet (•) for easy reading.

button A "hot spot" in a multimedia product that initiates an action when clicked.

calculator-based laboratory (CBL) An interface allowing a calculator to record data from probes.

case-based learning An approach in which students experience a series of realistic examples and supporting information as the means of presenting information to be learned.

CD-ROM *See* compact disc–read only memory.

cell Intersection of a row and a column in a spreadsheet; the point at which a number or formula is entered in the spreadsheet.

chat Form of telecommunications in which messages are exchanged in real time rather than stored for later reading.

client-server model A system design in which an individual's computer (the client) connects to a central computer (the server) to access certain resources. For example, the e-mail client software on your computer retrieves and sends messages by way of the server maintained by the company or institution that provides your e-mail service.

clipboard Computer memory buffer that can hold images and other information for convenient exchange among programs.

cognitive apprenticeship Learning within a relationship with a more expert practitioner of the skill to be learned.

cognitive load The various stresses imposed on short-term memory by individual capabilities, media resources, and learning tasks. When these stresses exceed the capacity of short-term memory, performance will deteriorate.

collaborative argumentation A form of structured online discussion in which participants offer proposals with supporting arguments, evaluate and compare the proposals, and then attempt to reach a consensus.

community access center A facility providing public access to computers, software, and the Internet (for example, a library).

compact disc–read only memory (CD-ROM) A high-capacity digital storage system. A CD-ROM disc can be read by a computer or other device but cannot be used for recording new data. In contrast, a CD-R disc can record new data, and a CD-RW disc can be rewritten multiple times.

compression Conversion to a file format that takes less disk space and consequently can be transmitted over the Internet more quickly.

computer-assisted instruction (CAI) Computer program intended to provide instructional experiences directly to the student.

computer-based instruction (CBI) *See* computer-assisted instruction (CAI).

computer-mediated communication (CMC) A form of communication that requires the exchange of information by computer, usually through the Internet.

conference Online discussion group.

Conference on Fair Use (CONFU) A series of meetings on copyright issues that produced guidelines in 1997 for teacher- or student-created multimedia and for distance education.

constructivism Theory proposing that students create a personal understanding (construct their own knowledge) by interpreting their experiences.

content standard A definition of what a student is expected to learn.

cooperative learning Situation in which students work together to accomplish an instructional goal.

copy To copy data from the active document to be temporarily stored in computer memory.

copyright The body of legal rights related to the reproduction, distribution, and performance of original works.

critical thinking Solving problems by gathering and interpreting information; as an instructional approach, it emphasizes the development of analytical skills that can be applied to a wide range of subject matter.

cross-platform Capable of functioning on computers with different operating systems, for instance, Microsoft Windows and Apple Macintosh computers.

cursor Symbol, usually a line or square, displayed on the computer screen indicating where the next symbol entered will appear.

cut To remove data from the active document for temporary storage in computer memory.

database Application program allowing the organization, storage, and search of information.

data logger A self-contained data collection device that includes a sensor, interface, and battery.

declarative knowledge Stored verbal information and facts.

delete (in word processing) To remove text at the location of the cursor.

design A tool developed to accomplish a purpose, or the process of creating that tool.

desktop publishing Programs that facilitate the entry and positioning of text and graphics to control precisely the appearance of printed documents.

dialog box A box that appears on a computer screen, on top of the information already displayed on the screen, and requests the user to provide input by entering text or clicking on a button.

digital divide The gap between those who are able to benefit from computer technology and those who are not. The phrase applies to group differences such as gender, socioeconomic status, and ability, and to even broader distinctions involving international economic and political differences.

digital format Recording format in which information is stored as a series of numbers, allowing exact duplication of the original information.

digital subscriber line (DSL) A digital technology for moving large amounts of digital information through existing copper phone lines. This is an alternative to the use of traditional modems, which send an analog signal over phone lines.

digital video disc (DVD) A storage method capable of putting from 4.7 GB to 17 GB of information on a disc the size of a CD-ROM. DVD is referred to as digital versatile disc in some sources to indicate the capacity to store any type of digital information.

discovery learning A method in which students discover important principles on their own.

document In multimedia creation, one multimedia file.

domain name A name that indicates a computer's address on the Internet; an easier-to-remember equivalent of the IP number.

dots per inch (dpi) Term describing the resolution of printers, monitors, and scanners. The use of the term *dot* can be confusing because the smallest elements a scanner can detect or a monitor can display are called pixels.

draw program A graphics program using object-oriented images rather than bitmaps. Mathematical descriptions are used to represent these objects.

drill Computer application designed to facilitate factual memorization.

dual-coding theory Theory proposing that imagery and verbal information are stored in different ways and that information stored in both forms will be easier to retrieve.

DVD-RAM A rewritable DVD format available to computer users.

edutainment Term for gamelike software that offers educational benefits.

electronic mail (e-mail) Personal message sent by the user of one computer to the user of another.

electronic portfolio A collection of artifacts, reflections, and artifact-related assessments assembled by an individual student.

embellished document A text document enhanced with graphics, video segments, or sound.

endorsement Official recognition that an individual has satisfied a designated set of requirements.

episodic memory Memory for an event usually connected with a specific time and place.

e-rate A subsidy for the costs of providing Internet connections to schools and libraries, established by the Telecommunications Act of 1996.

exploratory environment Setting providing elements for the learner to manipulate and learn as the result of this manipulation.

fair use Guidelines describing the conditions under which the copying of intellectual property is appropriate.

fidelity Extent to which a simulation mimics reality.

field (in a database) Category defined by the user of a database to contain a specified type of information, such as age, name, zip code.

file (in a database) Complete collection of related database records.

file transfer protocol (FTP) Standards allowing the transfer of files to and from a host computer.

FireWire A high-speed hardware system for connecting a computer with peripheral devices, such as a digital camcorder.

flash memory A memory storage device that retains information over an extended period of time in special memory chips.

font Standardized design of characters that determines the appearance of text (for example, Helvetica, Times).

formatting Determining the physical appearance of a document.

forum Online discussion group in which participants contribute comments to be read by all participants.

frame In a multimedia document, one image in a video or one screen image.

framework An educational document organizing standards, benchmarks, and instructional practices.

game Program that emphasizes competition and enjoyment. Certain games have educational benefits as well.

geocaching An activity in which enthusiasts hide or locate small "treasures" using the capabilities of global positioning technology.

Geographic Information System (GIS) Software for mapping data to precise map locations.

Global Positioning System (GPS) Hardware for determining longitude, latitude, and altitude based on data from multiple satellites.

graphic design The arrangement or layout of information on the computer screen, especially as it relates to informativeness, interpretability, and interest.

graphic user interface (GUI) System for interacting with a computer based on the manipulation of icons rather than the input of typed commands.

grid Method for organizing the computer screen using patterns of lines.

group investigation Cooperative learning method in which group members develop a project related to a general theme proposed by the teacher.

header In an e-mail message, the top portion that contains, at a minimum, the address for the sender, the address for the receiver, and a topic for the e-mail.

hierarchical design A form of website design in which the content is organized as a system of categories and subcategories.

higher-order thinking Thinking that is complex, effortful, self-regulated, and judgmental.

hypercomposition A form of composition that involves multiple media types and allows for nonlinear examination.

hypermedia Multimedia that a user can examine in a flexible, nonlinear fashion. The user can typically move from one information source to several others and can control which of these options to take.

hypertext Text that can be examined in a nonlinear manner. The user can typically move from one segment of text to several others by responding to options made available by the computer program controlling the text presentation.

hypertext markup language (HTML) A set of special codes and tags inserted in a document that inform a web browser how to display hypermedia elements (for example, text, graphics) and how to take specific actions (for example, branch to another World Wide Web document).

hypertext transfer protocol (HTTP) The protocol used by the World Wide Web for transmitting pages; abbreviated as "http" at the beginning of a website address.

icon A small image often used consistently to represent a specific program action or category of information.

incremental advantage Improvement due to increased efficiency.

individual accountability Requirement of cooperative learning demanding that individuals must achieve for the team to achieve.

inert knowledge Knowledge that students have acquired but fail to use.

insert (in word processing) To enter text at the position of the cursor.

instant messaging Synchronous communication between two individuals via the Internet.

instructional resource Information resource that has been prepared specifically for an instructional purpose.

integrated services digital network (ISDN) A digital technology for moving large amounts of digital information through existing copper phone lines. An alternative to the use of traditional modems, which send an analog signal over phone lines.

Internet International web of computer networks.

Internet service provider (ISP) Company providing individuals with modem access to the Internet.

IP number For every computer with a permanent connection to the Internet, the number designating its precise Internet address.

jaggies Staircase effect in the production of lines that are not perfectly horizontal or vertical. Jaggies appear when the individual units used to construct lines are large enough to be visible.

justification (of text) Alignment of lines of text to form a straight margin (for example, left-justified).

knowledge as design Knowledge that has been applied or adapted to a purpose.

learning community The collaborative group formed when teachers and students join together to work on long-term projects.

license An agreement that grants specific rights concerning the copying or reproduction of copyrighted material.

linear multimedia presentation Multimedia information presented in a standard sequence; a slide show.

linear tutorial Form of instruction in which all learners go through the same material in the same sequence.

link In the network model of memory, any connection between nodes.

listserv An alternative term for a mailing list.

list server Computer server hosting a mailing list.

local area network (LAN) Interconnected computers in one location, such as a school building or office.

long-term memory (LTM) Memory store allowing virtually permanent storage.

lossless compression File compression that relies totally on increased efficiency, generating a smaller file without reduction in image quality.

lossy compression File compression that approximates rather than exactly matches the original; produces a smaller file in which data and precision are lost during the process.

lurking Observing an e-mail or chat session without participating.

mailing list (*see also* listserv) Telecommunications process in which an e-mail message is sent to a designated address and then resent to every member subscribing to the list.

map Device that identifies the components of a hypermedia presentation and shows the main links among components.

margin Distance between the edge of text and the edge of the paper.

master slide The common color and visual elements held constant across all slides of a presentation.

meaningful learning Learning in which new experiences are linked with information already stored in long-term memory.

megabyte Approximately 1 million bytes. The capacity of a high-density floppy disk is between 1 and 1.5 megabytes.

menu List of available options.

metacognition Knowledge about your own thinking and learning.

metacognitive control functions Behaviors involved in planning, regulating, and evaluating mental behaviors.

metacognitive knowledge Knowledge about how tasks are performed, what makes tasks easy or difficult, and one's personal skills and limitations.

microcomputer-based laboratory (**MBL**) An interface allowing a computer to record data from probes.

mindtool A tool that encourages problem solving and learning by freeing the learner from tasks that require attention or significant storage capacity; some educators believe that powerful computer tools can serve this function.

modem Computer peripheral device allowing information to be exchanged over a telephone line between computers.

multimedia Communication format integrating several media (text, audio, visual); most commonly implemented with a computer.

navigation User-controlled movement through hypermedia content.

netiquette Conventions for appropriate online conduct.

network model A model of human memory representing the contexts of memory as interconnected nodes of information.

node Unit of information; an idea, picture, or sound.

object Individual components in an authoring environment that can be combined by the author/programmer to create a product.

object-oriented image Image in which objects are represented using mathematical equations rather than as maps of pixel colors.

online tutorial An Internet-based activity intended to deliver direct instruction mostly through the presentation of information and simple methods for the evaluation of understanding.

paint program Computer program designed to create and manipulate graphic information.

pasting Inserting data stored in the memory of the computer into an active document.

pedagogical content knowledge Instructional skills that are unique to the teaching of a discipline.

performance standard A definition of an acceptable level of achievement in terms of proficiency in performing an actual task.

personal data assistant (**PDA**) A hand-held device, typically pen operated, capable of data storage and some basic computation

pixel The smallest element a scanner can detect or a monitor can display.

plagiarism Representing someone else's work as your own.

plug-in An application that works within a browser to process certain types of files.

podcast Making audio files available in a way that allows the files to be downloaded for convenient listening.

point-to-point A pattern of communication involving information sent between two computers rather than among many computers.

point-to-point protocol (**PPP**) One of the standard protocols used for modem transmissions over the Internet.

portable document format (**PDF**) A format developed to allow sharing and display of documents across operating systems and when the application used to create the original document may not be available.

practice Computer application designed to facilitate the development of skill fluency.

presentation software A form of tool software intended for use in creating and delivering formal group presentations.

primary source A general information source prepared without consideration for student needs.

probe Device built to measure variations in a specific variable (for example, temperature, pH).

problem solving Thinking processes involved in overcoming an obstacle in order to reach a goal.

procedural knowledge Memory of how to do something.

protocol A set of rules and conventions governing how devices on a network exchange information.

query A request made to a search engine.

QuickTime Format allowing digital movies and sounds to be compressed, edited, and played on a computer.

QuickTime VR A three-dimensional, virtual reality format based on QuickTime.

reception learning A method in which concepts, principles, and rules to be learned are presented directly to the students.

record Meaningful collection of database fields representing one unit of storage.

resolution The amount of data stored in an image file measured in pixels per inch.

rote learning Learning with little attention to meaning.

sampling frequency Number of times per second, in kilohertz (kHz), that digitized sound is produced. More frequent sampling provides more realistic reproduction of original sound.

scaffolding External support for learning or problem solving.

scanner A device that captures a bitmapped representation of an image.

screen capture The process of saving the image appearing on the computer monitor as a graphics file.

screen reader software Software that reads the text and other screen information (for example, menu options) for visually impaired users.

search engine A program, used by a search service, that checks a user's request against the database of webpages tracked by the service and returns a list of matches.

select To identify material to which some action (such as underlining or deletion) is to be applied.

sensor A device capable of measuring a specific characteristic of the physical environment.

sequential design A form of website design in which the content is organized so that each element leads directly to the next in logical sequence.

short-term memory (STM) The limited capacity and duration store containing the thoughts, ideas, and images of which a person is aware; also known as working memory.

simulation Computer program that imitates the key elements of realistic experiences.

site license License offering certain privileges to users at a designated site; for instance, allowing a school district to make a number of copies of software from a single original.

slide show Linear multimedia; a fixed sequence of images, text segments, sounds, or video segments.

socioeconomic status (SES) A measure of prestige based on income, education, and occupation.

software piracy Copying software to avoid payment or without the appropriate approval.

spell checker Word processing feature that checks for spelling errors.

spreadsheet Application program resembling a ledger sheet, allowing numerical data to be entered into cells arranged as rows and columns. Calculations can be performed on these data by attaching formulas to cells.

standards Expectations for knowledge, performance capabilities, or the availability of resources.

storyboarding Process of roughing out the sequence of displays and activities to be incorporated into new instructional software or into a presentation.

streaming A web-based technology allowing the continuous reception of audio and/or video information.

style (of characters) Standardized modification in the appearance of text, such as underlining or italicizing.

synchronous (communication) Communication in which a message is sent and received almost simultaneously (for instance, Internet-based chat).

tab Predefined insertion point established in word processing. Setting a tab stop allows the user to move the insertion point to a specified column.

tag An HTML command.

task specialization methods Cooperative learning methods in which the goal is cooperative accomplishment of a task requiring the application of what group members have learned.

TCP/IP (transmission control protocol/Internet protocol) Standards that allow different computers to transfer data over the Internet.

TEACH Act Legislation intended to define the role that copyrighted digital media can play in distance education.

team rewards Recognition for a team's success in cooperative learning.

telementoring The use of the Internet to create a mentoring relationship.

template Organizational plan for a database or spreadsheet.

text object A framed segment of text treated as a unit by certain functions of word processing or desktop publishing programs.

thread A series of linked messages consisting of replies to previous messages.

thumbnail A small version of a larger image, often used on the Web as a link to a page containing the full-size image.

transfer Application of skills or knowledge learned in one situation to a different situation.

transformational advantage Improvement due to a qualitatively superior method.

translator A small utility added to an application that allows the conversion of files created with another program for use in the host application.

transmission control protocol/Internet protocol *See* TCP/IP.

tutorial A learning activity in which the computer primarily presents new information to the student and provides opportunities for the student to become proficient with this information.

universal resource locator (**URL**) An address for an FTP or World Wide Web file on the Internet.

user interface The way a computer application presents itself to the user; the means by which the user interacts with the contents of the application.

video projector Special hardware that projects a screen image onto a large screen.

virtual reality The simulation of an environment that can be experienced visually as having width, height, and depth and in some cases can allow interaction or manipulation.

virtual reality modeling language (**VRML**) A computer language used to create a virtual reality environment.

web design A form of website design that establishes a complex set of connections among webpages.

WebQuest A document (usually prepared as a webpage) consisting of a brief introduction to a topic, the description of an inquiry task related to that topic, a set of primary web resources students can use in performing the task, and suggestions for how students might use the web resources.

word processing Application allowing the entry, manipulation, and storage of text and sometimes graphics.

word wrap Characteristic of word processing programs allowing text that would extend beyond the right margin of a page to automatically move to the beginning of a new line.

working memory *See* short-term memory.

World Wide Web (**WWW**) System providing access to Internet resources based on hypertext-like documents.

writing process approach Method of writing instruction emphasizing planning, drafting, editing, revising, and publishing. This method emphasizes rewriting with guidance from the teacher and peers.

zone of proximal development Skills an individual can perform with some assistance.

References

Abdal-Haqq, I. (2001). Locating quality web sites: Rules, criteria, standards. *Technology Leadership News, 5* (1), 1–3.

Adaptive Computer Technology Centre. (1998). *Accessible Web page design* [Online]. Available: http://www.utoronto.ca/atrc/tutorials/actable/index.html

Albrecht, B., & Firedrake, G. (1998). Grabbing data: What you need to log and use real-world data. *Learning and Leading with Technology, 26* (1), 36–40.

Albrecht, B., & Firedrake, G. (1999). Blowin' hot and cold about my data. *Learning and Leading with Technology, 26* (5), 32–36.

Alessi, S. (1988). Fidelity in the design of instructional simulations. *Journal of Computer-Based Instruction, 15* (2), 40–47.

Alessi, S., & Trollip, S. (2001). *Multimedia for learning: Methods and development* (3rd ed.). Boston: Allyn & Bacon.

Althaus, S. (1997). Computer-mediated communication in the university classroom: An experiment with on-line discussions. *Communication Education, 46* (3), 158–174.

American Association of School Librarians and Association for Educational Communications and Technology. (1998). *Information power: Building partnerships for learning.* Atlanta: American Library Association and Association for Educational Communication and Technology. Available: http://www.ala.org/aasl/index.html

American Association of University Women Educational Foundation. (2000). *Tech-savvy: Educating girls in the new computer age.* Washington, DC: American Association of University Women Educational Foundation.

American Library Association. (2002). CIPA web site [Online]. Available: http://www.ala.org/cipa

American Psychological Association. (2001). *Publication manual* (5th ed.). Retrieved November 27, 2004, from http://www.apastyle.org/elecgeneral.html

American Psychological Association Board of Educational Affairs (APA/BEA). (1995). *Learner-centered psychological principles: A framework for school redesign and reform.* Washington, DC: American Psychological Association.

Anderson, J. (1976). *Language, memory, and thought.* Hillsdale, NJ: Erlbaum.

Anderson, J. (1983). *The architecture of cognition.* Cambridge, MA: Harvard University Press.

Ausubel, D. (1963). *The psychology of meaningful learning.* New York: Grune & Stratton.

Baker, L. (1985). Differences in the standards used by college students to evaluate their comprehension of expository prose. *Reading Research Quarterly, 20,* 297–313.

Bangert-Drowns, R. (1993). The word processor as an instructional tool: A meta-analysis of word processing in writing instruction. *Review of Educational Research, 63* (1), 69–93.

Bangert-Drowns, R. L., Hurley, M. M., & Wilkinson, B. (2004). The effects of school-based writing-to-learn interventions on academic achievement: A meta-analysis. *RER, 74,* 29–58.

Barrett, H. (2000). Create your own electronic portfolio: Using off-the-shelf software to showcase your own or student work. *Learning and Leading with Technology, 27* (7), 14–21.

Barrett, H. (2004). Differentiating electronic portfolios and online assessment management systems [Online]. Paper presented at the Society for Information Technology in Teacher Education Conference. Available: http://electronicportfolios.org/systems/concerns.html

Barron, B. (2000). Problem solving in video-based microworlds: Collaborative and individual outcomes of high-achieving sixth-grade students. *Journal of Educational Psychology, 92,* 391–398.

Bartz, W., & Singer, M. (1996). The programmatic implications of foreign language standards. In R. Lafayette (Ed.), *National standards: A catalyst for reform* (pp. 139–168). Lincolnwood, IL: National Textbook.

Bayraktar, S. (2001–2002). A meta-analysis of the effectiveness of computer-assisted instruction in science education. *Journal of Research on Technology in Education, 34* (2), 173–188.

Bebell, D., O'Dwyer, L., Russell, M., & Seeley, K. (2004). Estimating the effect of computer use at home and in school on school achievement [Online]. Paper presented at the annual meeting of the National Educational Computing Conference. Available: http://center.uoregon.edu/ISTE/NECC2004/handout_files_live/KEY_190226/neccachieve.pdf

Bebell, D., Russell, M., & O'Dwyer, L. (2004). Measuring teachers' technology uses: Why multiple-measures are more revealing. *Journal of Research on Technology in Education, 37,* 45–63.

Becker, H. (1999). *Internet use by teachers: Conditions of professional use and teacher-directed student use* [Online]. Available: http://www.crito.uci.edu/TLC/findings/Internet-Use/startpage.htm

Becker, H., & Ravitz, J. (1998). The equity threat of promising innovation: Pioneering Internet-connected schools. *Journal of Educational Computing Research, 19* (1), 1–26.

Becker, H., & Ravitz, J. (1999). The influence of computer and Internet use on teachers' pedagogical practices and perceptions. *Journal of Research on Computing in Education, 31* (4), 356–384.

Berge, Z. (1995). Facilitating computer conferencing: Recommendations from the field. *Educational Technology, 35* (1), 22–30.

Beyer, B. (1988). *Developing a thinking skills program.* Boston: Allyn & Bacon.

Black, S., Levin, J., Mehan, H., & Quinn, C. (1983). Real and non-real time interaction: Unraveling multiple threads of discourse. *Discourse Processes, 6,* 59–75.

Bransford, J., Sherwood, R., Hasselbring, T., Kinzer, C., & Williams, S. (1990). Anchored instruction: Why we need it and how technology can help. In D. Nix & R. Spiro (Eds.), *Cognition, education and multimedia: Exploring ideas in high technology* (pp. 115–141). Hillsdale, NJ: Erlbaum.

Bransford, J., & Stein, B. (1984). *The IDEAL problem solver.* New York: Freeman.

Brant, G., Hooper, E., & Sugrue, B. (1991). Which comes first—the simulation or the lecture? *Journal of Educational Computing Research, 7* (4), 469–481.

Brooks, J., & Brooks, J. (1999). *In search of understanding: The case for constructivist classrooms.* Alexandria, VA: Association for Supervision and Curriculum Development.

Brown, A. (1981). Metacognition: The development of selective attention strategies for learning from texts. In M. Kamil (Ed.), *Directions in reading: Research and instruction* (pp. 21–43). Washington, DC: National Reading Conference.

Brown, A. (1987). Metacognition, executive control, self-rejection and other more mysterious mechanisms. In F. Weinert & R. Kluwe (Eds.), *Metacognition, motivation, and understanding* (pp. 65–116). Hillsdale, NJ: Erlbaum.

Brown, A. (1992). Design experiments: Theoretical and methodological challenges in creating complex interventions in classroom settings. *Journal of the Learning Sciences, 2* (2), 141–178.

Brown, J., Collins, A., & Duguid, P. (1989). Situated cognition and the culture of learning. *Educational Researcher, 18,* 32–42.

Bruce, B., & Levin, J. (1997). Educational technology: Media for inquiry, communication, construction and expression. *Journal of Educational Computing Research, 17* (1), 79–102.

Bruning, R. H., Schraw, G. J., Norby, M. M., & Ronning, R. R. (2004). *Cognitive psychology and instruction* (4th ed.). Upper Saddle River, NJ: Merrill Prentice Hall.

Burke, E. (1993). Copyright catechism. *Educom Review, 28* (5), 46–49.

Bushweller, K. (1999a). *Digital deception: The Internet makes cheating easier than ever* [Online]. Available: http://www.electronic-school.com/199903/0399f2.html

Bushweller, K. (1999b). Generation of cheaters. *American School Board Journal, 186* (4), 24–30.

Business Software Alliance. (2002). *Anti-piracy* [Online]. Available: http://www.bsa.org/freetools/consumers/swandlaw_c.phtml

Carver, S., Lehrer, R., Connell, T., & Erickson, J. (1992). Learning by hypermedia design: Issues of assessment and implementation. *Educational Psychologist, 27* (3), 385–404.

Center for the Digital Future. (2004). *Surveying the digital future: Ten years, ten trends* [Online]. University of Southern California Annenberg School Center for the Digital Future. Available: http://www.digitalcenter.org/downloads/ DigitalFutureReport-Year4-2004.pdf

Center for Media Education. (2001). *TeenSites.com: A field guide to the new digital landscape* [Online]. Available: http://www.cme.org/teenstudy/ index.html

Champagne, A., Gunstone, F., & Klopfer, L. (1985). Instructional consequences of students' knowledge about physical phenomena. In L. West & A. Pines (Eds.), *Cognitive structure and conceptual change* (pp. 163–188). Orlando, FL: Academic Press.

Children's Internet Protection Act. (2001). [Online]. Available: http://ftp.fcc.gov/Bureaus/ Common_Carrier/Orders/2001/fcc01120.doc

Chomsky, C. (1990). Books on videodisc: Computers, video, and reading aloud to children. In D. Nix & R. Spiro (Eds.), *Cognition, education and multimedia: Exploring ideas in high technology* (pp. 31–47). Hillsdale, NJ: Erlbaum.

Christmann, E., Badgett, J., & Lucking, R. (1997). Progressive comparison of the effects of computer-assisted instruction on the academic achievement of secondary students. *Journal of Research on Computing in Education, 29,* 325–336.

Clark, R. (1985). Confounding in educational computing research. *Journal of Educational Computing Research, 1,* 137–148.

Clement, J. (1983). A conceptual model discussed by Galileo and used intuitively by physics students. In D. Gentner & A. Stevens (Eds.), *Mental models* (pp. 206–251). Hillsdale, NJ: Erlbaum.

Cochran-Smith, M. (1991). Word processing and writing in elementary classrooms: A critical review of related literature. *Review of Educational Research, 61* (1), 107–155.

Cochran-Smith, M., Paris, C., & Kahn, J. (1991). *Learning to write differently: Beginning writers and word processing.* Norwood, NJ: Ablex.

Cognition and Technology Group. (1990). Anchored instruction and its relationship to situated cognition. *Educational Researcher, 19* (6), 2–10.

Cognition and Technology Group. (1992). The Jasper Series as an example of anchored instruction: Theory, program description and assessment data. *Educational Psychologist, 27* (3), 291–315.

Cognition and Technology Group. (1996). Multimedia environments for enhanced learning in mathematics. In S. Vosniadou, E. De Corte, & R. Glaser (Eds.), *International perspectives on the design of technology supported learning environments* (pp. 285–305). Hillsdale, NJ: Erlbaum.

Cohen, M., & Riel, M. (1989). The effect of distant audiences on students' writing. *American Educational Research Journal, 26* (2), 143–150.

Collins, A., & Quillian, M. (1969). Retrieval time from semantic memory. *Journal of Verbal Learning and Verbal Behavior, 8,* 240–247.

CONFU. (1997a). *Educational fair use proposals for distance learning* [Online]. Available: http://www .ninch.org/ISSUES/COPYRIGHT/FAIR_USE_ EDUCATION/CONFU/DistanceLearning.html

CONFU. (1997b). *Fair use guidelines for educational multimedia* [Online]. Available: http://www .ninch.cni.org/ISSUES/COPYRIGHT/FAIR_ USE_EDUCATION/CONFU/Multimedia.html

Cooper, J., & Weaver, K. D. (2003). *Gender and computers.* Mahwah, NJ: Erlbaum.

Costa, A. (1990). Teacher behaviors that promote discussion. In W. Wilen (Ed.), *Teaching and learning through discussion* (pp. 45–77). Springfield, IL: Charles Thomas.

Covey, P. (1990). *A right to die? The case of Dax Cowart.* Paper presented at the annual meeting of the AERA, Boston, MA.

Crews, K. D. (2002). *New copyright law for distance education: The meaning and importance of the TEACH Act* [Online]. Available: http:// www.ala.org/ala/washoff/WOissues/copyrightb/ distanceed/distanceeducation.htm

Cuban, L. (2001). *Oversold and underused: Computers in the classroom.* Cambridge, MA: Harvard University Press.

Cuban, L., Kirkpatrick, H., & Peck, C. (2001). High access and low use of technologies in high school classrooms: Explaining an apparent paradox. *American Educational Research Journal, 38* (4), 813–834.

Culp, K. M., Honey, M., & Mandinach, E. (2003). *A retrospective on twenty years of education technology policy* [Online]. Available: http://www .nationaledtechplan.org/participate/20years.pdf

Daiute, C. (1983). The computer as stylus and audience. *College Composition and Communication, 34,* 134–145.

Daiute, C., & Taylor, R. (1981). Computers and the

improvement of writing. *Association for Computing Machinery Proceedings* (pp. 83–88).

Day, J. (1986). Teaching summarization skills. *Cognition and Instruction, 3,* 193–210.

de Jong, T., & van Joolingen, W. (1998). Scientific discovery learning with computer simulations of conceptual domains. *Review of Educational Research, 68,* 179–201.

Department of Education. (1998). *Discounted telecommunication services for schools and libraries* [Online]. Available: http://www.ed.gov/Technology/comm-mit.html

D'Ignazio, F. (1990). Restructuring knowledge: Opportunities for classroom learning in the 1990s. *Computing Teacher, 18* (1), 22–25.

D'Ignazio, F. (1996). Minimalist multimedia: Authoring on the World Wide Web. *Learning and Leading with Technology, 23* (8), 49–51.

Dillon, A., & Gabbard, R. (1998). Hypermedia as an educational technology: A review of the quantitative research literature on learner comprehension, control, and style. *Review of Educational Research, 68* (3), 322–349.

Dodge, B. (1995). *Some thoughts about WebQuests.* Available: http://edweb.sdsu.edu/courses/edtec596/about_webquests.html

Doherty, K., & Orlofsky, G. (2001). Student survey says. *Education Week, 20* (35), 45–48.

Doyle, C. (1999). *Information literacy in an information society: A concept for the information age* (2nd ed.). Collingdale, PA: DIANE.

Duffy, T., & Bednar, A. (1991, September). Attempting to come to grips with alternative perspectives. *Educational Technology, 32,* 12–15.

Dunkin, M., & Biddle, B. (1974). *The study of teaching.* New York: Holt, Rinehart & Winston.

Edelson, D. (1998). Learning from stories: An architecture for Socratic case-based teaching. In R. Schank (Ed.), *Inside multi-media case-based instruction* (pp. 103–174). Mahwah, NJ: Erlbaum.

Eisenberg, M., & Berkowitz, R. (1990). *Information problem-solving: The big six skills approach to library and information skills instruction.* Norwood, NJ: Ablex.

Ennis, R. (1987). A taxonomy of critical thinking dispositions and abilities. In J. Baron & R. Sternberg (Eds.), *Teaching thinking skills: Theory and practice* (pp. 9–26). San Francisco: Freeman.

Erikson, J., & Lehrer, R. (1998). The evolution of critical standards as students design hypermedia documents. *Journal of the Learning Sciences,* 351–386.

Erthal, M. (1998). Who should teach keyboarding and when should it be taught? *Business Education Forum, 53* (1), 36–37.

Federal Communications Commission (FCC). (1997). Report and order in the matter of Federal-State Joint Board on Universal Service [Online]. Available: http://www.fcc.gov/ccb/universal_service/fcc97157/97157.html

Flavell, J. (1987). Speculations about the nature and development of metacognition. In F. Weinert & R. Kluwe (Eds.), *Metacognition, motivation, and understanding* (pp. 21–30). Hillsdale, NJ: Erlbaum.

Fletcher-Flinn, C., & Gravatt, B. (1995). The efficacy of computer-assisted instruction (CAI): A meta-analysis. *Journal of Educational Computing Research, 12* (3), 219–242.

Flower, L., & Hayes, J. (1981). A cognitive process theory of writing. *College Composition and Communication, 32,* 365–387.

Fritz, M. (1992). Be juris-prudent. *CBT Directions, 5* (2), 6, 8–10.

Gagne, E. (1985). *The cognitive psychology of school learning.* Boston: Little, Brown.

Gagne, E., Yekovich, C., & Yekovich, F. (1993). *The cognitive psychology of school learning* (2nd ed.). New York: HarperCollins.

Gagne, R., & Glaser, R. (1987). Foundations in learning research. In R. Gagne (Ed.), *Instructional technology: Foundations* (pp. 49–83). Hillsdale, NJ: Erlbaum.

Gallup Organization. (1997). *U.S. teens and technology* [Online]. Available: http://www.nsf.gov/od/lpa/nstw/teenov.htm

Garner, R. (1987). *Metacognition and reading comprehension.* Norwood, NJ: Ablex.

Gay, G. (1986). Interaction of learner control and prior understanding in computer-assisted video instruction. *Journal of Educational Psychology, 78* (3), 225–227.

Gee, J. P. (2003). *What video games have to teach us about learning and literacy.* New York: Palgrave Macmillan.

Gee, J. P. (2004). Millennials and bobos, Blue's Clues and Sesame Street: A story for our times. In D. E. Alverman (Ed.), *Adolescents and literacies in a digital world* (pp. 51–67). New York: Lang.

Gehring, J. (2001). Not enough girls. *Education Week, 20* (35), 18–19.

George, Y., Malcolm, S., & Jeffers, L. (1993). Computer equity for the future. *Communications of the ACM, 36* (5), 78–81.

Gilster, P. (1997). *Digital literacy.* New York: John Wiley & Sons.

Global Reach. (2004). *Global Internet statistics* [Online]. Available: http://www.glreach.com/globstats

Goldberg, A., Russell, M., & Cook, A. (2003). The effect of computers on student writing: A meta-analysis of studies from 1992 to 2002. *Journal of Technology, Learning, and Assessment, 2* (1). Available: http://www.jtla.org

Goldman, S., Petrosino, A., Sherwood, R., Garrison, S., Hickey, D., Bransford, J., & Pellegrino, J. (1996). Anchored science instruction in multimedia learning. In S. Vosniadou, E. De Corte, & R. Glaser (Eds.), *International perspectives on the design of technology supported learning environments* (pp. 257–284). Hillsdale, NJ: Erlbaum.

Gordin, D., Gomez, L., Pea, R., & Fishman, B. (1997). *Using the World Wide Web to build learning communities in K–12* [Online]. Available: http://www.ascusc.org/jcmc/vol2/issue3/gordin.html

Gordon, J. (1996). Tracks for learning: Metacognition and learning technologies. *Australian Journal of Educational Technology, 12* (1), 46–55.

Graves, D. (1983). *Writing: Teachers and children at work.* Exeter, NH: Heinemann.

Greeno, J. (1998). The situativity of knowing, learning, and research. *American Psychologist, 52* (12), 5–26.

Hannafin, M., Hannafin, K., Hooper, S., Rieber, L., & Kini, A. (1996). Research on and research with emerging technologies. In D. Jonassen (Ed.), *Handbook of research for educational communications and technology* (pp. 378–402). New York: Simon & Schuster.

Hannafin, R., & Freeman, D. (1995). An exploratory study of teachers' view of knowledge acquisition. *Educational Technology, 35* (1), 49–56.

Harel, I. (1991). *Children as designers.* Norwood, NJ: Ablex.

Harel, I., & Papert, S. (1990). Software design as a learning environment. *Interactive Learning Environments, 1,* 1–32.

Harley, S. (1996). Situated learning and classroom instruction. In H. McLellan (Ed.), *Situated learn-ing perspectives* (pp. 113–122). Englewood Cliffs, NJ: Educational Technology Publications.

Harper, B., Hedberg, J., Corderoy, B., & Wright, R. (2000). Employing cognitive tools within interactive multimedia environments. In S. Lajoie (Ed.), *Computers as cognitive tools: No more walls* (pp. 227–245). Mahwah, NJ: Erlbaum.

Harper, G. (1997). *Copyright law and electronic reserves* [Online]. Available: http://www.utsystem.edu/ogc/intellectualproperty/ereserve.htm

Harris, J. (1995). Curricularly infused telecomputing: A structural approach to activity design. *Computers in the Schools, 11* (3), 49–59.

Hartson, T. (1993). Kid-appeal science projects. *Computers in Education, 20* (6), 33–36.

Hayes, J., & Flower, L. (1980). Writing as problem solving. *Visible Language, 14,* 388–399.

Hayes, J., & Simon, H. (1974). Understanding written problem instructions. In L. Gregg (Ed.), *Knowledge and cognition.* Hillsdale, NJ: Erlbaum.

Haynes, C., & McMurdo, C. (2001). *Structured writing: Using Inspiration software to teach paragraph development.* Eugene, OR: International Society for Technology in Education.

Healy, J. (1998). *Failure to connect: Why computers are damaging our children's minds.* New York: Simon & Schuster.

Henderson, L., Klemes, J., & Eshet, Y. (2000). Just playing a game? Educational simulation software and cognitive outcomes. *Journal of Educational Computing Research, 22* (1), 105–129.

Hirsch, E. (1988). *Cultural literacy: What every American needs to know.* New York: Vantage.

Howe, M. (1972). *Understanding school learning.* New York: Harper & Row.

Hsu, J., Chapelle, C., & Thompson, A. (1993). Exploratory learning environments: What are they and do students explore? *Journal of Educational Computing Research, 9* (1), 1–15.

International Society for Technology in Education. (1998). *National educational technology standards for students* [Online]. Available: http://cnets.iste.org

Interstate New Teacher Assessment and Support Consortium. (1992). *Model standards for licensing for beginning teacher licensing, assessment and development: A resource for state dialog* [Online]. Available: http://www.ccsso.org/projects/Interstate_New_Teacher_Assessment_and_Support_Consortium

Jansen, B., & Culpepper, S. (1996). Using the big six research process. *Multimedia Schools, 3* (5), 32–38.

Jennings, S. (2001). National keyboarding trends. *Business Education Forum, 55* (3), 46–48.

Jerald, C., & Orlofsky, G. (1999). Raising the bar on school technology. *Education Week, 19* (4), 58–69.

Johnson, D., & Johnson, R. (1989). Social skills for successful group work. *Educational Leadership, 47* (4), 29–33.

Johnson, D., & Johnson, R. (1999). *Learning together and alone* (5th ed.). Boston: Allyn & Bacon.

Johnson, D., Johnson, R., & Holubec, E. (1991). *Cooperation in the classroom* (rev. ed.). Edina, MN: Interaction.

Joinson, A. N. (2003). *Understanding the psychology of Internet behaviour.* New York: Palgrave Macmillan.

Jonassen, D. (1986). Hypertext principles for text and courseware design. *Educational Psychologist, 21,* 269–292.

Jonassen, D. (1991, September). Evaluating constructivistic learning. *Educational Technology, 32,* 28–33.

Jonassen, D. (1995). Supporting communities of learners with technology: A vision for integrating technology with learning in schools. *Educational Technology, 35* (4), 60–63.

Jonassen, D. (1996). *Computers in the classroom: Mindtools for critical thinking.* Englewood, NJ: Prentice Hall.

Jonassen, D. (2000). *Computers as mindtools for schools.* Upper Saddle River, NJ: Prentice Hall.

Jonassen, D., & Carr, D. (2000). Mindtools: Affording multiple knowledge representations for learning. In S. Lajoie (Ed.), *Computer as cognitive tool* (vol. 2, pp. 165–196). Mahwah, NJ: Erlbaum.

Jonassen, D., & Grabinger, R. (1990). Problems and issues in designing hypertext/hypermedia for learning. In D. Jonassen & H. Mandl (Eds.), *Designing hypermedia for learning* (pp. 3–25). New York: Springer-Verlag.

Jonassen, D., Peck, K., & Wilson, B. (1999). *Learning with technology: A constructivist perspective.* Upper Saddle River, NJ: Merrill.

Joyce, J. (1988). Siren shapes: Exploratory and constructive hypertexts. *Academic Computing, 3* (4), 10–14, 37–42.

Katz, L., & Chard, S. (1989). *Engaging children's minds: The project approach.* Norwood, NJ: Ablex.

Kemery, E. (2000). Developing online collaboration. In A. Aggarwal (Ed.), *Web-based learning and teaching technologies: Opportunities and challenges* (pp. 227–245). Hershey, PA: Idea Group.

Kendall, J., & Marzano, R. (1996). *Content knowledge: A compendium of standards and benchmarks for K–12 education.* Aurora, CO: Mid-Continent Regional Educational Laboratory.

Kimball, L. (1995). Ten ways to make online learning groups work. *Educational Leadership, 53* (2), 54–56.

Knapp, L., & Glenn, A. (1996). *Restructuring schools with technology.* Boston: Allyn & Bacon.

Kozma, R. (1991). Learning with media. *Review of Educational Research, 61* (2), 179–211.

Laboratory of Comparative Human Cognition. (1989). Kids and computers: A positive vision of the future. *Harvard Educational Review, 59,* 73–86.

Laboratory Network Program Frameworks Task Force. (1998). *Summary of analyzed state curriculum frameworks* [Online]. Available: http://www.mcrel.org/hpc/sum-cur-fram

Lawless, K., & Brown, S. (1997). Multimedia learning environments: Issues of learner control and navigation. *Instructional Science, 25* (2), 117–131.

Lee, M. J., & Tedder, M. C. (2004). Introducing expanding hypertext based on working memory capacity and the feeling of disorientation: Tailored communication through effective hypermedia design. *Journal of Educational Computing Research, 30,* 171–195.

Lehrer, R. (1993). Authors of knowledge: Patterns of hypermedia design. In S. Lajoie & S. Derry (Eds.), *Computers as cognitive tools* (pp. 197–227). Hillsdale, NJ: Erlbaum.

Lehrer, R., Erickson, J., & Connell, T. (1994). Learning by designing hypermedia documents. *Computers in the Schools, 10* (1/2), 227–254.

Lepper, M., & Gurtner, J. (1989). Children and computers: Approaching the twenty-first century. *American Psychologist, 44* (2), 170–178.

Lesgold, A. (2001). The nature and methods of learning by doing. *American Psychologist, 56* (11), 964–971.

Levin, D., & Arafeh, S. (2002). *The digital disconnect: The widening gap between Internet-savvy students and their schools* [Online]. Pew Internet and American Life Project. Available: http://www.pewinternet.org/pdfs/PIP_Schools_Internet_Report.pdf

Levin, S. (1991). The effects of interactive video enhanced earthquake lessons on achievement of seventh grade earth science students. *Journal of Computer Based Instruction, 18* (4), 125–129.

Liao, Y. (1992). Effects of computer-assisted instruction on cognitive outcomes: A meta-analysis. *Journal of Research on Computing in Education, 24* (3), 367–380.

Linn, M. C., Eylon, B., & Davis, E. A. (2004). The knowledge integration perspective on learning. In M. C. Linn, E. A. Davis, & P. Bell (Eds.), *Internet environments for science education* (pp. 29–46). Mahwah, NJ: Erlbaum.

Locatis, C., Letourneau, G., & Banvard, R. (1990). Hypermedia and instruction. *Educational Technology, Research and Development, 37* (4), 65–77.

Loving, C. (1997). From the summit of truth to its slippery slopes: Science education's journey through positivist-postmodern territory. *American Educational Research Journal, 34* (3), 421–452.

MacKinnon, G. (2000). The dilemma of evaluating electronic discussion groups. *Journal of Research on Computing in Education, 33,* 125–131.

Magid, L. (1998). *Child safety on the Information Highway* [Online]. Available: http://www.safekids.com/child_safety.htm

Major, A. (1998). Copyright law tackles yet another challenge: The electronic frontier of the World Wide Web. *Rutgers Computer and Technology Law Journal, 24* (1), 75–105.

Markman, E., & Gorin, L. (1981). Children's ability to adjust their standards for evaluating comprehension. *Journal of Educational Psychology, 73,* 320–325.

Martin, J. (1994). Are you breaking the law? *MacWorld, 11* (5), 125–129.

Mayer, R., Heiser, J., & Steve, L. (2001). Cognitive constraints on multimedia learning: When presenting more material results in less understanding. *Journal of Educational Psychology, 93,* 187–198.

Mayer, R. E. (2001). *Multimedia learning.* New York: Cambridge University Press.

Mayer, R. E. (2004). Should there be a three-strike rule against pure discovery learning? The case for guided methods of instruction. *American Psychologist, 59,* 14–19.

McCloskey, M. (1983). Naive theories of motion. In D. Gentner & A. Stevens (Eds.), *Mental models* (pp. 71–94). Hillsdale, NJ: Erlbaum.

McKenzie, J. (1997). Making the net work for schools: Online research modules. *From Now On: The Educational Technology Journal* [Online], *7* (1).

Available: http://fromnowon.org/sept97/online.html

McKeown, M. G., & Beck, I. L. (1990). The assessment and characterization of young learners' knowledge of a topic in history. *American Educational Research Journal, 27,* 688–726.

McLellan, H. (1996). Situated learning: Multiple perspectives. In H. McLellan (Ed.), *Situated learning perspectives* (pp. 5–17). Englewood Cliffs, NJ: Educational Technology Publications.

Means, B., Blando, J., Olson, K., Middleton, T., Morocco, C., Remz, A., & Zorfass, J. (1993). *Using technology to support education reform.* Washington, DC: Office of Educational Research & Improvement.

Meyer, L. (2001). New challenges. *Education Week, 20* (35), 49–64.

Milheim, W., & Martin, B. (1991). Theoretical bases for the use of learner control: Three different perspectives. *Journal of Computer-Based Instruction, 18,* 99–105.

Montague, M. (1990). Computers and writing process instruction. *Computers in the Schools, 7* (3), 5–20.

Moursund, D., & Bielefeldt, T. (1999). *Will new teachers be prepared to teach in a digital age?* [Online]. Available: http://www.milkenexchange.org/project/iste/ME154.pdf

Naisbitt, J. (1984). *Megatrends: Ten new directions transforming our lives.* New York: Warner.

Nash, G. B., Crabtree, C., & Dunn, R. E. (1997). *History on trial: Culture wars and the teaching of the past.* New York: Knopf.

National Center for Education Statistics. (2001). *The condition of education 2001: Teacher's readiness to use computers and the Internet* [Online]. Available: http://nces.ed.gov/programs/coe/2001/pdf/39_2001.pdf [May 2002].

National Center for Education Statistics, U.S. Department of Education. (2003). *Computer and Internet use by children and adolescents in 2001* [Online]. Washington, DC: National Center for Education Statistics. Available: http://nces.ed.gov/pubs2004/2004014.pdf

National Center for Missing and Exploited Children. (2000). *Online victimization: A report on the nation's youth* [Online]. Available: http://www.ncmec.org/download/nc62.pdf

National Commission on Excellence in Education. (1983). *A nation at risk.* Washington, DC: U.S. Department of Education.

National Council of Teachers of Mathematics. (2000). *Principles and standards for school mathematics* [Online]. Available: http://standards.nctm.org/document/index.htm

National Telecommunications and Information Administration. (2002). *A nation online: How Americans are expanding their use of the Internet* [Online]. Available: http://www.ntia.doc.gov/ntiahome/dn/index.html

National Telecommunications and Information Administration. (2004). *A nation online: Entering the broadband age* [Online]. Available: http://www.ntia.doc.gov/reports/anol

Niess, M. (1998). Using computer spreadsheets to solve equations. *Learning and Leading with Technology, 26* (3), 22–27.

Norris, C., Sullivan, T., Poirot, J., and Soloway, E. (2003). No access, no use, no impact: Snapshot surveys of educational technology in K–12. *Journal of Research on Technology in Education, 36,* 15–27.

Office of the Inspector General. (2004). *Semiannual report to Congress: October 1, 2003–March 31, 2004* [Online]. Available: http://www.e-ratecentral.com/FCC/SAR_31_FCC-OIG.pdf

Office of Technology Assessment. (1992). *Testing in American schools: Asking the right questions.* Washington, DC: U.S. Government Printing Office.

Olaniran, B., Savage, G., & Sorenson, R. (1996). Experimental and experiential approaches to teaching face-to-face and computer-mediated group discussion. *Communication Education, 45* (3), 244–259.

O'Neill, D. K., & Harris, J. B. (2004). Bridging the perspectives and developmental needs of all participants in curriculum-based telementoring programs. *Journal of Research on Technology in Education, 37,* 111–128.

O'Neill, E. T., Lavoie, B. F., Bennett, R. (2003). Trends in the evolution of the public web [Online]. *D-Lib Magazine, 9.* Available: http://www.dlib.org/dlib/april03/lavoie/04lavoie.html

Oppenheimer, T. (2003). *The flickering mind: The false promise of technology in the classroom and how learning can be saved.* New York: Random House.

Owston, R., Murphy, S., & Wideman, H. (1992). The effects of word processing on students' writing quality and revision strategies. *Research in the Teaching of English, 26* (3), 249–276.

Owston, R., & Wideman, H. (1997). Word processors and children's writing in a high-computer-access setting. *Journal of Research on Computing in Education, 30* (2), 202–220.

Paivio, A. (1986). *Mental representations: A dual coding approach.* New York: Oxford University Press.

Palincsar, A., & Brown, A. (1984). Reciprocal teaching of comprehension-fostering and comprehension-monitoring activities. *Cognition and Instruction, 1,* 117–175.

Panel on Educational Technology, President's Committee of Advisors on Science and Technology. (1997). *Report to the president on the use of technology to strengthen K–12 education in the United States* [Online]. Available: http://www.ostp.gov/PCAST/k-12ed.html

Papert, S. (1993). *The children's machine: Rethinking school in the age of the computer.* New York: Basic.

Paris, S., & Lindauer, B. (1982). The development of cognitive skills during childhood. In B. Wolman (Ed.), *Handbook of developmental psychology* (pp. 333–349). Englewood Cliffs, NJ: Prentice Hall.

Paris, S., & Winograd, P. (1990). How metacognition can promote academic learning and instruction. In B. Jones & L. Idol (Eds.), *Dimensions of thinking and cognitive instruction* (pp. 15–51). Hillsdale, NJ: Erlbaum.

Park, J., & Staresina, L. N. (2004). Tracking U.S. trends. *Education Week, 23,* 64–67.

Partnership for 21st Century Skills. (2003). *Learning for the 21st century: A report and MILE guide for 21st century skills* [Online]. Available: http://www.21stcenturyskills.org

Paulson, F., Paulson, P., & Meyer, C. (1991). What makes a portfolio a portfolio? *Educational Leadership, 48* (5), 60–63.

Pea, R., & Kurland, D. (1987a). Cognitive technologies in writing. In E. Rothkopf (Ed.), *Review of research in education #14* (pp. 277–326). Washington, DC: American Educational Research Association.

Pea, R., & Kurland, D. (1987b). On the cognitive effects of learning computer programming. In R. Pea & K. Sheingold (Eds.), *Mirrors of minds: Patterns of experience in educational computing* (pp. 147–177). Norwood, NJ: Ablex.

Pearlman, R. (1991, January). Restructuring with technology: A tour of schools where it's happening. *Technology and Learning,* 30–37.

Perkins, D. (1985). The fingertip effect: How information-processing technology shapes thinking. *Educational Researcher, 14,* 11–17.

Perkins, D. (1986). *Knowledge as design.* Hillsdale, NJ: Erlbaum.

Pogrow, S. (1996). HOTS: Helping low achievers in grades 4–7. *Principal, 76* (2), 34–35.

Pon, K. (1988). Process writing in the one-computer classroom. *Computing Teacher, 15* (6), 33–37.

Porter, C., & Cleland, J. (1995). *The portfolio as a learning strategy.* Portsmouth, NH: Heinemann.

Prensky, M. (2001). *Digital game-based learning.* New York: McGraw-Hill.

Pressley, M., Snyder, B., Levin, J., Murray, H., & Ghatala, E. (1987). Perceived readiness for examination performance (PREP) produced by initial reading of text and text containing adjunct questions. *Reading Research Quarterly, 22,* 219–236.

Quinn, C., Mehan, H., Levin, J., & Black, S. (1983). Real education in non-real time: The use of electronic message systems for instruction. *Instructional Science, 11,* 313–327.

Ravitz, J., Wong, Y., & Becker, H. (1999). *Teaching, learning, and computing: 1998—Report to participants* [Online]. Available: http://www.crito.uci.edu/tlc/findings/special_report

Read, J., & Barnsley, R. (1977). Remember Dick and Jane. *Canadian Journal of Behavioral Science, 9,* 361–370.

Resnick, L. (1987). *Education and learning to think.* Washington, DC: National Academy Press.

Resnick, M., Bruckman, A., & Martin, F. (1999). Constructional design. In A. Druin (Ed.), *The design of children's technology* (pp. 149–168). San Mateo, CA: Kaufmann.

Riel, M. (1997). *The Internet: A land to settle rather than an ocean to surf and a new "place" for school reform through community development* [Online]. Available: http://www.gsn.org/teach/articles/netasplace.html

Ring, G. (1993). The effects of instruction in courseware preview methodology on the predictive validity of teacher preview ratings. *Journal of Educational Computing Research, 9* (2), 197–218.

Russell, M., Bebell, D., O'Dwyer, L., & O'Conner, K. (2003). Examining teacher technology use: Implications for preservice and inservice teacher preparation. *Journal of Teacher Education, 54,* 297–310.

Salomon, G., & Perkins, D. (1987). Transfer of cognitive skills from programming? When and how? *Journal of Educational Computing Research, 3* (2), 149–169.

Salpeter, J. (1992). Are you obeying copyright law? *Technology and Learning, 12* (8), 14–23.

Sanders, J., & McGinnis, M. (1991). *Computer equity in math and science: A trainer's workshop guide.* Metuchen, NJ: Scarecrow Press.

Scardamalia, B., Bereiter, C., McLean, R., Swallow, J., & Woodruff, E. (1989). Computer-supported intentional learning environments. *Journal of Educational Computing Research, 5* (1), 51–68.

Schallert, D. (1980). The role of illustrations in reading comprehension. In R. Spiro, B. Bruce, & W. Brewer (Eds.), *Theoretical issues in reading comprehension* (pp. 503–524). Hillsdale, NJ: Erlbaum.

Schank, R. (1998). *Inside multi-media case based instruction.* Mahway, NJ: Erlbaum.

Schofield, J. W., & Davidson, A. L. (2004). Achieving equality of student Internet access within schools. In A. H. Eagly, R. M. Baron, & V. L. Hamilton (Eds.), *The social psychology of group identity and social conflict* (pp. 97–109). Washington, DC: American Psychological Association.

Sharan, Y., & Shachar, H. (1988). *Language and learning in the cooperative classroom.* New York: Springer-Verlag.

Sharan, Y., & Sharan, S. (1992). *Expanding cooperative learning through group investigation.* New York: Teachers College Press.

Shea, V. (1994). *Netiquette.* San Francisco: Albion Press.

Sheingold, K. (1991, September). Restructuring for learning with technology: The potential for synergy. *Phi Delta Kappan,* 28–36.

Shipstone, D. (1988). Pupils' understanding of simple electrical circuits. *Physics Education, 23,* 92–96.

Shulman, L. (1998). Teacher portfolios: A theoretical activity. In N. Lyons (Ed.), *With portfolio in hand* (pp. 23–38). New York: Teachers College Press.

Slavin, R. (1991). *Student team learning: A practical guide to cooperative learning* (3rd ed.). Washington, DC: National Education Association.

Slavin, R. (1995). *Cooperative learning: Theory, research, and practice* (2nd ed.). New York: Merrill.

Slavin, R. (1996). Research on cooperative learning and achievement. *Contemporary Educational Psychology, 21* (1), 43–69.

Smagorinsky, P. (1995). Constructing meaning in the disciplines: Reconceptualizing writing across the curriculum as composing across the curriculum. *American Journal of Education, 103,* 160–184.

Smilowitz, M., Compton, D., & Flint, L. (1988). The effects of computer mediated communication on an individual judgment. *Computers in Human Behavior, 14,* 311–321.

Squires, D. (1999). Educational software for constructivist learning environments: Subversive use and volatile design. *Educational Technology, 39* (3), 48–53.

Steinberg, S. (1989). Cognition and learner control: A literature review, 1977–1988. *Journal of Computer-Based Instruction, 16,* 117–121.

Susman, E. (1998). Cooperative learning: A review of factors that increase the effectiveness of cooperative computer-based instruction. *Journal of Educational Computing Research, 18* (4), 303–322.

Sutton, R. (1991). Equity and computers in schools: A decade of research. *Review of Educational Research, 61* (4), 475–503.

Taylor, R. (1980). *The computer in the school: Tutor, tool, tutee.* New York: Teachers College Press.

Technology, Education, and Copyright Harmonization Act of 2002. (2002). Available: http://www.copyright.gov/legislation/pl107-273.html

Tennyson, R. (1980). Instructional control strategies and content structure as design variables in concept acquisition using computer-assisted instruction. *Journal of Educational Psychology, 72,* 525–532.

Tennyson, R., & Buttrey, T. (1980). Advisement and management strategies as design variables in computer-assisted instruction. *Educational Communication and Technology Journal, 28,* 169–176.

Theodosakis, N. (2001). *The director in the classroom: How filmmaking inspires learning.* San Diego, CA: Tech4learning Publishing. Companion web site: http://www.thedirectorintheclassroom.com

Thomas, J., & Rohwer, W. (1986). Academic studying: The role of learning strategies. *Educational Psychologist, 21,* 19–41.

Thomas, L., & Knezek, D. (1991). Facilitating restructured learning experiences with technology. *Computing Teacher, 18* (6), 49–53.

Thomas, R., & Hooper, E. (1991). Simulation: An opportunity we are missing. *Journal of Research on Computing in Education, 23* (4), 497–513.

Tierney, R., Carter, M., & Desai, L. (1991). *Portfolio assessment in the reading-writing classroom.* Norwood, MA: Christopher-Gordon.

Tobin, K. (1986). Effects of wait time on discourse characteristics in mathematics and language arts classes. *American Educational Research Journal, 23,* 191–200.

Tobin, K. (1987). The role of wait time in higher cognitive level learning. *Review of Educational Research, 57,* 69–95.

Toomey, R., & Ketterer, K. (1995). Using multimedia as a cognitive tool. *Journal of Research on Computing in Education, 27* (4), 472–482.

Tulving, E. (1972). Episodic and semantic memory. In E. Tulving & W. Donaldson (Eds.), *Organization of memory.* New York: Academic Press.

UCLA Center for Communication Policy. (2000). *The UCLA Internet report: Surveying the digital future* [Online]. Available: http://www.ccp.ucla.edu/pages/ internet-report.asp

U.S. Department of Education. (2004a). Department to study technology's role in raising student achievement [Press release]. Available: http://www.ed.gov/news/pressreleases/2004/02/02132004.html

U.S. Department of Education. (2004b). *Toward a new golden age in American education: How the Internet, the law and today's students are revolutionizing expectations* [Online]. Washington, DC: Office of Educational Technology. Available: http://www.nationaledtechplan.org

U.S. Department of Education, Office of the Under Secretary, Policy and Program Studies Service. (2003). *Federal funding for educational technology and how it is used in the classroom: A summary of findings from the integrated studies of educational technology.* Washington, DC: U.S. Department of Education.

U.S. House of Representatives. (1994). *Goals 2000: Educate America Act* [Online]. Available: http://www.ed.gov/legislation/GOALS2000/TheAct/intro.html

Volman, M., & van Eck, E. (2001). Gender equity and information technology in education: The second decade. *Review of Educational Research, 71* (4), 613–634.

Voss, J. F., Carretero, M., Kennet, J., & Silfies, L. N. (1994). The collapse of the Soviet Union: A case study in causal reasoning. In M. Carretero & J. F.

Voss (Eds.), *Cognition and instructional processes in history and the social sciences* (pp. 403–429). Hove, UK: Erlbaum.

Vygotsky, L. (1978). *Mind in society: The development of higher mental processes.* Cambridge, MA: Harvard University Press.

Wakefield, J. (1996). *Educational psychology: Learning to be a problem-solver.* Boston: Houghton Mifflin.

Wallace, R. M. (2004). A framework for understanding teaching with the Internet. *American Educational Research Journal, 41,* 447–488.

Warschauer, M., Knobel, M., & Stone, L. (2004). Technology and equity in schooling: Deconstructing the digital divide. *Educational Policy, 18,* 562–588.

Waxman, H. C., Lin, M., & Michko, G. M. (2003). *A meta-analysis of the effectiveness of teaching and learning with technology on student outcomes* [Online]. Available: http://www.ncrel.org/tech/effects2

Weinman, J., & Haag, P. (1999). Gender equity in cyberspace. *Educational Leadership, 56* (5), 44–49.

Wenglinsky, H. (1998). *Does it compute: The relationship between educational technology and student achievement in mathematics* [Online]. Available: http://www.ets.org/research/pic/dic/techtoc.html

Wetzel, K. (1990). Keyboarding. In S. Franklin (Ed.), *The best of the writing notebook* (2nd ed., pp. 46–48). Eugene, OR: Writing Notebook.

Wheatley, G. (1991). Constructivist perspectives on science and mathematics learning. *Science Education, 75,* 9–21.

Whitehead, A. (1929). *The aims of education.* Cambridge, UK: Cambridge University Press.

Windschitl, M., & Sahl, K. (2002). Tracing teachers' use of technology in a laptop computer school: The interplay of teacher beliefs, social dynamics, and institutional culture. *American Educational Research Journal, 39* (1), 165–205.

World Wide Web Consortium. (1999). *Web Accessibility Initiative page author guidelines* [Online]. Available: http://www.w3.org/TR/WD-WAI-PAGEAUTH

Index

• • •

Ability, equity and, 375
Acceptable-use policies (AUPs), 396–397
Access to technology, 16–17
    adapting technology for equal access and, 375–378
    e-rate and, 373–374
    Internet and, 172–173
    See also Dangers of Internet access
Active learning, Web for, 232–237
Active student role, 13
Activity-based approaches, 32–35
    early use of, 34–35
    today's use of technology and, 35
Adaptations for equal access, 375–378
Adaptive Web page design, 376–378
Adventures of Jasper Woodbury, The (hypermedia environment), 139–140
AECT (Association for Educational Communication and Technology) standards, 28
AIFF (audio interchange file format), 306
Algebraic equations, solutions to, spreadsheets for understanding, 100–101
Alignment, 24
Analog format, 145–146
Analog modems, 176
Analog signals, 176
Applets, 206
AppleWorks, 276–278
Apprenticeship method, for hypermedia design, 339–340
Ask Jeeves for Kids, 229, 394
Assessment
    electronic portfolios for, 90–91
    learning related to, 15
    of performance, 55
    standards and, 14
Association for Educational Communication and Technology (AECT) standards, 28
Asynchronous communication, 181
Attitudes, of teachers, 32
Audio interchange file format (AIFF), 306
Audio recording, digital, 308–309
AUPs (acceptable-use policies), 396–397

Authentic activities, 58–60, 65
Authentic inquiry tasks, classroom example of, 202–204
Authentic learning
    activities for, 58–60, 65
    geography project for, 314–316
    multimedia support for, 153
Authoring, for Web. *See* Web authoring
Authors
    copyright law and, 378–390
    of Web information, 230–231
Automaticity, 132

Background music, 307
Bandwidth, 175
Benchmarks, 23
Big Six skills, 222–228
Bitmapped images, 275
Blogs, 95, 347–349
BMP (bitmap) file format, 283, 284
Bookmarks, 207–209
    changing titles of, 207, 209
    exporting, 208–209
Bots, 210
Brainstorming, 92–94
Branches, 320
Branching tutorials, 125
Browsers, 205–207
    keeping track of resources using, 207–209
Browsing the Web, 209–210
    combined with searching, 211
Builds, 253
Bulleted charts, 253
Buttons
    in EZediaMX, 262–263, 268
    in hypermedia, 325

CAI. *See* Computer-assisted instruction (CAI)
Calculator-based laboratories (CBLs), 106
Camcorders, 288, 295
    digital, 295–296

Camcorders (*cont.*)
  gathering video clips from, 298
  tips for, 300
Cameras, digital, 287–288
Canada project, 353–358
Carmen Sandiego series, 134–135
Case-based learning, 43
CBI (computer-based instruction), 121–122
CBLs (calculator-based laboratories), 106
CD burners, 146
CD-ROMs
  definition of, 145
  of reference sources, 149–150
  technology of, 145–146
Cells, in spreadsheets, 96
Chat, 181–182
Cheating, 391
Children's International Protection Act (CIPA),
  374
Citing Internet sources, 228
Clay animation, 302–304
Client-server model, 178
Clip art collections, as image source, 291
Clipboard, 280
CMC. *See* Computer-mediated communication
  (CMC)
Cognitive apprenticeships, 65–66
Cognitive load, 156–157
Cognitive models of school learning, 39
Collaborative augmentation, 193
Coloring books, as image sources, 290
Communication. *See* Computer-mediated communication
  (CMC)
Community access centers, 369
Compression, 283
Computer-assisted instruction (CAI), 121–122,
  157–165
  evaluation forms for, 160–163
  research on, 157–158
  software for, 160, 164–165
Computer-based instruction (CBI), 121–122
Computer control, 49
Computer-mediated communication (CMC), 174–191
  advantages of, 185–188
  chat and, 181–182
  conferencing using, 179–181
  e-mail and, 174–179
  instant messaging and, 182
  Internet tools for, 174
  mailing lists and, 179, 180, 181
  netiquette for, 188, 189–191
  online discussion and, 187–188
  potential problems with, 188

videoconferencing and, 182–184
  See also Online discussion
Conceptual models of school learning, 51–57
  constructivism and, 54–56
  meaningful learning and, 51–54
Concreteness, of simulations, 129
Conference on Fair Use (CONFU), 385–386
Conferences, electronic, 179–181
Construction, Internet tools for, 174
Constructivism, 54–56
Content-area learning, 118–165
  computer-assisted instruction and, 157–163
  computer-based instruction for, 121–122
  constructivism and cooperative learning and,
    163–165
  drill and practice for, 130–133
  educational games for, 133–137
  example of, 119–121
  exploratory environments for, 137–143
  hypermedia and, 138–139, 144–145, 152–157
  hypertext and, 144
  instructional process for, 122–123
  multimedia and, 144–150, 152–157
  project ideas for, 71
  simulations for, 125–130
  technology integrated into, 11–13
  tutorials for, 123–125
Content organization, 318–320
Content standards, 22
Control, offered by simulations, 130
Control functions, metacognitive, 48–49
Cooperative learning, 14–16, 66–67
  constructivitism with, 163–165
  hypermedia design and, 326–328
Copy function, with word processing programs, 84
Copying
  for creating multimedia, 385–386
  for distance education, 385–387
  multiple-copy fair use guidelines for books and
    periodicals, 384–385
  obtaining permission for, 388
  for one's own use, 384–385
  of software, 382
Copyright law, 378–390
  copying computer software and, 382
  establishing copyright, 380–381
  fair use, 382–387, 390
  issues and problems in education involving,
    378–380
  rights, licenses, and permissions, 381–382
  student work on websites and, 389
Cost-effectiveness, of simulations, 130
Crawlers, 210

Critical thinking, 61, 227
Cross-platform files, 285
Culture of practice, 59–60
Curriculum
    alignment of, 24
    frameworks for, 23–24
Cursors, with word processing programs, 84
Cut function, with word processing programs, 84

Dangers of Internet access, 390–398
    acceptable-use policies (AUPs) and, 396–397
    balancing freedom and protection from, 392–393
    filtering and, 394–396
    safe areas of Internet and, 393–394
    supervision and, 377–378
    types of, 390–392
Databases, 101–106
    components of, 101–102
    developing, 102–103
    digital portfolios and, 12–13
    of reviewed sites, 229
    wildflower identification project using, 103–105
Data collection, 106–111
    devices for, 106–107
    encouraging higher-order thinking using, 108–111
    examples of, 107–108
Data loggers, 62, 106, 110–111
Declarative knowledge, 44
Delete function, with word processing programs, 84
Design, 317
    of hypermedia, 317–326
    knowledge as, 316–317
    learning as, 338–339
    See also Hypermedia design
Desktop publishing, 249
Dial-on-demand connections, 175
Dial-up connections, 175
Digital audio recording, 308–309
Digital cameras, 287–288
Digital format, 146
Digital literacy, 222, 224
Digital portfolios, 12–13
Digital subscriber line (DSL), 175
Digital video discs. See DVDs (digital video discs)
Discovery learning, 52, 54
Distance education, fair use and, 385
DNSs (domain name servers), 171
Documents
    design of, with word processing programs, 85
    embellished, 244–245, 246, 248–250
    in eZediaMX, 261–262
Domain names, 171

Domain name servers (DNSs), 171
Dots per inch (dpi), 276
Draw programs, 274–278
Drill activities, 132
Drill and practice, 42, 130–133
    applications of, 130–133
    example of, 130–132
    focus of, 133
DSL (digital subscriber line), 175
Dual-agenda approach, 62
Dual-coding theory, 153–154
DVD-RAMs, 146–147
DVDs (digital video discs)
    characteristics of, 146–147
    definition of, 145
    uses of, 147

Editing, with word processing programs, 84
Educational games, 133–137
    classroom uses of, 137
    examples of, 134–137
Educational opportunity, equity of. See Equity of
    educational opportunity
Educational reform standards, 24. See also School reform
Educational Testing Service (ETS) mathematics study,
    369–370
Educational theories, common themes of, 56. See also
    specific theories
Edutainment, 133
Electronic portfolios, 10, 12–13, 90–91
Electronic thesaurus, with word processing
    programs, 85
E-mail (electronic mail), 174–179, 180
Embellished documents, 244–245, 246
    creating with word processing programs, 248–250
Encapsulated PostScript (EPS) file format, 284
Encyclopedias, multimedia, 150, 151–153
Engaging Students in American History
    web site, 219–220
EPS (Encapsulated PostScript) file format, 284
Equity of educational opportunity, 18–19, 365–378
    adapting technology for equal access and,
        375–378
    gender and, 371–375
    socioeconomic status and, 366–371
    student ability and, 375
    teachers and, 371
E-rate, 373–374
ETS (Educational Testing Service) mathematics study,
    369–370
Evaluating projects, 331–334
Evaluation forms, for CAI, 160–163

Executive mechanisms, 39
Exploratory environments, 137–143
    characteristics of, 138
    effectiveness of, 142–143
    hypermedia environments and, 138–139
Exploring the Nardoo (hypermedia environment),
        140–142
eZediaMX, 268, 302, 306
eZediaQT1, 265–266, 346

Facilitative teacher role, 14
Fair use, 382–387, 390
    copying for one's own use and, 384–385
    distance education and, 385
    factors determining, 383
    multimedia and, 385–386
    multiple copies for classroom use and, 384–385
    variations with different media, 383–384
Fidelity, of simulations, 128
Fields, in databases, 101
File formats, of graphics files, 282–284
Files, database, 102
File transfer protocol (FTP), 205
Filmmaking model, 337–338
Filtering, 394–396
    firewalls for, 394
    stand-alone software for, 394–395
Financial threats, as danger of Internet access, 392
Firewalls, 394
FireWire, 297
Flash memory, 288
Flatbed scanners, 286–287
Fonts, 82
Font styles, 82–83
Formatting, with word processing programs, 82
Forums, electronic, 179–181
Fractional T1s, 175
Frames, in eZediaMX, 260
Frameworks, 23–24
FTP (file transfer protocol), 205
Funding, to provide access to Internet, 373–374

Gaggle, 394
Games. See Educational games
Gender, equity and, 371–375
Geocaching, 113–114
Geographic Information System (GIS), 112–113
    geocaching using, 113–114
Geography project, 314–316
GIF (graphics interchange format), 283, 284, 351
Global Positioning System (GPS), 112–113
GLOBE Program, 112–113
Google, 212

Graphic design, 321–322
Graphics, in Web authoring, 351–352
Graphics file formats, 282–284
Graphics interchange format (GIF), 283, 284, 351
Graphics tools, 274–278
    for writing assignments, 279–282
Graphic user interface (GUI), 278
Grids, for screen layout, 321
Group investigation, 67, 327–328
GUI (graphic user interface), 278

Harassment, as danger of Internet access, 392
Hierarchical design, 319–320
Higher-order thinking, 60–64
    data collection to encourage, 108–111
Higher Order Thinking Skills (HOTS) Project, 62
High-road transfer, 63–64
Historical inquiry, 218–220
Hits, 209
HotBot, 213
HOTS (Higher Order Thinking Skills) Project, 62
HTML (hypertext markup language), 206, 342, 378
    example of, 344–345
    saving word processing documents in, 346
HTTP (hypertext transfer protocol), 205
Hypercomposition, 328
Hypercomposition design model, 328–338
    evaluating and revising in, 335–336
    planning and, 330
    transforming and translating and, 330–334
Hypermedia
    advantages of, 152–154
    concerns about, 154–157
    definition of, 144–145
    student-authored, 317
Hypermedia design, 317–326
    content organization for, 318–320
    cooperative learning and, 326–328
    filmmaking model and, 337–338
    focusing on, 317
    graphic design and, 321–322
    hypercomposition design model and, 328–335
    multimedia projects and, 242–268, 342–358
    teacher's role in, 338–341
    text presentation and writing style and, 323–324
    user interface and navigation and, 324–326
Hypermedia environments, 138–139
Hypermedia projects, 71–72, 246
    authoring environments for, 258–268
Hypertext, definition of, 144
Hypertext markup language (HTML), 206, 342, 378
    example of, 344–345
    saving word processing documents as, 346
Hypertext transfer protocol (HTTP), 205

Image collections, organizing and saving, 275, 291–294
Imagery, 42
Images, 273–284
    bitmapped, 275
    for capture, 284
    creating, 274
    draw programs for, 274–278
    file formats for, 282–284
    learning with, 309–310
    modifying existing, 274
    object-oriented, 276
    paint programs for, 274–278
    saving for use by application programs, 275
    sources of, locating, 289–294
    still, tools for capturing, 284–289
    for Web, 285–286
    Web authoring and, 351–352
    in writing assignments, graphics tools for, 279–282
iMovie, 298–299, 302
Incremental advantage, 221
Index search engines, 211–212
Individual accountability, 327
Individual needs, meeting using multimedia, 154
Inert knowledge, 58–59
Information creation, in hypercomposition design model, 334–335
Information gathering, in hypercomposition design model, 330–334
Information literacy, 222, 224
Information Literacy Standards, 224
Information problem solving, 222
Inquiry, Internet tools for, 174
Insert function, in word processing programs, 84
Inspiration (software program), 92–94
Instant messaging, 182
Instruction
    computer-assisted, 121–122, 157–165
    computer-based, 121–122
    verbal, multimedia support for, 152–153
Instructional materials, duplication by multimedia materials, 154–155
Instructional process, 122–123
Instructional resources, on Web, 217–221
Integrated approach, 14
Integrated services digital network (ISDN), 175
Integrating technology into content-area instruction, 11–13
Intellectual property, copyright law and. *See* Copyright law
International Society for Technology in Education (ISTE) standards, 24–25, 26–27, 28
Internet, 170–197, 201–238
    access to, 172–173
    for authentic activities, 65
    communication using, 174–191
    connecting to, 175–177

copyright and, 379–380
dangers of, 390–398
domain name servers and, 171
e-rate and, 373–374
growth of, 171
information seeking on, 225–226
locating and accessing resources, 226–227
netiquette and, 188, 189–191
publishing on, 89, 94
reliability of resources on, 215
role in education, 173–174
TCP/IP and, 171
telecomputing activity structures and, 184–185
using information from, 227–228
    See also Computer-mediated communication (CMC); Dangers of Internet access; World Wide Web (WWW)
Internet addresses, 205
Internet service providers (ISPs), 175
iPhoto, 292–294
IP numbers, 171
iPod, 309
ISDN (integrated services digital network), 175
ISPs (Internet service providers), 175
ISTE (International Society for Technology in Education) standards, 24–25, 26–27, 28

Jaggies, 277
JPEG (Joint Photographic Experts Group) file format, 284, 351
Justification, 84

"Keyboard" computers, 95–96
Keyboarding, 89–94
Kidlink, 394
KidPix Slideshow, 250–252, 278, 279–282, 305, 306
KidsClick!, 229
"Knowing Nature" course, as technology application example, 7–9
Knowledge
    declarative, 44
    generation of, in hypercomposition design model, 335
    inert, 58–59
    metacognitive, 47–48
    procedural, 44
Knowledge as design, 316–317

LANs (local area networks), 176
Layouts
    databases for creating, 102–103
    Web authoring and, 350
Learner control, 49
    with advisement, 49–50

Learning
   assessment related to, 15
   case-based, 43
   cognitive models of, 39
   conceptual models of, 51–57
   cooperative, 14–16, 66–67, 163–165, 326–328
   as design, 338–339
   discovery, 52, 54
   with graphics tools, 309–310
   meaningful, 51–54
   project-based, 68–70
   reception, 52
   rote, 51
   social context of, 64–68
   with sound tools, 309–310
   of word processing features, 87
Learning communities, 68
Learning experience, depth of, multimedia and, 153
Legal threats, as danger of Internet access, 392
Letter Sounds CD, 130–132
Licenses, 381
Linear multimedia presentation, 245–246
Linear organization of content, 318
Linear tutorials, 125
Links, 318, 337
   in network model of memory, 44
List servers, 179
Listservs, 179
Local area networks (LANs), 176
Logic, in eZediaMX, 264
Long-term memory (LTM), 42–46
   components of, 42–44
   network model of, 44–46
Lossless compression, 283
Lossy compression, 283
Low-road transfer, 63, 64

Mailing lists, 179, 180, 181
Maps, in hypermedia, 324
Margins, 84
Master slides, 253
MBLs (microcomputer-based laboratories), 106
Meaningful learning, 51–54
   knowledge as design and, 316–317
Media literacy, 222
Megabytes, 145
Memory, 39–46
   declarative, 44
   episodic, 42–44
   flash, 288
   long-term, 42–46

   procedural, 44
   short-term (working), 40–42
Memory stores, 40
Mental processes, 46
Mental tools, 46
Menus, in hypermedia, 324
Metacognition, 47–51
Metacognitive control functions, 48–49
Metacognitive knowledge, 47–48
Meta-index searches, 212
Microcomputer-based laboratories (MBLs), 106
Microsoft Encarta, 151
"Middle-School Curriculum and Methods" course, as technology application example, 9–11
Mindtool, 81
Missing Gerbil Case video, 271–273
Mobility impairments, adaptations of technology for, 376
Modems, 176
Motivation, multimedia and, 154
Movies. *See* Video
MP3 file format, 306
Multichoice, in eZediaMX, 264
Multidisciplinary approach, 14
Multimedia, 144–150
   advantages of, 152–154
   authoring environments for, 258–268
   CD-ROMs and, 145–146
   concerns about, 154–157
   definition of, 144–145
   DVDs and, 146–147
   fair use and, 385–386
   reference sources and, 149–150
   talking books and, 147–149
   See also Images; Sound; Video
Multimedia projects, 242–268, 342–358
   authoring environments for, 258–268
   classifying, 244–246
   collaborative, example of, 353–358
   in ninth-grade classroom example, 242–244
   questions to ask when considering, 246–248
   software tools for creating, 248–258
   on Web, 342–358

National Center for Accreditation of Teacher Education (NCATE) standards, 25, 27–29
National Educational Technology Plan, 33–34
National Geographic Wonders of Learning CD-ROM Library, 148
Navigation
   in hypermedia, 318, 324–326
   Web authoring and, 350

NCATE (National Center for Accreditation of Teacher Education) standards, 25, 27–29
Netiquette, 188, 189–191
Nodes, 318
    in network model of memory, 44

Object-oriented images, 276
Online discussion
    CMC's impact on, 187–188
    experience with, 197
    key issues for, 197
    teacher's roles in, 191–197
Online resources. *See* Primary sources; Web resources
Online tutorials, 217
Operation: Frog, 127–128
Oregon Trail, The (game), 134
Organizational structure, 319–320
Organization of content, 318–320
Organization sponsors, of Web information, 231
Outlining, with word processing programs, 84

Page layout, Web authoring and, 350
Paint programs, 274–278
Paste function, with word processing programs, 84
Path-based animation, in eZediaMX, 264
PDAs (personal digital assistants), 106
Pedagogical content knowledge, 214
Performance-based assessment, 14, 55
Performance standards, 22
Permission to copy, 388, 389
Physical molestation, as danger of Internet access, 392
Physics course, as technology application example, 4–7
PICT file format, 283, 284
Piracy, software, 382
Pixels, 275
Plagiarism, 391
Planets project, 329
Play phases, 41–42
Plug-ins, 206–207
PNG (portable Network graphic) file format, 284
Podcasts, 308–309
Point-to-point communication, 183
Point-to-point protocol (PPP), 177
Portable Network graphic (PNG) file format, 284
Portals, educational, resources identified by, 229
Portfolio assessment, 55
    electronic portfolios for, 90–91
PowerPoint, 254–258, 264–268, 305
PPP (point-to-point protocol), 177
Practice activities, 132. *See also* Drill and practice

Presentation software, 246, 252–257
Primary sources, 60, 217–221
    digitized, from reputable institutions, 229–230
    information literacy and, 222, 224
    strategies for using, 222–228
Private speech, 69
Probes, 106
Problem solving, 61
Procedural knowledge, 44
Processes, 46–51
Project-based learning, 68–70
Project evaluation, 331–334
Project quality, in hypermedia design, 340
Publishing, 89
    on Internet, 89, 94

Queries, 209
QuickTime format, 301, 306
QuickTime VR, 206

RAW file format, 284
Reception learning, 52
Reciprocal teaching, 65
Records, in databases, 101–102
Reference sources, multimedia, 149–150
Reform. *See* Educational reform; School reform
Rehearsal, 40–42
Research, on learning with technology, 72–73
Resolution, 285
Resources, and equity, 18–19
Restructuring schools, 21–22
    design projects and, 340–341
Retrieval, with word processing programs, 82
Rights, under copyright law, 381
Robots, 210
Rote learning, 51
Routers, 176

Safe areas of Internet, 393–394
Safety
    Internet and, 390–398
    of simulations, 130
Safety guidelines, for Internet use, 396, 398
Sampling frequency, 305
Scaffolding, 69, 204
    of Web exploration, 233–235
Scanners, flatbed, 287–287
School learning
    cognitive models of, 39
    conceptual models of, 51–57

School reform, 19–22
  key elements for, 19–21
  perspectives on, 29–31
  restructuring schools and, 21–22
  See also Educational reform
Schools, restructuring, 21–22
  design projects and, 340–341
Screen captures, 280
Screen layout, 321–322
Screen reader software, 376
Search engines, 209, 210–212
  choosing type to use, 212
  index, 211–212
Searching, 209, 210–213
  combined with browsing, 211
  developing skills for, 226–227
  meta-index searches and, 212
Select function, with word processing programs, 84
Sensors, 106
Sequential design, 319
Servers, 205
  client-server model, 178
  domain name servers (DNSs), 171
  list servers for e-mail, 179
SES (socioeconomic status), equity of educational
    opportunity and, 18, 366–371
Short-term memory (STM), 40–42, 156
SimCity (game), 135–137
Simulations, 125–130
  advantages of, 129–130
  attributes of, 128–129
  Operation: Frog, 127–128
  uses of, 126
Site licenses, 381
Slide shows, 245–246, 247
  creating, 250–258
  presenting, 257–258
"Sniffy, the Virtual Rat," 119–121
Snow Goose WebQuest, 235–237
Social context of learning, 64–68
Socioeconomic status (SES), equity of educational
    opportunity and, 18, 366–371
Software
  for CAI, 160, 164–165
  constructivism with, 163–165
  copying, 382
  for creating multimedia projects, 248–258
  filtering, 394–395
  hypermedia, developing, 317–326
  for image creation and manipulation, 274–278
  presentation, 246, 252–257
  screen reader, 376
  spreadsheet, 94, 96–101, 105–106
  video editing, 295, 297–298

Web authoring, 342–358
  word processing, 81–94
Software piracy, 382
Software site licenses, 381
Sound, 305–309
  background music as, 307
  learning with, 309–310
Sources, primary. *See* Primary sources
Speakme, in eZediaMX, 264
Speech, private, 69
Spell checkers, 85
Spiders, 210
Spreadsheets, 94–101, 105–106
  activities using, 98
  functions of, 97
  solutions to algebraic equations and, 100–101
  temperature comparison project using, 97–99
Standards
  AECT, 28
  content, 22
  educational equity and, 25
  ISTE, 24–25, 26–27, 28
  for learning with technology, 24–25
  NCATE, 25, 27–29
  performance, 22
  performance-based assessment and, 14
  recommended approach to, 22–24
  reform and, 24
STM (short-term memory), 40–42, 156
Storage, with word processing programs, 82
Storyboarding, 337
Streaming technologies, 206
Stress, measuring using data logger, 110–111
Student ability, equity and, 375
Student artwork, as image source, 291
Students
  access to technology, 16–17, 172–173, 373–374, 375–378
  active role of, 13
  dangers of internet access, 390–398
  inadequacy of skills for multimedia learning, 155–157
  productivity tools used in work of, 79–80
  use of computers, 17–18
Subscription information services, 222
Supervision, for Internet safety, 377–378
Synchronous communication, 181

Tables, in Web text presentation, 352
Tabs, 84
Tagged image file format (TIFF), 283, 284
Talking books, 147–149
Task specialization methods, 327
TCP/IP (transmissions control protocol/Internet
    protocol), 171

TEACH Act, 385, 387, 391
Teacher preparation, 31–32
    teacher attitudes and, 32
    training and, 31–32
Teachers
    equity and, 371
    facilitative role of, 14
    hypermedia design role of, 338–341
    perceptions of most helpful types of learning
        experiences, 370
    productivity tools used in work of, 79–80
    roles in online discussion, 191–197
Teaching, reciprocal, 65
Team rewards, 326–327
Telecomputing activity structures, 184–185
Telementoring, 186–187
Temperature comparison project using spreadsheet,
    97–99
Templates
    creating using databases, 102–103
    Web authoring and, 350
Text
    in hypermedia, 323–324
    input of, with word processing programs, 82
Text objects, in eZediaMX, 262
Text presentation, Web authoring and, 352–353
Theodosakis, Nikos, 337–338
Thesaurus, with word processing programs, 85
Thinking
    computer tools and, 70–71
    critical, 61
    higher-order, 60–64, 108–111
Threads, 179
Thumbnails, Web authoring and, 351
TIFF (tagged image file format), 283, 284
T1 lines, 175
Tools approach, 13, 80–81
Training, of teachers. *See* Teacher preparation
Transfer, 63–64
    with simulations, 129
Transformational advantage, 221
Translators, 283
Transmission control protocol/Internet protocol
    (TCP/IP), 171
Tutorials, 123–125
    branching, 125
    evaluating, 125
    function of, 123–124
    linear, 125
    online, 217

Universal resource locators (URLs), 205
User interface, in hypermedia, 324–326

Verbal instruction, multimedia support for, 152–153
Video, 295–304
    camcorders for, 295–296, 298–299, 300
    clay animation and, 302–304
    devices used for, 295
    exporting and storing, 299–301
    production and, 296–302
    sequencing images of clay characters for, 302–304
    Web authoring and, 351–352
Videoconferencing, 182–184
Video editing, 295, 297–298
Video imagers, 288–289
Video production, 296–302
    projects for, 300–301
Video projectors, 252
Virtual reality modeling language (VRML), 206
Visual impairments, adaptations of technology for, 376, 378
Volunteerism, and telementoring, 186–187
Vygotsky, Lev, 69

WAV (Waveform Audio) file format, 306
Weather data project, 232–233
Web. *See* World Wide Web (WWW)
Web authoring
    alternative Web page construction methods
        for, 345–349
    basic features and skills for, 343–345
    blogs and, 347–349
    design tips for, 349–353
    general purpose software for, 349
    projects, 342–358
    similarity of word processing to, 342–343
    software for students, 346, 349
Web designs, 320
WebQuests, 234, 235–237
Web resources, 216–221
    citing, 228
    classroom use of, 223–224
    historical inquiry using, 218–220
    instructional, 217–221
    keeping track of, 207–209
    online tutorials as, 217
    primary sources, 60, 217–221
    subscription information services as, 222
    using, 227–228
Who Wants to Be a Millionaire? (activity), 242–243
WiggleWorks, 148–149
Wildflower identification project, 103–105
Wireless connections, 176–177
Word processing programs, 81–94
    activities for all grade levels using, 83
    characteristics of, 82–86
    embellished documents created with, 248–250

Word processing programs *(cont.)*
keyboarding and, 89–94
learning features of, 87
saving documents as HTML, 346
similarity of Web authoring to, 342–343
value of, 85–86
writing process approach using, 88–89
writing using, 86–88
Word wrap, 82
Working memory, 40–42
World Wide Web (WWW), 204–209
for active learning, 232–237
adaptive Web page design and, 376–378
blogs on, 95, 347–349
browsers and, 205–207, 208
browsing and, 209–210
classroom uses of, 213–216
evaluating information on, 223, 229–231
graphics for, 285–286
as image source, 290
keeping track of resources on, 207–209
publishing on, 89, 94
resources on, 216–221
scaffolding projects using, 233–235
searching, 209, 210–213
student work on websites and, 389
See also Internet; Searching; Web resources
Writing, with word processing programs, 86–88
Writing process approach, 88–89
Writing style, in hypermedia, 323–324
WWW. *See* World Wide Web (WWW)

Yahoo!, 210
Yahooligans!, 229, 394

Zone of proximal development, 69